ANNUAL REVIEW OF INTELLECTUAL PROPERTY LAW DEVELOPMENTS

2010

ANNUAL REVIEW OF INTELLECTUAL PROPERTY LAW DEVELOPMENTS

2010

ABA Section of Intellectual Property Law

ABA

Defending Liberty
Pursuing Justice

Printed in the United States of America

15 14 13 12 11   5 4 3 2 1

Cataloging-in-Publication Data is on file with the Library of Congress

ISBN: 978-1-61632-892-4

Discounts are available for books ordered in bulk. Special consideration is given to state bars, CLE programs, and other bar-related organizations. Inquire at Book Publishing, ABA Publishing, American Bar Association, 321 North Clark Street, Chicago, Illinois 60654-7598.

www.ababooks.org

SUMMARY OF CONTENTS

CONTENTS

The framework of the Annual Review *consists of a master index of more than 600 topics, as shown below. Legal developments covered in this volume are italicized and referenced with page numbers.*

FOREWORD

The ABA Section of Intellectual Property Law (ABA-IPL) is pleased to present the third volume of the Section's *Annual Review of Intellectual Property Law Developments.* This book again provides to its readers a depth and breadth of coverage of the year's most significant developments in intellectual property law.

With more than 25,000 members, ABA-IPL is the largest intellectual property law organization in the world. The *Annual Review*, along with an array of other Section books and its *Landslide®* magazine, allow the Section to offer expert, balanced, and thoughtful content on all intellectual property matters, both to our members and to broader audiences.

We are grateful for the extraordinary group of volunteers who have contributed to this book. Our special thanks go to the Annual Review Editorial Board, led by Chair and Editor-in-Chief Liisa Thomas and Vice Chair and Deputy Editor-in-Chief Herb Hart. They have devoted countless hours of their time to this effort and have been assisted by more than one hundred authors, editors, and reviewers. Their collective expertise has created this authoritative and thoughtful review spanning the complex landscape of intellectual property law.

On behalf of the ABA Section of Intellectual Property Law, we are pleased indeed to be able to introduce this review.

Marylee Jenkins
Chair

Robert A. Armitage
Chair-Elect

PREFACE

On behalf of the Editorial Board for the ABA Section of Intellectual Property Law's (ABA-IPL) *Annual Review of Intellectual Property Law Developments*, I am pleased to provide to Section members and nonmembers alike the third volume of this collaborative publication.

Since its inception, the *Annual Review* has served as a resource reflecting thoughtful and balanced reporting on recent legal developments by ABA-IPL members. The *Annual Review* is a unique publication that combines the collective knowledge and insight of some of the leading practitioners in our area of law, and we have been proud to serve as the stewards of this joint and authoritative work. From a pool of hundreds of court decisions and other legal authority related to intellectual property law, the *Annual Review* provides dispassionate recitation of the legal developments that are most likely to impact your profession and practice. We know that you will find this work to be an invaluable tool for your practice.

We owe a debt of gratitude to the many authors, editors, and reviewers who contributed to this book—and to every member of our Board, particularly Deputy Editor-in-Chief and Board Vice Chair Herbert Hart. We are also indebted to the ABA staff team of Leslie Keros, Amy Mandel, Rick Paszkiet, and Bryan Kay, along with manuscript editors Erin Quinn and Ashlee Garcia. As in years past, special thanks also go to Kris Davis, chair of the Board's Editing Committee, who has done an impressive amount of work making sure that this volume gets into your hands; Tywanda Lord, vice chair of the Board's Production Committee; and Pete Peterson, chair of the Board's Intake Committee. All the Board members, both those who served last year and those who have newly joined our ranks, have my heartfelt thanks. Without the hard work of this great team, this volume would not exist.

I hope you enjoy this year's *Annual Review* and find it to be as helpful to your practice as I have for mine.

Liisa M. Thomas
Editor-in-Chief

Contributors

Robert A. Armitage*
Richard Abbott
Kevin N. Ainsworth
Cortney Alexander
Terese L. Arenth
Marjory G. Basile
Eric M. Bowen
Louis Campbell
Kevin R. Casey
Kimberly K. Cauthorn
Juliana M. Cofrancesco
Vince Cogan
Jessica L. Cox
Joyce Craig
Mirut Dalal
Michael Dallal
Nancy A. Del Pizzo
Amanda Joy Dittmar
Kenneth L. Dorsney
Joseph M. Drayton
Douglas N. Ellis
Kristen L. Fancher
David S. Fleming
Tanya L. Forsheit
Dana Garbo
David A. Gauntlett
Ivette Goldfrank
Melanie Grover
Zarema E. Gunnels
R. Mark Halligan
Gerald B. Halt, Jr.
Gina Hayes
Justin Hendrix
Bach V. Hoang
Randi Isaacs
Paul M. Janicke
Jan Jensen
Ben Kleinman

Jeffery P. Langer
Debra Kobrin Levy
Matthew A. Levy
Sue Liemer
Deborah L. Lively
Philippa Loengard
Shana K. Mattson
Monica P. McCabe
Eichakeem L. McClary
Adrienne Lea Meddock
Charles E. Miller
Corinne L. Miller
Jonathan A. Muenkel
Kevin E. Noonan
Suzanne K. Nusbaum
Jason Oliver
Nancy Olson
Susan Perng Pan
Kimberly Parke
Gail Podolsky
Malla Pollack
Stephanie Quick
Susan Linda Ross
Daniel H. Royalty
Eric W. Schweibenz
Doris Shen
Charles Edison Smith
Adam Z. Solomon
Michael D. Stone
David Sugden
Kelu L. Sullivan
David Swenson
Marc Temin
Peter J. Toren
Catherine A. Van Horn
Howard P. Walthall, Jr.
Mark H. Wittow
Jeremy A. Younkin

---

*   Author of chapter introduction

Reviewers

Liisa M. Thomas
Herbert D. Hart III
George W. Jordan III
Neil A. Smith
Erika Harmon Arner†
Brian C. Carroll†
Kristopher R. Davis
Adrienne Fields
David S. Fleming†
Alexa Hansen*
Mark D. Janis

Tywanda Harris Lord
Jennifer M. Mikulina
Robert H. Newman†
Pete R. Peterson
Richard L. Rainey*
Christina N. Scelsi
Raghu Seshadri
Armen Vartian†
Sabina Vayner*
Howard P. Walthall Jr.

---

*   Author of chapter introduction
†   Annual Review Vice Chair

ABA SECTION OF INTELLECTUAL PROPERTY LAW DIVISION CHAIRS

2009–2010
Patents: Robert O. Lindefjeld

Trademarks and Unfair
  Competition: Amy J. Benjamin

Copyrights: June M. Besek

IP-Related Legal
  Issues: Chris Steinhardt

Professional and Section
  Relations: Sharon A. Israel

Litigation, Alternative Dispute
  Resolution, and Related
  Issues: Marc K. Temin

Information Technology: Mark H. Wittow

Meetings and Resolutions: Susan E. McGahan

2010–2011
Patents: Robert O. Lindefjeld

Trademarks and Unfair
  Competition: Jonathan Hudis

Copyrights: June M. Besek

IP-Related Legal
  Issues: Chris Steinhardt

Litigation, Alternative Dispute
  Resolution, and Related Issues:
  Harrie Samaras

Information Technology:
  Mark H. Wittow

ABBREVIATIONS

ACPA	Anticybersquatting Consumer Protection Act
BPAI	Board of Patent Appeals and Interferences
CAN-SPAM Act	Controlling the Assault of Non-Solicited Pornography and Marketing Act
CDA	Communications Decency Act
DMCA	Digital Millennium Copyright Act
FDA	U.S. Food and Drug Administration
FTC	Federal Trade Commission
ISP	Internet Service Provider
ITC	International Trade Commission
JMOL	Judgment as a Matter of Law
TTAB	Trademark Trial and Appeal Board
USPTO	U.S. Patent and Trademark Office

PART I
PATENTS

CHAPTER 1

PATENT SYSTEM

Patent term restoration, the limitations of reissue practice, and the proper standard the USPTO should apply in construing claims and rendering obviousness determinations were all issues addressed by the Federal Circuit this past year.

In *In re Suitco Surface, Inc.* and *Koninklijke Philips Electronics N.V. v. Cardiac Science Operating Co.,* the Federal Circuit addressed the manner in which—and the extent to which—the USPTO claim-construction standard, the so-called broadest reasonable construction standard, is to apply in practice before the USPTO. In *Suitco,* the court chastised the USPTO for applying the standard in an *unreasonable* manner and the court found in *Koninklijke* that the USPTO had memorialized the standard into rulemaking in a context where the Federal Circuit deemed it inapplicable, indeed contrary, to Federal Circuit law. The court further reminded the agency that it lacked substantive rulemaking authority to simply disregard Federal Circuit jurisprudence.

Regarding patent term restoration, the Federal Circuit in *Ortho-McNeil Pharmaceutical, Inc. v. Lupin Pharmaceuticals Inc.* found in favor of the patent owner seeking patent term restoration under the Hatch-Waxman Act—and against the USPTO seeking to limit access to patent term restoration. *Ortho-McNeil* related to an extension sought for a later-approved, single-enantiomer drug for which the racemate form of the drug had previously been approved.

Similarly, in *Photocure ASA v. Kappos,* another second-patent-term restoration case, the Federal Circuit affirmed the district court's determination that the USPTO erred when it refused to grant the patentee a patent term extension on the grounds that the "active ingredient" for the drug at issue was a previously approved "active moiety." Instead, in view of the separate chemical compositions, separate patentability, and separate FDA approval processes that methyl aminolevulinate hydrochloride underwent, it qualified as a new active ingredient and therefore was eligible for a patent term extension, even though it was the methyl ester of previously approved aminolevulinic acid hydrochloride.

In *MBO Laboratories, Inc. v. Becton, Dickinson & Co.,* the Federal Circuit reminded patent practitioners of some of the limitations on patent reissue practice. It did so with an extensive discussion of those limits, pointing out that reissue is not a "panacea for all patent prosecution problems."[1]

Finally, in *In re Chapman,* the Federal Circuit vacated and remanded a BPAI determination that the claims of the patent at issue were obvious and in doing so addressed the proper obviousness standard that the BPAI must apply, as well as the proper standard of review the Federal Circuit applies regarding factual determinations by the USPTO.

---

1.   MBO Laboratories, Inc. v. Becton, Dickinson & Co., 602 F.3d 1306, 1313 (quoting *In re* Weiler, 790 F.2d 1576, 1582 (Fed. Cir. 1986)).

STRUCTURE

Judicial Review

Standard of Review for BPAI Obviousness Decisions Includes Harmless Error

In *In re Chapman,*[2] the Federal Circuit vacated and remanded a BPAI final decision that had found the claims of Chapman's patent application to have been obvious. Applying the harmless error rule, the Federal Circuit reviewed three factual findings of the BPAI, finding two of them to contain potentially harmful error.

The BPAI had found the claims at issue obvious in view of a prior patent to Gonzalez, alone or in combination with another reference. On appeal, Chapman and the government agreed that three of the BPAI's factual findings concerning the Gonzalez reference were erroneous. Because judicial review of agency decisions under the APA includes a harmless error rule, the Federal Circuit needed to consider whether the applicant had shown that the three errors were harmful in that they affected the decision below.[3]

According to the Federal Circuit, the first error—the BPAI's erroneous description of the examiner's position as to what Gonzalez disclosed—was harmless; the BPAI did not rely on the erroneous description. The second error, the BPAI's misunderstanding about a particular teaching in Gonzalez, was potentially harmful in that it increased the likelihood of an erroneous conclusion of obviousness. Likewise, the third error, an erroneous understatement of the number of alternatives disclosed in a reference, was potentially harmful because it affected whether selection from among the alternatives was obvious.

PROCEDURES

Single Enantiomer of Previously Marketed Racemate Is a New Drug Entitled to Patent Term Extension

In *Ortho-McNeil Pharmaceutical, Inc. v. Daiichi Sankyo Co.,*[4] the Federal Circuit affirmed the district court's judgment sustaining the extension of the patent term of Licensor Ortho-McNeil's U.S. Patent 5,053,407 (the '407 patent) and enjoining Defendant Lupin from infringement during the extended patent term of Ortho-McNeil's licensed '407 patent.[5]

The '407 patent was directed to levofloxacin, an enantiomer of its racemate ofloxacin and a new product for use as an antimicrobial agent. Pursuant to regulations, the FDA reviewed the drug product containing levofloxacin as its active ingredient, and the FDA granted Patentee Daiichi permission to sell and use the drug. Daiichi, who later licensed the '407 patent to Ortho-McNeil, subsequently filed for a patent term extension in view of the time to obtain regulatory approval.

---

2. 595 F.3d 1330 (Fed. Cir. 2010).
3. *Id.* at 1338 (citing Munoz v. Strahm Farms, Inc., 69 F.3d 501, 504 (Fed. Cir. 1995)).
4. 603 F.3d 1377 (Fed. Cir. 2010).
5. *Id.* at 1378.

Lupin then invoked litigation procedures in the district court, pursuant to 21 U.S.C. § 355(j)(2)(A)(vii)(IV), contesting whether the '407 patent was entitled to a patent term extension, while stipulating to the validity, enforceability, and infringement of the '407 patent. The district court upheld the USPTO's application of the patent term extension statute, and the Federal Circuit affirmed.

The Federal Circuit first rejected Lupin's contention that the USPTO and FDA's interpretation of the patent term extension statute was incorrect as far as enantiomers are concerned. Specifically, Lupin argued that, because an enantiomer is half of its racemate, the enantiomer levofloxacin was an "active ingredient" of the previously marketed racemate ofloxacin. On the basis that the enantiomer levofloxacin was already an active ingredient of a previously marketed drug ofloxacin, Lupin argued that levofloxacin was not the first permitted commercial marketing or use of the patented product and, therefore, was not eligible for a patent term extension under 35 U.S.C. § 156. The Federal Circuit noted the USPTO's long-standing and consistent practice of treating an enantiomer as a different product from its racemate. The Federal Circuit then rejected Lupin's view that a 2007 amendment to section 355 changed the fundamental interpretation of enantiomers by allowing a specific election of enantiomers for separate treatment. The Federal Circuit thus upheld the USPTO's and district court's determination that the enantiomer levofoxacin was a different drug from its racemate and therefore qualified as a new drug under the patent term extension statute.

Lupin also challenged the scope of the injunction, alleging that patent term extensions under section 156 apply only to the sale and use of infringing products, but do not apply to prevent parties from importing or making the otherwise infringing product. The Federal Circuit reviewed the injunction and its scope for an abuse of discretion. Here, the court noted that the patent term extension statute applied to pharmaceutical uses, meaning that nonpharmaceutical uses are not subject to the extension. However, Lupin did not allege any nonpharmaceutical uses of levofloxacin. Thus, although the injunction against Lupin prohibited Lupin from making, using, offering to sell, or importing levofloxacin in bulk or tablet form, the injunction was not deemed to be overbroad because it was commensurate with the patent rights granted by the patent term extension statute.

New Drug Was Entitled to Term Extension Even When "Active Moiety" Had Been Previously Approved

In ***Photocure ASA v. Kappos***,[6] the Federal Circuit affirmed the district court's determination that the USPTO erred in its interpretation of the patent term extension statute, which serves to lengthen the patent term for a "drug product" undergoing regulatory review. The term "drug product" is defined by statute to mean the "active ingredient" of "a new drug . . . including any salt or ester of the active ingredient."[7]

Patentee Photocure developed a new chemical compound for treating skin cancer, the active ingredient of which was methyl aminolevulinate hydrochloride (MAL), sold under the brand name Metvixia. Photocure obtained U.S. Patent No. 6,034,267 (the '267 patent) on the basis of the improved therapeutic properties of MAL, as compared with the previously known compound ALA. The specification of the '267 patent char-

---

6. 603 F.3d 1372 (Fed. Cir. 2010).
7. 35 U.S.C. § 156(a), (f).

acterizes MAL as better able to penetrate the skin, as a better enhancer of protoporphyrin IX production, and as providing improved selectivity for the target tissue to be treated as compared with ALA. ALA had also previously received FDA approval for the same therapeutic use as MAL.

According to the FDA, Photocure's MAL product was considered a "new drug" under the Federal Food, Drug, and Cosmetic Act, 21 U.S.C. § 321(p), and thus required full FDA approval—a process that consumed four and one-half years. After Photocure had obtained the required FDA approval, Photocure applied for the statutory extension of the term for the '267 patent. However, after consulting with the FDA as to the requirements of patent term extension, the USPTO denied Photocure's request, finding that the statute's requirement of a new "active ingredient" was not met. According to the USPTO, Photocure's MAL was the "same product" as ALA because the "underlying molecule" of MAL was ALA, and ALA was simply formulated differently in the two different drugs. The USPTO concluded that, because a drug product containing ALA was previously approved by the FDA, and because ALA had the same "active moiety" as MAL, Photocure's MAL drug product was directed to an "active ingredient" that was previously approved by the FDA. Consequently, the USPTO determined that the '267 patent was not entitled to the requested term extension under 35 U.S.C. § 156.

On appeal, the Federal Circuit agreed with the district court that the USPTO's interpretation of the patent term extension statute was incorrect. Citing the different biological properties, separate patenting, and separate FDA regulatory approval, the district court held, and the Federal Circuit agreed, that MAL and ALA were different "products" with different "active ingredients," explaining that a compound can only qualify as the "active ingredient" if that compound itself is present in the drug. The Federal Circuit compared this situation with the established precedent for extending patent term for separately patentable esters, even though salts of the same acid were previously approved.

Finally, the Federal Circuit rejected the USPTO's assertion that its interpretation was entitled to deference under *Chevron, U.S.A., Inc. v. Natural Resources Defense Council, Inc.*,[8] which held that, when a statute is ambiguous, the court should defer to the interpretation by the agency charged with administering the statute. The Federal Circuit agreed with the district court that *Chevron* did not apply because the patent term extension statute was unambiguous.

POST-PATENT ISSUANCE

Original Patent's Disclosure Controls in Patentee's Challenge to Applicant's Written Description in Interference Proceeding

In *Koninklijke Philips Electronics N.V. v. Cardiac Science Operating Co.*,[9] the Federal Circuit considered Philips's appeal from a district court's decision reviewing an interference decision under 35 U.S.C. § 146. In the interference, the BPAI had determined that Cardiac's application had priority over the Philips patent and canceled the claims of the

---

8.   467 U.S. 837 (1984).
9.   590 F.3d 1326 (Fed. Cir. 2010).

Philips patent. Philips filed suit in district court seeking review of the interference decision, but the district court sua sponte dismissed Philips's complaint with prejudice. The Federal Circuit reversed and remanded the case to the district court with instructions to construe the claims in accordance with the rule established in *Agilent Technologies, Inc. v. Affymetrix, Inc.*[10]

The interference proceeding had presented patentability issues in addition to priority issues. Among the patentability issues was a written description challenge: Philips argued that the interference count was not patentable to Cardiac because the properly construed count was not supported by an adequate written description under 35 U.S.C. § 112, ¶ 1. The key language of the count was "impedance-compensated defibrillation pulse." According to Philips, the Philips specification defined the language as connected to both patient impedance and the energy level, while the Cardiac specification disclosed only patient impedance. Thus, when the count was construed in light of the Philips specification, the written description of the Cardiac application did not adequately support the count. The BPAI had rejected this argument, asserting that, under the relevant USPTO regulation (37 C.F.R. § 41.200(b)), the count should be "given the broadest reasonable construction in light of the application or patent in which it appears,"[11] namely, the Cardiac application. The district court agreed.

On appeal, the Federal Circuit concluded that the district court and the BPAI had not properly applied the rule from *Agilent*. As the Federal Circuit explained, under *Agilent*, in interference proceedings where there is a written description challenge, the relevant specification for claim construction is the originating disclosure, i.e., the specification of the Philips patent. Accordingly, the claim construction rule in section 41.200(b) "does not apply in an interference proceeding when one party challenges another's written description."[12] Both the BPAI and the district court had erred by relying on the USPTO regulation and disregarding *Agilent*. The BPAI and the district court "must follow judicial precedent instead of section 41.200(b) when a party challenges another's written description during an interference proceeding because the USPTO lacks the substantive rulemaking authority to administratively set aside judicial precedent."[13]

In addressing the remaining issues on appeal, the court held that, because the district court did not give Philips a full and fair opportunity to present arguments and evidence that its patent had priority, and, because there were genuine issues of material fact as to anticipation and written description, the district court had improperly entered summary judgment. Additionally, if the district court were to conclude on remand that the application's written description was sufficient, the Federal Circuit instructed the district court to address Philips's arguments regarding the novelty and obviousness of the application's claims pursuant section 102 and section 103, respectively.[14]

---

10. 567 F.3d 1366 (Fed. Cir. 2009) (reported in ABA Section of Intellectual Property Law, Annual Review of Intellectual Property Law Developments, 2009 (2010)).

11. *Cardiac Science,* 590 F.3d at 1334.

12. *Id.* at 1336.

13. *Id.* at 1337.

14. *Id.* at 1338.

Reissue

Eligibility

ERROR

NONRECAPTURE RULE

Rule against Recapture Invalidates Only Reissue Patent Claims, Not Original Claims Included in Reissue Patent

In ***MBO Laboratories, Inc. v. Becton, Dickinson & Co.***,[15] the Federal Circuit affirmed the district court's judgment that claims 27, 28, 32, and 33 of MBO's U.S. Reissue Patent No. 36,885 (the RE '885 patent) were invalid based on the rule against recapture, reversed the district court's judgment that all other claims of the RE '885 patent were invalid, and remanded the case to the district court to address Becton's motion for summary judgment of noninfringement of original claims 13, 19, and 20.

MBO was the assignee of the RE '885 patent. The RE '885 patent, which was a reissue of U.S. Patent No. 5,755,699 (the '699 patent), disclosed a hypodermic safety syringe designed to protect against needle-stick injuries by covering a contaminated cannula or needle behind a blocking flange that snapped over the needle tip after removal from the patient.

On appeal, MBO argued that the district court erred in holding the RE '885 patent claims 27, 28, 32, and 33 invalid for violating the rule against recapture. Under that rule, reissue patent claims are invalid if broadened to cover subject matter that the patentee surrendered during prosecution of the original claims.[16] The Federal Circuit follows a three-step process to apply the rule: (1) the reissue claims are construed to determine if they are broader than the original claims; (2) if so, a determination is made as to whether the broadened claims cover surrendered subject matter; and (3) a determination is then made as to whether the reissued claims were materially narrowed in other respects to avoid the recapture rule.[17]

Here, the parties did not dispute that the reissued claims were broadened and were not otherwise materially narrowed to avoid the recapture rule. On the disputed issue of surrender, the Federal Circuit agreed with the district court that MBO violated the rule against recapture by claiming relative movement between the guard body and needle. The court reasoned that substantial evidence supported the district court's finding that, during prosecution of a related application, MBO surrendered claims to a guard body that moved relative to a fixed needle.

In reaching its decision, the Federal Circuit clarified that patentees can violate the rule against recapture by claiming in a reissue patent subject matter surrendered while prosecuting *any related application or patent in the family tree*. The court reasoned that "original patent" as used in 35 U.S.C. § 251, although it refers to the patent corrected by reissue,

---

15. 602 F.3d 1306 (Fed. Cir. 2010).
16. *Id.* at 1313 (citing Hester Indus., Inc. v. Stein, Inc., 142 F.3d 1472 (Fed. Cir. 1998)).
17. *Id.* at 1314 (citations omitted).

does not limit the patents and their prosecution histories that can be the basis for a patentee's surrender of subject matter. Thus, in the court's view, subject matter surrendered at any point in a patent family's entire prosecution history can trigger the rule against recapture.

The Federal Circuit next addressed the district court's holding invalidating the entire RE '885 patent based solely on MBO's violation of the rule against recapture. The parties did not dispute error in the district court's decision. The Federal Circuit reversed the district court's judgment relating to the original patent claims, holding that, when a reissue patent contains unmodified original patent claims, a court can invalidate only the reissue claims under the rule against recapture, not the original unmodified claims. Accordingly, it remanded the case for consideration of Becton's motion for summary judgment of noninfringement on claims 13, 19, and 20.

Reexamination

Ex Parte

Overly Broad Claim Construction Exceeds Scope of Claims and Specification

In ***In re Suitco Surface, Inc.,***[18] the Federal Circuit vacated-in-part and affirmed-in-part the BPAI's rejection of claims in Suitco's U.S. Patent No. 4,944,514 (the '514 patent).[19] In particular, the Federal Circuit found that the claim rejections, made during a reexamination proceeding, were based on an unreasonable claim construction. The Federal Circuit remanded the claim construction issue, with instructions.

The '514 patent generally was directed to a "floor finishing material" used for athletic courts, bowling alleys, and various other surfaces. In particular, the '514 patent claimed a thin plastic sheet which was connected to a floor surface by an adhesive layer. Originally, a district court had construed the meanings of the terms "material for finishing" and "uniform flexible film" as disclosed in the '514 patent. On appeal, the Federal Circuit remanded the case twice and, eventually, an ex parte reexamination was filed, and the BPAI was required to construe the above terms. The BPAI affirmed an earlier rejection by the examiner and construed certain limitations from the claims. Suitco appealed to the Federal Circuit on the grounds that the BPAI wrongly construed the "material for finishing the top surface of the floor" term and incorrectly rejected the claims on anticipation grounds, as no prior-art reference disclosed the "uniform flexible film" limitation.

The court first determined that the USPTO's construction of the "material for finishing" limitation was unreasonable. Here, the court held the language in the claims clearly indicated the material was a finishing material and therefore should be used on the final layer of the finished surface. The court specifically emphasized the meaning of the term "finishing" and its implications. As a result, the USPTO wrongly interpreted the "material for finishing" limitation to cover materials applied anywhere above the surface being finished, despite the fact that it might not be the top finishing layer. The USPTO maintained that it was required to give all the claims the broadest reasonable construction, especially given that "comprising" was used in the claims. Although the court acknowl-

---

18. 603 F.3d 1255 (Fed. Cir. 2010).
19. *Id.* at 1261.

edged this as the general principle for claim interpretation, the court found the USPTO's construction to be unreasonably broad, especially in light of the claims and the specification. Therefore, the court remanded the case with proper instructions for conducting a new claim construction and new invalidity analysis using this new claim construction.

The court then addressed the "uniform flexible film" limitation. Suitco did not challenge the USPTO's construction of this term, but instead argued that the prior-art references failed to disclose the limitation. The court swiftly dismissed Suitco's contention and found substantial evidence supporting the BPAI's ruling that the prior-art references anticipated this particular limitation.

CLAIM INTERPRETATION

Chapter 2 presents a diverse collection of Federal Circuit patent cases addressing a variety of claim construction issues concerning preambles, disclaimers, preferred embodiments, definitions, disclaimers, means-plus-function limitations, expert testimony, dictionary definitions, and general language in the specification.

One valuable reminder is that preambles are not to be taken lightly. In *Haemonetics Corp. v. Baxter Healthcare Corp.*, the Federal Circuit gave effect to a definition in a preamble. In *Marrin v. Griffin,* the Federal Circuit held that language in a preamble was not a claim limitation where it only added an intended use. In *In re Skvorecz*, the signal "comprising" in the preamble did not render the claim anticipated by a device containing less, rather than more, than what was claimed.

Other cases turned for the worse due to extrinsic evidence. In *General Protecht Group, Inc. v. International Trade Commission*, the expert testimony addressing corresponding structure for means-plus-function limitation fell short. In *Ultimax Cement Manufacturing Corp. v. CTS Cement Manufacturing Corp.*, the Federal Circuit relied on the context in which the claim term was used within the claim and the specification as compared to the district court's erroneous reliance on expert testimony and one of many dictionary definitions.

Cases considering the specification show the degree to which specificity counts. In *Silicon Graphics, Inc. v. ATI Technologies, Inc.*, the Federal Circuit credited specific language in the specification over general language. In *Baran v. Medical Device Technologies,* the Federal Circuit endorsed a claim construction that excluded one of the preferred embodiments of the invention. In *Pressure Products Medical Supplies, Inc. v. Greatbatch Ltd.*, merely mentioning prior art references did not suffice to identify corresponding structure for a means-plus-function limitation. In *Edwards Lifesciences LLC v. Cook Inc.*, an interchangeable use of two claim terms in the specification was akin to a definition. In *Pass & Seymour v. International Trade Commission*, which considered the claims, specification and prosecution history, plain meaning controlled the construction of the claim term "both."

Where potential disclaimers during prosecution are concerned, a lack of clarity continues to favor patentees. In *Schindler Elevator Corp. v. Otis Elevator Corp*, the Federal Circuit modified the lower court's claim construction in treating the patentee's prosecution disclaimer more narrowly. Similarly, in *Vizio, Inc. v. International Trade Commission,* a statement during prosecution explaining the benefits of the patented invention over the prior art did not result in a broad disclaimer.

Albeit in dicta, the Federal Circuit addressed the de novo standard of review for claim construction in *Trading Technologies International, Inc. v. eSpeed, Inc.* Finally, the Federal Circuit addressed yet another Google AdWords case in *Bid for Position, LLC v. AOL, LLC*, and the Northern District of Illinois promulgated Local Patent Rules (LPRs), effective October 1, 2009.

DEFERENCE

Federal Circuit Panel Criticizes De Novo Review of Claim Construction

In ***Trading Technologies International, Inc. v. eSpeed, Inc.,***[1] the Federal Circuit upheld all of the district court's findings regarding the validity and construction of two of Trading Tech's (TT) patents. TT filed suit alleging that two of its patents were infringed upon by three eSpeed software products. The district court held, after construing the patent claims, that: (1) one of eSpeed's products infringed the asserted claims of both patents and the infringement was not willful; (2) the remaining two accused products did not literally infringe and TT was precluded from asserting infringement under the doctrine of equivalents; (3) the on-sale bar of 35 U.S.C. § 102(b) did not apply; (4) there was not an indefiniteness problem in the asserted claims; and (5) there was no inequitable conduct. Also, the district court denied eSpeed's JMOL motion on validity, indefiniteness, priority date, and a patent misuse defense.

TT owned two patents that claimed software for displaying the inside market on commodities traders' screens of an electronic exchange. The inside market is the point between the best offer to buy an instrument (the bid) and the best offer to sell that instrument (the ask). The actual price of a spot trade will typically be at or between the bid and the ask. In a dynamic market, that price can change rapidly. In the prior art, the inside market was at a point on the center of a screen, and changes in the inside market were indicated by changing the values in a price axis. The invention was directed at keeping those prices constant and having the indicator for the inside market move up and down the screen, as appropriate, giving a more helpful indication of the current price of the inside market.

The parties disagreed about whether eSpeed's products satisfied limitations in TT's claims calling for "static display prices" and a "static price axis." Under the district court's claim construction, one eSpeed product infringed, but the other two (the redesigns) did not.

The Federal Circuit affirmed the district court's claim construction. Judge Rader's opinion commented that, although claim construction involves many "technical, scientific, and timing issues that require full examination of the evidence,"[2] the Federal Circuit's en banc ruling in *Cybor*[3] precluded the court from giving even "the slightest iota of deference"[4] to the district court's claim construction. Whereas *Cybor* had interpreted the U.S. Supreme Court's *Markman* decision as requiring claim construction to be reviewed de novo, the Court had, in fact, made many references to "the factual components" of claim construction, according to Judge Rader. For example, the Court had determined that claim construction falls "somewhere between a pristine legal standard and a simple historical fact."[5] The Court had also implied that the trial court had a better vantage point for resolving evidentiary disputes underlying claim construction. Taking into account these points from *Markman*, and the contrary command for de novo review in *Cybor*, Judge Rader found himself "stranded." Nonetheless, after a lengthy analysis, Judge Rader concluded that the district court's claim construction had been correct.

---

1. 595 F.3d 1340 (Fed. Cir. 2010).
2. *Id.* at 1351.
3. Cybor Corp. v. FAS Techs., Inc., 138 F.3d 1448 (Fed. Cir. 1998) (en banc).
4. *eSpeed*, 595 F.3d at 1351.
5. *Id.* at 1350.

District Judge Clark, sitting by designation, concurred to comment on the policy ramifications of the de novo review standard for claim construction. Judge Clark observed that the de novo review standard might discourage settlement at the trial level given that the party who receives an adverse construction ruling can simply renew the same arguments on appeal, hoping for a more sympathetic examination of complicated facts by the Federal Circuit. Judge Clark also noted that the de novo review standard might delay resolution of the case, especially if a litigant decided for strategic reasons to offer only skeletal claim construction arguments at trial, awaiting appeal before asserting the full-fledged arguments. Judge Clark opined that tactics such as these would be less likely to succeed if the Federal Circuit gave some deference to district court claim constructions, even if limited to claim constructions involving resort to extrinsic evidence. Judge Lourie concurred only in the result.

PERTINENT SOURCES

Intrinsic Sources

Quality Score Based on Numerous Additional Factors Other Than Price Held Not to Be Claimed "Value"

In ***Bid for Position, LLC v. AOL, LLC,***[6] the Federal Circuit affirmed the summary judgment of noninfringement by the U.S. District Court for the Eastern District of Virginia.

The plaintiff, Bid for Position, alleged that the district court erred in its claim construction of the patent-in-suit. The patent-in-suit, U.S. Patent 7,225,151, described a method for conducting a continuous auction for positions of priority in the auction and automatically adjusting the bidder's bid to maintain the chosen priority status. The claims at issue hinged upon the court's construction of two principle terms, one of which allowed the bidder to choose the position of priority, whereas the other required that the value of the bid be a monetary amount and not a quality score.

The accused products were two versions of Google's Internet advertising system, AdWords without Position Preference and AdWords with Position Preference. AdWords ran an auction for order of placement of advertisements that were triggered by keywords. The order of placement was based on an Ad Rank. The Ad Rank was the product of the maximum price that the advertiser is willing to pay whenever its advertisement is clicked and the likelihood that users will click the advertisements. The Ad Rank was recalculated whenever an advertisement was triggered by the keyword.

Position Preference is a feature where an advertiser can select a minimum desired bidding position. The advertiser's placement over a period of time (twenty-four hours) is averaged, and the bid is periodically adjusted as needed to maintain the minimum desired bidding position.

The Federal Circuit first examined the district court's claim construction. The Federal Circuit affirmed the district court's construction of "information for selecting one of the two or more positions of priority that the first bidder wishes to maintain in the auction" as

---

6. 601 F.3d 1311 (Fed. Cir. 2010).

meaning that the bidder chooses the position of priority,[7] as well as the district court's construction of "value" as meaning the monetary amount of the bid.

The Federal Circuit then affirmed summary judgment for both products. AdWords without Position Preference merely selects the highest ranking position based on the offered bid and, therefore, does not meet the element of allowing the bidder to choose the position of priority. AdWords with Position Preference product compares a quality score (Ad Rank), which is not a "value" or an equivalent under the doctrine of equivalents because the quality score has no consistent mapping with the monetary amount of the bid, but was instead based upon numerous other factors other than money.

The Federal Circuit did not address the district court's finding the AdWords with Position Preference also did not allow the bidder to choose the position of priority.

Expert Testimony Failed to Show Equivalency for Claimed Latching Means

In *General Protecht Group, Inc. v. International Trade Commission,*[8] the Federal Circuit affirmed the ITC's final determination that the appellants violated section 337 of the Tariff Act of 1930 (19 U.S.C. § 1337). The violation involved the importation, sale for importation, or the sale within the United States after importation of certain ground fault circuit interrupters (GFCIs). However, the Federal Circuit reversed and remanded a portion of the ITC's determination that certain devices manufactured by appellants General Protecht Group, Inc. (GPG), Wenzhou Trimone Science and Technology Electric Co., Ltd. (Trimone), and Shanghai ELE Manufacturing Corp. (ELE) infringed U.S. Patent Nos. 7,283,340 (the '340 patent), and 5,594,398 (the '398 patent).

ELE, GPG, and Trimone appealed the ITC's limited exclusion order in part based upon a claim construction rendered in the '340 patent. GPG also appealed based in part upon a means-plus-function construction rendered in the '398 patent.

Turning first to the '340 patent, the court determined that claims of the '340 patent included limitations of a detection circuit and an interruption contact assembly. The claimed assembly had four sets of interrupting contacts configured to provide electrical continuity between the line terminals and the load terminals in a reset state, with a detection circuit to determine if the assembly was properly wired. ELE, GPG, and Trimone argued that the ALJ and the ITC had improperly construed the terms "detection circuit" and "load terminals."

The Federal Circuit agreed with ELE that the ITC erred in adopting an administrative law judge's (ALJ) finding that ELE's 2006 and GPG's 2003 and 2006 GFCIs infringed the '340 patent, because the devices did not contain a "detection circuit." The court noted that expert testimony indicated that the detection circuit limitation required the device to detect a proper wire condition and generate a signal in response. ELE's and GPG's 2003 and 2006 GFCIs did not have a circuit that generated a predetermined signal when the circuit detected that the device was properly wired; instead, if it was properly wired, the circuit worked, and if it was not, the circuit did not work. Because the expert testimony was "plainly inconsistent"[9] with the ALJ's construction and the asserted claims, the testimony did not support a finding that ELE's and GPG's devices infringed the '340 patent.

---

7. *Id.* at 1313.
8. 619 F.3d 1303 (Fed. Cir. 2010).
9. *Id.* at 1308.

Not only did the Federal Circuit find that Trimone's 2006 GFCIs did not infringe the '340 patent, but it also found that the ALJ erred in construing the claim term "load terminals" to include receptacle outlets. Because the ALJ relied on expert testimony that did not mention receptacle outlets or user load terminals "at all,"[10] there was no evidence that a person of ordinary skill in the art would interpret the term "load terminals" to include receptacle outlets or user load terminals. Based on that construction, the GFCIs included two sets of interrupting contacts that contained receptacle outlets. Thus, Trimone's 2006 GFCI did not infringe.

Turning next to the '398 patent, the court reversed the ITC's determination that GPG's accused 2006 GFCI device infringed claims of the '398 patent. The claims of the '398 patent used means-plus-function language to define several elements pursuant to 35 U.S.C. § 112. In particular, the court found that the '398 patent disclosed a mechanical architecture for a GFCI receptacle with a "latching means" that can move between a circuit-making position and a circuit-breaking position.[11]

GPG's device used a magnet capable of retaining an armature attached to the device's mount. The Federal Circuit noted that expert testimony revealed only that magnets were well known as latches, which testimony goes to function and result, not that magnets performed the latching-means function in substantially the same way as the mechanical latch means described in the '398 patent. Thus, the court held that substantial evidence did not support the ITC's finding that the magnetic latching structure of GPG's device was equivalent to the mechanical structure disclosed in the '398 patent.

In a dissenting opinion, Judge Newman opined that the majority had ruled on the appealed issues without deference to the ITC and made de novo rulings based on theories not briefed by the parties.[12] She argued that substantial evidence supported each of the ITC's findings that appellants' GFCIs were infringing.

Intrinsic Evidence Supports Plain Meaning of Claim Term "Both"

In *Pass & Seymour, Inc. v. International Trade Commission*,[13] the Federal Circuit upheld the claim construction analysis and determination of the ITC that the accused products manufactured by General Protecht Group, Inc (GPG) and certain other Chinese manufacturers did not infringe patents owned by Pass and Seymour (P&S).

P&S is the owner of certain patents related to circuit interpreters for use with household electrical appliances, which are typically recognized by the characteristic "test" and "reset" button on household electrical outlets. The two patents at issue, U.S. Patent Nos. 5,594,398 (the '398 patent) and 7,212,386 (the '386 patent) are directed to improved safety features for circuit interrupters to protect users from electrical shock and protect appliances from electrical damage.

The parties disagreed over the term in the '398 patent "mounting means for said conducting member to permit movement thereof between a first position, wherein said pair of contacts are in respective, circuit-making engagement with said pair of terminals, and second position, wherein both of said pair of contacts are in spaced, circuit-breaking

---

10. *Id.* at 1311.
11. *Id.*
12. *Id.* at 1314 (Newman, J., dissenting).
13. 617 F.3d 1319 (Fed. Cir. 2010).

relation to said pair of terminals."[14] The administrative law judge adopted P&S's proposed definition that the claim was satisfied if either of the two contacts was moved into a spaced, circuit-breaking second position because, collectively, "both" contacts would be in a position that resulted in the circuit breaking. The administrative law judge also adopted P&S's proposed construction of the disputed term, "a unitary, electrically conducting member carrying a pair of spaced electrical contacts."[15] The term was construed to mean a "member that provides an electrical current carrying path between two or more spaced contacts."[16]

On appeal, the Federal Circuit agreed with the ITC's determination that the administrative law judge's constructions did not give meaning to the claim limitations that "both" contacts be in a spaced, circuit-breaking second position and the that electrically conducting member be "unitary" and "carry" the pair of spaced contacts. In agreeing with the ITC's definition, the court explained that "[t]he plain language of the claim requires that both of the pair of contacts move into spaced, circuit-breaking relation to the terminals" and if P&S sought to cover "devices where only one contact moved into spaced, circuit-breaking relation to the terminals, then it could have written its claims to read 'wherein at least one of said pair of contacts is in spaced, circuit-breaking relation to said pair of terminals.'"[17] The court then agreed with the ITC's factual finding that the accused products do not both move into a spaced second position and, thus, there was no infringement.

The court also agreed with the ITC that the proper construction of the limitation "a unitary, electrically conducting member carrying a pair of spaced electrical contacts" must give meaning to "unitary" which denotes "a single continuous structure." The court found that "the specification and prosecution history confirm that this plain meaning is appropriate in the context of this claim limitation."[18] According to the court, because the "accused products at issue here do not meet the 'mounting means' limitation as properly construed, and thus do not meet every limitation of the asserted claims, there can be no infringement."[19]

With regard to the '386 patent, the parties disagreed over the claim term "circuit interrupter coupled to the actuator assembly, the circuit interrupter being configured to disconnect the first conductive path from the second conductive path in response to the actuator signal in the reset state." The court found that the plain language of this claim requires that "the circuit interrupter be configured to trip in response to an actuator signal in the reset state."[20] Thus according to the court, "[c]onstruing this limitation to require generation of an actuator signal without respect to the state of the device does not conflict with any other limitation of the claim."[21] Accordingly, the court affirmed the ITC's determination of noninfringement with regard to the '386 patent.

---

14. *Id.* at 1321.
15. *Id.*
16. *Id.* at 1323.
17. *Id.* at 1324.
18. *Id.*
19. *Id.* at 1325.
20. *Id.* (emphasis in original).
21. *Id.* at 1326.

Federal Circuit Splits over Scope of Prosecution Disclaimer

In *Schindler Elevator Corp. v. Otis Elevator Corp.,*[22] the Federal Circuit held that the district court too narrowly construed the two terms at issue during claim construction, improperly adding a limitation to the asserted claims. On summary judgment, the district court had determined that Otis did not infringe the claims because Otis's elevator system did not meet the limitations of the two claims at issue.

The claims related to an elevator system that can be accessed by individuals who carry an "information transmitter," where the system recognizes the individual's elevator call using a "recognition device" and dispatches an elevator. The district court had construed those two limitations as being limited to devices that required no "personal action by the passenger" of any sort (other than walking into the elevator area). Otis' accused system required passengers to place an identification card at least within range of a card reader, and so fell outside the claims, according to the district court.

On appeal, Schindler argued that the intrinsic evidence did not support the district court's "without any personal action of any sort" limitation. The Federal Circuit agreed. The claim itself included language specifying that the information transmitter would be "carried by" the user, itself a type of personal action. Likewise, "the specification itself provides examples where a user would need to do more than just walk to bring his transmitter into recognition range,"[23] including pushing a cart or unlocking a door, according to the Federal Circuit. Whether the district court's limitation was supported by a disclaimer made during prosecution was a more complicated question. The applicant had added the "information transmitter" limitation in response to an obviousness rejection. The district court had found that, as a consequence of this amendment, the applicant had disclaimed coverage over systems that involved "the use of a passenger's hands for any and all purposes." The Federal Circuit disagreed. Although the applicant had disclaimed coverage as a result of the amendment, the disclaimer extended only to personal action taking place "after the passenger has brought the transmitter within range of the recognition device . . . ."[24] That was the only "clear and unmistakable disavowal" of the type that would trigger prosecution disclaimer.

The Federal Circuit modified the district court's construction of the two terms at issue by removing "without requiring any sort of personal action" from each construction, vacated the grant of summary judgment of noninfringement, and remanded the case.

Judge Dyk, in a separate opinion, concurred in the result but dissented in part. Judge Dyk agreed that the district court's "without requiring any sort of personal action" construction imposed an improper limitation on the scope of the claims, in view of the claim language and specification. He disagreed with the majority's analysis of the scope of the prosecution disclaimer, however. Judge Dyk argued that "[c]ontrary to the majority, it seems to me that the action of swiping a card to call the elevator separate from the action required to gain entry to the building is clearly within the disclaimer of both the specification and prosecution history."[25] According to Judge Dyk, the majority had artificially eliminated the disclaimer. In addition, Schindler's arguments for a narrow disclaimer also

---

22. 593 F.3d 1275 (Fed. Cir. 2010).
23. *Id.* at 1284.
24. *Id.* at 1285.
25. *Id.* at 1287 (Dyk, J., concurring).

had to be rejected, according to Judge Dyk, because they effectively were based on prosecution arguments that Schindler could have made to distinguish the prior art, as opposed to those arguments actually made. The law of prosecution disclaimer is based on the arguments that the applicant actually makes, Judge Dyk asserted.

Explanation of Invention's Benefits over Prior Art during Prosecution Did Not Amount to Disavowal of Claim Scope

In *Vizio, Inc. v. International Trade Commission,*[26] the Federal Circuit affirmed the ITC's construction of the term "channel map information" and its determination that U.S. Patent No. 6,115,074 (the '074 patent) was not invalid as anticipated or obvious. The Federal Circuit also affirmed the ITC's determination that the '074 patent was infringed by digital televisions being imported by Funai Electric Co., Ltd. and Funai Corporation (collectively, Funai), but reversed the ITC's determination that "work-around products" infringed the '074 patent.

By way of background, Funai initiated a section 337 investigation at the ITC against, inter alia, Vizio, alleging violations of 19 U.S.C. § 1337 through importation or sale of certain digital televisions that infringed the '074 patent. The ITC ruled in favor of Funai and issued a limited exclusion order and a cease-and-desist order directed to the named respondents.

On appeal, the Federal Circuit addressed three claim interpretation issues. First, the Federal Circuit held that, with respect to the claim term "channel map information," based on intrinsic evidence and the understanding of one of ordinary skill in the art, the claims reciting "MPEG compatible channel map information" referred to the MPEG-2 standard.[27] Second, regarding whether the claims precluded the use of information other than channel map information, particularly whether they precluded the use of the Moving Picture Experts Group Program Map Table (MPEG PMT) (i.e., the data used for decoding in the prior art), the Federal Circuit found that the cited statements from the '074 patent's prosecution history merely explained the benefits of the patented invention over the prior art, namely, that it did not require the use of the MPEG PMT. Thus, the Federal Circuit concluded that there had been no broad disclaimer of any and all use of the PMT, only a disclaimer of systems that required the use of the MPEG PMT. Third, regarding whether the claims required that the device and method be capable of utilizing the channel map information or whether mere receipt and storage of the channel map information is sufficient, the Federal Circuit held that the channel map information must be capable of being used and, further, that all four minimum data fields of the channel map information must be suitable for use in decoding.[28] Using this claim construction, the Federal Circuit affirmed the ITC's determination that the asserted claims were not invalid as anticipated or obvious.

Regarding infringement, the Federal Circuit found that, although the accused legacy products infringed under the proper claim construction, the accused "work-around products" did not. The Federal Circuit concluded that the work-around products did not convert all the necessary channel map information into a useable format and, thus, did not

---

26. 605 F.3d 1330 (Fed. Cir. 2010).
27. *Id.* at 1336–38.
28. *Id.* at 1339–42.

meet the requirements identified in the construction of the third claim construction issue discussed above.

In dissent, Judge Clevenger disagreed with the majority's finding of noninfringement with regard to the work-around products. Judge Clevenger noted that the third claim construction issue identified by the majority was not raised by the parties and, therefore, was not properly before the Federal Circuit.

Interchangeable Use of Two Claim Terms in Specification Was Akin to a Definition

In ***Edwards Lifesciences LLC v. Cook Inc.,***[29] the Federal Circuit affirmed the summary judgment entered by the U.S. District Court for the Northern District of California. The district court construed the asserted claims and found noninfringement of certain claims of U.S. Patent Nos. 6,582,458; 6,613,073; 6,685,736; and 6,689,158, which are directed to intraluminal grafts for treating aneurisms and occlusive diseases of blood vessels without open surgery.

The Federal Circuit first found that, in light of the common specification of the asserted patents, the claimed "graft" devices must be intraluminal. It noted that the specification consistently used the words "graft" and "intraluminal graft" interchangeably and frequently described an intraluminal graft as "the present invention." As such, the "interchangeable use" of the two terms was "akin to a definition."[30] Finally, the Federal Circuit observed that certain claims were limited to grafts that are attachable "while inside of a vessel." (Although intraluminal grafts are inserted inside of a vessel, traditional vascular grafts are not.) The Federal Circuit rejected the plaintiff's claim differentiation argument that intraluminal graft and graft must be construed differently, explaining that different words may be construed to cover the same subject matter where the evidence supports such a reading.

The Federal Circuit also found that the amendment to one claim deleting the modifier "intraluminal" did not mean that the claim was entitled to a broader reading because the accompanying remarks indicated that the claim defined an intraluminal graft. Further, the court found that declarations submitted by the inventors during prosecution describing a traditional vascular graft as a graft were irrelevant because they were submitted only for the purpose of provoking an interference, which the USPTO declined to declare. Accordingly, the Federal Circuit refused to infer that the Examiner relied on the declarations.

Additionally, the Federal Circuit found that the claims were limited to intraluminal grafts including wires, even though certain claims did not expressly recite wires, because Edwards admitted that the wires provide structure permitting grafts to attach in the manner required by the claims. Although certain dependent claims expressly recited wires, the Federal Circuit found that the doctrine of claim differentiation could not be used to contradict the clear import of the specification—that wires were essential to the invention.

The Federal Circuit further found that the wires recited by the claims must be malleable because the inventors disclaimed the use of resilient wires in the invention as described in the specification by: (1) disparaging prior-art resilient wires; and (2) specifically

---

29. 582 F.3d 1322 (Fed. Cir. 2009).
30. *Id.* at 1329.

describing the disclosed wires as malleable. Although the inventors canceled claims requiring "malleable wires" during prosecution and replaced them with claims requiring only "wires," the court found that this amendment did not show that the claims encompassed malleable wires because the inventors distinguished claims that did not explicitly require malleable wires by arguing that the inventors' wires were "malleable, deformable, non-springy material" and were not self-expanding.

The Federal Circuit concluded that, for the purposes of interpreting this claim, malleable wires and resilient wires were mutually exclusive because the specification defined "malleable" to exclude any substantial resilience, overriding any ordinary meaning that might encompass substantial resilience. The Federal Circuit rejected the plaintiff's argument that the inventors' definition of "malleable" did not limit the claim scope simply because it appeared in the context of the description of a preferred embodiment.

The Federal Circuit affirmed the district court's summary judgment of noninfringement because the accused devices included self-expanding (i.e., resilient) wires. Although a molding balloon could be used to smooth out the accused devices after self-expansion, the wires were primarily resilient, not malleable. Further, it held that the accused devices could not infringe under the doctrine of equivalents because the inventors disclaimed resilient wires, and that subject matter could not be recaptured using the doctrine of equivalents.

Pre-Phillips *Claim Construction Ignored Context in Which Claim Term Was Used*

In *Ultimax Cement Manufacturing Corp. v. CTS Cement Manufacturing Corp.*,[31] the Federal Circuit held that the term "soluble $CaSO_4$ anhydride," as used in the '556 patent claims for fast-setting, high-strength cement, should be construed to mean "soluble anhydrous calcium sulfate."[32] The court also held that the existence of a genuine issue of material fact precluded summary judgment that the '556 patent was unenforceable due to laches, and that claim 17 of the '684 patent was not indefinite.

The district court granted CTS's motion for summary judgment on the grounds that CTS did not infringe the asserted claims based on a construction of the word "anhydride," Ultimax's patent was unenforceable due to laches, and that claims of Ultimax's patent were indefinite, because the claimed compound "crystal X" encompassed over 5,000 possible compounds, and because "crystal Y" lacked a coma between "f" and "cl."

On appeal, the Federal Circuit agreed with Ultimax with respect to the construction of "anhydride." The court concluded that the district court, which construed the claims prior to the Federal Circuit's *Phillips* decision,[33] improperly relied on expert testimony and on a single dictionary definition, to the exclusion of other dictionary definitions, and, most importantly, the context in which the term was used within the claim and the specification.

According to the Federal Circuit, the term "anhydride," when placed next to "$CaSO_4$," served to modify the calcium sulfate term (calcium sulfate from which water has been removed). In support of its construction, the Federal Circuit noted: (1) other dictionaries

---

31. 587 F.3d 1339 (Fed. Cir. 2009).
32. *Id.*
33. Phillips v. AWH Corp., 415 F.3d 1303 (Fed. Cir. 2005) (en banc).

allowed such interpretation; (2) the context of the entire specification further supported such a construction; (3) interpreting the term in that way was not rewriting the claim or correcting a typographical error; (4) claim drafters could not have intended the alternative meaning as it would have been redundant; and (5) interpreting the claim in that way merely restated its plain meaning.

With respect to laches for the '556 patent, the Federal Circuit also agreed with Ultimax that summary judgment was improper, "as it is not clear that Ultimax knew or should have known of CTS's alleged infringement before it conducted discovery on the '684 patent in 2002."[34] Instead, the court noted that the only time relevant to the presumption of laches was that after Ultimax knew or should have known of the allegedly infringing product.

The Federal Circuit further agreed with Ultimax that claim 17 of the '684 patent was not indefinite. According to the court, "a claim to a formula containing over 5000 possible combinations is not necessarily ambiguous if it sufficiently notifies the public of the scope of the claims."[35] The court determined that drafting a claim broadly does not render it insolubly ambiguous, and it does not prevent the public from understanding the scope of the patent. Furthermore, a court can correct the obvious typographical error in the notation "(f cl)" because "(1) the correction is not subject to reasonable debate based on consideration of the claim language and the specification and (2) the prosecution history does not suggest a different interpretation of the claims."[36]

Because the Federal Circuit reversed the district court's claim construction, the court vacated the district court's holding of noninfringement and remanded the issue. The Federal Circuit also reversed the district court's grant of summary judgment of laches and remanded for a trial on laches. The Federal Circuit further reversed the summary judgment of indefiniteness, directing the district court to enter summary judgment that the claim at issue was not indefinite.

Claims

Claim Term Construed Based on Unambiguous Definition in Preamble

In *Haemonetics Corp. v. Baxter Healthcare Corp.*,[37] the Federal Circuit determined the lower court's construction of the claim term "centrifugal unit" was erroneous, emphasizing that claims must be construed with an eye towards giving effect to all of their terms, even if it renders the claims inoperable or invalid. Haemonetics and Fenwal are manufacturers and sellers of centrifuge products for separating red blood cells from human blood by aphaeresis. Haemonetics was assigned U.S. Patent 6,705,983 ('983 patent), which claims a compact blood centrifuge device for separating and collecting components in a liquid such a blood. Haemonetics brought suit against Fenwal alleging infringement of the '983 patent by Fenwal's ALYX centrifugal system. Following claim construction and summary judgment motions, Haemonetics narrowed its suit to infringement of only claim 16 of the '983 patent. Fenwal countered, asserting claim 16 was invalid as indefinite, anticipated by prior invention, and

---

34. *Ultimax,* 587 F.3d at 1349.
35. *Id.* at 1352.
36. *Id.* at 1353.
37. 607 F.3d 776 (Fed. Cir. 2010).

obvious. Claim 16 used the term "centrifugal unit" three times throughout the claim, once in the preamble and twice in the body. The district court construed the claim term "centrifugal unit," as used in the preamble, to mean "the combination of both the vessel and the tubing."[38] Based on dimensional limitations recited in the claim, the court reasoned that the remaining two references in the body of the claim excluded the tubing. The jury found claim 16 was valid and infringed, and Fenwal timely appealed the decision.

On appeal, Fenwal argued that the court erred when construing centrifugal unit in the body of claim 16 to refer to only the vessel, even though the preamble of the claim defined the term as including a vessel and a plurality of tubes. Haemonetics countered by arguing the claim preamble merely indicated the claimed invention's field of use, and the specification made it clear that centrifugal unit in the context of the dimensional limitations referred only to the vessel. The Federal Circuit agreed with Fenwal and held that claims should be construed with an eye toward giving effect to the unambiguous definition in the preamble, even if it renders the claims inoperable or invalid. Further, patent claims are used to give notice to the public of the scope of a claim invention, and this function would be undermined "if courts construed claims so as to render physical structures and characteristics specifically described in those claims superfluous."[39] Although Haemonetics's counsel indicated that an error may have occurred while drafting claim 16, the court refused to construe the disputed term to have differing meanings, in light of this possible error, because the original claim 16 is what the patentee claimed, and it was what the public was entitled to rely on. The court also refused to redraft a claim "to contradict their plain language in order to avoid a nonsensical result."[40] Similarly, the specification defined "centrifugal unit" in the context of two embodiments—one of which included a plurality of tubes tracking the language of claim 16.

The court vacated the district court's grant of JMOL and remanded the case to determine the meaning of some of the dimensional terms in the claim to determine whether claim 16 was definite. In response to Fenwal's appeal of the jury's finding that the patent was not invalid due to anticipation or obviousness, the court vacated the verdict and award of remedies due to the district court's incorrect claim construction.

PREAMBLE

Preamble Not a Claims Limitation Where It Only Added an Intended Use

In *Marrin v. Griffin,*[41] the Federal Circuit affirmed the district court's ruling that language in the preamble was not a claim limitation and that the asserted patent was invalid under section 102(b) as anticipated. The claimed invention was directed to a scratch-off label. The preamble of a representative claim read: "A scratch-off label for permitting a user to write thereon without the use of a marking implement, comprising . . . ."[42]

The Federal Circuit rejected Griffin's argument that the "for permitting" language in the preamble should have been construed as a claim limitation. The court found that the

---

38. *Id.* at 780.
39. *Id.* at 781.
40. *Id.* at 782.
41. 599 F.3d 1290 (Fed. Cir. 2010).
42. *Id.* at 1292.

preamble "only added an intended use, namely, that the scratch-off layer may be used for writing."[43] The court also held that the preamble was not relied on during prosecution to distinguish the claimed invention from the prior art. Indeed, during prosecution, the applicants attested that a "writing means," a term that appeared in an earlier claim, was not a limitation of the amended claims.

The court disagreed with the dissenting opinion's suggestion that "the presumption against reading a statement of purpose in the preamble as a claim limitation is inapplicable because the body of the claim makes no sense without the preamble's reference to a 'label.'"[44] The majority explained that "the mere fact that a structural term in the preamble is part of the claim does not mean that the preamble's statement of purpose or other description is also part of the claim."[45]

In a dissenting opinion, Judge Newman opined that the preamble should be construed as a claim limitation. She did not view the preamble as merely a statement of purpose or use because the features in the preamble were relied on in the specification and prosecution history to distinguish the claimed invention from the prior art. She also disagreed with the majority's suggestion that there is a presumption that preamble language is irrelevant to claim scope.

Specification

General Language Did Not Trump Specific Language

In *Silicon Graphics, Inc. v. ATI Technologies, Inc.,*[46] the Federal Circuit affirmed the jury's decision that certain claims of the patent-in-suit were not invalid but vacated and remanded the district court's decision of noninfringement on summary judgment.[47]

Silicon Graphics, Inc. (SGI) asserted that ATI Technologies, Inc. (ATI) indirectly infringed its patent, which teaches a graphics system and process that produces three-dimensional images, and is of the type used to animate movies such as Toy Story and Wall-E. The district court granted ATI's motion for summary judgment of noninfringement on certain claims because its construction of those claims precluded direct infringement by ATI's customers. The jury, however, found the rest of the asserted claims to be valid.

On appeal, SGI challenged the district court's decision to grant summary judgment in favor of ATI. In particular, SGI argued that the district court misconstrued three claim terms in the patent: (1) "a rasterization process"; (2) "scan conversion"; and (3) "s10e5." As to the first term, the Federal Circuit reversed the district court's construction because the patent's specification explicitly taught that "rasterization" consisted of multiple processes, whereas the district court had defined the term to constitute a single process. Given that "the specification define[s] the terms in controlling terms," the Federal Circuit reversed the district court's construction.[48] As to the second term, the Federal Circuit affirmed the district court's construction of "scan conversion" because it was supported by

---

43. *Id.* at 1294.
44. *Id.* at 1294–95.
45. *Id.* at 1295.
46. 607 F.3d 784 (Fed. Cir. 2010).
47. *Id.* at 786.
48. *Id.* at 790 (citing Phillips v. AWH Corp., 415 F.3d 1303, 1316 (Fed. Cir. 2005)).

the specification. As the Federal Circuit explained, "general language in the specification permitting some operations to be done in [a certain way] does not work to contradict the specific language that requires scan conversion in [another way]."[49] Beyond explaining what the specification taught, the Federal Circuit noted what the specification did not teach. For example, the specification never stated that the scan conversion permitted operation to be done along the same lines as the general language. As to the third term, the Federal Circuit reversed the district court's claim construction, because the district court improperly imported limitations into the claim from an embodiment, which is not permitted unless the specification makes it clear that the inventor intended to limit the claim.

ATI, meanwhile, argued on appeal that the jury's finding of validity was incorrect. Here, however, the Federal Circuit upheld the jury's finding of validity because the prior art failed to disclose each and every element of the claimed invention. Furthermore, the Federal Circuit held that the jury had sufficient evidence in the record to support its decision, especially in light of the fact that SGI was able to discredit the testimony of one of ATI's experts.

Extrinsic Sources

Prior Art

District Court Erred in Including Structures in Cited Prior Art When Construing Means-Plus-Function Claim

In ***Pressure Products Medical Supplies, Inc. v. Greatbatch Ltd.***,[50] the Federal Circuit held that the district court could revise its claim construction during trial, but found that, under the facts presented, the revised construction of the term "means for permitting removal" was erroneous.

The patents-in-suit related to a device known as an introducer, which the court described as "a device that permits a surgeon to place and remove catheters or pacemaker leads into blood vessels during surgical procedures."[51] The disputed limitation required "means for permitting removal of said hemostatic valve and introducer sheath from said lead or catheter disposed therethrough without requiring said introducer sheath and hemostatic valve to be removed from an end of said lead or catheter."[52] The magistrate judge ruled "means for permitting removal" required a claim construction under 35 U.S.C. § 112, ¶ 6, and that the claimed function corresponded to "score lines defined in the hemostatic valve and introducer sheath, and equivalents thereof."[53] The magistrate judge construed the term "score lines," which appeared in five dependant claims in one of the patents-in-suit, as "one or more line(s) defined in the hemostatic valve and introducer sheath."[54]

During trial, it became evident that there was a dispute over the district court's construction of the term "score line." Accordingly, at the close of the patentee's proof, the district

---

49. *Id.* at 791–92.
50. 599 F.3d 1308 (Fed. Cir. 2010). A five-judge panel heard the appeal.
51. *Id.* at 1311.
52. *Id.* at 1312.
53. *Id.*
54. *Id.* at 1313.

court revised the construction of "score line" and held that this term meant a "linear perforation; slit; slot; tab; line; severing; weakening; or tear that can be partial or complete."[55]

Although the Federal Circuit was "somewhat sympathetic" to Defendant Enpath's argument that this late adjustment in claim construction prejudiced its defense, the Federal Circuit noted that the district court's revision to its claim construction was made early enough in the trial to allow Enpath to adjust its arguments. Further, the Federal Circuit found that the district court's supplemental definition of a claim term during trial was not "a fundamental procedural flaw that jeopardizes the jury's verdict."[56] The Federal Circuit also found that the district court correctly determined that, absent a supplemental definition of "score line," the jury might improperly define this term on its own.

The Federal Circuit held that the district court erred in its revised construction of "score line." The Federal Circuit found that the district court erroneously included the structures disclosed within a "laundry list of prior art references" within its construction of "score line."[57] The Federal Circuit explained that "[t]rial courts cannot look to the prior art, identified by nothing more than its title and citation in a patent, to provide corresponding structure for a means-plus-function limitation."[58] Accordingly, the Federal Circuit remanded the case in light of the magistrate judge's construction of score line.

The patentee argued that the trial court's construction was proper under the doctrine of claim differentiation because the means-plus-function element must encompass structures other than score lines, which are claimed in other claims. The Federal Circuit disagreed, noting that "a means-plus-function claim element already includes structures other than the corresponding structure explicitly described in the specification, namely, equivalents of the corresponding structure."[59]

In a dissenting opinion, Judge Newman indicated that she would affirm the district court's claim construction. In her view, the district court properly construed "means for permitting removal" in light of the knowledge reflected in the prior-art references cited in the specification.

PROCEDURES

Northern District of Illinois Adopts Local Patent Rules

Local Patent Rules (LPRs) for the Northern District of Illinois (NDIL) were published with comments due on May 22, 2009. A modified set of LPRs was adopted on September 24, 2009, with an effective date of October 1, 2009. A committee that included Chief Judge James F. Holderman, Judge Matthew F. Kennelly, Judge James B. Zagel, Judge Amy J. St. Eve, and practitioners drafted the LPRs, which were adopted on September 24, 2009, and took effect on October 1, 2009.[60]

---

55. *Id.* at 1314.
56. *Id.* at 1316.
57. *Id.* at 1316–17.
58. *Id.* at 1317.
59. *Id.* at 1318.
60. A copy of the full set of rules is available at http://www.ilnd.uscourts.gov/home/
_assets/_documents/Rules/localpatentrules-preamble.pdf.

The NDIL LPRs were promulgated to permit greater predictability and planning for the court and litigants, and to anticipate and address many procedural issues that commonly arise in patent cases.[61] The new rules apply to all cases filed after October 1, 2009, and to earlier-filed cases at the court's discretion.[62] In general, the NDIL LPRs establish a schedule from initial disclosures to the completion of discovery that spans a period of approximately two years. A few of the new NDIL LPRs are summarized below.

(1) *Default Protective Order Provided.*[63] The NDIL LPRs provide for a default protective order that is deemed to be in effect as of the date for each party's Initial Disclosures. Either party can move the court to modify the protective order for good cause with no effect on the timing of disclosures required by the LPRs.

(2) *Meaningful Document Production to Accompany Meaningful Initial Disclosures.*[64] The NDIL LPRs generally require the exchange of initial disclosures within fourteen days after the defendant files its answer or other response. The initial disclosures include meaningful production of documents to allow the parties-in-suit to file appropriately detailed infringement contentions within fourteen days after the initial disclosures.

(3) *Detailed Initial Infringement Contentions Required.*[65] Among other things, the accuser's initial infringement contentions must include the identification of each claim allegedly infringed, matched with specific accused instrumentalities (identified by name) of the opposing party.

(4) *Claim Construction Proceedings toward the End of Fact Discovery.*[66] The NDIL LPRs generally deal with claim construction proceedings toward the end of fact discovery. Although the lawyers and judges who drafted the rules considered earlier and later timing, the decision to place the claims construction proceedings near the end of fact discovery reflects the belief that the rules will allow sufficient time for the parties to identify and focus on the outcome determinative claim terms. Consistent with this philosophy is the LPR's default limit of no more than ten disputed terms or phrases.

Another noteworthy rule concerns the requirement that an accused infringer must file the first and last claim construction briefs. This rule provides for consecutive, as opposed to simultaneous, briefs with the expectation that consecutive briefing is "more likely to promote a meaningful exchange regarding the contested points."[67]

---

61. N.D. Ill. Pat. R. Preamble.
62. N.D. Ill. Pat. R. 1.1.
63. N.D. Ill. Pat. R. 1.4. *See* N.D. Ill. Pat. R. Appendix B for a copy of the default protective order.
64. N.D. Ill. Pat. R. 2.1.
65. N.D. Ill. Pat. R. 2.2, & Preamble.
66. N.D. Ill. Pat. R. 4.1, 4.2, & Preamble.
67. N.D. Ill. Pat. R. 4.2, Comment.

FORMAT

Transitional Phrases

Signal "Comprising" Does Not Render Claim Anticipated by Device That Lacks the Claimed Limitation

In *In re Skvorecz*,[68] the Federal Circuit reversed a finding by the BPAI that claims in a reissue application were anticipated by a prior-art patent.

The reissue application at issue related to a wire chafing stand, which is used to support chafers (devices for maintaining hot food outside the kitchen). As the specification explained, wire chafing stands are nested together for transportation and storage. The nested stands frequently wedge into one another and are difficult to separate. The patent discloses an improved stand, which has an "indent" or "offset" at the upper end of the wire legs to prevent significant wedging.

After his patent application was allowed, Mr. Skvorecz filed a reissue application seeking reissuance of several claims. Claim 1 of the reissue application was to: "A wire chafing stand comprising a first rim of wire steel . . . and having at least two wire legs with each wire leg having two upright sections interconnected with one another . . . and further comprising a plurality of offsets located either in said upright sections of said wire legs on in said first rim for laterally displacing each wire leg relative to said first rim . . . ."[69]

The BPAI sustained the reissue examiner's rejection of claims 1 and 2 for anticipation based on a figure in the prior art. On appeal, the USPTO argued that claim 1 of the reissue application could be construed to include wire legs without offsets because the claim used the open-ended transition term "comprising." The USPTO argued that the use of the word "comprising" permitted the Skvorecz structure to include legs without offsets, although claim 1 indicated that "said wire legs" and "each wire leg" have offsets.

The Federal Circuit noted that, during examination, claims should be given their broadest reasonable interpretation "to facilitate exploring the metes and bounds to which the applicant may be entitled, and thus to aid in sharpening and clarifying the claims during the application stage, when claims are readily changed."[70] Furthermore, the Federal Circuit noted that this practice might also be useful during reissue examinations. However, the practice "does not include giving claims a legally incorrect interpretation."[71]

The Federal Circuit rejected the USPTO's reading of the claim, explaining that the signal "comprising" means that "the device may contain elements in addition to those explicitly mentioned in the claim," and the signal "does not render a claim anticipated by a device that contains less (rather than more) than what is claimed."[72] Because the Federal Circuit interpreted the claim to state that "each wire leg" has an offset, the Federal Circuit found that it was improper to interpret the signal "comprising" to mean that all of the wire legs in the Skvorecz claim need not have offsets. The prior art, which does not have an

---

68. 580 F.3d 1262 (Fed. Cir. 2009).
69. *Id.*
70. *Id.*
71. *Id.* at 1267.
72. *Id.* at 1267–68.

offset in each wire that serves as a leg, therefore does not anticipate the Skvorecz claim. Accordingly, the Federal Circuit reversed the anticipation rejection.

Common Terms

Claim Construction Properly Excluded a Preferred Embodiment

In ***Baran v. Medical Device Technologies, Inc.,***[73] the Federal Circuit reviewed a summary judgment of noninfringement for Medical Device and other defendants in a suit brought by Plaintiff Dr. Gregory Baran for infringement of patents for biopsy instruments.

The subject matter at issue was a biopsy needle having a needle-like structure, known as a stylet. The stylet is surrounded by a cylindrical structure, known as a cannula. The cannula is retractable against spring pressure to expose one end of the stylet. Once retracted, a clasp-like structure locks the cannula in the retracted position. The stylet can then be inserted into the patient's body. After the stylet is inserted in to the patient's body, the user can press the ends of the clasp-like structure causing the spring pressure to be released and the cannula to be push forward with sufficient force to also enter the patient. The entire biopsy needle is then removed from the patient, thereby extracting a biopsy sample.

The Federal Circuit's opinion reviewed the claim construction analysis underlying the grant of summary judgment. It first considered the district court's construction of the term "detachable." In the patent, the plaintiff claimed a cannula and "a stylet means . . . said stylet means being detachable from said cannula." The district court had construed the term "detachable" as meaning "capable of being separate or withdrawn from the cannula *without loss or damage.*"[74]

The plaintiff alleged error because the claim as construed did not cover one of the preferred embodiments disclosed in the patent. The patent disclosed both a multiple use biopsy needle and a single use biopsy needle. However, in the multiple-use biopsy needle, the stylet was described as detachably engaged and capable of easy removal. On the other hand, the description of the single use embodiment indicated that the stylet was adhesively bonded to the cannula. The Federal Circuit agreed that the use of "detachably engaged" with the multiple-use embodiment, and the use of "adhesively bonded" with the single-use embodiment, suggested that the patentee intended detachable to mean capable of removal or separation without breaking or causing damage. The Federal Circuit noted that its construction of detachable was consistent with the plain meaning of "detachable" reflected in several dictionary definitions. The Federal Circuit concluded that it was of no consequence that the claim construction excluded a preferred embodiment, noting that it is quite common that different claims in a patent cover different embodiments in the patent. Because the claim terms "detachable" and "releasably" were used interchangeably by the patentee, the Federal Circuit agreed with the district court that the claim terms had the same meaning.

---

73. 616 F.3d 1309 (Fed. Cir. 2010).
74. *Id.* at 1312.

The Federal Circuit also reviewed construction of the term, "release means for retaining." At issue was whether the "means for retaining" must also perform the function of releasing, or merely be capable of releasing (i.e., releasable). In the context of the patent, "release means for retaining" was held to tie both the release function and the retention function to the means-plus-function limitation. Accordingly, the Federal Circuit found no error in construction of "release means for retaining."

The Federal Circuit also considered whether there was a material issue of disputed fact that the accused structure was the same or equivalent to the corresponding structure set forth in the specification pursuant to section 112, paragraph 6. The Federal Circuit agreed with the district court that the accused structure and the corresponding structure were substantially different, and that summary judgment was appropriate. Therefore, the district court did not err in concluding that the accused structure was not equivalent to the disclosed structure.

The Federal Circuit further held that the district court did not err in striking expert opinion portions of the plaintiff's declaration in opposition to the motion for summary judgment. It found that the district court was justified in doing so because although the plaintiff may not have been required to prepare an expert report under Federal Rule of Civil Procedure 26(a)(2)(B), that did not exempt the plaintiff from the district court's case management deadlines once the plaintiff wrote such a report. Accordingly, the Federal Circuit agreed that the district court did not err in striking of most of plaintiff's declaration.

CHAPTER 3

CONDITIONS FOR PATENTABILITY

The prerequisites for patentability received renewed attention by courts this past year.

In *Bilski v. Kappos,* the long-awaited U.S. Supreme Court decision, the Court rejected the Federal Circuit's machine-or-transformation test as the sole test for patent-eligible subject matter under 35 U.S.C. § 101. Following the *Bilski* decision, the Court granted certiorari in *Prometheus Laboratories, Inc. v. Mayo Collaborative Services,* a case in which the Federal Circuit had applied the machine-or-transformation test to determine that methods for calibrating drug dosages were patentable subject matter. The Court vacated the Federal Circuit's decision and remanded the case back to the Federal Circuit for reconsideration in view of its discussion in *Bilski.*

Utility was at issue in *Association for Molecular Pathology v. USPTO.* The U.S. District Court for the Southern District of New York found that method and composition of matter claims directed to isolated human genes were unpatentable, nonstatutory subject matter.

Turning to the novelty requirement, courts examined a number of facets of 35 U.S.C. § 102. Patentees were cautioned against early publication and early sale in a number of cases. In *In re Lister,* the Federal Circuit held that a deposit copy filed with the U.S. Copyright Office in connection with obtaining a copyright registration became a "printed publication" under section 102(b) when the full title became keyword searchable in the Westlaw and Dialog databases. Furthermore, in *Iovate Health Sciences, Inc. v. Bio-Engineered Supplements & Nutrition, Inc.,* the Federal Circuit affirmed the district court's grant of summary judgment on the issue of invalidity because the claimed method for enhancing muscle growth was disclosed in a magazine advertisement more than one year before the critical date. In *Delaware Valley Floral Group, Inc. v. Shaw Rose Nets, LLC,* the Federal Circuit held that a patent for producing larger rose heads was invalid under the on-sale bar, where the only admissible evidence established that a product produced using the patented process was commercially sold, and the invention was ready for patenting more than one year prior to the filing date of the patent application.

Several courts found that patents were anticipated based upon disclosures in earlier patents. In *Therasense, Inc. v. Becton, Dickinson & Co.,* the Federal Circuit clarified that, for a claim to be anticipated, a single prior-art reference must expressly or inherently disclose not only each claim element, but also the claimed arrangement or combination of those elements. Further, in *Orion IP, LLC v. Hyundai Motor America,* the Federal Circuit, using the Fifth Circuit's de novo review standard of a denial of JMOL, reversed a jury determination that claims were not anticipated by the prior art.

The Federal Circuit also articulated the standard for the date at which a patent could be used as prior art against other applications. In *In re Giacomini,* the Federal Circuit held that a U.S. patent based on a provisional application is a reference against other applicants as of its provisional filing date.

The nonobviousness requirement under 35 U.S.C. § 103 was also addressed by the Federal Circuit. In *Fresenius USA, Inc. v. Baxter International, Inc.*, the Federal Circuit reversed the trial court's grant of JMOL setting aside a verdict of obviousness because there was substantial evidence in support of the jury's implicit conclusion that the combination of prior-art references taught the claimed invention. In *George M. Martin Co. v. Alliance Machine Systems International LLC*, the Federal Circuit affirmed the lower court's decision finding the disputed patent obvious at the time of invention in light of strong evidence of obviousness and near-simultaneous invention.

Conversely, in *B-K Lighting, Inc. v. Fresno Valves & Castings, Inc.*, the Federal Circuit partially reversed the district court's grant of summary judgment of invalidity based on obviousness, holding that the presence of conflicting expert affidavits created a genuine issue of material fact precluding summary judgment. Similarly, in *Source Search Technologies, LLC v. LendingTree, LLC*, the Federal Circuit vacated the district court's grant of summary judgment of infringement and invalidity for obviousness. The court, however, agreed with the district court's findings that LendingTree's Web site met the "goods and services" limitation and that the claim at issue was not indefinite.

In *King Pharmaceuticals, Inc. v. Eon Labs, Inc.*, the Federal Circuit concluded that, when prior art teaches taking an effective therapeutic amount of a drug with food, the prior art also inherently includes the natural effect of increased bioavailability of the drug. The Federal Circuit concluded that the additional step of informing a patient of the increased bioavailability effect cannot convert an otherwise known method into a new patentable method absent a nonobvious functional relationship of the informing step to the method.

The presence or lack of secondary indicia proved to be a common ground for making an obviousness determination. In *Media Technologies Licensing, LLC v. The Upper Deck Co.*, the Federal Circuit affirmed the district court's grant of summary judgment that two patents relating to sports/memorabilia trading cards were invalid under 35 U.S.C. § 103(a) and that secondary considerations did not overcome the prima facie case of obviousness. Similarly, in *Rolls-Royce v. United Technologies Corp.*, the Federal Circuit addressed the proper standard of obviousness regarding an interference-in-fact inquiry. In *In re Lackey*, the Federal Circuit found that, absent a showing of unexpected results or other indicia of nonobviousness, one of ordinary skill would easily substitute a known metal discussed in one reference to form the structure taught in a different reference.

Conversely, in *Trimed, Inc. v. Stryker Corp.*, the Federal Circuit held that the district court erred in summarily accepting the accused infringer's statement of facts, relying on "common sense" to support a conclusion of obviousness without articulating a basis for invalidating the patent based on obviousness.

Despite the decision in *Trimed*, common sense served as a basis for finding obviousness in a number of cases. In *Wyers v. Master Lock, Co.*, the Federal Circuit reversed a jury verdict of nonobviousness, resorting to common sense to make factual findings. Similarly, in *Perfect Web Technologies, Inc. v. InfoUSA, Inc.*, the Federal Circuit held that common sense may be used to invalidate a patent, provided the reasoning is articulated.

Turning to obviousness-type double patenting, in *Boehringer Ingelheim International GmbH v. Barr Laboratories, Inc.*, the Federal Circuit held that a retroactive terminal disclaimer was ineffective to cure a finding of invalidity based on obviousness-type double patenting. In *Sun Pharmaceutical Industries, Ltd. v. Eli Lilly & Co.*, the Federal Circuit held that a claim to a method of using a composition was invalid under obviousness-type double patenting because it was not patentably distinct from an earlier claim to the identical composition in a parent patent, where the specification of the earlier patent disclosed multiple uses of the compound, including the use claimed in the later patent. The court also found that, for purposes of undertaking such a comparison, a court should examine the specification of the issued patent, not the specification that existed as of the effective filing date of the issued patent. Further, in *Amgen, Inc. v. F. Hoffmann-La Roche Ltd.*, the Federal Circuit held that for purposes of overcoming obviousness-type double patenting, continuation patent applications are not entitled to the safe harbor provision of 35 U.S.C. § 121, which applies solely to divisional requirements.

Finally, the Federal Circuit addressed priority chains in patent continuation applications. In *Encyclopædia Britannica, Inc. v. Alpine Electronic of America, Inc.*, the Federal Circuit held that a proper priority claim is required for all applications in a priority chain, not just the final issued patent.

PATENTABLE SUBJECT MATTER

Processes and Methods

Machine-or-Transformation Test Is Not Sole Test for Patent-Eligible Subject Matter

In **Bilski v. Kappos,**[1] the U.S. Supreme Court affirmed a Federal Circuit ruling that Bilski's claimed invention was not patent-eligible subject matter under 35 U.S.C. § 101, but rejected the Federal Circuit's reasoning.

Bilski filed a patent application claiming an invention that would allow buyers and sellers of commodities to protect against the risk of price changes. The invention involved initiating a series of transactions between a commodity provider and consumers of the commodity and initiating a series of transactions between the commodity provider and those having a risk position that was opposite to the consumers. The invention could be used in the energy market to protect against fluctuations in energy demand.

The examiner rejected the application under section 101 as being directed to nonpatent-eligible subject matter. The BPAI and a divided Federal Circuit affirmed.

Under section 101, patent-eligible subject matter must fall into one or more of four categories, namely, processes, machines, manufactures, or compositions of matter. Thus, certain subject matter, by its nature, is not eligible for patent protection regardless of novelty and nonobviousness. In agreeing that Bilski's claimed invention was not directed to patent-eligible subject matter, the Federal Circuit used what has been referred to as the machine-or-transformation test. Under that test, a process is patent-eligible if it is either tied to a particular machine or apparatus or transforms a particular article to another state or thing. The machine-or-transformation test was developed out of concern that a patented process could be read to cover purely human activity, such as a mental process for solving a problem. Significantly, the Federal Circuit ruled that the machine-or-transformation test was the *only* test for determining patentability of a process under section 101.

---

1.   130 S. Ct. 3218 (2010).

In affirming the Federal Circuit's judgment, the U.S. Supreme Court explored three issues: (1) whether the machine-or-transformation test was the proper standard; (2) whether business method patents are patent eligible at all; and (3) whether Bilski's patent application claimed patent-eligible subject matter.

The Court first observed that the categories of section 101 were intended to be broad. In fact, the Court noted that there were only three categories of previously recognized exceptions to the broad scope of section 101: laws of nature, physical phenomena, and abstract ideas. Moreover, the Court majority noted that the categories enumerated in section 101 were to be interpreted according to their plain meaning. Additionally, "process" is defined in section 100(b). The courts are not to use the three categorical exceptions to deviate from the plain meaning of the statutory categories of inventions.

With those principles in mind, the Court held that the plain meaning of "process" was not restricted to passing the machine-or-transformation test. It concluded that the Federal Circuit had overly relied on *Cochrane v. Deener* for its reasoning that the machine-or-transformation test was exclusive.[2] Dictum in *Cochrane* noted that a "process" is "an act or a series of acts performed upon the subject matter to be transformed and reduced to a different state or thing."[3] However, the Court concluded that its later cases had limited the foregoing definition as a helpful but nonexclusive clue, explaining that the Federal Circuit remained free to develop "other limiting criteria that further the purposes of the Patent Act and are not inconsistent with its text."[4]

The Court next turned to whether business methods were altogether excluded from the statutory categories of patent-eligible subject matter. It again reasoned that the plain and ordinary meaning of the term "process" could include some business methods and exclude other business methods. Additionally, the Court reasoned that business methods themselves were a vague category that could include technological advances for conducting business more effectively.

The Court observed that the Patent Act explicitly recognized the existence of business method patents in 35 U.S.C. § 273. The Court noted that the Federal Circuit first recognized the validity of business method patents in *State Street Bank & Trust Co. v. Signature Financial Group, Inc.*[5] Shortly thereafter, Congress passed section 273, establishing a defense of prior use against assertion of a method patent. For only the purposes of this prior-use defense, "method" was defined as "a method of doing or conducting business."[6]

The Court reasoned that the later-passed section 273 could not change the meaning of section 101. However, interpretation of section 101 to categorically exclude business methods would render section 273 meaningless, contrary to a long established rule of statutory interpretation. The rule applies, the Court noted, even though section 273 was passed long after section 101. Additionally, although section 273 may very well have been passed in response to *State Street Bank*, the subjective intent of legislators cannot overcome such a long established rule. Accordingly, the Court concluded that business method patents could not be excluded from section 101.

---

2.   Cochrane v. Deener, 94 U.S. 780, 788 (1877).
3.   *Id.*
4.   *Bilski*, 130 S. Ct. at 3231.
5.   149 F.3d 1368 (Fed. Cir. 1998).
6.   35 U.S.C. § 273(a)(3) (1999).

Justice Scalia joined Chief Justice Roberts and Justices Kennedy, Thomas, and Alito in their reasoning that categorical exclusion of business method patents would render section 273 meaningless. Justice Scalia refused to join Justices Roberts, Kennedy, Thomas, and Alito in their reasoning rejecting a categorical rule limiting patents to only areas contemplated by Congress because section 101 is a "'dynamic provision designed to encompass new and unforeseen inventions,'"[7] regardless of section 273. Concurring in the judgment, Justices Stevens, Ginsburg, Breyer, and Sotomayor wrote a lengthy refutation of the "dynamic provision" arguments raised by Roberts, Kennedy, Thomas, and Alito. Because Justice Scalia did not join either side's opinion on the "dynamic provision" issue (leaving a four-to-four split among the Court), this portion of Kennedy, Roberts, Thomas, and Alito's opinion is not controlling.

Lastly, the Court examined whether the patent application in question fell into the recognized exceptions to section 101, by reviewing three prior cases, *Gottschalk v. Benson*,[8] *Parker v. Flook*,[9] and *Diamond v. Diehr*.[10]

The invention at issue in *Benson* was a process for converting binary coded decimal into pure binary form on a computer using a mathematical formula. The process, according to the Court, used no more than conventional processes. The Court concluded that the claimed process was not patent eligible because, as a practical matter, it resulted in a patent on the underlying formula.

The invention in *Flook* was a chemical conversion process in which the only distinguishing feature from the prior art was a mathematical formula. Although the invention was limited to the petrochemical industry, the invention apart from the mathematical formula was neither novel nor nonobvious. According to the Court, adding "insignificant postsolution activity" could not circumvent the prohibition of patenting abstract ideas.

The invention in *Diehr* was a previously unknown method for processing rubber that used a computer for calculating a mathematical formula to complete some of the steps. The Court concluded that although an abstract idea could not be patented, application of an abstract idea to a known structure or process could be patentable. The Court emphasized that rather than delineating the old and new elements of the invention, the claimed invention should be viewed as a whole. The Court held that the claimed invention was to an industrial process, rather than to a mathematical formula.

In view of those cases, the Court found Bilski's claimed invention was to a well-known abstract idea of hedging risk to the energy market. Accordingly, the majority concluded that Bilski's invention was directed to an abstract idea and therefore not patent eligible.

In conclusion, although the Court disagreed that the machine-or-transformation test is the sole test, it left open the door for the Federal Circuit to establish other limiting criteria, so long as they are consistent with the text of section 101.

Although the Court unanimously agreed that Bilski's claimed invention was not patentable, the Court was divided on a number of issues, particularly whether business meth-

---

7. *Bilski*, 130 S. Ct. at 3227 (quoting J.E.M. Ag Supply, Inc. v. Pioneer Hi-Bred Int'l, Inc., 534 U.S. 124, 135 (2001)).

8. 409 U.S. 63 (1972).

9. 437 U.S. 584 (1978).

10. 450 U.S. 175 (1981).

ods were patent eligible. Justice Stevens, joined by three others wrote in a concurring opinion that business methods should not be patent eligible. Justice Stevens wrote extensively about the historical understanding that business methods were not considered processes, up until the *State Street* decision. Justice Stevens wrote that the motivations for passing section 273 were relevant. In his view, section 273 expressly provides a *defense* to an assertion of a business method patent. Accordingly, Justice Stevens reasoned that Congressional intent was to *limit* the scope of the *State Street* decision. Therefore, in Justice Stevens's view, it would be counter-intuitive to interpret section 273, which was passed to limit the impact of business methods, to endorse business methods. According to Justice Stevens, Congress certainly would not have passed section 273 had Congress known at the time that section 273 would be later used to uphold business method patents.

Methods for Calibrating Drug Dosages Held to Be Patentable Subject Matter under the Machine-or-Transformation Test

In *Prometheus Laboratories, Inc. v. Mayo Collaborative Services*,[11] the Federal Circuit held that the claimed methods of calibrating thiopurine drug dosages constituted patent-eligible subject matter. The district court had granted summary judgment of invalidity under 35 U.S.C. § 101, finding that the claimed methods were unpatentable, natural phenomena. The Federal Circuit reversed the judgment, concluding instead that the claims were directed to patentable, transformative methods of treatment.

The patents-in-suit claimed methods of optimizing therapeutic efficacy and reducing toxicity by administering a thiopurine drug to a subject, and then determining the levels of the drug's metabolites in the subject. The amount of drug to be administered could then be increased or decreased based on the levels of the drug's metabolites in the subject.

Prometheus marketed a test that used the technology covered by the patents at issue. Mayo formerly purchased and used Prometheus's test, but in 2004, announced it would be using and selling its own test. Mayo's test measured the same metabolites as Prometheus's test, but used different levels to determine whether the amount of drug to be administered should be increased or decreased. On June 15, 2004, Prometheus sued Mayo for patent infringement, and shortly thereafter, Mayo rescinded its announcement and did not launch its own test.

Mayo filed a motion for summary judgment on the issue of patent invalidity under section 101, and the U.S. District Court for the Southern District of California granted the motion. Prometheus appealed the decision to the Federal Circuit, and on September 16, 2009, the Federal Circuit reversed the summary judgment, finding that the patent was directed to patent-eligible subject matter.

The Federal Circuit, following its machine-or-transformation analysis from *In re Bilski*,[12] noted that a method is patentable if: (1) the method is tied to a particular machine or transforms a particular article; and (2) the machine or transformation is central to the method's purpose. Applying the machine-or-transformation analysis to the claims at issue, the Federal Circuit first concluded that the administering and determining steps of the claimed methods were transformative, and not merely data gathering. The court reasoned

---

11.   581 F.3d 1336 (Fed. Cir. 2009), *vacated*, 130 S. Ct. 3543 (2010).
12.   545 F.3d 943 (Fed. Cir. 2008) (en banc), *cert. granted*, 129 S. Ct. 2735 (2009).

that, although mental steps alone are not patentable, the existence of a mental step in a claim, like the "wherein" clauses in the claims at issue, does not necessarily render a claimed method nontransformative. The Federal Circuit then concluded that the administering and determining steps were part of the treatment regimes and, therefore, central to the claimed methods' purpose of treating the human body.

Following these conclusions, the Federal Circuit held that the claimed methods "squarely [fell] within the realm of patentable subject matter because they 'transform[ed] an article into a different state or thing,' and this transformation [was] 'central to the purpose of the claimed process.'"[13] The Federal Circuit reversed the judgment of the district court, and remanded the case with instructions to deny the motion for summary judgment of invalidity under section 101.

The U.S. Supreme Court granted certiorari in this case, vacated the judgment, and remanded the case back to the Federal Circuit to reconsider the merits in light of its decision in *Bilski v. Kappos.*[14]

Exceptions

Laws of Nature

Method and Composition of Matter Claims on Human Genes Were Unpatentable

In *Association for Molecular Pathology v. USPTO,*[15] Judge Robert W. Sweet of the Southern District of New York ruled in favor of the plaintiffs, granting partial summary judgment that the claims of several patents on BRCA1 and BRCA2 were invalid as encompassing nonstatutory subject matter. In an extensive 156-page opinion, the district court entered a narrow ruling that, although damaging to the University of Utah and its licensee, Myriad Genetics, was not as far-reaching as plaintiffs and their backers, the American Civil Liberties Union and the Public Patent Foundation, had asked.

At issue in this litigation were patent claims reciting compositions of matter relating to isolated human genes, specifically DNA molecules coding for particular polypeptides, which in turn encoded particular amino acid sequences, and methods of detecting a mutation in the BRCA1 or BRCA2 genes for making a diagnosis relating to an increased likelihood of developing breast or ovarian cancer.

The district court granted summary judgment that the composition of matter claims are invalid based on its determination that U.S. Supreme Court precedent contains a prohibition on patenting "products of nature." The court rejected the defendants' argument that the claimed nucleic acids were distinct from the genes resident in human chromosomes by virtue of being "isolated," and the argument that the nucleic acids were not 'products of nature' because they were man-made copies of such genes. The court instead held that the claimed subject matter was unpatentable because genes are the "physical embodiment of [genetic] information."[16] In making its determination, the court seemed

---

13. *Prometheus*, 581 F.3d at 1345.
14. Mayo Collaborative Services v. Prometheus Labs., Inc., 130 S. Ct. 3543 (2010).
15. 702 F. Supp. 2d 181 (S.D.N.Y. 2010).
16. *Id.* at 229.

persuaded by the plaintiffs' arguments that the claims encompassed genetic information, and that this information should be freely available both to individual patients and researchers. The court's treatment of (and emphasis on) the informational aspects of isolated DNA is in marked contrast to how the USPTO and the Federal Circuit have treated these claims as drawn to a chemical compound ("albeit a complex one"[17]) and emphasized traditional notions that isolated and purified chemical compounds are patent eligible. The court disagreed with arguments from defendants and several amicus curiae that attempted to distinguish claims to isolated nucleic acids from genes as they reside in chromosomes, either as a composition of matter or a manufacture. In making its determination, the court was also careful to limit its decision to DNA, expressly avoiding the logical extension of a determination that DNA is an unpatentable "product of nature" to other biological molecules, including antibiotics, antibodies, and vitamins.

The method claims were found invalid under the Federal Circuit's machine-or-transformation test from *In re Bilski*.[18] In view of the U.S. Supreme Court's subsequent decision in *Bilski v. Kappos*, it is likely that the viability of this portion of the decision will await further explication by the Federal Circuit.

The district court declined plaintiffs' invitation to rule on constitutional issues, specifically that gene patents violated the plaintiffs' First and Fourteenth Amendment rights. The court dismissed the constitutional claims against the USPTO, invoking the principle that courts should avoid reaching constitutional questions.

SINGLE INVENTION

Obviousness-Type Double Patenting

Retroactive Terminal Disclaimer Is Ineffective in Overcoming Obviousness-Type Double Patenting Determination

In ***Boehringer Ingelheim International GmbH v. Barr Laboratories, Inc.,***[19] the Federal Circuit reversed the district court's finding of invalidity based on obviousness-type double patenting. The district court held that the filing of a terminal disclaimer after expiration of the parent patent was insufficient to overcome invalidity due to obviousness-type double patenting and that the safe harbor provision of 35 U.S.C. § 121 was inapplicable to remove the parent patent as an invalidating reference.

On appeal, Boehringer contended that its retroactive terminal disclaimer overcame a finding of invalidity based on obviousness-type double patenting. The Federal Circuit disagreed, stating that the "fundamental reason for the rule [of obviousness-type double patenting] is to prevent unjustified timewise extension of the right to exclude."[20] Because Boehringer did not disclaim its rights before the expiration of the parent patent, Boehringer

---

17.   Amgen v. Chigai, 927 F.2d 1200 (Fed. Cir. 1991).

18.   545 F.3d 943 (Fed. Cir. 2008).

19.   592 F.3d 1340 (Fed. Cir. 2010), *reh'g and reh'g en banc denied per curiam*, 603 F.3d 1359 (Fed. Cir. 2010).

20.   *Id.* at 1347 (emphasis and citation omitted).

enjoyed an improper extension of patent rights. The court noted that "[t]here is nothing that Boehringer can do now to 'un-exercise' the right that it has already improperly enjoyed."[21] The Federal Circuit, therefore, held that a retroactive terminal disclaimer was ineffective to cure a finding of invalidity.

The Federal Circuit also considered whether the safe harbor provision of section 121 precludes a finding of obviousness-type double patenting even though the patent resulted from a divisional of a divisional application in which a restriction requirement was entered. The court acknowledged that it had previously determined that "[section] 121 applies specifically to continuing applications deriving from a divisional application filed as a result of a restriction requirement."[22] Accordingly, the court found that the safe harbor provision applies equally to a divisional of a divisional application filed as a result of a restriction requirement. The court further found that section 121 "is not concerned with any overlap in non-elected inventions prosecuted within any particular divisional application or in how any such applications are filed." Instead, "[t]o prevent loss of the safe harbor in dividing out claims to non-elected inventions, what is required is consonance with the restriction requirement."[23]

Dissenting in part, Judge Dyk discussed the scope of the safe harbor provision of section 121. Judge Dyk agreed with the majority's interpretation that section 121 is not limited to the first divisional application filed as a result of the examiner's restriction requirement. However, Judge Dyk found that, in his view, the majority had "misinterpreted both the 'consonance' and 'as a result of' requirements" of section 121.[24]

Defendant Mylan Pharmaceuticals Inc. filed a combined petition for panel rehearing and rehearing en banc, both of which were denied.[25] Judge Gajarsa, joined by Judge Dyk, dissented from the denial of the petition for rehearing en banc stating that the "majority's decision improperly expands the statutory safe harbor provision of 35 U.S.C. § 121 beyond Congress's intended scope . . . is inconsistent with our longstanding precedent, and will work a major change in our jurisprudence."[26]

Use of Compound Not Patentably Distinct in View of Uses Disclosed in Specification of Earlier Patent

In *Sun Pharmaceutical Industries, Ltd. v. Eli Lilly & Co.*,[27] the Federal Circuit affirmed the district court's decision that the asserted claims of one Eli Lilly patent were invalid in view of an earlier-issued Eli Lilly patent under the doctrine of obviousness-type double patenting.

Eli Lilly asserted two patents covering the compound gemcitabine against Sun Pharmaceutical. The '614 patent claimed gemcitabine and a method of using gemcitabine to treat viral infections. In addition to disclosing gemcitabine's utility for antiviral purposes, the specification of the '614 patent included a description of gemcitabine's anticancer utility. The '826 patent claimed a method of using gemcitabine for treating cancer.

---

21. *Id.* at 1348.
22. *Id.* at 1352.
23. *Id.* at 1353–54.
24. *Id.* at 1356 (Dyk, J., dissenting in part).
25. 603 F.3d 1359 (Fed. Cir. 2010) (per curiam).
26. *Id.* at 1360 (Gajarsa, J, dissenting).
27. 611 F.3d 1381 (Fed. Cir. 2010).

The Federal Circuit explained that in prior cases it had found the "claims of a later patent invalid for obviousness-type double patenting where an earlier patent claimed a compound, disclosing its utility in the specification, and [the] later patent claimed a method of using the compound for a use described in the specification of the earlier patent."[28] The court rejected Eli Lilly's attempt to distinguish these cases on the grounds that "the antiviral use provided the essential utility necessary to the patentability of the '614 patent's claim to gemcitabine."[29] The Federal Circuit concluded that its holding in prior cases that a "claim to a method of using a composition is not patentably distinct from an earlier claim to the identical composition in a patent disclosing the identical use extends to any and all such uses disclosed in the specification of the earlier patent."[30]

Finally, the Federal Circuit held the district court did not err in consulting the specification of the issued '614 patent, rather than the specification of an earlier application, when conducting its obviousness-type double patenting analysis. The court found that, where a patent claims a compound, a court performing an obviousness-type double patenting analysis should examine the specification of the issued patent in order to ascertain the coverage of the claim. The court explained that, under those circumstances, "the specification that must be considered in that of the issued patent," not the specification that existed as of the effective filing date of the issued patent.

Continuation Patent Application Is Not Entitled to Safe Harbor Protection of 35 U.S.C. § 121 from Assertions of Double Patenting

In *Amgen, Inc. v. F. Hoffmann-La Roche Ltd.,*[31] the Federal Circuit held that continuation patent applications are not entitled to the safe harbor provision of 35 U.S.C. § 121. Amgen brought a declaratory judgment action against Roche alleging that Roche's product would infringe five Amgen patents if Roche's product were imported into the United States. Roche responded that Amgen's asserted patents were invalid and not infringed. The district court: (1) granted summary judgment of no obviousness-type double patenting on a group of asserted claims that Amgen claimed were entitled to the safe harbor provision; and (2) granted a preverdict JMOL of no obviousness-type double patenting on the remaining claims that the parties agreed were not entitled to the safe harbor provision. The Federal Circuit vacated the district court's JMOL for no obviousness-type double patenting for the claims in three of the five patents, remanding to the district court for further analysis, and affirmed the district court's judgment of no obviousness-type double patenting for the claims in the remaining two patents.

During prosecution, the USPTO subjected Amgen's '298 application to a six-way restriction requirement. Amgen elected one of the inventions for prosecution in the '298 application. However, instead of filing divisional applications directed to the nonelected inventions, Amgen filed two applications that it designated "continuation" applications. Eventually these matured into the five asserted patents. Roche contended that claims in some of the asserted patents were invalid for obviousness-type double patenting in view of

---

28. *Id.* at 1385.
29. *Id.* at 1386.
30. *Id.* at 1387 (internal quotation marks omitted).
31. 580 F.3d 1340 (Fed. Cir. 2009).

claims in other asserted patents. Amgen argued that the safe harbor provision of section 121 shielded the relevant patents from a charge of obviousness-type double patenting.

The safe harbor provision of section 121 protects a divisional application, the original application, or any patent issued on either of them from validity challenges based on a patent issuing on an application subjected to a restriction requirement or on another application filed as a result of a restriction requirement. Roche argued that the safe harbor provision did not apply to the relevant patents here because they issued from continuation applications, not divisional applications.

The court held that only divisional applications, and their descendants, can be eligible for the safe harbor protections under section 121, drawing on the reasoning in *Pfizer, Inc. v. Teva Pharmaceutical USA, Inc.*,[32] In *Pfizer*, the court held that continuation-in-part applications are not entitled to the safe harbor under section 121, based on the statutory text (which refers only to divisional applications) and the legislative history (which refers to divisional applications and makes no suggestion that the safe harbor provision is to be directed at other types of applications). In earlier cases, the Federal Circuit had held that continuation applications fell within the safe harbor, but the continuations at issue there had descended from divisional applications.[33] That was not true of Amgen's continuations. Amgen argued that its continuations should be treated as divisional applications because both applications are limited to the subject matter disclosed in the earlier application (consistent with MPEP § 201.06), unlike a continuation-in-part application. However, the court was not persuaded. As a result, the court vacated the grant of summary judgment of JMOL of no obviousness-type double patenting for the relevant patents and remanded to the district court to question whether the asserted claims of those patents were invalid for obviousness-type double patenting.

Even without the benefit of the safe harbor provision, Amgen still could defend against a double-patenting challenge by showing that the claims of the relevant patents were patentably distinct from the claims of the allegedly invalidating patents. However, the parties disagreed as to whether post-invention evidence could be used in the obviousness-type double patenting inquiry. In particular, Amgen argued that it should be able to prove that the claims at issue were patentably distinct by setting out evidence that there were alternative processes for making the claimed products, even though that evidence was dated after the filing date of the parent, but before the filing date of the continuation. Roche argued that it also should be permitted to present its own evidence from that time period to show the lack of patentable distinctness. The Federal Circuit accepted Amgen's argument, but rejected Roche's argument on the grounds that it contravened 35 U.S.C. § 120. The court did offer a qualification: to the extent that Amgen chose to rely on evidence of alternative processes, Roche would be allowed to rely on subsequent developments in the art in the relevant time period to show that the alternative processes offered by Amgen do not establish patentable distinctness. The court then examined the other claims, which the parties had already agreed were not protected by the safe harbor provisions, and affirmed the district court's JMOL of no obviousness-type double patenting because the claims were patentably distinct.

---

32. 518 F.3d 1353 (Fed. Cir. 2008).

33. Applied Materials, Inc. v. Advanced Semiconductor Materials Am., Inc., 98 F.3d 1563 (Fed. Cir. 1996); Symbol Tech., Inc. v. Opticon, Inc., 935 F.2d 1569 (Fed. Cir. 1991).

NOVELTY

Summary Judgment of Infringement and Invalidity Improper Where Genuine Facts Remained in Dispute

In *Source Search Technologies, LLC v. LendingTree, LLC,*[34] the Federal Circuit vacated and remanded the district court's summary judgment that the patent at issue was infringed but invalid as obvious. The Federal Circuit found that genuine issues of material fact precluded summary judgment on both infringement and invalidity.[35]

Source Search asserted U.S. Patent No. 5,758,328 (the '328 patent) against LendingTree, alleging that Lending Tree's Web site infringed the '328 patent. The invention of the '328 patent—directed to a computerized service for matching buyers with vendors—solved the "too much" or "too little" problem associated with popular search engines.[36] That is, it eliminated the problem of getting too many or too few hits by allowing purchasers to request a quote for standard goods or services through the selection of options in preset menus. Lending Tree's alleged infringing Web site matches prospective borrowers with potential lenders for home, auto, and personal loans.

Following a *Markman* hearing, both parties submitted summary judgment motions and cross motions. The district court granted motions on the issues of infringement and invalidity due to obviousness, but denied the motion on the issue of invalidity due to indefiniteness. Both parties appealed.

The Federal Circuit first considered whether the asserted claim was invalid as obvious. The district court had relied on three e-commerce prior-art references, one article published in the Association of Computing Machinery (ACM) magazine, and a pre-Internet reference known as the "bricks and mortar" prior art. Of the three e-commerce systems, two were parts-procurement services and the third was a document-searching system. The ACM article taught the need for a filtering system between information sources and their users. The "bricks and mortar" prior art related to referral systems, such as home contractor and social-service networks, which use a person rather than a computer to match clients with a goods or services provider.

As a preliminary matter, Source Search contended that estoppel prevented LendingTree from relying on the bricks and mortar prior art because it first cited the reference in a supplemental expert report. The Federal Circuit, however, disagreed, finding no "miscarriage of justice" that required estoppel. As the court noted, Source Search waited nine months to object, conducting full discovery on the reference during that time. Turning to the substance of the obviousness question, the Federal Circuit considered the claim term "quote," which was interpreted to mean "price and other terms of a particular transaction in sufficient detail to constitute an offer capable of acceptance."[37] Analyzing the prior art, the court found that none of the three e-commerce systems returned a "quote." Nor did the bricks and mortar prior art supply a quote; it simply matched clients with contractors and other service providers.

---

34. 588 F.3d 1063 (Fed. Cir. 2009).
35. *Id.* at 1066.
36. *Id.* at 1066–67.
37. *Id.* at 1071.

Furthermore, the court continued, the invention of the '328 patent was not simply a computerized version of the bricks and mortar prior art. Even after computerizing an attorney-referral network, for example, the client would still need to relay details before receiving a quote; these details would likely go directly to the attorney, not the referral service. And even if the prior art contained a quoting feature, the further step of "filtering" was required. Although the ACM article discussed filtering, it did not consider filtering in the purchaser and vendor context. Therefore, the court held, genuine issues of material fact precluded a grant of summary judgment of obviousness.

The Federal Circuit next considered infringement. LendingTree argued that its Web site lacked functions meeting the "request for a quotation" and "goods and services" limitations. Source Search countered that collateral estoppel barred LendingTree from arguing that its Web site did not return "quotes" because, in a prior case, it lost a similar argument relating to "bids." Here, the Federal Circuit agreed with the district court, which refused to apply collateral estoppel, because the prior litigation involved wholly different issues on an unrelated patent. Considering the merits of the question, the court again turned to the meaning of "quote." Some aspects of LendingTree's Web site indicated that the borrower must take further steps after being matched with a lender. Other evidence in the record, however, supported a finding that LendingTree's Web site returned an "offer capable of acceptance." Because genuine issues of fact remained in dispute, the court concluded that the district court erred in granting summary judgment on this specific issue.

The court ended its infringement discussion by considering the "goods and services" limitation, which the district court had construed to mean "standardized articles of trade and performances of work for another."[38] LendingTree argued that its Web site did not offer goods or services, and, even if it did, they were not "standard." The court rejected these arguments, holding that lenders offered a financial service through the Web site and a loan is a "standard" item. Summary judgment, therefore, was proper to the extent that LendingTree's Web site met the "goods and services" limitation.

Finally, the Federal Circuit considered whether the asserted claim was invalid as indefinite. According to LendingTree, the presence of the term "goods or services" added a subjective element to the claim at issue. Because one practicing the claimed invention would have to differentiate between standard and nonstandard goods or services, LendingTree argued, the claim was indefinite. The court disagreed, finding that once a person began practicing the invention and chose the specific market, the nature of the relevant goods or services would become clear. Furthermore, one of ordinary skill is not an automaton, but would understand the markets and system enough to determine what was "standard."[39] The court held, therefore, that the asserted claim was not indefinite and affirmed the district court's summary judgment as to that issue.

Accordingly, the Federal Circuit vacated the district court's grant of summary judgment regarding invalidity and infringement, but affirmed the district court's finding that LendingTree's Web site met the "goods and services" limitation and that the claim was not indefinite.

---

38. *Id.* at 1075.
39. *Id.* at 1076–77 (citing KSR Int'l Co. v. Teleflex Inc., 550 U.S. 398, 421 (2007)).

Technological Contents of Reference

Anticipatory Reference Must Disclose the Arrangement of the Claimed Elements

In ***Therasense, Inc. v. Becton, Dickinson & Co.***,[40] the Federal Circuit clarified what must be disclosed for a reference to anticipate a patent claim. The court held that for a claim to be anticipated, a single prior-art reference must expressly or inherently disclose not only each claim element, but also the claimed arrangement or combination of those elements.[41]

Abbott Diabetes Care, Inc. and Abbott Laboratories (collectively, Abbott) accused Becton, Dickinson & Co.'s and Nova Biomedical Corp.'s (collectively, BD/Nova) product of infringing claims 11 and 12 of Abbott's U.S. Patent No. 5,628,890 (the '890 patent). After a trial, the district court, over Abbott's objection, instructed the jury as follows regarding anticipation:

> [F]or anticipation to apply, it is not necessary that the prior-art reference expressly lay out the elements in the exact way laid out in the claim. Rather, for anticipation, it is sufficient if the single reference would have informed those skilled in the art that all of the claimed elements *could have been arranged* as in the claimed invention.[42]

The jury answered "Yes" in response to special verdict form questions "[h]ave defendants proven by clear and convincing evidence that Claims 11 and 12 of the '890 patent are invalid by reason of anticipation or obviousness?" and "[h]ave defendants proven by clear and convincing evidence that Claims 11 and 12 of the '890 patent are invalid by reason of inadequate written description?"[43] In accordance with the jury's verdict, the district court entered judgment in favor of BD/Nova. The court also denied Abbott's motions for JMOL and for a new trial. Abbott appealed the judgment of invalidity.

On appeal, Abbott argued that the district court's instruction on the law of anticipation was legally erroneous because anticipation requires a single prior-art reference to disclose the same elements in the same way as they are arranged in the claim. Abbott also argued that the jury could not have found the asserted claims obvious or invalid by reason of inadequate written description.

The Federal Circuit agreed with Abbott that the district court's instructions were erroneous because an anticipatory reference must disclose, either expressly or inherently, all of the elements in the same way they are arranged or combined in the claim. "Inherent disclosure" does not mitigate this disclosure requirement. An anticipatory reference inherently discloses an arrangement or combination only when the reference "*necessarily* includes" the unstated arrangement or combination.[44] The mere fact that a certain arrangement

---

40. 593 F.3d 1325 (Fed. Cir. 2010).

41. *Id.* at 1332–33.

42. *Id.* at 1331 (emphasis in original).

43. *Id.* at 1330.

44. *Id.* at 1332 (quoting Transclean Corp. v. Bridgewood Servs., Inc., 290 F.3d 1364, 1373 (Fed. Cir. 2002)).

or combination "could" or "may" result from a given set of circumstances is not suffi-cient.[45] The Federal Circuit therefore found the district court's instruction on the law of anticipation to be legally erroneous.

The court nonetheless upheld the district court judgment because the instruction could not have changed the result. The court found that the asserted claims would have been obvious over a prior-art reference, such that no reasonable jury could have returned a verdict that the claims were not obvious.

In this regard, Abbott argued that the prior art lacked all of the elements claimed in the '890 patent, which is directed to an electrode strip that channels a sample fluid through a directional flow. In particular, Abbott argued that the prior art was missing two claimed elements: (1) "said reference or counter electrode spaced downstream from said working electrode"; and (2) "said covering layer having an aperture for receiving sample."[46] Here, Abbott argued that the prior-art reference, which depicts a strip with three channels hav-ing counter electrodes and working electrodes, lacked the first contested element because the channels not filled up first—the reference or counter electrodes—are upstream from working electrodes. The court explained, however, that Abbott's arguments addressed only the scope of the claims, not the content of the prior art. The claims only required a single counter electrode spaced downstream of a single working electrode. Further, the claims' transitional phrase, "comprising," allows additional counter electrodes to be up-stream of working electrodes. Whichever channel is filled up first, the counter electrode in that channel will be downstream from a working electrode. The court therefore con-cluded that the first contested claim element was present in the prior art.

Abbott also argued that the second contested element—a covering layer having an aperture—was missing from the prior-art reference because one of the reference's figures depicted the aperture elsewhere. The court noted, however, that the claimed arrangement is disclosed and depicted elsewhere in the reference. The court therefore concluded that the second contested element was present in the prior art.

Abbott also argued that its claims were not obvious because the claimed sensor solves a problem still present in the prior art. The court noted, however, that the claims were broad enough to claim devices that do not solve that problem. The court therefore con-cluded that the asserted claims would have been obvious as a matter of law and affirmed the jury's verdict. Having affirmed the verdict of "anticipation or obviousness," the court did not reach Abbott's challenge to the jury's verdict that the patent contained an "inad-equate written description."[47]

Finally, the Federal Circuit dismissed BD/Nova's cross-appeal of the jury's determi-nation that the asserted claims were infringed by BD/Nova's product as improper, because even if the court accepted BD/Nova's arguments entirely, they would not reverse or modify the court's judgment.

45. *See id.* (quoting Cont'l Can Co. USA v. Monsanto Co., 948 F.2d 1264, 1269 (Fed. Cir. 1991)).
46. *See id.* at 1335.
47. *Therasense,* 593 F.3d at 1337.

Priority-Based Prior Art—Section 102(a)

Prior Disclosure in Printed Publication

Increased Bioavailability of Drug, When Taken with Food, Is Inherently Anticipated in Prior Art Recommending Taking Drug with Food, Albeit for a Different Reason

In *King Pharmaceuticals, Inc. v. Eon Labs, Inc.*,[48] the Federal Circuit affirmed the district court's summary judgment of patent invalidity. The Federal Circuit concluded that the asserted claims were inherently anticipated under 35 U.S.C. § 102.

Eon filed two Abbreviated New Drug Applications (ANDAs) seeking approval to market generic metaxalone, a muscle relaxant, prior to expiration of the patents-in-suit. Eon filed the first ANDA in 2001. Then patent owner Elan Pharmaceutical (Elan) marketed a branded version of metaxalone and counter-claimed for infringement of the first patent-in-suit. During pendency of the suit, Elan assigned its patent rights to King. In 2004, Eon filed the second ANDA. In response, King filed suit against Eon for infringing the second patent-in-suit.

Claim 1 of the first patent-in-suit was drawn to "a method of increasing the oral bioavailability of metaxalone" by "administering . . . a therapeutically effective amount of metaxalone . . . with food."[49] The inventors had found that ingesting metaxalone with food allowed better absorption by the body. That benefit was not otherwise known at the time the invention. Other independent claims also described increased bioavailability via administration of metaxalone with food, and dependent claims described limits on the effective amount and timing of metaxalone administration relative to food consumption. Claim 21 included an additional limitation of informing the patient that taking metaxalone with food would increase the drug's bioavailability. Claims of the second patent-in-suit were similar.

There were three prior-art publications in issue authored respectively by Fathie, Albanese and Abrams. Fathie disclosed that nausea resulting from the metaxalone might be reduced by taking the medication with food. Albanese disclosed that administration of metaxalone with meals reduced gastric upset. Abrams similarly disclosed that administering metaxalone three or four times daily with milk or food reduced "gastrointestinal distress."

Thus, Fathie, Albanese and Abrams described taking metaxalone with food but did not specifically describe increased bioavailability. The Federal Circuit agreed with the district court that the preamble of claim 1, describing increased bioavailability of metaxalone, was inherently anticipated by the prior art. Although the prior art did not disclose that taking metaxalone with food increased bioavailability, the patents-in-suit disclosed that increased bioavailability was the natural consequence of taking metaxalone with food. Accordingly, the Federal Circuit concluded that prior art disclosing taking metaxalone with food, albeit for a different purpose, i.e., to address nausea and gastric distress, inherently anticipated the asserted claims.

---

48.   616 F.3d 1267 (Fed. Cir. 2010).
49.   *Id.* at 1270–71.

The district court also had held that claim 21 was invalid under 35 U.S.C. § 101. Relying on *In re Bilski*,[50] the district court had held that "the act of informing another person of the food effect of metaxalone does not transform metaxalone into a different state or thing."[51] However, the Federal Circuit held that the district court had erred in applying *Bilski* by isolating its analysis to the "informing" step rather than construing the claim as a whole. Nevertheless, the Federal Circuit reviewed the remaining record and determined that claim 21 was invalid on alternative grounds. In particular, the Federal Circuit reasoned that "[t]he 'informing' limitation adds no novelty to the method, which is otherwise anticipated by the prior art."[52] In doing so, the Federal Circuit relied on its "printed matter" precedent and observed that "the relevant inquiry here is whether the additional instructional limitation of claim 21 has a 'new and unobvious functional relationship' with the known method of administering metaxalone with food."[53]

King contended that the new and unobvious functional relationship was that the "informing" step increased the likelihood that the patient would take metaxalone with food, thereby increasing efficiency of the method. The Federal Circuit disagreed. The Federal Circuit reasoned that merely informing the patient about the benefits of a drug did not transform the process of taking the drug with food.

Prior Patenting

Every Application in a Priority Chain Must Meet the Statutory Requirements to Be Effective

The Federal Circuit upheld a finding that the patentee's priority claim was defective, and the claims invalid, in *Encyclopædia Britannica, Inc. v. Alpine Electronic of America, Inc.*[54]

The patents-in-suit, U.S. Patent Nos. 7,051,018 and 7,082,437, recited a priority chain as follows:

> Continuation of application No. 10/103,814, filed on Mar. 25, 2002, which is a continuation of application No. 08/202,985, filed on Feb. 28, 1994, now Pat. No. 6,546,399, which is a continuation of application No. 08/113,955, filed on Aug. 31, 1993, now abandoned, which is a continuation of application No. 07/426,917, filed on Oct. 26, 1989, now Pat. No. 5,241,671.[55]

The district court found one application in this priority chain, U. S. Serial No. 08/113,995, to be defective and not entitled to priority to the earlier-filed applications. This application was filed without an oath or declaration or the filing fee, and without page one of the specification. The Office issued a Notice of Incomplete Application, and the applicant petitioned to have the application accepted as of its filing date, asserting that the first

---

50. 545 F.3d 943 (Fed. Cir. 2008), *aff'd sub nom.* Bilski v. Kappos, 130 S. Ct. 3218 (2010).
51. *King*, 616 F.3d at 1277.
52. *Id.* at 1278.
53. *Id.* at 1279.
54. 609 F.3d 1345 (Fed. Cir. 2010).
55. *Id.* at 1347.

page was not necessary to support the claims under 35 U.S.C. § 112. The Office rejected the petition because it was not accompanied by an oath or declaration of the inventors supporting this assertion. The applicant never remedied this defect, and the Office duly determined the application to be abandoned. Prior to receiving the Notice of Abandonment, applicant filed another application, U.S. Serial No. 08/202,985 that claimed priority to all prior applications including Serial No. 08/113,995.

The district court found the priority chain was broken for applicant's failure to recite, or amend the '955 application to recite, the priority claim to the earlier applications. Under these circumstances, the earliest filing date for the patents-in-suit was the '955 application filing date. However, this was more than one year after publication of an International Application corresponding to the earliest application in the priority chain, which the district court found was invalidating prior art under 35 U.S.C. § 102(b).

In an opinion by Judge Moore, joined by Judges Bryson and Gajarsa, the Federal Circuit affirmed, framing the issue as whether 35 U.S.C. § 120 requires an intermediate application in a priority chain to contain a specific reference to the earlier filed application, an issue of first impression for the court. On appeal, defendants proffered three grounds for affirming the district court: (1) that there was no specific reference in the '955 application to the earlier applications, contrary to the express language of section 120; (2) that the '955 application was not co-pending because it was filed on the grant date of the earlier patent in the priority chain; and (3) that the '955 application was not entitled to its filing date because applicant never paid the filing fees or provided the required oath/declaration. The panel identified the phrase "similarly entitled" in the statute as the key issue in its analysis; as used in context in the statute, an application can satisfy the requirement for co-pendency if it is "filed before the patenting or abandonment of or termination of proceedings on . . . an application similarly entitled to the benefit of the filing date of the first application."[56]

The opinion set out the four requirements for co-pendency under section 120: (1) the invention described in the new application must be "disclosed . . . in an application previously filed in the United States"; (2) the application must be "filed by an inventor or inventors named in the previously filed application"; (3) the application must be co-pending with the earlier application, or "filed before the patenting or abandonment of or termination of proceedings on the first application"; and (4) the application must "contain[] or [be] amended to contain a specific reference to the earlier filed application."[57]

The patentee argued these requirements were intended to be applied to the patents-in-suit as the "final" application in the priority chain, and that they are not required for intermediate applications that, in their interpretation of the statute, are "similarly entitled" to the earliest-claimed priority date. Britannica's argument depended on a semantic deconstruction of the statutory language, which interpreted the "specific reference" requirement to be separate from the other three; thus, this requirement was not applicable to applications "similarly entitled" to the asserted priority date.

The panel opinion expressly rejected this interpretation, saying that it contradicted the plain language of the statute. In the court's view, every application in the priority chain must satisfy each of the four statutory requirements for the priority chain to be effective. The opinion also rejected Britannica's contention that its interpretation of the statute occa-

---

56. *Id.* at 1349.
57. *See* 35 U.S.C. § 120 (2006).

sioned no public harm because it was included on the face of the patents-in-suit, noting that a later priority claim cannot be used to cure an earlier, defective one.

Because the panel affirmed the district court's priority determination on statutory grounds, the panel did not reach the other grounds for defective priority argued by defendants. Specifically, "[w]e therefore leave for another day whether filing a continuation on the day the parent issues results in applications that are co-pending as required by the statute."[58]

Prior Application by Another—Section 102(e)

Patent of Another Is Prior Art as of Its Provisional Filing Date

In *In re Giacomini,*[59] the Federal Circuit addressed the question of the effective date as prior art of a U.S. patent that began as a provisional application. Is it the date of the provisional filing, or the date of the later nonprovisional application? The court, in an opinion by Judge Rader, ruled that such a reference is prior art as of the filing date of the provisional application.

Giacomini's application, claiming a method of selectively storing sets of electronic data in a limited-size cache memory, was rejected as anticipated by a U.S. patent to Tran. There was no dispute that Tran disclosed and enabled the method claimed by Giacomini. Tran's nonprovisional U.S. filing date was after Giacomini's filing date, but it was based on a U.S. provisional application filed before Giacomini's filing date. Giacomini contended that, under principles enunciated by the Court of Customs and Patent Appeals' 1966 decision in *In re Hilmer,*[60] Tran's provisional filing date should be used to block other U.S. filers like Giacomini. As prior art, Giacomini contended, Tran should be effective only as of its nonprovisional filing date. The court disagreed.

Judge Rader first noted that any entitlement to the date of a provisional filing is restricted to situations where the provisional contains a disclosure that fully supports the nonprovisional claims at issue, in the sense of the first paragraph of 35 U.S.C. § 112. Section 119(e) provides that a provisional must contain such a disclosure in order to "have the same effect, as to such invention, as though filed on the date of the provisional application . . . ."[61] Here it was undisputed that Tran's disclosure met these requirements.

The court then discussed the rationale for allowing U.S. patents to be effective as prior art as of dates when they were still held secret as applications before the USPTO. Citing back to *Alexander Milburn Co. v. Davis-Bournonville,*[62] Judge Rader noted that the rule stems from the proposition that only the first inventor can obtain a valid patent, and if the subject matter is disclosed in an earlier-filed application of another, the later filer appears not to have been the first inventor and, thus, should not be entitled to a patent.[63] Although the reference in *Milburn* claimed priority from a nonprovisional United States filing date for the reference patent, whereas here the reference's priority was from a

---

58. *Id.* at 1352.
59. 612 F.3d 1380 (Fed. Cir. 2010).
60. 359 F.2d 859 (C.C.P.A. 1966).
61. 35 U.S.C. § 119(e)(1) (2006).
62. 270 U.S. 390, 402 (1926).
63. *Giacomini,* 612 F.3d at 1384.

provisional U.S. application, the court said that should make no difference. The apparent indication of earlier inventorship by the reference patentee is the same whether he has filed a traditional application or a provisional application, provided there is full disclosure in the priority document of the subject matter of interest.

The court next turned to distinguishing *In re Hilmer*, where the foreign priority date of a U.S. patent was ruled unavailable when the patent was sought to be used as prior art against a later filer; it was prior art only as of its U.S. filing date.[64] Here, the Federal Circuit said the situation was different for two reasons. First, Congress amended the patent statute in 1994, long after *Hilmer* was decided, to permit provisional applications to be filed and to have effect from their filing dates. Second, the reference patent in *Hilmer* had a priority date based on a foreign national filing, whereas here the Tran priority date arose from a U.S. filing, albeit a provisional U.S. filing. Foreign priority and priority based on a U.S. filing—whether provisional or nonprovisional—are two different things. The Court of Customs and Patent Appeals drew such a line of demarcation in *In re Klesper*,[65] in which it noted that *Hilmer* clarified that "domestic and foreign filing dates stand on entirely different footings."[66] The court in *Giacomini* relied on that distinction, limiting the *Hilmer* rule to situations where the reference patent's priority is based on a foreign filing. The court therefore affirmed the BPAI's holding that Giacomini's claims were anticipated by Tran.

Prior Art in Relation to Filing Date—Section 102(b)

Patent Invalid under the On-Sale Bar

In ***Delaware Valley Floral Group, Inc. v. Shaw Rose Nets, LLC***,[67] the Federal Circuit affirmed the district court's grant of summary judgment that the patent-in-suit was invalid under the on-sale bar under 35 U.S.C. § 102(b).[68] The Federal Circuit also held that the district court was not required to consider an errata sheet submitted by the inventor that contradicted his previous deposition testimony regarding the date of invention, and that the inventor did not offer sufficient explanation as to why the declaration that he submitted in opposition to summary judgment contradicted his deposition testimony.

In January 1996, Mr. Shaw, the inventor, applied for a patent that claimed a process for producing larger rose heads. In a declaratory judgment suit, Shaw answered the plaintiffs' interrogatories, asserting that he had invented the claimed process in August 1995 and first offered a product using the process around August/September 1995.[69] In a subsequent deposition, however, Mr. Shaw testified eighteen times that he invented the claimed process in 1994, explaining that his interrogatory answer was a "typo error."[70] Mr. Shaw also testified that he and his employees started commercially exploring the roses grown

---

64.   *See Hilmer*, 359 F.2d at 862.
65.   397 F.2d 882 (C.C.P.A. 1968).
66.   *Id.* at 885.
67.   597 F.3d 1374 (Fed. Cir. 2010).
68.   *Id.* at 1376.
69.   *Id.* at 1376–77.
70.   *Id.* at 1377.

using the patented process in September 1994. After Delaware Valley served Shaw with a motion for sanctions and demanded that Shaw withdraw its allegations of infringement due to patent invalidity based on the on-sale bar, Shaw submitted an employee's declaration, stating that the patented process was not refined until the end of 1995. Mr. Shaw also executed, fifty-seven days after his deposition, an errata sheet, where he asserted that the date of invention and commercial sale was 1995, not 1994. After Delaware Valley moved for summary judgment, Mr. Shaw submitted his own declaration, also insisting on 1995 as the date of invention and commercial sales. The district court excluded both declarations and the errata sheet from evidence, granted summary judgment of invalidity, and also denied Shaw's motion for reconsideration.

On appeal, Shaw argued that the district court had erred in excluding evidence that demonstrated genuine issues of material fact with respect to the date of invention and commercial sale and the date in which the claimed process was "ready for patenting." Shaw also challenged the district court's denial of its motion for reconsideration.

The Federal Circuit noted the U.S. Supreme Court's two-part test for the on-sale bar under section 102(b). Under the test, an inventor is barred from obtaining a patent where the patent application is filed more than one year after: (1) the product was sold or offered for sale; and (2) the invention was ready for patenting.

The Federal Circuit first concluded that that the district court did not abuse its discretion when it exclusively relied on Mr. Shaw's deposition testimony to determine the date of conception and commercial sales of products using the patented process. According to the court, Shaw did not attempt to submit an errata sheet to make substantive changes to the deposition testimony until well beyond the thirty days allowed under Federal Rule of Civil Procedure 30(e) and after Delaware Valley moved for sanctions.[71] The Federal Circuit also pointed out that Mr. Shaw, a seasoned deponent, testified eighteen times in his deposition that he had invented the patented process in 1994. With respect to Mr. Shaw's declaration, the court determined that it was submitted solely for the purpose of opposing the motion for summary judgment in an attempt to create a genuine issue of material fact.

The Federal Circuit also concluded that the district court did not abuse its discretion when it excluded the declaration by Shaw's employee, who lacked personal knowledge as to the timing of the invention's conception or commercial sales. According to the court, there was no dispute that the employee started working for Shaw after the commercial sales occurred, whether those sales took place in 1994 or 1995. Therefore, the only admissible record evidence did not raise an issue of fact with respect to the first prong of the on-sale bar test. As for the second prong of the test, the Federal Circuit concluded that Shaw failed to contest at the district court level whether the invention was ready patenting and, thus, waived that argument.

The Federal Circuit thus affirmed the district court's grant of summary judgment based on the on-sale bar under section 102(b), because Shaw failed to raise a genuine issue of material fact surrounding the dates of conception or commercial sales and further failed to dispute that the invention was "ready for patenting."

---

71. *Id.* at 1380.

Prior Public Disclosure

Prior Disclosure in Printed Publication

Deposit Copy with the U.S. Copyright Office Becomes "Publicly Accessible" When Its Entire Title Is Searchable through a Database

In *In re Lister,*[72] the Federal Circuit held that a reference could not constitute a "printed publication" under 35 U.S.C. § 102(b) absent evidence of when that reference became "publicly accessible" in a commercial database, i.e., when a researcher interested in the technology would be able to locate that reference. The BPAI affirmed the examiner's rejection of certain claims of Lister's application under section 102(b) because a reference authored by Lister and registered at the U.S. Copyright Office was considered "publicly accessible," meaning that an interested researcher could have found the reference by searching the Copyright Office's catalog title for relevant terms.

Lister raised two grounds for appeal: (1) the task of traveling to the Library of Congress to inspect the copyrighted reference was too burdensome and, therefore, negated the public accessibility of even a sufficiently indexed reference; and (2) the reference was not a printed publication because there was no evidence that the reference was included in a catalog or index as of the critical date, such that an interested researcher could discover it. Both grounds required the Federal Circuit to consider whether the reference was publicly accessible.

The Federal Circuit rejected Lister's first argument. The court noted that any member of the public, after submitting a proper request, may gain access to a "deposit copy" of a work submitted to the Copyright Office, without any special authorization. The court also reiterated its holding in *In re Hall*[73] that a reference may meet the requirement of being "publicly accessible" even if gaining access was burdensome, such as requiring a significant amount of travel. The Federal Circuit agreed with the board's finding that a local searcher could have been hired by an interested person to inspect a "deposit copy" on their behalf and that it is not necessary to show actual inspection once accessibility was shown.

Addressing the second argument, it was undisputed that there were three relevant databases: the Copyright Office's automated catalog and two commercial databases, Westlaw and Dialog. The automated Copyright Office catalog was not sorted by subject matter and could only be searched by either the author's last name or the first word of the title of the work. Westlaw and Dialog obtained the automated catalog data from the Copyright Office and entered it into their own databases. Users of the Westlaw and Dialog databases could perform keyword searches of the titles, but not the full texts, of the works.

The USPTO conceded at oral argument that the Copyright Office's automated database was insufficient to render the manuscript "publicly accessible" because of the limited search capabilities available. The first word of the title, for example, was "Advanced." With respect to the Dialog and Westlaw databases, unlike the Copyright Office, one could search key words in the title and, thus, search "handicap" and "golf." Dr. Lister argued such key words would have been insufficient to uncover his manuscript. The Federal Circuit disagreed, finding that "[a] reasonably diligent researcher with access to a database

---

72.   583 F.3d 1307 (Fed. Cir. 2009).
73.   781 F.2d 897, 899–900 (Fed. Cir. 1986).

that permits the searching of titles by keyword would be able to attempt several searches using a variety of keyword combinations."[74]

The Federal Circuit found evidence that the reference in question was available on Westlaw and Dialog; however, there was no evidence of when the reference was available, i.e., whether it was available more than one year prior to the critical date.[75] Accordingly, the Federal Circuit vacated and remanded the board's decision.

Claims for Enhancing Muscle Performance Invalid as Anticipated

In *Iovate Health Sciences, Inc. v. Bio-Engineered Supplements & Nutrition, Inc.,*[76] the Federal Circuit affirmed the district court's grant of summary judgment of invalidity, holding the asserted claims of U.S. Patent 6,100,287 (the '287 patent) invalid as anticipated under 35 U.S.C. § 102(b) because the claimed invention was disclosed in a printed publication more than one year before the critical date.[77]

Iovate asserted the '287 patent, which claimed a method of using a dietary supplement "for enhancing muscle performance or recovery from fatigue," against Bio-Engineered Supplements & Nutrition, Inc. (BSN), alleging infringement by certain BSN nutritional products.[78] The district court granted BSN's motion for summary judgment of invalidity, finding the claims anticipated by a prior publication. Specifically, the court found each and every element of the claims disclosed in advertisements for TwinLab Mass Fuel and Weider's VICTORY Professional Protein, both published in *Flex* magazine prior to the critical date.

On appeal, Iovate argued that: (1) issues of material fact, particularly whether the publication disclosed all the claim limitations, precluded the grant of summary judgment; and (2) the publication did not enable one of skill in the art to practice the claimed invention.

The Federal Circuit first considered whether the *Flex* ads disclosed each and every limitation of the claims of the '287 patent. Because it was undisputed that the Mass Fuel ad lacked a key limitation, the Federal Circuit focused solely on the Professional Protein ad. The court concluded that the Professional Protein ad disclosed each and every element of the asserted claims. In particular, the court found no discernible difference between increasing muscle *strength* and increasing muscle *performance*. Indeed, as the court noted, the specification of the '287 patent specifically describes increasing strength. Indeed, Iovate had relied on BSN's advertisements for increasing muscle strength to support its allegations of infringement. Although noting that only one of a claim's stated purposes need be disclosed for anticipation, the court bolstered its conclusion by finding that the Professional Protein ad also disclosed the "recovery from fatigue" element.

Iovate further argued that the Professional Protein ad did not anticipate the claims because it failed to disclose an effectiveness requirement. The court again disagreed, stating that the '287 claims were not limited to an effective amount or determination of any result achieved. But even if they were, the Professional Protein ad instructed one to take "2.0 g protein per 1 kg of body weight daily" as well as taking the supplement once

74. *Lister,* 583 F.3d at 1315.
75. *Id.* at 1316.
76. 586 F.3d 1376 (Fed. Cir. 2009).
77. *Id.* at 1383.
78. *Id.* at 1378.

before exercise and once after.[79] Therefore, the court held, regardless of any questions about false advertising, the Professional Protein ad disclosed each and every limitation of the asserted claims of the '287 patent.

The Federal Circuit next considered whether the Professional Protein ad enabled one of ordinary skill in the art to practice the claimed invention. According to Iovate, the district court erred by focusing on whether such a person could have made the advertised supplements, rather than on whether he could have practiced the claimed invention. Additionally, Iovate continued, the ad lacked any guidance on ingredient dosages. The court rejected Iovate's arguments, finding that the claims are not directed to any particular concentrations, ratios, or percentages. Even if the claims had been limited to an effective amount, the court continued, one of ordinary skill in the art would have been able to determine such an amount based on the ad and on the knowledge in the art at the time as disclosed in the specification.

Concluding that no reasonable fact-finder could find other than that the Professional Protein ad was enabling prior art, the Federal Circuit affirmed the district court's summary judgment of invalidity.

Prior Commercialization

Federal Circuit Reverses Jury Determination That Claims Are Not Anticipated

In *Orion IP, LLC v. Hyundai Motor America,*[80] the Federal Circuit reversed a jury determination that claims of the patent-in-suit were not anticipated and affirmed a district court finding that the claims were not unenforceable for inequitable conduct.

The patent-in-suit was drawn to a method for electronically providing a proposal to a customer for automotive parts. The claimed method recited steps of receiving information from a customer as to what part was desired, specifying the part information electronically, gathering the parts data, including the price information, from a database, and preparing a proposal to be given to the customer.

The Federal Circuit applied the law of the Fifth Circuit to review, de novo, the district court's denial of defendant's motion for JMOL on the jury's determination of no anticipation. The cited prior art was an electronic parts catalog that provided customers with price and availability information for automotive parts and was publicly available before the critical date. The jury found that the system did not anticipate the claimed method because the prior art included wholesale price information that would not have been provided in a proposal to a customer. The Federal Circuit reversed based on evidence that the system was used in a manner whereby the information, including wholesale price information, was in fact provided to customers using the prior-art system. In addition, the Federal Circuit found that Hyundai had submitted sufficient evidence that would have allowed the jury to conclude that the prior-art system anticipated the '627 patent claims and that Hyundai was therefore entitled to JMOL on this issue.

---

79.   *Id.* at 1382.
80.   605 F.3d 967 (Fed. Cir. 2010).

　　Defendant's inequitable conduct defense was based on prior "sales" activity by the inventor and his failure to disclose that activity to the USPTO. The Federal Circuit agreed with the district court that this evidence was not particularly material. More critical to its decision affirming the district court's determination of no inequitable conduct was the failure of the defendant to provide clear and convincing evidence of any intent to deceive.

NONOBVIOUSNESS

Claim Construction and Proper Standards for Determining Anticipation and Obviousness in an Interference-in-Fact Proceeding

　　In *Rolls-Royce v. United Technologies Corp.,*[81] the Federal Circuit affirmed the district court's decision that Rolls-Royce's '077 patent would not have been obvious in light of United Technologies Corp.'s (UTC) '931 application. Rolls-Royce and UTC both claimed priority to inventions related to fan blades for gas turbine engines. Therefore, the BPAI held an interference proceeding between the parties. The contested terms critical to adjudicating the interference included "translated forward" and "a sweep angle that causes the blade to intercept the shock."[82] Rolls-Royce, being the junior party, filed a preliminary motion, alleging no interference-in-fact under 37 C.F.R. § 1.633(b). The BPAI subsequently denied the motion on the grounds that Rolls-Royce failed to present adequate evidence proving that no interference-in-fact existed between its application and the UTC application. Rolls-Royce appealed to the district court, which overturned the BPAI's decision and entered judgment in favor of Rolls-Royce. UTC appealed the district court's claim construction and judgment in favor of Rolls-Royce to the Federal Circuit.

　　First, the Federal Circuit reviewed the district court's construction of the term "translated forward" to mean "moved forward toward the axial direction."[83] Because the claims themselves did not clearly define "translated forward," the Federal Circuit consulted the specification, which indicated that "forward" did not mean forward in the ordinary sense of the term, and rather meant the axial direction. Accordingly, the Federal Circuit affirmed the district court's claim construction.

　　Next, the Federal Circuit addressed the proper construction of "a sweep angle that causes the blade to intercept the shock." Based on the specification, the point of view of a person of ordinary skill in the art, and the prosecution history, the court construed this term to mean "a rearward sweep angle in the outer region that is constant or decreasing."[84] Thus, the Federal Circuit affirmed the district court's claim construction here as well.

　　Finally, the Federal Circuit addressed whether the pertinent limitations of the Rolls-Royce patent would have been obvious to one of skill in the art in view of the UTC application. The standard inquiries required for a finding of obviousness were considered, including: the scope and content of the prior art, the level of ordinary skill in the art, the differences between the prior art and the claimed invention as perceived before the time of invention, and the extent of any objective indicia of nonobviousness. The

---

81.　603 F.3d 1325 (Fed. Cir. 2010).
82.　*Id.* at 1330.
83.　*Id.* at 1331.
84.　*Id.* at 1337.

Federal Circuit found that these elements all favored a finding that UTC's application did not render the claimed invention obvious. Further, the secondary considerations, which may serve as independent evidence of obviousness, bolstered the court's finding of nonobviousness. In particular, the Federal Circuit cited significant evidence indicating "Rolls-Royce's invention fulfilled a long-felt but unresolved need, achieved commercial success, and also achieved industry acclaim from the inventor's peers."[85] Therefore, the court affirmed the district court's holding that Rolls-Royce's patent was not obvious in view of UTC's application, and, hence, there was no interference-in-fact between the two applications.

Question of Law

Conflicting Expert Opinions about the Prior Art Preclude Summary Judgment of Obviousness

In *B-K Lighting, Inc. v. Fresno Valves & Castings, Inc.,*[86] the Federal Circuit reversed the district court's summary judgment of invalidity due to obviousness.

The case concerned U.S. Patent No. RE39,084, which discloses a lighting fixture having angular adjustability in the mounting. On appeal, the dispute primarily focused on the claims that recited that the angular adjustability was obtained by use of a tapered hole in the base of the fixture and a correspondingly tapered post in the movable part of the fixture. This arrangement, known as "frictional pivoting," allowed the installer to step back and observe the light pattern at a given angular adjustment, and then to change the angle, if need be, without having to loosen a set of screws each time such an adjustment was made. The parties agreed that "frictional pivoting," as used in the claims, was shorthand for allowing, but limiting, free pivotal movement while the fixture stayed put.

The prior art included product literature on a prior fixture, which defendant's expert, in his declaration in support of the motion for summary judgment, opined had the frictional pivoting feature. Plaintiff's expert, in his opposing declaration, opined, based on the same product literature, that the earlier fixture did not have frictional pivoting but may instead have had a locking arrangement. The district court, finding that the plaintiff's expert's opinion was merely conclusory, proceeded to grant the defendant's motion for summary judgment on obviousness grounds.

On this issue, a divided panel of the Federal Circuit held that plaintiff's expert's opinion injected a fact issue that rendered summary judgment inappropriate and necessitated a trial on the obviousness question for the claims reciting this feature. Accordingly, the Federal Circuit reversed this part of the district court's decision and remanded the case back to the court for trial. Judge Newman dissented on this point. She opined that the majority, by requiring a trial due merely to the presence of conflicting expert opinions, was creating a sea change in the way patent cases were adjudicated in the district courts.

---

85. *Id.* at 1339.
86. No. 2008-1537, 2010 WL 1709293 (Fed. Cir. Apr. 28, 2010).

District Court Improperly Granted Summary Judgment without Articulating Basis When Disputed Issues of Fact Remained

In *Trimed, Inc. v. Stryker Corp.*,[87] the Federal Circuit reversed the district court's summary judgment of patent invalidity based on obviousness, concluding that the district court erred in summarily accepting Stryker's statement of facts, failing to consider Trimed's secondary indicia of nonobviousness, and relying on common sense to support a conclusion of obviousness without articulating a basis for the decision. The Federal Circuit also ordered the case be reassigned on remand because it had twice reversed summary judgment rulings for Stryker.

Trimed sued Stryker for infringing Patent No. 5,931,839 (the '839 patent). The '839 patent claims a device, including pins, fasteners, and a plate, that is surgically implanted in a patient to set broken bones. The pins secure a less stable bone fragment to a more stable fragment. One end of the plate is attached to the more stable fragment by fasteners, while the pins attach to the other end of the plate via holes in the plate and traverse the fracture to enter the stable fragment to be secured at a stable fixation site. The holes in the plate stabilize the pins against displacement.

Stryker based its motion for invalidity on individual prior-art disclosures by Leibovic and May, alleging that each reference taught every feature of the claims. Stryker also alleged that the claims would have been obvious in view of either Leibovic or May combined with an article by Clancey.

In response, Trimed filed a memorandum contesting almost every aspect of Stryker's motion. Trimed alleged that the purported pins of Leibovic did not pass through holes in a plate, and that the wires of May did not perform the function of fixation as claimed. Trimed also challenged Stryker's assertion that the combination taught all of the claim features and alleged that the claimed invention was not merely a logical common sense solution to a known problem. Trimed also submitted evidence of secondary considerations of nonobviousness, including initial skepticism of the invention, followed by praise in the relevant industry.

On appeal, the Federal Circuit noted a number of disputed issues of fact, including the teaching of the prior art, whether the claimed invention achieves predictable results, and whether the device uses prior-art elements according to their established functions. Additionally, the Federal Circuit noted that the district court summarily dismissed secondary considerations of nonobviousness without explanation.

The Federal Circuit acknowledged that common sense is a valid consideration in an obviousness determination and reliance on common sense does not require a specific evidentiary basis, but concluded that the district court must support its common-sense finding by articulating its reasoning with sufficient clarity for review. Moreover, even though the Federal Rules of Civil Procedure do not require a district court to state findings or conclusions when ruling on a summary judgment motion, the court held that a district court's reasoning must be stated somewhere in the record if its underlying holdings would otherwise be ambiguous or unascertainable. By simply signing Stryker's Uncontroverted Statement of Facts and Conclusions and stating that the patent simply encompasses a common-sense solution to a problem, the district court did not meet its burden of stating its reasoning somewhere in the record.

---

87.   608 F.3d 1333 (Fed. Cir. 2010).

Factual Determinations—Four *Graham* Factors

Nonobviousness Analysis of Bundle Breaker Machines

In *George M. Martin Co. v. Alliance Machine Systems International LLC*,[88] the Federal Circuit affirmed the lower court's decision finding the disputed patent obvious at the time of invention.

The Martin Family Trust (the Trust) was assigned U.S. patent 6,655,566 (the '566 patent). The '566 patent disclosed a machine for separating stacked sheets of corrugated board, which is typically called a "bundle breaker" in the industry. The '566 patent used compliance structures to allow simultaneously breaking multiple stacks of corrugated board (logs) of different heights. The compliance structures included a fluid-pressurized structure connected to a plurality of rigid members through a flexible member. The Trust and George M. Martin Co. (Martin), the company that sold machines incorporating the '566 patent, sued Alliance Machine Systems International LLC (Alliance), which sold machines in direct competition with Martin. Following a two-week trial and four days of jury deliberation, the jury could not reach a unanimous verdict. After each side filed renewed motions for JMOL, the district court granted Alliance's JMOL motion for invalidity. The district court found the evidence regarding the primary considerations, including the scope and content of the prior art, the differences between the prior art and the claims at issue, and the level of the person having ordinary skill in the art, and other secondary considerations "so lop-sided" in favor of obviousness that judgment must be entered in favor of Alliance.[89]

Alliance asserted three bundle breakers as prior art. The first bundle breaker, the Pallmac machine, used an air bag solution used for adjusting the logs when stacking. The Trust argued that Pallmac's machine clamped incoming logs using a structure at the bottom of the machine, whereas the '566 patent implemented this structure at the top of the machine. The second bundle breaker, the Visy machine, used both a fluid-pressurized structure and a flexible member for adjusting the logs. The Trust argued that this machine did not render the '566 patent obvious because it failed to disclose a working compliance structure. The final bundle breaker cited as prior art, the Tecasa machine, admittedly disclosed all the limitations of the '566 patent. However, the Trust swore behind the Tecasa machine by arguing that it reduced its invention to practice before the critical date for the Tecasa machine. Nevertheless, the court used this machine as an indicia of obviousness because it was a simultaneous invention.

At trial, the Trust's expert admitted that there were only a discrete number of possible design options for the compliance structure. Although Alliance's expert admitted that one could not simply flip the Pallmac machine upside down and achieve the '566 patent, the expert testified that flipping the Pallmac machine was simple "from [a] concept point of view."[90] In assessing the Visy machine, the court held the record definitively supported the trial court's conclusion that the Visy machine's components adequately taught a compliance structure. The Trust's own tests showed that the Visy machine contained a structure,

---

88.   618 F.3d 1294 (Fed. Cir. 2010).
89.   *Id.* at 1300.
90.   *Id.* at 1302.

which deformed to allow for a uniform distribution of force. Accordingly, Visy disclosed a compliance structure. Finally, the Trust argued the Visy machine did not fully work for its intended purpose. The Federal Circuit rejected this argument because obviousness analysis does not require that a reference must work in order to qualify as prior art. Citing *Beckman Instruments, Inc. v. LKB Produkter AB*,[91] the court emphasized that a reference can be an inoperative device and still qualify as prior art for all that it teaches.

The court then addressed the secondary considerations of nonobviousness. Although the Trust argued that a number of secondary considerations precluded a finding of obviousness, the district court held the secondary considerations did not outweigh the fact that a majority of the industry came up with the same general hydraulic design to manage compliance problems with bundle breakers. Evidence of the failure of others and commercial success carried little weight with the Federal Circuit. Additionally, evidence of a long-felt but unsolved need did not support the Trust's argument because the Pallmac and Visy machines proved the need had been met by prior-art machines. In an attempt to show industry praise for the '566 patent, the Trust presented an internal Alliance email written by an Alliance employee that documented a customer's praise regarding the machine incorporating the '566 patent. Further, the Trust presented internal plans from Alliance that discussed adding design features from the '566 patent into its own products. The court dismissed this evidence and found that copying is only equivocal evidence of nonobviousness when there is an absence of more compelling objective indicia of other secondary considerations. Accordingly, the court disregarded this evidence as "hardly compelling."[92]

After balancing the secondary considerations, the Federal Circuit agreed with the lower court that the '566 patent was obvious in light of the strong evidence of obviousness based on the Pallmac and Visy machines and the near-simultaneous invention of the Tecasa machine.

Federal Circuit Affirms Obviousness Summary Judgment Despite Patentee's Proffer of Expert Testimony and Secondary Considerations Evidence

In *Media Technologies Licensing, LLC v. Upper Deck Co.*,[93] the Federal Circuit affirmed the district court's grant of summary judgment that two patents relating to sports/memorabilia trading cards were invalid under 35 U.S.C. §103(a). Judge Rader dissented.

Media Technologies' patents at issue claimed trading cards depicting famous people, with a small piece of memorabilia attached to the card along with a certificate attesting to its authenticity. Some of the claims specified that the memorabilia item was connected to a sports or entertainment personality.

The district court had based its obviousness determination on combinations of four pieces of prior art: (1) a Marilyn Monroe card with a diamond attached; (2) a bed sheet allegedly slept on by a Beatle with an attached certificate of authenticity; (3) a card depicting a friar with a piece of fabric associated with him attached; and (4) a greeting card depicting James Dean and including an attached piece of denim, and humorously claiming that the denim came from jeans worn by Dean. Media Technologies attempted to

---

91. 892 F.2d 1547 (Fed. Cir. 1989).
92. *Martin*, 618 F.3d at 1305.
93. 596 F.3d 1334 (Fed. Cir. 2010).

distinguish the references on various grounds, but the Federal Circuit agreed with the district court that the differences between the claimed inventions and the prior-art references were too slight to weigh in favor of nonobviousness. The Monroe reference disclosed a card, the Dean reference disclosed the use of memorabilia (albeit not authentic memorabilia), and the other references disclosed the use of pieces of authentic memorabilia. Although none of the references disclosed the use of sports memorabilia, the court credited defendant Upper Deck's expert testimony that one of ordinary skill in the art of sports trading cards would have looked to references outside the sports card industry to borrow concepts for use in sports cards.

Media Technologies also argued that the combined references did not render the claimed inventions obvious because those of ordinary skill would not have predicted that consumers would accept the pieces of memorabilia as authentic, and because there were—and are—an infinite number of ways to design trading cards. The Federal Circuit made short work of these arguments. The court concluded that it was predictable that consumers would accept the memorabilia as authentic because of the credibility already associated with the card vendors. As for the infinite alternatives argument, the court decided that card content was not infinitely variable; it was limited by the theme and physical limitations of the card.

Media Technologies fared no better with its secondary considerations arguments. Media Technologies offered evidence of alleged long-felt but unmet need, initial skepticism, commercial success, unexpected results, and industry recognition. The Federal Circuit was unimpressed. The alleged need—to stimulate demand for trading cards—had been met by the use of other trading card inserts besides memorabilia. The claim of initial skepticism was not adequately supported, and the argument that some people would be outraged at the idea of destroying memorabilia did not establish that people would be skeptical that pieces of memorabilia could be combined with trading cards. With respect to commercial success, Media Technologies had not established the required nexus with the claimed invention. Indeed, the commercial success may have been attributable to the popularity of the depicted celebrities. Regarding unexpected results, the Federal Circuit dismissed this argument as a mere reiteration of the fact that the commercial success of the cards was unexpected. Unexpected commercial success is not part of the unexpected results inquiry, according to the Federal Circuit.

Dissenting, Judge Rader asserted that the obviousness question should not have been resolved on summary judgment. Judge Rader pointed to evidence from industry publications that reinforced Media Technologies' claims of unexpected results, initial skepticism, and commercial success. He also referred to countervailing factual evidence on differences between the claimed inventions and the prior-art references, and noted that the majority had resolved the case as a matter of law despite the fact that Media Technologies had proffered expert testimony. Judge Rader saw the case as one in which the majority had indulged a bias against nontechnical arts, leading the majority to ignore conflicts in the factual record that should have been left for the jury.

Scope and Content of Prior Art

MOTIVATION TO COMBINE PRIOR ART

Applying KSR *Substitution Rationale, Federal Circuit Affirms BPAI's Obviousness Analysis*

In *In re Lackey,*[94] the Federal Circuit affirmed the decision of the BPAI that the claims of Lackey's patent application for metallic air admittance valves for use in plumbing systems were obvious.[95]

Lackey's invention was generally directed to a check valve, attached near the trap of a fixture, which provides ventilation to plumbing drain lines while preventing gases from escaping the drain lines. Claim 1, which is illustrative of the claims at issue, recited in toto: "[a]n air admittance valve having a tubular body with a valve chamber integral to one end of the tubular body, said valve chamber having a valve and an air inlet, wherein the tubular body and the valve chamber are fabricated from metal."[96]

The Examiner applied two references to reject Lackey's claims. The primary reference, generally directed to an air valve device for ducts, disclosed a valve having a valve body connected to an air duct, a valve chamber, an air inlet, and a membrane or annular flap (or valve). In particular, the reference disclosed that the valve was to be used with a sanitary appliance to eliminate a vacuum that can lead to contaminated water from the sanitary appliance being sucked into the duct. The secondary reference, meanwhile, disclosed plumbing fixtures that could be fabricated from metal and produced a reliable drainage system. The BPAI found Lackey's claimed invention obvious over the combination of these two references.

On appeal, Lackey argued that the first reference discloses an air duct and, thus, did not disclose an air admittance valve as claimed, and that the second reference was nonanalogous art. The Federal Circuit disagreed. According to the court, the first reference taught a check valve having a valve body, a valve chamber, an air inlet, and a membrane or annular flap. It also taught the air valve is used in combination with a "sanitary appliance" or plumbing system. The court noted that the BPAI relied on a dictionary definition of "sanitary" as including "relating to, or used in the disposal of sewage" to support its finding that the valve of the first reference could be applied in a plumbing fixture.[97] The Federal Circuit also noted that the secondary reference was directed to the same field of endeavor—inventions used with plumbing fixtures—as the primary reference.

Thus, the Federal Circuit found that one of ordinary skill would easily substitute one known element for another known element to obtain predictable results. In this case, one could simply take the valve of the first reference and make it out of metal as taught by the second reference. As such, the Federal Circuit concluded that Lackey's invention was indeed obvious over the combination of the two references.

---

94. 370 F. App'x 80 (Fed. Cir. 2010).
95. *Id.* at 81.
96. *Id.*
97. *Id.* at 82.

Without any evidence showing unexpected results or secondary indicia of nonobviousness, the Federal Circuit affirmed the obviousness rejections made by the examiner and the BPAI.

Asserted Claims Held Obvious Where Prior Art Taught All Elements of the Asserted Claims and Suggested Combining the Prior-Art Elements

In *Fresenius USA, Inc. v. Baxter International, Inc.,*[98] the Federal Circuit held that Baxter's asserted patent claims were invalid where all elements of a claim were taught in the prior art and the prior art included a suggestion to combine the elements. Fresenius initially filed suit against Baxter seeking a declaratory judgment that it did not infringe three of Baxter's patents because the claims were obvious. Baxter counterclaimed that Fresenius infringed its patents. The district court granted Baxter's motion for JMOL, asserting the patent claims were not invalid as obvious and that substantial evidence did not support the jury's finding of obviousness. Additionally, the district court awarded Baxter damages, injunctive relief, and imposed an ongoing royalty payment against Fresenius for any articles sold after the trial and before the injunction took effect. The Federal Circuit overruled the district court's grant of a post-verdict JMOL of nonobviousness on all but six of the asserted claims, upholding the district court's finding of nonobviousness for the remaining six claims. Also, the court vacated and remanded the injunction and royalty award for the district court to revise or reconsider in light of the court's reversal of JMOL.

The Baxter patent claims at issue were directed to a hemodialysis machine that contained a touch screen user interface. All three of the patents derived from a parent patent application that was filed in 1991. At the time the parent application was filed, touch screens were well-known in the prior art and had been used on other medical devices, such as a heart-lung machine. However, touch screens had not been integrated with a hemodialysis machine. In 1991, Baxter introduced the System 1000 that embodied the patents at issue, and in 1998, Fresenius introduced the infringing device, a hemodialysis machine with touch screen interface.

The court overruled the district court's grant of JMOL for most of the claims because there was substantial evidence supporting the jury's verdict that the claims were invalid as obvious.[99] The jury was presented with evidence that the prior art taught hemodialysis machines and medical devices containing touch screen user interfaces, that the prior art suggested combining touch screen user interfaces with hemodialysis machines, and that an artisan of ordinary skill would be able to combine touch screen user interfaces with hemodialysis machines.

The court also addressed the district court's use of the teaching-suggestion-motivation (TSM) test to determine obviousness. The district court had conducted the trial and issued its JMOL opinion before the U.S. Supreme Court had decided *KSR International Co. v. Teleflex Inc.,*[100] thus applying the TSM test as it existed before it was modified by *KSR.* The court determined that it would not overturn the implicit factual findings of the jury's verdict so long as the findings were supported by substantial evidence because it remains appropriate "to determine whether there was an apparent reason to combine the known

---

98. 582 F.3d 1288 (Fed. Cir. 2009).
99. *Id.* at 1298–1300.
100. 550 U.S. 398 (2007).

elements in the fashion claimed by the patent at issue."[101] The jury was presented with evidence that a prior-art reference suggested combining a touch screen with a hemodialysis machine, testimony regarding the ease and prevalence of integrating a touch screen into some kind of computer-controlled machine, and that it would not have been difficult for one to integrate a touch screen interface into a hemodialysis machine. As a result, the court overruled the JMOL of nonobviousness because Fresenius presented substantial evidence to support the jury's implicit factual finding that the prior art suggested the combination of elements taught in the prior art.[102]

The court also examined whether the jury was presented with evidence that all elements of the asserted claims were present in the prior art. There is no requirement that a single expert testify that all elements of a claim were present in the prior art, but rather the evidence can come from the totality of the testimony presented by all the experts. Thus, the fact that two different experts testified regarding two different sets of elements of claim 11 of the '027 patent did not affect the court's holding that the claim was nonobvious. Moreover, there was substantial evidence supporting the jury's verdict that claims 1–3 of the '131 patent, drafted in *Markush* form, would have been obvious because the jury was presented with evidence that at least one of the *Markush* elements was present in the prior art. On the other hand, the jury was not presented with evidence that claims 26–31 of the asserted '434 patent were present in the prior art. Those claims included means-plus-function language, but Fresenius failed to present any evidence that the structure corresponding to the claimed function or equivalent structure existed in the prior art. Therefore, the court overruled the district court's post-verdict JMOL on all claims except the means-plus-function claims.

Finally, the court held that the district court did not abuse its discretion in determining that injunctive relief was appropriate.[103] The record contained support for the district court's factual determinations that injunctive relief was appropriate. However, the court vacated the injunctive relief and remanded for the district court to revise or reconsider based on the court's reversal of JMOL. In addition, the court held that the district court did not abuse its discretion on imposing a royalty payment against Fresenius to compensate Baxter for the infringement that did occur.[104] The court held that it would not decide whether the district court's royalty award was proper, but instead vacated the award and remanded for the district court to consider based on the court's reversal of JMOL.

COMMON SENSE AND ORDINARY CREATIVITY

Federal Circuit Reverses Finding of Nonobviousness, Construing Prior Art Broadly

In *Wyers v. Master Lock Co.*,[105] the Federal Circuit reviewed a judgment that the asserted patent was valid and infringed.

The plaintiff, Wyers, brought an action for infringement of two sets of patent claims related to trailer hitch pin locks. One of the sets of claims was directed to an enlarging sleeve

---

101. *Fresenius*, 582 F.3d at 1300–01 (quoting *KSR*, 550 U.S. at 418).
102. *Id.* at 1301–02.
103. *Id.* at 1302.
104. *Id.* at 1303.
105. 616 F.3d 1231 (Fed. Cir. 2010).

(the sleeve patents), whereas the other set of claims was directed to a contaminant-guarding seal (the seal patents). The district court granted Wyers' motion for JMOL of infringement, which was not appealed. The defendants argued on appeal that both sets of claims were obvious as a matter of law, and so invalid.

It was undisputed that the sole difference between the prior art and the sleeve patents was the enlarging sleeve, and that the sole difference between the prior art and the seal patents was the contaminant-guarding seal. Prior-art references introduced by the defendants disclosed an enlarging sleeve and contaminant-guarding seal. The district court nevertheless concluded that a reasonable jury could find that both references were outside the scope of the relevant art.

In reversing the judgment of the district court, the Federal Circuit reviewed three factual issues: (1) whether the prior-art references and the invention were analogous arts; (2) whether there was a sufficient motivation to combine the references; and (3) whether secondary considerations of nonobviousness rendered the asserted claims nonobvious.

The Federal Circuit concluded that both prior-art references were in the same field of invention and so relevant to the validity determination. For the seal patents, the Federal Circuit held that padlocks were within the relevant field of the invention, pointing to statements in the background section of the seal patents discussing prior-art padlocks. Additionally, the Federal Circuit found the prior art was reasonably pertinent to the problem solved by the invention. The court referred to the *KSR* decision as directing courts to construe the scope of analogous art broadly. Accordingly, the Federal Circuit concluded that the district court erred in finding prior-art references disclosing the enlarging sleeve and the contaminant guarding seal were not pertinent.

Next, the Federal Circuit concluded that as a matter of law there was a motivation to combine the references. According to the court, *KSR* and later Federal Circuit cases made clear that, while motivation to combine was typically a finding of fact, it could be resolved at the summary judgment stage in certain circumstances. For example, even though credibility determinations are to be avoided at summary judgment, expert testimony of nonobviousness does not necessarily create an issue of material fact. Obviousness could be determined on summary judgment by resorting to logic, judgment, and common sense in lieu of testimony — and even contrary to expert testimony.

With those principles in mind, the Federal Circuit determined that it was common sense to combine the references with the prior art to arrive at the invention. The court further determined that it was a matter of common sense that one of ordinary skill in the art would have had a reasonable expectation of success in making the combination.

Finally, the Federal Circuit rejected Wyers' evidence of secondary considerations as mainly conjecture and held that even if established, secondary considerations could not overcome such a strong prima facie case of obviousness.

Common Sense May Be Used in Determining Whether Claims of a Patent Are Obvious

In *Perfect Web Technologies, Inc. v. InfoUSA, Inc.*,[106] the Federal Circuit affirmed the district court's decision that Perfect Web's asserted patent claims relating to methods of managing and targeting bulk e-mail distributions were invalid. Specifically, the district

---

106. 587 F.3d 1324 (Fed. Cir. 2009).

court found the asserted claims to be obvious in light of the prior art and common sense. On appeal, the main issue was whether the final step of claim 1 was obvious.

Claim 1 recited a method for managing bulk e-mail distribution to groups of targeted consumers. The first three steps consisted of selecting a group of target recipients, transmitting a set of bulk e-mails to that group, and calculating the number of e-mails successfully transmitted. If the calculated number did not exceed a certain minimum quantity, then the final step called for repeating the previous steps until that minimum is exceeded. The district court found this last step to be obvious because it was "merely the logical result of common sense application of the maxim 'try, try again.'"[107]

The Federal Circuit affirmed the district court's ruling of obviousness. In considering obviousness, the U.S. Supreme Court has held that "the background knowledge, creativity, and common sense of the person of ordinary skill" is an appropriate source.[108]

In this case, Perfect Web argued that the district court improperly found obviousness because its common sense rationale was not based on the evidence, factual findings of the record, or expert testimony. In rejecting a patent for obviousness, the USPTO or a district court "must not only assure that the requisite findings are made, based on evidence of record, but must also explain the reasoning by which the findings are deemed to support the agency's [or court's] conclusion."[109] Here, the Federal Circuit determined the district court had sufficient evidence in the record to support its use of common sense to render the patent invalid. Given that the last step in Perfect Web's proposed method was merely a repetition of the first three steps, and only a few other solutions existed to address the problem, the Federal Circuit held that it would be obvious to a person of ordinary skill in the art to repeat the procedure. The Federal Circuit also held that the district court did not err in declining to consider the parties' expert testimony. Specifically, reliance on expert testimony in this case was not necessary because the person of ordinary skill in the art only required a high school education and limited marketing experience.

Perfect Web also argued that its invention was not obvious because it satisfied the secondary consideration of a long-felt and unmet need that existed prior to its invention. However, Perfect Web failed to provide supporting evidence, such as data that showed that the invention "actually reduced marketing costs, time or the number of consumers who opt out."[110] Perfect Web further contended the claims should have been construed prior to the finding of invalidity. The Federal Circuit disagreed, however, because Perfect Web could not identify a construction that would change the court's analysis of obviousness. Accordingly, the Federal Circuit found the asserted claims of the patent-in-suit obvious.

---

107. *Id.* at 1327.
108. *Id.* at 1329 (citing KSR Int'l Co. v. Teleflex, Inc., 550 U.S. 398, 418–21 (2007)).
109. *Id.* at 1328 (citing *In re* Lee, 277 F.3d 1338, 1344 (Fed. Cir. 2002)).
110. *Id.* at 1333.

CHAPTER 4

ADEQUATE PATENT DISCLOSURE

The adequacy of patent disclosures played a significant role in determining the validity of patents, with the Federal Circuit addressing several cases involving questions regarding adequate patent disclosure.

In *Bradford Co. v. Conteyor North America, Inc.,* the Federal Circuit concluded that arguments made to persuade an examiner to allow an application trump an ambiguous disclosure that might otherwise have supported an earlier priority date for the patent.

In *Robertson v. Timmermans,* the court held that when an applicant copies claims from another application or patent in order to provoke an interference proceeding and the claims are subject to a 35 U.S.C. § 112 challenge, the originating disclosure of the copied claims should be used for construing whether the claims have adequate support.

In *Yorkey v. Diab,* the court determined that, in the context of proving reduction to practice, data collection restraints required by a claim may be inferred collectively from the environment in which the data is collected, the collected data, and the content of the software code processing the data. The constraints need not be corroborated by "an over the shoulder" observer.

In *Harari v. Hollmer,* the Federal Circuit found that a patent applicant sufficiently incorporated an earlier application by reference, despite a lack of clarity in the applicant's transmittal statement and a preliminary amendment because a reasonable examiner could clearly identify the exact reference the applicant was attempting to incorporate solely by looking at all the documents provided by the applicant.

In *Anascape, Ltd. v. Nintendo of America, Inc.,* the Federal Circuit held the written description of the parent application failed to support the claims of a later-filed application seeking the benefit of the filing date of the parent application.

Addressing the interplay between the written description and enablement requirement, in *Ariad Pharmaceuticals, Inc. v. Eli Lilly & Co.,* the Federal Circuit held en banc that the written description requirement under section 112, paragraph 1 is a separate and distinct requirement from that of enablement. *ALZA Corp. v. Andrx Pharmaceuticals, LLC* and *In re '318 Patent Infringement Litigation* illustrate the distinction between the written description and enablement requirements.

In *ALZA Corp.,* the patent claimed a drug with two types of dosage forms with ascending rates of release, however, the district court and the Federal Circuit concluded that the specification fully enabled only one type of dosage. Although the second type of dosage was disclosed in the patent and one of ordinary skill in the art would know how to develop the second dosage, the technology was not fully mature and required an iterative trial-and-error process. The Federal Circuit concluded that the second type of dosage required undue experimentation given the limited guidance provided by the specification. Therefore, the Federal Circuit affirmed the district court's decision holding that the patent was invalid for lack of enablement. Similarly in *In re '318 Patent Infringement Litigation,* a divided Federal Circuit panel affirmed the district court's conclusion that the asserted claims, drawn to a method of treating Alzheimer's disease and related dementias by administering an effective amount of galanthamine, were invalid for lack of enablement. The Federal Circuit reasoned that the one-page specification, which lacked any in vitro or animal test results, did no more than "state a hypothesis" and "propose testing" of the hypothesis, which were insufficient to meet the enablement requirement.

The Federal Circuit also addressed the patentee's obligation to disclose the best mode. In *Ajinomoto Co., Inc. v. International Trade Commission,* the court held that the ITC correctly found two of Ajinomoto's patents on genetically engineered lysine invalid for failure to meet the best mode requirement of section 112, paragraph 1.

Turning to indefiniteness, the court in *Enzo Biochem Inc. v. Applera Corp.* found that the term "not interfering substantially" in a biochemical composition claim was not indefinite because the meaning could be deduced in part from narrower dependent claims and in part from examples given in the specification. On a motion for summary judgment of anticipation, the patentee's filing of an opposing expert declaration concerning the prior art precluded granting of the motion. Similarly, in *Yorkey v. Diab,* the Federal Circuit determined that, absent an express requirement in the claims or specification, a claim recitation requiring multiple functions be solved to determine a characteristic does not require solving those functions simultaneously or directly. A reference that allows for the characteristic to be approximated can therefore anticipate the claim limitation. Finally, in *Power-One, Inc. v. Artesyn Technologies, Inc.,* the Federal Circuit found that the district court's claim construction was not impermissibly vague where the specification and the prior art gave indications of the scope of the court's use of disputed terms.

ENABLEMENT

Breadth of Disclosure

Ultimately Confirmed Hypotheses Are Not Sufficient to Meet the Utility and Enablement Requirements for Patentability

In *In re '318 Patent Infringement Litigation,*[1] a divided Federal Circuit panel affirmed the findings of the U.S. District Court for the District of Delaware that claims were invalid for lack of enablement. Dissenting alone, Judge Gajarsa disagreed with the majority's finding based on what he perceived as a failure of the district court to establish a factual and legal basis sufficient for a determination that U.S. Patent No. 4,663,318 (the '318 patent) had an enabling disclosure.

Representative claim 1 was drawn to "[a] method of treating Alzheimer's disease and related dementias which comprises administering to a patient suffering from such a disease a therapeutically effective amount of galanthamine or a pharmaceutically-acceptable acid addition salt thereof."[2] At the time the '318 patent application was filed, there was evidence of a correlation between Alzheimer's disease symptoms and reduced levels of the neurotransmitter acetylcholine, which could be produced using galanthamine (also spelled

---

1.   583 F.3d 1317 (Fed. Cir. 2009).
2.   *Id.* at 1320.

galantamine). The '318 specification consisted of only a single page, but included short summaries of six scientific papers discussing the administration of galanthamine to humans and animals. During prosecution of the '318 patent, the examiner did not reject the claims on enablement grounds. Nevertheless, the examiner did reject the claims on the basis of indefiniteness and the failure to clearly identify which subject matter Dr. Davis sought to patent. Dr. Davis overcame the indefiniteness and obviousness rejections, in part, by stating that animal model experiments, expected to confirm that galanthamine could effectively treat the disease, were underway. Dr. Davis advised the USPTO that the results would be provided to the USPTO in two or three months, after conclusion of the experiments. The '318 patent issued before the results of the animal studies—which suggested that galanthamine could be an effective treatment for Alzheimer's disease—were known. The experimental results, which were never submitted to the USPTO, were not available until after several months and "considerable effort" by researchers.[3]

The '318 patent litigation occurred after the inventor, Dr. Bonnie Davis, licensed the '318 patent to Janssen Pharmaceutica N.V. and its subsidiaries (Janssen), who in turn obtained FDA approval for treatment of mild to moderate Alzheimer's using galanthamine. A number of generic drug manufacturers sought to market a generic version and filed Abbreviated New Drug Applications (ANDAs) with Paragraph IV certifications. At trial, the generic manufacturers conceded infringement, but contended that the '318 patent was invalid as either anticipated or obvious in view of the prior art. Alternatively, the generic manufacturers contended that the '318 patent was invalid due to lack of enablement.

After a bench trial, the district court found that the '318 patent was not anticipated or obvious, but concluded that the patent lacked an enabling disclosure. First, the district court concluded that the specification of the '318 patent did not demonstrate utility because it provided only "minimal disclosure" of any utility, and the animal trials were not complete when the '318 patent issued. Second, the district court found that the claims and specification were not sufficient for one of ordinary skill in the art to use the claimed method, pointing to the lack of guidance on galanthamine dosage information.

The Federal Circuit panel majority began by reviewing the requirements for enablement and pointed out that enablement and utility are "closely related," citing to its holding in *Process Control*.[4] In particular, the court noted that if a patent claim cannot meet the utility requirement, it also fails to meet the "how-to-use" aspect of the enablement requirement. The majority also pointed out that the "utility requirement prevents mere ideas from being patented" and reiterated the U.S. Supreme Court's discussion in *Brenner* that "a patent is not a hunting license," but is a reward only for successfully meeting the requirements for patentability.[5]

The Federal Circuit panel majority noted that the court had previously held in vitro or animal test results sufficient to satisfy the utility requirement for new compounds and methods of treatment using the same.[6] Nevertheless, because no test results were available prior to the '318 patent's issuance, the panel majority concluded that the district court had correctly found that later available test results could not be used to establish enablement.

---

3. *Id.* at 1322.

4. Process Control Corp. v. HydReclaim Corp., 190 F.3d 1350, 1358 (Fed. Cir. 1999).

5. Brenner v. Manson, 383 U.S. 519, 536 (1966).

6. *In re* Krimmel, 292 F.2d 948, 954 (C.C.P.A. 1961); *In re* Brana, 51 F.3d 1560, 1568 (Fed. Cir. 1995); Scott v. Finney, 34 F.3d 1058, 1063–64 (Fed. Cir. 1994).

The majority also concluded that the technical references summarized in the '318 patent specification did not provide a sufficient basis to establish enablement, and rejected Janssen's assertions that the papers, combined with the reasoning of one of ordinary skill in the art, would have lead one of ordinary skill in the art to the claimed method of treatment. Although Janssen offered expert testimony in support of its position, the court found that even in view of that testimony, the specification did no more than "state a hypothesis" and "propose testing" of the hypothesis, insufficient to meet the enablement requirement.[7] Thus, the panel majority concluded that the '318 patent specification failed to meet the enablement requirement because the inventor did not establish the requisite level of utility.

Dissenting alone, Judge Gajarsa focused on the district court's failure to perform an adequate legal analysis of whether sufficient utility would have been reached. He also expressed his view that the district court had failed to make sufficient factual findings to determine enablement. Rather than find nonenablement, he suggested that the proper course was a remand back to the district court to perform the requisite fact-finding and legal analysis.

Undue Experimentation

Patent Claiming Two Dosage Forms Held Nonenabling in Its Teaching of Dosage Type Known in the Art

In *ALZA Corp. v. Andrx Pharmaceuticals, LLC,*[8] the Federal Circuit affirmed a district court holding that asserted patent claims were invalid for lack of enablement.[9]

Plaintiffs ALZA Corporation and McNeil-PPC, Inc. (collectively, ALZA), held a patent to a drug that treated Attention Deficit Hyperactivity Disorder (ADHD) through a drug dosage form that had an ascending release rate over time. The patent claimed priority to a provisional patent application. Defendants Andrx Pharmaceuticals, LLC and Andrx Corporation (collectively, Andrx) developed a competing drug under an Abbreviated New Drug Application (ANDA).

At a *Markman* hearing, the sole independent claim was held to cover two different types of dosage forms; osmotic and nonosmotic. The district court concluded that the specification did not provide an enabling disclosure of the nonosmotic dosage form and, therefore, did not enable the full scope of the claim.

The first dosage form—osmotic dosage—involved a semi-permeable capsule and a fluid (known as a "push" layer) that expands when it comes into contact with bodily fluid, causing a push against the drug agent, in turn causing the drug agent to exit at increasing rates. The second dosage form, known as nonosmotic dosage, included oral tablets and capsules that did include a push layer.

ALZA argued that creating nonosmotic dosage forms and adjusting release rates was well known in the art as of the filing date of the application maturing into the patent-in-suit. However, ALZA conceded that one of ordinary skill in the art would have to engage in an iterative trial-and-error process.

---

7.   *'318 Patent Infringement Litig.*, 583 F.3d at 1327.
8.   603 F.3d 935 (Fed. Cir. 2010).
9.   *Id.*

It thus was not disputed that some degree of experimentation was required by one of skill in the art to develop the second type of dosage form of the invention. At issue was whether the degree of experimentation was undue. The Federal Circuit affirmed the holding of the district court that, at the time the application maturing into the patent-in-suit was filed, the field of ascending release rates was not fully developed, and that the specification provided only a starting point and direction for further trial-and-error research.

WRITTEN DESCRIPTION

Reconciling Written Description with Claim Language for Determining Priority Date

In *Anascape, Ltd. v. Nintendo of America, Inc.*,[10] the Federal Circuit held that the written description of a parent application failed to support the claims of a later-filed application seeking the benefit of the filing date of the parent application. Nintendo appealed the judgment of the district court, which found that Nintendo's video game controllers infringed U.S. Patent No. 6,906,700 ('700 patent) owned by Anascape.

The subject matter at issue related to videogame controllers allowing for multiple "degrees of freedom" for users to translate their hand motion to the graphic images in a video game. The '700 patent was a continuation-in-part of U.S. Patent No. 6,222,525 ('525 patent), and the validity of the '700 patent claims depended on whether its claims were entitled to the filing date of the '525 patent. In order to claim the benefit of the earlier filing date of a parent application, the claims of the later-filed application must have support in the written description of the parent "in sufficient detail that one skilled in the art can clearly conclude that the inventor invented the claimed invention as of the filing date sought."[11] Therefore, the scope of the '700 patent claims and the scope of the '525 patent specification were the principal issues on appeal. Specifically, the Federal Circuit addressed whether the description in the '525 patent supported controllers having multiple input members that could operate in six degrees of freedom, as claimed in the '700 patent.

On appeal, Anascape maintained that the '525 patent's specification, which described controllers having a single input member operable in six degrees of freedom, was not limited to a single input member. Nintendo's appeal was premised on the argument that the '525 patent's specification was directed to only a single input member. In order to resolve the dispute, the Federal Circuit addressed each component of the '525 patent, finding multiple examples in the background, summary, and drawings, all indicating that the '525 patent's specification supported only a single input member controller. Anascape responded by citing claim language in the '525 patent reciting more than a single input member, but Nintendo countered that this specific claim language was added in an amendment made after the critical filing date. Anascape also argued that the subject matter in the '525 patent described a preferred embodiment and that the '525 patent did not disclaim the broader claims of the '700 patent.

---

10. 601 F.3d 1333 (Fed. Cir. 2010).
11. *See* Lockwood v. Am. Airlines, Inc., 107 F.3d 1565, 1572 (Fed. Cir. 1997).

The Federal Circuit, in rejecting that argument, noted that a patentee is not deemed to disclaim every variant it fails to mention, just as a patentee is not presumed to support variants that are not mentioned.[12] The court stressed the importance of viewing each case as it would be understood by a person of ordinary skill in the field of the invention. After parsing conflicting expert testimony, the court concluded that the only reasonable reading of the '525 patent's specification was that it was directed to a controller having a single input member operable in six degrees of freedom, and the claims of the '700 patent were enlarged to cover more than a single input member operable in six degrees of freedom. Therefore, the Federal Circuit concluded that Anascape's '700 patent was not entitled to the '525 patent's filing date. The court found the district court erred in its ruling, and the judgments of validity, infringement, and damages were reversed.

En Banc Court Confirms Existence of Written Description

In *Ariad Pharmaceuticals, Inc. v. Eli Lilly & Co.,*[13] the Federal Circuit held en banc that 35 U.S.C. § 112, ¶ 1, contains a written description requirement separate from the enablement requirement. The patent at issue was directed to the regulation of gene expression. The claims in the patent were genus claims, encompassing the use of all substances that achieved the desired result of reducing the binding of NF-êB to NF-êB recognition sites. At trial, a jury found infringement and held that none of the asserted claims were invalid.

A Federal Circuit panel reversed the judgment of the U.S. District Court for the District of Massachusetts, which had denied Lilly's motion for JMOL and had held the asserted claims invalid for lack of written description support. The court also upheld the district court's finding of no inequitable conduct. Ariad petitioned for rehearing en banc, challenging the existence of a written description requirement separate from the enablement requirement.

On appeal, the en banc court began with the language of the statute itself. The court agreed with Lilly and "read the statute to give effect to its language that the specification 'shall contain a written description of the invention' and [held] that § 112, first paragraph, contains two separate description requirements: a 'written description [i] of the invention, *and* [ii] of the manner and process of making and using [the invention].'"[14] The court concluded that if Congress had intended enablement to be the sole description requirement of section 112, first paragraph, then the statute would have been written differently. The court further concluded that a separate requirement to describe one's invention was basic to patent law. The specification must then, the court explained, "describe how to make and use the invention (i.e., enable it), but that is a different task."[15]

The court also read U.S. Supreme Court precedent as recognizing a written description requirement separate from an enablement requirement. The Federal Circuit also found that a separate written description requirement did not conflict with the function of the

---

12. *See* Amgen Inc. v. Hoechst Marion Roussel, Inc., 314 F.3d 1313, 1330 (Fed. Cir. 2003).

13. 598 F.3d 1336 (Fed. Cir. 2010) (en banc).

14. *Id.* at 1344 (emphasis & alteration in original) (citing 35 U.S.C. § 112, ¶ 1 (2006)).

15. *Id.* at 1345.

claims. The court noted that "[c]laims define and circumscribe," while "the written description discloses and teaches."[16]

In addition to finding that both the statutory language and U.S. Supreme Court precedent supported the existence of a written description requirement separate from enablement, the Federal Circuit concluded that stare decisis compelled the court to find that section 112, first paragraph, included a separate written description requirement. "[T]o change course now," according to the court, "would disrupt the settled expectations of the inventing community, which has relied on [the precedent] in drafting and prosecuting patents, concluding licensing agreements, and rendering validity and infringement opinions."[17] The court explained that if the law of written description is to be changed, such a decision would rest with Congress.

The court rejected Ariad's argument that original claims, as part of the original disclosure, constitute a written description of the invention. The court noted that although many original claims will satisfy the written description requirement, certain claims may not. A generic claim, for example, may define the boundaries of a vast genus of chemical compounds, and yet the question may still remain whether the specification, including original claim language, demonstrates that the applicant has invented species sufficient to support a claim to a genus. The court pointed out that this case illustrated the problem of generic claims. The claims in this case recited methods encompassing a genus of materials achieving a stated useful result, i.e., reducing NF-κB binding to NF-κB recognition sites in response to external influences. But the specification did not disclose a variety of species that accomplished the result.

The court also recognized that there might be "little difference in some fields between describing an invention and enabling one to make and use it, but that is not always true of certain inventions, including chemical and chemical-like inventions. Thus, although written description and enablement often rise and fall together, requiring a written description of the invention plays a vital role in curtailing claims that do not require undue experimentation to make and use, and thus satisfy enablement, but that have not been invented, and thus cannot be described."[18] In other words, the Federal Circuit's view is that the written description requirement serves as a check on the scope of claims to subject matter that may be enabled but has not been fully described. Adopting the analysis of the original panel, the court concluded that the asserted claims were not supported by a written description because the patent's specification failed to adequately disclose how the claimed reduction of NF-κB activity was achieved. The court held that the patent disclosed no working or even prophetic examples of methods that reduced NF-κB activity and no completed syntheses of any of the molecules prophesized to be capable of reducing NF-κB activity. The court, therefore, concluded that there was not substantial evidence to support the jury's verdict that the asserted claims were supported by adequate written description and, thus, held the asserted claims invalid.[19] The court also reinstated Part II of the panel decision, concluding that the district court's finding of no inequitable conduct was correct.

---

16. *Id.* at 1347.
17. *Id.*
18. *Id.* at 1352.
19. *Id.* at 1358.

Judge Newman joined the majority, but wrote separately to add that the subject matter of this case was basic research, which was presented to the patent system before its practical application was demonstrated. In Judge Newman's view, the threshold in all cases required a transition from theory to practice.

Judge Gajarsa concurred, writing that, in his view, the text of section 112, first paragraph was a model of legislative ambiguity. Judge Gajarsa found the majority's interpretation of the statute reasonable, but disagreed that an independent written description requirement was a necessity of patent law. Judge Gajarsa explained that empirical evidence demonstrated that written description served little practical purpose as an independent invalidity device, and better served the goals of the Patent Act when confined to the priority context. He concluded that confining written description to the priority context would provide greater clarity to district courts and practitioners, "both of whom are currently left to trudge through a thicket of written description jurisprudence that provides no conclusive answers and encourages a shotgun approach to litigation . . . [but] only Congress wields the machete to clear it."[20]

Judge Rader, whom Judge Linn joined, dissented-in-part and concurred-in-part. Judge Rader concluded that the statute was unambiguous and had no separate written description requirement. Judge Rader noted that a proper reading of the statutory description requirement recognized that the enablement requirement identified the invention and told a person of ordinary skill what to make and use. Further, Judge Rader concluded that the written description doctrine had meaning only if the court ignored its own claim construction rules. That is, according to Judge Rader, the court has power to err twice—both in construing the claims so broad as to exceed the scope of the rest of the specification and then to invalidate those claims because the court reads the specification as failing to support the court's own broad conception of the claimed subject matter.

Judge Linn, whom Judge Rader joined, also wrote separately to dissent-in-part and concur-in-part. Judge Linn wrote that the statutory arguments failed to justify establishing a separate written description requirement apart from enablement and beyond the priority context, and failed to tether that written description requirement to a workable legal standard. Judge Linn believed the appeal should have been returned to the panel for resolution of the enablement question, but concurred in affirming a finding of no inequitable conduct.

Arguments Made during Prosecution Preclude Arguments over Ambiguous Disclosure That May Have Otherwise Established an Earlier Priority Date

In *Bradford Co. v. Conteyor North America, Inc.*,[21] the Federal Circuit concluded that arguments made to persuade an examiner to allow an application trump an ambiguous disclosure that might otherwise have supported an earlier priority date for the patent. The plaintiff-patentee sought to overcome prior-art defenses by asserting the benefit, under 35 U.S.C. § 120, of a copending parent application. The patent-in-suit issued on a continuation-in-part (CIP) of that application, which involved collapsible shipping containers having interior pockets, called "dunnage," for holding parts of the equipment being shipped.

---

20. *Id.* at 1361 (Gajarsa, J., concurring).
21. 603 F.3d 1262 (Fed. Cir. 2010).

The claims at issue required that the dunnage be accessible from the side of the container, rather than from the top.

To overcome an asserted obviousness defense the patentee attempted to argue for the benefit of the parent patent's filing date, contending that the parent disclosed a side-accessible arrangement. The district court refused to accord that date, noting that the applicant, in prosecuting the CIP before the USPTO, had specifically told the examiner that the parent application, which had become a patent, did not disclose the side-loading feature. The district court found the plaintiff was now estopped to contend differently in the litigation.

The Federal Circuit agreed. The panel first reiterated the court's longstanding doctrine that to obtain the benefit of an earlier U.S. filing date, each application in the chain must meet the requirements of 35 U.S.C. § 112, including the written description requirement.[22] The panel expressed the view that those requirements might well have been met here, i.e., that the parent application may have had a sufficient written description for the claims now in issue. However, the patentee was estopped to so argue, having earlier argued to the USPTO examiner that the parent application and patent had no such disclosure.

The appeal also involved two other issues. One was the meaning of the term "coupled to" in the claims. The district court ruled that meant a direct mechanical connection between the dunnage and the container frame. The panel viewed that construction as unduly narrow, holding instead that the term would embrace indirect connections through bars mounted in the frame. The summary judgment of noninfringement was accordingly reversed and the case remanded for further proceedings.

Written Description Requirement Satisfied When Reasonable Examiner Could Clearly Identify Patent Document Meant to Be Incorporated by Reference

In *Harari v. Hollmer,*[23] the Federal Circuit reversed and remanded a decision from the BPAI dismissing junior party, Harari's, '880 patent application from an interference with senior party, Hollmer's, patent. The BPAI's dismissal was based on its findings that Harari's claims failed to meet the written description requirement of 35 U.S.C. § 112 due to an insufficient incorporation by reference statement.

Harari's '880 application claimed priority to a chain of patent applications originating with the '566 application. At the time of its filing, the '566 application contained a statement incorporating by reference the '579 application. That statement declared that the application was filed on the same day and included only the application's title and named inventors. When filing the later '880 application, Harari submitted a preliminary amendment revising the earlier incorporation by reference statement. The preliminary amendment included the awarded filing date and actual serial number of the '579 application, as well as copies of text and drawings from the '579 application. By doing this, Harari sought to claim priority to the '566 application, including its reference to the '579 application.

---

22. *Id.* The court cited primarily its decision in *Lockwood v. Am. Airlines, Inc.,* 107 F.3d 1565, 1572 (Fed. Cir. 1997), for this proposition.

23. 602 F.3d 1348 (Fed. Cir. 2010).

The examiner conducting the interference rejected Harari's preliminary amendment as new matter in violation of 35 U.S.C. § 132, and found the original disclosure in the '566 application did not clearly identify the '579 application as being incorporated by reference. On appeal the BPAI affirmed the examiner's rejection. Harari subsequently appealed to the Federal Circuit.

The Federal Circuit reversed the BPAI's decision, and found the '880 application as filed adequately incorporated the '579 application by reference, and did not constitute new matter. According to the Federal Circuit, the BPAI should have reviewed the preliminary amendment in light of Harari's original disclosure. At the time of his initial filing, Harari only knew the title of the '579 application and that it was being filed on the same day. The Federal Circuit reasoned that Harari's inclusion of those facts in the '566 application's disclosure was sufficient to incorporate the '579 application by reference. Therefore, the Federal Circuit concluded that the preliminary amendment did not introduce new matter when it subsequently used the '579 application's language and drawings in a "cut and paste" format.[24] In fact, USPTO regulations strongly encouraged the applicant to amend the identifying information with any newly available serial number or filing date.

The Federal Circuit also clarified the standard for determining whether an applicant sufficiently and unambiguously incorporates an earlier application by reference. To do so, according to the Federal Circuit, a reasonable examiner must be able to clearly identify the exact reference the applicant is attempting to incorporate solely by looking at all the documents which the applicant presents. Alternatively, the examiner cannot be "so befuddled by the language of the original disclosure, despite the explanation provided in the transmittal and preliminary amendment, that he could not determine what document was intended to be incorporated by reference."[25] The Federal Circuit concluded that Harari's transmittal sheet and remarks within the preliminary amendment informed the examiner in objectively clear language that the disputed incorporation by reference statement was directed to the '579 application. Accordingly, the Federal Circuit held that Harari should not have been dismissed from the interference because he met the written description requirement of section 112 and did not include new matter in violation of section 132.

Written Description Challenges during Interference Proceedings and Which Written Description Should Prevail for Term Interpretations

In *Robertson v. Timmermans,*[26] the Federal Circuit held that when an applicant copies claims from another application or patent in order to provoke an interference proceeding and the claims are subject to a 35 U.S.C. § 112 challenge, the originating disclosure is to be used for construing the meaning of the pertinent claims.

In order to provoke an interference proceeding, Timmermans copied claims from a patent issued to Robertson. Timmermans claimed priority to a parent application which was filed before Robertson's patent. Robertson subsequently filed motions alleging the Timmermans application lacked sufficient written description for the claimed subject matter. At issue with these motions was the meaning of the term "solid," as used to

---

24. *Id.*
25. *Id.* at 1352–53.
26. 603 F.3d 1309 (Fed. Cir. 2010).

modify "rod" in the copied claims. Citing 37 C.F.R. § 41.200(b), the BPAI found that the term should be given the broadest reasonable meaning, "in light of the specification of the application or parent in which it appears."[27] Accordingly, the BPAI relied on the specification from the Timmermans application. However, Timmermans failed to disclose the term "solid" to describe any elements. Therefore, the BPAI held that when used to modify a rod, "solid" should be construed as "solid" in terms of the rod's physical state, in contrast to a liquid or gaseous state. After the BPAI denied Robertson's motions, citing failure to show Timmermans's claims were unpatentable for lack of written description support, Robertson appealed.

In the time period between the BPAI's decision and this case reaching the Federal Circuit, two important changes occurred regarding interference proceedings. First, in *Agilent Technologies, Inc. v. Affymetrix, Inc.,*[28] the Federal Circuit held that "when a party challenges written description support for an interference count or the copied claim in an interference, the originating disclosure provides the meaning of the pertinent claim language."[29] Second, *Agilent* clarified that section 41.200(b), which requires terms to be interpreted in view of the host disclosure, does not apply when one party copies a claim in order to provoke an interference proceeding if the opposing party challenges the written description of the copied claim.

In light of those developments, the Federal Circuit held the BPAI erred in construing the disputed terms in light of the written description from Timmermans. Instead, Robertson's written description should have been used for claim construction when the court addressed Robertson's motion alleging lack of support in the written description. Timmermans argued the recent change in the rule was immaterial because of the common dictionary meaning of "solid" and because the claim construction was consistent with the written descriptions in both Robertson and Timmermans. The Federal Circuit rejected both arguments, vacated the BPAI's judgment and remanded the case to the BPAI to construe Timmermans's claims in light of Robertson's patent.

Proof of Actual Reduction to Practice for a Claim Requiring Certain Constraints during Data Collection Need Not Be Corroborated but Can Be Inferred

In *Yorkey v. Diab,*[30] the Federal Circuit affirmed the BPAI decision in favor of the senior party Diab that its claims corresponding to the count satisfied the written description requirement under 35 U.S.C. § 112, first paragraph.[31] The court reversed the BPAI's

---

27. 37 C.F.R. § 41.200(b).

28. 567 F.3d 1366 (Fed. Cir. 2009).

29. *Id.* at 1375.

30. 601 F.3d 1279 (Fed. Cir. 2010).

31. An interference is a USPTO administrative proceeding between two parties to determine which party was first to invent and, thus, entitled to a U.S. patent. Procedurally, the party with the application having the earliest effective filing date will be designated as "senior party," and the other will be designated "junior party." *See* 37 C.F.R. § 41.207. The proceeding is centered around description(s) of the invention, which is designated as the "count(s)." 37 C.F.R. § 41.202(a)(2).

decision that junior party Yorkey failed to establish actual reduction to practice prior to Diab's priority date. [32] The Federal Circuit remanded the case to the BPAI for further determinations regarding Yorkey's actual reduction to practice.

The court found that the BPAI clearly erred in deciding that Yorkey did not establish, by a preponderance of the evidence, that the invention was actually reduced to practice.[33] In order to establish an actual reduction to practice, the inventor must prove that: (1) he constructed an embodiment or performed a process that met all the limitations of the interference count; and (2) he determined that the invention would work for its intended purpose.[34] Here, Yorkey produced evidence of computer software that performed similar calculations as described in the count. The software performed manipulations of the data but did not specify how the data was collected. Yorkey's witness testified that he collected the data for the software from patients in hospital and in-house clinical studies. The BPAI discounted the hospital data because it was "uncertain and speculative" whether the data Yorkey referred to included the dual wavelength and motion requirements of the count.

The court found that it is not necessary to produce an "actual over-the shoulder observer" to corroborate whether there was patient motion. Instead, the court looked to the data collected, the notations on the data and notations in the software code that supported Yorkey's view that two wavelengths were used in measurement and that there was patient movement during data collection. In combination with other evidence, the Federal Circuit concluded that it was sufficient that Yorkey explained where certain areas of the code corresponded to claim features. Thus, Yorkey met his burden of establishing a prima facie case of actual reduction to practice, and the court remanded the case to the BPAI for further proceedings.

Claim Recitation Need Not Require Simultaneous or Direct Solution

In *Yorkey v. Diab*,[35] the Federal Circuit affirmed the BPAI decision in favor of the senior party Diab that there was interference-in-fact and that Diab's specification supported the claim corresponding to the count as required by 35 U.S.C. § 112, first paragraph.[36]

With regard to the first issue, the court determined that Diab's claim anticipated each feature of Yorkey's claim, assuming that Diab's claim was prior art. The law of anticipation required the BPAI to interpret the claim language and make factual findings that the prior-art reference (Diab) included each limitation either expressly or inherently.

The invention at issue was a method for measuring the concentration of oxygen in blood. The language of the two parties' claims differed slightly. Yorkey's claim recited

---

32. *See* Cooper v. Goldfarb, 154 F.3d 1321, 1327 (Fed. Cir. 1998).

33. Whether an invention has been reduced to practice is a question of law based on underlying facts. Henkel Corp. v. Procter & Gamble Co., 485 F.3d 1370, 1374 (Fed. Cir. 2007). The BPAI's ultimate conclusion of reduction to practice is reviewed de novo, whereas its underlying factual finding is reviewed for substantial evidence.

34. *See Cooper*, 154 F.3d at 1327.

35. 605 F.3d 1297 (Fed. Cir. 2010).

36. *See supra* note 31.

that "*three* functions" must be solved to obtain a saturation value to measure oxygen in blood. By contrast, Diab's claim recited that "*the* functions" are solved to obtain a saturation value without reciting "three" functions explicitly. Yorkey contended that Diab's claim did not solve three equations for saturation; rather, it solved only two, and used a third signal for "approximating at least a portion of said first and second intensity signals based upon the third intensity signal."[37] Yorkey contended that the three functions in its own claim must be determined directly or simultaneously. In Yorkey's view, Diab's claim merely included steps to determine a noise reference value to be subtracted from the other intensity signals, which was not a third function. Yorkey also contended Diab's noise reference value did not include any component of saturation and, thus, could not comprise one of the three functions for saturation as claimed by Yorkey.

The court decided in favor of Diab on each point. The court found the BPAI's claim construction reasonable in that the claim did not specifically require simultaneous or direct determination of saturation from the three functions. The court observed that Yorkey did not point to any terms in the claim or specification that required the three equations to be solved directly or simultaneously.[38] Thus, the fact that the third signal of Diab was used to approximate the first and second signals as an intermediate step was still a function used to determine saturation. Based on Diab's specification, the court also determined that there was an interference-in-fact because Diab's claim did include each feature of Yorkey's claim.

With regard to the second issue, the court found that the three equations of Diab's specification each included a time-varying component of the concentration of oxygen-bound hemoglobin. Diab's claim, therefore, was adequately supported by its disclosure.

BEST MODE

Best Mode Requirement Not Satisfied and Conclusory Inequitable Conduct Allegations Are Deemed Waived

In ***Ajinomoto Co., Inc. v. International Trade Commission,***[39] the Federal Circuit affirmed the ITC's final determination that there was no violation of 19 U.S.C. § 1337 and held that: (1) U.S. Patent Nos. 5,827,698 (the '698 patent) and 6,040,160 (the '160 patent) were invalid for violating the best mode requirement of 35 U.S.C. § 112, ¶ 1; and (2) the '698 patent was unenforceable due to inequitable conduct.[40]

The '698 and '160 patents related to processes for manufacturing lysine. Lysine is an essential amino acid that livestock must obtain from their food sources. Because naturally

---

37. *Yorkey*, 605 F.3d at 1301.

38. Former provision 37 C.F.R. § 41.200(b) allowed the BPAI to give claims their broadest reasonable construction. A week after the April 7, 2010 court decision, the USPTO canceled the 37 C.F.R. § 41.200(b) provision in view of *Agilent Techs., Inc. v. Affymetrix, Inc.*, 567 F.3d 1366 (Fed. Cir. 2009). *See* 75 Fed. Reg. 72 (Apr. 15, 2010). The new provision is effective for interferences declared on or after April 15, 2010, and, thus, is not applicable to the subject case.

39. 597 F.3d 1267 (Fed. Cir. 2010).

40. *Id.* at 1277–78.

occurring lysine may be inadequate, feed manufacturers and farmers regularly added lysine as a dietary supplement to grass feed for livestock. The industry used microorganisms such as Eschericia coli (E. coli) to synthesize lysine from a carbon source. The methods that were the subject of the '698 and '160 patents improved the processes through which genetically engineered E. coli could synthesize lysine, thus allowing for the production of greater quantities of lysine than from naturally occurring E. coli strains.

On appeal, Ajinomoto did not dispute many of the ITC's underlying factual findings, but instead asserted error in the legal test employed by the ITC in defining the best mode requirement.[41] In particular, Ajinomoto asserted that the best mode requirement applies to "innovative aspects" or "inventive features" of the invention. The Federal Circuit, however, disagreed with Ajinomoto. The Federal Circuit held that the best mode inquiry related to the invention as claimed—in this case, processes for making lysine using a genetically altered E. coli bacterium—and was not limited to "innovative aspects" or "inventive features," which the Federal Circuit characterized as "vague" terms that "appear nowhere in our best mode case law."[42]

The Federal Circuit concluded that the ITC applied the correct test to the best mode analysis, and that, in accordance with section 112, paragraph 1, the inventors were obligated to disclose their preferred host strains to the USPTO.[43] The Federal Circuit also rejected Ajinomoto's alternative argument that it had satisfied the best mode requirement because it had publicly deposited a strain containing a lysic variant and disclosed the deposit in the patent specification. The Federal Circuit held that the strain deposited was not the strain preferred by the inventors; therefore, "the deposit failed to enable one skilled in the art to practice the inventors' preferred embodiment and, thus, concealed the best mode."[44]

With respect to inequitable conduct, the Federal Circuit noted that Ajinomoto failed to challenge the ITC's finding of intent to deceive and that Ajinomoto's sole argument on appeal of this issue was limited to a single sentence asserting that the inequitable conduct decision should be reversed because it was based upon erroneous best mode conclusions. The Federal Circuit characterized Ajinomoto's argument as "conclusory" and held that it was therefore waived on appeal. The Federal Circuit concluded that its decision not to address the ITC's inequitable conduct decision "does not affect the finding of no violation of section 337 in this case" based upon its conclusion that the asserted patents were invalid for failure to comply with the best mode requirement.[45]

---

41. Determining compliance with the best mode requirement requires a two-prong inquiry. First, it must be determined whether, at the time the application was filed, the inventor possessed a best mode for practicing the invention. This is a subjective inquiry which focuses on the inventor's state of mind at the time of filing. Second, if the inventor did possess a best mode, it must be determined whether the written description disclosed the best mode such that a person skilled in the art could practice it. This is an objective inquiry, focusing on the scope of the claimed invention and the level of skill in the art. Eli Lilly & Co. v. Barr Labs. Inc., 251 F.3d 955, 963 (Fed. Cir. 2001).

42. *Id.* at 1274.

43. *Id.*

44. *Id.* at 1276.

45. *Id.* at 1278.

INDEFINITENESS

Recitation of "Not Interfering Substantially" Does Not Render Patent Claim Indefinite

In *Enzo Biochem Inc. v. Applera Corp.*,[46] the Federal Circuit addressed the question of whether inclusion of the phrase "not interfering substantially" in connection with two biochemical features of interest rendered claims indefinite. Four patents were in suit, all relating to chemical labels, or tags, placed on strands of DNA or RNA to facilitate a determination of whether those strands later hybridized (stuck together) with other strands that are of interest.

According to the four specifications, properly chosen chemical labels had a number of advantages over the more traditional radioactive labeling of DNA or RNA strands. The labels recited in the claims included a detection moiety, detectable by chemical analysis. Each label also included a linkage portion referred to in the claims as a "linkage group," for holding the detection moiety firmly to its base. The definiteness issue revolved around two recitations appearing in various claims: (1) some claims recited that the linkage group must be chosen so as to be "not interfering substantially" with the ability of the base to hybridize with a complementary base in a nucleic acid strand; (2) other claims recited that the linkage group must, in addition, "not interfere substantially" with detection of the detection moiety.

The district court on summary judgment held that these recitations were indefinite, thus invalidating the claims, because the specifications failed to set forth any way to gauge "substantial interference." The district court also determined that any of several prior-art references anticipated the claims. Finally, the district court ruled that one of the four patents was not infringed.

On appeal, the Federal Circuit panel reversed the district court's judgment that the patents were invalid for indefiniteness.[47] The panel first noted the inconsistency between the lower court's indefiniteness ruling and its finding of anticipation because a claim that is indefinite is incapable of being assessed against the prior art. Moving to the merits of the indefiniteness question, the Federal Circuit started with the proposition that deciding the issue of indefiniteness required a determination of whether persons skilled in the art would understand the claim term at issue. The Federal Circuit noted that when a term of degree is used in a claim, the patent must provide some standard for measuring that degree. The word "substantially," said the court, can denote either approximation or magnitude; here it denotes magnitude because it was used in the context of *how much* interference can be tolerated.

Though the patents did not provide a precise numerical measure of interference, the Federal Circuit found that they contained several criteria for determining the degree of interference. First, the dependent claims specified particular chemical structures for the linkage groups. Those dependent claims provided some clues about the meaning of "substantial." The Federal Circuit reasoned that, given that the scope of the dependent claims was included within the scope of the independent claim, readers of the independent claim would know that the amount of interference caused by the structures recited in the depen-

46. 599 F.3d 1325 (Fed. Cir. 2010).
47. *Id.* at 1343.

dent claims was not "substantial." Second, the specifications provided examples of specific linkage groups that might be used. Those likewise provide clues as to how much interference could be permitted. Third, the patent specifications also taught that thermal denaturation profiles could be used to measure the degree of interference with hybridization. Finally, the prosecution history of one of the patents was helpful, in that it contained a Rule 132 declaration listing eight specific linkage groups that would not cause substantial interference. From these observations the Federal Circuit concluded that the intrinsic record provided sufficient guidance to a person of ordinary skill for determining the scope of "substantially."

Turning to the anticipation question, the court discussed an expert declaration, submitted in opposition to the summary judgment motion, in which the expert asserted that the teaching of one of the reference patents would not have resulted in a workable labeling compound. The panel ruled that the declaration, read in the light most favorable to the plaintiff, Enzo, created a genuine issue of material fact concerning anticipation. For that reason, the Federal Circuit held that the district court's grant of summary judgment of anticipation based upon that patent was in error.

The district court's summary judgment of noninfringement of one of the four patents in suit was affirmed. The claims in that patent recited a "nonradioactive moiety." The Federal Circuit found that the district court had correctly construed that phrase to mean that some form of indirect detection was involved. Given that the defendant's products did not utilize any indirect detection, the summary judgment of noninfringement of that patent was proper.

Claims Reciting "Point-of-Load Regulator" Were Not Indefinite; District Court's Construction of That Term Was Not Impermissibly Vague Despite Use of "Near" and "Adapted"

In *Power-One, Inc. v. Artesyn Technologies, Inc.,*[48] a case that involved the usual types of claim-construction and obviousness issues, the Federal Circuit also grappled with a question of indefiniteness of a claim term. The arguments on appeal were not only that the claim term was indefinite, but also that the district judge's construction of the term was itself fatally vague, leaving the meaning to the subjective judgment of the jury.

The patent in suit involved regulators for controlling the power supplied to various components and devices (loads) in an electronic system. In the prior art as well as in the involved patents, a distributed power arrangement was described, with a regulator located near each device being controlled (hence point-of-load or POL regulators). The term "point-of-load regulator" used in various asserted claims of the patents in suit was not defined in the patent. The district court construed it to mean:

> [A] dc/dc switching voltage regulator designed to receive power from a voltage bus on a printed circuit board and *adapted* to power a portion of the devices on the board and to be placed *near* the one or more devices being powered as part of a distributed board-level power system.[49]

---

48. 599 F.3d 1343 (Fed. Cir. 2010).
49. *Id.* at 1347 (emphasis added).

A jury then found direct infringement, and the district court denied JMOL. On appeal, defendant Artesyn challenged the district court's construction of POL regulator, particularly the court's use of the above-italicized terms "adapted" and "near," as being impermissibly vague, leaving it to the jury to determine the needed degree of adaptation and nearness. Alternatively, Artesyn contended the disputed claim term POL regulator was indefinite and hence incapable of construction.

On the first point, the Federal Circuit approved the district court's use of the terms "near" and "adapted to power" in its claim construction language, observing that "[c]laims using relative terms such as 'near' or 'adapted to' are insolubly ambiguous only if they provide no guidance to those skilled in the art as to the scope of that requirement,"[50] so a court's use of similar terms in its construction should be permissible. Here, the specification and drawings described known prior-art, multiregulator systems of the same general type, thereby conferring a measure of meaning to the terms. Moreover, the patent specification taught that the purpose in locating the regulators nearby was to hold power losses to a minimum. These facts overcame Artesyn's contention of vagueness in the district court's claim construction.

Moving to Artesyn's alternative contention on appeal that the term POL regulator in the claims was indefinite despite any attempt to construe it, the court used an analysis similar to what it had used to reject Artesyn's contention of vagueness in the court's claim construction, finding adequate guidance in the specification for what POL regulators were intended to do.

Artesyn also appealed the district court's refusal to grant JMOL, setting aside the jury's finding that the evidence did not establish obviousness. The court held that the jury was free to disregard the testimony of Artesyn's expert and to credit that of Power-One's expert in determining that the claims were nonobvious. The court therefore affirmed the district court's denial of Artesyn's motion for JMOL on validity.

---

50. *Id.* at 1348.

CHAPTER 5

PATENT INFRINGEMENT

The Federal Circuit addressed a wide variety of infringement-related issues this past year, including claim construction, proof of literal infringement for both utility and design patents, and proof of willful, induced, and contributory infringement. Statutory interpretation also played a pivotal role in defining infringement in various contexts this year.

On at least three occasions, the Federal Circuit addressed the fundamental issue of claim construction and its ramifications for the infringement analysis. In *Adams Respiratory Therapeutics, Inc. v. Perrigo Co.,* the court held it acceptable to compare the accused product to a commercial embodiment of the patent in order to show infringement when the commercial embodiment meets all of the claim limitations of the asserted claims. The court also held that a claim construction that excludes the preferred embodiment is rarely, if ever, correct. In *Becton, Dickinson & Co. v. Tyco Healthcare Group,* the Federal Circuit found erroneous the district court's denial of Tyco's request for JMOL, construing the relevant claims based on the patent specification and the plain language of the patent claims. In *Richardson v. Stanley Works, Inc.,* a design patent case, the Federal Circuit found that the district court did not err in eliminating the functional elements during claim construction because a narrow construction is necessary where a design contains numerous functional elements.

Proving infringement in utility patent cases remained an issue in hot contention, with the Federal Circuit confirming that a patentee must show actual, specific infringement. In *Intellectual Science & Technology, Inc. v. Sony Electronics, Inc.,* the Federal Circuit upheld a district court's summary judgment after finding that the patentee's expert made only conclusory statements of infringement and failed to identify which elements of the allegedly infringing products met the elements of the asserted claims. Similarly, in *Lincoln National Life Insurance Co. v. Transamerica Life Insurance Co.,* the Federal Circuit found error in a district court's denial of the alleged infringer's motion for JMOL, stating that the alleged infringer had to actually practice every step of the claimed method, not simply be contractually bound to do so. In *Oracle Corp. v. Parallel Networks, LLP,* the Federal Circuit reversed the district court's summary judgment of noninfringement because there was a dispute of material fact regarding whether the hardware, as opposed to the software examined by the district court, could meet the requisite claim limitation. Furthermore, the Federal Circuit found in *Transocean Offshore Deepwater Drilling, Inc. v. Maersk Contractors USA, Inc.* that "an offer made in Norway by a U.S. company to a U.S. company to sell a product within the U.S. for delivery and use within the U.S. constitutes an offer to sell within the U.S. under § 271(a)." Similarly, the agreement reached in Norway between the two U.S. companies constituted a sale under section 271(a).

The Federal Circuit also reaffirmed the use of the ordinary-observer test for design patents. In *Crocs, Inc. v. International Trade Commission,* the court declared that a side-by-side comparison of the patented design and the accused product is the proper procedure for determining infringement of a design patent. In *International Seaway Trading Corp. v. Walgreens Corp.*, the court held that the ordinary-observer test is the sole test of invalidity of a design patent.

In *i4i Limited Partnership v. Microsoft Corp.*, the Federal Circuit affirmed a judgment based on the jury's verdict of willful infringement and a $200 million damages award against Microsoft, constraining its review of damages to a "clear showing of excessiveness" because Microsoft did not file a preverdict motion for JMOL on that issue. The court also found no error in the issuance of a permanent injunction against the sale of Microsoft Word, but modified the effective date.

Additionally, the Federal Circuit addressed contributory and induced infringement. In *Vita-Mix Corp. v. Basic Holding, Inc.*, the court held that noninfringing uses are, for the purposes of the contributory infringement analysis, substantial when they are based on the defining features of the accused device. Regarding induced infringement, the court held that, where a product has substantial noninfringing uses, intent to induce infringement cannot be inferred, even when the defendant has actual knowledge that some uses of its product may be infringing.

In another inducement of infringement case, the Federal Circuit found in favor of the patentee. In *SEB S.A. v. Montgomery Ward*, the Federal Circuit held that a patentee had a viable claim for inducement of patent infringement under 35 U.S.C. § 271(b), even though the patentee had not produced direct evidence that the accused infringer actually knew of the patent-in-suit. The court determined that evidence of the alleged infringer's deliberate disregard of a known risk that the patentee had a patent covering the products at issue was sufficient to meet the "knowledge-of-the-patent" requirement in an inducement of infringement claim.

Finally, the Federal Circuit interpreted statutory provisions concerning patent term adjustments, which affect infringement analyses. In *Wyeth Holdings Corp. v. Sebelius*, the Federal Circuit held that the date of submission of an administrative New Animal Drug Application serves as a critical date for determining patent term extensions under the FDA's phased review. In *Wyeth v. Kappos*, the court found erroneous the USPTO's methodology for calculating patent term adjustments due to "Paragraph A" and "Paragraph B" delays under 35 U.S.C. § 154(b)(1). More broadly, in *Novo Nordisk A/S v. Caraco Pharmaceutical Laboratories, Ltd.*, the court analyzed case history, legislative history, and statutory language in order to interpret the counterclaim provision of the Hatch-Waxman Act. In doing so, it found that, for the purposes of Paragraph IV certification under the Act, the term "an approved method" may be construed as *any* approved method.

DIRECT INFRINGEMENT

Infringement of Method Claims Require Accused Infringer to Perform Every Step of the Method

In ***Lincoln National Life Insurance Co. v. Transamerica Life Insurance Co.***,[1] the Federal Circuit reversed a judgment rendered on a jury verdict of infringement, finding error in the district court's denial of JMOL.

---

1.   609 F.3d 1364 (Fed. Cir. 2010).

The patent-in-suit, U.S. Patent No. 7,089,201, relates to computerized methods for administering variable deferred annuity plans. The claimed method requires a minimum guaranteed payment regardless of market activity of the underlying annuity fund so that monies may be paid even if the fund has been reduced to zero. The defendants' product was a Guaranteed Minimum Withdrawal Benefit rider to its annuities, which guaranteed a minimum payment regardless of market activity.

The patentee added the clause, "even if the account value is exhausted before all payments have been made," to the final step (e) in the claimed method. The district court construed this clause to mean that there is a guaranteed payment during the period where payments are scheduled to be made. However, the court also construed the claim as not requiring that the account be exhausted, only that the "even if" clause "simply recites one of the circumstances in which the guaranteed payment must still be made . . . ."[2]

Defendant Transamerica challenged the jury determination of infringement on two grounds. The first was that it had never paid a guaranteed payment when the underlying fund did not have monies available to pay it. This interpretation requires step (e) to mandate that the fund be exhausted for a payment to be made. The second argument was that Transamerica had not implemented a computerized annuity system as claimed.

The Federal Circuit reversed and remanded in an opinion written by Judge Moore and joined by Judges Clevenger and Mayer. The court rejected Transamerica's first argument as being contrary to the district court's claim construction (where the exhausted situation is contingent, representing just one possible outcome). Thus, "[i]f Transamerica's computerized system makes a payment regardless of account value—i.e., if the system will make a payment to the owner of an exhausted account, should that circumstance arise—Transamerica performs step (e). Conversely, if the computerized system is configured such that it does *not* make a payment if an account is exhausted, Transamerica does not perform step (e)."[3]

Regarding the second argument Transamerica raised against the judgment below, the opinion characterizes as "undisputed" that when Transamerica's computer detects that the fund amount is less than the payment amount, it stops making payments. Payments are made, but manually. The account holder is notified that the fund has zero value; thereafter, guaranteed payments are made through means other than the computerized payment method employed by Transamerica. The panel agreed with Transamerica that the evidence established that it does not make guaranteed annuity payments after an account has become exhausted using its computerized system and, thus, does not infringe Lincoln's asserted claims. The court specifically held that a method claim can only be infringed by the practice of each step, not a contractual obligation to do so.

The court refused to reach the question of whether the district court had abused its discretion by denying Transamerica's motion to amend its pleadings to assert invalidity under 35 U.S.C. § 101 following the Federal Circuit's decision in *In re Bilski*, based on there being no remaining case or controversy between the parties. In a concurring opinion, Judge Clevenger opined that, although he agrees that the district court's decision in this regard was not an abuse of discretion, he believes the court should have ruled on the matter.

---

2. *Id.* at 1367.
3. *Id.* at 1368–69.

Considering Multiple Use Limitations in Motions for Declaratory Judgment

In *Oracle Corp. v. Parallel Networks, LLP*,[4] the Federal Circuit vacated and remanded the district court's summary judgment of noninfringement to Oracle in a lawsuit brought by Parallel, claiming infringement of Parallel's U.S. Patent Nos. 5,894,554 (the '554 patent) and 6,415,335 (the '335 patent).

Oracle had originally sued epicRealm, seeking a declaratory judgment for noninfringement of the '554 and '335 patents. In response, epicRealm counterclaimed for infringement by certain Oracle products. epicRealm later assigned the patents to Parallel, who, as a result, replaced epicRealm in the action.

The asserted claims each have three limitations requiring "releasing," "intercepting," and "dispatching" steps. In district court, Parallel presented two contentions of infringement. Under the first contention, the accused Web cache software is treated as the "Web server," and the Oracle HTTP Server (OHS) hardware is treated as the page server. Under the second contention, the OHS hardware is treated as the Web server, and either the software program Oracle Containers for Java (OC4J) or the software program Real Application Clusters (RAC) is treated as the page server. During claim construction, the district court construed "releasing" to mean "freeing the web server to process other requests."[5]

The district court granted Oracle's motion solely on the grounds that the accused products did not meet the releasing limitation. On appeal, the Federal Circuit determined that, because either the software or the hardware could act as the Web server, infringement could be shown by demonstrating that either the software or the hardware met the releasing limitation.

The Federal Circuit reasoned that the district court did not examine hardware infringement when it granted Oracle's motion for summary judgment of noninfringement. Based on the district court's claim construction, the Federal Circuit determined that the releasing limitation could be met under the hardware infringement theory so long as the Web server's hardware was made available for other uses. Oracle contended that the other uses must be for processing a new page request. However, based on claim construction, the Federal Circuit deemed this reading too narrow. Because the Web server handles multiple Web page requests simultaneously, it can use the freed processor cycles to process other Web page requests, thus meeting the releasing limitation.

Because a reasonable jury could find that Oracle's products meet the releasing limitation, the judgment of the district court was vacated and remanded.

Temporal Scope

Term Extensions for FDA-Regulated Goods

Patent Term Extensions and Determining When a Drug Is Initially Submitted to the FDA

In *Wyeth Holdings Corp. v. Sebelius*,[6] the Federal Circuit held that the date of sub-

---

4.   No. 2009-1183, 2010 WL 1709308 (Fed. Cir. Apr. 28, 2010).

5.   *Id.* at *3.

6.   603 F.3d 1291 (Fed. Cir. 2010).

mission of an administrative New Animal Drug Application (NADA) serves as a critical date for determining patent term extensions under the FDA's phased review.

The FDA's drug-approval process has two phases: a testing phase and an approval phase. Because approval of animal drug patents may take several years, patent term extensions are available, which may be added to the date on which an application initially was submitted. The extension period allows for patent holders to add half of the testing phase period plus the entire approval phase period, not exceeding five years, to the life of a patent. The testing phase ends and the approval phase commences upon submission of a NADA, which must include reports detailing the proposed drug's composition, safety, efficacy, manufacturing methods, and withdrawal periods.

Wyeth sought approval of Cydectin, a drug for treating parasites in cattle. During the testing phase of the approval process, Wyeth used a phased review option, which allows for a more streamlined process of drug approval. Phased review requires a sponsor to submit multiple technical reports on a rolling basis, detailing drug effectiveness, environmental safety, manufacturing methods and controls, public safety, residue chemistry and regulatory methods, and target animal safety. The FDA then reviews the technical sections and issues individual complete response letters for each received section. Once all the necessary complete response letters are compiled, an administrative NADA may be submitted, marking the end of the testing phase. Wyeth's final technical section was agreed to be submitted in three separate portions.

The FDA approved Wyeth's NADA sixteen days after it submitted its administrative NADA. In order to achieve the longest patent term extension, Wyeth argued that the approval phase should be considered to begin when it filed the first technical section of its NADA, or at least when it filed the first portion of its final technical section, because that began the regulatory review process. The Federal Circuit disagreed, approving the FDA's interpretation that a NADA must include all the information required by 21 U.S.C. § 360b(b) to start the application phase. Given that individual technical submissions do not include all the information required by the full NADA, the testing period continued to run until Wyeth filed its administrative NADA. The Federal Circuit concluded that the FDA's interpretation of when an application is initially submitted was within the permissible range of interpretations left open by 35 U.S.C. § 156(g). The court agreed that, under phased review, the FDA may not review an application for approval until a sponsor submits an administrative NADA. Further, the court explained that, although the phased review option offers a more fluid process than the traditional filing process for a NADA, an application is not officially submitted under phased review until the submission of an administrative NADA. Accordingly, the court affirmed the judgment for the FDA.

Patent Term Adjustment

Current USPTO Framework for Calculating Patent Term Adjustments Incorrect in Light of Congressional Intent

In *Wyeth v. Kappos,*[7] the Federal Circuit affirmed the district court's summary judgment for the plaintiffs, Wyeth and Elan Pharma International Ltd. (Wyeth). Wyeth filed suit against the USPTO, challenging the method used to calculate patent term adjustments

---

7.   591 F.3d 1364 (Fed. Cir. 2010).

due to delays in prosecuting patent applications. Both parties filed motions for summary judgment. The district court granted Wyeth's motion, and the Federal Circuit affirmed the resulting judgment.

Under 35 U.S.C. § 154(b)(1), patent applicants are guaranteed a term adjustment to compensate for delays caused by the USPTO during patent prosecution. Section 154(b)(1), paragraph A guarantees that patent holders receive a one-day extension for each day of USPTO delay beyond specified examination deadlines. Paragraph B guarantees a one-day term extension for each day of USPTO delay beyond three years after the application filing date. Section 154(b)(2)(A) provides that, if these two delay periods overlap, the term extension "shall not exceed the actual number of days the issuance of the patent was delayed." The USPTO promulgated a regulation, 37 C.F.R. § 1.703(f), setting out a methodology for calculating term extensions in cases of paragraph A and paragraph B overlap. Under the regulation, the USPTO used the greater of the paragraph A delay or the paragraph B delay to determine the term adjustment, but did not combine the two delay periods. Effectively, the USPTO treated paragraph B delay as starting at the application filing date for purposes of determining the amount of overlap.

Wyeth prosecuted two patent applications that had encountered both paragraph A and paragraph B delays. Applying its regulation, the USPTO calculated term adjustments of 462 and 492 days, respectively. For example, the second patent at issue experienced 336 days of A delay and 827 days of B delay, and the USPTO arrived at a 492-day term adjustment by calculating the delay as 827 days (taking the larger of the A and B delay and effectively ignoring the A delay) and subtracting 335 days for applicant-caused delay. Wyeth argued that the USPTO's calculation was incorrect because "overlap" should begin only after the three-year mark. Under that approach, the delay would be calculated as 336 days (A delay) + 827 days (B delay) – 106 days (the amount of A delay that had occurred after the three-year mark). After subtracting the applicant-caused delay of 335 days, Wyeth contended that it was entitled to a term adjustment of 722 days.

Reviewing the USPTO's regulation, the Federal Circuit concluded that the USPTO's methodology could not be "reconciled with the language of the statute."[8] The USPTO allowed B delays to occur at *any time* after the application filing, whereas the language of section 154(b) did not permit B delays to start running until three years *after* the application filing.[9] The Federal Circuit agreed with the district court's conclusion that the USPTO's methodology incorrectly "considers the application *delayed* under [the B guarantee] during the period *before it has been delayed.*"[10] Additionally, the Federal Circuit rejected the USPTO's contention that its interpretation was entitled to *Chevron* deference, concluding that the statutory language was unambiguous.[11] Finally, the court noted the imperfections of both the USPTO's interpretation and the statute itself, potentially producing slightly different consequences for similarly situated applicants, but concluded that it was not the court's role to attempt to correct potential statutorily created inequities.

---

8. *Id.* at 1370.
9. *Id.* (emphasis in original).
10. *Id.* at 1369 (emphasis in original).
11. *Id.* at 1372.

Commerciality of Infringing Activity

Requirements

OFFER FOR SALE

Negotiations between Two U.S. Companies for Product to Be Delivered to and Used in United States Constitutes Offer to Sell

In *Transocean Offshore Deepwater Drilling, Inc. v. Maersk Contractors USA, Inc.,*[12] the Federal Circuit found that "an offer made in Norway by a U.S. company to a U.S. company to sell a product within the U.S. for delivery and use within the U.S. constitutes an offer to sell within the U.S. under [35 U.S.C.] § 271(a)."[13]

Transocean alleged that a rig used in offshore drilling infringed its patents. Maersk A/S, the Danish parent of Defendant Maersk USA, contracted with Keppel FELS Ltd. to build the accused rig in Singapore. Maersk A/S later negotiated with Statoil ASA, a Norwegian company, for Statoil's use of the accused rig. The companies reached an agreement, and Maersk USA and Statoil Gulf of Mexico LLC, a Texas company, signed a contract in Norway. The contract provided that the "operating area" for the rig would be the U.S. Gulf of Mexico.

After the agreement was signed, but before the rig was delivered, Maersk USA modified the rig to avoid infringement of Transocean's patents. Transocean nonetheless brought suit against Maersk USA for infringement of its patents.

The district court granted Maersk USA's motion for summary judgment of noninfringement on the grounds that there was no sale or offer to sell under 35 U.S.C. § 271(a). As the Federal Circuit explained, the district court "relied on the undisputed facts that the negotiation and signing of the contract took place outside the U.S. and that the contract gave Maerk the option to alter the rig to avoid infringement."[14]

Before the Federal Circuit, Maersk USA argued that the offer itself must be made in the United States to constitute an offer for sale under section 271(a). The Federal Circuit disagreed, holding that Maersk USA made an offer to sell in the United States for purposes of 35 U.S.C. § 271(a), even though the negotiations and execution of the agreement between Maersk USA and Statoil Gulf of Mexico took place outside of the United States. The court explained that, when determining whether an offer for same constitutes an offer to sell an infringing product in the United States, "[t]he focus should not be on the location of the offer, but rather the location of the future sale that would occur pursuant to the offer."[15] The Federal Circuit noted that other courts have concluded that an offer for sale constitutes infringement when the contemplated sale would occur in the United States. The court "agree[d] that the location of the contemplated sale controls whether there is an offer to sell in the United States."[16] The court explained that to hold otherwise "would

---

12. No. 2009-1556, 2010 U.S. App. LEXIS 17181 (Fed. Cir. Aug. 18, 2010).
13. *Id.* at *27.
14. *Id.* at *24.
15. *Id.* at *27.
16. *Id.*

exalt form over substance by allowing a U.S. company to travel abroad to make offers to sell back into the U.S. without any liability for infringement."[17]

Similarly, the Federal Circuit found that the contract between Maersk USA and Statoil Gulf of Mexico was a sale under section 271(a). The court explained that "a contract between two U.S. companies for the sale of the patented invention with delivery and performance in the U.S. constitutes a sale under § 271(a) as a matter of law."[18] The Federal Circuit noted that, when determining whether a sale in the United States has occurred, courts may take into account factors other than the location of negotiation and contracting. For example, the place of performance may be considered. In this case, the U.S. Gulf of Mexico was identified as the "operating area" in the contract, and the rig was delivered to U.S. waters.

Although the contract gave Maersk USA the right to alter the final design of the rig, the court found that "the potentially infringing article is the rig sold in the contract, not the altered rig that Maersk USA delivered to the U.S."[19] The Federal Circuit also rejected Maersk USA's claim that there was no sale because the entire rig was not constructed and ready for use at the time of contracting. The court noted that "[a] 'sale' is not limited to the transfer of tangible property; a sale may also be the agreement by which such a transfer takes place."[20] Here, the court found that Transocean's argument that schematics included in the contract show sale of the patented invention raised a genuine issue of material fact sufficient to withstand summary judgment of noninfringement.

Technological Scope

Literal Infringement

Safety Needle Device Did Not Literally Infringe When It Lacked a Spring Means

In ***Becton, Dickinson & Co. v. Tyco Healthcare Group,***[21] Becton, Dickinson and Company (Becton) sued Tyco, alleging infringement of U.S. Patent 5,348,544 (the '544 patent). The '544 patent is directed to a safety needle intended to avoid accidental needle sticking. The safety needle includes a safety shield which is initially located at the base of the needle. A hinged arm, which is in a folded position prior to use, is pushed by a health care worker after injection, causing the hinged arm to unfold and the safety shield to move down the needle cannula toward the needle tip. After injection and removal of the needle, the health care worker then slides the safety shield down from the base of the needle to the needle tip in order to prevent any further injections. The '544 patent uses "spring means" to help with the movement of the shield from the base to the tip of the needle. Tyco's safety needle uses living hinges to connect the safety shield to the needle base. Although Tyco's devices lack any separately defined spring,

---

17. *Id.* at *28.
18. *Id.* at *32–*33.
19. *Id.* at *33.
20. *Id.*
21. Nos. 2009-1053, 2009-1111, 2010 WL 2977612 (Fed. Cir. July 29, 2010).

Becton argued that the hinges acted as springs to move the safety shield down the length of the needle. Becton maintained that Tyco's living hinges contained stored energy, and, when the hinged arm was unlatched, the stored energy transferred from the hinges to the safety shield to move the safety shield down the needle cannula.

Tyco argued before the trial court that the '544 patent's "spring means" required a separate spring from the hinged arm structure. A jury disagreed and returned a verdict finding that Tyco literally infringed the '544 patent. Tyco appealed the case to the Federal Circuit and again argued that its devices did not literally infringe the '544 patent because they lacked the separate spring means required by the '544 patent. Based on the plain language of the claims and the specification, the Federal Circuit agreed and reversed the lower court's judgment entered on the jury's verdict.

In reaching its decision, the court found that the asserted claim of the '544 patent disclosed four separate elements in a list following its preamble. Because the claim listed the elements separately, the court determined that the elements were distinct components of the patented invention. The court found that the specification confirmed this interpretation because the specification did not contain any description of the hinges themselves as moving the safety shield. Further, nothing in the specification indicated that the hinges contained stored energy that would enable them to force the safety shield toward the needle tip. The court found that Becton's interpretation rendered the claim limitations nonsensical because the asserted claim described the spring means as being "connected to" a hinged arm. If the hinged arm and spring means were one structure, the claim should not have recited the two structures as being *connected to* each other. Additionally, the court found that, if the spring means and hinged arm were not separate structures, then the asserted claims would be invalid as obvious over the prior art.

The court then focused on Becton's failure to produce sufficient evidence establishing that the living hinges contained stored energy, which would result in the hinges acting as springs. The court cited Tyco's repeated demonstrations during trial indicating that the hinges did not exert any force on the safety shield once they were latched. Becton had argued that the jury's verdict should nevertheless stand because the accused devices were submitted as evidence, and the jury could examine and inspect the living hinges themselves. The Federal Circuit disagreed, citing an overwhelming record of evidence that showed that no movement of the safety shield occurred after unlatching due to the hinges. The court concluded "[a] jury verdict based on inferences wholly unsupported by the record cannot stand."[22]

Finally, the court addressed Becton's argument that Tyco's devices inherently disclosed springs as separate structures within the hinged arm. Becton argued that the hinges in the hinged arm structure were separate from the hinged arm itself. The court summarily dismissed this argument and held that a hinged arm by definition must include at least one hinge.

Expert's Conclusory Affidavit Insufficient to Create Issue of Material Fact

In *Intellectual Science & Technology, Inc. v. Sony Electronics, Inc.,*[23] the Federal Circuit affirmed the district court's judgment of noninfringement because the patentee,

---

22. *See id. at *9* (citing Lightning Lube, Inc. v. Witco Corp., 4 F.3d 1153, 1166 (3d Cir. 1993)).

23. 589 F.3d 1179 (Fed. Cir. 2009).

Intellectual Science, had not identified specific structures in the accused products that corresponded to the claim elements of the asserted claims. The court further held that a patentee's expert declaration that failed to specifically identify the allegedly infringing structure was insufficient to justify denial of summary judgment of noninfringement.

The only claim at issue on appeal was a means-plus-function claim that required a "data transmitting means."[24] Before the district court, the patentee's expert identified several "off-the-shelf" components and declared that several items in circuit diagrams acted in combination as a data transmitting means. The special master's opinion, adopted by the district court, found that the expert's declaration was insufficiently detailed to raise a genuine issue of material fact and recommended granting summary judgment of noninfringement. In turn, the district court granted the accused infringer's motion for summary judgment of noninfringement.

On appeal, Intellectual Science argued that the required features of the means element were "off-the-shelf" components that its expert identified in the accused products by stating that the components performed the same function in the same way and produced the same result as the means of the asserted claims. Intellectual Science argued that these expert statements were sufficient for establishing infringement.

The Federal Circuit rejected this argument, holding that a "patentee [cannot] survive summary judgment of noninfringement on an apparatus claim without specifically identifying the allegedly infringing structure in the accused device."[25] In this case, the patentee was required to analyze the structures in the "off-the-shelf" components in order to demonstrate that they actually contained the accused structures. An expert's conclusory statements to that effect are insufficient. As a result, the court affirmed the district court's grant of summary judgment of noninfringement.

Doctrine of Equivalents

Existence of Numerical Range in Claim Does Not Necessarily Foreclose Equivalency

In *Adams Respiratory Therapeutics, Inc. v. Perrigo Co.,*[26] the Federal Circuit vacated the district court's summary judgment of noninfringement with respect to Adams' patent-in-suit (the '252 patent) and remanded the case consistent with its opinion. The issues on appeal included whether the district court: (1) correctly granted summary judgment of noninfringement based on its construction of the claim term "equivalent;" (2) correctly denied summary judgment of noninfringement based on its construction of the term "bioavailable;" and (3) correctly granted summary judgment of noninfringement on the doctrine of equivalents.

In 2007, Adams brought an action against Perrigo for infringement of Adams's '252 patent covering an extended release form of Mucinex, a prescription expectorant used to help expel mucus that causes congestion. The claims of the '252 patent recited a modified release drug product having two portions: a first, immediate release portion and a second, sustained release portion. Perrigo's alleged infringement was based on its efforts to seek

---

24. *Id.* at 1181.
25. *Id.* at 1187.
26. No. 2010-1246, 2010 WL 3064010 (Fed. Cir. Aug. 5, 2010).

approval from the FDA to market and sell a generic version of the extended release Mucinex product that contained the active ingredient guaifenesin. Adams asserted that Perrigo's proposed generic drug product infringed dependent Claims 26, 33, 34, and 39 of the '252 patent.

The first issue on appeal was whether the district court correctly granted summary judgment of no infringement based on its construction of the term "equivalent." Claim 24 of the '252 patent, on which the asserted patent claims against Perrigo depended, contained a limitation that the ratio between the immediate release portion and sustained release portion have a C_{max} value (the maximum or peak concentration of a drug) "equivalent" to the C_{max} value for three doses of a standard immediate release drug product containing one-third the amount of guaifenesin when dosed every four hours. The district court construed the term "equivalent" as "within 80% to 125% of the value with which it is being compared, at a 90% confidence interval."[27] It based this construction on Adams's reliance on FDA bioequivalence guidelines during reexamination of the '252 patent. On appeal, Adams challenged the district court's decision requiring proof of a 90 percent confidence interval because the specification of the '252 patent did not require, or even mention, such a limitation. The Federal Circuit agreed with Adams and ruled that the term "equivalent" did not include the 90 percent confidence interval element because the Adams claim did not contain such a limitation.

Based on this corrected claim construction, the Federal Circuit disagreed with the district court's finding that Adams failed to present evidence of equivalence sufficient to create an issue of material fact concerning infringement. The Federal Circuit also ruled that Adams was not precluded from comparing the commercial embodiment of the '252 patent with the accused product in order to prove infringement. The Federal Circuit noted, however, that this is allowed only when the commercial product itself meets all of the claim limitations.

Next, the Federal Circuit addressed the issue of whether the district court properly denied summary judgment of noninfringement based on its construction of the term "bioavailable." On this issue, Perrigo argued that Adams could not prove infringement of Claim 24 of the '252 patent, which contained the limitation that the immediate release portion of guaifenesin to become "fully bioavailable in the subject's stomach." Perrigo based this argument on the premise that the term "bioavailable" meant absorption, as opposed to release, requiring Adams to show that Perrigo's proposed generic drug product was fully "absorbed" in the subject's stomach, not fully "released." The district court, however, disagreed with Perrigo's construction and found that the term "immediate release form which becomes fully bioavailable" means "a form intended to rapidly release in the stomach substantially all of the active ingredient for absorption."[28] The Federal Circuit agreed with the district court, finding that such construction was supported because the claim as so construed covered the preferred embodiment in the '252 patent. Perrigo's construction, by contrast, excluded the preferred embodiments and essentially all guaifenesin formulations. Accordingly, the Federal Circuit agreed with the district court's decision to deny summary judgment of noninfringement as to Claim 24.

Finally, the Federal Circuit vacated the district court's summary judgment of noninfringement under the doctrine of equivalents of claim 34 of the '252 patent. Claim

---

27. *Id.* at *3.
28. *Id.* at *6.

34 recited that the total amount of guaifenesin released into the patient must be "at least 3500 hr*ng/mL." Through discovery, four mean values were obtained for the rate of release of Perrigo's accused drug product. Each was less than 3500 hr*ng/mL, with the highest value calculated as 3493.38 hr*ng/mL, only a 0.189 percent difference from 3500 hr*ng/mL. The district court construed the term "at least" to indicate an absolute lower limit of the range of values permitted. Given that allowing Adams to prove infringement under the doctrine of equivalents would effectively vitiate the 3500 hr*ng/mL claim limitation, the district court granted summary judgment of noninfringement. The Federal Circuit, however, disagreed with the district court, concluding that infringement under the doctrine of equivalents may apply to patent claims containing specific numeric ranges. According to the Federal Circuit, "[t]he mere existence of a numerical value or range in a claim, absent more limiting language in the intrinsic record, does not preclude application of the doctrine of equivalents."[29] Here, use of the claim term "at least" did not foreclose application of the doctrine of equivalents. The proper inquiry, the court explained, was whether the accused value was insubstantially different from the claimed value. Given that Adams introduced evidence sufficient to raise an issue of fact in this regard, summary judgment of noninfringement was improper.

INDIRECT INFRINGEMENT

Inducement

Claim for Inducement of Infringement under 35 U.S.C. § 271(b) Viable Even Where Patentee Has Not Produced Direct Evidence That Accused Infringer Actually Knew of the Patent-in-Suit

In *SEB S.A. v. Montgomery Ward,* the Federal Circuit held that a claim for inducement of infringement "is viable even where the patentee has not produced direct evidence that the accused infringer actually knew of the patent-in-suit."[30] In the district court, a jury found Defendant Pentalpha liable for inducement of infringement. Pentalpha then renewed its motion for JMOL and also moved for a new trial, arguing that the plaintiff, SEB, did not adequately prove inducement under 35 U.S.C. § 271(b). The district court denied the motions.

On appeal, Pentalpha argued that the district court erred in its JMOL rulings because Pentalpha did not have any actual knowledge of the patent-in-suit during part of the time that it sold the alleged infringing products. Before analyzing the factual record, the court emphasized that "inducement requires a showing of 'specific intent to encourage another's infringement.'"[31] In discussing the elements to prove inducement of infringement, the Federal Circuit invoked its holding in *DSU Medical Corp. v. JMS Co.*[32] that "[t]he re-

---

29. *Id.* at *8.
30. 594 F.3d 1360, 1377 (Fed. Cir. 2010).
31. *Id.* at 1376.
32. 471 F.3d 1293, 1304 (Fed. Cir. 2006) (en banc).

quirement that the alleged infringer knew or should have known his actions would induce actual infringement necessarily includes the requirement that he or she know of the patent."[33] However, as the Federal Circuit recognized, its decisions had not set out "the metes and bounds of the knowledge-of-the-patent requirement." Drawing from nonpatent cases, the court held that the knowledge-of-the-patent requirement is met where the alleged infringer was deliberately indifferent to the existence of a patent.[34] The standard is a subjective one, so if an alleged infringer shows that it was genuinely unaware of even an obvious risk that a patent exists, the knowledge standard is not met. The court also cautioned that it was not purporting to establish the "outer limits of the type of knowledge needed for inducement."[35] The court opined that "constructive knowledge, with persuasive evidence of disregard for clear patent markings," might suffice, comparable to the showing of constructive knowledge required under the marking provision, 35 U.S.C.§ 287(a).

Applying its standard, the Federal Circuit found that the trial record contained adequate evidence to support a conclusion that Pentalpha deliberately disregarded a known risk that SEB had a patent covering the products at issue. Pentalpha had purchased SEB's product overseas and "copied all but the cosmetics" to make the alleged infringing product[36] and then hired an attorney to conduct a right-to-use study without informing the attorney that the Pentalpha product was based on SEB's product. According to the Federal Circuit, the failure to inform one's counsel of copying is "highly suggestive of deliberate indifference in most circumstances,"[37] especially where the accused infringer has experience with the patent system.

Moreover, the Federal Circuit concluded that Pentalpha had offered no exculpatory evidence at trial to establish that it actually believed that a patent covering the accused product did not exist. The court dismissed Pentalpha's argument that the SEB fryer it had purchased was not marked with a U.S. patent number, noting both that a product purchased overseas would not be expected to bear U.S. patent markings and that there was no evidence that Pentalpha had relied on the lack of markings in any event.

The Federal Circuit found that the district court correctly denied Pentalpha's renewal of its motion for JMOL and motion for a new trial.[38] The court held that the trial record sufficiently supported the conclusion that Pentalpha deliberately ignored the risk that SEB had a patent that covered its product.

Contributory Infringement

Noninfringing Uses Are "Substantial" for Section 271(c) Purposes When the Uses Are Based on Defining Features of the Accused Devices

In ***Vita-Mix Corp. v. Basic Holding, Inc.,***[39] the Federal Circuit addressed several patent and trademark issues. Of particular interest were the court's decisions to affirm the

---

33. *SEB,* 594 F.3d at 1376.
34. *Id.* at 1376–77.
35. *Id.* at 1378.
36. *Id.*
37. *Id.*
38. *Id.* at 1365, 1378.
39. 581 F.3d 1317 (Fed. Cir. 2009).

district court's summary judgment of no inducement of infringement, no contributory infringement, and no Lanham Act violation.

Vita-Mix sold blenders under the name VITA-MIX 5000. Vita-Mix's patent-in-suit related to a method for preventing the formation of an air pocket around the blades of a consumer blender using, among other things, a "plunger." Basic also sold blenders, including the Blender Solutions 5000. Basic's blenders included a "stir stick." Vita-Mix argued that Basic's customers directly infringed the claimed method when using Basic's blenders (with the stir sticks), and that Vita-Mix facilitated this infringement in violation of sections 271(b) and (c).

Regarding the section 271(c) contributory infringement allegation, the court noted that the accused devices were undisputedly capable of noninfringing use, so the question of contributory infringement turned on whether the noninfringing use was substantial.[40] In general, noninfringing uses are deemed insubstantial when they are unusual, far-fetched, illusory, impractical, occasional, aberrant, or experimental. According to Vita-Mix, the noninfringing uses here (e.g., stirring the stir sticks in a noninfringing manner) were insubstantial because they were based on additional features separate from the infringing features. Under *Ricoh Co. v. Quanta Computer, Inc.,* one cannot "evade liability by bundling an infringing device with separate and distinct components that are capable of noninfringing use."[41] The Federal Circuit rejected Vita-Mix's argument, distinguishing *Ricoh* on the grounds that the additional features on Basic Holding's stir stick are "defining features of the device, are directly related to the use of the stir stick, and are useful only if the stir stick is used"[42] for noninfringing purposes. The court found that no reasonable jury could find these uses insubstantial and affirmed the district court's grant of summary judgment of no contributory infringement.

Regarding the inducement allegation under section 271(b), Vita-Mix argued that Basic Holding's product instructions, and the design of Basic's products, support an inference that Basic had a "specific intent to encourage another's infringement of the patent"[43] as required under the Federal Circuit's inducement standard. The Federal Circuit was not persuaded. Basic's original instructions taught a stirring action which Basic could have reasonably believed was noninfringing,[44] and its amended instructions taught a clearly noninfringing alternative. In regards to Vita-Mix's argument that the design itself supports an inference of intent, the court concluded that the fact that the default position of Basic's stir stick may lead to infringement in some circumstances does not give rise to an inference that Basic intended for users to practice the patented method. The court cited *Warner-Lambert Co. v. Apotex Corp.* for the proposition that "[e]specially where a product has substantial non-infringing uses, intent to induce infringement cannot be inferred even when the defendant has actual knowledge that some users or its product may be infringing."[45]

As for the trademark issue, the court found that the number "5000" as used in connection with the Vita-Mix products serves as a grade designation rather than an indication of

---

40. *Id.* at 1327.
41. Ricoh Co. v. Quanta Computer Inc., 550 F.3d 1325, 1337 (Fed. Cir. 2008).
42. *Vita-Mix*, 581 F.3d at 1328.
43. *Id.*
44. *Id.* at 1329.
45. Warner-Lambert Co. v. Apotex Corp., 316 F.3d 1348, 1365 (Fed. Cir. 2003).

the source of the goods.[46] Accordingly, Vita-Mix owned no common law trademark rights in "5000" on which to base its Lanham Act claim.

WILLFUL INFRINGEMENT

Where No Preverdict JMOL on Damages Is Filed, Jury's Damages Award Is Reviewable Only for "Clear Excessiveness" and Must Be Affirmed if Any Evidence Supports the Verdict

In *i4i Limited Partnership v. Microsoft Corp.,*[47] the Federal Circuit affirmed the district court's judgment of willful infringement and its $240 million damages award. The court also affirmed the permanent injunction entered against Microsoft, but modified its effective date.

i4i owns U.S. Patent No. 5,787,449 (the '449 patent) and alleged that certain versions of Microsoft Word produced since 2003 contained an infringing custom XML editor. Before submission of the case to the jury at trial, Microsoft moved for JMOL on the issues of infringement, willfulness, and validity. The district court denied the motions, and the jury returned a verdict of willful infringement and assessed damages of $200 million. Microsoft renewed its motions and also moved for a new trial. The district court again denied the motions, awarded enhanced damages of $40 million for willful infringement, and entered a permanent injunction against Microsoft. On appeal, Microsoft challenged the court's construction of the claim term "distinct," the jury's validity finding, the jury's infringement finding, the damages award, and the district court's decision to enter a permanent injunction.

The Federal Circuit first considered the district court's construction of the claim term "distinct." Microsoft argued that the claims, which recite "distinct map storage means" and "distinct storage means," are limited to both storage of the metacode map and mapped content in separate files as well as the ability to independently edit the document's content and its metacode map. The court disagreed, finding that the claim language did not restrict storage to a "file," nor did that term appear anywhere in the patent. Furthermore, as explained in the prosecution history, the invention of the '449 patent was distinguishable over the prior art because of its separation of the content and structure of a document, not because of where it stored information. With regard to whether the term "distinct" meant that the metacode map and mapped content were independently manipulated, the court noted that the claims themselves did not recite "independent manipulation," and neither the specification nor prosecution history restricted the invention in such a way. "Independent manipulation" was a benefit of separate storage, not a limitation. The court, therefore, rejected Microsoft's arguments and agreed with the district court's construction.

The Federal Circuit then considered Microsoft's invalidity arguments—in particular, that either the '449 patent was invalid as obvious, or JMOL or a new trial on validity was warranted because it was invalid as anticipated. At trial, Microsoft moved for JMOL on invalidity based on i4i's precritical date sales of a software program called S4. The court, however, held that the preverdict JMOL was insufficient to preserve Microsoft's right to a

---

46. *Vita-Mix*, 581 F.3d at 1331.
47. 598 F.3d 831 (Fed. Cir. 2010).

post-verdict JMOL on obviousness or other prior art. Microsoft, therefore, waived its right to challenge the factual findings underlying the jury's verdict on other references. And, because all of Microsoft's obviousness arguments on appeal related to the sufficiency of the facts, the court concluded that the obviousness issue had to be resolved in favor of i4i.

Regarding Microsoft's on-sale bar argument, the court first noted that i4i undisputedly sold the S4 software more than one year before filing the '449 patent application. At issue was whether S4 anticipated the '449 claims. S4's creators testified it did not because it lacked the "metacode map" limitation. However, the S4 source code had been destroyed, and apparently there was no other documentary corroboration of S4's content. Microsoft argued that its evidence of the precritical date sales created a prima facie case of anticipation and that i4i's testimony of the S4 developers failed to rebut the prima facie case because the testimony was uncorroborated. The court disagreed, holding that corroboration is required in certain circumstances, but not in a case like this where the testimony was offered in response to an anticipation attack and pertained to whether the prior art included the elements of the claimed invention.

Microsoft also challenged the jury instructions pertaining to the validity defenses. According to Microsoft, the jury should not have been instructed to apply the clear and convincing standard for overcoming the presumption of validity as to prior art that the USPTO had not considered during prosecution. In the Federal Circuit cases imposing the clear and convincing standard, Microsoft noted, the court has not distinguished between prior art that was before the USPTO and prior art that was not. In response to Microsoft's argument, the Federal Circuit invoked those cases and rejected the argument without additional comment.

Microsoft also challenged the infringement determinations. Regarding the jury instructions on contributory infringement, the court found no error in using the term "component" rather than the terms "material or apparatus" as used in 35 U.S.C. § 271(c). The instructions properly guided the jury, and the court found the slight deviation from the statute's wording immaterial in this case. Additionally, the court found no error in instructing the jury to focus on the XML editor, rather than all of Word, when deciding whether there were any substantial noninfringing uses. As the court explained, if a tool within a larger software package is a separate and distinct feature, as the evidence showed here, then that tool may be the relevant "material or apparatus."[48]

Turning to the sufficiency of the evidence for infringement, the court considered Microsoft's argument that the general verdict must be set aside unless both of i4i's alternative legal theories—contributory infringement and inducement—were supported by substantial evidence. The court found that it would uphold the verdict if sufficient evidence existed to support either theory so long as neither was legally defective. After considering the evidence presented at trial, the court found the jury could have reasonably concluded that Microsoft contributorily infringed the '449 patent. As the court saw it, the evidence established that at least one Word user would have carried out the claimed method, so the underlying direct infringement existed. In addition, Word's custom XML editor had no substantial noninfringing uses (there were three noninfringing uses, but none were sub-

---

48. *Id.* at 849 (citing Lucent Techs., Inc. v. Gateway, Inc., 580 F.3d 1301, 1320–21 (Fed. Cir. 2009)).

stantial), and the circumstantial evidence demonstrated that a reasonable jury could have found that Microsoft knew about i4i's patent and knew that the use of the custom XML editor would infringe. For the sake of completeness, the Federal Circuit also reviewed the inducement allegation and concluded that it, too, was supported by substantial evidence because Microsoft's custom XML instructions evinced the requisite intent and Microsoft possessed the required knowledge of the patent and the probable infringement.

The Federal Circuit then considered damages. At trial, i4i's expert opined that $200 million was a reasonable award based on a $98 royalty rate and 2.1 million infringing uses of Word. Microsoft countered on appeal that a $98 royalty rate was unreasonable because some versions of Word sold for as little as $97. Furthermore, $200 million greatly exceeds the one to five million dollars Microsoft paid to license other patents. Acknowledging the weaknesses Microsoft identified in the damages calculations, the court noted that Microsoft's disagreement was with the expert's conclusions, not his methodology. *Daubert*[49] and Federal Rule of Evidence 702 are safeguards against unreliable opinions, but do not guarantee correctness. Given the expert's credentials and explanations, the court found that the district court did not abuse its discretion in allowing him to apply the methodology, and that his opinion was "based on sufficient facts or data."

The court next addressed admissibility of the survey offered by i4i. To determine infringing use, i4i's survey expert had randomly selected 988 businesses from a pool of 13,000,000 U.S. companies. He received forty-six responses, of which nineteen reported they used Word in an infringing manner. To be conservative, he assumed that everyone who did not respond did not use Word in an infringing manner. As a result, he calculated that 1.9 percent of Word copies sold to businesses between 2003 and 2008 infringed, resulting in 1.8 million infringing uses.[50] Given the conservative assumptions of the survey, the court held that the district court did not abuse its discretion by admitting it over Microsoft's objections.

Regarding the reasonableness of the $200 million award, the court found that, under the procedural posture of the case, which differed from *Lucent*,[51] it could not even address the issue. At trial, Microsoft chose not to file a preverdict JMOL on damages. As a result, the court could not consider on appeal whether $200 million was "grossly excessive or monstrous," but found itself constrained to apply a more deferential standard and affirm unless no evidence existed to support the jury's verdict. Although noting that the amount was high, the court nonetheless found it supported by the evidence.

Following a jury finding of willfulness, the district court, although statutorily authorized to treble damages, enhanced damages by $40 million. After reviewing the district court's analysis of the *Read*[52] factors, the Federal Circuit found no abuse of discretion in enhancing damages. Although the court agreed with Microsoft that it would have been improper to enhance damages based on litigation misconduct alone, the court concluded that the district court had considered litigation misconduct only after finding the other *Read* factors favored an enhanced award.

---

49. Daubert v. Merrell Dow Pharms., Inc., 509 U.S. 579 (1993).
50. i4i's expert reached the ultimate number of 2.1 million infringing uses at the time of trial by considering sales of Word between the end of the survey and the beginning of trial. *i4i*, 598 F.3d at 855 n.4.
51. *Lucent Techs.*, 580 F.3d at 1301.
52. Read Corp. v. Portec, Inc., 970 F.2d 816 (Fed. Cir. 1992).

Turning to Microsoft's final challenge on appeal, the Federal Circuit considered the district court's decision to grant a permanent injunction. Although the injunction applied to Word products that could open an XML file containing custom XML, the court noted that its scope was narrow, applying only to users who purchased Word after the date the injunction took effect. After reviewing the district court's analysis of each *eBay*[53] factor, the court found no error in the issuance of the injunction, but modified the injunction's effective date. Because the evidence indicated that it would take approximately five months for Microsoft to comply, the court accordingly extended the effective date of the injunction from sixty days to five months from the date of the order.

Following the decision, Microsoft petitioned for a panel rehearing and a rehearing en banc. The court granted the request for panel rehearing for the limited purpose of addressing Microsoft's contention with the jury's willfulness verdict. In a reissued opinion,[54] the court again held that Microsoft challenged only the award of enhanced damages, not the willfulness verdict itself. But even accepting Microsoft's position that it had challenged the willfulness verdict, the court continued, it was reasonable for the jury to find Microsoft willfully infringed. The Federal Circuit subsequently denied the petition for rehearing en banc.

HATCH-WAXMAN

Method of Use Labeling Counterclaims Permitted under the Hatch-Waxman Act in Limited Circumstances

In *Novo Nordisk A/S v. Caraco Pharmaceutical Laboratories, Ltd.,*[55] the Federal Circuit held that the Hatch-Waxman Act authorizes a counterclaim only if the listed patent in the *Orange Book* does not claim any approved methods of using the listed drug.[56]

The *Orange Book* is an FDA publication that lists drugs along with the applicable patents and associated use codes. Use codes along with use code narratives disclose descriptions of the patent claims for the associated drug. The *Orange Book* allows generic drug manufacturers to rely on the safety and efficacy studies found in the *Orange Book* to quicken the FDA approval process.

Novo marketed and distributed a drug under the brand name of "Prandin," which is "an adjunct to diet and exercise to improve glycemic control" in adults with diabetes.[57] There are two patents listed in the *Orange Book* for Prandin. The first patent, U.S. Patent No. RE 37,035 ('035 patent), expired on March 14, 2009. The second patent, U.S. Patent No. 6,677,358 ('358 patent), expires on June 12, 2018.

The Hatch-Waxman Act outlines the process for filing Abbreviated New Drug Applications (ANDA). Under the ANDA process, generic manufacturers must make certifications for each patent from the *Orange Book* associated with the drug for which it is

---

53. eBay Inc. v. MercExchange, L.L.C., 547 U.S. 388, 391 (2006).

54. i4i Ltd. P'ship v. Microsoft Corp., 589 F.3d 1246 (Fed. Cir. 2009), *withdrawn & superseded by* 598 F.3d 831 (Fed. Cir. 2010).

55. 601 F.3d 1359 (Fed. Cir. 2010).

56. *Id.*

57. *Id.* at 1362.

seeking approval. Accordingly, generic manufacturer must meet one of the four listed paragraphs contained in the Act in order to use the patented product or process. Pertinent to this case, Paragraph III certification requires that the patent is set to expire on a certain date. Paragraph IV certification requires that the patent is invalid or will not be infringed by the manufacture, use, or sale of the generic drug. Here, Caraco filed an ANDA for the drug repaglinide, the generic name for Prandin. The application relied on Paragraph III certification for the '035 patent and Paragraph IV certification for the '358 patent.

Caraco then proposed a section viii statement for the '358 patent. A section viii statement is required if a generic manufacturer wishes to seek FDA approval for a use not covered by a method-of-use patent for a listed drug. In support of its section viii statement, Caraco submitted a proposed label to the FDA that did not contain the patented method of using the listed drug. This is conventionally called a "carve-out."

Under the FDA's guidelines, there must be no overlap between the proposed carve-out label by a generic manufacturer and the use code narrative submitted by the pioneering manufacturer. The FDA approved Caraco's proposed carve-out label, and Novo moved for reconsideration, arguing that the use of the drug in accordance with the proposed label would make the drug less safe and effective. Novo also sued Caraco for infringement in district court. Novo subsequently submitted a new use code for the '358 patent to replace the existing code in the *Orange Book* for Prandin. Following the approval of the new use code, the FDA denied Novo's request for reconsideration and denied Caraco's section viii statement because the label overlapped the new use code for the '358 patent. Caraco counterclaimed and requested an order requiring Novo to use the previous use code for the '358 patent on the grounds that the new use code was overbroad and that it suggested that the '358 patent covered more approved methods than it claimed. The district court granted an injunction directing Novo to have the FDA replace Novo's current patent use code in the *Orange Book* with its former listing. Novo then filed a stay of the injunction pending its appeal of the district court's decision.

The Federal Circuit vacated the injunction, beginning its analysis by scrutinizing the statute prescribing the language of the Paragraph IV certification. This provision allows generic manufacturers to assert counterclaims "on the ground that the patent does not claim either (aa) the drug for which the application was approved; or (bb) an approved method of using the drug."[58] Both parties agreed that the '358 patent claimed only one of the three approved methods of using Prandin. In interpreting the provision cited above, Caraco argued that "an approved method" means "all approved methods." In contrast, Novo argued "an approved method" means "any approved method." The court agreed with Novo. Relying on the dictionary, the language of the counterclaim provision, the legislative history, and the case history, the court found that the statute authorizes a counterclaim only if the patent does not claim *any* approved method of using that specific drug.

Caraco also claimed that the patent misuse doctrine should be used to uphold the district court's injunction. However, because the district court expressly declined to address the patent misuse issue, the Federal Circuit similarly declined to adjudicate the issue.

Judge Dyk issued a relatively lengthy dissent disagreeing with the majority's interpretation of the statutory language of the Hatch-Waxman Act. Judge Dyk expressed the view that the majority had erred in interpreting the role of the *Orange Book* and the legislative history of the Hatch-Waxman Act. Further, Judge Dyk found Novo's actions to be ma-

---

58. *Id.* (quoting 21 U.S.C. § 355(j)(5)(C)(ii)(I)).

nipulative and suggested that the legislative history of the Hatch-Waxman Act indicates it was intended to stop such manipulations. Therefore, Judge Dyk asserted that the district court was correct in its ruling, and Caraco had been entitled to an injunction reinstating the previous use code.

DESIGN PATENT INFRINGEMENT

Design Patent Infringement Determined by Side-By-Side Comparison of Patented Design and Accused Product

In *Crocs, Inc. v. International Trade Commission,*[59] the Federal Circuit criticized the ITC's "excessive reliance" on the detailed verbal description and instead declared that a side-by-side comparison of the patented design and the accused product is the proper procedure for determining infringement of a design patent. The court also performed a similar comparison between the complainant's product and the patent to determine whether the complainant met the domestic industry requirement.

Crocs is the assignee of U.S. Patent No. D517,789 (the '789 patent), which claims an ornamental footwear design as depicted in several figures. Crocs is also the assignee of U.S. Patent No. 6,993,858 (the '858 patent), entitled "Breathable Footwear Pieces." Crocs filed a complaint against several importers, alleging unfair competition under 19 U.S.C. § 1337 due to the importers' importation of foam footwear into the United States. Specifically, Crocs asserted that the imported footwear infringes the design of the '789 patent and Claims 1 and 2 of the '858 patent.

On cross motions for summary determination concerning infringement, the presiding administrative law judge (ALJ) granted the respondents' motions, finding no infringement. On review, the ITC vacated and remanded the decision for further review.

After an evidentiary hearing, the ALJ concluded that the respondents did not violate section 1337 because the respondents' products did not infringe the '789 patent. The ALJ also found that the Crocs products did not satisfy the technical prong of section 1337's domestic industry requirement, i.e., the Crocs products did not practice the invention of its patent. Further, the ALJ found that the '858 patent was obvious and invalid. The ITC upheld the ALJ's findings, and Crocs appealed the ITC's final determination.

The ALJ and the ITC reached their conclusions concerning infringement of the '789 patent by using a detailed verbal claim construction: a detailed description of the specific features depicted in the patent figures. The ALJ found that none of the accused products infringed because they were missing one or more features listed in the verbal description. The ALJ also found that the Crocs products were also missing a feature listed in the verbal description. Thus, because Crocs failed to practice the patent, Crocs failed to satisfy the technical prong of the domestic industry requirement. The ITC affirmed the ALJ's findings, noting an additional feature from the description that Croc's products were missing.

The Federal Circuit reversed both the infringement and domestic industry findings. According to the Federal Circuit, the ITC's findings show the dangers of reliance on a detailed verbal claim construction. Previously, the Federal Circuit had cautioned trial courts about excessive reliance on detailed verbal description in design patent cases. In

---

59. 598 F.3d 1294 (Fed. Cir. 2010).

this case, the claim construction focused on particular features of the '789 patent and led the ALJ and the ITC away from consideration of the design as a whole. Further, the Federal Circuit noted that some features used to evince noninfringement are not even present through all of the '789 patent figures. Therefore, the patent is not necessarily limited to products having those features.

The Federal Circuit reaffirmed the "ordinary observer" test as the proper standard for finding infringement. To show design patent infringement, the patentee must establish that an ordinary observer familiar with the prior art designs would be deceived into believing that the accused product is the same as the patented design. This test must be adapted to a pictorial setting because design patents typically are claimed as shown in drawings. The proper comparison thus requires a side-by-side comparison of the patent drawings and the accused products.

The Federal Circuit compared the figures of the '789 patent with pictures or computer models of the accused products placed in similar positions and found that all of the accused products appear nearly identical to the patented design. In particular, the Federal Circuit highlighted two "overall effects" present in both the claimed design and the accused products. One overall effect is a convergence of major design lines and curves at a specific focal point. Another overall effect is a specific visual theme. Finding that the accused products "embody the overall effect of the '789 design in sufficient detail and clarity to cause market confusion," the court held that the accused products infringe the '789 patent.[60]

The Federal Circuit then turned to the issue of establishing domestic industry. Section 1337 requires that a domestic industry "relating to the articles protected by the patent . . . exists or is in the process of being established."[61] In order to meet this "technical prong" of the domestic industry requirement, "the complainant must practice its own patent."[62] The test for this technical prong is "essentially the same as that for infringement," i.e., the ordinary observer test.[63] This test "applies best" in a side-by-side comparison of the patent drawings and the patentee's products. After comparing, side-by-side, the '789 patent drawings and the Crocs products, the court found that an ordinary observer familiar with the prior art designs would consider the Crocs shoes to be the same as the patented design. The court also noted the "overall effects" of the patented design present in the Crocs products. The court therefore found that the technical prong was satisfied.

Finally, the Federal Circuit turned to the issue of obviousness of the invention of the '858 patent. The '858 patent claims a footwear piece including shoe straps made of a specific material and joined in a specific way. The ALJ found that two pieces of prior art show every element of the asserted claims, including the use of the specific claimed material; therefore, the asserted claims were obvious under 35 U.S.C. § 103. The ITC upheld the ALJ's findings. Regarding secondary considerations of nonobviousness, the ITC found that Crocs did not establish a nexus between the shoes claimed and their commercial success. The ITC did find that at least one respondent copied the Crocs shoe, but held that this evidence of copying did not rebut the prima facie case of obviousness.

---

60. *Id.* at 1306.
61. 19 U.S.C. § 1337(a)(2) (2006).
62. *Crocs*, 598 F.3d at 1307.
63. *Id.* (quoting Alloc, Inc. v. Int'l Trade Comm'n, 342 F.3d 1361, 1375 (Fed. Cir. 2003)).

The Federal Circuit reversed, finding that the specific claimed material was missing from the prior art. The court observed that the prior art actually taught away from using the specific claimed material, especially using that material for the claimed shoe straps, because it yields unpredictable beneficial results. The footwear works even though it uses a material previously thought unacceptable for shoe straps.[64]

The Federal Circuit also noted that Crocs had shown secondary indicia of commercial success indicative of nonobviousness. A patentee makes a prima facie showing of a nexus between commercial success and a patent when the patentee shows that there is commercial success for a product that is the invention disclosed and claimed in a patent. Not only were the Crocs shoes the invention disclosed in the '858 patent, but it was the patent's inventive aspect that influenced the commercial success of the Crocs. The court also considered the ALJ's findings of industry praise and copying to be additional indicators of nonobviousness.[65]

Separation of Functional and Ornamental Aspects Proper for Design Patent Claim Construction

In *Richardson v. Stanley Works, Inc.*,[66] the Federal Circuit held that the district court properly construed the asserted claim of Richardson's design patent by separating the functional aspects from the ornamental aspects of the claimed design. The Federal Circuit also upheld the district court's determination of no infringement. After conducting a bench trial, the district court found that Stanley Works did not infringe the asserted claim of the patent because the overall visual effect of the two products was not substantially similar to an ordinary observer if that observer ignored the functional aspects of the claimed design. The Federal Circuit agreed.

In *OddzOn Products, Inc. v. Just Toys, Inc.*, the Federal Circuit held that when a design contains both functional and nonfunctional elements, "the scope of the claim must be construed in order to identify the nonfunctional aspects of the design as shown in the patent."[67] Subsequently, in its en banc decision in *Egyptian Goddess*, the Federal Circuit discouraged district courts from engaging in any detailed verbal claim construction in design patent cases, but also suggested that courts may find it helpful to guide the fact finder by offering guidance on a number of claim scope issues, for example, by "distinguishing between those features of the claimed design that are ornamental and those that are purely functional."[68]

Richardson and Stanley Works took contrary views on the effect of *Egyptian Goddess*. Stanley Works argued that *Egyptian Goddess* permits courts to factor out all functional features from the claimed design, thereby giving them no effect in the subsequent infringement analysis. Richardson argued that *Egyptian Goddess* demands that the infringement analysis take account of the claimed design as a whole, as it would be viewed by an ordinary observer. Under this approach, factoring out individual features, even functional features, would be impermissible in claim construction. Instead, the function-

---

64. *Crocs*, 598 F.3d at 1309.

65. *Id.* at 1311.

66. 597 F.3d 1288 (Fed. Cir. 2010).

67. OddzOn Prods., Inc. v. Just Toys, Inc., 122 F.3d 1396, 1405 (Fed. Cir. 1997).

68. Egyptian Goddess, Inc. v. Swisa, Inc., 543 F.3d 665 (Fed. Cir. 2008) (en banc) (citing *OddzOn,* 122 F.3d at 1405).

ality doctrine would govern whether a design patent claim extended beyond the realm of ornamentality, and a finding of functionality would be warranted only where the *overall* appearance of an article is dictated by function.

The Federal Circuit adopted Richardson's approach. In the Federal Circuit's view, the issue was "not very different from that in *OddzOn*," and nothing in *Egyptian Goddess* compelled a different outcome.[69] According to the court, given that protection for a design patent is limited to the ornamental design, "[a] claim to a design containing numerous functional elements, such as here, necessarily mandates a narrow construction."[70] The district court therefore did not err in factoring out functional elements in the course of its claim construction.

Having upheld the district court's claim construction, the Federal Circuit readily dispensed with the infringement allegation. Once the functional features of the claimed device were ignored, the visual appearance of the claimed device was not substantially similar to that of the accused device. Accordingly, the court affirmed the judgment of no infringement.

"Ordinary Observer" Test Is Sole Test for Anticipation of Design Patents

In **International Seaway Trading Corp. v. Walgreens Corp.,**[71] the Federal Circuit agreed with the district court's holding that the ordinary-observer test is the sole test of invalidity of a design patent.

Courts historically have applied two tests to determine whether a design patent is infringed. Under the ordinary-observer test, a jury compares the accused device to the patented design to see whether, in the eyes of an ordinary observer, the two designs are the same. Under the point-of-novelty test, a jury asks if the accused device appropriates the portion of the patented design that distinguishes it from the prior art. In *Egyptian Goddess, Inc. v. Swisa, Inc.,*[72] the en banc Federal Circuit held that the point-of-novelty test should no longer be used to determine design patent infringement and that the ordinary-observer test should be the sole test. The Federal Circuit had not ruled, however, on whether both tests still apply to invalidity determinations.

On summary judgment, the district court held that the ordinary-observer test was the sole test of patent invalidity under 35 U.S.C. § 102. Applying the ordinary-observer test, the district court held that the patents were invalid as anticipated by the prior art, a patent assigned to Crocs, Inc. The district court did not consider the point-of-novelty test.

The Federal Circuit agreed with the district court's conclusion that the ordinary-observer test is the sole test of invalidity, citing the U.S. Supreme Court's decision in *Peters v. Active Manufacturing Co.,* which declared that "[t]hat which infringes, if later, would anticipate, if earlier."[73] The Court reasoned that, because the ordinary-observer standard is the correct standard for infringement, it therefore must also be the correct standard for anticipation.

---

69. *Richardson*, 597 F.3d at 1293.
70. *Id.* at 1294.
71. 89 F.3d 1233 (Fed. Cir. 2009).
72. 543 F.3d 665 (Fed. Cir. 2008) (en banc).
73. Peters v. Active Mfg. Co., 129 U.S. 530, 537 (1889).

The Federal Circuit then applied the ordinary-observer test and concluded that no genuine issues of material fact existed as to whether the exterior features of the patented designs precluded a finding of anticipation. The Federal Circuit observed that the exterior features of the patented designs differed only slightly from the corresponding features in the prior art. The Federal Circuit held that these variations were insufficient to preclude an anticipation finding because they do not alter the shoe's overall visual impression. The court concluded, however, that the district court had erred in disregarding the design of the shoe's insole, concluding that because the insole was visible to the consumer purchasing the shoe, it is a relevant part of the design. The court thus remanded the case to the district court to consider whether the differences in the insole patents between the prior art and the patented designs precluded a finding of anticipation or obviousness.

The Federal Circuit then turned to the question of whether the design of the asserted patent was obvious as a matter of law. The court concluded that obviousness, like anticipation, requires application of the ordinary-observer test. Given that this issue presented questions of material fact, the court remanded for the district court to consider obviousness.

CHAPTER 6

PATENT DEFENSES

The Federal Circuit examined several cases involving patent defenses, with inequitable conduct, inventorship, patent misuse, and estoppel at the forefront.

The Federal Circuit provided guidance in several cases on the types of activities that could give rise to inequitable conduct. In *Advanced Magnetic Closures, Inc. v. Rome Fastener Corp.*, the court concluded that a pattern of deception regarding inventorship supported a finding of inequitable conduct. Similarly, in *Avid Identification System, Inc. v. Crystal Import Corp.*, the court found no clear error when the district court applied the duty of candor and disclosure to people other than the inventor and attorney involved in the prosecution of the patent-at-issue. In that case, the district court had found that the company president's substantial involvement in the preparation or prosecution of patent applications gave rise to a duty of candor and disclosure to the USPTO.

Finding inequitable conduct often turns on adequate proof of intent to deceive the patent examiner. Several cases confirmed that mere failure to disclose prior art does not automatically constitute inequitable conduct. In *Golden Hour Data System, Inc. v. emsCharts, Inc.*, the Federal Circuit remanded the case to the district court for additional findings as to whether the intent prong of inequitable conduct was satisfied when the patent applicant failed to disclose a prior-art brochure during prosecution of the patent-at-issue. Similarly, in *Leviton Manufacturing Co., Inc. v. Universal Security Instruments, Inc.*, the Federal Circuit remanded the case to determine whether the explanation offered by the patentee for withholding the application was unreasonable. And, in *Optium Corp. v. Emcore Corp.*, the court held that withholding a reference of high materiality cannot, by itself, prove the deceptive intent element of an inequitable conduct claim.

The Federal Circuit also examined several lower-court findings of inequitable conduct. In *AstraZeneca Pharmaceuticals LP v. Teva Pharmaceuticals USA, Inc.*, the court affirmed the lower court's finding that AstraZeneca's failure to synthesize and test prior-art compounds did not constitute a material misrepresentation. In *Ring Plus v. Cingular Wireless*, the Federal Circuit overturned a finding of inequitable conduct because the inference of good faith was as reasonable as the inference of deceptive intent. In addition, in *Taltech Ltd. v. Esquel Enterprises Ltd.*, the Federal Circuit affirmed a finding of inequitable conduct on remand from an earlier appeal. Interestingly, the different interpretations by the majority and the dissent regarding questions of materiality and intent illustrate the difficulty and uncertainty of inequitable conduct determinations.

Cases involving inventorship were also examined by the Federal Circuit. In *Applera Corp.-Applied Biosystems Group v. Illumina, Inc.*, the Federal Circuit found that, under the terms of an employee invention agreement between a named inventor and his former employer, the inventor was entitled to retain ownership of his inventions. In *Vanderbilt University v. ICOS Corp.*, the Federal Circuit rejected the district court's interpretation of the law of joint inventorship, explaining that coinventors are not required to have a complete conception of the claimed subject matter. It affirmed, however, the district court's holding that Vanderbilt's researchers were not coinventors because Vanderbilt had not provided clear and convincing evidence that they contributed to the invention.

The court also decided cases involving estoppel and laches. In *Aspex Eyewear Inc. v. Clariti Eyewear, Inc.,* the Federal Circuit affirmed a grant of summary judgment dismissing the plaintiff's infringement claim based on the doctrine of estoppel, finding that the plaintiff waited three years after initially accusing the defendant of patent infringement to bring a lawsuit.

In *Hearing Components, Inc. v. Shure Inc.,* the Federal Circuit held that the laches defense does not apply where the accused infringer fails to prove evidentiary and/or economic prejudice caused by the patentee's delay in filing a patent enforcement action. Here, evidentiary prejudice could not take the form of missing evidence further proving delay, nor could economic prejudice be proven because the defendant did not make any significant increased expenditures during the delay period and in direct reliance of the delay.

In *Intervet Inc. v. Merial Ltd.,* the Federal Circuit reversed the district court's claim constructions, finding that the claim terms relating to DNA sequences should not be restricted to sequences disclosed in the specification. In addition, the court found that insertion of a phrase into a claim by a narrowing amendment to obtain allowance during USPTO prosecution did not entirely foreclose recourse to the doctrine of equivalents for the inserted phrase.

Finally, the court decided cases involving other patent defenses, including patent exhaustion, patent misuse, and indefiniteness. In *Fujifilm Corp. v. Benun,* the Federal Circuit ruled that the U.S. Supreme Court's decision in *Quanta Computer, Inc. v. LG Electronics, Inc.* did not eliminate the territoriality requirement for patent exhaustion.

In *Princo Corp. v. International Trade Commission,* the Federal Circuit, sitting en banc, held that patent misuse is a doctrine that should be narrowly construed and sparingly applied. In particular, the court held that patent misuse requires proof that a patentee has impermissibly broadened the physical or temporal scope of a patent-in-suit and resulted in an anticompetitive effect.

In *Telcordia Technologies v. Cisco Systems,* the Federal Circuit held that, for determining indefiniteness of means-plus-function limitations, the written description must disclose adequate defining structures to render the bounds of the claim understandable to the skilled artisan.

Lastly, in *Alfred E. Mann Foundation for Scientific Research v. Cochlear Corp.,* the Federal Circuit reaffirmed the principle that an exclusive licensor who retains the ability to sue third parties for infringement has standing to sue, even if its rights are secondary to the exclusive licensee's right to sue.

MISUSE

Application of Patent Misuse Doctrine Narrowed

In ***Princo Corp. v. International Trade Commission,***[1] the Federal Circuit, sitting en banc, narrowed the scope of the patent misuse doctrine over a vigorous dissent by Judge Dyk, joined by Judge Gajarsa.

---

1.   616 F.3d 1318 (Fed. Cir. 2010) (en banc).

The case arose over patents relating to compact disc (CD) technology and standard-setting for such technology. Philips Corp., an intervenor and the patentee in the complaint to the ITC, developed technology for making writable (CD-R) and rewritable (CD-RW) compact discs, as did Sony. The companies established a standard that encompassed the Philips patented technology (which "worked very well"), which the ITC found was superior to the Sony patented technology (which "was prone to error"). Philips administered a package license regime for patents protecting CD technology, involving its own patents along with at least one Sony patent. As part of the license, licensees agreed to produce compact discs according to the industry standard. Licensees also agreed to use Philips technology and not to produce discs using the Sony technology, which was nevertheless part of the package license.

Philips filed a complaint in the ITC against Princo, which had entered into a package license and then refused to pay royalties. An administrative law judge found the Philips patents to be valid and infringed but unenforceable due to patent misuse for requiring licensees to license a package of patents, including other CD technology-related patents that were not required to avoid infringement. The ITC affirmed, but a Federal Circuit panel reversed, holding that the package license was not patent misuse because it charged a uniform royalty no matter which or how many of the patents were involved in the manufacture of the licensed CDs.

On remand, the ITC ruled against Princo on its allegations of price-fixing and restraint of trade. Princo contended that a particular Sony patent should not have been included in the license package, and further, that the agreement to produce only industry standard CDs was equivalent to prohibiting licensees from using the Sony technology to produce competing CDs. The ITC rejected these arguments on the grounds that Princo had made no showing that CDs produced using the Sony patented technology were competitive with CDs made using the licensed Philips technology.

A second Federal Circuit panel vacated and remanded on the issue of whether Sony and Philips had agreed to "suppress" the Sony technology, which the panel said would not have the procompetitive effects that shielded the package license from antitrust liability and patent misuse unenforceability.

This decision was vacated in favor of en banc review, and the en banc majority affirmed the ITC's decision that the Philips patents were not unenforceable for patent misuse. In a decision by Judge Bryson (who dissented from the panel's decision to remand), joined by Judges Rader, Lourie, Newman, Linn, and Moore, and by Judges Prost and Mayer in part, the court found that, even assuming an agreement between Sony and Philips to promote the Philips technology rather than the Sony technology as an industry standard, the "conduct alleged in this case is not the type of conduct that would give rise to the defense of patent misuse."[2]

The majority reached this decision by interpreting U.S. Supreme Court precedent to establish a general rule that a patentee cannot impermissibly expand the physical or temporal scope of a patent, such as by tying the sale of unpatented articles to a license for a patented article, or requiring royalty payments after expiration of a licensed patent. However, the majority noted the law permits conditional sales, such as licenses containing field of use limitations, but those limitations cannot include price-fixing restrictions, tying, or

---

2. *Id.* at 1326.

other limitations that are against public policy. The majority also noted that a patentee has the right to license or refuse to license its patents.

To show patent misuse, there must be evidence of anticompetitive effects associated with the restrictions. Mere allegations of "some kind of wrongful conduct" are not sufficient to establish patent misuse; even proof of an antitrust violation does not mandate a finding of patent misuse "unless the conduct in question restricts the use of that patent and does so in one of the specific ways that have been held to be outside the broad scope of the patent grant."[3] Finally, the majority referenced the 1988 amendments to the Patent Act, codified at 35 U.S.C. § 271(d), as evidence that Congress intended to limit the scope of the patent misuse doctrine.

The majority distinguished the conduct at issue from this standard of patent misuse. According to the majority, even if an alleged horizontal Philips-Sony agreement existed to suppress the Sony patent, that agreement would not constitute misuse of the Philips patents-in-suit. The en banc opinion posed the question before it to be "[w]hen a patentee offers a license to a patent, does the patentee misuse that patent by inducing a third party not to license its separate, competitive technology?"[4] The majority said Princo had provided no compelling authority to support an affirmative answer to that question, other than a decision involving a license that included a twenty-year covenant not to compete. The referenced decision indicated that there must be "leverage" of the patent right that imposed "overbroad conditions" for use of the patent-in-suit, which required at a minimum that the licensed patent rights "contribute significantly" to the alleged misuse. That was not the case here, because there was no link between the Philips-Sony agreement to restrict the availability of the unasserted Sony patents and the patents-in-suit. Even if the effect or intent of the agreement between Sony and Philips was to suppress the Sony technology, this conduct placed no conditions on the availability or use of the licensed Philips patents. The majority distinguished impermissible conditions and limitations that a licensee might impose from restrictions on Sony's activities under the standard-setting agreement; the latter did not involve "an exploitation of the [Philips] patents against Philips's licensees" and is thus not patent misuse "under any court's definition of the term."[5] In part because Princo was unable to demonstrate anticompetitive effects resulting from the alleged agreement, attributable to the patents-in-suit, the court found that a finding of patent misuse was unwarranted.

Princo also raised antitrust allegations concerning the purported Philips-Sony agreement. Citing *United States v. Penn-Olin Chemical Co.*,[6] the majority held that, under the "reasonable probability" standard, Princo had not shown that the Sony technology could have competed but for the allegedly anticompetitive conduct. There was no evidence that the Sony technology could have competed with the Philips technology and ample evidence that the Sony technology could not, so there was an adequate basis for the ITC's finding.

Judges Prost and Mayer concurred in the judgment, but opined that the misuse doctrine is neither as narrow in scope as the majority believes nor as expansive as the dissent contends. However, Judge Prost believed that whether a party has committed an antitrust

---

3. *Id.* at 1329.
4. *Id.* at 1331.
5. *Id.* at 1333
6. 378 U.S. 158, 175–76 (1964).

violation is at least probative of whether there is also patent misuse, thereby parting company with the majority. In addition, in her opinion the court need not have reached the issue of the extent to which refusing to license the Sony technology has an effect on the scope of the Philips technology.

In stark contrast, Judge Dyk, the author of the original panel opinion, dissented, joined by Judge Gajarsa. The dissenting judges asserted that the case "presents important questions concerning the scope of the doctrine of patent misuse," and specifically that the "critical question is whether the existence of an antitrust violation—in the form of an agreement to suppress an alternative technology designed to protect a patented technology from competition—constitutes misuse of the protected patents."[7] Judge Dyk believed that the U.S. Supreme Court's decision in *Illinois Tool Works Inc. v. Independent Ink, Inc.*[8] controls and mandates that an antitrust violation warrants a finding of patent misuse. Here, the existence of an agreement to suppress the Sony technology is, in his view, subject to the application of a "vigorous patent misuse defense." He also contended that there is a presumption (based on U.S. Supreme Court precedent such as *Ethyl Gasoline Corp. v. United States*[9]) that an agreement not to compete is anticompetitive and that the burden was on Philips to establish it was not. This contrasted starkly with the majority's finding that the burden was on Princo to prove anticompetitive effects of the agreement.

Judge Dyk framed the majority's holding as resting, in part, on the proposition that the purported Philips-Sony agreements cannot "infect" the patents-in-suit because the Sony patent was not asserted in the ITC action. Under the majority's rubric, there likely would be no opportunity for an accused infringer to raise a patent misuse defense if it must be in response to an assertion of the suppressed patented technology, which would (almost by definition) never be asserted. He further noted that it is important that "monopolists" not be able to "squash nascent, albeit unproven, competitors at will," especially in new technology markets, which would be permissible according to the majority's holding given that patent misuse could not be asserted as a defense.[10]

EXHAUSTION

Patent Exhaustion Territoriality Requirement Not Eliminated

In *Fujifilm Corp. v. Benun,*[11] the Federal Circuit affirmed the district court's finding of willful infringement of Appellee Fujifilm Corp.'s patents by the defendants, including Jazz Products LLC and Polytech Enterprise Ltd., which are controlled by Defendant Jack Benun.

The case concerned single-use cameras, also known as lens-fitted film packages (LFFPs). Fuji participates in the LFFP market and owns U.S. patents directed to LFFPs. Once used, LFFPs are opened by a film processor to process the film inside. The empty LFFP shell is

---

7. *Princo*, 616 F.3d at 1341 (Dyk, J., dissenting).
8. 547 U.S. 28, 42 (2006).
9. 309 U.S. 436, 456–57 (1940).
10. *Princo*, 616 F.3d at 1356–57 (Dyk, J., dissenting).
11. 605 F.3d 1366 (Fed. Cir. 2010).

not returned to the consumer. Jazz bought used LFFPs, refurbished them, and sold them as new. In 2005, Fuji sued the defendants for refurbishing and selling LFFPs.

Jazz purchased 1.4 million LFFPs refurbished by Polytech, which were detained pursuant to ITC orders prohibiting the importation of LFFPs that infringe Fuji's patents. Based on the ITC orders, Jazz exported most of the detained LFFPs. However, from October 2005 to January 2006, Polytech sold almost one million of the previously detained LFFPs back to Jazz in the United States. Customs released these reimported LFFPs based on an October 14, 2005 letter from the defendants' counsel. During the district court proceedings, Fuji moved for partial summary judgment of infringement. The defendants similarly moved for summary judgment that, inter alia, a prior sale of the LFFPs in bankruptcy was a patent-exhausting first sale and that the LFFPs were permissibly repaired.

On appeal the Federal Circuit examined whether *Quanta Computer, Inc. v. LG Electronics, Inc.*[12] eliminated the first sale rule's territoriality requirement. The defendants argued that Quanta created a rule of "strict exhaustion" and that the court's failure to recite the territoriality requirement eliminated it. However, the Federal Circuit noted that *Quanta* did not involve foreign sales and that the Defendants relied on phrasing that supported rather than undermined the exhaustion doctrine's territoriality requirement. As a result, the Federal Circuit determined that intervening law did not eliminate the first-sale rule's territoriality requirement for patent exhaustion.

The Federal Circuit next addressed Defendants' contention that "the court invoked non-mutual collateral estoppel and precluded Polytech from presenting its permissible repair and first sale defenses on the basis of court proceedings to which Polytech was not a party."[13] The Federal Circuit reasoned that this estoppel argument was waived because the defendants failed to raise this argument in either their Federal Rule of Civil Procedure 50(a) or 50(b) motions.

The third issue addressed by the Federal Circuit was whether a new trial on damages was warranted. The defendants argued that the damages were excessive because in calculating the royalty rate Fuji experts included both infringing and noninfringing LFFPs. Fuji's experts included all of the LFFPs in their calculation because of the defendants' inability to separate infringing and noninfringing LFFPs. Fuji responded to the defendants' argument by showing that the royalty could have been higher than the amount awarded by the jury. The Federal Circuit rejected the defendants' contention, noting that the jury was entitled to rely on evidence of bundling and conveyed sales in determining the proper scope of the royalty base.

The final issue addressed by the Federal Circuit was whether the district court properly held the defendants in contempt of a preliminary order enjoining the importation of infringing LFFPs. The defendants argued that there was insufficient evidence of infringement, that the imported cameras were redesigned, and that Fuji's patent rights were terminated during the bankruptcy sale. Finding the appellant's first two arguments unconvincing, the Federal Circuit reasoned that the district court did not abuse its discretion in finding contempt of the preliminary injunction. The Federal Circuit did not address the bankruptcy argument because it was waived in appellant's failure to raise it in either their 50(a) or 50(b) motions.

---

12. 553 U.S. 617 (2008).
13. *Fujifilm*, 605 F.3d at 1370.

INEQUITABLE CONDUCT

Inequitable Conduct Extended to Include Duties of Substantially Involved Parties

In *Avid Identification System, Inc. v. Crystal Import Corp.,*[14] the Federal Circuit affirmed the district court's holding that Avid's U.S. Patent No. 5,235,326 (the '326 patent) was valid and infringed by Crystal Import Corporation (Datamars), but unenforceable for inequitable conduct.

Avid is the assignee of the '326 patent. The '326 patent discloses a multimode encrypted chip and reader system for use in identifying lost animals. Dr. Hannis Stoddard is the president and founder of Avid. In April 1990, Dr. Stoddard demonstrated Avid's technology at a trade show. Thereafter, in August of 1991, Avid filed for the '326 patent which was granted in August 1993. The district court held that the trade-show demonstration was material to the application that led to the '326 patent and that Dr. Stoddard had a duty to disclose it to the USPTO.

A party may show inequitable conduct by producing clear and convincing evidence of: (1) material prior art; (2) knowledge chargeable to the patent applicant of prior art and its materiality; and (3) the applicant's failure to disclose the prior art to the USPTO with intent to mislead. On appeal, Avid challenged the district court's finding that the trade show demonstration was material and that Dr. Stoddard, Avid's president, had a duty of candor to disclose this information.

The Federal Circuit held that the district court's analysis of materiality was not clearly erroneous. The court first determined that Dr. Stoddard owed a duty of candor in his dealing with the USPTO. 37 C.F.R. § 1.56 imposes a duty of candor and good faith in dealing with the USPTO on all individuals associated with the filing and prosecution of a patent application. To have a duty to disclose to the USPTO, an individual must: (1) be associated with the filing and prosecution of a patent application such that he owes a duty of candor to the USPTO; and (2) know that the information in question is material. USPTO Rule 56 defines individuals associated with the filing or prosecution of a patent application as: (1) each named inventor; (2) each attorney or agent that prepares or prosecutes the application; and (3) every other person who is substantively involved in the preparation or prosecution of the application and who is associated with the inventor or assignee.

The district court determined that Dr. Stoddard was substantially involved and associated under C.F.R. § 1.56(c)(3) and therefore owed a duty of candor to the USPTO. Dr. Stoddard's substantial involvement was established by: (1) his position in which he was involved in all aspects of the company's operation; (2) two communications he had with an inventor regarding European patent applications; and (3) his lack of credibility at trial. Dr. Stoddard's association with the inventors of the patent was established through the nature of his position as president and founder of Avid, through which he hired inventors to reduce his ideas to practice. As a result of Dr. Stoddard's substantial involvement and association, as well as through a review of the entire record and relevant case law, the Federal Circuit found that Stoddard owed a duty of candor to the USPTO.

---

14. 603 F.3d 967 (Fed. Cir. 2010).

The court then determined that the district court's materiality finding was not clearly erroneous because, although the precursor product did not invalidate the asserted patent, it was the closest prior art and was, therefore, highly material to patentability.

Failing to Disclose Prior-Art Brochure Might Be Inequitable Conduct

In *Golden Hour Data System, Inc. v. emsCharts, Inc.,*[15] the Federal Circuit affirmed the district court's finding of no joint infringement of Golden Hour's U.S. Patent No. 6,117,073 (the '073 patent) but vacated and remanded to the district court the charge of inequitable conduct to make additional fact findings with respect to the intent prong of inequitable conduct.

The '073 patent claims a computerized system and method for information management service in connection with emergency medical transport. This system provides for the integration of dispatch, clinical services, and billing data. Golden Hour brought an infringement suit against emsCharts and Softech, LLC (Softech) alleging infringement of the '073 patent. The accused infringers, emsCharts, which produces a Web-based medical charting program, and Softtech, which produces computer aided flight dispatch software, had formed a strategic partnership, enabling their two products to work together, and had collaborated to sell the two programs as a unit.

After a jury found in favor of Golden Hour, the district court held a bench trial to consider the issue of inequitable conduct. A central feature of the inequitable-conduct trial was an undated brochure that described Air Medical Software (the AeroMed system). Neither of the parties dispute that the brochure would have been anticipatory of some of the claims of the '073 patent if it had been prior art. Based on the brochure, prosecution counsel prepared and filed an Information Disclosure Statement (IDS). The description of the AeroMed system in the IDS is identical to what was presented on the front cover of the brochure. However, the IDS did not disclose the integrated billing system that was described inside the brochure. Additionally, at no time during prosecution of the application was the brochure or the billing system information provided to the examiner. The defendants argued that prosecution counsel committed inequitable conduct by intentionally failing to disclose the brochure or the information contained in the brochure. Finding materiality and an intent to deceive the USPTO, the district court concluded that Golden Hour had committed inequitable conduct, rendering the '073 patent unenforceable.

On appeal, the Federal Circuit affirmed the district court's finding that the evidence did not show joint infringement because there was insufficient evidence that one party exercised "control or direction" over the entire process such that all steps can be attributed to the controlling party.

The Federal Circuit remanded the inequitable-conduct decision. It first agreed that the withheld brochure was material because a reasonable examiner would likely wish to inquire into the prior-art status of the system disclosed in the AeroMed brochure in light of the representations as to the system appearing in the specification. Additionally, the Federal Circuit found that the brochure and the information it contained were material because they contradicted other representations to the USPTO regardless of whether the brochure was or was not prior art. By not correcting the false statement in the specification, Golden Hour continued to maintain its truth in direct contradiction to the AeroMed brochure.

---

15. Nos. 2009-1306, 2009-1396, 2010 WL 3133539 (Fed. Cir. Aug. 9, 2010).

The Federal Circuit found the district court's findings insufficient to show that the applicant intended to deceive the examiner. The Federal Circuit reasoned that two possible explanations existed for the failure to advise the USPTO about the integrated billing disclosed in the brochure: (1) Golden Hour and their counsel failed to read the brochure; or (2) one or both read the brochure and deliberately withheld the information. Examining the testimony before the district court, the Federal Circuit concluded that it was necessary to remand the case back to the district court to make detailed factual findings, particularly concerning whether Golden Hour or their counsel in fact read the brochure and deliberately decided to withhold damaging information from the USPTO.

Failure to Disclose Material Patent Application Can Constitute Inequitable Conduct

In *Leviton Manufacturing Co., Inc. v. Universal Security Instruments, Inc.,*[16] the Federal Circuit agreed with the lower court that a material patent application was withheld during prosecution of the patent-in-suit. At issue was U.S. Patent Application No. 10/690,776 (the Germain application), filed in October 2003 by Leviton, which listed Germain and five other inventors as coinventors. The Germain application claimed priority to a February 2003 provisional application. In April 2004, Leviton filed another application, later issued as U.S. Patent No. 6,864,766 (the '766 patent), which was a third-generation continuation of U.S. Patent No. 6,246,588 (the '588 patent). The '588 patent claimed priority to an application filed in 1999. The '766 patent and the Germain application had many claims that were nearly identical, yet neither had common inventors or priority references to one another. Leviton also failed to disclose the Germain application during the prosecution of the '766 patent. Leviton disclosed the '766 patent in the prosecution of the Germain application only after the '766 patent was issued. In response to a subsequent double-patenting rejection, Leviton canceled the claims from the Germain application containing similar subject matter as the '766 patent.

In March 2005, Leviton filed suit against Universal and Meihao alleging infringement of the '766 patent. A reexamination of the '766 patent was then requested in June 2005. During the reexamination period, Leviton did not disclose the Germain application or litigation related to the application to the USPTO examiner. The examiner subsequently confirmed all of the claims. The requestor of the reexamination appealed the decision.

In view of Leviton's apparent failure to adequately disclose information, the district court dismissed the infringement case with prejudice and gave Meihao leave to file a motion for fees and costs. The magistrate judge held that Leviton committed inequitable conduct, engaged in a strategy of vexatious litigation and awarded attorneys' fees to Meihao. The district court entered a judgment in favor of Meihao for over $1 million in costs and reasonable attorneys' fees.

On appeal, the Federal Circuit began its discussion by stating the Patent Act allows for awarding of attorneys' fees in exceptional cases to the prevailing party.[17] Because the district court granted the attorneys' fees on both inequitable conduct and vexatious litigation, the Federal Circuit focused its review on these two elements. In reviewing the ineq-

16. 606 F.3d 1353 (Fed. Cir. 2010).
17. 35 U.S.C. § 285.

uitable conduct element, the court found that the Germain application was material because "a reasonable examiner would want to consider the Germain application with respect to inventorship and double patenting."[18]

Leviton also challenged the district court's conclusion that its failure to disclose related litigation during prosecution of the '766 patent was material. Citing MPEP § 2001.06(c) and Federal Circuit precedent, the court held that Leviton should have disclosed the related litigation, including suits relating to the validity of the patent, fraud, and inequitable conduct. Thus, the court concluded the failure to disclose the litigation was material.

Next, the court addressed whether Leviton withheld the Germain application and related litigation with the intention to deceive the USPTO examiner. The Federal Circuit noted that intent to deceive is rarely proven through direct evidence and can be generally inferred by facts and circumstances regarding an applicant's conduct. The applicant is also allowed to offer a good faith explanation when information of a relatively high level of materiality is found to be withheld. Meihao argued that Claude Narcisse, one of the attorneys responsible for filing and prosecuting the Germain application, failed to provide a credible explanation for not notifying the USPTO about copying the claim language. Meihao maintained that Leviton had a strong motive to deceive the USPTO and that Narcisse's experience and knowledge indicated that he should have known about his duty to disclose. Further, Meihao argued there was an absence of good faith on Leviton's part. Leviton responded by arguing that the judge erroneously inferred the intent to deceive and Narcisse did not believe the Germain application was prior art because the '766 patent's priority date was three years before the filing of the Germain application. The Federal Circuit found there to be genuine issues of material fact regarding the finding of intent to deceive and remanded the issue for an evidentiary hearing.

Regarding Leviton's failure to disclose the related litigation, the court held that although Narcisse did not provide any explanation for not disclosing the information, "the failure to provide an explanation is not independently dispositive of whether a patent prosecutor intended to deceive the USPTO."[19] Accordingly, because the court found genuine issues of material fact existed regarding the inequitable conduct finding, the court vacated the district court's holding and remanded the case for a bench trial.

Finally, the court reached the vexatious litigation issue. Because the district court based the vexatious litigation holding on its positive finding of inequitable conduct, the Federal Circuit vacated and remanded the lower court's decision regarding this element. Additionally, the court expressed concern over the district court's rejection of Leviton's work-product objections. The lower court found that Meihao satisfied the rare exceptions to producing work product of "substantial need" and "undue hardship."[20] However, the Federal Circuit concluded the lower court erred in its vexatious litigation finding, which was based in part on Leviton's numerous work-product objections. Accordingly, the district court's judgment was vacated and remanded.

In a relatively lengthy dissent, Circuit Judge Prost departed with the majority and would have affirmed the district court's findings of inequitable conduct and deceptive intent. Prost emphasized certain facts and circumstances surrounding Narcisse's prosecu-

---

18. *Leviton*, 606 F.3d at 1361–62.
19. Larson Mfg. Co. v. Aluminart Prods. Ltd., 559 F.3d 1317, 1341 (Fed. Cir. 2009).
20. *Leviton*, 606 F.3d at 1365.

tion of the Germain application to argue the lower court correctly found inequitable conduct on summary judgment. Judge Prost believed the majority's holding will result in a more difficult burden for others trying to establish deceptive intent.

Materiality

Failure to Provide Data for Less Similar Compounds Does Not Constitute Inequitable Conduct

In *AstraZeneca Pharmaceuticals LP v. Teva Pharmaceuticals USA, Inc.,*[21] the Federal Circuit affirmed the district court's summary judgment of no inequitable conduct.[22] The district court found insufficient evidence to show that AstraZeneca made a material misrepresentation or omission with the intent to deceive the patent examiner during prosecution, and the Federal Circuit agreed.

The Federal Circuit noted that inequitable conduct, which may render a patent unenforceable, requires threshold findings of materiality and deceptive intent. Although no uniform standard of materiality has been applied, the court noted that the test used most often is "whether a reasonable examiner would have considered the information important in deciding whether to grant the patent."[23] Even if a reference meets the materiality test, it need not be disclosed if it is cumulative to, or less material than, the other references disclosed. Deceptive intent requires that the conduct demonstrate sufficient culpability and cannot be inferred from the mere withholding of information. Once materiality and deceptive intent are established by clear and convincing evidence, they are balanced with cognizance of the underlying facts in order to make a determination about inequitable conduct.

Teva argued that AstraZeneca committed inequitable conduct by failing to synthesize and test additional prior-art compounds having potential atypical antipsychotic activity, which was the property AstraZeneca argued was unexpected in the claimed drug during prosecution. The court disagreed with Teva, concluding that, although failure to conduct tests may be criticized in some situations, AstraZeneca's provision of existing internal data on certain compounds in place of the preparation and testing of other less similar compounds did not constitute a material misrepresentation. In considering the deceptive intent prong, the court noted that Teva did not provide evidence of bad faith concerning AstraZeneca's nondisclosure of data.

The Federal Circuit affirmed the district court's summary judgment of no inequitable conduct, concluding that Teva did "not provide[] evidence sufficient to establish the threshold facts of material withholding with the intent to deceive."[24]

---

21. 583 F.3d 766 (Fed. Cir. 2009).
22. *Id.* at 777.
23. *Id.* at 773.
24. *Id.* at 777.

Intent to Deceive

Inequitable Conduct Determination Supported by Finding of Actual Deceit over Inventorship

In *Advanced Magnetic Closures Inc. v. Rome Fastener Corp.*,[25] the Federal Circuit affirmed the district court's conclusion that Advanced Magnetic Closure's (AMC) patent-in-suit, drawn to magnetic snap fasteners commonly used in women's handbags, was unenforceable because of inequitable conduct. The court also affirmed in part an award of attorneys' fees and costs under section 285 against AMC and its attorneys based on inequitable conduct and litigation misconduct under 28 U.S.C. § 1927. The Federal Circuit affirmed the award as to AMC, but reversed as to counsel involved in the case, except for one firm that settled during the appeal.

AMC had, inter alia, submitted reconstructed evidence and had engaged in evasive litigation tactics. For example, AMC submitted an expert report opining that the patent-in-suit covered the accused fasteners, and that the expert had performed a test confirming the same. The defendant later uncovered that the expert had not, in fact, performed that test, but instead the test had been conducted by another individual who had reached the opposite conclusion. AMC then elected not to use that expert.

The asserted inequitable conduct concerned allegations that AMC's president, Bauer, had misrepresented to the USPTO that he was the sole inventor of the patent-in-suit. A former employee, Riceman, claimed that he had invented the fastener of the patent-in-suit. In a previous lawsuit, Riceman had settled the claims of inventorship with AMC and had agreed not to voluntarily assist anyone litigating against AMC. Deposed pursuant to a subpoena, Riceman contradicted Bauer's explanation of how he had allegedly invented the fastener of the patent-in-suit. AMC then submitted two documents in an effort to corroborate Bauer's claim of inventorship. One was an invoice that demanded payment for snap fastener prototypes. Bauer admitted at trial that the invoice was not the original but one that he had drafted and reconstructed. The second was an invoice from a law firm for patent prosecution services. AMC later conceded that invoice had also been "reconstructed," but that admission came after Rome had identified the document's defect in its summary judgment reply brief. Also, according to the Federal Circuit, AMC submitted other reconstructed evidence at trial.

The district court found that the inventorship question was material to patentability and information regarding inventorship had been withheld from the USPTO with an intent to deceive.

The Federal Circuit affirmed the district court's inequitable conduct determination. The court first noted that information regarding inventorship was always material. The court also found that the intent to deceive was "the single most reasonable inference able to be drawn from the evidence."[26]

The Federal Circuit, however, overturned joint and severable liability against AMC's counsel who had not settled during the appeal, because the district court had failed to comply with controlling regional circuit requirements to support sanctions.

---

25. 607 F.3d 817 (Fed. Cir. 2010).

26. *Id.* at 830 (citing Star Scientific, Inc. v. R.J. Reynolds Tobacco Co., 537 F.3d 1357, 1365 (Fed. Cir. 2008)).

Judge Rader filed a concurring opinion noting that he would refrain from reviewing inequitable conduct cases until after the *en banc* court issue an opinion in *Therasense v. Becton Dickinson.*

Failure to Disclose a Material Reference Does Not Prove Deceptive Intent for Inequitable Conduct

In ***Optium Corp. v. Emcore Corp.***,[27] Emcore brought suit against Optium alleging infringement of patents directed to reducing interference over fiber-optic lines through the use of two-tone phase modulation. Optium countered by filing a separate suit alleging the relevant patents were unenforceable due to inequitable conduct. Optium's inequitable conduct claim rested on Emcore's failure to disclose an alleged "highly relevant" reference (the Willems reference) to the patent examiner. Emcore acknowledged the inventors knew of Willems and that the reference was cited in the background section of an internal research report. On appeal, none of the inventors or prosecuting attorneys could adequately explain why Willems had not been submitted to the patent examiner during prosecution, perhaps partly due to the ten-year period between prosecution and the appeal. Optium's expert asserted that Willems, in view of a combination of other references, would establish a prima facie case of obviousness. However, because there was no evidence presented establishing deceptive intent, the district court held there was no inequitable conduct.

On appeal, the Federal Circuit reiterated its longstanding view that proof of intent to deceive or mislead the patent examiner is necessary to prove inequitable conduct. Further, "clear and convincing evidence must show that the applicant made a deliberate decision to withhold a known material reference" when an applicant omits a reference during prosecution.[28] The court rejected Optium's argument that circumstantial evidence, in particular, the high level of materiality of Willems, could be used in the absence of direct evidence of intent to deceive. The court cited Federal Circuit precedent in rejecting "the notion that the materiality of a reference alone can suffice to prove deceptive intent."[29] The court also rejected Optium's argument that its evidentiary burden should be lessened because the applicant had failed to provide an explanation for not disclosing Willems, holding that the challenger always carries the burden to meet a threshold level of evidence establishing deceptive intent.

In a detailed concurrence, Judge Prost expressed concern over the majority's language regarding the proper utility of a reference of high materiality. Judge Prost stressed that materiality and intent are separate elements under inequitable conduct. Judge Prost explained that materiality is not per se irrelevant in establishing deceptive intent. Instead, materiality might be probative of intent.

---

27. 603 F.3d 1313 (Fed. Cir. 2010).
28. *Id.* at 1320–21 (citing Molins PLC v. Textron, Inc., 48 F.3d 1172, 1181 (Fed. Cir. 1995)).
29. *Id.* at 1321.

Inequitable Conduct Finding Is Inappropriate When Inference of Good Faith Was as Reasonable as Inference of Deceptive Intent

In *Ring Plus v. Cingular Wireless*,[30] the Federal Circuit overturned the lower court's ruling of unenforceability due to inequitable conduct but affirmed its judgment of noninfringement.

The plaintiff brought a patent infringement claim against the defendant of a patent related to software for enabling message presentation during a telephone ringing period. The telephone ringing period refers to the time after a phone call is routed from the calling party to the called party, where the calling party is waiting for the called party to answer. The plaintiff's invention allows the called party to hear a sound presentation, such as a voice message or music, during the ringing period.

To prove inequitable conduct, a party must establish: (1) affirmative misrepresentation of material fact, failure to disclose material information, or submission of false material information; and (2) intent to deceive the USPTO. On appeal, the underlying factual findings of materiality and intent are reviewed for clear error, whereas the ultimate holding of inequitable conduct is reviewed for abuse of discretion.

The alleged misrepresentations of fact were made in the background of the application and in an amendment submitted during prosecution. In the background section of the application, the applicants characterized certain prior art references as missing an algorithm or software for operating a phone system. In the amendment, the applicants asserted that their invention was the only system that only generated a message when the phone line between the caller and the called party was not busy.

On appeal, the Federal Circuit agreed with the district court that the prior art references disclosed software for operating a telephone system, and accordingly found no error in the district court's determination that the Applicants' statement in the background of the invention was a material misrepresentation. However, the Federal Circuit determined that the district court had clearly erred in concluding that the statement in the amendment was a misrepresentation, in view of the fact that disclosures in the references contradicted the district court's position.

As to intent to deceive, the Federal Circuit concluded that the district court's finding of intent to deceive had been based almost entirely on a finding that the references *unambiguously* disclosed software. The Federal Circuit noted that the references did not explicitly disclose software, but described components that would be understood by those skilled in the art to be associated with software. From the foregoing, coupled with the other evidence of record, the court concluded that an inference of good faith was as reasonable as an inference of deceptive intent and overturned the determination of inequitable conduct.

Next, the court reviewed the district court's summary judgment of noninfringement. The asserted claims in the patent recited a series of steps which included determining whether the called number was busy and allowing the sound presentation if not busy. At issue was whether the steps applied during only the telephone-ringing period. The accused product played the sound presentation prior to determining whether the line was busy. The plaintiffs argued that "allowing" should be constructed as "allowing to continue or to begin." Therefore, the claim limitation "allowing for a sound presentation if the telephone is busy" would cover a product that played a sound presentation prior to determining

---

30. 614 F.3d 1354 (Fed.Cir. 2010).

whether the phone line was busy, and permitting the voice presentation to continue upon determination that the line was not busy.

The Federal Circuit affirmed the claim construction construing "allowing" as "allowing to begin," as opposed to "allowing to begin or continue." Given that the foregoing claim construction was the sole alleged error underlying the grant of summary judgment, the Federal Circuit affirmed summary judgment of noninfringement.

Role of Different Interpretations of Materiality and Intent in Inequitable Conduct Determinations

In **Taltech Ltd. v. Esquel Enterprises Ltd.,**[31] the Federal Circuit affirmed the district court's inequitable conduct finding. Of particular importance, however, are the starkly different interpretations of both materiality and intent seen in the majority and dissenting opinions. The issue, involving U.S. Patent No. 5,568,779, directed to seams containing thermal adhesive that are used to reduce seam puckering in dress shirts, arose from the patentee's failure to disclose a "raincoat seam" during patent prosecution that the inventor testified was his "inspiration" for the invention.

In an earlier appeal, the Federal Circuit had reversed and remanded an inequitable-conduct determination specifically on the issue of whether this "undisclosed raincoat seam (URS)" was cumulative over the prior art of record, specifically, a German patent issued to Rober. On remand, the district court found that the URS was not cumulative, was material prior art and that the patentee exhibited an intent to deceive by not disclosing the URS and by making affirmative misrepresentations during patent prosecution. In turn, the court found this to be an exceptional case, under 35 U.S.C. § 285, of both inequitable conduct and litigation misconduct, and, consequently, awarded defendants attorneys' fees and costs. The district court set the post-judgment interest rate at the time its initial inequitable conduct determination had been made.

In the latest appeal, in an opinion by Judge Mayer and joined by Judge Friedman, the Federal Circuit affirmed the inequitable conduct determination but reversed the post-judgment interest rate used below. The majority agreed that the translation of the Rober patent, as presented by the patentee during prosecution, was sufficiently inadequate that the teachings of the reference were not properly before the examiner. Thus, the URS disclosure was not cumulative over the deficient presentation of the Rober patent. The majority also agreed that failure to disclose the importance of the best mode thermal adhesive, as incorporated into the URS, was material. Likewise, the majority noted, as the district court previously found, that positions taken by the plaintiff at trial were contrary to affirmative statements made during patent prosecution, and thereby constituted misrepresentations. Included in these misrepresentations was evidence that types of stitches characterized by the patentee as being inadequate for use in dress shirts were used in 5 percent of the dress shirts sold by patentee during the time the patent-in-suit was being prosecuted. The majority also found evidence of misrepresentations made by the plaintiff's patent attorney, who indicated that the prior-art stitch had only recently come to his (and by attribution, the inventor's) attention, even though the inventor previously testified that he was aware of the stitch prior to the time the plaintiff's attorney made that statement.

---

31. 604 F.3d 1324 (Fed. Cir. 2010).

Regarding the intent to deceive prong of the inequitable conduct showing, the majority affirmed the district court's reliance on "indirect and circumstantial evidence" of an
intent to deceive, inferred from conduct including disclosure of other, less material prior
art seams than the URS and the absence of any contrary evidence of good faith. The
majority expressly rejected the argument that the purported misrepresentations were irrelevant because they had no bearing on the reasons why the patent claims were allowed,
stating that "TAL's assertion of unequivocal untruths about a reference, simultaneous with
presentation of the reference, in order to minimize the reference's impact on the examiner
shows TAL's intent to deceive."[32]

Regarding litigation misconduct, the majority refused to disturb the district court's
determination, stating that as an appellate court it was "ill-suited" to weigh the evidence,
which, being "context-specific," was better decided by the district court. Specifically, the
majority opined: "it ill-behooves an appellate court to overrule a trial judge concerning
litigation misconduct when the litigation occurred in front of the trial judge, not the
appellate court."[33]

Regarding the interest rate determination, the majority held that reversal of the district court's prior inequitable conduct determination rendered that judgment "legally insufficient." Instead, the proper interest rate should be set from the date of the district
court's more recent judgment, which was affirmed by the Federal Circuit in this opinion.

In dissent, Judge Gajarsa took an almost diametrically opposite view of the evidence of
both materiality and intent. He noted first that the "URS" was a drawing made by the
inventor during his deposition in response to a question about what had been his "inspiration" for the claimed invention, and because there is no requirement that an applicant disclose evidence of his "inspiration," he was under no duty to disclose the URS during
prosecution. In Judge Gajarsa's view, the majority defined the URS, the Rober patent, and
the disclosures of each in a way that minimized the considerable overlap between them,
going so far as to set forth the stitch disclosed in the URS, the Rober patent, and the patent-
in-suit, and comparing the similarities and differences. In Judge Gajarsa's view, such a
comparison made it clear that the Rober patent disclosed features of the claimed invention
missing from the URS, rendering the URS cumulative to the disclosure of the Rober patent.
He also disagreed with the relevance of the particular thermal adhesive used in the URS and
the majority's reliance on this thermal adhesive as the best mode to support its determination
that the URS was not cumulative. Here, Judge Gajarsa asserted that the thermal adhesive was
irrelevant, because even the broadest claims did not contain any limitations directed to the
species of thermal adhesive. Judge Gajarsa also found alternative explanations for the patentee's
statements that both the district court and the majority characterized as misrepresentations.
For example, instead of finding, as the majority did, that the patentee's characterization of
certain prior art seams (as being inadequate) was inconsistent with the patentee's use of such
seams in 5 percent of the dress shirts it sold at the time, Judge Gajarsa believed the statement
was consistent with the patentee using such seams in *only* 5 percent of it shirts.

Judge Gajarsa was even more forceful in his assessment of how the majority addressed the intent to deceive prong, finding that "the majority has approved a deceptive
intent finding that lacks any support in law or fact and represents a dangerous departure

---

32. *Id.* at 1334.
33. *Id.* (quoting Nilssen v. Osram, 528 F.3d 1352, 1359 (Fed. Cir. 2008)).

from our precedent."[34] In his view, the inferred intent depended almost entirely on the failure to disclose the URS, which is improper because there must be some quantum of evidence for both materiality and intent. Moreover, Judge Gajarsa argued that the majority ignored evidence of good faith, including that the inventor had produced the URS drawing during a deposition, indicating that he had nothing to hide.

DEFENSES TO DOCTRINE OF EQUIVALENTS

Estoppel

Prosecution History Estoppel

AMENDMENT-BASED ESTOPPEL

Narrowing Amendment Does Not Limit Doctrine of Equivalents to Only Then-Known Viruses

In ***Intervet Inc. v. Merial Ltd.,***[35] the Federal Circuit remanded Intervet's declaratory judgment action back to the district court to examine whether Intervet infringed Merial's patent, based upon a new claim construction and directed guidance regarding the doctrine of equivalents.

The patent-at-issue involved a particular type of porcine circoviruses (PCVs) and the DNA encoding them. There are two types of PCVs: PCV1, which does not cause diseases in pigs, and PCV2, which causes a wasting syndrome disease in pigs. The patent specification described five representative strains of PCV2, giving their full DNA sequences. The specification also set out, for comparison purposes, the DNA sequence of a representative PCV1 virus. To further distinguish PCV1 from PCV2, the specification flagged thirteen protein-producing stretches of DNA called open reading frames (ORFs), designated ORFs 1–13, within the PCV2 viruses. These ORFs seemed to be common to PCV2 viruses, but not common to PCV1 viruses.

In dispute were two claim terms, specifically the meaning of "Porcine Circoviruses Type II" and "ORFs 1–13." The district court limited the meaning of Porcine Circoviruses Type II to the five described in the specification. It also limited the meaning of ORFs 1–13 to the thirteen ORFs given in the specification. On these bases, the district court found no infringement because Intervet's products differed from the five described viruses and did not use any of the thirteen ORFs.

The Federal Circuit disagreed with both constructions. First, the panel noted that the specification said the five described PCV2 viruses were "representative of" a "type of porcine circovirus."[36] Further, the specification gave guidance for identifying other viruses based upon the degree of homology with the five examples. The specification made clear that a 96 percent homology with one of the samples would place a virus in the PCV2 family, whereas a homology of 76 percent or less did not. Intervet's virus was 99.6 percent homologous to one of the five samples and hence was within the claimed PCV2 family.

---

34. *Id.* at 1340 (Gajarsa, J., dissenting).
35. No. 2009-1568, 2010 WL 3064311 (Fed. Cir. Aug. 4, 2010).
36. *Id.* at *4.

Second, with regard to the term "ORFs 1–13," the panel noted that the specification described these ORFs as appearing in only one of the five deposited samples, and that small variations were seen among the other samples. The court concluded that persons skilled in the art would not read the phrase "ORFs 1–13" as strictly limited to the exact ORFs appearing in that sample, but rather would expect small natural variations among the PCV2 viruses. The new interpretations of the claims suggested that on remand literal infringement would be found.

The Federal Circuit also provided guidance as to how the doctrine of equivalents should be applied, which would likely be invoked on remand. The district court had permitted no range of equivalents for the phrase "porcine circovirus type II" because Merial had inserted that phrase to overcome a prior art rejection. Intervet's vector contained an ORF that was derived from a non-PCV2 source but was apparently 99 percent homologous to one of the PCV2 viruses described in the patent's specification.

The Federal Circuit instructed that Merial was not completely estopped from asserting the doctrine of equivalents. The panel explained that the U.S. Supreme Court's decision in *Festo Corp. v. Shoketsu Kinzoku Kogyo Kabushiki Co.* indicated prosecution history estoppel should be applied flexibly and determined that there was "no reason why a narrowing amendment should be deemed to relinquish equivalents . . . beyond a fair interpretation of what was surrendered."[37] Here there was a narrowing amendment made to procure allowance of the claim, but the surrender should not have been deemed to exclude from the claim every ORF except those physically derived from a then-known PCV2 virus. Merial was thus not estopped from asserting equivalents for Intervet's highly homologous virus.

Judge Dyk dissented in part, raising serious reservations regarding whether DNA isolates are eligible for patent protection at all, noting:

Thus, it appears that in order for a product of nature to satisfy section 101, it must be qualitatively different from the product occurring in nature, with "markedly different characteristics from any found in nature." It is far from clear that an "isolated" DNA sequence is qualitatively different from the product occurring in nature such that it would pass the test laid out in *Funk Brothers* and *Chakrabarty.* The mere fact that such a DNA molecule does not occur in isolated form in nature does not, by itself, answer the question.[38]

EQUITABLE ESTOPPEL

Long Silence after Exchange of Letters Leads to Equitable Estoppel

In *Aspex Eyewear Inc. v. Clariti Eyewear, Inc.*,[39] the Federal Circuit affirmed the district court's dismissal of the case, on summary judgment, because of equitable estoppel. The Federal Circuit also affirmed the district court's denial of the defendant's request for attorneys' fees.

---

37. 535 U.S. 722, 737–38 (2002).

38. *Intervet*, 2010 WL 3064311, at *11 (Dyk, J., dissenting-in-part) (citing Funk Bros. Seed Co. v. Kalo Inoculant Co., 333 U.S. 127, 130 (1948); Diamond v. Chakrabarty, 447 U.S. 303, 309 (1980)).

39. 605 F.3d 1305 (Fed. Cir. 2010).

The case arose out of two cease-and-desist letters sent by Aspex's lawyers in 2003. The letters mentioned five patents relating to magnetically attachable auxiliary eyeglass lenses (such as sunshades), including the '207 patent and its reissue. Clariti's lawyers asked for particulars of Aspex's contentions; two months later, Aspex responded with another letter, this time specifying only two of the patents, not including the '207 or its reissue. In response, Clariti asserted that it was not infringing any valid claim of either of the two specified patents. There the matter stood for the next three years.

In 2006, Aspex sent a new letter to Clariti. This letter indicated that Clariti's products, which had not changed since the last letter, were infringing both the '207 patent and its reissue. After a further exchange of letters in which Clariti refused to cease selling the accused products, Aspex filed suit against Clariti, claiming infringement of the '207 patent and its reissue. Clariti defended on the ground of equitable estoppel, contending it had been misled by Aspex's silence regarding the two patents now in suit and, therefore, thought no claim would be asserted against them based on these patents.

The district court granted Clariti's motion for summary judgment based on equitable estoppel and dismissed the case. The judge found the three prongs for equitable estoppel were established beyond reasonable dispute: (1) Aspex's failure to mention the two patents in its detailed assertion letter, coupled with over three years of silence thereafter, was misleading conduct; (2) Clariti's president, according to her declaration, relied upon that conduct to continue and expand her company's business; and (3) Clariti would be materially prejudiced if the suit were allowed to go forward, in that if it had known about Aspex's contentions, it would likely have discontinued the products and pursued other lines of business.

On appeal, the Federal Circuit affirmed. The Federal Circuit panel majority found no abuse of discretion on any of the equitable estoppel prongs, despite Apex's argument that its letters had been merely tentative, using phrases such as "may" infringe and "some" of Clariti's products. The Federal Circuit panel majority characterized Aspex's initial letters as aggressive and concluded that, under the circumstances, Clariti could reasonably have construed the ensuing three years of silence as a signal that no suit would be brought. The Federal Circuit panel majority also concluded that the reliance prong needed for equitable estoppel did not require that the defendant establish precisely what other business paths it would have taken if it had not been misled or that all of its marketing decisions were based on the patentee's misleading conduct.

Chief Judge Rader dissented, stating the court was extending prior law on equitable estoppel. Here, there was no direct threat of legal action in the initial exchange of letters, which he said prior decisions had required. Therefore, he concluded that Aspex's letters did not create any clear duty to speak about the patents after the initial exchange of letters.

Federal Circuit Reviews Claim Construction and Affirms Judgment Entered by District Court from Ambiguous Jury Form

In *Telcordia Technologies v. Cisco Systems,*[40] the Federal Circuit reviewed three issues: (1) claim construction of an asserted patent; (2) indefiniteness of another asserted patent; and (3) the damages awarded by the trial court based on the jury verdict.

---

40. 612 F.3d 1365 (Fed. Cir. 2010).

Plaintiff Telcordia, asserted three patents, including U.S. Patent Nos. 4,893,306 (the '306 patent); 4,835,763 (the '763 patent); and RE 36,633 (the '633 patent), against Defendant Cisco. Only the '306 and '763 were challenged on appeal.

The '306 patent relates to a technology for facilitating transition of a public switched telephone network to a packet switched network using "Dynamic Time Division Multiplexing" (DTDM). The '763 patent relates to a communication ring with nodes connected in a circular loop by a ring and a redundant ring, wherein a destination node can determine whether to use the signal from the ring or the redundant ring.

The district court found that the '306 patent was valid but not infringed and both the '633 and '763 patents were valid and willfully infringed. A verdict of $6.5 million plus prejudgment interest was entered. Telcordia appealed the construction of the '306 patent. Cisco cross-appealed the district court's findings and judgment as to the '306 and the '763 patents.

The Federal Circuit first reviewed the claim construction of the '306 patent. Agreeing with the construction of at least one term that formed the basis for finding that the '306 patent was not infringed, the Federal Circuit affirmed the district court's holding of noninfringement of the '306 patent.

For purposes of Cisco's invalidity appeal, the Federal Circuit reviewed construction of the term "empty payload field." In digital signal processing in the context of the '306 patent, there is no such thing as "no signal." The bits of the empty payload field have to be either a "0" or "1." The Federal Circuit considered whether the empty payload field included "a payload field that is empty of source data, but including *bits that serve no purpose other than place-holding*" or "a payload field that is empty of source data, but including *bit signals of some kind*."[41] The former, adopted by the district court, emerged as a result of misunderstanding Telecordia's claim construction position in a previous action involving the '306 patent. The Federal Circuit agreed with the latter construction and remanded for further consideration.

The Federal Circuit next reviewed whether the '763 patent was valid under 35 U.S.C. § 112, paragraph 2. The '763 patent used a means-plus-function limitation: "monitoring means." At issue was whether the written description clearly "link[ed] or associate[d]" a structure to the claimed function from the perspective of a person skilled in the art.[42] The written description described a controller, in this case a "black box," as the structure performing the function. Finding that Telecordia's expert showed that the specification met the requirement of disclosing adequate defining structures to render the bounds of the claim understandable to a skilled artisan, the Federal Circuit held that the written description was sufficient and affirmed denial of Cisco's motion for judgment of invalidity as a matter of law. This issue was the subject of a dissenting-in-part opinion. The dissent argued that the written description did not rise to the level of *clearly* linking a particular structure with claimed function.

Finally, the Federal Circuit reviewed the jury verdict and the resultant amount of damages entered. The verdict form asked "[i]f you have found any claim . . . valid and infringed by Cisco, please identify the amount of monetary damages that will compensate Telcordian for Cisco's infringement."[43] The jury entered $6.5 million. Although the jury

---

41. *Id.* at 1372.
42. *Id.* at 1377.
43. *Id.* at 1378.

form was ambiguous, the district court held that the figure was for past infringement only and did not include prejudgment interest. The Federal Circuit gave broad deference to the district court's interpretation of the jury verdict and affirmed.

LACHES

Laches Does Not Apply Unless the Patentee's Delay in Filing Suit Results in Evidentiary or Economic Prejudice

In *Hearing Components, Inc. v. Shure Inc.,*[44] Hearing had alleged that Shure's straight- and barbed-nozzle earphone products infringed three of Hearing's patents. The parties filed separate appeals from the judgment of the district court on several issues, and the Federal Circuit affirmed-in-part and reversed-in-part.

One issue in particular was Shure's appeal of the district court's denial of Shure's motion for JMOL for application of the laches defense based on Hearing's delay in filing its action. The district court specifically rejected the application of laches because Shure did not suffer any economic prejudice as a result of Hearing's delay in bringing suit.

On appeal, the Federal Circuit found that the district court correctly determined that laches did not apply. To prevail on laches, the accused infringer must prove that: (1) the delay in filing suit was for an unreasonable and inexcusable length of time, as measured from the time the patentee knew, or reasonably should have known, of its claim against the alleged infringer; and (2) such delay operated to the prejudice or injury of the alleged infringer. The Federal Circuit also noted that a delay of more than six years raised a presumption of laches, at which time the burden shifted to the patentee to show that its delay was reasonable under the circumstances or that the alleged infringer suffered no prejudice as a result of the delay.

Given that Shure proved a delay by Hearing of six years minus a day, the presumption of laches technically did not apply. Even if it did, however, the Federal Circuit agreed with the district court that Hearing successfully rebutted any presumption of laches that might otherwise have been created because Shure did not suffer prejudice from the delay in bringing suit. The Federal Circuit explained that two types of prejudice could result from delay: (1) evidentiary prejudice; and (2) economic prejudice.

Evidentiary prejudice includes, for example, loss of records or unavailability of evidence that prevents the accused infringer from proving a claim or defense. Shure argued that it suffered evidentiary prejudice in the form of lost evidence of further delay that could have been used to prove laches. The Federal Circuit, however, rejected Shure's argument, stating that "[i]f the only missing evidence is evidence of further delay, that does not amount to a showing of evidentiary prejudice."[45]

The Federal Circuit also agreed with the district court that Shure did not suffer any economic prejudice through Hearing's delay. Here, the Federal Circuit explained that "[t]he proper inquiry is whether there has been a 'change in the economic position of the alleged infringer during the period of delay.'"[46] Although capital investment was not re-

---

44. 600 F.3d 1357 (Fed. Cir. 2010).
45. *Id.* at 1376.
46. *Id.* (quoting A.C. Aukerman Co. v. R. L. Chaides Constr. Co., 960 F.2d 1020, 1033 (Fed. Cir. 1992) (en banc)).

quired to show economic prejudice, Shure did not make any significant increased expenditures during the delay period and in direct reliance of the delay (e.g., increased marketing and/or development expenses). Indeed, Shure knew of the Hearing patents long before any action was filed and relied on noninfringement opinions of counsel, thus, demonstrating that it would not have acted any differently had it been sued earlier. The Federal Circuit also made clear that the increase in damages caused by delay does not qualify as economic prejudice. Given that Hearing proved there was no real change in Shure's economic position as a result of the delay in Hearing filing suit, laches did not apply.

OWNERSHIP

Licensor Retaining Capacity to Sue for Infringement, Even If Secondary to Exclusive Licensee, Has Standing

In *Alfred E. Mann Foundation for Scientific Research v. Cochlear Corp.,*[47] the Federal Circuit analyzed the effects of an exclusive license on a licensor patent owner's standing to sue for infringement. The district court granted defendant's motion dismissing the case for lack of standing, based on an exclusive license of U.S. Patent Nos. 5,609,616 and 5,938,691 from the plaintiff Alfred Mann Foundation (AMF) to Advanced Bionics (AB), a third party who declined to exercise its right to sue under the license.

At the outset, the Federal Circuit, in an opinion written by (then) Chief Judge Michel and joined by Judges Newman and Linn, set forth the rule that a patent owner can transfer "all substantial rights" in a patent to an exclusive licensee, making the transfer "tantamount to an assignment," with the result that standing to sue resides solely with the licensee.[48] To determine whether the license did so, a court looks to the substance of the rights conferred in the license and the intention of the parties to the license agreement.

The court declined to set out an exhaustive list of license characteristics that must be transferred to constitute an assignment, but did recognize that "the nature and scope of the licensor's retained right to sue accused infringers is the most important factor in determining whether an exclusive license transfers sufficient rights to render the licensee the owner of the patent."[49] Indeed, "[w]here the licensor retains a right to sue accused infringers, that right often precludes a finding that all substantial rights were transferred to the licensee."[50] Of course, this factor can be "rendered illusory by the licensee's ability to settle licensor-initiated litigation by granting royalty-free sublicenses to accused infringers."[51]

With these principles in mind, the court reviewed the license between AMF and AB. In particular, the license granted AB an exclusive, worldwide right to practice the patented invention throughout the full term of the patents-in-suit; the first right to enforce the patents against any infringer, including the right to select counsel and to make unilateral litigation decisions; the right to settle such lawsuits without prior authorization from, but with prior consultation with, AMF; the right to grant sublicenses, provided they included

---

47. 604 F.3d 1354 (Fed. Cir. 2010).
48. *Id.* at 1358.
49. *Id.* at 1361.
50. *Id.*
51. *Id.*

certain license terms, as found in the license between AMF and AB, and, specifically, pass-through royalty provisions; and the right to terminate sublicenses if the license between AMF and AB terminated. The court concluded that the license permitted AMF to retain a secondary right to sue infringers if AB declined to pursue an infringement lawsuit, including the same rights to unilateral control of such litigation.

Thus, the court determined that, under the license, AMF retained sufficient rights to have standing to sue, comparing the license here with the license granted in *Abbott Laboratories v. Diamedix Corp.,* where the right of the licensor to sue if the exclusive licensee declined to do so "prevented the licensee from 'enjoy[ing] the right to indulge infringements, which normally accompanies conveyance of the right to sue.'"[52] Accordingly, the Federal Circuit reversed the district court's grant of the defendant's motion to dismiss and remanded the case.

Assignment of Patent Rights Not Required under Employment Agreement

In *Applera Corp.-Applied Biosystems Group v. Illumina, Inc.,*[53] the Federal Circuit affirmed the district court's denial of Applera's motion for JMOL or new trial on ownership of the two patents-in-suit. A jury had found that the inventor, Dr. Stephen Macevicz, had not assigned any patent rights to his former employer, Applera, under the terms of his Employee Invention Agreement (EIA).

Dr. Macevicz was a former in-house patent attorney at Applera. When he joined Applera, Dr. Macevicz signed an EIA. Under the EIA, Dr. Macevicz was required to assign to Applera any patent rights for inventions that he developed while employed by Applera, unless:

(1) the invention was developed entirely on his own time;
(2) "no equipment, supplies, facility, or trade secret of the Company was used in its development"; and
(3) "(i) it does not relate to the business or actual or demonstrably anticipated research or development of the Company, or (ii) it does not result from any work performed by [him] for the Company."[54]

While employed by Applera, Dr. Macevicz developed a method of sequencing DNA. He described his inventions in a personal laboratory notebook and he used his home computer to prepare a patent application directed to his inventions. Dr. Macevicz did not inform Applera about his inventions or patent application. The patents-in-suit issued from Dr. Macevicz's patent application and were acquired by Solexa.

The Federal Circuit found that substantial evidence supported the jury's conclusion that Dr. Macevicz had not assigned his invention to Applera under the EIA.[55] The first exception criterion of the EIA was met because it was undisputed the invention was developed entirely on Dr. Macevicz's own time. The Federal Circuit held that substantial evi-

---

52. *Id.* at 1363 (quoting Abbott Labs. v. Diamedix Corp., 47 F.3d 1128, 1132 (Fed. Cir. 1995)).
53. Nos. 2009-1253, 2009-1260, 2010 WL 1169936 (Fed. Cir. Mar. 25, 2010).
54. *Id.* at *7.
55. *Id.* at *8.

dence supported the jury's finding that the second exception criterion was met, and rejected Applera's argument that Dr. Macevicz used Applera's trade secrets in developing his invention.

Finally, the Federal Circuit interpreted the EIA under California law and found that the third exception criterion was met if Dr. Macevicz's invention met either of the two conditions set forth in that criterion, namely that it: (1) did not relate to Applera's business or actual or demonstrably anticipated research or development; *or* (2) did not result from any work performed by Dr. Macevicz for Applera.[56] The court thus rejected Applera's argument, based on the California Court of Appeal's interpretation of a similarly worded statute, that both conditions had to be met. The Federal Circuit found that there was substantial evidence that Dr. Macevicz's invention met the second of the two conditions: that it did not result from any work performed by Dr. Macevicz for Applera. In view of this finding, the Federal Circuit did not consider whether substantial evidence supported the first condition: that Dr. Macevicz's inventions did not relate to Applera's business.

INVENTORSHIP

Joint Inventorship

Coinventorship Does Not Require Complete Conception by Each Coinventor

In *Vanderbilt University v. ICOS Corp.*,[57] Vanderbilt filed suit to have three of its professors added as coinventors on a patent held by the defendant, ICOS. The patent claimed compounds known as PDE5 inhibitors, previously known to be useful for treating erectile dysfunction. One particular such inhibitor, called GR37273x, was specifically claimed in the patent and was the center of the inventorship controversy. ICOS had acquired the patent from Glaxo, which had had a research relationship of several years with the three Vanderbilt scientists. Glaxo had determined that one of its own scientists, Dr. Daugan, was the sole inventor, and he alone was named on the patent.

In the search for more powerful PDE5 inhibitors than were known before, the Vanderbilt scientists had developed a scheme for modifying such compounds. They took a known PDE5 inhibitor and substituted a phenyl ring at the eight position of one of its rings, finding that the modified compound was much more powerful. They theorized that other PDE5 inhibitors could be modified and improved in the same manner. They established an ongoing research relationship with ICOS's assignor, Glaxo, passing on their findings. During that relationship, Glaxo discovered the claimed compound GR37272x. There appears to be no dispute that the first person to develop and determine the structure of GR37272x was someone at Glaxo. However, Vanderbilt contended that its scientists provided the methodology for modifying PDE5 inhibitors in the manner that led to GR37272x and for that reason should be regarded as coinventors of that compound.

The district judge ruled for ICOS. She reasoned that, because the Vanderbilt scientists at no time had a full conception of GR37272x, they could not be regarded as coinventors.

---

56. *Id.* at *12–*13.
57. 601 F.3d 1297 (Fed. Cir. 2010).

She relied on the Federal Circuit holding in *Board of Education ex rel. Board of Trustees of Florida State University v. American BioScience Inc.*,[58] in which the court declined to accord coinventor status to workers who merely provided the starting materials for a claimed chemical compound. The district judge also found the evidence inconclusive concerning a connection between the Vanderbilt scientists' methodology and the actual development steps that led Glaxo to GR37272x. Given that inventorship changes must be supported by clear and convincing evidence, and Vanderbilt's evidence did not rise to that level, the district court refused to add the Vanderbilt scientists as coinventors.

On appeal, the Federal Circuit ruled that, although each coinventor must contribute in some way to the claimed subject matter, there is no minimum quantum of contribution required. It was error for the district court to require that each coinventor must at some time have a complete conception of the claimed compound; rather, each must engage with the others in some significant way toward that end. However, the error here was harmless, because the evidence on the basic fact question of whether the Vanderbilt methodology was used at all at Glaxo in finding the claimed compound was balanced, with neither side's theory being more plausible than the other's. Vanderbilt had thus failed to establish coinventorship by clear and convincing evidence.

Judge Dyk concurred in part and dissented in part. He agreed that each coinventor need not have a complete conception of the claimed compound, but he opined that the error infected the district judge's assessment of the evidence of the parties' respective contributions. Accordingly, he would have remanded the case for a new determination under the correct rule.

---

58. 333 F.3d 1330 (Fed. Cir. 2003).

CHAPTER 7

PATENT REMEDIES

The Federal Circuit addressed several patent remedies issues related to false marking, enhanced damages, and the calculation of compensatory damages.

The court decided several important cases that involved standing and the intent to deceive necessary for, and the damages resulting from, false patent marking. In *Stauffer v. Brooks Bros., Inc.,* the Federal Circuit confirmed that a qui tam plaintiff has standing to assert false marking claims on behalf of the United States, but the government's interest in seeing its laws enforced warrants its intervention in false marking suits.

In *Pequignot v. Solo Cup Co.,* the court held that marking a product with an expired patent number creates a rebuttable presumption of an intent to deceive. This presumption can, however, be rebutted by showing a good faith reliance on counsel. Marking a product that "may be covered" by a patent, coupled with an opinion of counsel, does not constitute an intent to deceive in a false marking case.

Regarding damages resulting from false patent marking, the court in *Forest Group, Inc. v. Bon Tool Co.* found error in the district court's fine of $500 for a single offense of false marking and held that the statutory fine under 35 U.S.C. § 292 should be assessed per article.

The court also decided cases involving claims for enhanced damages under 35 U.S.C. § 285. In *Medtronic Navigation, Inc. v. BrainLAB Medizinische Computersystems GmbH,* the Federal Circuit held that the district court erred in awarding attorneys' fees under section 285, as the action was not exceptional and the prosecuting attorneys did not unreasonably and vexatiously multiply the proceedings. In contrast, in *Gentile v. Sun Products, Inc.,* a treble-damages award was upheld where a pro se defendant withheld or destroyed evidence, offered evasive and misleading testimony, and otherwise engaged in dilatory litigation tactics.

The court also addressed compensatory damages in a few significant cases. In *Lucent Technologies, Inc. v. Gateway, Inc.,* the Federal Circuit held that Lucent had presented sufficient evidence to support jury verdicts regarding validity and infringement, but that it failed to present sufficient evidence to support the jury's calculation of damages, which had resulted in a total award of nearly $358 million dollars.

In *ResQNet.com, Inc. v. Lansa, Inc.,* the Federal Circuit rejected the 12.5 percent reasonable royalty rate adopted by the district court to calculate a damages award in a software patent infringement case. The Federal Circuit determined that the expert testimony on which the award's reasonable royalty rate was based had relied too heavily on 25 percent to 40 percent royalty rates received by the patentee for "rebundled" software and source code licenses as opposed to "straight" licenses covering just the patents at issue.

Finally, the court addressed the issue of standing in claims brought under the Invention Secrecy Act. In *Honeywell International, Inc. v. United States,* the Federal Circuit found that Honeywell had standing to make a claim for just compensation under the Act and was not precluded from recovering damages based on the first-sale doctrine.

DAMAGES

Court Permitted to Speculate on Damages Where Defendant Destroyed Evidence

In *Gentile v. Sun Products, Inc.,*[1] the Federal Circuit found no error in the denial of a motion for new trial. The district court found patent infringement and no invalidity on summary judgment. After a bench trial, the district court awarded damages and found the defendants, Sun and its sole shareholder, John Gill, willfully infringed the plaintiff, Robert Gentile's (Gentile) patent. The defendants moved for a new trial on several grounds, including laches and improper factual findings by the district court.

The Federal Circuit reviewed denial of a motion for new trial under the law of the applicable regional circuit, the First Circuit. The applicable First Circuit standard of review was "manifest abuse of discretion." The Federal Circuit also limited its review to the alleged errors on which the motion for new trial was based.

The Federal Circuit first held that there was no abuse of discretion in rejecting the laches defense because Gentile had a valid excuse for delay: Gentile was asserting the patent against another party. The Federal Circuit next held that Gill's argument that the district court improperly adopted findings and analysis of the same patent from another action (*Gentile I*) was improper because Gill failed to object at the time.

The Federal Circuit also affirmed the damage award. The district court was forced to estimate the number of infringing products that were produced by Gill because Gill either destroyed or withheld the relevant records. For that reason, the Federal Circuit rejected Gill's contention that there was insufficient evidence to support the damage award.

The Federal Circuit could not address whether Gentile had already been compensated for some of the infringing products by the settlement in *Gentile I*. A suit was brought against another party that may have purchased infringing products from Gill. However, given that Gill failed to provide any evidence of how many of Gill's infringing products were covered by the *Gentile I* settlement, Gill was precluded from claiming Gentile was not entitled to "double" compensation.

Lastly, the Federal Circuit affirmed the treble damage award, even though Gill was a pro se litigant. Although agreeing that Gill's pro se status was relevant, the Federal Circuit also pointed to numerous instances of bad faith. Such instances included Gill's announcement that he had "no intention of giving [Gentile] one dime," covering up evidence, offering trial testimony that was either evasive or misleading, and failing to appear at an agreed-upon mediation session. Accordingly, the Federal Circuit concluded that the district court did not abuse its discretion by trebling the damage award, notwithstanding Gill's pro se status.

---

1.   No. 2009-1529, 2010 WL 1303481 (Fed. Cir. Apr. 6, 2010).

First-Sale Doctrine Does Not Preclude Damages When Seller Lacked Rights in Patent at Time of Sale

In ***Honeywell International, Inc. v. United States,***[2] the Federal Circuit found that Honeywell had standing to make a claim for just compensation under the Invention Secrecy Act and was not precluded from recovering damages based on the first-sale doctrine.

The patent-in-suit relates to passive night vision goggles (NVGs) that can be used in airplane cockpits that have full color displays. Allied Corporation filed the application that issued as the patent-in-suit on October 10, 1985. A secrecy order was later imposed on the application pursuant to the Invention Secrecy Act. Every year until 2000, the USPTO imposed secrecy orders on the application, which prevented the patent from issuing. By 2000, Allied Corporation had become AlliedSignal Inc., which merged with Honeywell, Inc. to create Honeywell International, Inc. Honeywell International, Inc. amended the patent application that issued as the patent-in-suit.

After the patent issued, Honeywell International, Inc. and Honeywell Intellectual Properties, Inc. (collectively, Honeywell) sued the United States for patent infringement and just compensation under the Invention Secrecy Act for preissuance use of the invention. The Court of Federal Claims found that three accused systems infringed one of the asserted claims, but that this claim was invalid as obvious and because it lacked sufficient written description. The Court of Federal Claims also found that Honeywell lacked standing to seek just compensation under the Invention Secrecy Act and that the first-sale doctrine precluded Honeywell from recovering damages based on the government's use of systems that Honeywell Inc. manufactured and sold.

The Federal Circuit reversed the trial court's ruling on invalidity and held that the infringed claim is valid. Turning to Honeywell's claim for just compensation under the Invention Secrecy Act, the Federal Circuit rejected the Court of Federal Claims' conclusion that Honeywell lacked standing to assert this claim. The Invention Secrecy Act provides a right of action, in certain circumstances, to the owner of a patent "issued upon an application that was subject to a secrecy order issued pursuant to section 1981."[3] The Court of Federal Claims noted that, when the secrecy order issued on the application that later issued as the patent-in-suit, the claims in the pending application were different from the claims in the issued patent. Accordingly, the Court of Federal Claims found that patent-in-suit did not issue "upon" or "on" the application "as there was no contiguous relationship of dependence between the two."[4]

The Federal Circuit rejected the trial court's "contiguous relationship or dependence test," finding that it "lacks any foundation in the text of the statute itself."[5] The Federal Circuit found that because Honeywell owned the patent-in-suit, and the patent-in-suit issued from an application that was subject to a secrecy order, Honeywell had standing to assert a claim for just compensation under the Invention Secrecy Act.

The Federal Circuit also found that the first-sale doctrine did not apply to the accused systems that were manufactured and sold by Honeywell Inc. The first-sale doctrine ap-

---

2.   609 F.3d 1292 (Fed. Cir. 2010).

3.   35 U.S.C. § 183.

4.   *Honeywell,* 609 F.3d at 1303 (quoting Honeywell Int'l, Inc. v. United States, 81 Fed. Cl. 224, 233 (2008)).

5.   *Id.*

plies when there has been an authorized first sale. Because AlliedSignal—not Honeywell Inc.—owned the patent-in-suit when Honeywell Inc. sold the systems, Honeywell Inc.'s sales were not authorized. The Federal Circuit explained that "[t]he fact that Honeywell now owns the patent does not retroactively authorize the earlier sale."[6]

Judge Mayer dissented-in-part. He would have affirmed the trial court's decision that the infringed claim is invalid as obvious and lacking adequate written description. He also believed that the first-sale doctrine precluded Honeywell from recovering damages for infringement by products sold by Honeywell Inc. In his view, "[b]ecause Honeywell received compensation for the sales, through Honeywell Inc., its patent rights in those products are extinguished."[7] Judge Mayer noted that the court's decision allowed Honeywell to earn profits from the sale of the infringing product as well as damages for infringement by those products.

Reasonable Royalty

Patent Holder Must Present Sufficient Evidence to Prevent Jury Speculation as to Reasonable Royalty

In *Lucent Technologies, Inc. v. Gateway, Inc.,*[8] the Federal Circuit held that Lucent had presented sufficient evidence to support the jury verdicts regarding validity and infringement, but failed to supply sufficient evidence to support the jury's damages calculation.

Lucent owned U.S. Patent No 4,763,356 (the '356 patent), which claimed a method of entering information into fields on a computer screen without using a keyboard. Lucent accused a calendar date-picker tool incorporated into Microsoft Outlook, Microsoft Money, and Windows Mobile of infringing two claims of the '356 patent. Finding the patents valid and infringed, the jury awarded Lucent almost $358 million dollars, amounting to approximately 8 percent of the sales price of Outlook.

The Federal Circuit first affirmed the jury verdicts on validity and infringement. Regarding direct infringement, the Federal Circuit concluded that although the direct evidence offered in the case might not support a finding of infringement, the "circumstantial evidence was just adequate" to permit a jury to find that at least one person, other than an expert witness, had performed the claimed method.[9] As direct evidence, Lucent had relied on testimony from its expert that he and his wife both used the accused feature. That alone was not enough to prove infringement. However, the Federal Circuit opined that direct evidence of actual use may not be necessary in some cases because "[c]ircumstantial evidence is not only sufficient, but may also be more certain, satisfying and persuasive than direct evidence."[10] In this case the Federal Circuit found the circumstantial evidence from Lucent's experts' testimony, the extensive sales of the products, and instruction manuals for the products sufficient, albeit barely, to establish direct infringement.

---

6.   *Id.* at 1304.
7.   *Id.* at 1308.
8.   580 F.3d 1301 (Fed. Cir. 2009).
9.   *Id.* at 1318.
10. *Id.*

With respect to indirect infringement, the Federal Circuit rejected Microsoft's argument that contributory infringement did not apply because the products had substantial noninfringing uses. The Federal Circuit held that the proper inquiry was whether the particular tool that performed the claimed method had substantial noninfringing uses, not whether the entire software package had substantial noninfringing uses. To find otherwise, the Federal Circuit reasoned, would permit an infringer "to escape liability as a contributory infringer merely by embedding the infringing apparatus in a larger product with some additional, separable feature before importing and selling it."[11]

Turning to the jury's calculation of damages, the Federal Circuit concluded the damages award was not supported by substantial evidence. The court came to this conclusion using the *Georgia-Pacific*[12] framework, which instructs the court to imagine a hypothetical negotiation between the two parties and determine the royalty that the parties would have agreed upon before any infringement began.

The Federal Circuit first analyzed the evidence under *Georgia-Pacific* factor two, which considers the rates paid by licensees for the use of other patents comparable to the patent-in-suit. The Federal Circuit found several problems with the evidence Lucent had presented to support the jury award. First, the Federal Circuit pointed to the lack of any evidence on expected usage of the patented method by consumers, which was relevant because more frequently used inventions are generally deemed more valuable. Without evidence on expected usage of the feature, the Federal Circuit determined that a jury could not reasonably conclude that the date-picker feature would be so frequently used or valued that it would command approximately 8 percent of the price of Outlook.

Second, the Federal Circuit found that Lucent had presented insufficient evidence to allow the jury to compare the four lump-sum license agreements in evidence to the hypothetical negotiation presupposed by the *Georgia-Pacific* framework. One agreement Lucent relied on was a license for an entire patent portfolio related to PC-related technologies. The Federal Circuit viewed that agreement as differing vastly from the hypothetical licensing scenario of the present case, which involved only one narrow patent. Without further information, the Federal Circuit reasoned that the jury could only speculate as to how the two could be compared. Regarding three other lump-sum licensing agreements, the Federal Circuit faulted Lucent for merely offering "a recitation of royalty numbers," concluding that Lucent had only presented superficial testimony regarding the differences between those license agreements and the hypothetical license negotiations and that Lucent failed to clearly show that the technology of those agreements was similar to the technology being litigated.

Third, the Federal Circuit rejected Lucent's reliance on four running-royalty license agreements to support the jury's award. The Federal Circuit reasoned that, although a running-royalty license could be relevant to a lump-sum damages award, such license applied only when some basis for comparison existed, such as a means for recalculating the value of the running royalty agreement to arrive at a lump-sum award. Lucent had produced no such evidence. The Federal Circuit then discussed several examples of Lucent's evidentiary failures: Lucent had neglected to present testimony on whether the patented technology of the four running-royalty license agreements was essential to the licensed

---

11. *Id.* at 1320.
12. Georgia-Pacific Corp. v. U.S. Plywood Corp., 318 F. Supp. 1116 (S.D.N.Y. 1970).

product being sold or was merely a small component or feature of the licensed product; Lucent had omitted the value of cross-license rights in a cross-license agreement; Lucent had failed to explain how an agreement for multiple patents could be compared to negotiations over one patent; Lucent had neglected to offer any explanation of the types of products covered by an agreement or the various royalty rates set forth in the agreement; and Lucent had failed to offer evidence about how the rates corresponded to a percentage of the cost of the product sold under the license. The Federal Circuit concluded that the dearth of evidence regarding the second *Georgia-Pacific* factor could not support an award three to four times the amount of the average lump-sum agreements in evidence.

Although the Federal Circuit criticized the lack of evidence presented with regard to the license agreements, the court did not hold, as a matter of law, that the license agreements themselves could not support the damages award. Instead, the Federal Circuit reasoned that the evidence of record did not meet the substantial evidence threshold needed to support the jury award.

Turning to *Georgia-Pacific* factors ten and thirteen, which focus on how parties would value the patented feature, the Federal Circuit concluded that "[t]he evidence can support only a finding that the infringing feature contained in Microsoft Outlook is but a tiny feature of one part of a much larger software program" and could not constitute a substantial portion of the value of Outlook.[13] The Federal Circuit reasoned that the evidence could only support an award of an "exceedingly small" portion of the profit from Outlook and, therefore, *Georgia-Pacific* factors ten and thirteen provided little support for the damages award.

The Federal Circuit also considered the evidence presented in support of *Georgia-Pacific* factor eleven, which focuses on the degree to which the patented invention was used. Rejecting Microsoft's characterization of evidence of use occurring subsequent to the time of the hypothetical negotiation as irrelevant, the Federal Circuit reiterated that post-infringement evidence of use may be probative in some circumstances. Although the court acknowledged that there was no requirement that damages be limited to proven instances of direct infringement, the court reasoned that "[t]he damages award ought to be correlated, in some respect, to the extent the infringing method is used by consumers."[14] In this case, the Federal Circuit found the record devoid of data on how often consumers used the date-picker and, therefore, concluded that the evidence, relative to this factor, failed to support a large royalty rate.

After briefly stating that the remaining *Georgia-Pacific* factors offset one another, the Federal Circuit concluded the jury award was "based mainly on speculation and guesswork" and against the clear weight of the evidence.[15] In turn, the court held that the evidence simply could not support a royalty of approximately 8 percent of Microsoft's revenues for the sale of Outlook.

Finally, the Federal Circuit discussed the entire market value rule, concluding that its application in this case would constitute legal error for two reasons. First, for the entire market value rule to apply the patentee must prove that the feature is the basis for customer demand, and the court saw no evidence demonstrating that the date-picker was the basis for consumer demand for Outlook. Second, the Federal Circuit found that the evi-

---

13. 580 F.3d at 1332.
14. *Id.* at 1334.
15. *Id.* at 1335.

dence did not support a rate of 8 percent of the value of the Outlook product. Although "the base used in a running royalty calculation can always be the value of the entire commercial embodiment," the court reasoned, "the magnitude of the rate [must be] within an acceptable range."[16]

Responding to criticism by commentators of the application of the entire market value rule, the Federal Circuit reaffirmed the continued viability of the rule, pointing out "[t]here is nothing inherently wrong with using the market value of the entire product, especially when there is no established market value for the infringing component or feature, so long as the multiplier accounts for the proportion of the base represented by the infringing component or feature."[17]

Licensing Factors

COMPARABLE LICENSES

Royalty Rates from License Agreements Unrelated to the Claimed Invention Cannot Support a Reasonable Royalty Rate Calculation under 35 U.S.C. § 284

In *ResQnet.com, Inc. v. Lansa, Inc.*,[18] the Federal Circuit held that royalty rates from license agreements unrelated to the patents-in-suit or their claimed technology cannot support a reasonable royalty rate calculation under 35 U.S.C. § 284. After a bench trial, the district court found that a 12.5 percent reasonable royalty rate applied to the revenues of Lansa from the sale of infringing software.[19] In arriving at the rate, the district court relied on the opinion testimony of the expert offered by ResQnet.com because Lansa had provided no expert testimony on the issue of damages.[20]

On appeal, Lansa challenged the district court's damages award and, specifically, the methodology used by ResQnet's expert.[21] The Federal Circuit found that ResQnet's expert relied primarily on the first factor of the *Georgia-Pacific* framework, which requires "considering past and present royalties received by the patentee 'for the licensing of the patent in suit proving or tending to prove an established royalty.'"[22] ResQnet's expert relied on six licenses: one "straight" license that arose out of litigation over the patents in suit and five rebranding or rebundling software and source code licenses (the rebundled licenses).[23] The trial record demonstrated that the rebundled licenses were based on royalty rates between 25 percent and 40 percent, substantially higher than 12.5 percent, and did not "even mention[] the patents in suit or show[]any other discernible link to the claimed technology."[24]

---

16. *Id.* at 1338–39.
17. *Id.* at 1339.
18. 594 F.3d 860 (Fed. Cir. 2010).
19. *Id.* at 868.
20. *Id.* at 870, 872.
21. *Id.* at 868.
22. *Id.* at 869, 872.
23. *Id.* at 870.
24. *Id.*

The Federal Circuit concluded that ResQnet's expert "used unrelated licenses on marketing and other services—licenses that had a rate nearly eight times greater than the straight license—to push the royalty up into the double figures."[25] This was the same error that the court had criticized in *Lucent v. Gateway.*[26] According to the Federal Circuit, ResQnet's expert offered "little to no evidence of a link between the rebundling licenses and the claimed invention."[27] In fact, "[the expert's] downward shift from the rebundling royalties is an admission that his calculations are speculative without any relation to actual market rates at all."[28] The Federal Circuit vacated the damages award "[b]ecause the district court's award relied on speculative and unreliable evidence divorced from proof of economic harm linked to the claimed invention."[29]

Judge Newman dissented-in-part, accusing the majority of diverging from precedent as to the calculation of damages. Judge Newman concluded that the majority had erred in determining that "it is improper to consider, for the purpose of understanding the value of the infringed patents, any licenses involving the technology of those patents bundled with additional technologies, such as software code."[30] *Lucent* was distinguishable, according to Judge Newman, because the damages in *Lucent* corresponded to the value of a system of which the infringing component was a small part, whereas here, "the patented technology was a large part of the 'bundled' licenses, and these licenses were fairly considered for their content and value."[31]

Marking

Good-Faith Reliance on Counsel May Rebut Intent to Deceive Shown by False Statement in Patent Marking Claim

In *Pequignot v. Solo Cup Co.,*[32] the Federal Circuit affirmed the district court's summary judgment decision that patent holder Solo did not have the requisite intent to deceive the public to support violation of the false marking statute. Reviewing the decision de novo, the Federal Circuit followed its precedent in *Clontech Laboratories, Inc. v. Invitrogen Corp.,*[33] in holding that the combination of a false statement and knowledge that the statement was false creates only a rebuttable presumption of intent to deceive the public. The Federal Circuit determined that Solo successfully rebutted the presumption because it followed advice of counsel and implemented a business policy based on that advice.

Solo makes plastic hot drink cup lids, which are formed using thermoforming stamping machines. The machines contain mold cavities that can stamp out plastic lids repetitively for fifteen to twenty years before replacement. Solo added the patent numbers of

25. *Id.*
26. Lucent Techs., Inc. v. Gateway, 580 F.3d 1301, 1327–28 (Fed. Cir. 2009).
27. *Id.* at 871.
28. *Id.*
29. *Id.* at 868, 873.
30. *ResQnet*, 594 F.3d at 876 (Newman, J., dissenting).
31. *Id.* at 879 (Newman, J., dissenting).
32. 608 F.3d 1356 (Fed. Cir. 2010).
33. 406 F.3d 1347 (Fed. Cir. 2005).

patents that cover the plastic cup lids to the mold cavities in order to satisfy the marking requirements of 35 U.S.C. § 287.

Pequignot sued Solo alleging that Solo falsely marked nearly twenty-two billion articles pursuant to the false marking statute, 35 U.S.C. § 292. The basis of the plaintiff's false marking claim resulted from 1) Solo's marking of products with two expired patent numbers and 2) Solo's applying a notice to both patented and unpatented product packaging that the contents of the package "may be covered" by one or more patents.

As to the marking with expired patents, Solo sought advice of counsel, who indicated that Solo was not required to remove the expired patent numbers from its products. However, counsel noted that false marking liability hinges on intent to deceive the public and, thus, informed Solo that it was important that Solo not further any unintentional falsity in product literature, etc. Thereafter, Solo developed a policy whereby when mold cavities need to be replaced due to wear, Solo would remove the expired patent numbers from the new molds. Solo concluded that wholesale replacement of mold cavities would be too costly and burdensome.

As to the "may be" patented packaging notices, Solo had also relied on outside counsel's recommendation to change its packaging in order to provide sufficient notice of patent marking. Solo's attorney testified that she believed the language was not false marking even if placed on packing for unpatented products. During pendency of the case, Solo discontinued the package marking to avoid further claims under the false marking statute.

The district court granted summary judgment in favor of Solo, finding that Solo did not have the requisite intent to deceive. The district court concluded that Solo's evidence was sufficient to rebut the presumption of intent to deceive. Specifically, the court determined that when false markings at issue are numbers of expired patents that previously covered the marked products, the presumption of intent to deceive is weaker because the possibility to deceive and the benefit to the false marker are diminished. The Federal Circuit agreed with the district court's assessments on this point, requiring a showing of preponderance of the evidence of no intent to deceive the public. Moreover, the Federal Circuit emphasized that the intent that must be demonstrated is intent to deceive the public, and not intent to falsely mark an unpatented article. In addition, the district court found that Solo relied in good faith on advice of counsel and acted out of a desire to reduce costs and business disruption.

Regarding the "may be covered" language, the district court found that, although this was a closer case, Solo added the language at the suggestion of its outside counsel and that it was done for logistical and financial reasons. Thus, there was no intent to deceive. The Federal Circuit agreed with the district court analysis on this point as well.

False Marking Statute (35 U.S.C. § 292) Is a Qui Tam Action and Operates as a Statutory Assignment of the United States' Rights

In *Stauffer v. Brooks Bros., Inc.*,[34] the Federal Circuit reversed the district court's judgment that Stauffer, an individual asserting a false marking claim under 35 U.S.C.

---

34. Nos. 2009-1428, 2009-1430, 2009-1453, 2010 U.S. App. LEXIS 18144 (Fed. Cir. Aug. 31, 2010).

§ 292, lacked standing in a qui tam action against Brooks Brothers. The Federal Circuit also determined that the district court erred in denying the United States' motion to intervene in the suit.

Brooks Brothers and its parent company manufacture and sell bow ties. Some of these bow ties contain an "Adjustolox" mechanism, and are marked with U.S. Patent Nos. 2,083,106 and 2,123,620. These patents expired in 1954 and 1955, respectively. In December 2008, Raymond E. Stauffer brought a qui tam action under section 292 in the U.S. District Court for the Southern District of New York, alleging that Brooks Brothers had falsely marked its bow ties with expired patents. Brooks Brothers moved to dismiss Stauffer's complaint under Rule 12(b)(1) for lack of standing and under Rule 12(b)(6) for failure to allege an intent to deceive the public with sufficient specificity. The district court granted Brooks Brothers' 12(b)(1) motion, finding that Stauffer had not sufficiently alleged that the United States had suffered an injury from Brooks Brothers' false marking. Because the 12(b)(1) motion was granted, the district court did not reach the merits of the 12(b)(6) motion. After the district court's decision on Stauffer's lack of standing, the United States moved to intervene under Rules 24(a)(1)–(2) and also under Rule 24(b)(1). The district court denied the government's motion.

Reviewing the standing decision de novo, the appellate court applied the U.S. Supreme Court precedent of *Vermont Agency of Natural Resources v. United States*.[35] According to *Vermont Agency,* a qui tam plaintiff, or relator, can establish standing based on the United States' implicit partial assignment of its damages claim to "any person." In other words, even though a relator may suffer no injury himself, a qui tam provision operates as a statutory assignment of the United States' rights, and the assignee of a claim has standing to assert the injury in fact suffered by the assignor. Thus, in order to have standing, Stauffer must allege that the United States has suffered an injury in fact causally connected to Brooks Brothers' conduct that is likely to be redressed by the court. Congress, by enacting section 292, defined an injury in fact to the United States. Because the government would have standing to enforce its own law, Stauffer, as the government's assignee, also has standing to enforce section 292.[36] The Federal Circuit remanded the case to the lower court to determine the merits of the case, including Brooks Brothers' Rule 12(b)(6) motion to dismiss for failure to state a claim.

The Federal Circuit reviewed the lower court's decision denying the United States' motion to intervene under Federal Rule of Civil Procedure 24(a)(2) for an abuse of discretion. The Federal Circuit agreed with the government's position that it had an interest in seeing its patent statute enforced and in receiving half the statutory damages. The government also alleged that, without intervention, this would prejudice the government's ability to protect its interests which may not be adequately represented by Stauffer. Brooks Brothers did not challenge the latter point. The Federal Circuit noted that res judicata would attach to the government's claims against Brooks Brothers for the particular marking issues involved in the suit. Thus, regardless of the United States' ability to bring its own suit under section 292, the government's ability to protect its interest in this particular case would be impaired by disposition of the action without

---

35. 529 U.S. 765 (2000).
36. *Stauffer,* 2010 U.S. App. LEXIS 18144, at *11–*13.

the government's intervention.[37] The Federal Circuit determined that the district court committed an error of law in denying the United States' motion.

Fines for False Marking under Section 292 Are Assessed Per Article

In *Forest Group, Inc. v. Bon Tool Co.,*[38] the Federal Circuit held that, under 35 U.S.C. § 292, each article that is falsely marked with an intent to deceive is a separate offense under the statute. Forest sued Bon Tool for infringement of its patent. Bon Tool counter-claimed, alleging false marking and a Lanham Act violation and seeking declaratory judgment that Forest's patent was invalid. The district court granted summary judgment of noninfringement in favor of Bon Tool. The district court then conducted a bench trial on Bon Tool's counterclaims and found that Forest had falsely marked its product, assessing Forest with a $500 fine for a single offense of false marking. The Federal Circuit agreed with the district court's decision that Forest falsely marked its product, but found erroneous the district court's $500 fine.[39]

For a false marking claim under section 292, there are two elements: (1) the marking of an unpatented article; and (2) the intent to deceive the public. The Federal Circuit upheld the district court's determination that both elements had been satisfied. As for intent to deceive, the Federal Circuit agreed that Forest had lacked intent to deceive until the date of a summary judgment of noninfringement in another case involving the same patent.

The Federal Circuit then considered whether the fine assessed by the district court was appropriate. On appeal, Bon Tool argued that based on the language of section 292, Forest should be fined for each separate instance of false marking rather than a single fine covering all falsely marked articles. The Federal Circuit agreed, finding that the plain language of section 292 requires a fine to be imposed on a per-article basis.[40] The court noted that "injuries occur each time an article is falsely marked" and "[t]he more articles that are falsely marked the greater the chance that competitors will see the falsely marked article and be deterred from competing."[41] Accordingly, the court reasoned that a per article fine is appropriate in light of the purpose behind the false marking statute.[42] However, the court noted that the statute does not require a full $500 fine per marked article because "[i]n the case of inexpensive mass-produced articles, a court has the discretion to determine that a fraction of a penny per article is a proper penalty."[43]

Accordingly, the court upheld the district court's finding of false marking, but vacated the $500 fine imposed by the district court and remanded the case with instructions to assess a fine on a per article basis.[44]

---

37. *Id.* at *21–*22.
38. 590 F.3d 1295 (Fed. Cir. 2009).
39. *Id.* at 1300, 1305.
40. *Id.* at 1301.
41. *Id.* at 1303.
42. *Id.*
43. *Id.* at 1304.
44. *Id.*

Attorneys' Fees

District Court Award of Attorneys' Fees Reversed Because Case Was Not "Exceptional" within Meaning of 35 U.S.C. § 285

In *Medtronic Navigation, Inc. v. BrainLAB Medizinische Computersystems GmbH,*[45] the Federal Circuit reversed the district court's award of approximately $4.4 million in attorneys' fees, costs, expenses, and interest to BrainLAB.

Medtronic alleged infringement of U.S. Patent Nos. 5,383,454 (the Bucholz patent), 4,722,056 (the Roberts patent), and 5,389,101 and 5,603,318 (the Helibrun patents). The accused devices included BrainLAB's image-guided surgical navigation devices that used cameras to detect the position of surgical instruments through triangulation. After claim construction, Medtronic moved for summary judgment, arguing infringement under the doctrine of equivalents for the Bucholz and Roberts patents as well as literal infringement and infringement through the doctrine of equivalents for the Helibrun patents. Before trial, BrainLAB moved for summary JMOL. Both parties' motions were denied by the court. The jury returned a verdict in favor of Medtronic, finding that BrainLAB had infringed the Bucholz, Roberts, and Heilbrun patents. However, after the trial, BrainLAB renewed its motion for JMOL, which was granted by the court. The district court found that the theory of infringement of the Bucholz patent through the doctrine of equivalents was barred by prosecution history estoppel, the Roberts patent was not infringed under the doctrine, and the Helibrun patent was not infringed either literally or by equivalents. After trial the district court granted BrainLAB's petition and awarded attorneys' fees under section 285 and 28 U.S.C. § 1927.

On appeal, Medtronic argued that the district court erred in awarding attorneys' fees. Under section 285, a court may award attorneys' fees when it determines that either the patentee's infringement claims were frivolous or that there was litigation misconduct at trial. Under section 285, awards of attorneys' fees are reviewed under a highly deferential standard. Here, the Federal Circuit held that the case was not exceptional and that attorneys' fees were awarded in error.[46] The Federal Circuit reasoned that the district court's characterization of Medtronic's claims as frivolous was baseless considering that BrainLAB's motions for summary judgment and JMOL were denied during the trial. In addition, upon examination of Medtronic's infringement claims, the court reasoned that each was sufficiently reasonable to warrant being litigated, despite the fact that they were all ultimately rejected by the district court in its JMOL ruling. Further, the Federal Circuit found no evidence of litigation misconduct at trial.

The Federal Circuit next examined the district court's grant of attorneys' fees under section 1927. Under section 1927, any attorney who unreasonably and vexatiously multiplies the proceedings in any case may be required by the court to pay attorneys' fees and any other resulting excess costs. The Federal Circuit reasoned that because it was not unreasonable for Medtronic to seek relief despite the district court's claim construction, McDermott, counsel to Medtronic, could not be found liable for continued representation of Medtronic in that effort. Additionally, the Federal Circuit found that McDermott was not guilty of any litigation misconduct.

Finding no violation of either sections 285 or 1927, the Federal Circuit found the district court's award of attorneys' fees to BrainLAB to be in error.

45. 603 F.3d 943 (Fed. Cir. 2010).
46. *Id.* at 966.

CHAPTER 8

PATENT LITIGATION

The Federal Circuit, district courts, and the ITC addressed procedural issues related to jurisdiction, standing, venue, and more substantive issues such as the proof required to demonstrate infringement, invalidity, and the domestic industry requirement.

Subject matter jurisdiction received a fair amount of attention this past year, confirming that the question often turns on whether the case involves substantive issues of patent law. In *HIF Bio, Inc. v. Yung Shin Pharmaceuticals Industrial Co.*, the court concluded that, where a cause of action presents sufficiently substantial questions of federal patent law, federal subject matter jurisdiction is proper. However, because this case involved inventorship of an unissued patent application, the federal court did not have subject matter jurisdiction.

Similarly, in both *Clearplay, Inc. v. Max Abecassis & Nissim Corp.* and *Tiger Team Technologies, Inc. v. Synesis Group, Inc.*, the Federal Circuit emphasized the importance of the complaint on the issue of appellate jurisdiction. In *Clearplay*, the court found that, for appellate jurisdiction to exist, resolution of a patent law issue must be necessary to every theory of relief under at least one claim in the plaintiff's complaint. Likewise, in *Tiger Team*, the Federal Circuit concluded that it had appellate jurisdiction over the case because the operative pleading included a claim that raised a substantial question of patent law even though no patent claims were at issue on appeal.

In *Davis v. Brouse McDowell, L.P.A.* and *Premier Networks, Inc. v. Stadheim & Grear, Ltd.*, the Federal Circuit and Illinois appellate court, respectively, affirmed the judgment of lower courts holding that federal courts had exclusive jurisdiction over legal malpractice claims where the attorney's alleged actions arose out of or were related to substantive patent issues.

Claims that only tangentially relate to patents, however, will not trigger the Federal Circuit's appellate jurisdiction. *Laboratory Corp. of America Holdings v. Metabolite Laboratories, Inc.* involved an appeal of the district court's grant of summary judgment of no breach of a know-how and patent license agreement. Because the underlying claim was for breach of contract, not patent infringement, the Federal Circuit did not have jurisdiction over the appeal.

Although a contract claim will not trigger Federal Circuit jurisdiction, the terms of a contract can serve to divest the court of jurisdiction. In *Dow Jones & Co. v. Ablaise Ltd.*, the Federal Circuit ruled that an offer of a covenant not to sue for infringement is sufficient to divest the district court of subject matter jurisdiction in a suit for declaratory judgment of invalidity.

Declaratory judgment jurisdiction was also an issue the Federal Circuit addressed. In *Innovative Therapies, Inc. v. Kinetic Concepts, Inc.*, the Federal Circuit held that whether declaratory judgment jurisdiction exists in a patent action must be examined on the facts of each case, and acts that occur *after* the filing of the declaratory plaintiff's original complaint cannot establish declaratory jurisdiction as of the date when that original complaint was filed.

The Federal Circuit also addressed jurisdiction under 28 U.S.C. § 1498(a). In *Advanced Software Design Corp. v. Federal Reserve Bank of St. Louis,* the Federal Circuit held that patent infringement claims against a third party acting with the authorization and consent of the United States can only be pursued in the Court of Federal Claims.

In addition to subject matter jurisdiction, the Federal Circuit addressed personal jurisdiction issues. In *Patent Rights Protection Group, LLC v. Video Gaming Technology, Inc.,* the court found that it was reasonable for a district court to exercise personal jurisdiction over the defendants because the defendants' attendance at trade shows within the forum provided minimum contacts with that forum for personal jurisdiction, and the burdens of defending the case in that forum in view of the availability of modern transportation and communications were not so compelling as to outweigh the plaintiff's and several states' interests in an efficient patent adjudication.

Standing was a hot button issue before the Federal Circuit as well. In *Tyco Healthcare Group LP v. Ethicon Endo-Surgery, Inc.,* the court affirmed the district court's entry of JMOL and dismissal without prejudice because Tyco failed to establish ownership of the patents-in-suit and thus lacked standing. In *AsymmetRx, Inc. v. Biocare Medical, LLC,* the court held that a mere licensee, who has no right to exclude others from making, using, or selling the licensed products, has no legally recognized interest that entitles it to bring or join an infringement action. In *Enovsys LLC v. Nextel Communications Inc.,* the court concluded that final judgment in a divorce proceeding, which provided that the spouse and would-be co-owner of the patent-at-issue disclaimed any interest in the patent, controls standing to sue under comity and res judicata principles.

In *Board of Trustees of the Leland Stanford Junior University v. Roche Molecular Systems, Inc.,* another case involving standing, the Federal Circuit vacated the district court's grant of summary judgment of invalidity and remanded the case with instructions to dismiss the claim for lack of standing. In that case, the court held that Stanford University lacked standing to sue because an inventor's agreement to "hereby assign" future inventions to Roche trumped an earlier agreement by the inventor agreeing to assign future inventions to Stanford University.

In *Sky Technologies LLC v. SAP AG & SAP America, Inc.,* the Federal Circuit was presented with another case involving the assignment of rights and standing to sue. In that case, the plaintiff had standing to bring a patent infringement claim because he had been transferred title of the patents through operation of law, despite the absence of a written assignment.

The Federal Circuit also continued its recent trend of transferring cases on mandamus petitions. In *In re Hoffman-La Roche Inc.,* the court ordered the Eastern District of Texas to transfer the case to the Eastern District of North Carolina because that court had a meaningful local interest in adjudicating the dispute, whereas no meaningful connection existed with the Eastern District of Texas. In *In re Nintendo,* the Federal Circuit vacated a district court order denying the defendant's motion to transfer venue because of the drastic difference between the two venues in terms of convenience, relevance, and fairness.

Several cases also presented issues related to the proof needed to demonstrate infringement or invalidity. In *Verizon Services Corp. v. Cox Fibernet Virginia, Inc.,* the Federal Circuit held that jury determinations of infringement and invalidity will be upheld when there is substantial evidence to support the verdict.

In *Martek Biosciences Corp. v. Nutrinova, Inc.,* the Federal Circuit held that a plaintiff is not necessarily required to perform testing of an accused process to prove infringement where it provides other substantive evidence—in particular, expert testimony as to the operation of the accused process.

In *Nystrom v. Trex Co.,* claim preclusion barred an infringement action against the defendant's new products, which were unchanged from the previously adjudicated claim limitations, notwithstanding that the new products were different from the old ones in other respects.

In *Comaper Corp. v. Antec, Inc.,* the court found that a new trial was required when a jury had reached inconsistent verdicts on the validity of the asserted claims.

The Federal Circuit also decided a few issues concerning counsel and litigation behavior. In *In re Deutsche Bank Trust Co. Americas,* the court held that the test of whether to apply a patent prosecution bar to a party's litigating attorney requires a fact-specific inquiry by the court. In *Carter v. ALK Holdings, Inc.,* the court held that claims asserted against the patent prosecutor under Article I, Section 8, Clause 8 of the U.S. Constitution and 35 U.S.C. § 122 were frivolous, but found a claim alleging breach of fiduciary duty not to be frivolous.

The ITC remained a prominent venue for patent litigation, deciding several major cases related to the domestic industry requirement. In *Certain Coaxial Cable Connectors & Components Thereof & Products Containing Same*; *Certain Short-Wavelength Light Emitting Diodes, Laser Diodes, & Products Containing Same*; and *Certain Computer Products, Computer Components & Products Containing Same,* the ITC shed light on how litigation expenses, attorneys' fees, and activities of patent engineers, licensing representatives, and intellectual property attorneys can be considered in establishing the domestic industry requirement of 19 U.S.C. § 1337.

The Federal Circuit in *SiRF Technology, Inc. v. International Trade Commission* affirmed the ITC's finding that SiRF infringed patents asserted by Global Positioning, concluding that a patent assignment is presumed valid once recorded with the USPTO and that the burden to show invalidity was on SiRF.

Finally, courts addressed some interesting issues related to the duty to preserve documents in *Pension Committee of the University of Montreal Pension Plan v. Banc of America Securities, LLC*; the enforceability of a recorded settlement agreement in *MedPointe Healthcare, Inc. v. Kozachuk*; and secrecy orders related to patents in *Hornback v. United States.*

JURISDICTION

Subject Matter Jurisdiction

Resolution of Patent Law Issue Is Necessary to Every Theory of Relief under at Least One Claim in Plaintiff's Complaint

In *ClearPlay, Inc. v. Max Abecassis & Nissim Corp.,*[1] the Federal Circuit held that, in order to establish appellate jurisdiction under 28 U.S.C. § 1295(a) over the underlying

---

1. No. 2009-1471, 2010 WL 1838949 (Fed. Cir. Apr. 21, 2010).

action, it is not enough that a well-pleaded complaint allege a single theory under which patent law is essential, but that where plaintiff has alleged alternative theories, patent law must be essential to each of those theories.[2]

On appeal, Nissim Corp. and Max Abecassis (collectively, Nissim) asserted that the Federal Circuit had jurisdiction because the issue of patent infringement was essential to defending against six state law tort claims brought by ClearPlay against Nissim for violating the terms of a license agreement that was part of the settlement of the underlying patent infringement action.[3] The disputed license agreement permitted ClearPlay to distribute allegedly infringing products upon payment to Nissim.

The Federal Circuit noted that, under the U.S. Supreme Court's decision in *Christianson v. Colt Industries Operating Corp.*,[4] section 1338 jurisdiction extends to those cases where: (1) patent law creates the cause of action; or (2) "that the plaintiff's right to relief necessarily depends on resolution of a substantial question of federal patent law, in that patent law is a necessary element of one of the well-pleaded claims."[5]

Here, the Federal Circuit determined that the first part of the test clearly is not satisfied.[6] With regard to the second part of the test, the court found that, although questions of patent infringement are at issue and such patent law issues could arise in the course of litigating each of ClearPlay's claims, "it is equally clear that none of those claims necessarily turns on an issue of patent law."[7]

The Federal Circuit agreed with Nissim that its threats against ClearPlay's customers would be meaningful only if the products actually infringed Nissim's patents, and the issue of patent infringement could arise in the course of litigating ClearPlay's claims. However, such theoretical possibility is not enough to provide jurisdiction because Clearplay could prevail solely on its state law tort claims without a court having to reach the question of patent infringement. The court examined each of ClearPlay's six claims for relief and found that, in the case of each asserted claim, "there is at least one theory of relief that would not require the resolution of a patent law issue."[8] The court emphasized that "resolution of a patent law issue must be necessary to every theory of relief under at least one claim in the plaintiff's complaint. And that is not so in this case."[9] Based on this understanding, the Federal Circuit transferred the case to the Eleventh Circuit.

---

2.   *Id.* at *10.

3.   More specifically, ClearPlay accused Nissim of tortious interference with a contractual relationship, tortious interference with potential advantageous business relationships, breach of the license agreement, breach of the covenant of good faith and fair dealing, and violation of Florida's Deceptive and Unfair Practices Act. *Id.* at *7.

4.   486 U.S. 800 (1988).

5.   *Id.* at 809.

6.   The court found that "ClearPlay's second amendment complaint . . . is entirely devoted to state law causes of action. Thus, federal patent law does not 'create the cause of action' as to any of the claims in the complaint." *ClearPlay*, 2010 WL 1838949 at *9.

7.   *Id.* at *8.

8.   *Id.*

9.   *Id.* at *10.

Federal District Court Properly Exercised Jurisdiction over Legal Malpractice Case Related to Patent Prosecution

In *Davis v. Brouse McDowell, L.P.A.,*[10] the Federal Circuit held that it had jurisdiction over an appeal of an action for legal malpractice.

Plaintiff Heather Davis alleged an attorney she hired to prepare utility and Patent Cooperation Treaty (PCT) applications committed malpractice. Davis claimed the attorney failed to file a timely PCT application. Further, with respect to the U.S. application, she claimed that the attorney failed to draft adequate claims, did not include information sufficient to comply with 35 U.S.C. § 112, ¶1, and did not use his own legal expertise to create a cohesive specification. The defendants removed the action to federal court.

Under 35 U.S.C. § 1338(a), federal district courts have exclusive jurisdiction over actions "arising under any Act of Congress relating to patents." The Federal Circuit explained that jurisdiction under section 1338(a) extends to cases where federal patent law creates the cause of action or where "the plaintiff's right to relief necessarily depends on resolution of a substantial question of federal patent law, in that patent law is a necessary element of one of the well-pleaded claims."[11] Further, if the complaint "presents multiple theories supporting a claim, that claim 'may not form the basis for § 1338(a) jurisdiction unless patent law is essential to each of those theories.'"[12]

Because Davis's cause of action for legal malpractice arose under state law, the Federal Circuit examined whether Davis's right to relief necessarily depended on resolution of a substantial question of federal patent law. Davis argued that her complaint presented only a single claim for legal malpractice supported by alternative theories based on allegations related to the PCT application and allegations related to the U.S. application. There was no dispute that Davis's allegations regarding the PCT application did not raise any issues of U.S. patent law. The Federal Circuit therefore recognized that, if Davis's complaint merely presented a single malpractice claim based on alternative theories, one of which did not require an assessment of federal law, the district court did not have jurisdiction over this case.

However, the Federal Circuit found that Davis's complaint did not present only a single claim for malpractice. Explaining that "[a] claim is broadly defined as the 'aggregate of operative facts giving rise to a right enforceable by a court,'" the Federal Circuit concluded that Davis's malpractice allegations arose out of different sets of operative facts.[13] One set of facts related to the preparation of filing of the PCT application, and another set of facts related to the preparation of the U.S. application. Thus, the Federal Circuit held that Davis's complaint presented at least two distinct claims.

The Federal Circuit also held that patent law was a necessary element of Davis's claim that her attorney committed malpractice in connection with the U.S. application. To prevail on this claim under Ohio law, Davis was required to show that she would have obtained patents on her inventions but for her attorney's alleged negligence. Whether Davis's

---

10. 596 F.3d 1355 (Fed. Cir. 2010).
11. *Id.* at 1359 (quoting Christianson v. Colt Indus. Operating Corp., 486 U.S. 800, 808–09 (1988)).
12. *Id.* (quoting *Christianson*, 486 U.S. at 810).
13. *Id.* (quoting BLACK'S LAW DICTIONARY 264 (8th ed. 2004)).

inventions were patentable was a question of U.S. patent law. Accordingly, the district court properly exercised jurisdiction.[14]

Covenant Not to Sue Divests Court of Subject Matter Jurisdiction

In ***Dow Jones & Co. v. Ablaise Ltd.***,[15] the Federal Circuit reversed the district court's denial of Ablaise's motion to dismiss Dow Jones's invalidity claim against U.S. Patent No. 6,295,530 (the '530 patent) and affirmed the district court's grant of summary judgment that the asserted claims of U.S. Patent No. 6,961,737 (the '737 patent) were invalid as obvious.

Both the '737 and '530 patents-in-suit claim a method for generating computer Web pages that are created and customized for the specific individual viewer based on information encoded in the signal sent to the location generating the pages. Ablaise accused Dow Jones of infringing the patents and offered a license. Dow Jones refused the offer and brought a declaratory judgment action for invalidity of the patents. Ablaise counterclaimed for infringement.

Following the district court's claim construction order, Albaise offered Dow Jones a covenant not to sue as to the '530 patent if Dow Jones dismissed its invalidity claim. Dow Jones refused unless the covenant included Dow Jones's parent corporation. Albaise bulked at the request and moved to dismiss the invalidity claim on the basis that the offer of a covenant not to sue deprived the district court of subject matter jurisdiction.

The district court denied Ablaise's motion to dismiss, reasoning that, although a covenant not to sue eliminated any case or controversy between the parties, jurisdiction could be established for sound prudential reasons and for judicial efficiency. The district court analogized the situation to one in which a federal trial court asserts supplemental jurisdiction under 28 U.S.C. § 1367(a), noting that the relationship between the '767 and '530 patents was so close that the validity or invalidity of one may be said to form part of the same "case or controversy" as the other. The district court furthered reasoned that Ablaise had asserted the '530 patent in at least nine other actions, and that resolving the validity of the '530 patent would help move those cases forward.

The Federal Circuit disagreed with the district court. Citing *MedImmune, Inc. v. Genentech*, the Federal Circuit noted that subject matter jurisdiction in a declaratory judgment suit depends on the existence of "a substantial controversy, between the parties having adverse legal interests, of sufficient immediacy and reality to warrant the issuance of a declaratory judgment."[16] The Federal Circuit found that the denial of Ablaise's motion to dismiss was contrary to the court's jurisprudence established in the relevant case law. The covenant not to sue extinguished any controversy between the parties and divested the district court of subject matter jurisdiction. The court reasoned that no amount of "prudential reasons" or perceived increases in efficiency can empower a federal court to hear a case where there is no existing case or controversy.

Dow Jones argued that the covenant not to sue did not extinguish the controversy because it did not include Dow Jones's parent company. However, the Federal Circuit rejected this argument because the parent company is a legally distinct entity and, there-

---

14. *Id.* at 1362.
15. 606 F.3d 1338 (Fed. Cir. 2010).
16. *Id.* at 1345 (citing MedImmune, Inc. v. Genentech, Inc., 549 U.S. 118, 127 (2007)).

fore, is not liable for acts of its subsidiaries, less a piercing of the corporate veil. Because the covenant not to sue proffered by Ablaise eliminated any controversy between Ablaise and Dow Jones, the district court lacked subject matter jurisdiction over Dow Jones's claim of invalidity of the '530 patent.

Lastly, the Federal Circuit examined the district court's finding of invalidity of the '737 patent for obviousness under 35 U.S.C. § 103. Finding Ablaise's arguments irrelevant and nonsupportive, the Federal Circuit affirmed the district court's grant of summary judgment of invalidity of the '737 patent.

Cause of Action That Necessarily Depends on Resolving Substantial Questions of Federal Patent Law Is Sufficient to Support Federal Jurisdiction under 28 U.S.C. § 1338(a)

In *HIF Bio, Inc. v. Yung Shin Pharmaceuticals Industrial Co.*,[17] the Federal Circuit decided that the district court erred when it remanded to California state court an action that concerned a patent inventorship dispute, as well as a dispute over title to two pending patent applications. Specifically, the Federal Circuit determined that the district court abused its discretion by not exercising supplemental jurisdiction because two of the causes of action—declaratory judgment of inventorship and slander of title—necessarily depended on resolving substantial questions of federal patent law sufficient to support federal jurisdiction under 28 U.S.C. § 1338(a).

The action was initially commenced in California state court by HIF and BizBiotech Co., Ltd. (BizBiotech), assignees of rights from patent applicants Jong-Wan Park (Park) and Yang-Sook Chun (Chun). From 1999 through 2002, Park and Chun discovered that a chemical called YC-1 could be used to inhibit the growth of cancerous tumors. Park and Chun shared their findings—including prepublication experimental data and nonpublic, prepublication scientific journal drafts—with the defendant, Che-Ming Teng (Teng), who provided Park and Chun with YC-1 for their experiments. Unknown to Park and Chun, Teng disclosed this information to defendant, Yung Shin Pharmaceuticals (Yung Shin), a Taiwanese drug manufacturer. On March 29, 2002, without the knowledge or approval of Park and Chun, Yung Shin filed a U.S. Provisional Patent application covering Park and Chun's discovery. The application identified Teng and defendant, Fang-Yu Lee, president of Yung Shin, as the inventors. In March 2003, Yung Shin filed a Patent Cooperation Treaty (PCT) application claiming priority to the U.S provisional application.

In April 2003, Park and Chun filed an application with the USPTO covering their discovery that YC-1 inhibited tumor growth. In July 2003, Park and Chun assigned these patent rights to BizBiotech, which in turn assigned them to HIF in February 2005.

After becoming aware of the defendants' patent application, HIF and BizBiotech filed suit in September 2005 in California state court. In November 2005, the action was removed to the U.S. District Court for the Central District of California, and in March 2006, the plaintiffs filed their first amended complaint, asserting twelve separate causes of action.[18] Sometime thereafter, the district court dismissed the plaintiffs' RICO cause of

---

17. 600 F.3d 1347 (Fed. Cir. 2010).
18. These twelve claims included: (1) declaratory judgment for ownership; (2) declaratory judgment for inventorship; (3) violations of the Racketeer Influenced and Corrupt Organization Act (RICO); (4) slander of title; (5) conversion; (6) actual and constructive fraud; (7) intentional

action and remanded the matter to the state court. In its decision to remand, the district court held that the plaintiffs' first and second causes of action concerned "rights of inventorship and ownership of inventions [which] are valid state law claims."[19] As a result, it refused to exercise supplemental jurisdiction and remanded all remaining state law claims. The defendants appealed.

The Federal Circuit dismissed the defendants' appeal for lack of jurisdiction, holding that 28 U.S.C. § 1447(d) precluded appellate review of a district court remand order based on a refusal to exercise supplemental jurisdiction. The defendants then appealed to the U.S. Supreme Court, which remanded the case to the Federal Circuit for further proceedings,[20] holding that section 1447(d) did not bar appellate review under the circumstances. Accordingly, the remaining issue to be decided by the Federal Circuit was whether the district court abused its discretion in remanding the plaintiffs' amended complaint to the state court.

On remand, the Federal Circuit concluded that the district court abused its discretion by failing to exercise supplemental jurisdiction because two of the remanded causes of action arose under 28 U.S.C. § 1331(a). Specifically, it found that the plaintiffs' claim for declaratory judgment of inventorship was not a state law claim because issues of inventorship present sufficiently substantial questions of federal patent law to support jurisdiction under section 1338(a).[21] Similarly, the Federal Circuit found that the plaintiffs' claim for slander of title created jurisdiction under section 1338(a) because patent law was essential to that claim, and no other nonpatent theory was available as a basis for the plaintiffs claim for their requested relief.[22]

Despite the existence of jurisdiction for the above two claims, however, the Federal Circuit found that both claims should be dismissed by the district court under Federal Rule of Civil Procedure 12(b). Specifically, given that the claims concerned inventorship of *pending* patent applications, there was no private right of action available by which the plaintiffs could seek relief from the district court. Rather, the plaintiffs' requested relief, a declaration about who is the true inventor of the subject matter sought patented, could be granted only by the director of the USPTO under 35 U.S.C. §§ 116 and/or 135(a). Noting that some district courts had previously held that section 116 created a private right of action, the Federal Circuit made clear that, here, section 116 "does not provide a private right of action to challenge inventorship of a pending patent application. Once the patent issues, however, 35 U.S.C. § 256 provides a right of action to challenge inventorship, and such challenge arises under § 1338(a)."[23]

---

interference with contract and prospective economic advantage; (8) negligent interference with contract and prospective economic advantage; (9) breach of implied contract; (10) unfair competition and fraudulent business practices; (11) unjust enrichment-constructive trust; and (12) permanent injunction. *Id.* at 1351 n.1.

19. HIF Bio, Inc. v. Yung Shin Pharms. Indus. Co., Ltd., No. 05-07976, 2006 WL 6086295, at *4 (C.D. Cal. June 9, 2006).

20. *See* Carlsbad Tech., Inc. v. HIF Bio, Inc., 129 S. Ct. 1862, 1867 (2009).

21. *HIF Bio*, 600 F.3d at 1353 (Fed. Cir. 2010) ("This court has held that 'the field of federal patent law preempts any state law that purports to define rights based on inventorship.'") (quoting Univ. of Colo. Found. v. Am. Cyanamid Co., 196 F.3d 1366, 1372 (Fed. Cir. 1999)).

22. To prove slander of title, the plaintiffs had to show that: (1) they invented the invention first; (2) the defendants' public statements of inventorship were false; and (3) such statements caused the plaintiffs damage. *Id.* at 1355.

23. *Id.* at 1354.

As to the remaining eight causes of action, the Federal Circuit found that the district court correctly remanded them to state court because none necessarily depended on the resolution of a substantial question of federal patent law.

Federal Circuit Clarifies the Scope of Its Jurisdiction under 28 U.S.C. § 1338

In ***Laboratory Corp. of America Holdings v. Metabolite Laboratories, Inc.***,[24] the Federal Circuit held that it lacked jurisdiction over an appeal from a declaratory judgment in a case that concerned an alleged breach of a license agreement. The license agreement stemmed from a previous judgment entered in a prior patent infringement and breach of contract proceeding.

The district court, on summary judgment, held that LabCorp did not breach the license agreement; thus, no further royalties were due because "'a plain reading of the verdict form [from the prior case], coupled with the language of the License Agreement, leads to the conclusion that the License Agreement was both breached and terminated,' and resulted in a loss of all rights (both patent and know-how) under the contract."[25]

On an appeal by Metabolite, LabCorp filed a motion for transfer of the appeal to the Tenth Circuit, arguing that the Federal Circuit lacked jurisdiction. In assessing its jurisdiction, the Federal Circuit employed the two-part test outlined by the U.S. Supreme Court in *Christianson v. Colt Industries Operating Corp.*,[26] where the Court examined "arising under" jurisdiction conferred by 28 U.S.C. § 1338(a). In *Christianson*, the Court held that such jurisdiction "extend[s] only to those cases in which a well-pleaded complaint establishes either that federal patent law creates the cause of action or that the plaintiff's right to relief necessarily depends on resolution of a substantial question of federal patent law, in that patent law is a necessary element of one of the well-pleaded claims."[27] The Federal Circuit then turned to *Grable & Sons Metal Products, Inc. v. Darue Engineering & Manufacturing*,[28] which it characterized as refining the *Christianson* test "by requiring a determination of whether 'a state law claim necessarily raise[s] a stated federal issue, actually disputed and substantial, which a federal forum may entertain without disturbing any congressionally approved balance of federal and state judicial responsibilities.'"[29]

Applying that analysis, the Federal Circuit found that "Metabolite's hypothetical claim would have been a breach of contract claim premised on LabCorp's continued referral of homocysteine-only assays to a third party without paying know-how royalties on its post-judgment 'Net Sales of Licensed Assays.'"[30] To prevail on that claim, Metabolite would need to prove the elements of a breach of contract claim under New Jersey law. The Federal Circuit reasoned that, because the issue of infringement was determined in the prior lawsuit, Metabolite's hypothetical action would not "require resolution of a disputed question of patent law central to the disposition of the breach of contract claim."[31] Finding

---

24. 599 F.3d 1277 (Fed. Cir. 2010).
25. *Id.* at 1281.
26. 486 U.S. 800 (1988).
27. *Id.* at 808–09.
28. 545 U.S. 308 (2005).
29. *Lab. Corp.*, 599 F.3d at 1282 (quoting *Grable*, 545 U.S. at 314).
30. *Id.* at 1283.
31. *Id.*

that Metabolite did not show that the court had proper jurisdiction pursuant to section 1338, the Federal Circuit transferred the appeal to the Tenth Circuit.

Judge Dyk filed a dissenting opinion. In dissent, Judge Dyk asserted that "[a]t its heart, this case involves the question whether the res judicata effect of our earlier decision . . . requires that the contract provision here be treated as terminated."[32] He argued that the case belongs in the Federal Circuit for two reasons: (1) the Federal Circuit has jurisdiction "because a suit to enforce or determine the res judicata effect of a prior judgment 'arising under' the federal patent laws is itself a suit that arises under federal patent law";[33] and (2) "the determination of a contract entitlement rests on a substantial question of patent law,"[34] specifically whether the patent covered the outsourced assays and, thus, fell under the scope of the license agreement.

State Deceptive Trade Practices Act Claim Requiring Proof of Noninfringement Raises Substantial Question of Patent Law

In *Tiger Team Technologies, Inc. v. Synesi Group, Inc.*,[35] a nonprecedential decision, the Federal Circuit affirmed the District Court of Minnesota's grant of summary judgment and dismissal of various state law claims and entry of a default judgment without damages in favor of Defendant Synesi. Notably, the Federal Circuit accepted appellate jurisdiction, despite the appeal being limited only to state law claims because the operative district court pleading included a claim that raised a substantial question of patent law.

Tiger Team Technologies, Inc. (TTT) originally brought suit against Synesi and two of its shareholder officers, Tim Olish and Rod Miley, asserting various claims, including a declaration that it did not infringe Synesi's patents. By its second amended complaint, TTT had dropped its declaratory judgment patent claims, but left several other state law claims, including breach of contract (Count I); promissory estoppel (Count II); deceptive trade practices under Minnesota Statute § 325D.44 (Count III); unfair competition (Count IV); and common law fraud by misrepresentation and/or omission (Count V).

The district court either dismissed or granted summary judgment in favor of the shareholder defendants on all counts. TTT appealed only the grant of summary judgment of Counts I, II, IV, and V; it did not appeal the dismissal of Court III for violation of the Minnesota Deceptive Trade Practices Act (MDTPA).

Before addressing the substantive issues of the appeal, the Federal Circuit examined whether it had jurisdiction to hear the appeal because TTT appealed only state law claims. The court explained that it had jurisdiction over the appeal because the operative pleading in the district court case contained a claim, the resolution of which raised a substantial question of patent law. Specifically, TTT's MDTPA claim was based on an assertion that the defendants made disparaging remarks about TTT by alleging that it committed patent infringement. In order to prevail on a claim for MDTPA, one must prove the falsity of the alleged disparaging statement In this case, TTT was required to prove that it had not infringed Synesi's patents. Thus, although TTT's MDTPA claim was a state law claim, it raised a substantial question of patent law, and the Federal Circuit had appellate jurisdic-

---

32. *Id.* at 1286–87 (Dyk, J., dissenting).

33. *Id.* at 1287.

34. *Id.*

35. No. 2009-1508, 2010 WL 1439062 (Fed. Cir. Apr. 12, 2010).

tion. The court further explained that TTT's failure to appeal the dismissal of its MDTPA claim was irrelevant because appellate jurisdiction is defined by a well-pleaded complaint, rather than the issues raised on appeal.

The court then addressed whether the district court erred in granting summary judgment given its refusal to pierce the corporate veil for claims of breach of contract and promissory estoppel. The district court found that TTT's allegations lacked evidentiary support to pierce the corporate veil. Finding no clear error in the facts, the Federal Circuit affirmed the grant of summary judgment on these two counts.

TTT also claimed the district court erred in refusing to consider facts TTT first presented in its opposition to the defendant's motion for summary judgment on TTT's fraud count. The district court found that the defendants would be prejudiced by TTT's inclusion of new factual allegations and granted summary judgment on the fraud count. The Federal Circuit found no error in the rule of prejudice and affirmed the grant of summary judgment.

Lastly, TTT appealed the district court's order entering a default judgment without awarding damages. The district court, after denying TTT's original request for damages, had instructed TTT to support the judgment with documentation. TTT then submitted an expert affidavit containing an opinion as to the judgment amount. In response, the district court found that the affidavit did not meet the requirement of establishing a "sum certain." The Federal Circuit found no error in the decision and affirmed the district court's entry of default judgment without damages.

Section 1498 Applies When a Third Party, with the Authorization and Consent of the Government, Acts on Behalf of the Government

In ***Advanced Software Design Corp. v. Federal Reserve Bank of St. Louis***,[36] the Federal Circuit affirmed the district court's decision to grant summary judgment against Advanced Software, holding that, because the Federal Reserve Banks used the allegedly infringing technology, in this case Treasury checks, with the authorization and consent of the United States, the plaintiff's infringement claims against the United States could be pursued only in the Court of Federal Claims under 28 U.S.C. § 1498(a).[37]

Section 1498(a), when applicable, relieves a third party from patent infringement liability and acts as a waiver of sovereign immunity and consent to liability by the U.S. government.[38] For section 1498(a) to apply, the third party must act for, and with the authorization and consent of, the government. When section 1498(a) does apply, the only remedy is an action against the United States in the Court of Federal Claims for reasonable compensation.

Advanced Software owns patents for methods of detecting fraudulent bank checks. The methods require the check draftee to encode check information at the time the check is issued. Three Federal Reserve Banks used this method to detect altered checks before they made the funds available, which, in turn, enabled them to avoid losses due to fraudulent checks. At the request of the Reserve Banks, the Treasury also adopted the system for

---

36. 583 F.3d 1371 (Fed. Cir. 2009).
37. *Id.* at 1372–73.
38. *Id.* at 1375.

checks it drafts. This allowed the Treasury to reduce the amount of time and resources previously necessary to discover and investigate fraudulently altered checks.

Although Advanced Software asserted section 1498(a) did not apply because the government did not provide unequivocal authorization or consent, the Federal Circuit disagreed, finding unequivocal authorization unnecessary because the government's authorization and consent may be express or implied, and it need not appear on the face of a particular contract.[39] In particular, the Federal Circuit noted several facts supporting its conclusion that section 1498(a) applied in this case: the Treasury's agreement to participate in the system, statements on behalf of the Treasury concerning its use of the technology, an amicus curiae brief from the United States supporting the finding of government authorization, and the statements of U.S. counsel at oral arguments. The court reasoned that all this evidence supported the conclusion that the Reserve Banks acted on behalf of, and with the authorization and consent of, the United States.

The Federal Circuit also found that Fiserv, a defendant supplying the accused technology to the Reserve Banks, acted for the government as required by section 1498(a). Although the government was not a party to the contract between Fiserv and the Reserve Banks, and the contract had been modified at the request of the Treasury to indicate the Reserve Banks were not acting on its behalf, the panel held "that § 1498(a) does not require the government to be a party to any contract, but may apply to activities by any person, firm, or corporation for the benefit of the government."[40]

The Federal Circuit also rejected Advanced Software's argument that section 1498(a) should not apply because the government was not the principal beneficiary of the accused infringement. Advanced Software argued that, because the Reserve Banks, not the Treasury, bear the risk of loss from fraudulently altered checks, the Reserve Banks benefit the most from preventing the fraud. In rejecting Advanced Software's argument, the court noted that it was not necessary for the government to be the sole beneficiary for the purposes of section 1498(a).[41] The court found that it was enough that the Treasury had received significant benefits because the technology saved the Treasury significant detection and investigation resources. The Federal Circuit also rejected the argument that the Treasury only received incidental benefits from the technology because the technology required the Treasury to participate every time it issued checks.[42] Therefore, it found that the Treasury had more than a general interest in the fraud prevention method.[43]

Finally, the Federal Circuit held that an agency relationship need not exist in order for section 1498(a) to apply.[44] Advanced Software argued that the Treasury requested the Reserve Banks avoid using the term "on behalf of the Treasury" in the contracts with Fiserv, negating any intent to have the Reserve Banks act as the Treasury's agent. The court held that it need not resolve this issue because an agency relationship was not required for section 1498(a) to apply.

---

39. *Id.* at 1377.
40. *Id.* at 1378.
41. *Id.*
42. *Id.* at 1379.
43. *Id.*
44. *Id.*

Personal Jurisdiction

Court May Reasonably Exercise Jurisdiction over Defendants Who Repeatedly Attended Trade Shows in Venue State

In *Patent Rights Protection Group, LLC v. Video Gaming Technology Inc.*,[45] the Federal Circuit vacated the district court's dismissal of a patent infringement case against Defendants Video Gaming Tech (VGT) and SPEC for lack of personal jurisdiction and determined that the district court abused its discretion in denying Plaintiff Patent Rights jurisdictional discovery.

The Federal Circuit first reviewed, de novo, the lower court's determination that it would be unreasonable for the U.S. District Court for the District of Nevada to exercise jurisdiction over VGT and SPEC. The Federal Circuit concluded that VGT and SPEC's limited contacts with the state of Nevada, which occurred at gaming trade shows in the late 1990s, the early 2000s, and in 2007 and 2008, were sufficient to find personal jurisdiction. Although the Federal Circuit acknowledged that defending a lawsuit in Nevada would place a burden on VGT and SPEC given their respective home states of Tennessee and Michigan, it concluded that exercising jurisdiction nevertheless was reasonable. The court noted that compelling cases where jurisdiction would be unreasonable even though a defendant has purposefully directed activities at forum residents "are limited to the rare situation in which the plaintiff's interest and the state's interest in adjudicating the dispute in the forum are so attenuated that they are clearly outweighed by the burden of subjecting the defendant to litigation within the forum."[46] In view of their trade show activities, the Federal Circuit determined that if VGT and SPEC could transport people and documents to Nevada to participate in trade shows, the parties could surely do the same for a trial, especially because "modern transportation and communications have made it much less burdensome for a party sued to defend [itself] outside its home state."[47]

Because patent infringement is a matter of federal law, the Federal Circuit also noted the shared interest of each of the several states. By providing the forum for Patent Rights' claims against the defendants, Nevada spares the two other states the burden of providing the forum, thereby providing an efficient resolution. Otherwise, Patent Rights might face the substantial burden of pursuing separate, largely similar actions against the defendants in two different home states.

Weighing these factors, the Federal Circuit determined that the district court erred by declining to exercise jurisdiction over SPEC and VGT solely on the grounds that to do so was unreasonable.

The Federal Circuit then reviewed the district court's denial of the plaintiff's motion for jurisdictional discovery. In support of its motion, Patent Rights submitted a declaration alleging that SPEC and VGT had exhibited infringing gaming machines at a Las Vegas gaming show. SPEC and VGT did not deny their presence at the show. Here, the Federal Circuit determined that the defendants' contention that their attendance at the show was not for commercial purposes lacked credibility. Given that additional discovery

---

45.   603 F.3d 1364 (Fed. Cir. 2010).

46.   *Id.* at 1369 (quoting Beverly Hills Fan Co. v. Royal Sovereign Corp., 21 F.3d 1558, 1568 (Fed. Cir. 1994)).

47.   *Id.* at 1370 (quoting Burger King Corp. v. Rudzewicz, 471 U.S. 462, 474 (1985)).

may reveal facts sufficient to support personal jurisdiction, the Federal Circuit determined that the district court abused its discretion in denying discovery on this matter.

VENUE

Venue Transfer

District Court Required to Transfer Patent Infringement Case to Another Venue

In *In re Hoffmann-La Roche Inc.*,[48] the Federal Circuit granted a petition for a writ of mandamus, directing the U.S. District Court for the Eastern District of Texas to vacate its order denying a motion to transfer venue to the Eastern District of North Carolina. The Federal Circuit held that the district court clearly abused its discretion in denying the motion.

The petition granted by the Federal Circuit stemmed from a patent infringement suit brought by Novartis Vaccines and Diagnostics, Inc., headquartered in California, against the makers of the HIV-inhibitor drug, Fuzeon, which had been developed and tested in North Carolina. Novartis brought suit in the Eastern District of Texas, and Hoffmann-La Roche moved to transfer the suit to the Eastern District of North Carolina.

In its motion, Hoffmann-La Roche contended "that there were no witnesses or any sources of proof within 100 miles of the Eastern District of Texas," "that the bulk of the key documentary evidence was present in the Eastern District of North Carolina," and "that a trial in the Eastern District of North Carolina would be far more convenient for [witnesses] who reside[d] within 100 miles of the district and [who] said their attendance in the Eastern District of Texas would be inconvenient and unlikely."[49] Novartis responded by arguing that "the parties, the sources of proof, and witnesses were spread throughout the country," and that 75,000 pages of relevant documents were already located in the Eastern District of Texas.[50]

The district court denied the motion to transfer venue, holding that the case was "'decentralized' . . . given the various locations of the potential witnesses" and "that neither venue had a localized interest in [the] matter."[51] The district court also held that "transfer would merely shift inconveniences from those witnesses closer to the Eastern District of Texas to those witnesses closer to the Eastern District of Texas . . . ."[52]

The Federal Circuit disagreed with the district court, finding a substantial difference between the two venues in terms of convenience, relevance, and fairness. The court explained that "[t]he accused drug was developed and tested within the Eastern District of North Carolina and documents and sources of proof remain[ed] there," that "the Eastern District of North Carolina's local interest in the case remain[ed] strong because the cause of action call[ed] into question the work and reputation of several individuals residing in

---

48.   587 F.3d 1333 (Fed. Cir. 2009).
49.   *Id.*
50.   *Id.*
51.   *Id.*
52.   *Id.*

or near that district," that "at least four non-party witnesses resid[ed] within 100 miles of the Eastern District of North Carolina [who] could be compelled for both deposition and trial testimony," and that "the district's less congested docket suggests that [it] may be able to resolve [the] dispute more quickly."[53] The court noted that, on the contrary, "there appear[ed] to be no connection between this case and the Eastern District of Texas except that in anticipation of [the] litigation, Novartis's counsel in California . . . transferred [75,000 pages of electronic documents] to the offices of its litigation counsel in Texas."[54]

The Federal Circuit found that the district court ignored the significant contrast between the two venues and found that, "because the Eastern District of North Carolina has a meaningful local interest in adjudicating the dispute and no meaningful connection exists with the Eastern District of Texas, this factor also favors transfer."[55] The Federal Circuit thus granted the petition and ordered the district court to "promptly transfer the case to the Eastern District of North Carolina."[56]

District Court Ordered to Transfer Venue of Patent Infringement Case

In *In re Nintendo Co.,*[57] the Federal Circuit granted a petition for a writ of mandamus, directing the U.S. District Court for the Eastern District of Texas to vacate its order denying a motion to transfer venue to the Western District of Washington. The Federal Circuit held that the district court clearly abused its discretion in denying the motion.[58]

The petition for a writ of mandamus stemmed from a patent infringement suit brought by Motiva, existing under the laws of Ohio with a principal place of business in Dublin, against Nintendo Co., existing under the laws of Japan with a principal place of business in Kyoto, and Nintendo of America, existing under the laws of Washington with a principal place of business in Redmond. Motiva brought suit in the Eastern District of Texas, and Nintendo Co. and Nintendo of America (collectively, Nintendo) moved to transfer the suit to the Western District of Washington.

In its motion, Nintendo contended that "the physical and documentary evidence was mainly located in the Western District of Washington and Japan," and that "no meaningful connection linked the Eastern District of Texas to [the] case."[59] Motiva argued that "the Eastern District of Texas was the proper venue even in the absence of any of the witnesses or evidence relevant to the cause of action."[60]

The district court denied the motion to transfer venue, and Nintendo appealed to the Federal Circuit. The Federal Circuit disagreed with the district court, finding "a stark contrast in relevance, convenience, and fairness between the two venues."[61] Following Fifth Circuit law, the Federal Circuit applied the "private" and "public" factors for deciding a motion to transfer venue: (1) the relative ease of access to sources of proof; (2) the

---

53. *Id.*
54. *Id.* at 1337.
55. *Id.*
56. *Id.* at 1338.
57. 589 F.3d 1194 (Fed. Cir. 2009).
58. *Id.* at 1196.
59. *Id.*
60. *Id.*
61. *Id.* at 1198.

availability of compulsory process to secure the attendance of witnesses; (3) the cost of attendance for willing witnesses; (4) all other practical problems that make a trial easy, expeditious, and inexpensive; (5) the administrative difficulties flowing from court congestion; (6) the local interest in having localized interests decided at home; (7) the familiarity of the forum with the law that will govern the case; and (8) the avoidance of unnecessary problems of conflicts of law or in the application of foreign law.

The Federal Circuit held that the district court "clearly abused its discretion in denying transfer from a venue with no meaningful ties to the case."[62] The Federal Circuit therefore granted the petition for a writ of mandamus and ordered the district court to vacate its order and transfer the case to the U.S. District Court for the Western District of Washington.

STANDING

State Divorce Decree Controls Standing to Sue

In *Enovsys LLC v. Nextel Communications Inc.,*[63] the Federal Circuit affirmed a jury determination of infringement. In a decision by Judge Prost, joined by Judge Bryson and, in part, by Judge Newman, the court considered Nextel's challenges to Enovsys's standing to bring the lawsuit and the jury's determination of infringement. Judge Newman dissented in part, agreeing with the majority on the procedural issue, but not on the infringement question.

The patents-in-suit involved global positioning systems (GPSs) for determining the location of mobile devices, wherein a user selects security settings that permit other users or entities to determine the position of the user's mobile device. That feature was used in applications for finding nearby restaurants, theaters, etc.

Nextel challenged the plaintiff's standing to sue on the grounds that Enovsys failed to join an indispensible party, namely, the wife of one of the inventors. That inventor had assigned his rights to the plaintiff for patents on an invention that was conceived (and patent applications filed that resulted in the patents-in-suit) while he was still married. Because California was the situs of the marriage, Nextel contended that the patents were community property in which the inventor's wife retained an interest (one that she assigned to Nextel). The inventor and his wife had obtained summary disposition of their marriage under California law and, under those provisions, had disclaimed the existence of any community property. This disclaimer rebutted the presumption that all assets acquired during a marriage are community property, according to the district court, which found that California law controlled the ownership status of the patents, and that the plaintiff had both title and standing to sue without joining the inventor's ex-wife.

The Federal Circuit affirmed, based on comity and res judicata principles. Under California law (which the court found was controlling), the inventor's ex-wife retained no residual interest in the patents-in-suit at the time the lawsuit was filed. Under those circumstances, the Federal Circuit reasoned that the judgment was entitled to full faith and credit by statute. In addition, the court found that Nextel was attempting to relitigate the

---

62. *Id.* at 1200.
63. 614 F.3d 1333 (Fed. Cir. 2010).

married parties' rights after a divorce decree in California state court that constituted a "complete and final adjudication of their property rights." Because Nextel had obtained the assignment from the inventor's ex-wife, the court found sufficient privity with one of the parties to that final adjudication that res judicata precluded further challenge in the patent infringement lawsuit.

Turning to the merits, the Federal Circuit panel majority found that Nextel's challenge to the jury's infringement determination was actually an attempt to change the district court's claim construction. Given that Nextel had not objected to the district court's claim construction at trial (indeed, the court found that the district court had substantially adopted Nextel's proposed construction for one of the terms), the Federal Circuit panel majority concluded that Nextel had waived any objection and affirmed the judgment.

Judge Newman dissented from this portion of the judgment. Judge Newman urged that Nextel's challenge to the jury's infringement determination involved how the jury had applied the accused infringing articles to the construed claims, rather than objecting to claim construction per se.

Recordation of Patent Assignment Shifts Burden of Proof of Issue of Standing to Challenger

In *SiRF Technology, Inc. v. International Trade Commission*,[64] the Federal Circuit affirmed the ITC's finding that Appellant SiRF infringed patents related to Global Positioning's technology in violation of section 1337 of the Tariff Act of 1930 (19 U.S.C. § 1337).[65] In doing so, the Federal Circuit found that recording an assignment with the USPTO creates a presumption of validity as to the assignment and places the burden to rebut this presumption on the challenger.

The inventions of the asserted patents were conceived in October 1999 while the inventor was employed at Magellan. In 1996, the inventor had entered into an employee invention assignment agreement with Magellan's predecessor, Ashtech, Inc. The assignment agreement applied to "all inventions . . . which are related to or useful in the business of the Employer[.]"[66] Although not clear from the record, this agreement appears to have been assigned to Magellan following its merger with Ashtech. In 2000, the inventor separated from Magellan and joined Global Locate. While at Global Locate, the inventor and his coinventor applied for the patent, which was then assigned to Global Locate.

The Federal Circuit reviews a question of standing de novo because the issue is jurisdictional, while the court reviews the underlying factual findings to determine if they are supported by substantial evidence. At issue was whether all co-owners were joined in the action so as to support a finding of standing under the rule that a co-owner, acting alone, lacks standing to maintain an infringement action. In particular, the court considered whether one of the inventors (Abraham) previously assigned his interest in the patent to his former employer, Magellan Corporation, which was not joined in the underlying ITC investigation.

The parties all agreed that Global Locate had the burden of establishing standing. They disagreed, however, as to whether Global Locate also had the burden of showing

---

64. 601 F.3d 1319 (Fed. Cir. 2010).
65. *Id.*
66. *Id.* at 1326.

that an interest in the patent had not been previously assigned by Abraham to Magellan. The Federal Circuit found that the ITC properly determined that the burden did not rest with Global Locate. In reaching its decision, the Federal Circuit determined that, although the recording of an assignment with the USPTO is not a determination of validity of the assignment, it creates a presumption of validity as to the assignment and places the burden to rebut such a showing on one challenging the assignment. The Federal Circuit then held that the ITC's determination that appellants did not sustain their burden was supported by substantial evidence.

The Federal Circuit next addressed SiRF's contention that the ITC erred in finding direct infringement. SiRF argued that infringement of the method claims at issue, which required joint infringement with the customers and end users, was not satisfied because SiRF neither controlled nor directed the customers or end users. The Federal Circuit disagreed, however, on the grounds that the claims did not require any specific action by the customers; therefore, the claims at issue only required action by a single party. Given that this requirement was satisfied, the Federal Circuit, like the ITC, found direct infringement of the asserted claims.

Lastly, the Federal Circuit considered whether the asserted method claims comprised patentable subject matter. In determining whether the claims were patentable, the Federal Circuit considered its decision in *In re Bilski*, in which it held that "a claimed process is surely patent-eligible under § 101 if: (1) it is tied to a particular machine or apparatus . . . ."[67] Finding that the claims were tied to a particular machine—the GPS unit—and that the claims could not be performed without it, the Federal Circuit reasoned that the method claims comprised patentable subject matter.

Patent Licensee Did Not Have Standing without Patent Owner's Participation

In *AsymmetRx, Inc. v. Biocare Medical, LLC*,[68] the Federal Circuit did not address the substantive license issues raised by the parties, but instead held that AsymmetRx, the licensee, did not have statutory standing without the participation of the president and fellows of Harvard College, the owners of the patents at issue.

On a motion for summary judgment, the district court held in favor of Biocare, concluding that Biocare either had a license that covered the infringing activity or, in the alternative, had an implied license.[69]

On appeal, AsymmetRx and Biocare argued the merits of the district court's interpretation of the language of the Biocare license. The Federal Circuit, however, resolved the case by deciding whether AsymmetRx had standing to bring the action against Biocare without Harvard's participation. Because neither party raised the issue of standing or addressed the issue of whether Harvard should be joined, the Federal Circuit was constrained to vacate the district court's decision and remand the case.

The Federal Circuit first discussed AsymmetRx's license with Harvard, which gave AsymmetRx "the right to prosecute in its own name and at its own expense any infringement" within the commercial diagnostic field, so long as AsymmetRx still had an exclu-

---

67. *Id.* at 1332 (citing *In re* Bilski, 545 F.3d 943, 954 (Fed. Cir. 2008)).
68. 582 F.3d 1314 (Fed. Cir. 2009).
69. AsymmetRx, Inc. v. Biocare Med. LLC, 578 F. Supp. 2d 333 (D. Mass. 2008).

sive license at the time the action was commenced and gave "careful consideration to the views of Harvard and to potential effects on the public's interest in making its decision whether or not to sue."[70] The license further provided that, if AsymmetRx chose to exercise this right, Harvard could seek to join as a party in that action.

The Federal Circuit then discussed the case law related to the assignment of the right to bring an infringement action in the licensee's own name. The Federal Circuit reiterated its holding from *Abbott Laboratories v. Diamedix Corp.* that "a bare licensee, who has no right to exclude others from making, using or selling the licensed products, has no legally recognized interest that entitles it to bring or join an infringement action," with the possible exception to this rule being "[i]f the owner of the patent, being within the jurisdiction, refuses or is unable to join."[71] The court also discussed its holding in *Vaupel Textimaschinen KG v. Meccanica Euro Italita S.P.A.*, in which the court found the assignee had the right to bring an infringement suit because the only rights the patent owner maintained were a reversionary right in the event of bankruptcy and the rights to veto sublicensing, to obtain patents in other countries, and to receive infringement damages. Additionally, in *Speedplay, Inc. v. Bebop, Inc.*, the court also found the assignee had standing because "the license grant was not subject to any prior granted licenses of any retained rights by the licensor to practice the patent."[72]

The Federal Circuit found that this case was "more similar" to *Abbott* than to *Vaupel* or *Speedplay*. The court concluded that Harvard retained "substantial interests" under the patents at issue, one of these being Harvard's right to sue for infringement. It also cited Harvard's retained rights to make and use the invention at issue for its own academic research purposes; to provide the invention to nonprofit or governmental institutions for research purposes; to require AsymmetRx to meet commercial use, availability, and FDA filing benchmarks; to require AsymmetRx to grant sublicenses suggested by Harvard; and to require AsymmetRx to enable Harvard to apply for, prosecute, and maintain patent applications.

The Federal Circuit therefore held that AsymmetRx did not have standing unless Harvard was also a party. Given that it was unclear whether Harvard was ever given the opportunity to join the suit in district court, the Federal Circuit did not address whether Harvard should be made an involuntary plaintiff, but vacated the summary judgment and remanded the case.

Present Assignment of Patent Rights Overrides Assignment of Future Interest in Matters of Ownership Despite Proper Recorded Assignment and Failure to Licensee

In *Board of Trustees of the Leland Stanford Junior University v. Roche Molecular Systems, Inc.*,[73] the Federal Circuit held that an inventor's agreement to "hereby assign" future inventions trumped the inventor's earlier agreement to "agree to assign" future inventions; therefore, the patentee lacked standing to bring its infringement claim. On

---

70. *AsymmetRx*, 582 F.3d at 1317.
71. Abbott Labs. v. Diamedix Corp., 47 F.3d 1128, 1130 (Fed. Cir. 1995).
72. Speedplay, Inc. v. Bebop, Inc., 211 F.3d 1245, 1251 (Fed. Cir. 2000).
73. 583 F.3d 832 (Fed. Cir. 2009).

summary judgment, the district court concluded that Roche's claim for ownership of the asserted patents was only a counterclaim, not an affirmative defense, and was therefore barred by the applicable statute of limitations and the Bayh-Dole Act.

One of the co-inventors, Holodniy, had signed multiple conflicting patent assignment agreements. At Stanford, Holodniy signed an agreement that recited "I agree to assign or confirm in writing to Stanford and/or Sponsors that right, title, and interest in . . . such inventions as required by Contracts or Grants."[74] Subsequently, Holodniy began collaborative work at Cetus, Roche's predecessor-in-interest. That work eventually gave rise to the patents-in-suit. As a condition of working at Cetus, Holodniy had signed another agreement providing that he "will assign and do[es] hereby assign to Cetus, my right, title, and interest in each of the ideas, inventions and improvements that Holodniy may devise as a consequent of his work at Cetus." The Federal Circuit held that the Stanford contract language "agree to assign" reflected a promise to assign in the future, not an immediate transfer of expectant interests, whereas the Cetus contract language "do hereby assign" effected a present assignment of Holodniy's future inventions to Cetus. Thus, at the time of invention, Cetus's equitable title converted to legal title, and Holodniy had no remaining rights in the invention when he executed an assignment to Stanford during prosecution of the asserted patents.

Although the Federal Circuit agreed that Roche's counterclaim for ownership was barred by the applicable statute of limitations, the court concluded that it was an abuse of discretion for the district court to strike Roche's affirmative defense of lack of standing. The statute of limitations was not fatal to the standing defense because, under California law, a defense may be raised at any time even if it would be barred by the statute of limitations as a counterclaim. Likewise, under California law, laches does not bar affirmative defenses. Moreover, the Federal Circuit held that "it is well settled that questions of standing can be raised at any time and are not foreclosed by, or subject to, statutes of limitations."[75]

The Federal Circuit also held that Stanford's election to take title under the Bayh-Dole Act did not void Roche's title to the Holodniy's invention. For inventions developed under federally funded research, the Bayh-Dole Act allows the government to take title to "subject inventions" under certain circumstances, but allows the "contractor" universities or inventors to retain ownership if the government chooses to not take title.[76] Furthermore, the Act allows an inventor to retain title to a subject invention only if the contractor does not elect to retain title to a subject invention.[77] The Federal Circuit held the Act inapplicable to these facts because Stanford's election to retain title did not void any prior, otherwise-valid assignments of patent rights, such as Holodniy's assignment to Cetus. Therefore, the Federal Circuit reasoned, the Bayh-Dole statutory scheme did not automatically void the patent rights that Cetus received from Holodniy.

Prior, unrecorded assignments like Cetus's can be overcome by subsequent bona fide purchasers who lack knowledge of the prior assignment.[78] However, in this case, the Fed-

---

74. *Id.* at 841.
75. *Id.*
76. 35 U.S.C. § 202(a), 202(b).
77. 35 U.S.C. § 202(d).
78. 35 U.S.C. § 261.

eral Circuit held that, even though the assignment to Cetus was not recorded in the USPTO, Stanford was not a bona fide purchaser because it had at least constructive or inquiry notice of the assignment agreement with Cetus.

Patent Ownership and Standing Vest by Operation of Law

In *Sky Technologies LLC v. SAP AG & SAP America, Inc.,*[79] the Federal Circuit addressed the issue of whether a transfer of title through operation of law without a written assignment may apply when a security interest in a patent is foreclosed.

The patent owner granted a security interest in several patents to a secured creditor and then another security interest to a second secured creditor. Both security interests were recorded at the USPTO. Subsequently, the prior secured creditor assigned its security interest to the second secured creditor, thus resulting in the second secured creditor holding all security interests in the patents. The second secured creditor's security agreement provided specifically that it had the right to purchase the collateral, including the patents, at any public sale resulting from the foreclosure of the security interest.

The patent owner defaulted on the debt secured by the patents. The secured creditor followed all procedures under Massachusetts law to foreclose on the patents, including bidding on the patents at public sale and winning the bid. Subsequently, the secured creditor who purchased the patents at the public sale assigned them to a third party. The third party sued the defendants for patent infringement. The defendants filed a motion to dismiss the complaint for lack of standing, arguing that the Patent Act requires that all assignments of a patent interest be in writing, and given that the transfer of the Patents from the patent owner debtor to the second creditor was not in writing, the plaintiff lacked standing. The plaintiff disagreed, arguing that Massachusetts law controlled the subject of transfer of patent ownership.

The court first examined the statutory requirement that all assignments of an interest in a patent must be in writing. The rationale behind the requirement is that a creditor cannot reach incorporeal property, such as a patent, due to its intangible nature; therefore, the transfer (either voluntary or involuntary by way of a judgment lien) to a purchaser must be done by written assignment in order to vest the purchaser with a complete title to the property. Relying on Federal Circuit precedent, the court expressed that, despite the writing requirement for patent assignments (under 35 U.S.C. § 261), "there is nothing that limits assignment as the only means for transferring patent ownership."[80] The court concluded that ownership of a patent may be changed by operation of law and supported this proposition by referring to the passage of title through intestacy. The court was not persuaded by the defendants' argument that 35 U.S.C § 154 requires that patents can only be owned by three categories of individuals—the patentee, his or her heirs, or his or her assigns—and instead concluded that section 154 did not restrict patent ownership to these three classes of individuals. Moreover, the court determined that the language of section 154 failed to specifically address transfers, by assignment or operation of law, of patent ownership. For these reasons, as well as several public policy reasons discussed by the court, the court held that, by following proper state foreclosure procedures, the predecessor in interest to the plaintiff held title to the patents; therefore, the assignment to the

---

79.   576 F. 3d 1374 (Fed. Cir. 2009).
80.   Akazawa v. Link New Tech. Int'l, Inc., 520 F.3d 1354,1356 (Fed. Cir. 2008).

plaintiff made the plaintiff the owner of the patents and the proper party to bring the underlying infringement action.

Standing Is Insufficient Where Plaintiff Fails to Establish Ownership of Patents-in-Suit

In *Tyco Healthcare Group LP v. Ethicon Endo-Surgery, Inc.,*[81] Tyco commenced suit against Ethicon for infringement of three patents involving medical instruments employing ultrasonic energy to cut and coagulate vessels in surgery. Ethicon moved for JMOL on the issue of standing, asserting that Tyco Healthcare did not own the patents-in-suit. Finding that Tyco had failed to establish ownership of the patents-in-suit and lacked standing to sue, the district court entered JMOL and dismissed the case without prejudice.

Tyco appealed the district court's dismissal without prejudice. Ethicon cross-appealed on the basis that the district court should have dismissed the action with prejudice. The Federal Circuit affirmed the district court's judgment because Tyco failed to establish ownership of the patents-in-suit and ultimately lacked standing to bring suit.

Prior to bringing its suit for patent infringement, Tyco had obtained an interest in the patents-in-suit by means of a contribution agreement that transferred title of all of the transferor's patents to Tyco, except for any patents related to pending litigation involving the transferor. To maintain standing in an action for patent infringement, the plaintiff must possess title to the patents-in-suit at the time of filing. The Federal Circuit reasoned that ownership of the patents-in-suit rested on interpretation of the contractual phrase "related to pending litigation."[82] Therefore, in its assessment of standing, the Federal Circuit concluded that, if the patents-in-suit were related to any pending litigation involving the transferor before it entered into the agreement, then the agreement did not transfer those patents to Tyco; if, however, the patents-in-suit were not related to any pending litigation, then Tyco would own the patents-in-suit and thus have standing to sue.

Based on the record before it, the Federal Circuit concluded that it was not possible to determine whether the patents-in-suit were related to any litigation ongoing at the time of the agreement and ultimately determined that the district court had properly dismissed Tyco's suit. The Federal Circuit held: "In sum, Tyco Healthcare bore the burden of proving that the patents-in-suit [were] not 'related to' any litigation pending at the time the Contribution Agreement was executed. Tyco failed to do this."[83] Turning to Ethicon's cross-appeal, the Federal Circuit determined that the district court did not abuse its discretion by dismissing the action without prejudice because, at some future time, Tyco could establish standing by showing that it owned the asserted patents, or it may be able to obtain ownership of the patents. Moreover, the Federal Circuit concluded that, because the evidence, testimony, and rulings developed during trial should be applicable to a subsequent action between the parties, the district court's dismissal without prejudice did not unduly prejudice Ethicon.

Dissenting, Judge Newman opined that, although the majority affirmed the judgment of the district court, it failed to adopt the district court's reasoning. Furthermore, Judge Newman determined that Tyco had established that the patents-in-suit were not related to any litiga-

---

81.   587 F.3d 1375 (Fed. Cir. 2009).
82.   *Id.* at 1378.
83.   *Id.* at 1380.

tion pending at the time the agreement was made, which Ethicon did not dispute; therefore, the patents-in-suit were transferred to Tyco. Based upon this reasoning, Judge Newman concluded that "the court's denial of standing is without support in law and fact."[84]

PLEADING

Declaratory Judgment

Neither the Existence of an Adverse Patent Nor Events Occurring after the Filing of a Complaint Can Automatically Create Declaratory Judgment Jurisdiction

In *Innovative Therapies, Inc. v. Kinetic Concepts, Inc.,*[85] the Federal Circuit affirmed the judgment of the district court dismissing for lack of jurisdiction a declaratory judgment action brought by Innovative Therapies, Inc. (ITI).

The district court concluded that the circumstances relied on by ITI did not establish declaratory judgment jurisdiction at the time ITI filed its complaint seeking a declaration that five Kinetic Concepts, Inc. (KCI) patents were invalid and/or not infringed by a medical device ITI planned to sell to treat chronic wounds. Moreover, the district court determined that events subsequent to the filing of ITI's complaint, namely, the filing of separate actions against ITI by KCI for patent infringement and trade secret misappropriation, could not change the fact that no actual controversy existed at the time ITI's original complaint was filed.

On appeal, ITI again argued that three specific facts, taken together, created an actual controversy sufficient for declaratory jurisdiction as enunciated under *MedImmune, Inc. v. Genentech, Inc.*[86] The first was the expedited approval that ITI received from the FDA for its medical device based on ITI's representations that such device has the "same technological characteristics" as KCI's previously approved device and as other FDA-approved devices that KCI claimed infringed its patents. This, ITI argued, demonstrated a reasonable belief that KCI would consider the ITI device to infringe KCI's patents. The Federal Circuit disagreed, however, ruling that "representations to a third person about 'technological characteristics' do not establish a justiciable controversy with the patentee."[87] It agreed with the district court that the existence or absence of KCI's awareness of ITI's representations to the FDA, a fact disputed by the parties, would have no bearing on the determination of the jurisdictional issue.

The second fact relied on by ITI consisted of statements made by KCI employees about ITI's medical device during two phone conversations with ITI executives. Here, ITI described its medical device to KCI executives and asked how KCI might react should ITI sell this device. During the first call, a KCI executive responded that "KCI will act aggressively" and would sue ITI, but only "if [KCI] first determined that the [ITI] product

84. *Id.* at 1385 (Newman, J., dissenting).
85. 599 F.3d 1377 (Fed. Cir. 2010).
86. 549 U.S. 118 (2007).
87. *Innovative Therapies*, 599 F.3d at 1380.

infringed KCI patents."[88] During the second call, another KCI executive said that the odds that KCI would sue ITI were "100% no doubt about it," and that there was no way the two companies could peacefully coexist with ITI's product on the market.[89] The Federal Circuit again agreed with the district court, finding that these informal conversations did not constitute a real threat of legal action, especially when KCI had neither seen nor evaluated ITI's device. The Federal Circuit also noted, but did not comment on, the district court's description of these phone calls as "a 'sub rosa' effort to create jurisdiction 'by initiating telephone conversations to employees of the patentee who were not in decision-making positions and who were not informed of the real purpose behind the conversations.'"[90]

The third fact claimed by ITI to create declaratory jurisdiction was KCI's known history of aggressively enforcing its patents. ITI argued that this circumstance should be given special consideration in view of the telephone conversations with KCI executives. Here again, however, the Federal Circuit disagreed. Specifically, the Federal Circuit found that, ITI did not meet the minimum standard discussed in *MedImmune* because, although that court held that a reasonable apprehension of suit was not always required for declaratory judgment jurisdiction, it "did not hold that a patent can always be challenged whenever it appears to pose a risk of infringement."[91] Moreover, although a patentee's prior litigation history may be a factor to consider when determining if declaratory jurisdiction exists, the fact that KCI filed infringement actions against third parties on wholly unrelated products does not meet the minimum standard announced in *MedImmune*.

ITI also argued that events that occurred after the filing of its original complaint verified that an actual controversy existed between ITI and KCI at the time of the original complaint. Specifically, ITI relied on the fact that KCI filed two actions against ITI after ITI filed its original complaint for declaratory judgment: (1) in Texas state court for, inter alia, misappropriation of trade secrets; and (2) in federal court in North Carolina for patent infringement. The Federal Circuit, however, discounted these events, and it agreed with the district court that acts that occurred after the filing of ITI's original complaint could not establish declaratory jurisdiction as of the date when ITI filed its original complaint. It further agreed with the district court that ITI's filing of an amended complaint did not change this result because the amended pleading was, in reality, a supplemental pleading under Federal Rule of Civil Procedure 15, and jurisdiction based on subsequent events cannot relate back to the date of an original pleading.

Finally, the Federal Circuit agreed that the district court properly exercised its discretion in dismissing the suit for lack of declaratory jurisdiction and that the objectives of the Declaratory Judgment Act were not served through ITI's actions in this case.

Standard for Declaratory Judgment Jurisdiction in Patent Cases Has Been Lowered

In *Hewlett-Packard Co. v. Acceleron, LLC,*[92] the Federal Circuit reversed a district court's decision to grant Acceleron's motion to dismiss for lack of declaratory judgment

---

88. *Id.*
89. *Id.*
90. *Id.* at 1381.
91. *Id.* at 1382 (citing SanDisk Corp. v. STMicroelectronics, Inc., 480 F.3d 1372, 1380–81 (Fed. Cir. 2007)).
92. 587 F.3d 1358 (Fed. Cir. 2009).

jurisdiction. HP had filed a declaratory judgment suit in the U.S. District Court for the District of Delaware. The district court granted Acceleron's motion to dismiss the case for lack of subject matter jurisdiction. Upon appeal, the appellate panel court reviewed the motion de novo.

The court, relying on *MedImmune, Inc. v. Genentech, Inc.*, noted that, under the Declaratory Judgment Act, subject matter jurisdiction can only be found if "the facts alleged, under all the circumstances, show that there is a substantial controversy, between parties having adverse legal interests, of sufficient immediacy and reality to warrant the issuance of a declaratory judgment."[93] The court found that HP and Acceleron had adverse legal interests, and that a definite dispute existed between them. Therefore, the court held that there was declaratory judgment jurisdiction.

The court recognized that its decision marked a shift from past declaratory judgment cases. Its reasoning for this shift was based on the precedent set in *MedImmune*, which the court explained "has altered the way in which the Declaratory Judgment Act applies to patent law cases, requiring that legal interests be evaluated in patent cases under the general criteria of the Act."[94] The court felt that, "[i]ntentionally or not, *MedImmune* may have lowered the bar for determining declaratory judgment jurisdiction in all patent cases."[95]

The court noted that, to receive a declaratory judgment, the plaintiff must show that a dispute is "definite and concrete, touching the legal relations of parties having adverse legal interests; and that it be real and substantial and admit of specific relief through a decree of a conclusive character, as distinguished from an opinion advising what the law would be upon a hypothetical state of facts."[96]

Acceleron wrote two letters to HP. In its first letter, Acceleron identified itself as the owner of the patent, claimed that the patent related to a particular type of HP server, imposed a two-week deadline on HP to respond, and indirectly requested that HP not file suit. In response, HP delivered a written counter proposal requesting a 120-day standstill period, during which both parties would agree not to pursue any legal action. Acceleron then sent its second letter, giving another two-week deadline, after which Acceleron said it would assume that HP had nothing to say regarding the merits of its patent or its relevance to HP's server product.

HP asserted that the letters Acceleron wrote were sufficient to show declaratory judgment jurisdiction. Acceleron, however, argued that jurisdiction did not exist because it never specifically asserted its rights under the patent and did not threaten to sue for infringement. The appeals court sided with HP and noted that "the purpose of a declaratory judgment action cannot be defeated simply by the stratagem of correspondence that avoids magic words such as 'litigation' or 'infringement.'"[97]

The court explained that "conduct that can be reasonably inferred as demonstrating intent to enforce a patent can create declaratory judgment jurisdiction."[98] Acceleron argued that its correspondence with HP could be viewed simply as a patent holder contacting another party in order to sell the patent or to suggest incorporating the patented

---

93. *Id.* at 1361 (quoting MedImmune, Inc. v. Genentech, Inc., 549 U.S. 118, 127 (2007)).

94. *Id.* at 1364.

95. *Id.* at 1361.

96. *Id.* at 1362 (quoting *MedImmune*, 549 U.S. at 127 (internal quotation marks and brackets omitted)).

97. *Id.*

98. *Id.* at 1363.

technology into the party's product. The court reasoned that, in those types of situations, the patent holder would probably not assert his or her patent was relevant to the other party's product, insist on a two-week deadline for a response, and ask that the other party not file suit.

The Federal Circuit also agreed with the district court that "the receipt of such correspondence from a non-competitor patent holding company . . . may invoke a different reaction than would a meet-and-discuss inquiry by a competitor, presumably with intellectual property of its own to place on the bargaining table."[99] It was also noted that Acceleron was solely a licensing entity and that, without enforcement of its patent, it derives no benefit from the patent. This added to the significance of Acceleron's refusal to agree to HP's 120-day mutual standstill. The court concluded that, given the totality of the circumstances, it was reasonable to interpret Acceleron's actions as implicitly asserting its rights.

The court further noted that the test for declaratory judgment jurisdiction in patent cases is objective. Acceleron attempted to argue that, at the time HP filed its complaint, HP had not determined if its interests were adverse to those of Acceleron. The court rejected this argument, finding that subjective belief was irrelevant, and that objective action is the controlling factor.

DISCOVERY

Attorney-Client Privilege

Counsel-by-Counsel Factual Inquiry and Balancing Test Needed to Determine Whether Patent Prosecution Bar Is Appropriate

In *In re Deutsche Bank Trust Co. Americas,*[100] the Federal Circuit articulated new standards to be used when a party seeks to include a prosecution prohibition in a protective order. The Federal Circuit remanded the case to the district court for reconsideration under the new standards discussed in the court's decision and in light of the full evidentiary record.

Plaintiff Island Intellectual Property, LLC (Island) brought an action against Deutsche Bank for infringement of three of Island's patents. During discovery, Deutsche Bank moved for a protective order to bar Island's litigation counsel from prosecuting any patents relating to the subject matter in dispute during, and for a limited time after the conclusion of, the litigation. The magistrate granted Deutsche Bank's request as to all of Island's trial counsel except its lead counsel. Deutsche Bank took issue with lead counsel's exemption from the prosecution bar, but the district court adopted the magistrate's order. Deutsche Bank subsequently petitioned the Federal Circuit for mandamus.

On appeal, the Federal Circuit began by determining that the questions presented were unique to patent law, such that Federal Circuit precedent would govern instead of that of the Second Circuit. The Federal Circuit then noted that the issue of whether a court properly exempted an attorney from a patent prosecution bar involves a counsel-by-coun-

99. *Id.*
100. 605 F.3d 1373 (Fed. Cir. 2010).

sel determination and turns on "the extent to which counsel is involved in 'competitive decisionmaking' with its client."[101] The Federal Circuit noted that the regional circuits were split on whether patent prosecution was "competitive decision making." Some circuits have found any involvement in prosecution subsequent to litigation to be inherently competitive, while others have found that patent prosecution did not constitute "competitive decision making" because such activity did not raise a presumption of an unacceptable risk of disclosure. Rigid rules either way, however, were not appropriate given the vast range of responsibilities and tasks undertaken by attorneys responsible for patent prosecution. Accordingly, the Federal Circuit emphasized that assessing the propriety of an exemption from a patent prosecution bar requires examination of "all relevant facts surrounding counsel's actual preparation and prosecution activities" and must be done on a counsel-by-counsel basis.[102]

Even if an unacceptable risk of disclosure or competitive use exists, the district court must also "balance this risk against the potential harm to the opposing party from restrictions imposed on that party's right to have the benefit of counsel of its choice."[103] In conducting such a balancing test, the court should consider a number of factors, including: (1) the extent and duration of counsel's past history in representing the client before the USPTO; (2) the potential difficulty the client may face if forced to rely on other counsel to represent it in litigation or before the USPTO; (3) whether the type of information that will trigger the bar is relevant to the preparation and prosecution of patent applications before the USPTO; (4) the scope of activities prohibited by the bar; (5) duration of the bar; and (6) definition of the subject matter covered by the bar.

Electronic Discovery

Southern District of New York Defines Document Preservation and Collection Obligations When Litigation Is Anticipated

In *Pension Committee of the University of Montreal Pension Plan v. Banc of America Securities, LLC,*[104] U.S. District Court Judge Shira A. Scheindlin, who six years earlier had written the *Zubulake* e-discovery decisions,[105] addressed the issue of a party's obligations with respect to document preservation and collection. In the most significant part of its eighty-eight-page opinion, the court held that a party who fails to institute a written litigation hold as soon as litigation is reasonably anticipated, or who fails to identify and preserve records of "key players" in the controversy underlying the litigation, is to be deemed grossly negligent and exposes itself to serious sanctions, including monetary sanctions and adverse jury inference instructions to presume that the lost evidence was relevant, and that its destruction was prejudicial to the requesting party.

---

101. *Id.* at 1378 (quoting U.S. Steel Corp. v. United States, 730 F.2d 1465, 1468 (Fed. Cir. 1984)).

102. *Id.* at 1380.

103. *Id.*

104. 685 F. Supp. 2d 456 (S.D.N.Y. 2010).

105. Zubulake v. UBS Warburg LLC, 220 F.R.D. 212 (S.D.N.Y. 2003); Zubulake v. UBS Warburg LLC, 229 F.R.D. 422 (S.D.N.Y. 2004).

In February 2004, ninety-six investors sued a number of former hedge fund directors, administrators, the auditor, and the prime broker and custodian led by Banc of America Securities LLC, asserting claims under federal securities laws and under New York law based on alleged losses of nearly $500 million resulting from the defendants' liquidation of two British Virgin Islands-based hedge funds and the defendants' subsequent bankruptcy. The case was initially brought in the U.S. District Court for the Southern District of Florida, but was stayed until 2007 pursuant to the Private Securities Litigation Reform Act. The case was later transferred to the Southern District of New York. In October 2007, during pretrial discovery, Defendants Citco NV, the Citco Group Ltd., and a group of Citco officers (collectively, the Citco defendants), noticed substantial gaps in the document production of thirteen of the plaintiffs. Depositions were taken and declarations were submitted regarding the plaintiffs' document preservation efforts, searches, and production. After the close of discovery in June 2008, the Citco defendants moved for sanctions, arguing that each of the thirteen plaintiffs had failed to preserve and produce documents, and that they had submitted false and misleading declarations regarding their collection and preservation efforts. The Citco defendants requested dismissal of the complaint and/or any other sanctions deemed appropriate by the court. Because of the plaintiffs' negligence—and in some instances gross negligence—in failing to preserve and produce (in response to discovery requests) electronic and paper documents, the court imposed monetary sanctions and issued adverse jury instructions. The court did not find that the plaintiffs' discovery conduct was willful.

In its decision, the court explained the differences between and elements of negligence, gross negligence, and willfulness in the pretrial discovery context. In doing so, the court stressed the importance of determining the relevance of documents lost as a result of a party's failure to implement a litigation hold. In particular, the court emphasized that "[t]he innocent party must . . . show that the evidence would have been helpful in proving its claims or defenses, i.e., that the innocent party is prejudiced without that evidence.[106]

The court also explained the types of sanctions that could be imposed, ruling that the sanction of dismissal of the complaint would be too harsh in this case. The court also discussed adverse jury instructions and how they could range from a charge of spoliation to a presumption of spoliation, which allows the jury to take into account the misconduct of the spoliating party and the prejudice to the innocent party.

The court noted that none of the plaintiffs had initiated a proper litigation hold until 2007, despite knowing that they should have done so in late 2003 when defense counsel contacted the plaintiffs. The court held that the grossly negligent plaintiffs would face an adverse jury instruction that would permit the jury to presume the relevance of the missing documents and that their loss resulted in prejudice to the requesting defendants. However, such plaintiffs would be allowed to rebut the presumption of relevance and prejudice. With respect to the plaintiffs who were only negligent, the burden of proof would be shifted so that the Citco defendants would need to demonstrate that the documents were relevant and that they were prejudiced by the loss of such documents.

The court held that the duty to preserve documents is triggered as soon as a party reasonably anticipates litigation, and that the following may support a gross negligence finding: failure to institute a timely written litigation hold; failure to identify all of the key players and to ensure that their electronic and paper records are preserved; failure to

---

106. *Pension Comm.*, 685 F. Supp. 2d at 467.

stop the deletion of e-mail messages or failure to preserve former employees' records that are in a party's possession, custody, or control; and failure to preserve backup tapes when they are the sole source of relevant information or when they relate to key players if the relevant information maintained by those players is not alternatively obtainable from readily accessible sources. In contrast, the court held that, after a litigation hold is in place, the failure to collect records from all employees involved with issues raised in the litigation, as opposed to only the key players, may constitute only negligence.

The court found that certain of the plaintiffs had been grossly negligent and had conducted discovery in an "ignorant and indifferent fashion."[107] The appropriate sanction would be an adverse inference instruction to the jury based on the fact that the plaintiffs had destroyed documents after the duty to preserve arose. The jury would be instructed to presume that the destroyed documents were relevant, and that their loss was prejudicial to the defendants (the plaintiffs would have the opportunity to rebut the presumption). On the other hand, Judge Scheindlin held that, where a responding party is merely negligent, the innocent party must prove both relevance and prejudice. The moving defendants were awarded their attorneys' fees and costs in making the motion.

SETTLEMENT

Settlement Agreement Held Enforceable Despite Party's Refusal to Sign

In *MedPointe Healthcare, Inc. v. Kozachuk*,[108] the Federal Circuit affirmed the district court, holding that an unwritten settlement agreement of material terms (Settlement) was enforceable after the defendant refused to execute it.

Defendant Walter Kozachuk worked for Plaintiff MedPointe. After Kozachuk resigned from MedPointe, Kozachuk filed a series of patent applications resulting in patents. Claiming Kozachuk breached his employment agreement by failing to assign the patents to MedPointe, MedPointe brought suit in the District of New Jersey against Kozachuk, asserting ownership of the patents. The parties agreed to settle the matter during a settlement conference before a Magistrate Judge, and the agreed-upon terms were recorded on a transcript of the proceedings. Under the settlement, the patents were to be assigned to MedPointe for a cash payment to Kozachuk. However, when presented with a written agreement to sign a month later, Kozahuck refused to sign, alleging that his counsel had inadequately represented him and coerced him into agreeing to the settlement. When Kozachuk failed to sign the written settlement, MedPointe moved for enforcement of the settlement, which the district court granted.

Kozachuk appealed the order enforcing the settlement. The Federal Circuit found that the district court's legal determinations were not unique to patent law and, therefore, were to be reviewed under Third Circuit law, and factual findings were reviewed under the Third Circuit's "clearly erroneous" standard. In particular, the Federal Circuit found that New Jersey law governed the enforceability of the settlement.[109] The parties did not dispute the choice-of-law issues.

---

107. *Id.* at 496.
108. No. 2009-1500, 2010 WL 1303480 (Fed. Cir. Apr. 6, 2010).
109. *Id.* at *4.

The Federal Circuit first explored whether the parties had entered into an enforceable contract. MedPointe and Kozachuk negotiated and assented to the settlement during a settlement conference before a magistrate judge where the material terms were recorded on transcript. Under New Jersey law, the Federal Circuit held that "where parties agree upon the essential terms of a settlement, so that the mechanics can be fleshed out in a writing to be thereafter executed, the settlement will be enforced notwithstanding the fact the writing does not materialize because a party later reneges."[110]

The Federal Circuit found ample evidence supporting the parties' requisite intent to agree to the settlement. The evidence included the transcript record as well as communications by Kozachuk before and after the settlement was reached. Despite Kozachuk's arguments to the contrary, the Federal Circuit held that the district court did not err in adopting the recommendations of the magistrate, nor in refusing to undertake live testimony to determine whether there was requisite intent to settle.[111] The Federal Circuit also held that there was no evidence establishing that the settlement was unconscionable and, regardless, that Kozachuk had failed to preserve this error. Finally, the Federal Circuit rejected Kozachuk's argument that Kozachuk's attorney coerced Kozachuk into agreeing to the settlement.

TRIAL

Evidence

Testing of Accused Process Is Not Required to Show Infringement Where Other Substantive Evidence Provided

In ***Martek Biosciences Corp. v. Nutrinova, Inc.,***[112] a five-judge panel of the Federal Circuit affirmed the U.S. District Court for the District of Delaware's denial of the defendants' JMOL motions asserting invalidity of Martek's U.S. Patent No. 5,340,594 (the '594 patent) and noninfringement of U.S. Patent No. 6,410,281 (the '281 patent). The Federal Circuit reversed the grant of JMOL of invalidity of claims 4 and 5 of U.S. Patent No. 6,451,567 (the '567 patent) and the district court's construction of the claim term "animal" in Martek's U.S. Patent No. 5,698,244 (the '244 patent).

The Federal Circuit held that substantial evidence supported the jury's finding that the claims of the '594 patent were entitled to the priority date of an earlier application (the 1988 application) because Martek's expert testified that one of ordinary skill in the art would understand certain passages of the 1988 application to disclose the relevant claim terms. The Federal Circuit rejected the defendants' argument that the jury could not rely on Martek's expert testimony because the 1988 application contained no working examples performing the relevant claim steps, noting that a claim is not invalid for lack of an adequate written description simply because it is broader than the specific examples disclosed. The Federal Circuit also rejected the defendants' argument that the 1988 application taught away from the claims' requirement that two types of cells be grown together,

---

110. *Id.* at *5–*6.
111. *Id.* at *7.
112. 579 F.3d 1363 (Fed. Cir. 2009).

finding that the specification's disclosure of different growth conditions for the two types of cells did not indicate that the cells could not be grown together.

The Federal Circuit also held that substantial evidence supported the jury's finding that the defendants infringed the asserted claims of the '281 patent, rejecting the defendants' argument that the evidence of infringement was insufficient because Martek did not conduct comparative testing to demonstrate that the defendants' accused process satisfied the claims. Although Martek did not conduct comparative testing, it presented testimony from two experts who testified that the defendants satisfied the claims based on their conceptual analysis of the accused process. The Federal Circuit rejected the defendants' argument that its holding in *Kim v. ConAgra Foods, Inc.* articulated a rule requiring that the plaintiffs alleging infringement of a claim containing functional limitations must perform actual tests or experiments on the accused product or method to show that the claimed functions are, in fact, performed.[113]

Applying a higher, "abuse of discretion" standard on the question of exclusion of evidence, the Federal Circuit held that the district court properly excluded the defendants' section 102(g)(2) evidence of prior invention because the alleged prior inventor's testimony regarding reduction to practice was not sufficiently corroborated. Although the defendants alleged that an abandoned patent application provided corroboration of reduction to practice, the Federal Circuit explained that an abandoned patent application can only corroborate conception, not reduction to practice. Although the defendants also cited a post hoc replication of experiments cited in the abandoned patent application, these experiments did not qualify as evidence of reduction to practice because they were not from a time prior to or contemporaneous with the alleged prior invention.

Regarding claim construction, the Federal Circuit held that the district court properly construed the term "non-chloride sodium salt" in the '281 patent to encompass sodium hydroxide (NaOH). Although the '281 patent does not discuss NaOH, the prosecution history expressly revealed that NaOH is a nonchloride sodium salt. Martek also presented two treatises teaching that NaOH can be considered a salt. Although the Federal Circuit acknowledged that selected statements from the prosecution history arguably supported the defendants' position, those statements were undercut by: (1) the explicit statement that NaOH is a nonchloride sodium salt; and (2) the applicant's statements distinguishing the prior art on grounds unrelated to NaOH. Thus, Martek committed no clear and unmistakable disavowal of claim scope.

Additionally, the Federal Circuit held that the district court erred in overturning the jury's verdict that claims 4 and 5 of the '567 patent were enabled. The district court relied primarily on the testimony of the defendants' expert, who testified that the patent did not enable one of ordinary skill in the art to practice an element of claim 1 directed to growing euryhaline organisms having certain characteristics. Specifically, the defendants' expert testified that it would require an enormous amount of research to select a euryhaline organism meeting the recited criteria among the approximately 10,000 possible euryhaline organisms. However, dependent claims 4 and 5 were narrower than claim 1 because they were directed to a class of organisms comprising only twenty-two possibilities. The defendants' expert did not testify that it would require undue experimentation to select a euryhaline organism from among these twenty-two that met the recited criteria, and the jury's verdict that defendants failed to prove invalidity by clear and convincing evidence was justified.

---

113. *Id.* at 1373 (citing Kim v. ConAgra Foods, Inc., 465 F.3d 1312, 1320 (Fed. Cir. 2006)).

The Federal Circuit also held that the district court erred in construing the term "animal" in the '244 patent to mean "any member of the kingdom Animalia, except humans." The specification defined the term "animal" as "any organism belonging to the kingdom Animalia." Although the specification disclosed preferred nonhuman animals, the Federal Circuit held that this did not constitute a clear disavowal of human animals. Further, the specification's identification of "economic food animal[s]" as "[p]referred animals" supported a broad construction of the unmodified term "animal" to include humans. The fact that the specification discussed "raising" and "feeding" animals did not show a clear intent to disclaim humans because these generic terms can apply to humans. The Federal Circuit held that the defendants' extrinsic evidence supporting its construction was irrelevant in view of the specification's express definition.

However, Judge Lourie, joined by Judge Rader, dissented from the majority's conclusion with respect to the construction of the term "animal." Judge Lourie contended that this was one of the rare cases where the specification, read as a whole, contradicted the specification's express definition of a term. Judge Lourie cited the fact that the specification is directed to raising nonhuman animals. For example, the specification read that "[t]he present invention concerns a method for raising an animal having [] high concentrations of omega-3 highly unsaturated fatty acids (HUFA) and food products derived from such animals." Judge Lourie contended that, because food products are not derived from humans, this description of the invention indicated that it did not encompass human animals.

Jury Instructions

Patentee Compensation under Invention Secrecy Act Applies Only to Pre-grant Secrecy Orders

In ***Hornback v. United States,***[114] the Federal Circuit affirmed dismissal of pro se plaintiff Hornback's claim for compensation for the government's use of his patent that was subject to a secrecy order under 35 U.S.C. § 181. The opinion by Judge Rader, joined by Chief Judge Michel and Judge David Folsom, Chief Judge of the U.S. District Court for the Eastern District of Texas, sitting by designation, construed the meaning of the term "use of the invention by the Government" in the statute, specifically the provisions of the statute that entitle a patentee to compensation for such government use.[115]

The patent-in-suit, U.S. Patent No 6,079,666, relates to boresight error slope sensors, which are used in missile guidance systems. Shortly after the application was filed, the application was deemed classified by the Air Force and, as a result, the USPTO imposed a secrecy order under 35 U.S.C. § 181. The secrecy order remained in effect for almost twelve years, but was eventually lifted and the patent subsequently issued. Hornback sued for compensation for the government's use of his invention for the period after the patent issued; compensation for the use during the time period before grant was barred by res judicata and was therefore not an issue in this case. Hornback brought suit under the provisions of section 183 in the U.S. District Court for the Southern District of Califor-

114. 601 F.3d 1382 (Fed. Cir. 2010).
115. 35 U.S.C. § 181.

nia, which dismissed the complaint under Federal Rule of Civil Procedure 12(b)(6) for failure to state a claim upon which relief could be granted. The Federal Circuit reviewed the district court's dismissal de novo under the procedural law of the Ninth Circuit.

Turning to section 183, the Federal Circuit set forth the "two avenues" provided for a patent applicant subject to a secrecy order to obtain compensation for "use of the invention by the Government": (1) directly from the head of the government department or agency that sought the secrecy order; and (2) by suit in the Court of Federal Claims or the district court where the applicant resides. However, pursuing the second avenue without attempting the first is available only after the patent has issued.

This case provided the Federal Circuit with its first opportunity to construe the meaning of the statutory language "use of the invention by the Government" with regard to whether this includes use of the invention after the patent for the invention has issued. The Federal Circuit noted that the phrase "use of the invention" is not expressly limited by the language of the statute to a use that occurs before the patent issues. Using statutory construction rubrics[116] that require provisions of the law to be considered as a whole, including "its object and policy," the Federal Circuit looked to the provisions of "related" statute 28 U.S.C. § 1498(a) to clarify the language. That statute provides that the remedy for use or manufacture by the United States of a patented article "shall be by action against the United States in the United States Court of Federal Claims for the recovery of his reasonable and entire compensation for such use and manufacture." The court also characterized section 181 to be limited to nonpublic use by the government, which does not apply for use after the patent grants. Finally, section 183 has a six-year limitation on the time for filing suit for recovery, which the Federal Circuit found must apply to preissuance use as the patent law already contains a six-year statute of limitations for bringing suit for patent infringement.[117]

Based on this analysis, the Federal Circuit held that section 183 provides for compensation only during the time when the secrecy order is in place. Therefore, there is no cause of action for use after the secrecy order was lifted and the patent granted.

"Substantial Evidence" Standard Makes Overturning Jury Verdicts Difficult

In *Verizon Services Corp. v. Cox Fibernet Virginia, Inc.,*[118] the Federal Circuit affirmed the jury's verdict, finding that substantial evidence supported the jury's conclusions that the asserted claims of two patents (U.S. Patent Nos. 6,282,574 and 6,104,711) were invalid, and claims of four other patents (U.S. Patent Nos. 6,430,275, 6,292,510, 6,137,869, and 6,636,597) were not infringed. The patents-in-suit involved packet-switched telephony technology, defined in the opinion as the practice of breaking signals, such as voice transmissions, into data packets and transmitting them nonsequentially.

The Federal Circuit held that the trial court did not err in not construing certain claim terms according to their ordinary and customary meaning. In doing so, the court rejected Cox's argument that the claims should be construed according to the inventors' intent. The court also distinguished *O2 Micro International Ltd. v. Beyond Innovation Technology*

116. U.S. Nat'l Bank of Or. v. Indep. Ins. Agents of Am., Inc., 508 U.S. 439, 455 (1993).
117. 35 U.S.C. § 286.
118. 602 F.3d 1325 (Fed. Cir. 2010).

Co.,[119] cited by Verizon for the proposition that claim terms not expressly construed should be remanded for construction. The court found that, unlike in *O2 Micro,* the scope of the claims was not at issue in this case. Using a "totality of the circumstances" standard, the Federal Circuit determined that there was not a reasonable probability that Cox's arguments "subverted the jury's reasoning," citing the sparse incidence of Cox's arguments, the propriety of the court's jury instructions, and that Verizon neither objected to these arguments nor argued to the contrary at trial.[120]

The panel affirmed all other appealed grounds because substantial evidence existed to support the jury's verdict. First, the Federal Circuit affirmed the jury's verdict of invalidity with respect to two of the patents. Although at trial the parties had introduced competing and contradictory expert testimony regarding anticipation of the asserted claims of the '711 and '574 patents, the jury was entitled to resolve the conflict between competing expert witness testimony by "looking at the record as a whole."[121] On this basis, the court found that Cox's expert, by testifying as to how the prior art disclosed each element of the asserted claims, provided the jury with substantial evidence to support a finding that the prior art anticipated the asserted claims of these patents. Second, the Federal Circuit affirmed the jury's verdict of noninfringement with respect to four of the patents. Here, the factual disputes over whether practice of the accused methods constituted infringement were properly decided by the jury. Based on the district court's proper construction of the claims, the court found that substantial evidence supported the jury's conclusion that Cox's method did not utilize or practice several limitations of the claims at issue.

The court also rejected Cox's argument that the trial court improperly excluded testimony from the named inventors on the grounds of assignor estoppel. The panel found that the trial court "properly allowed testimony from the witnesses about the patents they invented based on their personal knowledge, and properly excluded these same witnesses from providing expert testimony on invalidity for which they had not previously provided expert reports or been qualified as an expert."[122] This, the court held, was not an abuse of discretion. Finally, the court rejected the parties' motions, and arguments pertaining thereto, for a new trial.

Form of Verdict

New Trial Warranted after Jury Rendered Inconsistent Verdicts

In *Comaper Corp. v. Antec, Inc.,*[123] the Federal Circuit reversed the district court's denial of Antec's motion for a new trial based on inconsistent obviousness verdicts rendered by the jury.

Comaper alleged that Antec infringed claims 1, 2, 7, 12, and 13 of U.S Patent No. 5,955,955, which is directed to "a cooling device designed to mount within the drive bay

---

119. 521 F.3d 1351 (Fed. Cir. 2007).
120. *Verizon,* 602 F.3d at 1325.
121. *Id.* at 1335.
122. *Id.* at 1339
123. 596 F.3d 1343 (Fed. Cir. 2010).

of a computer."[124] After a five-day trial, a jury found that independent claims 1 and 12 were not obvious. It also found that claims 2 and 7, which depend on claim 1, and claim 13, which depends on claim 12, were invalid as obvious. As the district court and Comaper recognized, these verdicts are inconsistent because "[a] broader independent claim cannot be nonobvious where a dependant claim stemming from that independent claim is invalid for obviousness."[125]

The Federal Circuit affirmed the district court's conclusion that Antec waived its right to JMOL because it failed to move for JMOL under Rule 50(a) of the Federal Rules of Civil Procedure following the close of evidence. The Federal Circuit, however, rejected Comaper's argument that Antec waived its right to challenge the inconsistent verdicts because it did not object before the jury was dismissed. Applying Third Circuit law, the Federal Circuit explained that, when a jury returns a special verdict, as it did here, the verdict may be challenged on appeal as inconsistent even if an objection is not made before the jury is dismissed. By seeking a new trial on the grounds of inconsistent verdicts in its post-verdict motion, Antec preserved the issue for appeal.

The Federal Circuit found that, under Third Circuit law, "when faced with inconsistent verdicts and [. . .] evidence [that] would support either of the inconsistent verdicts, the district court must order a new trial."[126] The district court in *Comaper* denied Antec's motion for a new trial on the grounds that the evidence did not support verdicts of obviousness of dependant claims 2, 7, and 13 because the asserted prior art was not analogous to the invention of the asserted patent, nor was it sufficiently similar to the claims of the asserted patent. The Federal Circuit disagreed with both conclusions. First, the Federal Circuit found the asserted prior art references related to the same field of endeavor as the asserted patent. Second, the Federal Circuit held that "there is no question that there is ample evidence in the record supporting the jury's verdict that claims 2, 7, and 13 of the '955 patent would have been obvious."[127] Accordingly, the Federal Circuit remanded the case for a new trial on invalidity.[128]

INTERNATIONAL TRADE COMMISSION

"All or Substantially All" Test in Gray Market Trademark Infringement Cases Clarified to Mean Whether All or Substantially All Authorized Sales Are Materially Different

In *Deere & Co. v. International Trade Commission,*[129] the Federal Circuit vacated the ITC's final determination that U.S. sales of John Deere-branded forage harvesters intended for sale in Europe by Intervenors Bourdeau Brothers, Inc., OK Enterprises, and Sunova Implement Co. (collectively, Bourdeau) did not violate section 337 of the Tariff

---

124. *Id.* at 1345.
125. *Id.* at 1350 (quoting Callaway Golf Co. v. Acushnet Co., 576 F.3d 1331, 1344 (Fed. Cir. 2009)).
126. *Id.*
127. *Id.* at 1353.
128. *Id.* at 1355.
129. 605 F.3d 1350 (Fed. Cir. 2010).

Act of 1930 as amended.[130] The Federal Circuit remanded the case to the ITC to determine whether 96.6 to 96.9 percent—the ratio of North American forage harvesters sold by Deere in the United States divided by the sum of the authorized North American and European forage harvesters sold by Deere in the United States—is "substantially all" under the "all or substantially all" test in gray market trademark infringement cases, thereby entitling Deere to an ITC exclusion order.[131]

The ITC instituted an investigation in February 2003 based on a complaint filed by Deere alleging that Bourdeau and other Deere dealers unlawfully imported and sold Deere's European forage harvesters in the United States in violation of section 337. In May 2004, the ITC determined there were material differences between Deere's North American and European forage harvesters, supporting a finding of trademark infringement and, therefore, a general exclusion order. In March 2006, the Federal Circuit vacated in part and remanded the ITC's determination based on the additional requirement that Deere also show that all or substantially all of its authorized domestic forage harvesters are materially different from the accused gray market forage harvesters.

On remand, the administrative law judge (ALJ) issued an initial determination of infringement, finding that the original record demonstrated that Deere did not authorize the sales of the European forage harvesters in the United States, that new evidence of alleged Deere financing of the European forage harvesters sold by its dealers did not show authorization, and that the number of sales Bourdeau alleged were authorized were, in any event, so small that "substantially all" of Deere's authorized U.S. sales were of the North American forage harvesters.

In August 2008, the ITC reversed the ALJ, finding substantial evidence that Deere's U.S. and European dealers had apparent authority to sell the European forage harvesters, that Deere itself sold and/or facilitated the sale of the European forage harvesters in the United States, and that not "all or substantially all" of the authorized harvesters sold in the United States were the North American forage harvesters. The ITC noted that, because the total number of authorized sales of the North American forage harvesters in the United States was approximately 4,400, the introduction of even a small number of the European forage harvesters could cause substantial consumer confusion. The ITC then found such confusion based on its determination that at least 141 European forage harvesters sold in the United States were sold by official Deere dealers. The ITC considered 141 to be a "substantial quantity" of nonconforming goods because it constituted 40 to 57 percent of the 247 to 347 European forage harvesters sold in the United States by both official and independent (in some cases, accused) dealers. The ITC did not use as its denominator the total number of authorized forage harvesters sold in the United States, which would have been the number of authorized North American forage harvesters (4,400), plus the number of authorized European forage harvesters (141), or 4,541.

The Federal Circuit found that substantial evidence supported the numerator determined by the ITC. In particular, the Federal Circuit held that: (1) sales by official Deere dealers of the European forage harvesters in the United States were authorized based on buyers' reasonable belief, given Deere's actions that such sales were authorized; (2) substantial evidence supports the ITC's finding that Deere's official dealers, including its official European dealers, had apparent authority to sell the European version; (3) the ITC did not

---

130. 19 U.S.C. § 1337 (2004).
131. *Deere*, 605 F.3d at 1361–62.

err in including sales by Deere's official European dealers in the United States in its calculation; and (4) Deere had an opportunity to introduce evidence regarding authorization of its official European dealer sales.

With respect to the ITC's denominator, the Federal Circuit held that the ITC misapplied the "all or substantially all" test, and that the denominator should have been the total authorized sales in the United States, not the total European forage harvester sales in the United States. Using the ratio dictated by its remand instructions as well as the ITC's lower-end and upper-end findings, the Federal Circuit concluded that a total of 3.1 to 3.4 percent of the authorized forage harvesters sold in the United States were the European forage harvesters, or, conversely, that 96.6 to 96.9 percent of the authorized forage harvesters sold in the United States were the North American version. The Federal Circuit observed that those figures may be insubstantial, but that is for the ITC to determine on remand based on all of the relevant facts, noting that "[t]he cutoff as to what is to be considered 'substantially all' is a question of fact."[132]

Judge Newman concurred in the remand but dissented in part from the majority's holding that the importation and sales of the European forage harvester were deemed to be authorized by Deere, noting that "it is incorrect to hold that the infringing sales are 'authorized' by a concoction of 'apparent authority'" because to do so "improperly requires the trademark owner to prove that it tried and was unable to impose restrictions on its independent official dealers in the United States and overseas."[133]

"Substantial Investment" in Licensing Includes Enforcement Activities and Associated Legal Expenses Relating to Satisfaction of Section 337's Domestic Industry Requirement

In *Certain Coaxial Cable Connectors & Components Thereof & Products Containing Same,*[134] Administrative Law Judge Gildea found complainant John Mezzalingua Associates, Inc., d/b/a PPC, Inc. (PPC), made substantial investment in the exploitation of the asserted patent such that the domestic industry requirement under 19 U.S.C. § 337(a)(3)(C) was satisfied through enforcement activity. Although PPC designs, develops, tests, manufactures, and markets its coaxial cable connectors, Judge Gildea found the domestic industry requirement was satisfied through PPC's substantial investments in licensing activities. Judge Gildea considered expenses incurred in enforcing the asserted patent as attempts to obtain a license and treated them like licensing negotiations. This approach flatly rejected the position that enforcement activity does not constitute exploitation of a patent. He opined that enforcement activities and licensing are intertwined because "a company informed that it may be infringing a patent may seek to have that matter litigated in court rather than immediately negotiate a license agreement[;] . . . the post-litigation license is more dearly bought."[135] The enforcement activity Judge Gildea considered included cease and desist letters, engagement in licensing discussions, and litigation related to the asserted patent.

---

132. *Id.* at 1361.
133. *Id.* at 1362–63.
134. Inv. No. 337-TA-650, Initial Determination (U.S.I.T.C. Oct. 13, 2010).
135. *Id.* at *187–*88.

Although the issue was "a close one," Judge Gildea found substantial investment in licensing as evidenced by PPC's enforcement activity. Judge Gildea noted that it was a "reality of the marketplace" that PPC had to wield the threat of litigation and engage in actual litigation to obtain licenses. Even though Judge Gildea noted it was unclear if the litigation resulted in any proceeds or royalties, he found PPC's efforts were evidence of substantial investment in the exploitation of the patent such that the domestic industry under section 337(a)(3)(C) was satisfied.

The Commission gave notice that it would review Judge Gildea's determination and requested briefing on whether legal costs constituted "substantial investment" in the exploitation of intellectual property. The Commission also inquired about what weight legal fees paid in litigation with targeted licenses/infringers should be given when determining substantial investment, directly examining Judge Gildea's opinion that enforcement costs could be considered investment in licensing. In its notice, the Commission took the unusual step of requesting public comment on these domestic industry issues, thereby signifying the significance of this issue to ITC jurisprudence.

The Commission's opinion heightened the requirement for showing the relationship between litigation expenses and licensing activities for the purposes of domestic industry. Although licensing-related litigation expenses can be evidence of a domestic industry, "[a]llowing patent infringement litigation activities alone to constitute a domestic industry would place the bar for establishing a domestic industry so low as to effectively render it meaningless."[136]

After interpreting the statutory framework for section 337 investigations, the Commission concluded that "patent infringement litigation activities alone, i.e., patent infringement litigation activities that are not related to engineering, research and development, or licensing, do not satisfy the requirements of section 337(a)(3)(C)."[137] The Commission examined the language of section 337(a)(3)(C), finding that "Congress specifically identified three types of activities . . . that constitute exploitation. Patent infringement litigation was not among them."[138]

The Commission also examined the legislative history of the statute, discussing how the provisions of the statute were meant to cover universities and intellectual property owners engaging in extensive licensing with *manufacturers*. The Commission found that Congress's intent was to "identify instances in which licensing activities encourage practical applications of the invention or bring the patented technology to the market."[139] However, the Commission declined to require a showing that a licensee actually practices or intends to practice the licensed patent to establish a licensing domestic industry.

Although the Commission concluded that litigation unrelated to licensing cannot satisfy the domestic industry inquiry, "litigation activities (including patent infringement lawsuits) may satisfy [the domestic industry] requirements if a complainant can prove that these activities are related to licenses and pertain to the patent at issue."[140] In relying on

---

136. *Certain Coaxial Cable Connectors and Components Thereof and Prods. Containing Same*, Inv. No. 337-TA-650, Comm'n Op., 2010 ITC LEXIS 570 at *43–44, 46 (U.S.I.T.C. Apr. 14, 2010).
137. *Id.*
138. *Id.* at *45.
139. *Id.* at *49.
140. *Id.* at *43–*44.

litigation as substantial investment in licensing, a "complainant must prove that each asserted activity is related to licensing," whether those activities actually result in a license or not.[141] The Commission expressly stated that "in assessing whether the domestic industry requirement has been met, we will also consider licensing activities for which the sole purpose is to derive revenue from existing production."[142] In other words, the activities of entities whose sole purpose in licensing is to obtain revenue from manufacturers of the patented product can satisfy the domestic industry requirement.

The Commission remanded Judge Gildea's finding of domestic industry to more fully develop the record as to PPC's "litigation activities and costs," which would include circumstances surrounding any negotiations to license the patent, settlement costs, license drafting costs, and the existence of an established licensing program. The Commission made it clear that PPC would need substantive and documented evidence that the litigation activity it was relying on was related to licensing and not just a "broad allegation" that its litigation costs were related to licensing. For example, the Commission reversed Judge Gildea's consideration of litigation expenses related to a case in which the PPC had neither "shown that a license issued, nor asserted that [the] litigation was in pursuit of a license."[143]

The Commission also settled a longstanding ambiguity in the case law regarding the point in time at which the Commission determines whether a domestic industry exists. Specifically, the Commission found: "[w]e note that only activities that occurred before the filing of a complaint with the Commission are relevant to whether a domestic industry exists or is in the process of being established under sections 337(a)(2)–(3)."[144]

On remand, Judge Gildea found that no domestic industry exists.[145] Important to his analysis was the absence of clear evidence showing that no cease and desist letters or license offers preceded the filing of suits to enforce the asserted patent. However, based on the testimony of the PPC that settlement negotiations concerning those suits were intended to result in a license for the asserted patent, Judge Gildea found that expenses relating to settlement or licensing negotiations should be counted in the domestic industry analysis. Further, based on his analysis that the terms of the settlement and licensing agreement include the asserted patent, Judge Gildea concluded that drafting costs should also be counted. Accordingly, the judge examined individual entries within billing statements of PPC's outside attorneys to determine the number of attorney work hours devoted to licensing and settlement efforts. Nevertheless, Judge Gildea concluded that PPC's evidence did not support a substantial investment in licensing because the PPC received only one license for the asserted patent "of which only a portion actually relates to the patent at issue," it had no established licensing program for the asserted patent, and PPC made no effort to send cease and desist letters or licensing offers to anyone aside from the efforts involved with the single license. Commission review of the remand is pending.

---

141. *Id.* at *50–*51 n.16.

142. *Id.* at *49–50.

143. *Id.* at *55.

144. *Id.* n.17 (citing Bally/Midway Mfg. Co. v. U.S. Int'l Trade Comm'n, 714 F.2d 1117, 1121 (Fed. Cir. 1983)).

145. *Certain Coaxial Cable Connectors and Components Thereof and Prods. Containing Same*, Inv. No. 337-TA-650, Remand Initial Determination on Violation of Section 337 (May 27, 2010).

In-House Legal Costs Can Be Considered for the Domestic Industry Requirement of Section 337 of the Tariff Act of 1930

In *Certain Computer Products, Computer Components & Products Containing Same*,[146] Judge Essex of the ITC held that the complainant, International Business Machines Corp. (IBM), met the domestic industry requirement of 19 U.S.C. § 1337(a)(3)(c), based on the activities of its patent engineers, licensing representatives, and intellectual property attorneys.

Under section 1337(a)(3)(c), a domestic industry exists if there is "substantial investment" in "exploitation, including engineering, research and development, or licensing." In expanding what constitutes a "substantial investment" for the economic prong of the domestic industry, the ITC has included legal expenses associated with licensing and revenue from complainant's licenses, including the efforts of in-house counsel involved in licensing programs related to the asserted patent.

IBM asserted that it satisfied the domestic industry requirement based on its licensing activities. In recognizing IBM's domestic industry, Judge Essex explained that "entities that are actively engaged in licensing their patents in the United States can meet the domestic industry requirement."[147] His consideration of IBM's active engagement in licensing included legal expenses incurred to obtain license agreements. Moreover, IBM's employment and compensation of "patent engineers, licensing representatives and intellectual property attorneys" supported the conclusion that IBM met the domestic industry requirement.[148] IBM's licensing personnel and legal department invested substantial amounts of time to research and communicate with potential licensees and negotiate license agreements. Those investments generated millions of dollars in income and revenue for IBM. As a result, the domestic industry requirement was satisfied through IBM's systemic patent licensing program, which included substantial legal costs. Judge Essex's analysis was adopted by the Commission.

Attorneys' Fees and Post-Complaint Licenses Are Factors When Analyzing Domestic Industry under Section 337 of the Tariff Act of 1930

In *Certain Short-Wavelength Light Emitting Diodes, Laser Diodes, & Products Containing Same*,[149] Administrative Law Judge Luckern held that Complainant Gertrude Rothschild satisfied the domestic industry requirement through licensing activities, which included attorneys' fees relating to the consummation of pre- and post-complaint licenses. Ms. Rothschild requested summary determination that her substantial investment in the exploitation of her patent satisfied the domestic industry requirement. Ms. Rothschild is the inventor and owner of the asserted patent. Ms. Rothschild does not

---

146. Inv. No. 337-TA-628, Initial Determination, 2009 ITC LEXIS 667 (U.S.I.T.C. Mar. 16, 2009). The Commission determined not to review the Initial Determination. *See* 74 Fed. Reg. 34785 (July 17, 2009).

147. *Id.* at *271 (citing *Certain Digital Processors and Digital Processing Sys., Components Thereof, and Prods. Containing Same*, Inv. No. 337-TA-559, Initial Determination, at 93 (U.S.I.T.C. May 11, 2007)).

148. *Id.* at *274.

149. Inv. No. 337-TA-640, Order No. 72, 2009 ITC LEXIS 1021 (U.S.I.T.C. May 8, 2009).

manufacture a product covered by the asserted patent; however, she is active in efforts to license her patents by expending resources, such as legal fees, to consummate licenses and generate revenue through those licenses.

Judge Luckern noted that "the scope of the domestic industry in an investigation is determined on a case by case basis . . . and proof of substantial investment may include . . . the number of employees involved in the licensing process, legal fees, and whether licensing activities are active and on-going."[150] Judge Luckern rejected the argument by the respondents and the investigative attorney from the Office of Unfair Import Investigations (OUII) that "legal and litigation expenses together with royalty income cannot, in and of themselves, satisfy the domestic industry standard" and found that "legal fees related to litigation and licensing regarding the patent(s) at issue are a factor to consider with respect to the substantial investment requirement."[151]

Judge Luckern found that Rothschild made a substantial investment in exploitation of her patent by hiring attorneys and other licensing personnel that resulted in consummated licenses. Judge Luckern also determined that Rothschild's legal expenses were related to her proactive licensing campaign rather than as defensive bargaining chips in litigation. Consequently, Judge Luckern credited the legal expenses associated with obtaining licenses when analyzing substantial investment.

Judge Luckern also considered licenses Rothschild entered into during the investigation as evidence of substantial investment. Judge Luckern considered Rothschild's post-complaint licenses to be part of the "pattern of licensing" upon which he based his finding of substantial investment in the exploitation of the asserted patent.

The Commission determined to review this Initial Determination and requested briefing on three issues related to whether attorneys' fees constituted a substantial investment in licensing under section 337(a)(3)(C): (1) whether payment to outside counsel could qualify as a substantial investment in licensing at all; (2) whether investments in licensing in the form of in-house employees should be treated differently than outside counsel; and (3) the relationship between licensing and enforcement expenses.[152] To address the issue presented by pre- and post-institution licenses, the Commission also requested briefing on whether investments and royalties associated with licenses entered into prior to litigation are entitled to more weight in the analysis of substantial investment.

The parties and several amici submitted briefs, but the investigation was terminated through settlements before the Commission issued its decision.

---

150. *Id.*

151. *Id.* at *16.

152. *Certain Short-Wavelength Light Emitting Diodes, Laser Diodes, and Prods. Containing Same*, Inv. No. 337-TA-640, Comm'n Notice, 2009 ITC LEXIS 1148, at *3–*4 (U.S.I.T.C. June 11, 2009).

PRECLUSION

Claim Preclusion

Claim Preclusion Applies to Accused Product with Respect to Previously Adjudicated Noninfringing Features

In *Nystrom v. Trex Co.,*[153] the patent involved floorboards having slightly convex top surfaces, so shaped to allow water runoff to the side edges of the boards, and slightly concave bottom surfaces to facilitate stacking. In an earlier litigation against one of the current defendants, the patentee lost the case in both the district court and the court of appeals on noninfringement grounds. The courts found the defendant's product (an extrusion of sawdust and fibers made by compression) did not meet the limitation "board" or the limitation "manufactured by" as construed by both courts.[154]

After the prior judgment was final, the defendant introduced several new products—concededly different from the earlier ones in terms of texture and other parameters, but the same as the prior ones in terms of whether the products were "boards" or were "manufactured by" the process stated in the patent claim. The district court dismissed the second suit on various estoppel-type grounds, not including claim preclusion. On appeal, the Federal Circuit panel upheld the dismissal on claim-preclusion grounds. The court characterized the case as presenting a "slightly new angle" on claim preclusion. Prior cases had held that, for this doctrine to apply, the accused infringing products must be substantially the same as those involved in the earlier litigation.[155] The court explained that, for claim preclusion to apply in a patent case, the accused products or processes must be essentially the same in the second action as in the first, but mere colorable variations will not prevent the preclusion. However, those cases did not concentrate on whether the products needed to be substantially the same in all respects, or only in those respects that led to the prior judgment. The present case squarely presented that question.

The Federal Circuit decided claim preclusion applies even if the later product is significantly different from the earlier one, provided those differences are not the features on which the prior judgment was based. If the products are the same with respect to the adjudicated noninfringing features, there is no point in going forward again with litigation about the new products. The appellate court noted that, to allow the present case to go forward would be to allow relitigation of the same claim-limitation issues: "In essence, Nystrom would be attempting to prove infringement of the same claim limitations as to the same features of the accused devices. As such, this case presents the exact situation that *res judicata* seeks to prevent."[156]

---

153. 580 F.3d 1281 (Fed. Cir. 2009).

154. The trial court construed "board" to mean a "piece of elongated construction material made from wood cut from a log" and the term "manufactured to have" to mean "a manufacturing process utilizing woodworking techniques." *See id.* at 1284. The court of appeals in the earlier case affirmed both of these constructions and concluded noninfringement. *See id.*

155. *See id.* at 1284–85 (citing Foster v. Hallco Mfg. Co., 947 F.2d 469, 480 (Fed. Cir. 1991)).

156. *Id.* at 1286.

MALPRACTICE

Certain Claims against Patent Prosecutor Held Frivolous While Others Found Nonfrivolous

In *Carter v. ALK Holdings, Inc.,*[157] the Federal Circuit reversed the district court's decision that one of the counts in the complaint was frivolous, affirmed the district court's decision that two other counts were frivolous, and remanded for reconsideration of the appropriateness of sanctions.

Plaintiff Randall Carter alleged that, while he was employed by Acme Security, he developed a high security locking assembly for a safe deposit box door. The invention allegedly was made by Carter on his own time and using his own resources. The President of Acme Security, Michael Hassebrock, proposed a "50/50 partnership" with Carter and retained a patent attorney to draft a patent application for the invention. Although the provisional patent application named Carter and Curtis Taylor as coinventors, the nonprovisional application named Carter and Hassebrock as inventors. Hassebrock allegedly demanded that Carter assign his rights in the patent to Acme Security and, when Carter refused, Acme Security terminated Carter's employment.

Carter filed suit in federal court against ALK Holdings, Hassebrock, and the patent attorney who drafted the patent application (referred to in the court's decision as John Doe I.) All of Carter's claims related to the allegedly improper naming of Hassebrock as an inventor on the patent application.

The district court dismissed Carter's federal claims for failure to state a claim and declined to exercise supplemental jurisdiction over his state-law claims. The district court also ruled, sua sponte, that Counts I, VIII, and XI of Carter's complaint were frivolous and imposed sanctions of $30,356.89 on Carter's counsel pursuant to Federal Rule of Civil Procedure 11.

The Federal Circuit reviewed the district court's Rule 11 determination under the law of the Eleventh Circuit. The Federal Circuit began its analysis with Count VIII, which alleged a breach of fiduciary duty by John Doe I "in violation of 35 U.S.C. *et seq.*, 37 CFR *et seq.*, and the Manual of Patent Examination Procedure (MPEP)."[158] The district court found that "[t]he gravamen of Count VIII is that Defendant John Doe I breached the fiduciary duty owed to Plaintiff by representing two parties with conflicting interests and by sacrificing the interests of one party for another."[159] The district court found that this claim was an attempt "to manufacture a federal cause of action by couching a garden-variety malpractice claim in terms of patent law."[160]

The Federal Circuit found that Count VIII was not a frivolous federal claim. The court explained that a federal district court has jurisdiction pursuant to 28 U.S.C. § 1338(a) over cases in which "a well-pleaded complaint establishes either that federal patent law creates the cause of action or that the plaintiff's right to relief necessarily depends on the

---

157. 605 F.3d 1319 (Fed. Cir. 2010).

158. *Id.* at 1323 (quoting from the complaint).

159. *Id.* (quoting Carter v. ALK Holdings, Inc., 510 F. Supp. 2d 1299, 1308 (N.D. Ga. 2007)).

160. *Id.* (quoting *Carter*, 510 F. Supp. 2d at 1305).

resolution of a substantial question of federal patent law, in that patent law is a necessary element of one of the well-pleaded claims."[161] The Federal Circuit ruled that Count VIII involves a substantial question of federal patent law and was not frivolous because "determination of John Doe I's compliance with the MPEP and the CFR is a necessary element of Carter's malpractice cause of action because the CFR and the MPEP establish John Doe I's expected fiduciary duties to his client."[162]

At the same time, the Federal Circuit found that Count I, which alleged a violation of Article I, Section 8, Clause 8 of the U.S. Constitution, was frivolous. The court explained that the Patent Clause does not create private rights of action for inventors and that the argument regarding Count I advanced by Carter's counsel "contains no legal merit and is not supported by any reasonable explanation."[163]

The Federal Circuit found that Count XI, which alleged a violation of 35 U.S.C. § 122, was also frivolous. Section 122(a) provides that "applications for patents shall be kept in confidence by the Patent and Trademark Office." The Federal Circuit ruled that section 122 applies only to the actions of the USPTO. The Federal Circuit reasoned that, to the extent that any parties became aware of the contents of Carter's patent application, they did so because of a disclosure by attorney John Doe I, not the USPTO. Because Carter's counsel "failed to proffer any reasonable explanation for bringing Count XI," the Federal Circuit found that it was frivolous.

The Federal Circuit remanded for reconsideration of whether sanctions were appropriate. The court noted that the district court's imposition of sanctions appeared to have been based on its concern that Carter's counsel attempted to improperly claim federal jurisdiction. The Federal Circuit held that this concern no longer exists in view of the court's decision that Count VIII contains a nonfrivolous allegation of federal jurisdiction.

Jurisdiction of State Law Claim for Malpractice That Necessarily Involves Resolution of Substantial Question of Patent Law Resides in Federal Courts

In *Premier Networks, Inc. v. Stadheim & Grear, Ltd.,*[164] an Illinois appellate court affirmed the trial court's dismissal without prejudice of Premier's legal malpractice claim against Stadheim because it would have required determination of substantive matters of patent law, and exclusive jurisdiction therefore rested in the federal court. The appellate court also affirmed the trial court's dismissal with prejudice of Premier's claims challenging the parties' contingent fee agreement.

Premier had entered into a contingent fee agreement with Stadheim to provide all legal representation concerning certain patents, including a patent on a system that amplified telephone signals transmitted by individual telephones to telephone companies' central offices (the '805 patent), in return for costs, plus 40 percent of all future income derived from the patents. Premier had the final authority concerning license agreements and infringement lawsuits. Either party could terminate the agreement at any time, with provisions for quantum meruit payments to Stadheim for work performed.

---

161. *Id.* at 1323 (quoting Christianson v. Colt Indus. Operating Corp., 486 U.S. 800, 808–09 (1988)).
162. *Id.* at 1325.
163. *Id.* at 1325–26.
164. 918 N.E.2d 1117 (Ill. App. Ct. 2009).

Stadheim had sued Alcatel-Lucent on the '805 patent, but the federal district court granted summary judgment to Alcatel-Lucent on grounds of noninfringement, a judgment affirmed by the Federal Circuit, which noted that Premier had failed to rebut evidence that, unlike Premier's system, Alcatel-Lucent's system did not couple the receiver and transmitter of the telephone to the telephone lines. Premier sued Stadheim in Illinois state court for legal malpractice, alleging that Stadheim had failed to use scientific evidence that Premier had given to Stadheim that would have rebutted Alcatel-Lucent's evidence.

The appellate court observed that the federal courts' exclusive jurisdiction over patent cases extended to cases in which the plaintiff's right to relief necessarily depended on the resolution of a substantial question of patent law.[165] After discussing several state appellate court decisions applying that principle, and declining to follow a Nebraska decision refusing to defer to federal court jurisdiction,[166] the court concluded that, in this case, "the issues of legal malpractice are necessarily inextricably bound to determinations of substantive issues of patent law," so federal jurisdiction was exclusive.[167]

The appellate court also affirmed the trial court's dismissal with prejudice of Premier's claims that the contingent fee agreement created a prohibited business transaction between lawyer and client and violated the Illinois professional conduct rule that attorneys' fees shall be "reasonable." Premier alleged that the 40 percent contingent fee was unreasonable. The appellate court held that, to the extent that the contingent fee agreement could be construed as granting Stadheim a proprietary interest in the patents, the agreement was nonetheless permissible under the Illinois Rules of Professional Conduct as part of a contingent fee agreement if the fee were reasonable. The court concluded that, because the facts suggested a need for highly skilled representation in a very technically narrow area of patent practice, and Premier was free to terminate the agreement at any time, subject to reasonable compensation in quantum meruit for work performed, the fee agreement was not unreasonable, and the trial court did not err in dismissing Premier's claims.

---

165. *See, e.g.,* Christianson v. Colt Industries Operating Corp., 486 U.S. 800, 808–09 (1988).

166. New Tek Mfg., Inc. v. Beehner, 702 N.W.2d 336 (Neb. 2005) (holding reaffirmed after remand in New Tek Mfg., Inc. v. Beehner, 751 N.W.2d 135 (Neb. 2008)). The *Premier* court observed that "the Nebraska Supreme Court's analysis clearly went to the very heart of patent law," so the case was clearly within exclusive federal jurisdiction. *Premier*, 918 N.E.2d at 1123.

167. *Premier*, 918 N.E.2d at 1124.

PATENT TRANSACTIONS

Chapter 9 covers noteworthy cases involving arbitration agreements as well as a patent licensing case.

The U.S. Supreme Court addressed two cases involving arbitration. In *Stolt-Nielsen v. AnimalFeeds International Corp.*, the Court considered the effect of the absence of a contract on class arbitration proceedings. On the other hand, in *Rent-A-Center, West, Inc. v. Jackson*, a divided Court confirmed its support for enforcing arbitration agreements as written.

The District Court for the District of Minnesota also weighed in on an arbitration issue in *In re Arbitration Between Wells Fargo Bank, N.A. & WMR e-PIN, LLC*, finding that an arbitration panel did not exceed its authority in awarding fees to Wells Fargo.

The Eighth Circuit provided guidance on the interpretation of alternative estoppel in the context of arbitration provisions in *PRM Energy System Inc. v. Primenergy*.

Lastly, in *Imation Corp. v. Koninklijke Philips Electronics, N.V.*, the only nonarbitration-related opinion discussed in this chapter, the Federal Circuit interpreted the patent license term "agrees to grant and does hereby grant" rights in the patent to the licensee and its subsidiaries to include all subsidiaries of the licensee, even those that became subsidiaries after the license expired.

LICENSING

License Grant

Use of "Agrees to Grant and Does Hereby Grant" and "Now or Hereafter" Gave License to Later-Created Subsidiaries

In *Imation Corp. v. Koninklijke Philips Electronics, N.V.*,[1] the Federal Circuit reversed and remanded a district court holding that two of Licensee Imation's subsidiaries were not licensed under a license agreement. The plaintiff, Koninklijke Philips Electronics (Philips), entered into a cross license (License) with Imation's predecessor, Minnesota Mining and Manufacturing (3M).

The License cross-licensed patents related to magneto-optical information storage and retrieval technology among the parties and their subsidiaries. The licensed patents included those that, among other things, had "a filing date, or claim priority from a date, or are or were entitled to claim priority from a date, on or before the expiration date (March 1, 2000) of this Agreement," except that any patent license that had been granted

---

1. 586 F.3d 980 (Fed. Cir. 2009).

continued for the term of the patent.[2] The issue in this case was whether patents that had a filing date/priority date/entitled to a priority date *before* March 1, 2000, but *after* the date of the agreement were licensed to subsidiaries *after* March 1, 2000, such as Moser Baer.

The Federal Circuit reviewed the district court ruling based on the procedural law of the regional circuit (Eighth Circuit, de novo) and the state law designated in the License (New York). Critical to the decision was whether the License for future inventions was a present grant of rights or only an expectant interest. The court held that the language "agrees to grant and does hereby grant" created a present grant, not an expectant interest.[3]

Next, the Federal Circuit determined that, because the License used the phrase "now or *hereafter*" in the definition of "Subsidiary" and did not make reference date to the expiration of the agreement, the term included business entities that could come into existence at a future unspecified date. Therefore, the court held that patents that had a filing date or priority date, or were entitled to a priority date, prior to March 1, 2000, were licensed to Imation and its subsidiaries, regardless of when such subsidiary came into existence, including after the License agreement expired, for the life of such patents.

ALTERNATIVE DISPUTE RESOLUTION

Arbitration

U.S. Supreme Court Rules Unconscionability Challenge to Arbitration Agreement Was an Issue for the Arbitrator

In *Rent-A-Center, West, Inc. v. Jackson,*[4] a divided U.S. Supreme Court confirmed its support for enforcing arbitration agreements as written. The majority held that, where parties delegate to an arbitrator the authority to decide questions of enforceability of an arbitration agreement, the Federal Arbitration Act (FAA) prevents courts from considering general challenges to the enforceability of that agreement as a whole. Courts can consider, however, specific challenges to the enforceability of the delegation clause.

Antonio Jackson filed an employment-discrimination action under 42 U.S.C. § 1981 against his former employer, Rent-A-Center, in the U.S. District Court for the District of Nevada. The defendant-petitioner, Rent-A-Center, filed a motion under the FAA to dismiss or stay the proceedings and to compel arbitration based on the Mutual Agreement to Arbitrate Claims (Agreement), which Jackson signed as a condition of his employment. The Agreement to arbitrate, which was separate from Jackson's employment agreement, included two relevant arbitration provisions. The first provided for arbitration of all disputes arising out of Jackson's employment, including discrimination claims. The second required that an arbitrator also settle any challenge to the validity of the arbitration agreement. Specifically, the Agreement delegated to an arbitrator "exclusive authority to resolve any dispute relating to the [Agreement's] enforceability . . . including . . . any claim that all or any part of this Agreement is void or voidable."[5] Jackson opposed the motion to

---

2. *Id.* at 983.
3. *Id.* at 986.
4. 130 S. Ct. 2772 (2010).
5. *Id.* at 2777.

compel arbitration on the grounds that the Agreement as a whole was unenforceable because it was unconscionable under Nevada law. Jackson did not raise a specific challenge to the enforceability of the delegation clause itself. In response, Rent-A-Center sought enforcement of the second provision, seeking to have an arbitrator decide the "gateway" question of enforceability. The district court, enforcing the delegation clause, refused to consider all of Jackson's arguments for unconscionability and granted Rent-A-Center's motion to dismiss and to compel arbitration.

The Ninth Circuit reversed-in-part, affirmed-in-part, and remanded. The Ninth Circuit held that, where a party challenges an arbitration agreement as unconscionable, the threshold question of unconscionability is for the court, regardless of the delegation clause. The Ninth Circuit remanded the case for full consideration of Jackson's arguments of unconscionability. The U.S. Supreme Court granted certiorari.

The Court, by a 5–4 margin, reversed the judgment of the Ninth Circuit and decided the dispute in favor of arbitration. The Court held that, because Jackson's challenge to the enforceability of the arbitration Agreement was directed to the entire Agreement as a whole, and not specifically to the delegation provision, it was up to the arbitrator, not the court, to determine the unconscionability challenge. The Court ruled that, under the FAA, where an agreement to arbitrate includes a delegation clause providing that an arbitrator will determine challenges to the enforceability of the agreement, challenges specifically to the enforceability of the delegation clause are considered by a district court, whereas challenges to the enforceability of the agreement as a whole are considered by an arbitrator.

The Court also held that section 2 of the FAA places arbitration agreements on an equal footing with other contracts and requires courts to enforce them according to their terms, except upon such grounds existing under law or in equity for the revocation of any contract.

The Court's decision identified two distinct types of validity challenges under section 2: one "challenges specifically the validity of the agreement to arbitrate," and "[t]he other challenges the contract as a whole."[6] The Court held that only the first may be considered by a court in determining the enforceability of an arbitration agreement because, under section 2, an arbitration provision is severable from the remainder of the contract. Therefore, if a party challenges the validity under section 2 of the precise clause or provision containing the agreement to arbitrate, the federal court must consider the challenge before ordering compliance with the agreement under section 4.

In reaching its decision, the Court relied on its prior decision in *Prima Paint v. Flood & Conklin,*[7] holding that courts would not consider a challenge to the unconscionability of an employment agreement, as a whole, where the agreement contained a provision delegating such claims to an arbitrator. According to the Court in this case, the holding in *Prima Paint* is no less applicable when the clause or provision containing the agreement to arbitrate is itself part of a larger arbitration agreement, as opposed to another agreement, such as an employment agreement.

In this case, Jackson did not raise a specific challenge to the agreement to arbitrate enforceability (the delegation provision). Instead, he raised general challenges to the enforceability of the Agreement as a whole. The Court held that, because the delegation is severable from the remainder of the Agreement, unless Jackson also specifically chal-

---

6. *Id.* at 2778 (internal citation omitted) (alteration in original).
7. Prima Paint Corp. v. Flood & Conklin Mfg. Co., 388 U.S. 395 (1967).

lenged the delegation provision, it must be treated as valid under section 2 and enforced under sections 3 and 4.

Accordingly, the Court held that the district court correctly concluded that Jackson challenged only the validity of the contract as a whole. The Court noted that, in his opposition to Rent-A-Center's motion to compel arbitration, Jackson did not even mention the delegation provision. In his response to Rent-A-Center's motion to compel arbitration, Jackson argued that "the entire agreement seems drawn to provide [Rent-A-Center] with undue advantages should an employment-related dispute arise."[8] In Jackson's brief to the Court, he raised for the first time a challenge to the delegation provision, but the Court held that the challenge was too late and refused to consider it.

In a dissenting opinion, Justice Stevens, joined by Justices Ginsberg, Breyer, and Sotomayor, challenged the majority's application of the Court's ruling in *Prima Paint* to the present case. Specifically, the dissent does not recognize *Prima Paint* as permitting the severance of a potentially invalid delegation clause from the potentially invalid arbitration agreement that contains the delegation clause.

According to the dissent, there are two lines of cases that extend to the challenge presented by the respondent. The first line suggests that the intent of the parties must be determined in order to determine who is to decide a question relating to arbitrability. The second line concerns how challenges to arbitrability must be pled in order to be heard by the court. The dissent asserts that the question in the present case is clearly answered in the negative from the application of rule handed down in *First Options*. Justice Steven asserted that *Prima Paint* does not allow an arbitration agreement to clearly and unmistakably validate itself, but that a general challenge to a stand-alone arbitration agreement goes to the making of that agreement; therefore, the courts must decide the challenge.

The dissent aligns its analysis with that of the Ninth Circuit, finding that a good-faith challenge to the formation of an arbitration agreement controverts any assertion that both parties clearly and unmistakably demonstrated the requisite intent to assign any question of arbitrability to arbitration. As such, challenges of this nature warrant further judicial review and a determination prior to compelling arbitration.

Class Action Arbitration Must Be a Matter of Consent

In *Stolt-Nielsen v. AnimalFeeds International Corp.*,[9] the U.S. Supreme Court held that the Federal Arbitration Act (FAA) does not authorize the imposition of class arbitration where the parties never agreed to class proceedings. AnimalFeeds, a multinational corporation, brought a class action antitrust suit against petitioners, predominately foreign corporations that operate parcel tankers, for price fixing, and that suit was consolidated with similar suits brought by other charters, including one in which the Second Circuit subsequently reversed a lower court ruling that the charters' claims were not subject to arbitration. Consequently, the parties agreed that they must arbitrate their antitrust dispute. AnimalFeeds sought arbitration on behalf of a class of purchasers of parcel tanker transportation services. The parties agreed to submit the question of whether their arbitration agreement allowed for class arbitration to a panel of arbitrators who would be bound

---

8. *Jackson,* 130 S. Ct. at 2779.
9. 130 S. Ct. 1758 (2010).

by Class Rules developed by the American Arbitration Association (AAA) following *Green Tree Financial Corp. v. Bazzle*.[10] The FAA authorizes courts to enforce arbitration agreements only in accordance with their agreement.[11] Rule 3 of AAA Supplementary Rules provides that an arbitrator shall determine as a threshold matter whether the applicable clause permits the arbitration to proceed on behalf of or against a class. The parties selected an arbitration panel and stipulated that their arbitration clause was "silent" on the class arbitration issue. The arbitrators ruled that, by its silence, the applicable arbitration clause permitted class arbitration. The panel concluded that petitioners had failed to establish that the parties to the charter agreements intended to preclude class arbitration.

Petitioners sought review in the U.S. District Court for the Southern District of New York. The district court vacated the award, holding that the arbitrators' award was made in manifest disregard of a well-defined rule of governing maritime law. The district court ruled that, had the arbitrators conducted a choice-of-law analysis, they would have applied the federal maritime rule requiring contracts to be interpreted in light of custom and usage. Alternatively, the district court held that the result would be the same even if there were no established maritime rule and New York law then governed. The district court, however, did not reach the petitioner's contention that the arbitrators had exceeded their powers because the FAA does not permit the imposition of class arbitration on parties whose contract was silent on that question.

The Second Circuit reversed, holding that, because the petitioners had cited no authority applying a maritime rule of custom and usage *against* class arbitration, the arbitrators' decision was not in manifest disregard of maritime law. The Second Circuit also concluded that errors the district court identified in the arbitrators' award did not rise to the level of manifest disregard of the law because nothing in New York case law established a rule against arbitration.

The U.S. Supreme Court held that imposing class arbitration on parties who had not agreed to authorize class arbitration is inconsistent with the Federal Arbitration Act, 9 U.S.C. § 1 *et seq.* The Court's opinion emphasized the facts of this case. First, the parties' stipulation that there was "no agreement" on the issue of class arbitration eliminated both any ambiguity about their intent and any consideration of extrinsic factors such as parol evidence.

The Court noted that arbitration clauses by their nature are premised on agreements made between parties. Further, the Court ruled that the arbitrators' decision compelled the ocean couriers to proceed with class arbitration absent a contractual basis to support the decision.[12] Therefore, according to the Court, instead of identifying and applying a rule of decision of the FAA or either maritime or New York law, the arbitrators' award imposed its own policy choice and, thus, went beyond the scope of their power. The Court noted that the arbitrators regarded the agreement's silence on the question of class arbitration as dispositive. The Court added that the arbitration panel's conclusion is fundamentally at odds with the foundational FAA principle that arbitration is a matter of consent.

Second, although the Court acknowledged that an arbitrator may, in some contexts, infer the implicit consent of the parties notwithstanding silence in the contract on an issue, it made clear that it was not deciding what contractual basis could support a finding that

---

10. 539 U.S. 444 (2003).
11. Federal Arbitration Act, 9 U.S.C. § 2 (2006).
12. *Stolt-Nielsen*, 130 S. Ct. at 1775.

the parties agreed to authorize class arbitration.[13] The Court noted that it may be appropriate to presume that parties that enter into an arbitration agreement implicitly authorize the arbitrator to adopt such procedures as are necessary to give effect to the parties' agreement. Thus, the Court determined that procedural questions that grew out of a dispute and bear on its final disposition are presumed for an arbitrator to decide, rather than the judge. On the other hand, the Court noted that an implicit agreement to authorize class action arbitration is not a term that may be inferred solely from the fact that the parties agreed to arbitration of their disputes. This is so, the Court explained, because class-action arbitration changes the nature of arbitration to such a degree that it cannot be presumed the parties consented to it by simply agreeing to submit their disputes to an arbitrator.

The Court noted that the contract was silent as to the permissibility of class arbitration proceedings. The Court determined that federal maritime law, the Federal Arbitration Act (FAA), or New York law would govern the contract. In review of the arbitration award, the Court determined that the arbitrators based its decision on post-*Bazzle* arbitral decisions and did not include any reference to relevant legal frameworks that governed the contracts between the parties. In the Court's opinion, the arbitration panel went beyond its scope of authority by developing a rule not based on existing law, but solely based upon what the panel considered best for the present situation.[14]

In her dissent, Justice Ginsburg embraced an argument that the petition should be dismissed because the issue is unripe.[15] In Justice Ginsburg's view, the decision to permit class arbitration was "highly interlocutory" and, thus, inconsistent with the federal courts' general adherence to the final judgment rule, as it remained to be seen whether the arbitrators would have certified a class and found the particular antitrust claims at issue to be suitable for class resolution.

Moreover, Ginsburg continued, even on the merits, respondents should prevail. She disagreed with the Court's characterization of the panel's decision as policy-driven, pointing to evidence that the panel had, in fact, considered New York law and maritime law on contract interpretation. She also expressed skepticism that the parties had stipulated to the absence of any agreement at all on class arbitration. Rather, she suggested, the parties had merely stipulated that the contract contained no agreement to prohibit class arbitrations.

The dissenting opinion also suggested that the parties' referral of the question regarding class arbitration to the arbitration panel resulted in providing the panel with the prerequisite power to make a determination on the instant issue. Justice Ginsburg noted that the FAA section 10 provisions pertain to whether the arbitrator possessed the power to make a determination on the instant issue and not whether the arbitrator correctly determined the issue. In addition, Ginsburg cited *Burchell v. Marsh*, which provides that, so long as an arbitration "award is within the submission, and contains the honest decision of the arbitrators after a full fair hearing of the parties . . . [the award] will not [be set] aside for error, either in law or fact."[16]

Further, Ginsburg pointed out that there is no language in the arbitration clause that bars or allows class arbitration. The dissenting position is that the arbitration panels' acts were consistent with the contractual terms concerning the use arbitration, the parties to the

---

13. *Id.*
14. *Id.* at 1169.
15. *Id.* at 1777 (Ginsburg, J., dissenting).
16. Burchell v. Marsh, 58 U.S. 344, 349 (1854).

arbitration, and the appropriate subject matter for arbitration. Specifically, if the proposed class were certified, the arbitrators would then adjudicate only the rights of persons with whom Stolt-Nielsen agreed to arbitrate and only on those issues that may be subject to arbitration.

Finally, Justice Ginsburg expressed concern about the potential incongruities created by the Court's approach: although the class-action mechanism is available in courts, those parties who opt for arbitration can suddenly be stripped of their ability to bring claims as a class, whether in arbitration or in court.

Eighth Circuit Affirms Enforcement of Arbitration Provision Involving Nonsignatory

In **PRM Energy System Inc. v. Primenergy,**[17] the Eighth Circuit affirmed a district court decision granting a nonsignatory's enforcement of an arbitration provision. In 1999, PRM Energy (PRM) and Primenergy entered into a patent licensing agreement involving gasification technology patents. The agreement granted Primenergy the right to use the technology and to sublicense the technology in certain countries.

In 2002, Kobe Steel began to negotiate with PRM for a license to their technology in Japan. Kobe Steel's discussions with PRM stalled, but simultaneously Kobe Steel was discussing the possibility of a sublicense with Primenergy in violation of Primenergy's 1999 agreement with PRM. Primenergy and Kobe Steel entered into a sublicense agreement, but did not report it to PRM.

Subject to the arbitration provision in the 1999 agreement, PRM and Primenergy entered into arbitration in 2004. While the arbitration was ongoing, PRM filed a separate action against Kobe Steel for tortious interference and conspiracy. Later, PRM amended its complaint against Primenergy to include specific allegations concerning interactions between Primenergy and Kobe Steel. The district court consolidated PRM's action against Primenergy with PRM's action against Kobe Steel, but ruled that all of the claims, including those against Kobe Steel, were subject to arbitration. The district court held that Kobe Steel could enforce the arbitration provision because "all of PRM's claims either make reference to or presume the existence of the 1999 Agreements, and allege substantially interdependent and concerted misconduct by both the nonsignatory [Kobe Steel] and one or more of the signatories [Primenergy] to the contract."[18]

On appeal, the Eighth Circuit addressed: (1) whether a nonsignatory could compel an arbitration agreement; and (2) whether PRM's claims against Kobe Steel were outside the scope of the arbitration provision in the 1999 agreement. The appellate court recognized that, under the theory of alternative estoppel, Kobe Steel could enforce the provision.

Under the alternative estoppel theory, the claims must be so intertwined with the agreement containing the arbitration clause that it would be unfair to allow the signatory to rely on the agreement to formulate its claims, but to then disavow the application of the arbitration provision. Because the "alleged collusive action [between Kobe Steel and Primenergy] not only arose out of and targeted the 1999 Agreements, they were 'inti-

---

17. 592 F.3d 830, 832 (8th Cir. 2010).

18. *Id.* at 833; PRM Energy Sys. v. Primenergy, L.L.C., 2006 U.S. Dist. LEXIS 40831, at *10 (W.D. Ark. June 19, 2006) (quoting MS Dealer Serv. Corp. v. Franklin, 177 F.3d 942, 947 (11th Cir. 1999)) (internal quotation marks omitted).

mately founded in and intertwined' with Primenergy's underlying contract obligations[,]"[19] the Eighth Circuit affirmed the district court's order granting Kobe Steel's motion to compel arbitration.

Next, the appellate court addressed whether PRM's claims against Kobe Steel were outside the scope of the arbitration provision in the 1999 agreement. The arbitration provision covered "all disputes arising under" the agreement; however, PRM argued that the arbitration agreement was narrow and only applied to contract disputes, not tort disputes. The Eighth Circuit rejected that argument, explaining that it generally does not matter whether the claim arose out of a contract dispute or a tort dispute. Because PRM's claims against Kobe Steel arose under the 1999 agreements, the district court's decision was affirmed.

In a dissenting opinion, Judge Beam criticized the majority for compelling arbitration where "according to PRM, the tortious activities of Kobe Steel deal with transactions beyond the scope, and purposefully outside of, the licensing authority granted Primenergy."[20] Judge Beam distinguished this case from the facts in *Ross v. American Express Co.*[21] because the PRM/Primenergy agreements do not mention Kobe Steel, and Kobe Steel was never a participant in the PRM/Primenergy deal. Moreover, Judge Beam noted that, unlike in *Donaldson Co., Inc. v. Burroughs Diesel, Inc.*,[22] PRM's allegations against Kobe Steel did not involve interdependent and concerted misconduct.

Arbitration Panel Did Not Exceed Its Authority in Awarding Attorneys' Fees over a Patent Licensing Dispute

In *In re Arbitration Between Wells Fargo Bank, N.A. & WMR e-PIN, LLC*,[23] the U.S. District Court for the District of Minnesota upheld an arbitration award in favor of Claimant Wells Fargo following a dispute over Wells Fargo's licensing agreement with Respondent WMR directed to patents on central check-clearing system technology.[24] In its decision, the district court also awarded Wells Fargo $1,265,000 in attorneys' fees and $600,000 in costs associated with an underlying patent case. Additionally, the district court enjoined WMR from disclosing or using Wells Fargo's trade secrets.[25]

One of Wells Fargo's subsidiaries, Wells Fargo Services Corporation, had entered into a patent license agreement with WMR in 2004. The agreement included a covenant not to sue, a license, and an arbitration provision. The parties entered into an arbitration proceeding pursuant to the arbitration provision in the patent licensing agreement, and the panel entered an award in favor of Wells Fargo. The arbitration panel also granted a permanent injunction in favor of Wells Fargo and determined "inventorship" regarding technology disclosed in multiple patent applications currently pending before the USPTO.

---

19. *PRM Energy*, 592 F.3d at 836.

20. *Id.* at 837.

21. 547 F.3d 137, 148 (2d Cir. 2008).

22. 581 F.3d 726, 733–34 (8th Cir. 2009).

23. No. 08-5472, 2009 WL 2461518 (D. Minn. Aug. 10, 2009) (hereinafter Wells Fargo Arbitration). This decision has been appealed to the Eighth Circuit.

24. *See* DataTreasury Corp. v. Wells Fargo & Co., 490 F. Supp. 2d 756, 759 (E.D. Tex. 2007).

25. Wells Fargo Arbitration, 2009 WL 2461518, at *2.

Wells Fargo ultimately instituted an action against WMR (and fellow respondents Synoran, LLC and e-Banc, LLC) in October 2008 to force judgment on the arbitration award and to protect its trade secrets. More specifically, Wells Fargo sued to correct and confirm the award; the respondents moved to vacate or modify the award. The respondents argued that the arbitration panel exceeded or imperfectly executed its authority in the course of rendering its award for Wells Fargo.

After reviewing the parties' positions, the magistrate judge issued a Report and Recommendation (Report). The magistrate adopted the findings of the arbitration panel, advising that Wells Fargo's motion to correct and confirm the award as corrected be granted and that the respondents' motion to vacate or modify the award be denied. The district court adopted the Report despite objections by WMR, creating an important precedent regarding the scope of arbitrators' authority in the context of patent license agreements.

The respondents objected to the Report, challenging: (1) the finding that the respondents waived their rights to object to the award of injunctive relief; (2) the conclusion that "manifest disregard" is no longer a viable basis for vacatur; (3) the refusal to consider the public disclosure of certain trade secrets; and (4) the finding that the arbitration panel did not exceed its authority by awarding attorneys' fees to Wells Fargo as the prevailing party. In response to these objections, the district court reached several conclusions. First, it explained that the respondents had waived their right to object to the panel's award of injunctive relief because they had requested injunctive relief from the panel.[26] Second, the district court held that "manifest disregard," an extra-statutory ground to vacate an arbitral award, was no longer a viable basis for vacatur. Third, the district court denied the respondents' argument that the fee award was improper due to the public disclosure of trade secrets. Fourth, the court concluded that the respondents, with their own request for an award of fees, effectively waived their right to argue that the panel lacked authority to award attorneys' fees. Accordingly, the court found that the panel did not exceed its authority in awarding fees to Wells Fargo.

Furthermore, WMR objected to the Report on two additional grounds: (1) the magistrate's acceptance of the panel's adoption of the award; and (2) the panel's determination that Wells Fargo is the rightful inventor of the disputed technology. Accordingly, the district court explained that the panel corrected the award in October 2008 after giving the respondents an opportunity to reply to Wells Fargo's request for correction, and, in doing so, the panel did not reevaluate the basis of the claims. In regard to the panel's decision on inventorship, the district court explained that the parties' dispute regarding ownership of the trade secrets necessitated a determination of inventorship.

WMR and Synoran have appealed the orders of the U.S. District Court for the District of Minnesota to the Eighth Circuit.

---

26. *Id.*

PART II
TRADEMARKS

CHAPTER 10

NATURE OF TRADEMARKS

The central question of whether a term was capable of indicating source and thus worthy of trademark protection received some attention from courts this past year. Courts also considered the often-argued line between suggestiveness and descriptiveness of marks, as well as a number of procedural issues, including acceptable specimens of use in the USPTO.

In *Advertise.com, Inc. v. AOL Advertising, Inc.,* the Ninth Circuit reversed and vacated in part a preliminary injunction based on the district court's finding that the mark ADVERTISING.COM was not generic and, thus, protectable. The Ninth Circuit held that it was in error to find that the term "advertising.com" was not generic and concluded that AOL was unlikely to establish that the term was protectable as a trademark.

In *Amazing Spaces, Inc. v. Metro Mini Storage,* the Fifth Circuit went further and held that the plaintiff's logo, which consisted of a raised, five-pointed star set within a circle, by its intrinsic nature did not serve to identify a particular source and, therefore, was not legally protectable as a trademark. Likewise, in *In re T.S. Designs, Inc.,* the TTAB affirmed the final refusal of an application on the ground that the material sought to be registered—a "Clothing Facts" label that looked like a nutritional information label, but with information about the item of clothing—would be perceived by the public as merely informative rather than indicative of source.

In a decision favoring trademark protection, *Brooks v. Creative Arts By Calloway, LLC,* the TTAB held that Cab Calloway's grandson had created protectable rights in THE CAB CALLOWAY ORCHESTRA mark, and that those rights predated an application to register the CAB CALLOWAY mark by another party. In reaching its decision, the TTAB noted that a personal name may function as a mark and be inherently distinctive, provided that it does not function primarily merely as a surname.

Turning to the question of suggestiveness versus descriptiveness, in *Zobmondo Entertainment, LLC v. Falls Media, LLC,* the Ninth Circuit reversed the district court's holding, finding questions of material fact to exist regarding whether the disputed trademark WOULD YOU RATHER . . . ? was suggestive or merely descriptive. The Ninth Circuit discussed a number of tests for distinguishing between suggestive and descriptive marks and found that, where the "imagination" test is inconclusive and the "competitors' needs" test favors suggestiveness, the "extent-of-use" test cannot support summary judgment on its own; the factual issues must be resolved by a jury.

In *Great Clips Inc. v. Hair Cuttery of Greater Boston LLC,* the First Circuit affirmed the plaintiff's request for declaratory judgment, holding that a settlement agreement between the parties releasing each other from "claims that arise from the application and registration" of each other's respective marks (GREAT CUTS and GREAT CLIPS) also applied to use of the marks in the marketplace, and that the defendants' infringement counterclaim was therefore precluded.

In *In re Quantum Foods Inc.,* the TTAB held that a Web page printout is not an acceptable specimen of use for a trademark registration covering goods unless it provides a means to order the goods; mere inclusion of the mark holder's contact information is insufficient.

Finally, in *In re Sones,* the Federal Circuit vacated and remanded a decision by the TTAB, holding that a picture of the product is not a mandatory requirement for an electronic display (Web site) specimen of use. The court explained that acceptable Web-site-based specimens do not need to include a picture if they otherwise show that the mark is "associated" with the goods and serve as an indicator of source.

FORMS OF TRADEMARKS

Designs, Images

Five-Pointed Star Logo Not Entitled to Trademark Protection in Texas

In ***Amazing Spaces, Inc. v. Metro Mini Storage,***[1] the U.S. District Court for the Southern District of Texas held that "a logo consisting of a raised, five-pointed star set within a circle," used by a self-storage company in Texas, was not entitled to trademark protection.[2] Plaintiff Amazing Spaces, Inc. sued Metro Mini Storage and Landmark Interest Corporation, a self-storage company and general contractor also located in Texas, for trademark infringement in connection with prominent use of a star inside a circle design on building storage facilities. The defendants moved for summary judgment, alleging that the mark was not entitled to trademark protection.

In ruling in favor of the defendants, the court was persuaded by the argument that the five-pointed star within a circle symbol was ubiquitous throughout the entire state as a representation of Texas pride, especially because Texas was known as the "Lone Star" state. Though the parties disputed whether Amazing Spaces was the first business of its kind to use the symbol, the court considered this point immaterial to the ultimate disposition. The court took notice that "a drive on a highway, a walk along a downtown street, or a visit to a shopping center drives home just how common the five-point star within a circle design is."[3] Given its extent of use within the state of Texas, the court held that the common logo of a five-pointed star set within a circle was not inherently distinctive.

Additionally, the court held that Amazing Spaces had failed to demonstrate that its logo had acquired secondary meaning as a source identifier. In contrast, the summary judgment record provided evidence that at least twenty-eight other self-storage businesses utilized a star or star-within-a-circle on their buildings. The court further noted that Amazing Spaces had failed to offer survey evidence, which the Fifth Circuit has recognized as "the most direct and persuasive way of establishing secondary meaning."[4] Accordingly, the court held that the evidence submitted by Amazing Spaces did not address the ultimate issue as to whether the consuming public would associate the five-pointed star with the trademark owner and granted summary judgment in favor of the defendants.

---

1. 665 F. Supp. 2d 727 (S.D. Tex. 2009).
2. *Id.* at 730.
3. *Id.* at 738.
4. *Id.* at 741–42 (internal citation omitted).

Spectrum of Distinctiveness

Inherently Distinctive

Personal Name Used as Mark to Identify Orchestra Held to Be Inherently Distinctive

In *Brooks v. Creative Arts by Calloway, LLC,*[5] the TTAB sustained an opposition filed by the grandson of the late, well-known musician Cab Calloway against an attempt by Creative Arts, a company formed by Calloway's widow and daughters, to register the name "Cab Calloway" as a service mark.

In this case, the parties stipulated that the only issue before the TTAB was whether Brooks could establish protectable trademark rights in the mark THE CAB CALLOWAY ORCHESTRA prior to the date on which Creative Arts filed its intent-to-use application to register the CAB CALLOWAY mark. The TTAB found that Brooks had first used the Orchestra's name in connection with live and recorded musical performances, CDs, and videotapes more than six months before Creative Arts applied to register Calloway's name as a service mark, and that the Orchestra had given at least three additional live performances under that name within the six-month period preceding Creative Arts' filing. Moreover, the parties stipulated that, if Brooks established prior protectable rights in the Orchestra's name, Creative Arts' application would create a likelihood of confusion between the parties' marks. Thus, the only remaining question was whether the nature of the Orchestra's prior use was sufficient to establish "prior service mark use or, in the alternative, trade name use or use analogous to trademark use" sufficient to preclude Creative Arts' application.[6]

The question of whether the prior use was sufficient to establish prior protectable rights turned on the resolution of a dichotomy between common law and the Lanham Act as to whether a personal name mark is merely descriptive and, therefore, must acquire secondary meaning to merit protection, or inherently distinctive and, therefore, protectable without a showing of secondary meaning. Under the Lanham Act, a personal name mark (other than one that is primarily merely surname) is registrable on the Principal Register without a showing of secondary meaning and, therefore, is deemed to be inherently distinctive so long as it has been used in a way that would indicate to consumers that it served to identify the goods or services with which it was used. Given the foregoing, the TTAB held that there was no logical basis for requiring a personal name mark that is sufficiently distinctive for registration purposes also to have acquired secondary meaning before it could be relied upon in an opposition proceeding, especially because, under a settled interpretation of the Lanham Act that has been followed by the USPTO for more than fifty years, personal name marks are considered to be inherently distinctive. A contrary conclusion, the TTAB explained, would result in the application of different standards to the opposer and the applicant and thereby create a "first to file" system for personal names, "in direct conflict with the basic underpinning of trademark law" that "rights are obtained through use and not by being the first to file an application."[7] Accordingly, the

---

5. 93 U.S.P.Q.2d (BNA) 1823 (T.T.A.B. 2010).
6. *Id.* at 1828
7. *Id.* at 1830.

TTAB expressly held that, "when a plaintiff is asserting prior rights based on a personal name, not a surname, the personal name trademark is inherently distinctive."[8]

With that issue resolved, the TTAB found that the mark THE CAB CALLOWAY ORCHESTRA was inherently distinctive, that Brooks had established use of that name as a trade name and service mark prior to the date of Creative Arts' application, and that Creative Arts' application created a likelihood of confusion with Brooks' protectable mark. Accordingly, the TTAB sustained Brooks' opposition to Creative Arts' application.

Descriptive

Summary Judgment Finding of Mere Descriptiveness Reversed and Remanded Where Imagination Test Was Inconclusive and Competitors' Needs Test Favored Suggestiveness

In *Zobmondo Entertainment, LLC v. Falls Media, LLC,*[9] the Ninth Circuit reversed the district court's grant of summary judgment in favor of Zobmondo, finding that a question of fact existed regarding whether the mark at issue was inherently distinctive to consumers. The appeal arose after a persistent dispute between two competitors who both use the WOULD YOU RATHER . . .? mark on board games and books. In deciding the trademark infringement claim, the district court held that Falls Media's federally registered trademark, WOULD YOU RATHER . . .?, was not entitled to protection because it was merely descriptive and lacked secondary meaning.

On appeal, the Ninth Circuit reviewed the different tests used by the district court for differentiating between a suggestive mark and a merely descriptive mark: the imagination, competitors' needs, and extent-of-use tests.

The imagination test asks whether imagination or a mental leap is required in order to reach a conclusion about the nature of the product. Under the imagination test, the district court found the mark WOULD YOU RATHER . . .? to be descriptive because no leap of imagination was required to understand that this phrase denoted the main aspect of the game, which asked "would you rather" questions. The Ninth Circuit explained that the imagination test does not ask what information about a product *could* be derived from a mark, but rather whether a mental leap is *required* to understand the mark's relationship to the product. However, the court concluded that the district court erred in finding the mark merely descriptive as a matter of law because the record lacked comprehensive consumer surveys that could have shed light on how the average consumer perceives the mark. Thus, the court concluded that the imagination test, by itself, was inconclusive.

Next the court turned to the competitors' needs test, which focuses on the extent to which a mark is actually needed by competitors to identify their goods or services. If there is a great need, the mark is probably descriptive. The district court declined to apply this test because it found the test difficult to apply in this case. Drawing all inferences in favor of Falls Media, the Ninth Circuit concluded that the competitors' needs test strongly favored the argument that the WOULD YOU RATHER . . .? mark is suggestive. Notably, during development, Zobmondo itself identified 135 other possible names for its own game and

---

8.   *Id.*
9.   602 F.3d 1108 (9th Cir. 2010).

it marketed the game without the question mark for a period of time. Thus, the court found that the competitors' needs test favored Falls Media's distinctiveness argument.

The court then turned to the third test employed by the district court, the extent-of-use test, which evaluates the extent to which other sellers have used the mark on similar merchandise. The court noted that it was not aware of any other Ninth Circuit case applying the extent-of-use test as a controlling measure of trademark validity, and it declined to do so in this case. According to the court, if summary judgment is disfavored by both the imagination test and the competitors' needs test, the extent-of-use test would be, at most, one factor to be considered, and, on its own, would not support summary judgment.[10] Having found that the imagination test was inconclusive and that the competitors' needs test favored suggestiveness, the court was not persuaded that the extent-of-use test could render the WOULD YOU RATHER . . .? mark merely descriptive as a matter of law. Thus, the court reversed and remanded.

Generic

Addition of Top-Level Domain to a Generic Term Does Not Create a Protectable Mark

In *Advertise.com, Inc. v. AOL Advertising, Inc.*,[11] the Ninth Circuit reversed and vacated-in-part a preliminary injunction, which was based on the district court's finding that the mark ADVERTISE.COM is protectable. The court held that it was error for the district court to find that the term "advertise.com" is not generic and concluded that AOL is unlikely to establish that the term is protectable.

AOL secured registrations of the trademark ADVERTISE.COM and stylized versions of that mark for services relating to online advertising (including services that assist Web site operators in hosting third-party advertisements and services that assist Web marketers in online advertising efforts). AOL successfully fended off requests from the USPTO that it disclaim the term "advertising.com," arguing that the term is distinctive.

AOL later filed suit against Advertise.com, seeking a preliminary injunction against its use of the mark ADVERTISE.COM and a stylized variation of that mark. The district court granted the preliminary injunction, enjoining Advertise.com from using the mark ADVERTISE.COM or any mark or logo confusion similar to AOL's ADVERTISE.COM marks. The district court based its ruling on a finding that AOL was likely to show that ADVERTISE.COM is at least descriptive and, therefore, potentially protectable under trademark law.

On appeal, the Ninth Circuit considered whether the district court correctly determined that AOL was likely to succeed on the merits of its claim. The court held that the district court applied the wrong legal standard for considering genericness and, therefore, abused its discretion by entering a preliminary injunction.

After reviewing the substantive standards for genericness and noting that AOL enjoyed a presumption of validity due to its registration, the Ninth Circuit first identified "online or Internet advertising" as the relevant genus of services, and then considered whether AOL's mark merely restated that genus.

---

10. *Id.* at 1118.
11. 616 F.3d 974 (9th Cir. 2010).

The court considered the impression conveyed by the two elements of the mark—"advertising" and ".com"—when viewed separately. The term "advertising" was generic and conveyed the action of calling something to the public's attention. The term ".com" is a top-level domain indicator and reflected an online commercial organization. The court concluded that, considering the meaning of these terms taken separately, "advertising" and ".com" reflected only the genus of the services offered by AOL and suggested that the mark ADVERTISE.COM for online advertising services is generic.

The Ninth Circuit then acknowledged that even where the individual components of a mark may be considered generic, those components in combination may not be. Accordingly, the court analyzed whether ADVERTISE.COM, examined as a whole, was generic.

According to the Ninth Circuit, the "who-are-you/what-are-you" test strongly suggested that the mark as a whole was generic, because any online advertising company could be called "an advertising.com" or "an advertising dot-com." The court reasoned that these designations could be applied just as easily to one of AOL's online advertising competitors. The court noted that a modern dictionary defines a "dot-com" as relating to a business conducted on the Internet and that the definition provides "dot-com advertising" as an example. The court considered this dictionary usage as strongly suggesting that the phrase "advertise.com" was generic.

The Ninth Circuit relied on several other factors to support its finding of genericness. The court observed that the Federal Circuit, in rulings on registrability of marks, has held that the addition of ".com" or another top-level domain to an otherwise unprotectable term will result in a distinctive composite only in rare cases. The court also noted that there are many examples of domain names that include "advertising.com," such as "travel-advertising.com," "aplusadvertising.com," and "domainadvertising.com."

The court rejected AOL's argument that marks that communicate domain names intrinsically denote a source because only one entity can hold a domain name. The court commented that accepting AOL's logic would result in a per se rule that the addition of a top-level domain to a generic term would, in all cases, result in a protectable mark. This has been rejected by the USPTO, the TTAB, the Federal Circuit, and now by the Ninth Circuit. The court also observed that the main reason a consumer is likely to associate a domain name with a source is when the second level indicator (the portion to the left of the top-level domain name) is distinctive, which was not the case here.

The court concluded that this was not the rare case in which the addition of a top-level domain to a generic term resulted in a distinctive mark. Instead, the court held that Advertise.com was likely to rebut the presumption of validity and prevail on its claim that AOL's ADVERTISE.COM mark was generic.

Federal Registration

Principal Register

Term "Clothing Facts" Denied Registration; Functions as Informational Matter Rather Than as Trademark

In *In re T.S. Designs, Inc.,*[12] the TTAB affirmed the examining attorney's final refusal of an application to register the mark CLOTHING FACTS for clothing on the grounds

---

12. 95 U.S.P.Q.2d (BNA) 1669 (T.T.A.B. 2010).

that the matter sought to be registered did not function as an indication of origin. The TTAB agreed with the examining attorney that the public would be likely to perceive the matter as merely informative.

The TTAB relied upon the specimens submitted by the applicant. Both showed the same design, though one displayed the design printed on a sewn-in label and the other showed the design printed directly on a t-shirt. The application, however, was not for registration of the entire design, but only for the phrase "clothing facts."

The design as a whole mimicked the "Nutrition Facts" label that FDA regulation has made ubiquitous on packaged food. The overall shape of the design was a vertically oriented rectangle with rounded corners. Inside this shape, on the top line, "Clothing Facts" appeared in heavy lettering, but without the "TM" symbol. The next line read "amount per shirt." The design then listed either "0%" or "100%" of the "Daily Values" for the following categories: Sweatshop Labor, Pesticides Used, Plastic Prints, Harsh Resins, Certified Organic Cotton, and Water Based Inks. The bottom two lines of the design read "tsdesigns.com printing [line break] t-shirts for good™ © 2007."[13]

Based on the design as a whole, the TTAB found that the public would be less likely to view the phrase "Clothing Facts" as an indication of origin because two other elements of the design were displayed in a manner suggesting that they were intended to function as marks ("tsdesigns.com" and "t-shirts for good").

The TTAB, although emphasizing that the specimen as a whole was relevant, refused to assume that the public would recognize the words "Clothing Facts" as a conscious attempt to call to mind the FDA-required label titled "Nutrition Facts." The TTAB also refused to assume, even if the public recognized this reference, such recognition would result in the general public viewing "Clothing Facts" as an indication of origin. The TTAB also noted that the design made use of the "TM" symbol, but did so for other elements of the label.

The TTAB also rejected the applicant's argument that "Clothing Facts" should be considered a secondary indication of origin. The TTAB explained that designs on clothing had been characterized as secondary indications of origin only in situations where the design matter had already acquired secondary meaning (i.e., in the case of promotional goods). The TTAB decided that the applicant could not rely upon the doctrine of secondary source because the record included no evidence that the phrase "Clothing Facts" had acquired secondary meaning for another good or service. Therefore, the TTAB affirmed the refusal to register the mark.

Specimens

Web-Site-Based Specimen of Use Need Not Include a Picture of Goods

In *In re Sones*,[14] the Federal Circuit vacated and remanded a decision by the TTAB and held that a picture is not a mandatory requirement for a Web-site-based specimen of use. The Federal Circuit further clarified that "the test for an acceptable Web-site-based specimen, just as any other specimen, is simply that it must in some way evince that the mark is 'associated' with the goods and serves as an indicator of source."[15]

---

13. *Id.* at 1670.
14. 590 F.3d 1282 (Fed. Cir. 2009).
15. *Id.* at 1288.

Michael Sones filed an intent-to-use trademark application with the USPTO for the mark ONE NATION UNDER GOD for use in connection with charity bracelets. The application was allowed in August 2006. Within six months of the allowance, Sones filed a statement of use supported by a specimen that consisted of printouts of two Internet pages. Although the Internet pages displayed "shopping cart" functionality with respect to online ordering, the pages did not include pictures of the charity bracelets offered by Sones, as he was not in possession of pictures at the time the statement of use was submitted. The USPTO rejected the statement of use, citing that the specimen did not show a picture of the goods in close proximity to the mark. In July 2007, Sones filed a response to the rejection, but his arguments were not accepted, and the USPTO issued a final office action. In particular, the USPTO emphasized that a Web page display is "acceptable 'only if' it includes 'a picture of the relevant good.'"[16] Sones appealed the final rejection to the TTAB, which affirmed the examiner's objections to Sones' statement of use. Accordingly, Sones appealed the TTAB's decision to the Federal Circuit.

In reversing the TTAB, the Federal Circuit refused to follow the TTAB's prior bright-line rule that would require every Web-site-based specimen of use to contain a picture. The Federal Circuit noted that, by requiring the submission of a picture, the examining attorney and the TTAB improperly applied a *Trademark Manual of Examining Procedure* (*TMEP*) rule concerning the submission of catalog specimens to the Web page specimen as set forth in Sones' application. Further, the Federal Circuit declined to read the "picture" requirement into existing district court case law that was submitted to bolster the USPTO's and TTAB's reasoning with respect to a Web-site-based specimen of use. Specifically, the appellate court examined *Lands' End, Inc. v. Manback,*[17] which the TTAB used to support its decision, and found that this decision did not require a picture of the goods. Rather, the Federal Circuit noted that the *Lands' End* decision hinged on an analysis of "whether the customer had 'the opportunity to look to the displayed mark as a means of identifying and distinguishing the source of goods.'"[18]

Similarly, the Federal Circuit found no support for the USPTO's and TTAB's reasoning in trademark statute or policy. The appellate court was careful to clarify that "it is well established . . . that the purpose of a trademark is to distinguish goods and to identify the source of goods."[19] The Federal Circuit reasoned that to show use in commerce as required by the Lanham Act, the mark must be "placed in any manner on the goods or their containers or the displays associated therewith or on the tags or labels affixed thereto."[20] Accordingly, because the Lanham Act does not specify a particular requirement to demonstrate source of origin for display specimens, the mark need only be "associated" with the goods.

The Federal Circuit was also unable to differentiate Internet businesses from "brick-and-mortar" stores that do not need to submit pictures in connection with specimens of use where use of the mark on commercial packaging is acceptable. Specifically, the

---

16. *Id.* at 1285 (citing U.S. Trademark Appl. Serial No. 78/717,427, Final Office Action, at 2–3 (July 23, 2007)).

17. 797 F. Supp. 511 (E.D. Va. 1992).

18. *In re Sones*, 590 F.3d at 1287 (quoting *Lands' End*, 797 F. Supp. at 514 (noting that "a crucial factor in the analysis is if the use of an alleged mark is at a point of sale location.")).

19. *Id.* (citing *In* re Int'l Flavors & Fragrances Inc., 183 F.3d 1361, 1367 (Fed. Cir. 1999)).

20. *Id.* (quoting 15 U.S.C. § 1127).

appellate court noted that even the USPTO recognizes that "[i]n effect, the website is an electronic retail store, and the web page is a shelf-talker or banner which encourages the consumer to buy the product. A consumer using the link on the Web page to purchase the goods is the equivalent of a consumer seeing a shelf-talker and taking the item to the cashier in a store to purchase it."[21] Accordingly, the Federal Circuit held that "a picture is not a mandatory requirement for a Web-site-based specimen of use, and that the test for an acceptable Web-site-based specimen, just as any other specimen, is simply that it must in some way evince that the mark is 'associated' with the goods and serves as an indicator of source."[22] The appellate court disapproved of the bright-line rule that the TTAB applied and explained in the reversal that a picture is not the only way to show association between a mark and the goods.

On remand, the Federal Circuit charged the USPTO with the role of determining if Sones' specimen associates the mark sufficiently with the offered charity bracelets so as to identify and distinguish the goods. The appellate court further offered guidance with respect to a review of the submitted evidence and determined that relevant factors for consideration included the use of the "TM" designation, whether Sones' Web pages have a "point of sale nature," and whether the "actual features or inherent characteristics of the goods are recognizable from the textual description."[23]

Web Page Printouts Insufficient as Specimens of Use for Application Covering Goods Where Printouts Did Not Include Means to Order Goods

In *In re Quantum Foods Inc.*,[24] the TTAB affirmed the examining attorney's refusal to register the applicant's mark, finding that a Web page printout was not acceptable as a specimen of use for a mark covering goods. The mark at issue was PROVIDING PROTEIN AND MENU SOLUTIONS for goods described as precooked entrees.

After the applicant's intent-to-use application had already been published for opposition, and no opposition had been filed, the examining attorney found both the original and substitute specimens submitted in connection with applicant's statement of use to be unacceptable. The applicant then appealed the final refusal.

The substitute specimen was a printed copy of a Web page that showed the mark in close proximity to pictures of various cooked entrees. The Web page also described services available from the host. With its appeal brief, the applicant submitted a further printed Web page, along with an explanation that: (1) if a viewer placed the cursor over "for foodservice" on the Web page, the viewer would be presented with a menu which included "contact us"; and (2) choosing "contact us" caused display of a Web page which included both an e-mail address and a toll-free telephone number for the applicant's customer service department. The TTAB found this submission and explanation to be untimely and did not consider this argument in reaching a decision on appeal.

The TTAB found that the specimen of record failed to meet the three-part criteria required for an acceptable Web page specimen of use for a trademark (as opposed to a

---

21. *Id.* at 1288 (quoting TRADEMARK MANUAL OF EXAMINING PROCEDURE § 904.03(i)).
22. *Id.*
23. *Id.* at 1288–89.
24. 94 U.S.P.Q.2d (BNA) 1375 (TTAB 2010).

service mark). For a Web page specimen to be acceptable for a trademark, the TTAB requires: (1) display of the mark; (2) in close proximity to a picture of the goods; and (3) with a visible means for ordering those goods. Only the last element was at issue in this case.

In affirming the refusal, the TTAB explained that, although the applicant's Web page might allow one to order goods, that ability was not clear from the content of the printed Web page specimen. The Web page did not instruct one to choose "for foodservice" and then "contact us" if one wished to place an order for goods. It did not provide an order form, pricing information, or any material indicating that one could order goods by using the "contact us" link. Although the Web page could be viewed as encouraging the purchase of goods, that did not distinguish it from mere advertising material, which is not acceptable as a specimen of use for a trademark.

The TTAB explained that all advertising encourages recipients to order the advertised goods, but a mere advertisement is not an acceptable specimen of use. Web pages and catalogs have been accepted as specimens only to the extent they function in the same manner as shelf-talkers and banners do in brick-and-mortar stores. In particular, the TTAB clarified that, if a consumer visiting a Web page is unable to order the goods promoted, then the use of the proposed mark in connection with a depiction of those goods on the Web page is mere advertising and is not evidence of use of a trademark in connection with goods.

Proper Use

Settlement Agreement Language Held to Bar Claims of Trademark Infringement and Limitations on Geographic Scope of Use for Mark

In *Great Clips, Inc. v. Hair Cuttery of Greater Boston, LLC*,[25] the First Circuit affirmed the district court's grant of declaratory judgment of no trademark infringement. The court also held that the settlement agreement between Great Clips, Inc. and the defendant's predecessor-in-interest, Dalan Corporation, entitled Great Clips to use its federally registered mark without geographic limitation. The court rejected Hair Cuttery's and Great Cuts' counterclaims for damages and injunctive relief.

Great Clips, owner of the registered mark GREAT CLIPS for hair cutting and styling services, and Dalan entered into a settlement agreement after Dalan sought to register the mark GREAT CUTS for hair care services and products with the USPTO. The settlement agreement stipulated that each party released the other from "any and all claims that arise or may arise from the application and registration of its own respective mark(s)."[26]

Nineteen years after the agreement and sometime after Dalan had transferred its rights and interest in the GREAT CUTS mark to Hair Cuttery and Great Cuts, Great Clips entered into agreements to open franchises in Massachusetts and New Hampshire under the GREAT CLIPS mark. Thereafter, Hair Cuttery informed Great Clips of its intention to prevent Great Clips from using the GREAT CLIPS mark in New England, as continued use would allegedly impair Hair Cuttery's use of the GREAT CUTS mark. In response, Great Clips filed

---

25. 591 F.3d 32 (1st Cir. 2010).
26. *Id.* at 36.

a lawsuit seeking a declaration that it was entitled to use the GREAT CLIPS mark in the United States, that use in New England would not infringe upon any rights of Hair Cuttery and Great Cuts, and that the settlement agreement precluded Hair Cuttery and Great Cuts from asserting claims against Great Clips for infringement.

Hair Cuttery and Great Cuts attempted to limit the settlement agreement to claims arising from the application and registration proceedings at the USPTO. The court rejected this interpretation of the agreement, which indicated that the parties released each other from "any and all claims that arise from the application and registration."[27] The court determined that the settlement agreement precluded Hair Cuttery and Great Cuts from bringing infringement claims against Great Clips because "trademarks are registered in order to be used and the substance of the agreement was that each side conceded the other's registration and anticipated use of the registered marks."[28]

Other provisions in the agreement also led the court to apply the agreement to disputes outside the application and registration process. For example, Dalan agreed it would not use the phrase "great cuts for hair," preserving Great Clips' right to file a claim against Dalan. This provision, prohibiting Dalan's use of the GREAT CUTS FOR HAIR mark, contradicted the argument by Hair Cuttery and Great Cuts that the agreement was limited to the application and registration process. The agreement further preserved each party's right to bring claims against third parties for use of the other's mark. The court thus concluded that, absent clear language or evidence to the contrary, this prohibition logically applied to the parties' use claims against each other.

Therefore, the court affirmed Great Clips' right to use the mark GREAT CUTS in the United States, including in New England. The court also affirmed that the settlement agreement between the parties precluded Hair Cuttery and Great Cuts from asserting claims of infringement.

---

27. *Id.* at 35–36.
28. *Id.* at 36.

CHAPTER 11

TRADEMARK ACTIONS AND DEFENSES

Courts and the TTAB considered a wide array of trademark issues, including trademark "use," fair use, abandonment, fraud, the likelihood-of-confusion factors, contributory infringement, dilution, and various procedural issues arising in trademark actions. Some decisions simply expanded on well-settled principles, while others provided new twists.

A few courts, considering the bounds of trademark "use" in various contexts, determined that a plaintiff had not established use sufficient to support its action. In *Howard Johnson International, Inc. v. Vraj Brig, LLC*, the U.S. District Court for the District of New Jersey held that the "use" requirement of the Lanham Act was not satisfied where the defendant merely failed to remove the plaintiff's marks from a billboard advertising a decommissioned hotel.

In considering the "use in commerce" requirement of the Lanham Act in *Sensient Technologies Corp. v. SensoryEffects Flavor Co.*, the Eighth Circuit affirmed a summary judgment finding of no liability where the goods at issue were never sold or transported in commerce and therefore never were "used in commerce" as required for a Lanham Act infringement claim.

In *Pfizer Inc. v. Sachs,* the Southern District of New York determined that a plaintiff had established use sufficient to support a trademark action. In that case, the court held that the defendant's use of the plaintiff's VIAGRA and VIVA VIAGRA trademarks in promotional activities constituted use in commerce, trademark infringement, and dilution by tarnishment.

Use of a trademark under a statute other than the Lanham Act also received attention. In *Frayne v. Chicago 2016*, the U.S. District Court for the Northern District of Illinois denied Chicago 2016's and the U.S. Olympic Committee's (USOC) motion for summary judgment on its Ted Stevens Olympic and Amateur Sports Act (Stevens Act) and Anticybersquatting Consumer Protection Act claims, brought as a result of Frayne's operation of the www.chicago2016.com Web site. The court held that there was a question of fact as to whether Frayne "used" a trademark, in this case the Internet domain name, for commercial purposes, as required by the Act. Furthermore, the court determined that CHICAGO 2016 was not a trademark that automatically fell under the protections of the Stevens Act, given that there was no immediate false representation of association with the USOC.

In another decision, the nature of use dictated whether a mark was entitled to trademark protection. In *Autodesk, Inc. v. Dassault Systems SolidWorks Corp.,* the U.S. District Court for the Northern District of California granted Autodesk's motion for summary judgment and held that a "DWG" (drawing) file extension, when used as a word mark and not as a file extension, was not considered to be functional or generic.

On a related topic, courts also considered whether particular trademark uses constituted fair use. In *Toyota Motor Sales, U.S.A., Inc. v. Tabari*, the Ninth Circuit vacated the district court's permanent injunction as overbroad where the court failed to apply the nominative fair use test and placed the burden of showing no fair use on the plaintiff. The

Ninth Circuit declined to rule that use of a trademark in a domain name is presumptively not nominative fair use and remanded the case for further consideration of an appropriately narrowed remedy.

In *Hensley Manufacturing, Inc. v. ProPride, Inc.*, the Sixth Circuit held that a trademark owner's complaint should be dismissed where the allegations that the defendants' use of the marks at issue was likely to cause confusion did not satisfy the heightened pleading standard of *Ashcroft v. Iqbal*. In its decision, the court held that the defendant did not use the Hensley name as a trademark, and that the defendant's use of the Hensley name in its advertisements (to identify the inventor's name) constituted fair use.

Conversely, in *Yeager v. Cingular Wireless LLC*, the U.S. District Court for the Eastern District of California rejected the defendant's arguments in its summary judgment motion that use of a famous test pilot's name in an advertisement was protected by the First Amendment and constituted a nominative fair use.

Courts also considered cases involving the issue of abandonment. In *Crash Dummy Movie, LLC v. Mattel, Inc.*, the Federal Circuit held that an assignee's recordation of its assignment, negotiations for a possible retail contract for sale of products, and research and development activities were sufficient to overcome a statutory presumption of abandonment. On the same topic, the U.S. District Court for the Northern District of Illinois in *Metropolitan Life Insurance Company v. O'M Associates, LLC* found that use of a mark by a third party after abandonment by the prior mark owner does not constitute infringement under the Lanham Act.

The TTAB considered a few cases regarding fraud and deception on the USPTO. In *Asian & Western Classics B.V. v. Selkow*, the TTAB held that intent is a specific element of a fraud claim that must be pleaded with the same degree of particularity as is required of all other elements of fraud; therefore, an allegation that a trademark registrant "knew or should have known" that a statement was false was insufficient to state a claim for fraud on the USPTO. Similarly, in *DaimlerChrysler Corp. v. American Motors Corp.*, the TTAB explained that intent to deceive the USPTO in obtaining a trademark must be proved by clear and convincing direct, indirect, or circumstantial evidence.

District courts also weighed in on the issue of fraud and deception in the USPTO. In *Salu, Inc. v. Original Skin Store*, the U.S. District Court for the Eastern District of California denied the defendant's motion for summary judgment on a fraud claim where the defendant failed to meet the "heavy burden" of establishing the plaintiff's intent to deceive the USPTO. A statement of misrepresentation, alone, was not enough to meet the standard.

Also discussing fraud, in *City of New York v. Tavern on the Green, L.P.*, the U.S. District Court for the Southern District of New York found that the city of New York had prior rights to the mark TAVERN ON THE GREEN for restaurant services and cancelled an incontestable registration held by a licensee because the registration was fraudulently obtained.

Courts also explicitly addressed the role of the likelihood-of-confusion factors. In *Lapine v. Seinfeld*, the Second Circuit affirmed summary judgment in favor of the defendants as to both likelihood of confusion and likelihood of dilution on the sole ground that the marks at issue were extremely dissimilar, without considering the other likelihood-of-confusion or likelihood-of-dilution factors. In *Sabinsa Corp. v. Creative Compounds, LLC*, the Third Circuit reversed the district court's finding of likelihood of confusion following a bench trial, where the district court applied only three out of ten relevant factors and committed clear error on those three factors. Because any reasonable juror would have found likelihood of confusion, the court determined that remand to weigh the relevant factors was unnecessary.

Two cases involving constitutional issues relating to the U.S. Constitution and to the Pennsylvania Constitution produced noteworthy decisions. In *General Conference Corp. of Seventh-Day Adventists v. McGill*, the Sixth Circuit held that applying trademark law to a dispute between two church groups did not violate the First Amendment or the Religious Freedom Restoration Act. The court also found that the defendant failed to establish, for purposes of a summary judgment response, that the term "seventh-day adventist" was a generic reference to a particular religion.

In *Commonwealth v. Omar*, the Supreme Court of Pennsylvania held that the Commonwealth's criminal trademark counterfeiting law was unconstitutionally overbroad and violated the First Amendment to the U.S. Constitution. The Supreme Court of Pennsylvania construed the law to prohibit the use of an unauthorized reproduction of terms or words on items to identify a person's goods or services, which covered a considerable amount of speech protected by the First Amendment. Thus, the court held that sections 4119(a) and (i) unconstitutionally prohibited protected speech, including the use of words on a sign praising or protesting against any entity whose name consisted of a protected trademark.

The issue of contributory infringement also was the topic of a few cases. In *Tiffany (NJ) Inc. v. eBay Inc.*, the Second Circuit concluded that, notwithstanding the presence of counterfeit Tiffany merchandise among products sold on eBay, eBay did not directly or contributorily infringe Tiffany's trademark and did not dilute the distinctiveness of or tarnish the TIFFANY mark. With respect to false advertising, the court concluded that eBay's advertisements were not literally false, but it also found that the district court failed to support properly its conclusion that the advertisements were not misleading.

In *Georgia-Pacific Consumer Products LP v. von Drehle Corp.*, the Fourth Circuit vacated the grant of summary judgment where there existed issues of fact concerning contributory infringement, arising from possible confusion among the nonpurchasing public.

Motions to dismiss based on a lack of standing also received some attention. In *Fiat Group Automobiles S.p.A. v. ISM Inc.*, the TTAB granted the applicant's motion to dismiss for failure to state a claim, holding the opposer had no standing to bring a dilution claim in the absence of use or an allegation of use of its mark in the United States.

In *United Food Imports, Inc. v. Baroody Imports, Inc.*, the U.S. District Court for the District of New Jersey applied the prudential standing doctrine in granting the plaintiff's motion to dismiss the defendants' counterclaims where the counterclaims were premised on the superior rights of a third party. However, the district court found that the counterclaims could be asserted instead as affirmative defenses where the defendants could show they were in privity with the third party holding the superior trademark rights, such that the general rule disfavoring *jus tertii* defenses did not apply.

Some cases did not even make it beyond a finding that the court lacked personal jurisdiction. In *uBID, Inc. v. GoDaddy Group, Inc.*, the U.S. District Court for the Northern District of Illinois dismissed a claim brought under the Anticybersquatting Consumer Protection Act by Illinois-based online auction company uBID against the Arizona-based Internet domain name registrar GoDaddy, after declining to exercise personal jurisdiction over GoDaddy. The court found that GoDaddy's Illinois advertising and sales were insufficient to establish general jurisdiction, that GoDaddy was not subject to specific jurisdiction because its contact with Illinois customers was automated "unilateral activity" initiated by the customers, and that the "effects test" was inapplicable because there was no evidence that GoDaddy expressly aimed its conduct at Illinois.

In *Love v. Sanctuary Records Group, Ltd.*, the Ninth Circuit held that California's right of publicity law and the Lanham Act did not apply extraterritorially to actions occurring outside of the United States, and that there was no personal jurisdiction where the plaintiff had no losses in the United States related to the alleged actions.

Dilution also was a topic of interest in some notable cases. In *Starbucks Corp. v. Wolfe's Borough Coffee, Inc.*, the Second Circuit held that substantial similarity between competing marks is not required in order to prove a claim for dilution by blurring, but rejected a tarnishment claim where the plaintiff's survey evidence failed to show that the defendant's mark affected the positive impression of the plaintiff's mark. The court also rejected the defendant's parody defense because the defendant used its mark as an identification of source for its own goods.

In *Visa International Service Association v. JSL Corp.*, the Ninth Circuit held that dilution by blurring occurs when a party uses a common word that has become a famous and distinctive trademark for a new trademark meaning other than the word's dictionary definition. Also addressing dilution by blurring, in *National Pork Board v. Supreme Lobster & Seafood Co.*, the TTAB considered an opposition to the mark THE OTHER RED MEAT (referring to salmon) by the owner of the mark THE OTHER WHITE MEAT (referring to pork). The TTAB sustained the opposition on the basis of likelihood of dilution by blurring without reaching the opposer's alternative ground, likelihood of confusion.

Many other issues arose in trademark actions as well. In *Flagstar Bank, FSB v. Freestar Bank, N.A.*, the U.S. District Court for the Central District of Illinois held that the testimony of a proffered expert on "social linguistics and rhetorical criticism" was unreliable and inadmissible because it was not presented with any "proposal, theory, or technique" supporting its conclusions. Additionally, the court held that no genuine issue of material fact existed with respect to likelihood of confusion and found in favor of the defendant on summary judgment.

In *Express Scripts, Inc. v. Intel Corp.*, the U.S. District Court for the Eastern District of Missouri held actual and ongoing use of an allegedly infringing mark, coupled with a letter charging infringement, sufficient to support a declaratory judgment action.

Finally, a few cases decided at the summary judgment phase hinged on the evidence of disputed material facts. In *MetroPCS Wireless, Inc. v. Virgin Mobile USA, L.P.*, the U.S. District Court for the Northern District of Texas denied the defendant's motion for summary judgment on trademark infringement and dilution claims, holding that these claims largely centered on whether the plaintiff's reconfigured mobile handsets created a "new product," which presented a genuine issue of material fact.

In *Vantage, Inc. v. Vantage Travel Services, Inc.*, the U.S. District Court for the District of South Carolina denied the defendant's motion for summary judgment on the grounds of: (1) likelihood of confusion, finding factual disputes that were well-suited for a jury; and (2) damages, finding that the plaintiff introduced sufficient circumstantial evidence of a drop in business. However, the court granted the motion with respect to the common law trademark infringement claim because the plaintiff conceded that it was not the owner of the mark.

INFRINGEMENT

Eighth Circuit Analyzes "Use in Commerce" Requirement for Infringement Actions

In *Sensient Technologies Corp. v. SensoryEffects Flavor Co.,*[1] the Eighth Circuit affirmed a summary judgment, finding no liability where the goods at issue were never sold or transported in commerce and therefore were never "used in commerce" as required for a Lanham Act infringement claim. The court discussed at length whether the section 45 definition of "use in commerce" is applicable to infringement claims, but then assumed without holding that the definition applied because the issue was not properly raised on appeal.

Sensient sells flavor delivery systems. It has continuously used the trade name and mark SENSIENT FLAVORS, which has appeared in its advertising, marketing, and other materials since 2006.

A former employee of a Sensient sister company started his own business, which he called Performance Chemicals and Ingredients (PCI). PCI later purchased the assets of a flavor delivery systems company that owned the mark SENSORYEFFECTS and a registration of that mark. After further expansion in the flavor systems business, PCI changed its name to SensoryFlavors, building on the SENSORYEFFECTS trademark that it had acquired and was already using.

After changing its name to SensoryFlavors, the company sent an announcement to contacts in the food ingredients industry featuring the new name and mark. It also sent a media release and gave two presentations, all using the SensoryFlavors name and mark. However, SensoryFlavors made no sales under its new mark, no packages were sent bearing labels with the new mark, and no goods were transported under the new mark. SensoryFlavors did begin construction of a Web site at the domain name www .sensoryflavors.com, but it did not complete construction of the site.

Sensient filed suit against SensoryFlavors, asserting various claims, including trademark infringement under federal and Missouri law. SensoryFlavors changed its name once again to SensoryEffects Flavor Company as a result of the suit.

The district court granted summary judgment in favor of SensoryEffects and dismissed the case. The court declined to enter a permanent injunction concerning use of SensoryEffects' former mark—SENSORYFLAVORS—because it concluded that mark was never "used in commerce," preventing any finding of liability. With respect to the SENSORYEFFECTS mark, the district court concluded that confusion was not likely. The Eighth Circuit affirmed summary judgment as to both the SENSORYFLAVORS and SENSORYEFFECTS marks.

With respect to the SENSORYFLAVORS mark, the court focused on two issues relating to use in commerce: (1) whether section 45 of the Lanham Act, which defines "use in commerce," is applicable to infringement claims, or whether it applies only to registration of a mark; and (2) assuming that the section 45 definition is applicable, whether the use of SENSORYFLAVORS mark satisfied that definition.

Sensient argued against application of the section 45 definition. The Eighth Circuit observed that the Lanham Act's provisions for infringement of both registered and unregistered marks—section 32 and 43(a)—require, among other things, that the defendant use its mark in commerce. However, use in commerce is not defined in these provisions.

---

1.   613 F.3d 754 (8th Cir. 2010).

The only Lanham Act definition of "use in commerce" appears in section 45. A mark is used in commerce, with respect to goods (as opposed to services), when it is placed on the goods or their containers, on displays associated with the goods, on tags or labels affixed to the goods, or on documents associated with the goods if placement is impracticable, and when the goods are sold or transported in commerce.

A 1988 amendment to section 45 added a preliminary sentence immediately before this definition, providing that "use in commerce" means the bona fide use of a mark in the ordinary course of trade, "and not [use] made merely to reserve a right in a mark." This additional language raised the question of whether section 45 is intended to limit the subsequent definition to use in commerce solely for purposes of registration.

The Eighth Circuit recounted an extensive discussion of this issue from the Second Circuit's *Rescuecom*[2] decision. The Second Circuit envisioned two possible interpretations of section 45 in infringement cases. Under the first, no aspect of the section 45 definition would apply in infringement cases. Under the second (and more preferable, according to the Second Circuit), all of the section 45 definition would apply in infringement cases, except for the first clause relating to bona fide uses. The Second Circuit urged Congress to clarify the issue.

Although discussing this issue at length, the Eighth Circuit ultimately expressed no view as to whether section 45's use in commerce definition applies to infringement cases. Noting that Sensient did not raise this issue until oral argument, the court assumed, without holding, that section 45 does apply to infringement cases and then proceeded to determine whether SensoryEffects' use of the SENSORYFLAVORS mark met the section 45 definition of "use in commerce."

The Eighth Circuit observed that goods must have been sold or transported in commerce, among other requirements, in order to have been "used in commerce" under the section 45 definition. In this case, SensoryEffects' efforts to advertise and market its goods through an announcement, a press release, two customer presentations, and a Web site did not rise to the level of use in commerce as defined in section 45.

Maintaining a Billboard Displaying a Registered Trademark Is Not "Use"

In *Howard Johnson International, Inc. v. Vraj Brig, LLC,*[3] the U.S. District Court for the District of New Jersey held that the "use" requirement of the Lanham Act did not extend to a situation where a defendant merely displays a registered mark but does not use the subject mark in connection with the offer or provision of any goods or services.

Plaintiff Howard Johnson International, Inc. (HJI) operated a lodging facility franchise system and licensed individual franchisees to use HOWARD JOHNSON registered trademarks. In 2001, HJI and Defendant Vraj Brig, LLC entered into a fifteen-year license agreement whereby Vraj Brig would utilize the HOWARD JOHNSON trademarks and pay HJI certain recurring fees. Because Vraj Brig did not own the facility, Northeast Hospitality Services, LLC (Northeast), a nonparty to the action, leased the facility from Vraj Brig and property owner Peter Tucci and contracted with Vraj Brig to manage the facility as a hotel. Under the terms of the license agreement, HJI could terminate the agreement if Vraj Brig stopped operating the hotel as a HJI guest lodge. According to the

---

2.   Rescuecom Corp. v. Google, Inc., 562 F.3d 123 (2d Cir. 2009).
3.   Civ. No. 08-1466, 2010 WL 215381 (D.N.J. Jan. 14, 2010).

agreement, Vraj Brig would cease use of all HOWARD JOHNSON trademarks upon termination.

By 2006, the facility was decommissioned as a hotel and was severely vandalized. In August 2006, Tucci commenced a summary dispossess action against Northeast and took physical possession of the hotel. As a result, Vraj Brig ceased operating the property, and HJI terminated the license agreement. Tucci refused to remove a billboard on the facility bearing the name "Howard Johnson" that was clearly visible from the local highway. Because Tucci did not operate the facility as a guest lodge, HJI filed a lawsuit against Vraj Brig and Tucci alleging, inter alia, violations of sections 32(1) and 43(a) of the Lanham Act. Both HJI and Tucci brought summary judgment motions with respect to the Lanham Act claims.

In granting summary judgment in favor of Tucci on the issue of whether Tucci made "use of the mark to identify goods or services," the court first turned to the express language of Sections 32(1) and 43(a) of the Lanham Act, which require "'use' [of] a protected mark 'in connection' with the offer or provision of 'goods or services.'"[4] The court concluded that the Lanham Act did not apply to the case because Tucci did not use the mark, nor was there a connection to goods or services as required by the statute. In reaching this conclusion, the court noted that, although relatively few courts have faced this issue, cases on point illustrate that, even where confusion exists with respect to associations with goods or services, a "defendant must take some affirmative action to create or enhance confusion . . . ."[5] Further, the district court cited to instances where courts held that use of registered marks in the course of criticizing the owner's goods or services was not actionable conduct under the Lanham Act's "use" requirement because such speech bears no connection to the provision of goods or services. The court clarified its holding by stating that the "use" provision "only prohibits the affirmative use of a protected mark, and only when that use is in connection with the defendant's offer or provision of goods or services."[6] Accordingly, the court held in favor of Tucci, finding no evidence in the record that Tucci did anything other than passively allow the billboard with the HOWARD JOHNSON marks to remain on the property, or that he ever provided goods or services associated with the lodging facility.

With respect to the dilution claim under section 43 of the Act, the court reasoned that HJI's claim for summary judgment should also be dismissed because this section requires a plaintiff to show "use" of the mark "in commerce." For the same reasons identified in the trademark infringement context, the court held that dilution claims also require a showing that the defendant used the mark in offering or providing its goods or services.

AutoCad Company's "DWG" Word Mark Survives Summary Judgment Validity Challenge When Not Used as File Extension and Not Considered Functional or Generic

In *Autodesk, Inc. v. Dassault Systems SolidWorks Corp.,*[7] the U.S. District Court for the Northern District of California granted Plaintiff Autodesk's motion for summary judg-

---

4.   *Id*. at *5 (citing 15 U.S.C. §§ 1114(1), 1125(a)).

5.   *Id*. at *6 (citing Holiday Inns, Inc. v. 800 Reservation, Inc., 86 F.3d 619 (6th Cir.1996); AG v. Bloom, 315 F.3d 932, 939 (8th Cir. 2003)).

6.   *Id*. at * 7.

7.   685 F. Supp. 2d 1001 (N.D. Cal. 2009).

ment and held that a "DWG" (drawing) file extension, when used as a word mark and not as a file extension, was not functional and/or generic.

Plaintiff Autodesk is a leader in the field of computer-aided design (CAD) software that utilizes AutoCAD brand software to create detailed architectural and engineering drawings. Autodesk's AutoCAD software was introduced in 1982 and was designed to store files in the DWG file format with a ".dwg" extension. A RealDWG software library was available as of 1996. Autodesk claimed that it had used DWG as an unregistered word mark since the introduction of the software in 1982 and that it had also utilized a logo with DWG on its Web site, product packaging, and computer file icons. Moreover, Autodesk claimed that it promoted its business with the tagline "Experience It Before It's Real" as early as 2006. Autodesk also utilized an orange frame outline on its "Inventor" product's software DVD cases and marketing materials since 2007.

Defendant Dassault is a competitor in the field of CAD software that incorporates a reverse-engineered format of Autodesk's DWG file platform. Dassualt released programs named DWGeditor, DWGgateway, DWGseries, DWGviewer, and DWGnavigator, and utilized these names in the domain names of its various Web sites. Subsequently, Dassault obtained federal trademark registrations for the DWGeditor programs, which Autodesk petitioned to cancel, and the DWGgateway programs, which Autodesk opposed. In addition, Dassault utilized the AutoCAD word mark on its Web sites and marketing materials and featured a design that Autodesk alleged combined the "real" element of the REALDWG mark and "Experience It Before It's Real" tagline with Autodesk Inventor's trade dress.

Autodesk sued for, inter alia, trademark infringement, unfair competition, false designation of origin, trademark cancellation, and false advertising under federal law. In response, Dassault filed counterclaims for false advertising and for declaratory judgment of the ownership of the DWG mark. The parties each filed summary judgment motions that addressed, the following issues: (1) whether the DWG word mark was entitled to trademark protection or whether it was functional and/or generic; (2) whether Autodesk's real/orange frame design was protectable trade dress; (3) whether Dassault's use of the Autodesk marks qualified as nominative fair use; and (4) whether Autodesk's false advertising claims failed as a matter of law.

With respect to the validity of the DWG mark, the court held in favor of Autodesk, finding that the word mark was not generic or functional. Given that DWG was unregistered, the court noted that Autodesk bore the burden of proving nongenericness. Autodesk therefore argued that consumers associated DWG with Autodesk, and the primary significance of the mark was to describe the producer and not the product itself. The court denied Dassualt's summary judgment motion on the issue of genericness because of multiple genuine issues of material fact related to the primary purpose of the mark.

The court also granted summary judgment in favor of Autodesk and rejected Dassault's functionality defense. In reaching this conclusion, the court recognized that functionality generally does not apply to word marks because it is unclear how a word mark would be essential to an article's purpose or use, or how a word mark would affect an article's cost or quality. Although the court noted that the use of .dwg as a file extension is functional, Autodesk had agreed to disavow any ownership of "any even arguably functional use of DWG," including its desired use it as a file extension.[8] The court was ultimately persuaded that Autodesk claimed no monopoly over the .dwg extension and that the word mark was

---

8. *Id.* at 1009.

not functional. Finally, following Ninth Circuit precedent, the court refused Dassault's argument that Autodesk was not the senior user of the mark because "a third party's prior use of a trademark is not a defense in an infringement action."[9]

The court ruled in favor of Autodesk on Dassualt's claim of nominative fair use as a defense to trademark infringement. Utilizing the Ninth Circuit's three-pronged test from *New Kids on the Block v. News America Publishing, Inc.*,[10] the court held that, although the first prong was satisfied by Dassault, there were material issues concerning whether Dassault had used more of the marks than necessary to identify Autodesk's products and "whether such use suggests sponsorship or endorsement" under Ninth Circuit precedent.[11]

On the issue of protectable trade dress, Dassault's motion for summary judgment was granted. Here, Autodesk argued that the combination of an orange frame design, "Experience It Before It's Real" slogan, and the REALDWG trademark constituted protectable trade dress. The court refused to accept that an ordinary shape such as a rectangle could be inherently distinctive, even when combined with the color orange. To the contrary, Autodesk's evidence illustrated that it had used a rectangular frame in different colors and proportions. Additionally, the court held that Autodesk's advertising does not feature the orange frame alone or in combination with the "real" element in any way that could be used to establish secondary meaning. The court further found it significant that Autodesk did not have survey evidence of secondary meaning, nor did it possess sufficient evidence of intentional copying.

With respect to Autodesk's false advertising claim, Autodesk alleged that Dassualt had falsely advertised in the following statements: (1) "DWGgateway is the first free data translation plug-in that lets AutoCAD users work easily with DWG files created by any version of AutoCAD software;" (2) "save DWG files to any version of AutoCAD software;" and (3) "open, edit, and share DWG data more effectively with others."[12] In response, Dassault contested the falsity and materiality of the statements and claimed that the first and third statements were not actionable due to puffery. The court agreed with Dassault with regard to statement three, but concluded that there were triable issues of fact on the falsity and materiality of statements one and two and denied Dassault's motion for summary judgment.

Finally, Dassault asserted a counterclaim for false advertising against AutoDesk regarding its cartoon advertisement, which included language related to the general superiority of AutoDesk's products. The court determined that general superiority claims, rather than specific verifiable allegations of what risks might occur with a competitor's products, were nonactionable puffery.

---

9. *Id.* at 1011 (citing Comm. for Idaho's High Desert v. Yost, 92 F.3d 814, 820 (9th Cir. 1996)).

10. 971 F.2d 302, 306 (9th Cir. 1992) (explaining that, to prevail on a defense of nominative fair use, a defendant must prove the following three elements: "First, the product or service in question must be one not readily identifiable without use of the trademark; second, only so much of the mark or marks may be used as is reasonably necessary to identify the product or service; and third, the user must do nothing that would, in conjunction with the mark, suggest sponsorship or endorsement by the trademark holder").

11. *Autodesk*, 685 F. Supp. 2d at 1017.

12. *Id.*

Likelihood of Confusion

Dissimilarity of Marks Is Dispositive in a Trademark Infringement Matter

In *Lapine v. Seinfeld,*[13] the Second Circuit affirmed summary judgment for the defendants on claims of copyright infringement, trademark infringement, and trademark dilution. The case concerned two cookbooks recommending use of vegetable purees as a source of nutrition in children's food. In rejecting all three claims, the court rested its decision on the major dissimilarities between the books.

The claims for trademark infringement and dilution were based on Lapine's assertion of common law trademark rights in the title and cover of the book at issue. Lapine's book was titled *The Sneaky Chef: Simple Strategies for Hiding Healthy Foods in Kids' Favorite Meals*, with cover art consisting of a "stylized image of a female chef winking and 'shushing' while concealing carrots behind her back."[14] The defendants' book was titled *Deceptively Delicious: Simple Secrets To Get Your Kids Eating Good Food*, with cover art consisting of "realistic depictions of (a) a winking woman standing near carrots and holding a plate of brownies and (b) the same woman 'shushing' in a head-and-shoulder cameo."[15]

The Second Circuit rejected Lapine's argument that a district court must apply all of the standard likelihood-of-confusion factors before granting summary judgment, instead agreeing with the district court that, in this case, the similarity of the marks factor was dispositive. The court agreed with the district court that the colorfulness, realism, and detail of the artwork of the defendants' book was too dissimilar to the stylized, simplified, black-and-white rendering of Lapine's artwork for likelihood of confusion to exist. Any similarity between the trade dresses was held to "lack[] the uniqueness that would cause a consumer to disregard all differences between [the] marks."[16] Finally, the court found that the defendants' use of the famous "Seinfeld" name on their book weighed against any likelihood of that book being confused with Lapine's book. This lack of similarity between the marks also denied Lapine the benefit of a presumption of likelihood of confusion arising from allegedly intentional copying.

The dilution cause of action was also fatally undermined by the dissimilarity of the two parties' purported marks.

Addressing the copyright claim, the court held that the concepts of stockpiling vegetable purees and of using the purees in children's food in ways not apparent to the children were merely ideas and, therefore, uncopyrightable. The court applied the more discerning ordinary-observer test to conduct an independent consideration of whether the books were substantially similar, finding the books to be quite different in overall concept and feel. For example, one of the books included long discussions of child behavior and parenting; the other did not. Likewise, one book assumed knowledge of cooking and presented complex recipes; the other provided more basic instructions for simpler preparations. Moreover, the court characterized the similarities between the books as uncopyrightable ideas or stock elements.

---

13. 375 F. App'x 81 (2d Cir. 2010).

14. *Id.* at 84

15. *Id.*

16. *Id.* (quoting Physicians Formula Cosmetics, Inc. v. W. Cabot Cosmetics, Inc., 857 F.2d 80, 84 (2d Cir. 1998)).

Defense Judgment Reversed Where Likelihood-of-Confusion Factors Favored Plaintiff as a Matter of Law

In *Sabinsa Corp. v. Creative Compounds, LLC,*[17] the Third Circuit reversed the district court's holding, finding that Creative Compound's FORSTHIN mark was likely to create confusion in the marketplace with supplier Sabinsa's FORSLEAN mark. Both marks refer to *Coleus forskohlii* extract, a member of the mint family found primarily in India that is used as an ingredient in weight management products. The Third Circuit held that the district court erred in its findings on the *Lapp*[18] factors and in its ultimate finding of likelihood of confusion after a bench trial.

Specifically, the Third Circuit explained that the district court erred in considering only three of the relevant *Lapp* factors and by failing to discuss most of Sabinsa's evidence. The district court did not explain whether it viewed the remaining factors as neutral or irrelevant or how it weighed and balanced the combined factors. Further, its reasoning regarding the three factors it did analyze was flawed.

Regarding mark similarity, the district court erred in focusing on minute differences in the products' logos where the evidence showed that both marks are often used in plain text. Moreover, the district court compared the words "thin" and "lean" without comparing the overall impression of the marks. The Third Circuit found that the marks share all but three letters, have the same number of syllables, the same dominant syllable, and the same last letter. The Third Circuit concluded that it was clear error to find these marks not visually similar.

Regarding strength of the mark, there was no evidence submitted to support the district court's conclusion that "fors" is a generic term for forskohlin. The Third Circuit found that the district court erred by collapsing the "actual confusion" and "sophistication of customers" factors into its analysis of strength of the mark.

The Third Circuit found FORSLEAN to be a suggestive and commercially strong mark, and that the district court erred in concluding that manufacturers of neutraceuticals (i.e., the direct buyers) are the only relevant consumers. The degree of care exercised by customers should have been equal to that of the least sophisticated consumer in the class, which in this case is the individual consumer to which Sabinsa also markets its product.

Because Sabinsa did not submit evidence of actual confusion, the district court did not err in finding that this factor, along with length of time without confusion, favored Creative Compounds. The Third Circuit disagreed that "there [wa]s nothing in the record to suggest that Creative Compounds attempted to pass off its goods as Sabinsa's."[19] Inconsistent and false employee testimony, combined with the timing and marketing strategy of Forsthin all suggest that Creative Compounds intended to trade on Sabinsa's goodwill. However, this is not enough to tip the factor in Sabinsa's favor; the court concluded that the intent factor involved disputed factual issues that could not be resolved in favor of either party as a matter of law.

The Third Circuit found channels of trade and similarity of sales efforts to weigh in favor of Sabinsa. The court also found the products physically identical, clearly favoring Sabinsa. The court found no evidence that the public might expect Sabinsa to manufacture both products.

---

17. 609 F.3d 175 (3d Cir. 2010).
18. Interpace Corp. v. Lapp, Inc., 721 F.2d 460, 463 (3d Cir. 1983).
19. *Sabinsa,* 609 F.3d at 187.

Notwithstanding the question of fact as to intent, the court concluded that it would be clear error to allow the two factors that favored Creative Compounds to outweigh Sabinsa's strong showing on mark similarity and on the remaining factors. The Third Circuit concluded that remand to reweigh the *Lapp* factors would be a waste of resources because any reasonable juror would find that Sabinsa demonstrated likelihood of confusion.

Court Denies Motion for Summary Judgment on Trademark Infringement Claims, Finding Genuine Issues of Material Fact as to Likelihood of Confusion

In *Vantage, Inc. v. Vantage Travel Services, Inc.,*[20] the U.S. District Court for the District of South Carolina granted in part and denied in part Vantage Travel Services, Inc.'s (VTSI) motion for summary judgment on Vantage, Inc.'s (Vantage) claims for unfair competition, trademark infringement, and violation of the state Unfair Trade Practices Act. The underlying dispute involved the use of the trademark VANTAGE.

Vantage is a travel agency specializing in custom trips to international locations. Most of Vantage's customers are travel agents who earn commissions booking trips through Vantage. However, some customers also book directly with Vantage. VTSI sells prepackaged cruises directly to consumers.

The court recognized that Vantage must show likelihood of confusion to prevail on its claims. A likelihood of confusion exists if the defendant's actual practice is likely to produce consumer confusion over the origin of the goods or services in question. The court listed seven factors relevant to a likelihood-of-confusion determination and noted that actual confusion is the most significant factor. It also recognized that likelihood of confusion typically must be resolved by a jury because it is an inherently factual determination.

Although Vantage argued that its VANTAGE mark is suggestive, the court found genuine issues of material fact with respect to the strength of the mark. It held the parties' respective VANTAGE marks were similar. Both parties use VANTAGE alone as well as in combination with other nearly identical words (e.g., VANTAGE WORLD TRAVEL compared to VANTAGE DELUXE WORLD TRAVEL).

Next, the court found evidence of an overlap in services because both parties operate in the travel industry selling trips to consumers. Although both parties use the Internet to advertise their services, the court noted that Vantage did not really advertise directly to consumers. The court found no evidence that VTSI intended to cause confusion or acted in bad faith.

Vantage also provided evidence of several instances of customer confusion. However, the court determined that the record was unclear regarding whether the evidence of confusion was de minimis. It concluded that genuine issues of material fact remained with respect to likelihood of confusion, and that a jury would be particularly amenable to resolving the issue. Thus, the court denied VTSI's motion for summary judgment on this ground.

Turning to damages, the court found that Vantage had provided sufficient circumstantial evidence regarding a drop in business around the time it learned of misdirected travel agent inquiries. The court denied VTSI's motion on this ground as well.

---

20.   No. 6:08-2765-HMH, 2010 WL 1427965 (D.S.C. Apr. 8, 2010).

The court then turned to the question of laches—whether Vantage knew of the infringing use, whether Vantage's delay in filing suit was inexcusable or unreasonable, and whether VTSI was unduly prejudiced by Vantage's delay. The court recounted the history between the parties and found that VTSI failed to establish a defense of laches because it was on notice of Vantage's position with respect to the mark at least since the USPTO published Vantage's registration.

Lastly, the court granted the motion as to the common law trademark infringement claim because Vantage conceded it is not the owner of the VANTAGE marks. Rather, the marks are owned by the owner of Vantage, who was not a party to the suit. Because Vantage could not prove ownership, it could not succeed on its common law infringement claim.

Social Linguistics Expert Testimony Deemed Inadmissible under Daubert Test

In *Flagstar Bank, FSB v. Freestar Bank, N.A.,*[21] the U.S. District Court for the Central District of Illinois, deciding a *Daubert* motion, held that the testimony of a proffered expert on "social linguistics and rhetorical criticism" was unreliable and inadmissible because it was not presented with any "proposal, theory, or technique" supporting its conclusions. Additionally, on the summary judgment record before the court, the court held that there was no genuine issue of material fact regarding likelihood of confusion with respect to the trademark infringement claim, finding in favor of the defendant.

In June 2006, Freestar, a small community bank with thirteen branches located in the tri-county area of central Illinois, filed an application with the USPTO to register a trademark containing a slogan that closely resembled two of Flagstar's registered trademarks. At the time, Flagstar, a Michigan-based bank with 175 banking centers in Michigan, Indiana, and Georgia, was the owner of four registered trademarks and had expended over $12 million in advertising in 2008. Freestar utilized the applied-for logo and slogan in advertisements limited to the tri-county area, but both Flagstar and Freestar offered identical products and banking services, which included personal and business checking, savings and money market accounts, certificates of deposit, home mortgage loans, home equity lines of credit, online banking, and online mortgage applications. In 2008, Flagstar brought suit against Freestar for trademark infringement under the Lanham Act, and Freestar moved to strike Flagstar's expert report. The parties then filed cross-motions for summary judgment on the issue of likelihood of confusion.

Dr. Edward Lee Lamoureux was proffered by Flagstar as an expert on social linguistics and rhetorical criticism. The purpose of Dr. Lamoureux's report was to illustrate that the words "flag," "free," and "star" each were "strongly associated with some of the most broadly shared values in American culture: Patriotism, loyalty, national identity, and individual rights."[22] Thus, Lamoureux concluded that, in light of the September 11th terrorist attacks and due to the "significant and overlapping metaphorical associations" of these words, a substantial portion of banking customers would likely confuse the Flagstar and Freestar names in the common marketplace. In granting Freestar's motion to strike, the court noted that Dr. Lamoureux failed to present any "proposal,

---

21. 687 F. Supp. 2d 811 (C.D. Ill. 2009).
22. *Id.* at 819.

theory or technique" supporting the conclusions of likelihood of confusion. The court reasoned that, although Lamoureux noted that his theories relied on the consultation of classic texts, he included no reference to, supplements of, or discussion of the texts in the report and, therefore, left the court to speculate as to how he had applied such theories and how they related to his conclusions. Likewise, Dr. Lamoureux proposed no theory to explain how his patriotism-based metaphor concerning the words "flag," "free," and "star" would dominate other possible metaphorical associations in connection with those words. The court also viewed Dr. Lamoureux's failure to rely on any qualitative research or polls supporting his conclusions about patriotic metaphorical associations as a fatal flaw under the *Daubert* reliability standards. Furthermore, the court found that the absence of any reliable theory was exemplified by Dr. Lamoureux's inability to "explain the procedure by which he could evaluate whether the words 'freedom,' 'America,' 'liberty,' and 'patriot' [fell] under the same metaphorical umbrella of 'patriotism' that also [covered] the terms 'flag,' 'free,' and 'star.'"[23]

Finally, the court concluded that Dr. Lamoureux's expert report and proposed testimony were not relevant because the jury was equally as competent as an expert in drawing conclusions by evaluating the meaning of the words comprising the marks in question. The report, therefore, did not aid the trier of fact in determining "how the similarities of these words lead to confusion, or conversely, how the differences among the words may negate the likelihood of confusion."[24]

With respect to the parties' cross-motions for summary judgment on the issue of likelihood of confusion, the court held that Freestar's use of its logo and slogan did not create a likelihood of confusion with Flagstar's registered marks. In reaching this conclusion, the court was chiefly persuaded by the record evidence that there was no concurrent use of the marks in the same region and noted that, "consumers cannot become confused by a mark they will never encounter in the marketplace."[25] In addition, the court held that Flagstar could not show that it was reasonable to believe that it might have expanded into Freestar's territories. The court also examined the physical qualities of the marks in question and recognized that the differences were not minor stylistic differences. Specifically, the court noted that, because the marks had different names, displayed different graphical imagery, and had completely different colors and slogans, a customer was not likely to be confused as to the origin of the marks. Finally, although the products and services were identical, the court was careful to note that, in the area of banking services, prospective customers exhibit a high degree of care when making purchasing decisions, and that Flagstar presented no evidence to demonstrate that Freestar somehow lured away Flagstar's customers to its products or Web site.

---

23.   *Id*. at 820.

24.   *Id*. at 821 (citing Patsy's Italian Rest., Inc. v. Banas, 531 F. Supp. 2d 483, 485 (E.D.N.Y. 2008) (excluding expert testimony where the testimony would not aid the jury on the likelihood-of-confusion question)).

25.   *Id*. at 833.

Trial Will Determine Whether MetroPCS's Reconfiguration of Virgin Cell Phones Constitutes Trademark Infringement and Dilution

In *MetroPCS Wireless, Inc. v. Virgin Mobile USA, L.P.,*[26] the Northern District of Texas denied Defendant Virgin Mobile's motion for summary judgment on trademark infringement and dilution claims, holding that these claims largely hinged on whether Plaintiff MetroPCS's reconfigured mobile handsets created a "new product," which presented a genuine issue of material fact. The court granted MetroPCS's motion for summary judgment on contributory infringement.

MetroPCS reconfigures cell phones from other providers so that they will operate on its wireless network. This process is called "reflashing." At consumers' request, MetroPCS reflashed Virgin Mobile cell phones. The headsets of Virgin Mobile cell phones bear the VIRGIN MOBILE trademark and show the logo on the electronic display. MetroPCS sued Virgin Mobile for a declaration of noninfringement, and Virgin Mobile cross-sued for direct and contributory trademark infringement, dilution, and tortious interference with contract.

In addressing Virgin Mobile's direct trademark infringement claim, the court considered whether MetroPCS's reconfiguration constituted "use in commerce" of Virgin Mobile's trademark. The court noted that the purpose of trademark law is to aid consumers by assuring the same products with the same trademarks come from the same sources, and to protect a trademark owner's economic investments. The court also explained that, in the context of altered products: (1) if an alteration is so significant that it results in a new product, the original trademark should be removed to prevent deception; and (2) courts are less likely to require the removal of a trademark where the alteration is done at the request of the product owner.

The court concluded that resolution of Virgin Mobile's direct infringement claim turned on whether MetroPCS's reconfiguration service transformed the handsets into a new product. Both parties presented conflicting evidence on the issue. MetroPCS argued that its reconfiguration service was a mere alteration to the mobile handset at the owners' request; therefore, handset owners would not be confused. In contrast, Virgin Mobile argued that MetroPCS's reconfiguration sometimes damaged handsets and that, in those instances, the resulting handset is a completely new product. The court declined to hold as a matter of law that MetroPCS's reconfiguration services did not create a new product and constitute "use" of Virgin Mobile's mark.

As to likelihood of confusion, the court found that there could be two theories of confusion in this case, post-sale confusion and initial interest confusion. The court balanced the typical factors of likelihood of confusion with the additional factors that apply to altered goods: "the extent and nature of changes made to the product," "clarity and distinctiveness of the labeling on the reconditioned product," and "the degree to which any inferior qualities associated with the reconditioned product would likely be identified by the typical purchaser with the manufacturer."[27] The court held that a reasonable jury could find in favor of Virgin Mobile after evaluating and balancing all of the factors.

With regard to dilution, MetroPCS argued that a trademark owner like Virgin Mobile does not control the aftermarket use of its products and compared itself to a second-hand

---

26. No. 3:08-1658, 2009 WL 3075205 (N.D. Tex. Sept. 25, 2009).
27. *Id.* at *8.

repair shop. Virgin Mobile responded that MetroPCS was not an innocent second-hand repair shop; rather, MetroPCS was creating a different market of inferior products that still bear the Virgin Mobile trademarks. The district court held that the issue of whether MetroPCS was like a second-hand repair shop turned on whether MetroPCS traded in genuine, trade-marked goods, or whether it created new products through its reconfiguration service, an issue already found to be a genuine issue of material fact precluding summary judgment.

Finally, the court granted MetroPCS's summary judgment motion in regard to con-tributory infringement because the court found Virgin Mobile did not allege or provide any evidence of direct infringement or the intentional inducement of Virgin Mobile cus-tomers to resell their handsets.

Prior Owner of an Abandoned Mark Cannot Claim Infringement by a Subsequent User

In *Metropolitan Life Insurance Co. v. O'M Associates, LLC,*[28] the U.S. District Court for the Northern District of Illinois granted defendant's motion for summary judg-ment on trademark infringement and false advertising claims, holding that Plaintiff MetLife had abandoned its rights in the trademark at issue.

Michel O'Malley managed a MetLife agency located in Downers Grove, Illinois, which operated under the name "O'Malley & Associates." MetLife replaced O'Malley and changed the name of the agency to Preferred Planning Group. After the name change, MetLife's director of operations sent memoranda and e-mails informing all employees to stop using the O'Malley & Associates name in everyday business, as well as in letterheads and on business cards. MetLife's director of operations later testified that, at the time of those communications, MetLife had no intention of resuming use of the name.

After leaving MetLife, O'Malley joined a competing agency in Downers Grove and began operating under the name O'Malley & Associates. O'Malley & Associates then hired former MetLife agents and contacted MetLife clients, sending them announcements that stated they were "pleased to announce we [are] moving our offices to a larger loca-tion" and "I am moving my Downer Grove office and expanding the services available to you . . . sign where indicated and return as soon as possible to insure uninterrupted service on your accounts."[29]

MetLife sued O'Malley & Associates for trademark infringement and false advertising. O'Malley claimed that MetLife abandoned the O'Malley & Associates name before it began using it. The court agreed, rejecting MetLife's continued use and residual goodwill argu-ments. MetLife's evidence of continued use was limited to one internally faxed resignation letter on old letterhead; this single use was insufficient to show continued use of the mark. The court also explained that residual goodwill would preclude a finding of abandonment only when the abandoned mark is confusingly similar to the newly adopted mark. That was not the case here where the newly adopted mark was "Preferred Planning Group."

The court also rejected MetLife's false advertising claim, which was based on O'Malley & Associates' communications with MetLife clients. The court found that the letters from O'Malley and Associates were not "false or misleading 'commercial advertising or pro-

28.   No. 06-5812, 2009 WL 3015210 (N.D. Ill. Sept. 16, 2009).
29.   *Id.* at *2.

motion'"[30] because they were not directed to anonymous recipients. Although the communications were not actionable under the Lanham Act, they potentially could be considered a deceitful business practice.

Motion for Summary Judgment Granted for Trademark Infringement and Dilution Arising from Unauthorized Use of Trademark by an Advertisement Company

In *Pfizer Inc. v. Sachs,*[31] the U.S. District Court for the Southern District of New York held, on a motion for summary judgment, that Defendant Sachs and his company infringed and diluted Plaintiff Pfizer's VIAGRA and VIVA VIAGRA trademarks.

The court found that Sachs's use of Pfizer's VIAGRA and VIVA VIAGRA trademarks on a twenty-foot decommissioned missile at various locations—including in front of Pfizer's world headquarters in Manhattan and at adult entertainment expositions—was a use in commerce that was likely to cause confusion as to sponsorship and association.

In his defense, Sachs argued that: (1) Pfizer's VIAGRA and VIVA VIAGRA marks had become generic for erectile dysfunction medication; and (2) his use of the marks was protected under the First Amendment. To support his claim that the marks at issue had become generic, Sachs introduced a genericism survey, which was conducted by a surveyor he identified through an ad on Criagslist. The court found that Sachs's ad hoc genericism survey was flawed in methodology and did not show the mark to be generic. The court went on to find, based on the *Polaroid* likelihood-of-confusion factors,[32] that there was a likelihood of confusion between Sachs's use of the VIAGRA mark on the missile and Pfizer's registered and common law rights in the VIAGRA and VIVA VIAGRA marks. Specifically, the court found that: (1) Pfizer had strong marks; (2) the marks at issue are identical; (3) consumers were likely to be confused as to whether Sachs was engaged in marketing activities for Pfizer; and (4) even sophisticated consumers were likely to confuse the two uses.

In addition, the court found that Sachs's actions diluted Pfizer's marks by tarnishment. Sachs's exhibition of the missile with the marks at an adult entertainment exhibition, along with Sachs's notification to Pfizer that the missile would be displayed with models riding the missile and distributing condoms, would likely harm Pfizer's reputation by diluting and tarnishing its marks.

The court also rejected Sachs's claim that his use of the marks were protected by the First Amendment. Sachs urged that his use of the marks was protected speech about erectile dysfunction. The court determined that, even if such a message could be inferred from Sachs's actions, Sachs failed to show that using the marks was necessary to make his point.

The district court did not grant summary judgment on the issues of false advertising and deceptive acts because Pfizer was not able to show any actual injury.

Finally, the court awarded Pfizer reasonable attorneys' fees because Sachs acted in bad faith. The court cited several acts of bad faith, including Sachs's failure to comply

---

30.   *Id.* at *6 (quoting ISI Int'l, Inc. v. Borden Ladner Gervais LLP, 316 F.3d 731, 733 (7th Cir. 2003)).

31.   652 F. Supp. 2d 512 (S.D.N.Y. 2009).

32.   Polaroid Corp. v. Polarad Elecs. Corp., 287 F.2d 492, 495 (2d Cir. 1961).

with two cease-and-desist letters from Pfizer, his failure to seek advice of counsel, threats of continued infringement to Pfizer, and his attempts to capitalize on Pfizer's goodwill.

Contributory Infringement

Summary Judgment Vacated Where Reasonable Jury Could Find Contributory Infringement Involving Confusion among the Nonpurchasing Public

In *Georgia Pacific Consumer Products, LP v. Von Drehle Corp.,*[33] the Fourth Circuit vacated summary judgment where there were issues of fact concerning contributory infringement arising from possible confusion among the nonpurchasing public.

Plaintiff Georgia Pacific introduced a touchless paper towel dispenser called enMotion designed for use both in private homes and in public settings such as restrooms in hotels, stadiums, and restaurants. The Georgia Pacific enMotion dispenser was designed to be used with paper toweling specifically designed for use with the enMotion dispenser. That paper had a high-quality, fabric-like feel. Georgia Pacific sold the enMotion toweling to janitorial supply distributors, who then sold the products to their customers, such as hotels, stadiums, and restaurants. However, Georgia Pacific only leased the enMotion dispensers to distributors, who then subleased the dispensers to their customers. The leases and subleases stated that only enMotion toweling may be used in enMotion dispensers, and the same limitation was disclosed on the inside of the dispensers. Members of the public who used an enMotion dispenser could see various Georgia Pacific marks on the outside of the dispensers.

The requirement that only enMotion toweling be used with enMotion dispensers differentiated this product from most dispensers made by Georgia Pacific and other companies. Other dispensers were referred to as universal dispensers, which meant that they were designed to accept paper toweling from multiple manufacturers. With the enMotion dispenser, Georgia Pacific sought to create a branded dispenser that a user would expect to dispense only genuine Georgia Pacific towels. The enMotion dispenser was designed to work only with nonstandard, ten-inch enMotion toweling. Georgia Pacific intended that branding strategy to be similar to that used by companies such as soda manufacturers that dispensed soda in branded soda fountain dispensers.

Georgia Pacific discovered that one of its competitors, Defendant von Drehle, was selling paper toweling to distributors specifically made by von Drehle for use with Georgia Pacific's enMotion dispensers. That toweling was inferior to Georgia Pacific's enMotion toweling. Von Drehle's sales staff encouraged distributors to sell its toweling to their customers and to "stuff" the von Drehle paper in enMotion dispensers.

Georgia Pacific responded by suing von Drehle for unfair competition and contributory trademark infringement under the Lanham Act and unfair competition and tortious interference with contractual relationships under North Carolina common law. Von Drehle counterclaimed for violation of North Carolina's Unfair and Deceptive Trade Practices Act.

Following the parties' filing of cross-motions for summary judgment, the district court granted summary judgment in favor of von Drehle on all of Georgia Pacific's claims and in favor of Georgia Pacific on von Drehle's counterclaim. The Fourth Circuit affirmed the

---

33. 618 F.3d 441 (4th Cir. 2010).

grant of summary judgment in favor of Georgia Pacific with respect to von Drehle's counterclaim. However, the court vacated the award of summary judgment in favor of von Drehle on Georgia Pacific's claims and remanded the case for further proceedings.

The Fourth Circuit focused on the issue of contributory trademark infringement because von Drehle did not itself physically insert its replacement paper in enMotion dispensers. The court applied the contributory infringement analysis first articulated by the U.S. Supreme Court in *Inwood Laboratories*.[34] Based on *Inwood Laboratories* and later cases, a defendant is liable for contributory infringement only if it intentionally induces a merchant down the distribution chain to pass off its product as that of the trademark owner, or if it continues to supply a product that could readily be passed off to a particular merchant that it knew was mislabeling the product with the trademark owner's mark. Applying this test to von Drehle, the court observed that, assuming the stuffing of enMotion dispensers with von Drehle's toweling constituted trademark infringement, there was ample evidence in the record for a reasonable jury to find von Drehle liable for contributory infringement. The evidence indicated that von Drehle directly induced distributors to have their customers (such as restaurants) use von Drehle toweling in enMotion dispensers.

The Fourth Circuit then turned to the question of whether using von Drehle toweling in enMotion dispensers constituted direct infringement because contributory infringement can be found only when there is direct infringement. The court concluded there was sufficient evidence in the record for a reasonable jury to find direct infringement based on application of the multifactor test used in the Fourth Circuit to determine whether there was a likelihood of confusion.

The main area of dispute concerning the likelihood-of-confusion analysis was whether the entities that placed von Drehle paper in enMotion dispensers were using Georgia Pacific's marks in a manner likely to cause confusion in the relevant universe of consumers. The Fourth Circuit concluded that the relevant public was neither the distributors who purchased von Drehle toweling, nor those end-users (e.g., restaurants) who purchased von Drehle toweling from the distributors and placed the toweling in enMotion dispensers. The court concluded that the relevant public included those who used the toweling that had been placed in enMotion dispensers.

The court noted that those consumers need not be purchasers of the von Drehle toweling. Confusion among the nonpurchasing public may be considered in the likelihood-of-confusion analysis if it can be shown that public confusion will adversely affect the trademark owner's ability to control its reputation among lenders, investors, employees, and others with whom it interacts. The court then considered: (1) whether confusion among the nonpurchasing public was likely; and (2) whether such confusion would have an adverse impact. On the first question, the court concluded there was sufficient evidence for a reasonable jury to find likely confusion among restroom visitors. For example, three surveys found that high percentages of participants (over 45 percent) expected that the paper towel dispenser and toweling dispensed from it would come from the same source. On the second question, the court concluded that a reasonable jury could find such confusion likely to have an adverse impact on Georgia Pacific's reputation.

---

34. Inwood Labs., Inc. v. Ives Labs., Inc., 456 U.S. 844, 853–54 (1982).

eBay Not Liable for Infringement or Dilution, but Case Remanded for False Advertising Claim

In *Tiffany (NJ) Inc. v. eBay Inc.*,[35] the Second Circuit affirmed the district court's judgment against Plaintiff Tiffany's claims of trademark infringement and dilution but remanded the case for further proceedings on Tiffany's false advertising claim. The U.S. District Court for the Southern District of New York found that Defendant eBay, an online marketplace, did not engage in trademark infringement, trademark dilution, or false advertising with respect to counterfeit Tiffany jewelry that was sold through eBay's Web site. The Second Circuit concluded that eBay neither directly nor contributorily infringed Tiffany's mark, that eBay's actions did not dilute Tiffany's mark, and that eBay's advertisements of Tiffany products on its Web site and in keyword advertisements were not literally false. The Second Circuit, however, found that the district court failed to support properly its conclusion that the advertisements were not misleading, and the court remanded the case for further consideration of that issue.

eBay's procedures and anti-counterfeiting efforts were important factors in the district court and Second Circuit decisions. eBay itself does not sell items listed for sale, does not take possession of those goods, and does not know if and when an item is delivered to the purchaser. eBay spends twenty million dollars every year on anti-counterfeiting tools to promote safety on its Web site. Some of these measures include an internal Trust and Safety Department, a fraud engine dedicated to discovering illegal listings, and a Verified Rights Owner Program, or VeRO, allowing intellectual property owners to report violations. eBay also cancels suspicious transactions and suspends thousands of sellers every year for engaging in infringing conduct.

In addition, eBay allows intellectual property owners to create "About Me" Web pages on the eBay Web site detailing their products and intellectual property legal positions. Tiffany provided such a page, which warned shoppers about counterfeit Tiffany products and urged them to shop at Tiffany retail stores, through the Tiffany Web site, or by using the Tiffany catalog.

Tiffany argued that eBay directly infringed its mark by using the Tiffany mark in advertisements on the eBay Web site that promoted the sale of Tiffany merchandise and by purchasing sponsored links containing the mark on various search engines. The Second Circuit held that eBay's use of Tiffany's mark was lawful, although the court declined expressly to apply the nominative fair-use doctrine, which had been applied by the district court. The court explained that eBay's use of Tiffany's mark accurately described the genuine Tiffany goods offered for sale on its Web site, and that eBay's use did not imply affiliation between eBay and Tiffany. The Second Circuit further noted that, to impose liability because eBay could not guarantee the genuineness of all Tiffany products offered on its Web site would unduly inhibit the lawful resale of genuine Tiffany goods.

The Second Circuit then considered application of the U.S. Supreme Court's test for contributory trademark infringement set forth in *Inwood Laboratories, Inc. v. Ives Laboratories, Inc.*[36] In *Inwood*, the Court held that a manufacturer or distributor is liable for contributory trademark infringement if it intentionally induces another to infringe or if it continues to supply its product to one whom it knows or has reason to know is engaging in

---

35.　600 F.3d 93 (2d Cir. 2010).
36.　456 U.S. 844 (1982).

infringement. Tiffany argued that eBay was liable for contributory infringement because it continued to offer its services to sellers of counterfeit goods whom eBay knew or should have known were infringing Tiffany's mark. The Second Circuit concluded that eBay was not liable for contributory infringement under the *Inwood* test because: (1) eBay terminated listings once it learned they contained counterfeit goods, warned sellers and buyers, cancelled fees it earned from those particular listings, and directed buyers not to consummate the sale of the disputed items; and (2) although eBay possessed general knowledge regarding counterfeiting on its Web site, such generalized knowledge was insufficient under *Inwood* to impose an affirmative duty on eBay.

In order to establish eBay's contributory liability, Tiffany had to show that eBay knew or had reason to know of specific instances of actual infringement beyond those that eBay addressed upon learning of them. Tiffany argued that there was sufficient direct and circumstantial evidence to show that eBay knew or should have known that its service was being used to further counterfeiting activity, pointing to evidence that eBay was aware generally of counterfeit Tiffany sales. The Second Circuit disagreed, explaining that *Inwood* requires knowledge of specific instances of infringement, such as particular listings that are infringing or will infringe in the future. The Second Circuit also observed that the U.S. Supreme Court, in a later copyright case, described *Inwood*'s "narrow standard" for contributory trademark infringement as requiring knowledge of "identified individuals" engaging in infringing conduct.[37]

The Second Circuit agreed with Tiffany that a service provider may not act with willful blindness concerning knowledge of particular infringing transactions. However, the court found that eBay did not ignore the general information it received about counterfeit sales and, thus, was not willfully blind to the issue of counterfeit Tiffany products on its Web site. In fact, upon learning that specific sellers were selling counterfeit Tiffany products, eBay removed the sellers' listings and suspended the repeat offenders from the Web site.

The Second Circuit affirmed the district court's rejection of Tiffany's dilution-by-blurring and dilution-by-tarnishment claims. The court explained that, because eBay only used the Tiffany mark to advertise the availability of authentic Tiffany products on the eBay Web site and did not use the Tiffany mark to refer to eBay's own services, there could be no dilution by blurring or tarnishment of the Tiffany mark. The court found that there was no second mark or product at issue that blurred the distinctiveness of or tarnished the Tiffany mark. The court also found that, because eBay itself did not sell the goods at issue, eBay did not engage in dilution by counterfeiting.

Tiffany also claimed that eBay engaged in false advertising when it advertised the sale of Tiffany goods through hyperlinks on its Web site and by purchasing advertising space on search engines, among other things. Tiffany argued that, because many of the goods sold on eBay's Web site were, in fact, counterfeit, eBay should be liable for false advertising. The district court rejected Tiffany's argument, concluding first that the advertisements were not literally false because authentic merchandise was also available on eBay's Web site. The district court also found that the advertisements were not misleading because: (1) the advertisements constituted permissible nominative fair uses; (2) there was no proof that eBay had specific knowledge that specific advertisements related to counter-

---

37. *Tiffany*, 600 F.3d at 108 (citing Sony Corp. of Am. v. Universal City Studios, Inc., 464 U.S. 417, 439 (1984)).

feit goods; and (3) any falsity was the responsibility of the third-party seller and not of eBay. The Second Circuit agreed with the district court's finding that the advertisements were not literally false, as genuine Tiffany merchandise was offered for sale. However, the Second Circuit held that it could find, based on the record before it, that the advertisements were not likely to mislead or confuse consumers, and it rejected all of the district court's reasons for finding no false advertising. Even if eBay's advertisements were nominative fair uses, the court believed they could still be false or misleading. Whether eBay was aware of specific instances of counterfeit goods might be relevant to the contributory infringement analysis, but not to whether the advertisements were misleading for purposes of false advertising. Likewise, the possibility that the advertisements were misleading because of conduct by the seller rather than by eBay might be relevant to the infringement analysis, but less relevant to the false advertising claim. Rather than vacate the judgment as to the false advertising claim, the court remanded the case for reexamination of the false advertising issues.

DILUTION

Likelihood of Dilution

"The Other Red Meat" Likely to Dilute "The Other White Meat"

In *National Pork Board v. Supreme Lobster & Seafood Co.*,[38] the TTAB sustained an opposition on the basis of likelihood of dilution by blurring without reaching the opposer's alternative ground: likelihood of confusion. The mark applied for was THE OTHER RED MEAT (referring to salmon). The opposer relied on several registered service marks, which included the slogan THE OTHER WHITE MEAT (referring to pork).

The applicant, Supreme Lobster, is a private wholesaler of seafood and fish. In 2004, Supreme Lobster filed an intent-to-use application to register THE OTHER RED MEAT as a trademark for fresh and frozen salmon. The lead opposer, the National Pork Board (NPB), operates the pork industry generic advertising campaign funded by industry members. The NPB holds several incontestable registrations that include the phrase "The Other White Meat." Although the reference is to pork, none of the marks are trademarks for pork. The registration primarily relied on is a service mark for "association services namely, promoting the interests of members of the pork industry."[39]

The TTAB rejected several attacks on NPB's registrations, both as procedurally unallowable collateral attacks and on the merits. First, Supreme Lobster attempted to introduce evidence of meat recalls to demonstrate that the NPB had failed to control quality. The TTAB pointed out that Supreme Lobster was confusing an association service mark with a product certification mark. The NPB had no legal duty as a mark holder to police the quality of the products sold by association members. Second, Supreme Lobster argued that, because the NPB uses its marks for generic advertising, its marks were invalid as generic. The TTAB explained that the mark was not for a generic product (pork); rather, it was a service mark for association services. Supreme Lobster had introduced no evi-

---

38. 96 U.S.P.Q.2d (BNA) 1479 (T.T.A.B. 2010) (precedential).
39. *Id.* at 1493.

dence that the public did not recognize all THE OTHER RED MEAT advertising as emanating directly or indirectly from one, even if unknown, source. Third, Supreme Lobster argued that the NPB was not in control of all advertising using its registered slogan and, therefore, had lost rights in its marks for some variation of naked licensing. The TTAB found, however, that the NPB had controlled the relevant advertising.

Regarding the dilution claim, the TTAB first found that the NPB's slogan became famous before Supreme Lobster filed its application. Although NPB's mark was not registered for goods, the TTAB considered the mark's fame to be supported by the substantial sale of pork products by members of the promoted industry. The mark was proven to have been used as the central focus of the industry's marketing campaign for over twenty-five years. The relevant associations had spent over $550 million dollars during this campaign, averaging some $25 million per year. Furthermore, the mark had been used in extensive cooperative advertising, the cost of which was not included in these figures. Tracking surveys demonstrated "awareness rates at eighty to eighty-five percent of the general adult population and rates of correct source recognition at nearly seventy percent of the population."[40] A study performed by academics demonstrated the slogan to be the fifth most recognized slogan by the adult American population. The fame of the slogan was also supported by evidence of third-party coverage and by expert testimony. Furthermore, most of the evidence relied on predated Supreme Lobster's intent-to-use application.

As to the similarity of the marks, the TTAB relied on its own comparison of the slogans. Additionally, the TTAB credited a survey conducted by the NPB, which reported that THE OTHER RED MEAT trigged 35 percent of the subjects to conjure up THE OTHER WHITE MEAT, rejecting several attacks on its methodology. The survey had been conducted by a recognized expert for the purposes of this litigation. Supreme Lobster objected that the survey used leading questions, an inappropriate control question, and an overly broad universe, and that it failed to replicate market conditions. The TTAB rejected these objections because they neither explained how any of these flaws was likely to have biased the results, nor specified a reasonable alternative. For example, the study qualified participants by asking if they had in the past purchased fish or seafood. Supreme Lobster's objection was that the screening question should have asked if they intended to purchase salmon in the near future. Each participant then heard a recording of "The Other Red Meat." The interviewer then asked:

(4) "Thinking about the slogan you just heard [THE OTHER RED MEAT], do any other advertising slogans or phrases come to mind?" [If answered "yes" continue to Q5]

(5) "What other advertising slogan or phrase comes to mind?"[41]

The TTAB found this survey to be probative evidence that the public was likely to associate the two slogans with each other.

The next statutory factor, the degree of distinctiveness, favored the NPB because its slogan was inherently distinctive and commercially strong. The next two factors also favored the NPB: its use of the slogan had been "virtually exclusive," and the proof of fame also demonstrated a very high degree of public recognition.

---

40. *Id.* at 1496.
41. *Id.* at 1490.

Supreme Lobster's intent was also found to favor the NPB. Although the TTAB refused to find that Supreme Lobster had acted in bad faith, it did find incredible the testimony of Supreme Lobster's witness that the slogan had not been created as an echo of THE OTHER WHITE MEAT. The TTAB relied on the familiarity of the witness with the NPB's slogan. It also relied on the testimony of the witness that he chose his slogan to evoke health and variety, the same qualities raised by the NPB's slogan.

The final statutory factor, existence of actual association between the two marks, was ruled to be neutral. Because Supreme Lobster had filed its application based on an intent to use the mark, the TTAB recognized that the association survey conducted by the NPB's expert had been unable to model Supreme Lobster's actual usage. The survey, therefore, was found to be relevant on likelihood of association, but not on actual association.

The TTAB concluded that the record supported sustaining the NPB on the basis of likelihood of dilution by blurring. It declined to reach the pleaded alternative of likelihood of confusion.

Famous Marks

Fame Must Be Shown in the United States; Fame Outside the United States Is Insufficient

In *Fiat Group Automobiles S.p.A. v. ISM Inc.*,[42] the TTAB granted ISM's motion to dismiss Fiat's dilution claim for failure to state a claim, holding Fiat had no standing to bring a dilution claim in the absence of use or an allegation of use of its mark in the United States. The TTAB also held that Fiat satisfied its claim against ISM for lack of bona fide intent to use its mark in commerce.

Fiat is the owner of an application for the mark FIAT PANDA for automobiles, which was provisionally refused by the USPTO because it was likely to be confused with ISM's mark PANDA for automobiles, which had an intent-to-use application pending. Fiat filed an opposition with the TTAB, alleging that ISM's use of the PANDA mark for automobiles diluted its internationally famous unregistered marks FIAT PANDA and PANDA, and that ISM lacked a bona fide intent to use its mark in commerce.

Fiat based its dilution claim on the fact that it had used FIAT PANDA and PANDA continuously since 1980 in Europe and other countries. Fiat, however, presented no evidence of ownership or use of these marks in the United States. The TTAB rejected Fiat's contention that, because its marks were famous outside the United States, they were ipso facto well known in the United States.

The TTAB confirmed that "activity solely outside the United States is ineffective to create or maintain rights in marks within the United States."[43] Therefore, Fiat lacked standing to bring a dilution claim under the Trademark Dilution Revision Act (TDRA).[44] The statute provides a dilution cause of action for the protection of famous unregistered marks in use in the United States.

The TTAB relied on the plain meaning of the TDRA, which states that a mark is famous if it "is widely recognized by the general consuming public of the United States as

---

42.   94 U.S.P.Q.2d (BNA) 1111 (T.T.A.B. 2010).
43.   *Id.* at 1115.
44.   *Id.*

a designation of source of the goods or services of the mark's owner."[45] The TTAB further clarified that the provisions of the TDRA do not provide a cause of action for protection of famous unregistered marks "in absence of a specific pleading of intent to use, the filing of an application for registration, and some basis for concluding that the recognition of the mark in the United States is sufficiently widespread as to create an association of the mark with particular products or services, even if the source of the same is anonymous and even if the products or services are not available in the United States."[46]

The TTAB noted that Fiat could establish standing to bring an opposition on the grounds of dilution through ownership of its application that was provisionally refused by the USPTO because ISM's prior pending application was cited as a potential bar to registration of Fiat's mark. Therefore, the TTAB granted ISM's motion to dismiss with respect to the dilution claim, but granted Fiat thirty days to amend its notice of opposition to properly plead its standing and, consequently, granted Fiat leave to replead its dilution claim.

Blurring

Dilution By Blurring Occurs When Common Word Is Used with a New Trademark Meaning

In *Visa International Service Ass'n v. JSL Corp.,*[47] the Ninth Circuit affirmed the district court's decision to grant summary judgment to Plaintiff Visa, agreeing with the lower court that Defendant JSL's use of the mark eVISA for a multilingual education and information company on the Internet was likely to cause dilution by blurring of Visa's mark, VISA, for credit cards. The court noted that blurring by dilution occurs "when a mark previously associated with one product also becomes associated with a second [which] weakens the mark's ability to evoke the first product in the minds of consumers."[48]

The court also noted that relief under antidilution law requires a plaintiff to demonstrate that its mark is not only famous and distinctive but also that the defendant's use of the mark in commerce occurred after the plaintiff's mark had become famous, and that the defendant's use is likely to dilute the plaintiff's mark. The parties did not dispute that VISA is a famous and distinctive mark and that JSL began using eVISA after VISA had achieved its renown. The issue before the court was whether eVISA was likely to dilute VISA.

Recognizing that likelihood of dilution generally is a factual question not appropriate on summary judgment, the court noted that, in appropriate cases, a court may still conclusively determine before trial one or more of the requisite factors for dilution. These factors include the similarity of the marks and the recognition and distinctiveness of Visa's mark.

The court found eVISA "effectively identical" to VISA, noting that use of the prefix "e" does no more to distinguish the two marks than would the addition of words like "Corp." and "Inc."[49] The court also found VISA a strong trademark. For one, although the VISA mark

---

45. *Id.* at 1119.
46. *Id.* at 1117.
47. 610 F.3d 1088 (9th Cir. 2010).
48. *Id.* at 1090.
49. *Id.*

may draw from associations with travel visas, those associations are sufficiently remote that the word "visa" would not make consumers think of credit cards in the absence of the Visa brand.[50] This, the court noted, suggested that any association resulted from goodwill and deserved broad protection. Additionally, Visa introduced uncontroverted evidence that VISA was the world's top brand, used for online purchases almost as often as every other credit card combined.

JSL contested the validity of market surveys and expert testimony introduced by Visa. The court, however, noted that Visa could rely solely on the characteristics of the VISA mark and was not required to produce surveys or expert testimony to establish a likelihood of dilution. The court noted that such evidence could be needed where a defendant introduced evidence that dilution was unlikely, but, in this case, JSL's sole rebuttal to any inference of likely dilution was that there was no intention to dilute. The court stated that this was not enough to negate a showing of likelihood of dilution.[51]

The court further explained that it is not the use of the common word that causes dilution; rather, it is the way the word is used in a particular context. Using a word in a context similar to its dictionary meaning cuts against a finding of dilution.[52]

Second Circuit Rejects "Substantial Similarity" Requirement for Federal Dilution By Blurring Claims

In *Starbucks Corp. v. Wolfe's Borough Coffee, Inc.,*[53] the Second Circuit affirmed the district court's determination that Starbucks failed to establish dilution by tarnishment, but vacated and remanded the district court's finding that Starbucks failed to prove dilution by blurring. In deciding to remand the case with respect to dilution by blurring, the Second Circuit held that a plaintiff is not required to prove "substantial similarity" between the plaintiff's and defendant's marks.[54]

The district court found that the marks at issue—STARBUCKS and CHARBUCKS—were only minimally similar, and that this minimal similarity alone was sufficient to defeat Starbucks's dilution by blurring claim. The Second Circuit held that the district court erred to the extent that it required that there be substantial similarity between the marks. The court observed that, prior to enactment of the TDRA, the court had required that a plaintiff show substantial similarity in order to establish a federal or state dilution claim. However, the TDRA provided the court with "a compelling reason to discard the 'substantially similar' requirement for federal . . . dilution" by blurring actions.[55] The court focused its analysis on the statute's nonexhaustive list of factors to consider in deciding whether dilution by blurring is likely. First, although similarity is listed as an integral element in the definition of dilution by blurring, the Second Circuit emphasized that Congress "[did] not use the words 'very' or 'substantial' in connection with the similarity factor."[56] Instead, the statute directs courts to consider the degree of similarity. The court

---

50. *Id.*
51. *Id.* at 1091.
52. *Id.*
53. 588 F.3d 97 (2d Cir. 2009).
54. *Id.* at 107.
55. *Id.* at 108.
56. *Id.*

reasoned that consideration of the degree of similarity was inconsistent with a requirement that similarity be substantial. Second, the court explained that imposing a requirement of substantial similarity for all dilution-by-blurring claims would materially diminish the significance of the remaining five factors. The remaining factors would have no relevance unless the degree of similarity was found to be substantial.[57]

The Second Circuit held that the district court erred in considering two other dilution-by-blurring factors: whether the defendant intended to create an association with the famous mark, and whether there was evidence of any actual association between the subject marks. With respect to intent, the district court found that Starbucks failed to establish that Wolfe's Borough Coffee acted in bad faith and, consequently, that intent to create an association was not demonstrated. The Second Circuit rejected this finding, explaining that the determination of an intent to associate does not require a showing of bad faith. Where an allegedly diluting mark was created with an intent to associate with the famous mark, the intent factor should be found to favor a finding of a likelihood of dilution by blurring.

The district court also found that Starbucks's evidence on the "actual association" factor was insufficient. Starbucks had submitted telephone survey evidence indicating that 3.1 percent of respondents considered Starbucks as the possible source of Charbucks coffee and that 30.5 percent answered "Starbucks" when asked for the first thing coming to mind upon hearing the word "Charbucks." In referring to this evidence, the district court noted absence of actual confusion. The Second Circuit rejected this reasoning, holding that "the absence of actual or even of a likelihood of confusion does not undermine evidence of trademark dilution."[58]

Although remanding the dilution-by-blurring claim, the Second Circuit affirmed the district court's finding that Starbucks had failed to establish dilution by tarnishment. Starbucks had relied on survey evidence showing that 30.5 percent of respondents immediately associated Charbucks with Starbucks, and 62 percent of those respondents thought they would have a negative impression of a coffee called Charbucks. The Second Circuit held that a mere association between the two marks, coupled with a negative impression of the CHARBUCKS mark, is insufficient to establish a likelihood of dilution by tarnishment. The fact that a consumer "may associate a negative-sounding junior mark with a famous mark says little of whether the consumer views the junior mark as harming the reputation of the famous mark."[59] The court observed that the survey should have focused on how a hypothetical coffee using the junior mark "would affect the positive impressions about the coffee" sold under the senior mark.[60] The court refused to assume that a negative-sounding junior mark would likely harm the reputation of the famous mark by mere association "when the survey conducted by the party claiming dilution could have easily enlightened [the court] on the matter."[61]

---

57. *Id.* The Second Circuit noted that, in contrast to federal law under the TDRA, a showing of substantial similarity is still required in order to establish dilution under New York law. *Id.* at 114.

58. *Id.* at 109.

59. *Id.* at 110.

60. *Id.*

61. *Id.*

Finally, with respect to the dilution claims, Wolfe's Borough Coffee argued that it could not be liable for dilution by blurring or dilution by tarnishment because its use of CHARBUCKS marks was a parody falling within the statutory exceptions to liability. The Second Circuit held that use of CHARBUCKS marks by Wolfe's Borough Coffee could not qualify under the parody exception because they were used as a designation of source for the defendant's own goods.

The Second Circuit also affirmed the district court's finding that Starbucks had failed to establish a likelihood of confusion in support of its trademark infringement and unfair competition claims.

DEFENSES

Defendant Permitted to Assert the Allegedly Superior Trademark Rights of a Third Party in Privity with Defendant as an Affirmative Defense to a Claim of Infringement

In *United Food Imports, Inc. v. Baroody Imports, Inc.,*[62] the U.S. District Court for the District of New Jersey granted United Food's motion to dismiss Baroody's counterclaims based on the prudential standing doctrine, but transformed the counterclaims into affirmative defenses based on Baroody's privity with the holder of the superior trademark rights.

The underlying dispute arose when United Food, a wholesale distributor of packaged food products imported from Egypt, alleged that Defendants Paradise Halal Meat, LLC (Paradise Halal) and its owner, Abdelgawad Elsayed, infringed United Food's rights in the BASMA trademark. United Food filed suit, alleging trademark infringement, unfair competition, and contributory infringement. In response, Baroody counterclaimed, asserting that third-party Orouba Agrifoods Processing Co. (Orouba), the goods supplier, was the rightful owner of the BASMA mark, not United Food. In the past, Orouba had been a distributor to United Food. After that relationship ended, however, United Food began using nearly identical packaging to that of Orouba. When United Food obtained a registration for the BASMA mark, Orouba petitioned the USPTO for cancellation of the mark. Baroody then counterclaimed for a judgment declaring Orouba the rightful owner of the mark, for cancellation of United Food's trademark registration, and for damages.

The court rejected Baroody's attempt at bringing counterclaims that affirmatively asserted Orouba's rights rather than its own.[63] The court recognized that to bring a claim, a party must have standing. Here, however, all of the counterclaims simply adopted Orouba's claims against United Food in the USPTO cancellation proceeding. The court reviewed the exceptions to the general rule against third-party standing, which stem from prudential concerns, finding that none applied because Orouba could assert its own rights and had already done so before the USPTO. Thus, the court dismissed the counterclaims for lack of standing.

Nevertheless, the court allowed Baroody to transform the counterclaims into affirmative defenses under Federal Rule of Civil Procedure 8(c)(2), which allows a party who

62. No. 09-2835, 2010 U.S. Dist. LEXIS 33585 (D.N.J. Apr. 6, 2010).
63. *Id.* at *7.

mistakenly asserts a defense as a counterclaim to treat that claim as an affirmative defense. The court found the defenses were not precluded as *jus tertii* (i.e., defenses that only assert a third-party's rights).

Although *jus tertii* defenses usually are disfavored in trademark law because they could expand many trademark disputes far beyond a two-party conflict, the court recognized that the Third Circuit had not yet addressed the question of whether to allow *jus tertii* defenses in trademark cases. In reviewing cases where such defenses were disallowed, the court noted that no relationship existed between the defendant and the third-party whose rights were at issue. In this case, on the other hand, Orouba and Baroody appeared to have a contractual relationship because Orouba supplied Baroody with the allegedly infringing goods. Thus, the court concluded that, if a defendant can show privity with the relevant third party, it may claim some entitlement to the priority of that party's rights. The court thus declined to bar the affirmative defenses on United Food's motion to dismiss.

Fraud

Misstatements and Omissions in Application Constitute Fraud Resulting in the Cancellation of an Incontestable Registration

In *City of New York v. Tavern on the Green, L.P.*,[64] the U.S. District Court for the Southern District of New York granted the city's motion for summary judgment, holding that it had rights in the name "Tavern on the Green" that predated the defendants' incontestable registration for that name. In addition, the court ordered the incontestable registration cancelled, finding that it had been fraudulently procured.

In 1973, the city entered into a license agreement with Warner LeRoy to operate the "Tavern on the Green" as a restaurant and cabaret. LeRoy later transferred his interest in the agreement to Tavern on the Green, L.P. In 1978, LeRoy filed a trademark application to register the mark TAVERN ON THE GREEN for restaurant services with the USPTO on behalf of a joint venture that had been formed to operate the restaurant (Joint Venture). In the application, LeRoy claimed that the mark was first used on August 31, 1976. LeRoy did not disclose the 1973 agreement with the city to the USPTO. Rather, he signed a declaration stating that the Joint Venture had the right to use the mark and that "to the best of his knowledge and belief, no other person, firm, corporation or association has the right to use said mark in commerce . . . ."[65] LeRoy did not inform the city that he had filed the application or successfully registered the mark with the USPTO. In 1986, the Joint Venture filed a section 15 affidavit of incontestability pursuant to 15 U.S.C. § 1065 based on five years of continued use. In 2007, the Joint Venture filed another application to register the mark TAVERN ON THE GREEN for cooking oils, dressings, and dipping oils. The city, then aware of the prior registration and this application, filed two extensions of time to oppose the application, but never did.

The claim before the court arose out of the bankruptcy protection sought by Tavern on the Green, L.P. and LeRoy Adventures, Inc., which were referred to collectively in the

---

64.   427 B.R. 233 (S.D.N.Y. 2010).
65.   *Id.* at 238.

court's opinion as "Debtors." The city and Debtors each sought a declaration of rights to the mark, precipitated by the city's plan to reopen the restaurant with a new operator and Debtors' plans to auction the TAVERN ON THE GREEN restaurant service mark to the highest bidder.[66] The city also sought to cancel both registrations of the mark TAVERN ON THE GREEN, arguing that it had prior rights in the mark and that the registration for restaurant services was fraudulently procured.

Because the registration for restaurant services was incontestable, the court noted that it could not be cancelled except under one of the statutory exceptions to incontestability. The court found that there were two statutory exceptions applicable in this case: prior state law rights in the registered mark and fraudulent procurement.

First, the city established priority under New York law to the mark TAVERN ON THE GREEN and proved that the mark was closely associated in the mind of the public with the building and the location owned by the city in Central Park. The city had continuously operated restaurants at that location through numerous licensees since 1934, well before the Debtors' operation of the restaurant beginning in the mid-1970s.

Second, the court found undisputed facts that the 1981 application for the mark contained deliberate material misstatements and omissions about the relationship of the City and the applicant, which was not disclosed to the USPTO to be one of licensor and licensee. The applicant's statements and omissions evidenced "a deliberate attempt to mislead the PTO,"[67] which more than met the heightened evidentiary burden required to find fraud. Accordingly, the district court had the authority to cancel the mark pursuant to 15 U.S.C. § 1119 without regard to laches or time-limited defenses asserted by the Debtors.[68]

Additionally, the fraudulent behavior amounted to "unclean hands" that served to bar the Debtors' numerous equitable affirmative defenses, which meant that summary judgment was proper in all matters but one: the court did not grant the City's motion to cancel the TAVERN ON THE GREEN mark for cooking oils, as that matter was held to be "premature."

Standard for Proving Fraud on the USPTO Is Clear and Convincing Evidence of an Intent to Deceive

In *Salu, Inc. v. Original Skin Store,*[69] the U.S. District Court for the Eastern District of California denied Defendant The Original Skin Store's (TOSS) motion to dismiss for partial summary judgment as to its affirmative defense of fraud on the USPTO because it had not established Plaintiff Salu's intent to deceive the USPTO. TOSS sought cancellation of Salu's mark, SKINSTORE, alleging that it had been procured by fraud in that Salu made a "knowingly false representation of a material fact by stating that it had substantially exclusive use" of SKINSTORE five years prior to its declaration supporting its registration application.[70]

The court disagreed, finding that TOSS was obligated to demonstrate by "clear and convincing" evidence that Salu procured its mark by fraud and must "identify a deliberate

---

66.   The court noted that such a transfer would be barred as an assignment in gross, but acknowledged that the matter was not before the court. *Id.* at 239 n.4.

67.   *Id.* at 243.

68.   *Id.* at 244 (citing Marshak v. Treadwell, 240 F.3d 184, 192–94 (3d Cir. 2001)).

69.   No. S-08-1035, 2010 WL 1444617 (E.D. Cal. Apr. 12, 2010) (not for publication).

70.   *Id.* at *3.

attempt by the registrant" to mislead the USPTO.[71] The court noted that a false statement or representation alone may be caused by a misunderstanding or inadvertence and is not the same as a fraudulent statement, which requires proof of an intent to deceive.

Salu had acquired rights to a two-word mark, SKIN STORE, by assignment, which was not registered on the Principal Register (due to mere descriptiveness), but was successfully registered on the Supplemental Register on May 30, 2000, by the prior owner of the mark. Approximately four years after Salu acquired the rights to the two-word mark, it filed a trademark application for a one-word version, SKINSTORE, on May 2, 2005. Its application claimed that the mark had been used exclusively and continuously in commerce for at least five years prior. TOSS argued that this statement was deceptive.

TOSS claimed that Salu also failed to disclose a prior action and previous uses of the mark. Specifically, before filing its one-word trademark application, Salu was involved in a dispute with a company having the mark ESKINSTORE and the domain name www.eskinstore.com, which was argued before the World Intellectual Property Organization (WIPO). WIPO concluded that it did not have evidence to establish a "clear case of cybersquatting" and could not assess an infringement action under U.S. law.[72]

TOSS relied primarily on the WIPO decision, contending that it reflected substantial, non-infringing use by another party that Salu had failed to disclose. However, the court noted that WIPO had "pointedly" not decided that ESKINSTORE was noninfringing; therefore, Salu's failure to disclose that decision or the ESKINSTORE mark did not "demonstrate willful deception by clear and convincing evidence."[73] The court also pointed to Salu's evidence of actions that it had taken to prevent third parties from using its mark.

Salu said it had sent more than 300 cease and desist letters to alleged infringers, but the USPTO neither required nor asked for Salu to submit evidence of inconsequential or infringing uses. Additionally, Salu contended that the USPTO did not request additional evidence of acquired distinctiveness when it prosecuted Salu's application for SKINSTORE. The court noted that, although Salu may have provided more evidence that third-party uses were inconsequential or infringing, TOSS failed to prove that Salu was required to provide such evidence.

TTAB Denies Motion for Summary Judgment Finding Insufficient Evidence of Intent to Deceive

In *DaimlerChrysler Corp. v. American Motors Corp.*,[74] the TTAB denied Petitioner DaimlerChrysler's motion for summary judgment on its claim of fraud. The law governing fraud claims changed during the pendency of DaimlerChrysler's motion. DaimlerChrysler had relied on *Medinol Ltd. v. Neuro Vasx, Inc.*,[75] in which the TTAB required only an objective intent to prove fraud. The new and stricter standard set out by the Federal Circuit in *In re Bose Corp.*[76] requires a finding that an applicant or registrant knowingly made a false, material representation with the intent to deceive the USPTO in

---

71. *Id.* at *3.
72. *Id.* at *4.
73. *Id.*
74. 94 U.S.P.Q.2d (BNA) 1086 (T.T.A.B. 2010).
75. 67 U.S.P.Q.2d (BNA) 1205 (T.T.A.B. 2003).
76. 580 F.3d 1240 (Fed. Cir. 2009).

obtaining a registration. Finding intent to deceive requires clear and convincing evidence, a standard stricter than that for negligence or gross negligence.

Where a pleading asserts that a knowing misrepresentation on a material matter is made to procure a registration, the element of intent is sufficiently pled. The TTAB noted that DaimlerChrysler successfully pled a claim of fraud by alleging that: (1) Respondent American Motors Corp. (AMC) knowingly and falsely represented to the USPTO in its statement of use that it was using the AMC mark in commerce in connection with automobiles and structural parts thereof; (2) this material misrepresentation was made to induce the USPTO to issue a registration; and (3) this misrepresentation was relied on by the USPTO in the issuance of the subject registration.

Although DaimlerChrysler pled a claim of fraud, the TTAB clarified: "The preferred practice for a party alleging fraud in a Board opposition or cancellation proceeding is to specifically allege the adverse party's intent to deceive the USPTO, so that there is no question that this indispensable element has been pled."[77] Intent to deceive must be specifically pled. DaimlerChrysler did not point to evidence to support the inference of deceptive intent. Therefore, it failed to satisfy the clear and convincing evidence standard required to prove fraud. In its reply brief, DaimlerChrysler recognized that its reliance on the lower standard from *Medinol* was no longer appropriate. However, DaimlerChrysler did not direct the TTAB to any previously submitted evidence that would have met the new *Bose* standard.

The TTAB denied summary judgment, finding that the question of AMC's intent was an issue of genuine dispute with respect to a material fact, and observing that issues of intent usually are unsuitable for determination in pretrial motions.

TTAB Adopts In re Bose *Standard for "Fraud on the USPTO" Claims*

In *Asian & Western Classics B.V. v. Selkow*,[78] Asian and Western filed a petition to cancel Selkow's trademark registration on the grounds that Selkow committed fraud on the USPTO when she filed a registration application and declarations asserting that the mark had been used in commerce and no such use had actually occurred. The allegations of fraud were based solely on "information and belief" unsupported by any statement of the facts on which that belief was based and, as to intent to commit fraud, merely asserted generally that Selkow "knew or should have known" that her statements of use were false. The TTAB undertook a review of the sufficiency of the petition's allegations in connection with Asian and Western's motion for summary judgment. The TTAB concluded that, in light of the Federal Circuit's recent decision in *In re Bose Corp.*,[79] an allegation that a trademark registrant "knew or should have known" that a statement was false was not sufficient to state a claim for fraud on the USPTO.

First, the TTAB noted that, in claims of fraud on the USPTO, as in all other fraud claims, the petitioner must plead each element of the alleged fraud with particularity, pursuant to Federal Rule of Civil Procedure 9(b). Under that standard, the TTAB has long held that fraud claims based on information and belief, unsupported by allegations as to the specific facts on which that belief is based, fail to state a claim for fraud with the

---

77. *See DaimlerChrysler*, 94 U.S.P.Q.2d at 1089 n.2.
78. 92 U.S.P.Q.2d (BNA) 1478 (T.T.A.B. 2009).
79. *Id.* (citing *In re* Bose Corp., 580 F.3d 1240 (Fed. Cir. 2009)).

requisite particularity. However, the TTAB had not previously considered "intent to commit fraud" as a separate element of fraud subject to the Rule 9 particularity requirement and, therefore, had previously found allegations that a party "knew or should have known" a statement was false to be sufficient for fraudulent intent.

However, the landscape had recently changed. In *Bose*, the Federal Circuit overturned a TTAB decision granting a petition for trademark cancellation based on an allegation that Bose "knew or should have known" it made a false statement regarding commercial use in connection with a trademark renewal. The Federal Circuit examined the petition's allegation that Bose "knew or should have known" its statement to the USPTO regarding commercial use was false and concluded that an allegation based on a "knew or should have known" standard failed to satisfy the particularity requirement of Rule 9. The court concluded such an allegation would never be sufficient to support a fraud claim and expressly held that such an allegation implies mere negligence, not a specific intent to deceive.

In light of the Federal Circuit's ruling in *Bose*, the TTAB's decision in this case recognized, for the first time, that "intent is a specific element of a fraud claim." Accordingly, the TTAB also concluded "an allegation that a declarant 'should have known' a material statement was false" did not "make out a proper pleading" of intent in support of a claim for fraud on the USPTO.[80] The TTAB thus dismissed the cancellation petition with leave to amend and deemed Asian and Western's summary judgment motion to be moot.

First Amendment

First Amendment Does Not Prevent Application of Trademark Law to Disputed Use of "Seventh-Day Adventist"

In *General Conference Corp. of Seventh-Day Adventists v. McGill*,[81] the Sixth Circuit affirmed the judgment of the district court, holding that enforcement of one church's trademark rights against a breakaway church did not violate the Free Exercise Clause of the First Amendment or violate the Religious Freedom Restoration Act (RFRA).

The General Conference Corporation of Seventh-day Adventists (General Conference) was formed in 1863. The church grew out of several congregations that believed that Jesus Christ's second coming, or advent, was imminent and that the Sabbath should be observed on the seventh day of the week. The name "Seventh-day Adventist" reflects these two core beliefs, but it was not used by the early congregations. The name was first adopted by the General Conference after its formation. The General Conference has since registered several marks that include the term "Seventh-day Adventist," as well as related marks such as ADVENTIST and SDA.

McGill was a member of the official Seventh-day Adventist church, but decided to leave the church because of a theological dispute. He formed a small breakaway church called, variously, "Creation Seventh Day Adventist Church" and "Creation Seventh Day & Adventist Church." He also registered domain names incorporating elements of the General Conference's SEVENTH-DAY ADVENTIST mark, such as 7th-day-adventist.org.

---

80. *Id.* at 1479.
81. 617 F.3d 402 (6th Cir. 2010).

The General Conference sued McGill under the Lanham Act and Tennessee law, alleging, among other claims, trademark infringement, unfair competition, dilution, and cybersquatting. McGill asserted various affirmative defenses in his answer, including the Free Exercise Clause of the First Amendment, that the name "Seventh-day Adventist" is a generic reference to a religion rather than a source identifier for the General Conference, and that the General Conference lost its right to trademark protection of the Seventh-day Adventist name because it had strayed from the original doctrine of the church. In a motion to dismiss, McGill also argued that the RFRA rendered trademark law inapplicable to him because Seventh-Day Adventism is a religion and therefore is inherently generic and incapable of protection as a trademark. The district court denied McGill's motion to dismiss, finding that trademark law was applicable despite the Free Exercise Clause, that McGill had waived the RFRA defense by failing to include it in his answer, and that whether a trademark term is generic is a factual issue that could not be decided on a motion to dismiss.

The district court also granted partial summary judgment to the General Conference on various grounds. The court found that the marks SEVENTH-DAY ADVENTIST and ADVENTIST were incontestable and presumptively valid, a finding that shifted the burden to McGill to prove invalidity. The court concluded that McGill could not overcome this presumption with respect to the SEVENTH-DAY ADVENTIST mark, although it found a fact issue concerning the genericness of the term "Adventist." The district court also rejected McGill's affirmative defenses. The court later entered a default judgment against McGill on all remaining claims as a result of his failure to participate in a court-ordered mediation.

The Sixth Circuit addressed four issues raised in McGill's motion to dismiss and his opposition to the motion for partial summary judgment. First, the court rejected McGill's argument that the First Amendment precluded the district court from exercising subject matter jurisdiction. McGill contended that a court could not apply neutral principles of trademark law without resolving an underlying theological dispute about the meaning of Seventh-day Adventism. The Sixth Circuit reasoned that it was not required to decide any issue of church doctrine because there was no theological issue in dispute. Both the General Conference and McGill accepted the same core theological principles that the second advent is imminent and that the Sabbath should be celebrated on the seventh day. Neutral principles of trademark law could be applied to decide whether McGill was properly using the General Conference's marks to promote his church's services and materials.

Second, the Sixth Circuit refused to apply the RFRA to this case. The RFRA was enacted in order to require that courts apply a strict-scrutiny test in reviewing the burdens that governments place on the free exercise of religion. The statute prohibits any substantial burden on the exercise of religion, unless that burden furthers a compelling governmental interest and is the least restrictive means of furthering that interest. McGill argued that enforcement of the General Conference's trademarks would violate his free exercise rights because his religion requires him to use the term "Seventh Day Adventist" in the name of his church. The Sixth Circuit held that McGill cannot claim the benefit of the RFRA because it applies only to suits against the government and not to suits between private parties. With this decision, the Sixth Circuit joined the Seventh and Ninth Circuits, and it disagreed with the Second Circuit, which has found the RFRA applicable to private disputes.

Third, the Sixth Circuit rejected McGill's argument that Seventh-day Adventist is the name of a religion and is, therefore, a generic term that cannot be protected as a trademark. The court acknowledged that well-known terms that are understood as referring in general to a particular faith are generic. However, the court concluded it would be inappropriate to conclude as a matter of law that McGill met his burden of proving that the public considers "Seventh-day Adventist" to refer generically to a religion.

Finally, the Sixth Circuit concluded that summary judgment was proper as to the SEVENTH-DAY ADVENTIST mark. The mark was presumptively valid, and, based on the evidence presented, there was no genuine issue that McGill's use of the mark was likely to cause confusion.

First Amendment, Incidental Use Doctrine, and Nominative Fair-Use Defense Did Not Protect Use of Name in Commercial Publication

In *Yeager v. Cingular Wireless LLC,*[82] the U.S. District Court for the Eastern District of California denied Cingular's motion for summary judgment on right-of-publicity and Lanham Act claims arising from its use of the name of former Air Force pilot Chuck Yeager in an advertisement concerning Cingular's wireless services. Yeager, a famous test pilot, was the first to break the sound barrier.

Following the 2006 hurricane season, Cingular prepared a publication touting its emergency preparedness program. In that publication, Cingular included a sentence noting that, sixty years earlier, Yeager had broken the sound barrier and achieved a speed of Mach 1. Cingular went on to say that it had broken "another kind of barrier" with its MACH 1 and MACH 2 mobile command centers. The publication made no other mention of Yeager, did not propose a commercial transaction, and did not offer for sale any specific products or services.

Yeager sued Cingular, asserting a right-of-publicity claim under California law and a false endorsement claim under section 43(a) of the Lanham Act. Cingular moved for summary judgment on these claims, arguing that the First Amendment protected its use of Yeager's name because the publication was not commercial speech and it reported on newsworthy matters of public interest.

In analyzing Cingular's defense, the court first considered Cingular's argument that the publication was noncommercial speech. Even though it did not propose any commercial transactions or offer any products or services, the court concluded that Cingular's publication was commercial speech because its central theme was how Cingular's emergency preparedness program enhanced its wireless services. The court rejected Cingular's argument that the publication was noncommercial because its commercial aspects were intertwined with expressive aspects. The court explained that the publication's sole purpose was to promote Cingular's services and that it provided no editorial comment on public safety issues.

The court similarly rejected Cingular's second First Amendment argument that the publication was issued following the devastating 2006 hurricane season and reported on newsworthy matters of public interest. The court observed that the context of the publication and the nature of the information it conveyed showed that Yeager's name and accomplishments were used to attract attention to Cingular's unrelated wireless services. This was part of a carefully crafted strategy to promote the Cingular brand. Even though

---

82. 673 F. Supp. 2d 1089 (E.D. Cal. 2009).

Yeager's achievements may have been newsworthy, Cingular was not entitled to use Yeager's identity in the context of an unrelated commercial piece.

Cingular also argued that the incidental use doctrine protected its fleeting reference to Yeager. The court concluded that Cingular's use of Yeager's name was not incidental because it uniquely enhanced the marketability of Cingular's services.

Finally, Cingular sought summary judgment on Yeager's section 43(a) claim, arguing that: (1) Yeager could not demonstrate triable issues of fact regarding actual confusion; and (2) its use of Yeager's name was a permissible nominative fair use. With respect to confusion, the court concluded that a jury could infer that Cingular intended to capitalize upon positive associations with Yeager's name by implying endorsement. Even though there was scant specific evidence of actual confusion, the court held that it could not find that Cingular was entitled to JMOL at this stage of the proceedings.

Similarly, with respect to nominative fair use, the court noted that Cingular used Yeager's name and accomplishments to support its own product. This use was sufficient to create a triable issue of fact regarding implied endorsement, which, if found, would defeat application of the nominative fair-use defense.

Nominative Fair Use

Permanent Injunction Vacated as Overbroad Where Court Failed to Apply Nominative Fair-Use Test

In *Toyota Motor Sales, U.S.A., Inc. v. Tabari,*[83] the Ninth Circuit vacated the district court's permanent injunction against the pro se defendants' use of Toyota's LEXUS mark.

The case arose when Toyota sued Farzad and Lisa Tabari, independent auto brokers, for using the domain names buy-a-lexus.com and buyorleaselexus.com. During a bench trial, the district court applied the eight-factor *Sleekcraft* test and found infringement.[84] The court ordered the Tabaris to stop using the domains and enjoined them from using the LEXUS mark in any other domain names. The Tabaris appealed. The Ninth Circuit reversed, finding the *Sleekcraft* test inapplicable where a defendant uses a mark to refer to the trademarked good itself. Here, the Tabaris used the LEXUS mark to describe their business of brokering genuine Lexus vehicles. The court noted that this type of use is nominative fair use, which by definition is not an infringement.

Where a nominative fair-use defense is raised, the test is whether: (1) the product was "readily identifiable" without use of the mark; (2) the defendant used more of the mark than was necessary; or (3) the defendant falsely suggested that he or she was sponsored or endorsed by the trademark holder.[85] If the nominative use does not satisfy all three factors, the district court may order the defendant to modify its use in order to satisfy the factors. The court may not enjoin nominative fair use of a mark altogether.

The district court enjoined the Tabaris from using any "domain name, service mark, trademark, trade name, meta tag or other commercial indication of origin that includes the mark LEXUS."[86] The Ninth Circuit cautioned that a trademark injunction involving nomina-

---

83. 610 F.3d 1171 (9th Cir. 2010).
84. AMF, Inc. v. Sleekcraft Boats, 599 F.2d 341, 348–49 (9th Cir. 1979).
85. *Tabari,* 610 F.3d 1175–76.
86. *Id.* at 1176.

tive fair use can raise serious First Amendment concerns because it can interfere with truthful communication between buyers and sellers in the marketplace. To uphold the broad injunction, the court found that it would have to be convinced that consumers are likely to believe Web sites are sponsored or endorsed by a trademark holder whenever the domain name contains the trademark. In this case, the court was not convinced.

The court identified the relevant marketplace to be the online marketplace and the relevant consumer to be one who is accustomed to shopping online. The court found the injunction plainly overbroad because it prohibits domain names that dispel any confusion as to endorsement or sponsorship. Sites such as we-are-definitely-not-lexus.com would be barred, even though a reasonable consumer would not believe that Toyota sponsored the site. Prohibition of this type of truthful, nonmisleading speech does not advance the Lanham Act's purpose of protecting consumers and preventing unfair competition; rather, it undermines the rationale because the Tabaris cannot honestly communicate with their customers.

The court noted that consumers who use the Internet for shopping are generally quite sophisticated and are not likely to be confused that a domain name is sponsored by a trademark owner just because it contains the string of letters making up the trademark in the domain name (e.g., comcastsucks.org). The court declined to sanction the wholesale prohibition of nominative fair use as requested by Toyota. Outside the case of "trademark.com" (e.g., Lexus.com) or domains that actively claim affiliation with a trademark holder (e.g., we-are-lexus.com), the court concluded that consumers do not form any firm expectation about domain sponsorship.

Turning to the Tabaris' domain names, the court found that: (1) it was necessary to incorporate the LEXUS mark to communicate that the Tabaris specialize in Lexus vehicles; and (2) even assuming a limited injunction may be proper to prevent relapse of infringing conduct such as the use of the stylized LEXUS mark, the district court is in a better position to determine the scope of the remedy.

The court instructed the district court on remand to bear in mind that a trademark injunction should be tailored to prevent ongoing violations, not punish past conduct. The court also instructed the district court to analyze the case under the test for nominative fair use, not under the *Sleekcraft* test. It was error for the district court to treat nominative fair use as an affirmative defense. "[N]ominative fair use 'replaces' *Sleekcraft* as the proper test for likely confusion whenever defendant asserts to have referred to the trademarked good itself."[87] On remand, Toyota bears the burden of establishing that the Tabaris' use of the LEXUS mark was *not* nominative fair use. A finding of nominative fair use equates with a finding that the plaintiff failed to establish a likelihood of confusion as to sponsorship or endorsement.[88] Recognizing that earlier Ninth Circuit precedent held the opposite and placed the burden on the defendant, the court clarified that the relevant precedent had been "effectively overruled."[89] A defendant seeking to assert nominative fair use need only show that it used the mark to refer to the trademarked good; the burden then reverts to the plaintiff to show likelihood of confusion under the nominative fair-use test.

The court upheld the district court's ruling that Toyota's delay of six months in first contacting the Tabaris, and a subsequent two-year delay while the parties actively tried to resolve the dispute, were reasonable. Therefore, the Tabaris' laches defense failed.

---

87. *Id.* at 1182.
88. *Id.* at 1183.
89. *Id.*

Finally, the court ruled that the district court did not err by not empanelling a jury because Toyota sought only equitable relief in the form of a permanent injunction. The court also found the district court's bifurcation of the Tabaris' counterclaims to be harmless error because the district court did not rely on any factual findings made at the bench trial; it could have granted summary judgment on the same basis before the bench trial.

Owner of Internet Domain www.chicago2016.com Survives Summary Judgment Motion

In *Frayne v. Chicago 2016*,[90] the U.S. District Court for the Northern District of Illinois denied Chicago 2016's and the United States Olympic Committee's (USOC) motion for summary judgment on its Ted Stevens Olympic and Amateur Sports Act (Stevens Act) and Anticybersquatting Consumer Protection Act (ACPA) claims, brought as a result of Plaintiff Stephen Frayne's operation of the www.chicago2016.com Web site. The Stevens Act, which "grants the USOC exclusive rights over the use of certain words and symbols" and specifies requirements for its member national governing bodies for individual sporting events, differs from trademark protection under the Lanham Act.[91] Unlike ordinary trademark protection, Stevens Act protection of words and symbols differs in that "the USOC need not prove that a contested use is likely to cause confusion, and an unauthorized user of the word does not have available the normal statutory defenses."[92]

Frayne registered the Chicago2016.com domain in 2004 for the purpose of providing a forum for discussion about the pros and cons of hosting the Olympic games.[93] After registration of the domain name to Frayne, the domain registrar maintained a parked page on the site, which included several advertising links. All revenues for the links, however, went to the registrar, not to Frayne. In 2006, Chicago 2016 filed for trademark protection of the phrase "Chicago 2016," which the USPTO registered on April 22, 2008. Subsequently, Chicago 2016 assigned its rights in the trademark to the USOC. Following the assignment, the defendants filed a Uniform Domain-Name Dispute-Resolution Policy (UDRP) action against Frayne, seeking the immediate transfer of the Chicago2016.com domain name. After resolution of the UDRP action, Frayne sued Chicago 2016 and the USOC, seeking declaratory relief stemming from the trademark allegations made in the UDRP action.

Chicago 2016 and the USOC brought a motion for summary judgment under the Stevens Act, arguing that the mark falsely represented an association with the USOC and that Frayne used it to induce his sale of goods and services. In denying the defendants' motion for summary judgment on the Stevens Act claim, the court held that there was a question of fact as to whether Frayne "used" the trademark, in this case the Internet domain, for commercial purposes as required by the Act. In reaching this conclusion, the court looked to the fact that Frayne did not receive revenues from the parked page and that it was unclear that he had even consented to the registrar's use of the parked page. Furthermore, the court determined that "Chicago 2016" was not a mark that automatically fell

---

90. 92 U.S.P.Q.2d (BNA) 1454 (N.D. Ill. 2009).

91. *Id.* at 1456 (citing 36 U.S.C. § 220506(a)).

92. *Id.* (quoting San Francisco Arts & Athletics, Inc. v. U.S. Olympic Comm., 483 U.S. 522, 531 (1987)).

93. *Id.* at 1455–56.

within the protections of the Stevens Act, as there was no immediate false representation of association with the USOC. Rather, the court reasoned that a city-plus-Olympic-year combination could acquire an association with the USOC and the Olympics over time, but because the defendants had not proffered this argument, the determination required further proceedings.

Similarly, the court denied the defendants' motion for summary judgment on the ACPA claim, holding that it was not ripe because it depended on a determination that Chicago 2016 was a protected mark pursuant to the Stevens Act. Additionally, the court held that a question of fact existed as to whether Frayne had a bad-faith intent to profit from the Chicago 2016 mark, an element necessary to prove liability under the ACPA.

Abandonment

Trademark Assignee Overcame Statutory Presumption of Trademark Abandonment Despite Six Years of Nonuse and Cancellation of Its Registrations

In *Crash Dummy Movie, LLC v. Mattel, Inc.,*[94] the Federal Circuit affirmed a decision by the TTAB that trademark assignee Mattel had overcome a statutory presumption that it abandoned the "Crash Dummies" trademarks (CRASH DUMMIES and THE INCREDIBLE CRASH DUMMIES) despite six years of nonuse and the cancellation of its registrations.

Under the Lanham Act, a trademark is deemed to be abandoned if "use has been discontinued with intent not to resume such use."[95] Three consecutive years of nonuse is prima facie evidence of abandonment, creates a rebuttable presumption that the mark owner has abandoned the mark, and shifts the burden to the mark owner to show either use of the mark or an intent to resume use of the mark during the statutory period.

Tyco Industries, Inc. (Tyco) had produced a line of Crash Dummies toys from 1991 to 1994, granted forty-nine licenses for use of the marks that expired in 1995, and granted an option to produce a Crash Dummies movie to appellant The Crash Dummy Movie, LLC (CDM) in 1995, which expired in 1996. Tyco registered the Crash Dummies marks in 1993.

Mattel acquired the Crash Dummies marks by assignment in 1997 when it purchased Tyco. Mattel recorded the assignment in 1998, but, because of a need to retool Tyco's toys to meet its more stringent safety requirements and to research, develop, and market the retooled toys, Mattel did not use the marks in commerce until December 2003. Meanwhile, the USPTO cancelled Mattel's registrations for failure to file a declaration of use in 2000. In March 2003, CDM filed an intent-to-use application to register Crash Dummies for use with games and playthings. Mattel opposed CDM's application, asserting that it was entitled to common law trademark rights in Crash Dummies that predated CDM's application. CDM asserted that Mattel had abandoned the Crash Dummies marks through nonuse.

The TTAB sustained Mattel's opposition, and the Federal Circuit affirmed, finding that three factors provided "substantial evidence" that Mattel had, at all times, intended to

---

94.   601 F.3d 1387 (Fed. Cir. 2010).
95.   15 U.S.C. § 1127 (2006).

resume use of the marks: (1) Mattel's 1998 recordation of the trademark assignment; (2) Mattel's 1998 talks with KB Toys about a possible retail contract for Crash Dummies toys; and (3) Mattel's research and development activities between 2000 and 2003 and its ultimate shipment of toys to market in December 2003. The court also held that the cancellation of the registrations was not dispositive, as a registrant's failure to file a use declaration does not necessarily indicate an intent to abandon the mark or its common law trademark rights, nor does it establish a lack of intent to use the mark. Accordingly, the court affirmed the TTAB's decision sustaining Mattel's opposition to CDM's application to register the Crash Dummies marks.

PROCEDURAL MATTERS

Trademark Infringement Complaint Dismissed Where Defendant's Advertisements Involved Only a Descriptive Fair Use of an Individual's Name and Were Unlikely to Cause Confusion

In *Hensley Manufacturing, Inc. v. ProPride, Inc.,*[96] the Sixth Circuit held that a trademark owner's complaint should be dismissed where the allegations that the defendants' use of the marks was likely to cause confusion did not satisfy the heightened pleading standard of *Ashcroft v. Iqbal.*[97]

Plaintiff Hensley Manufacturing, Inc. (HMI) manufactured and sold the "Hensley Arrow," a trailer hitch designed by Jim Hensley. Jim Hensley sold his hitch business to HMI in 1994. Additionally, HMI registered a trademark for Jim Hensley's name and sold trailer hitches using the Hensley name. Subsequently, Mr. Hensley ceased business with HMI, designed a new trailer hitch, and licensed the new design to a competitor, ProPride, Inc. ProPride promoted the new hitch in various print, Web site, and mail advertisements identifying Mr. Hensley as the designer of the hitch.

HMI sued ProPride and Jim Hensley for federal and common-law trademark infringement and unfair competition and requested a preliminary injunction. The district court granted ProPride's motion to dismiss the complaint, finding that its use of the Hensley name constituted a descriptive fair use of an individual's name, other than as a mark, to describe ProPride's goods.

The Sixth Circuit affirmed the district court's holding that ProPride did not use the Hensley name in a true "trademark" manner.[98] The Sixth Circuit held that the complaint did not allege facts sufficient to show that ProPride's use of the Hensley name created a likelihood of confusion regarding the source of its products. Although the complaint did refer to content in ProPride's advertisements (attached as exhibits), the Sixth Circuit determined that the trademark infringement claims failed because the advertisements did not create a likelihood of consumer confusion regarding the source of the competitor's products. The advertisements identified the inventor as the designer of the new hitch

---

96.   579 F.3d 603, 609–11 (6th Cir. 2009).

97.   129 S. Ct. 1937, 1949–50 (2009) (holding that "a claim has facial plausibility when the plaintiff pleads factual content that allows the court to draw the reasonable inference that the defendant is liable for the misconduct alleged.").

98.   *Hensley*, 579 F.3d at 611.

system, identified the competitor as the seller, and stated that the inventor was no longer affiliated with the trademark owner.

Additionally, the Sixth Circuit held that, even if the trademark claims were properly pled, the affirmative defense of fair use precluded the trademark infringement claims because the complaint and attached exhibits showed that the competitor's uses of the inventor's name were merely descriptive.[99] The Sixth Circuit found that the record established that ProPride's advertisements used Jim Hensley's name only to identify him as a designer of trailer hitches, describe his relationship with ProPride, and tell the story of his success in the industry.

Jurisdiction

Lanham Act and State Right-of-Publicity Claim Do Not Apply to Actions Occurring Outside the United States

In *Love v. Sanctuary Records Group, Ltd.*,[100] the Ninth Circuit affirmed the lower court, holding that neither the Lanham Act nor California's common law right of publicity applied extraterritorially to actions that occurred in Great Britain. The court also held that Plaintiff Mike Love's allegations against the defendant for acts directed entirely at markets in Ireland and the United Kingdom were properly dismissed with prejudice for lack of personal jurisdiction because the plaintiff had no losses in the United States related to that defendant's actions.

Love, a founding member of the band known as *The Beach Boys*, acquired the right to use the band's trademark in live performances. When the band's founding member, Brian Wilson, released a solo album and began touring, a British newspaper began promoting Wilson's work. The newspaper distributed a compact disc (CD) of Wilson's performances in 2.6 million copies of its newspaper in the United Kingdom and Ireland. A small number of newspapers without the CD were distributed in the United States. The CD featured photographs that included images of Love. The photographs were prominently advertised in the newspaper. Love sued various parties, including Wilson and a British company that licensed and recorded the CD, for violations of the Lanham Act and Love's right of publicity under California law.

The Ninth Circuit affirmed the district court's dismissal of the right-of-publicity claim based on its de novo review of the lower court's ruling as to choice of law, noting that California recognizes a statutory and common law right of publicity, but England does not. The court applied California's three-part governmental interest test: (1) examining the laws of each jurisdiction to determine if they differ; (2) if they differ, determining whether a true conflict exists in that both jurisdictions have an interest in its law being applied; and (3) where more than one jurisdiction has a legitimate interest, identifying and applying the law of the jurisdiction whose interest would be more impaired.

The court found that there was no true conflict between the law of California and England because California had no interest in applying its law to the alleged conduct, given that no party remaining in the suit was a citizen of California, and given that the claimed misappropriation occurred nearly exclusively in Ireland and Great Britain. The

---

99. *Id.* at 612.
100. 611 F.3d 601 (9th Cir. 2010).

court considered de minimis the handful of copies of the newspaper that were distributed in California without the CD.

The court rejected Love's argument that, because he owned property in California, he was not an out-of-state party. Love had not cited a single case in which a California court recognized that injury relevant to a choice-of-law analysis is suffered anywhere other than the domicile of the celebrity or the location where the image is exploited. The court noted that, even if Love's commercial interests in California created a true conflict, Great Britain's interest would be more impaired if English law were not applied because England has demonstrated a significant policy decision favoring unrestricted competition in "commercial exploitation of names and likenesses."[101]

The court found that the Lanham Act claims were properly dismissed because the Act cannot be applied extraterritorially to acts that were committed in Europe. The court set forth the three-part test for coverage of the Lanham Act for foreign acts: (1) the alleged acts must have an effect on foreign commerce in the United States; (2) the effect must be great enough to present a cognizable Lanham Act injury; and (3) the interests of and links to commerce in the United States "must be sufficiently strong in relation to those of other nations."[102]

The Ninth Circuit noted that the first two criteria are met even where all of the alleged acts occurred outside of the United States so long as an American plaintiff can claim monetary damage in the United States. In this case, it was undisputed that all relevant acts occurred outside of the United States. Love's only monetary damages claim was that his ticket sales in America were lower after distribution of the newspaper and CD, which he claimed caused Europeans to mistakenly associate the CD and Wilson's works with Love's touring band. The court found this argument unavailing, holding it unlikely a jury would believe confusion overseas resulted in decreased ticket sales in the United States.[103]

The court dismissed Love's claim against the British company that had licensed and recorded the CD for lack of personal jurisdiction because that defendant "did not purposefully direct any of the relevant intentional acts at California."[104]

The court upheld the district court's award of attorneys' fees to the defendants based on several findings. The court found that California's right-of-publicity statute provides for attorneys' fees to the prevailing party. Even though the statute was held not to apply, the fact that Love brought an action under that statute mandated the award. The court also found that attorneys' fees were warranted under the Lanham Act, which provides for such award in exceptional cases. The court found that an exceptional case under trademark law is one where the defendant acted maliciously, fraudulently, deliberately, or willfully. An exceptional case was demonstrated here because Love asserted groundless and unreasonable claims, had not presented any evidence of any "United States effect," and all cases cited to support Love's extraterritorial application were readily distinguishable and of no persuasive value.[105]

---

101. *Id.* at 611.

102. *Id.* at 613 (citing Star-Kist Foods, Inc. v. P.J. Rhodes & Co., 769 F.2d 1393, 1395 (9th Cir. 1985)).

103. *Id.*

104. *Id.* at 609.

105. *Id.* at 615.

Actual and Ongoing Use of a Mark, Coupled with a Letter Charging Infringement, Held Sufficient to Support a Declaratory Judgment Action

In *Express Scripts, Inc. v. Intel Corp.*,[106] the U.S. District Court for the Eastern District of Missouri denied Defendant Intel's motion to dismiss for lack of subject matter jurisdiction and its request for dismissal under the Declaratory Judgment Act, holding that a real and immediate controversy between the parties existed and thus satisfied the actual controversy requirement of the Declaratory Judgment Act.

After Plaintiff Express Scripts, Inc. (ESI) filed a federal trademark application with the USPTO for the mark INTELLACT, Intel sent a letter to ESI alleging that its use of the INTELLACT mark: (1) was likely to confuse or deceive consumers as to the source of the goods and services or suggest a relationship between the parties that did not exist; (2) was likely to dilute the famous INTEL mark; (3) constituted infringement of Intel's established trademark rights; and (4) violated Intel's rights under the laws of trademark dilution and unfair competition. Intel's letter requested a written response from ESI by May 22, 2009. Instead, on May 22, 2009, ESI filed a lawsuit seeking a declaratory judgment that its INTELLACT mark did not infringe or dilute the INTEL mark.

In evaluating the circumstances of the case, the court relied on the U.S. Supreme Court's decision in *MedImmune, Inc. v. Genentech, Inc.*, requiring "a controversy of sufficient immediacy and reality to warrant the issuance of a declaratory judgment."[107] Prior to *MedImmune*, the Federal Circuit used a two-part test that required a plaintiff to establish a reasonable apprehension of imminent suit and an ongoing or meaningful preparation toward potentially infringing activity.[108] *MedImmune* eliminated the first element. Since the decision, courts applying *MedImmune* have determined that jurisdiction to enter a declaratory judgment is warranted "where the defendant has taken a position that puts the declaratory judgment plaintiff in the position of either pursuing arguably illegal behavior or abandoning that which he claims a right to do."[109]

Intel argued that its letter demanding that ESI abandon its intent-to-use application failed to create a case or controversy under Article III. During briefing of the motion, however, ESI presented evidence of current use of the mark. Therefore, the court held that the letter put ESI in the position of either pursuing arguably illegal behavior or abandoning that which it claimed a right to do under *MedImmune*. Evidence of use of the mark by ESI extended jurisdiction outside the USPTO, as registration does not afford protection against an infringement action.

The court denied Intel's motion to dismiss and concluded that declaratory judgment was required to "clarify and settle the legal relations in issue" and to grant ESI "relief from the uncertainty, insecurity, and controversy giving rise to the proceedings."[110] Nevertheless, the court warned that ESI presented minimal evidence of use and that the issue would be revisited if refuted by Intel after further discovery.

---

106. No. 4:09-cv-00796, 2010 U.S. Dist. LEXIS 18933 (E.D. Mo. Mar. 3, 2010).

107. *Id.* at *7.

108. *Id.* at *6.

109. *Id.* at *8 (quoting SanDisk Corp. v. STMicroelectronics, Inc., 480 F.3d 1372, 1381 (Fed. Cir. 2007)).

110. *Id.* at *16.

District Court Declines to Exercise Personal Jurisdiction over Out-of-State Domain Name Registrar in ACPA Suit

In *uBID, Inc. v. GoDaddy Group Inc.*,[111] the U.S. District Court for the Northern District of Illinois declined to assert either general or specific personal jurisdiction over GoDaddy, an Arizona-based Internet domain name registrar, and dismissed a suit brought under the Anticybersquatting Consumer Protection Act (ACPA).[112] The decision, which has been appealed to the Seventh Circuit, represents a continued retrenchment of the *Zippo* sliding scale test,[113] commonly invoked to assert personal jurisdiction over out-of-state Internet merchants that operate interactive Web sites.

GoDaddy provides a number of automated domain name services to customers: it registers domain names, provides an auction service through which persons can buy or sell domain names, hosts "parked pages" to which visitors of GoDaddy-registered domain names are directed until an active Web site is created, and shares advertising revenue from parked pages with the pages' registrants. These services are available to anyone, regardless of residence. Several GoDaddy customers, including two Illinois residents, used its services in relation to domain names similar to or including the trademarks of uBID, an Illinois-based online auction company. uBID sued, contending that, by providing services to those registrants, Go Daddy trafficked in or used uBID's trademarks with bad-faith intent to profit from those marks in violation of the ACPA. GoDaddy moved to dismiss for lack of personal jurisdiction.

The court held that GoDaddy's Illinois activities did not subject it to general personal jurisdiction. Although GoDaddy advertised at Illinois sporting venues and sponsored drivers and athletes that competed in Illinois events, the court characterized these activities as "part of a national advertising campaign" and found them devoid of the "Illinois-specific focus" necessary to support general jurisdiction.[114] Nor were GoDaddy's sales to Illinois residents—from which GoDaddy derived 3.19 percent of its revenue—sufficient for the assertion of general jurisdiction. The court held that due process would not allow the assertion of general personal jurisdiction over GoDaddy because the company "has never demonstrated a desire to create an Illinois presence through an Illinois-specific advertising campaign or direct solicitations of Illinois customers."[115]

Notably, the court rejected the reasoning of its own 2006 ruling, which found the "continuous and systematic" contacts necessary to support general jurisdiction in a modest number of sales to, and donations from, Illinois residents in combination with maintenance of an interactive Web site.[116] The court also rejected uBID's attempt to apply the *Zippo* sliding scale test to general jurisdiction.

The court likewise declined to assert specific personal jurisdiction over GoDaddy, finding that the Arizona company had not purposefully availed itself of Illinois law. The court acknowledged that GoDaddy entered into agreements with, sold services to, and

---

111. 673 F. Supp. 2d 621 (N.D. Ill. 2009).

112. 15 U.S.C. § 1125(d) (2009).

113. Zippo Mfg. Co. v. Zippo Dot Com, Inc., 952 F. Supp. 1119, 1123–27 (W.D. Pa. 1997).

114. *uBid*, 673 F. Supp. 2d at 627.

115. *Id.* at 628.

116. *See* George S. May Int'l Co. v. Xcentric Ventures LLC, 409 F. Supp. 2d 1052, 1060 (N.D. Ill. 2006).

collected revenue from two Illinois residents who had registered and parked domain names containing uBID's marks. However, the court pointed out that GoDaddy's interaction with these customers was completely automated. It reasoned that the contacts were initiated by the customers, not GoDaddy, and thus were best characterized as "unilateral activity" of third persons that could not satisfy due process under *Helicopteros*.[117] The court also cited GoDaddy's contractual attempts to avoid being haled into Illinois courts by including Arizona choice-of-forum clauses in its customer agreements as another factor weighing against purposeful availment.

Finally, the court rejected applicability of the *Calder* "effects test," which allows for assertion of personal jurisdiction over a nonresident defendant who expressly aims his or her actions at a plaintiff in the forum state knowing that harm is likely to result from these actions.[118] Citing again the automation of GoDaddy's services, the court found no evidence that suggested GoDaddy expressly aimed its conduct at Illinois. The court acknowledged GoDaddy's "general awareness" that its customers registered domain names similar to trademarked terms. However, neither that general knowledge nor anything in the record suggested that GoDaddy had particular knowledge that its practices harmed uBID in Illinois, making the "effects test" inapplicable.

Conspicuously absent from the court's ruling on specific jurisdiction was any discussion of *Zippo* or its progeny.

LEGISLATION

Pennsylvania Criminal Law on Trademark Counterfeiting Held Unconstitutionally Overbroad

In *Commonwealth v. Omar*,[119] the Supreme Court of Pennsylvania held that the Commonwealth's criminal trademark counterfeiting law, 18 PA. CONS. STAT. § 4119, was unconstitutionally overbroad and violated the First Amendment to the U.S. Constitution. During a traffic stop, a police officer discovered that Defendant Omar was in possession of allegedly counterfeit Nike brand sneakers. Similarly, Defendant O'Connor was arrested for selling hats bearing the "Penn State" logo on the Pennsylvania State University campus. The Centre County Court of Common Pleas (Pennsylvania) dismissed the charges filed by the Commonwealth, alleging violations of the Pennsylvania Trademark Counterfeiting Statute, 18 PA. CONS. STAT. § 4119, based on the Centre County criminal trial court's prior decision striking the statute as unconstitutionally vague and overbroad.[120] The Commonwealth then appealed a series of consolidated cases involving the constitutionality of the Pennsylvania Trademark Counterfeiting Statute to the Supreme Court of Pennsylvania.

The provisions of the Pennsylvania Trademark Counterfeiting Statute criminalized the acts of "[a]ny person who knowingly manufactures, uses, displays, advertises, distrib-

---

117. *uBid,* 673 F. Supp. 2d at 629 (citing Heliocopteros Nacionales de Colombia, S.A. v. Hall, 466 U.S. 408, 412 (1984)).

118. *See* Calder v. Jones, 465 U.S. 783, 790 (1984).

119. 981 A.2d 179 (Pa. 2009).

120. *See id.* at 181.

utes, offers for sale, sells or possesses with intent to sell or distribute any items or services bearing or identified by a counterfeit mark."[121] In affirming the lower court's ruling, the Supreme Court of Pennsylvania construed the law to prohibit "the use of any items bearing an unauthorized reproduction of terms or words used by a person to identify that person's goods or services," which covered a considerable amount of speech protected by the First Amendment.[122] Thus, the court held that sections 4119(a) and (i) unconstitutionally prohibited protected speech, including the use of words on a sign praising or protesting against any entity whose name consisted of a protected trademark.

In making its decision, the court rejected the Commonwealth's attempt to apply the limiting phrase "with intent to sell or distribute" as an amendment to the entire list of verbs in the definition of the offense in section 4119(a). Rather, the court held that the limiting phrase applied solely to the word "possesses."[123] Thus, the court's decision hinged on the rules of ordinary statutory construction, which provide that words and phrases shall be construed according to the rules of grammar. The court further rejected the Commonwealth's position that the Pennsylvania Trademark Counterfeiting Statute was limited only to use of a counterfeit mark deceptively for profit. The court noted that, as drafted, "even our use of the words 'Nike' and 'Penn State' in this opinion without the permission of the company or the university would fall" within the statute's overbroad prohibition.[124]

---

121. 18 PA. CONS. STAT. ANN. § 4119(a) (2009).
122. *Omar,* 981 A.2d at 187.
123. *Id.* at 187.
124. *Id.*

CHAPTER 12

TRADEMARK REMEDIES

This past year, courts issued notable decisions in cases concerning damages, attorneys' fees, injunctions, and even criminal counterfeiting. Most of the decisions benefited plaintiffs.

In a number of cases, for example, courts awarded damages or fees to successful intellectual property plaintiffs. In *Rexall Sundown, Inc. v. Perrigo Co.,* the U.S. District Court for the Eastern District of New York held that, where a plaintiff successfully alleges false advertising, it is the defendant's burden to show what portion of its profits are not attributable to the alleged false and misleading promotions. In *LaQuinta Corp. v. Heartland Properties LLC,* the Sixth Circuit held that a franchisee who breaches a franchise contract and continues to use the franchisor's trademarks may be assessed not just liquidated damages for breach of contract, but also treble damages for willful infringement of the franchisor's marks. In a fees case dealing with bad faith by the defendant, *Lahoti v. Vericheck, Inc.,* the U.S. District Court for the Western District of Washington held that a pattern and practice of cybersquatting and related abusive litigation may support classifying a suit as exceptional for purposes of granting attorneys' fees to the prevailing party.

Courts were generous in granting injunctive relief as well. In *Miche Bag, LLC v. Marshall Group,* the U.S. District Court for the Northern District of Indiana granted a preliminary injunction based on a product configuration trade dress infringement claim, even though one element of the claimed trade dress was functional and the plaintiff's advertising emphasized only the functional features of the product. In *Pacific Sunwear of California, Inc. v. Kira Plastinina Style, Ltd.,* the Ninth Circuit affirmed the district court's judgment issuing an injunction restricting certain uses of an individual's personal name in a trademark dispute.

One court was unsympathetic to the plaintiff, however. In *United States v. Xu,* the Fifth Circuit granted the defendant's post-verdict motion for judgment of acquittal on a criminal counterfeiting charge. In that case, the court found that the government had failed to prove an element of the crime, namely, that the trademark at issue was registered on the principal register of the USPTO.

STATUTORY DAMAGES

Appropriateness of Enhanced Damages

In *La Quinta Corp. v. Heartland Properties LLC,*[1] the Sixth Circuit affirmed a judgment awarding $111,325.37 in liquidated damages for breach of contract and treble defendants' damages (another $117,866.16) for willful trademark infringement.

---

1. 603 F.3d 327 (6th Cir. 2010).

Defendants Heartland were franchisees of a Budgetel Inn in Shepherdsville, Kentucky. The franchisor, Baymont Franchises International, LLC, was a wholly owned subsidiary of the plaintiff, La Quinta. La Quinta, however, was not a party to the franchise contract.

Under the franchise agreement: (1) Heartland was required to adopt computer system updates as implemented by Baymont; (2) Heartland had the right to terminate the franchise on written notice after ten years of the contract's twenty-year term; and (3) the incorporated trademark licenses terminated immediately upon any termination of the franchise agreement. When Baymont implemented reservation system changes that involved a major investment by its franchisees, Heartland failed to adopt those changes. Despite notices from Baymont, Heartland neither adopted the new reservation system nor ceased use of Baymont's trademarks.

Baymont sued Heartland in federal court, while Heartland sued Baymont and La Quinta in state court. La Quinta removed the state court case to federal court, where the suits were consolidated and the parties were realigned so that the Heartland parties became defendants. The parties cross-moved for summary judgment after an extended discovery period. Heartland simultaneously filed several discovery motions, including a request to reopen the discovery period. In the meantime, the court had, by agreement of the parties, entered a preliminary injunction.

Based on recommendations by the magistrate judge, and over Heartland's objections, the trial court granted La Quinta's and Baymont's motions for summary judgment and denied Heartland's motion for summary judgment. The court also denied all of Heartland's discovery motions on the grounds that Heartland had been dilatory during the discovery period. Applying Wisconsin law, as required by the franchise agreement, the court held that the original contract permitted Baymont to demand implementation of the new reservation system and to require Heartland to pay the entire cost of the upgrade even if Heartland exercised its right to terminate the franchise after only a brief use of the new system. The court ruled that the liquidated damages provision in the contract was reasonable, and it awarded liquidated contract damages in the amount of $111,325.37.

In light of the contract language, the multiple written notices sent by Baymont to Heartland, and Heartland's violation of the preliminary injunction, the district court held that Heartland had willfully infringed Baymont's trademarks during the almost one-year period Heartland had operated the hotel as a Budgetel Inn after its breach of the franchise contract. The court calculated Baymont's trademark damages by using the royalty provisions in the franchise contracts, although it made many factual determinations in favor of Heartland's positions during calculation of the amount. The court then trebled the damages award for willfulness, awarding $117,866.16 for trademark infringement. The claims against La Quinta were dismissed because it was not a party to the franchise contract. Heartland appealed. The Sixth Circuit, reviewing the damages awards for abuse of discretion, affirmed the trial court's judgment.

As to the award of both treble damages for willful trademark infringement and liquidated damages for breach of contract, the appellate court rejected the franchisees' claim that this was unreasonable, punitive, or otherwise inappropriate. The court noted that many courts had affirmed similar awards against hold-over, breaching franchisees. Although the court noted that the items included within the two damages calculations might overlap to some extent, it pointed out that the underlying legal claims were distinct.

Furthermore, it opined that accepting the franchisees' position would encourage breaching trademark franchisees to continue to use their former franchisor's marks after breach.

DEFENDANT'S LOST PROFITS

Apportionment

Defendant Has Burden to Show Profits Not Attributable to False Advertising

In ***Rexall Sundown, Inc. v. Perrigo Co.***,[2] the United States District Court for the Eastern District of New York held that, in an action alleging false advertising, the plaintiff is required to prove the amount of the defendant's sales, but the defendant must demonstrate all of its costs and deductions, "including any portion of sales that was not due to the allegedly false advertising."[3] The court's written opinion was intended to memorialize its oral ruling at trial as to the parties' dispute over their burdens in identifying profits.

Both parties sold nutritional supplements, specifically, glucosamine chondroitin. Plaintiff Rexall sued Perrigo for false and misleading promotional statements on its packaging, and Perrigo brought a similar counterclaim. Rexall's claim against Perrigo was based on Perrigo's use of "compare to" statements on its packaging, such as "Compare to Osteo Bi-Flex Ingredients" or "Compare Osteo Bi-Flex," which statements referred to Rexall's product.[4] Rexall alleged that these statements implied that Perrigo's product contained the same ingredients as that of Rexall, or were as effective. Rexall also alleged that neither claim was accurate. Rexall sought profits from the sales of the Perrigo products that were advertised with these statements.

The issue before the court was which party bore the burden of establishing the amount of profits that were due to the alleged false advertising statements under the Lanham Act, in particular, 15 U.S.C. § 1117(a). The court held that both case law and the plain language of the Lanham Act require that, where a plaintiff in a false advertising case has proven all of the required elements as to liability (including causation) and established that it is entitled to the defendant's profits, the plaintiff need only demonstrate the total amount of the defendant's sales. The defendant must show, however, how much should be deducted, including costs and an apportionment of profits that were not caused by the alleged false or misleading statements.

Recognizing that a party may not be able to separate the amount of profits directly related to the allegations from those profits that are unrelated, the court found that such an instance would not result in a windfall to the movant. To the contrary, the court noted that, even if Perrigo were unable to apportion its profits, Rexall would not be entitled to all profits because the Lanham Act is subject to principles of equity and requires that mon-

---

2. 707 F. Supp. 2d 357 (E.D.N.Y. 2010) (not for publication).
3. *Id.* at 359.
4. *Id.* at 358.

etary awards serve "as compensation and not a penalty."[5] The court would rule accordingly even though it had the discretion to award the full amount of profits.

EXCEPTIONAL CASE REMEDIES

Attorneys' Fees Award Supported in Part by a History of Cybersquatting

In *Lahoti v. Vericheck, Inc.,*[6] the trial court ruled that the case was "exceptional" and granted attorneys' fees to the prevailing party, Vericheck.

Vericheck offers financial services, including Internet-supported check verification services. It discovered that Lahoti had registered the domain name "ericheck.com" after a Canadian firm had allowed its prior registration of that domain name to lapse. Vericheck filed a complaint under ICANN's Uniform Dispute Resolution Procedure with the National Arbitration Forum (the NAF) seeking the transfer of the domain name from Lahoti. The NAF ordered the disputed domain name to be transferred to Vericheck. Rather than transfer the domain name, Lahoti filed an action in federal court requesting a declaratory judgment that its use and registration of the domain name did not violate any provision of the Lanham Act. The trial court granted Vericheck partial summary judgment, and Lahoti appealed. The appellate court agreed with the trial court's ruling that Lahoti was not entitled to the good-faith safe harbor provision of the federal cybersquatting statute,[7] but it disagreed with other rulings, so it remanded the case for further proceedings. On remand, the court granted judgment for Vericheck on both Lahoti's claims and Vericheck's counterclaims, holding that Lahoti's actions related to the ericheck.com Web site had violated the federal cybersquatting statute, infringed Vericheck's common law trademark rights, and violated a Washington state unfair competition statute.

The court held that the mark at issue was suggestive, rather than merely descriptive. First, the mark is composed of two parts. "Veri" has no established meaning; "check" has a multiplicity of meanings. The mark as a whole does not convey any information about the nature of the related business. Second, a third party had previously registered the mark without the USPTO requiring proof of secondary meaning. The court acknowledged that a third party's registration does not provide a presumption of secondary meaning, but considered this to provide some evidence of inherent distinctiveness.

The court found the evidence of third-party use insufficient to weaken the mark because of the low number of registrations in a related business and the lack of evidence that the third-party marks had been widely used. Lahoti argued that the prior existence of a third-party federal registration of the VERICHECK mark precluded Vericheck from raising its counterclaims. The court rejected this as an invalid *jus tertii* defense.[8] Furthermore, the record included evidence of a number of incidents of actual confusion involving Vericheck

---

5. *Id.* at 362; *see* Pedinol Pharmacal, Inc. v. Rising Pharms., Inc., 570 F. Supp. 2d 498, 506 (E.D.N.Y. 2008).

6. 708 F. Supp. 2d 1150 (W.D. Wash. 2010). See discussion of Ninth Circuit decision at pp. 308–310 *infra*.

7. 15 U.S.C. §1125(d)(1)(B)(ii) (2006).

8. 708 F. Supp. 2d at 1166. *See, e.g.,* LOUIS ALTMAN & MALLA POLLACK, CALLMANN ON UNFAIR COMPETITION, TRADEMARKS AND MONOPOLIES § 23:29 (4th ed.) (discussing courts' rejection of third-party priority as a defense in infringement actions).

customers stating that they had visited Lahoti's Web site and were confused by the absence of standard Vericheck forms. As for Lahoti's intent, the trial court had found in an earlier opinion that he had acted in bad faith because he had been adjudged a cybersquatter in regard to thousands of domain names and had continued to register large quantities of domain names for services that he might offer in the future.

The court ordered the transfer of the domain name to Vericheck, ordered Lahoti to pay the maximum statutory damages allowable for cybersquatting, and awarded attorneys' fees and costs.

The Lanham Act allows an award of attorneys' fees to the prevailing party if the judge deems the case "exceptional." The court listed numerous reasons supporting its decision to classify the case as exceptional, including Lahoti's registration and use of an illicit domain name, his attempts to obtain thousands of dollars from Vericheck in return for the domain name, his knowing disregard of Vericheck's trademark rights, his pattern and practice of both cybersquatting and related abusive litigation, and his willingness to submit inaccurate answers to interrogatories during the current lawsuit.

SPECIAL COUNTERFEIT REMEDIES

Conviction for Criminal Counterfeiting Vacated Where Government Failed to Prove Federal Registration of Mark at Issue

In *United States v. Xu*,[9] the Fifth Circuit granted Xu's post-verdict motion for judgment of acquittal on the criminal charge of trafficking in counterfeit goods, finding that the government had failed to show that the trademark at issue was the subject of a federal registration. In the lower court proceeding, a jury found Xu guilty of conspiring to traffic in counterfeit pharmaceutical drugs and introducing misbranded drugs into interstate commerce with intent to defraud. Xu was also convicted of trafficking in counterfeit goods, which Xu appealed. On appeal, the district court granted his motion except as to one count for trafficking in counterfeit versions of the drug Zyprexa. Xu then appealed that ruling to the Fifth Circuit.

In reviewing Xu's conviction for trafficking in counterfeit goods, the Fifth Circuit viewed the evidence in light most favorable to the prosecution and examined whether any rational trier of fact could have found the essential elements of the crime proven beyond a reasonable doubt. Specifically, to establish a violation of trafficking in counterfeit goods under 18 U.S.C. § 2320, the government must have proven that: (1) the defendant trafficked (or attempted to traffic) in goods or services; (2) the trafficking (or attempt) was intentional; (3) the defendant used a counterfeit mark in connection with such goods or services; and (4) the defendant knew the mark was counterfeit.[10] Xu challenged the third element, that he used a counterfeit mark. To be counterfeit, a mark must be "identical with, or substantially indistinguishable from, a mark registered on the principal register in the [USPTO] and in use."[11] Xu argued that the government did not establish that the

---

9. 599 F.3d 452 (5th Cir. 2010).
10. *Id.* at 452 (citing U.S. v. Hanafy, 302 F.3d 485, 487 (5th Cir. 2002)).
11. *Id.* at 453.

ZYPREXA trademark was registered on the USPTO's principal register and was in use at the time of the offense.

The Fifth Circuit noted that no cases in the circuit had addressed the quantum of proof sufficient to show trademark registration under section 2320.[12] The court found this "unsurprising," as trademark registration typically is simply proven by offering a registration certificate.[13] Here, the government had not introduced a trademark registration certificate or any authentic samples of the drug from which the jury could have inferred that the mark was registered. In addition, an employee of the drug's manufacturer did not testify that the ZYPREXA mark was registered. The employee testified that the counterfeit product bore a trademark symbol, but no effort was made to demonstrate that authentic product carried the same symbol.

Furthermore, the court held that a statement that the trademark at issue was "registered" is insufficient to sustain a conviction because a trademark may be registered in a number of ways, not just on the principal register, as required by the language of the statute. For example, a trademark may be registered on the USPTO's supplemental register or recorded with federal customs or state agencies. The panel found evidence suggesting compliance with FDA rules inapposite, however. In conclusion, the appellate court found that the government failed to show that one of the allegedly counterfeited trademarks, ZYPREXA, was registered on the principal register of the USPTO and granted Xu's post-verdict motion for judgment of acquittal. The court declined to reach the question of whether the mark was currently in use.

INJUNCTIONS

Preliminary Injunctions

Preliminary Injunction Restricting Trademark Use of Individual Designer's Name Affirmed

In *Pacific Sunwear of California, Inc. v. Kira Plastinina Style, Ltd.,*[14] the Ninth Circuit affirmed the lower court's grant of a preliminary injunction restricting Kira Plastinina Style, Ltd.'s (KP Style) use of the name of its designer, Kira Plastinina, in audio and video media advertisements. Pacific Sunwear of California, Inc. (Pac Sun) had alleged that KP Style's use of the KIRA PLASTININA mark infringed Pac Sun's KIRRA mark. The Ninth Circuit held that the injunction against KP Style's use of the designer's name properly reflected "a consideration of the reluctance to preclude an individual's business use of his name" and did not reflect "an injunction against nontrademark use."[15]

The court noted that its review of the district court's decision to grant a preliminary injunction was "limited and deferential" and would only be reversed "if the district court

---

12. *Id.* at 454.
13. *Id.*
14. 364 F. App'x 330 (9th Cir. 2010).
15. *Id.* at 331 (quoting E. & J. Gallo Winery v. Gallo Cattle Co., 967 F.2d 1280, 1288, 1297 (9th Cir. 1992)).

abused its discretion."[16] Moreover, the court noted that it would be an abuse of discretion if the lower court based its decision on either "clearly erroneous findings of fact" or "an erroneous legal standard."[17] The court held that the preliminary injunction was "sufficiently clear" to protect the interests of Pac Sun and provide adequate notice to KP Style, and held that the lower court's decision was not clearly erroneous because the district court had properly identified the likelihood of confusion legal standard, and "did not clearly err in finding that there was a likelihood of confusion between the parties' marks."[18] As a result, the court found no abuse of discretion in the district court's ultimate holding that Pac Sun was likely to succeed on the merits of its claim.

Consideration of Trade Dress Functionality in Preliminary Injunction Motion

In *Miche Bag, LLC v. Marshall Group,*[19] the U.S. District Court for the Northern District of Indiana granted a preliminary injunction based solely on a claim of trade dress infringement even though one element of the claimed dress was functional.[20]

Miche is the only large U.S. distributor of ladies' handbags with detachable covers. A complete handbag consists of a shell and a detachable cover. A user may adapt her handbag to match a different ensemble by merely changing detachable covers.

Miche is a major marketing success. It entered the market in July 2007 by selling handbags in one mall kiosk. In 2009, Miche had sales of $27 million; its 2010 projection is $50 million. Most sales are by Internet or through sales parties held by Miche's 4,000 associates. These associates are largely recruited from Miche's customer network. Both Miche and its associates spend substantial sums on advertising. The court defined Miche's trade dresses as follows:

> Miche Bag's Classic Bag trade dress consists of a handbag with a two-tone appearance, a rigid and specifically depicted polygonal-shaped body with inset sides, a specifically depicted slightly-curved upper aspect; specifically depicted curved straps, oval chrome buckles, trapezoidal-shaped zipper ends, and removable covers with both full-wrap and side-wrap variations. [Footnote omitted] Miche Bag's Big Bag trade dress consists of a handbag with a two-toned appearance, specifically depicted flexible straps, round chrome buckles, and removable covers with fold-over flaps.[21]

Marshall argued that the claimed trade dresses were not protectable because they were functional. It relied in large part on Miche's application for a utility patent on detachable covers for handbags.

---

16. *Id.*

17. *Id.*

18. *See* AMF Inc. v. Sleekcraft Boats, 599 F.2d 341, 348–49 (9th Cir. 1979), *abrogated in part on other grounds*, Mattel, Inc. v. Walking Mountain Prods., 353 F.3d 792 (9th Cir. 2003).

19. No. 10-129, 2010 WL 2539447 (N.D. Ind. June 16, 2010).

20. The preliminary injunction hearing also involved patent issues, but the court did not reach them. *See id.* at *9.

21. *Id.* at *4. In the footnote omitted from the quotation, the court rejected Miche's proposal that cuteness be one element of the claimed dresses.

Although emphasizing that its rulings were provisional and made on a scant record, the court decided that neither trade dress was functional. As for the patent application, the court noted that it knew of no case basing a presumption of functionality on the application for (as opposed to the grant of) a utility patent. However, the court also noted that Miche admitted the functionality of combining a handbag shell with a removable cover. Furthermore, Miche's advertisements stressed this functional aspect of its products, rather than any trade dress. Nevertheless, the court agreed with Miche that the trade dresses claimed were for a combination of elements, most of which were not even argued to be functional. Many alternative appearances were possible for handbags with detachable covers. Therefore, the court concluded that neither trade dress was functional.

Regarding secondary meaning, the lack of a survey supported Marshall. However, that was outweighed by evidence regarding sales volume, advertising, market penetration, and the rapid amassing of a 4,000-person network of associates/customers. The court also ruled that secondary meaning was strongly evidenced by Marshall's intentional copying of Miche's designs. Marshall had supplied its off-shore manufacturer with samples of Miche's products, but not with specifications (even though specifications were standard in the industry).

Likelihood of confusion was found based on a likelihood-of-confusion survey and Marshall's intentional copying.

The balance of irreparable harms was held to strongly favor Miche. Marshall Group's handbags were less expensive and of lower quality than Miche's products. Unaddressed likelihood of confusion, therefore, was likely to harm both Miche's sales and its reputation, especially with its consumer/sales associates. Marshall had other lines of products that would not be restricted by the preliminary injunction. The court, therefore, granted a preliminary injunction against handbags resembling either of Miche's trade dresses, specifying that the injunction did not reach sales of other handbags with detachable covers.

CHAPTER 13

TRADEMARK PROSECUTION AND TRANSACTIONS

Significant cases involving trademark transactions touched on a number of legal fields, including the antitrust status of the National Football League with regard to trademark licensing, the status of a trademark license as an "executory contract" under bankruptcy law, and contract law generally. A number of procedural issues related to trademark prosecution and proceedings before the TTAB also were decided, including acceptable specimens of use, requirements for use in commerce, evidence required to show third party use, and defamatory and scandalous marks.

In *American Needle, Inc. v. National Football League,* the U.S. Supreme Court unanimously held that the National Football League (NFL) was not immune from antitrust liability as a "single entity" under section 1 of the Sherman Antitrust Act when it granted an exclusive license to Reebok International Ltd. to manufacture and sell NFL team headwear.

The Third Circuit's *In re Exide Technologies* decision overturned decisions of the bankruptcy and district courts permitting a debtor-in-possession to reject a ten-year-old trademark license on the ground that it was an "executory contract," holding that the lower courts had applied the wrong test in analyzing the issue. Judge Ambro wrote separately to provide an analytical framework under which to analyze the currently unresolved question of what rights a licensee retains in the event that a trademark license is rejected as executory under bankruptcy law.

In *Sunstar, Inc. v. Alberto-Culver Co.,* the Seventh Circuit held that sophisticated parties that use a technical legal term in a license agreement are deemed to intend the term's technical meaning. In that case, the parties used the Japanese term *senyoshiyoken* to describe the license, and the court used Japanese law to determine the meaning of the term and its effect on the interpretation of the licensee's ability to make small changes to licensed marks.

In *In re Mighty Leaf Tea,* the Federal Circuit held that third party use of marks incorporating an element common to both the applied-for and the cited marks does not negate a likelihood of confusion when no evidence is supplied regarding either the extent to which these third party marks are used in the marketplace or that the common element between the marks at issue has a recognized meaning.

In *University of South Carolina v. University of Southern California,* the Federal Circuit affirmed the TTAB's refusal of an application to register a logo including the letters "SC," and also affirmed the TTAB's grant of summary judgment against the University of South Carolina on its petition to cancel a registration owned by the University of Southern California. Despite affirming the grant of summary judgment against the University of South Carolina, however, the court reversed the TTAB on the issue of standing, finding that the University of South Carolina had standing to seek the cancellation.

In *American Express Marketing & Development Corp. v. Gilad Development Corp.,* the TTAB held, as a matter of first impression, that the noncommercial use exception to a dilution claim does not apply in inter partes proceedings, which require by law that the mark be currently in use in commerce. Given that it cannot be true both that a mark is in use in commerce and that the same use is noncommercial, the noncommercial use defense cannot be asserted in response to an opposition to an application or to a petition to cancel an existing registration.

In *John W. Carson Foundation v. Toilets.com, Inc.,* the TTAB sustained an opposition to an intent-to-use application based on both res judicata and lack of a bona fide intent to use grounds. Because previous litigation had resulted in an injunction against the applicant's use of the mark at issue, continued legal use of the mark was impossible.

In *Cold War Museum, Inc. v. Cold War Air Museum, Inc.,* the Federal Circuit held that the evidence of record in an inter partes trademark cancellation proceeding automatically included the entire registration file, overruling a portion of its prior decision in *British Seagull Ltd. v. Brunswick Corp.* The court held that it was plain error for the TTAB to refuse to consider evidence in the form of "documents and other things filed in connection with the [trademark] application," as such an approach conflicted with the language of 37 C.F.R. § 2.122(b).

Several other decisions also touched on various procedural issues. For example, in *Dating DNA, LLC v. Imagini Holdings, Ltd.,* the TTAB held that, in order to reopen an expired discovery period, the moving party must establish "excusable neglect," and in *In re Lebanese Arak Corp.,* the TTAB clarified that refusals of applications to register marks which tie a religious group to something officially disfavored by that group are properly based on the statutory bar against registration of defamatory, not scandalous, matter.

In *Odom's Tennessee Pride Sausage Inc. v. FF Acquisition LLC,* the Federal Circuit held that the TTAB may decide not to consider pleadings amended by consent of the parties in an opposition. Furthermore, the court held that the TTAB may grant summary judgment on likelihood of confusion grounds even when all but one of the likelihood of confusion factors favors the losing party. Additionally, in *Promgirl, Inc. v. JPC Co.,* the TTAB held that a full discovery conference is mandatory unless the parties agree to settlement, and in *Qualcomm Inc. v. FLO Corp.,* the TTAB denied a motion for summary judgment as premature where the opposer had not yet served its initial disclosures.

TRADEMARK TRIAL AND APPEAL BOARD

Procedure

Initial Disclosures Are Required before Filing Motion for Summary Judgment

In ***Qualcomm Inc. v. FLO Corp.,***[1] the TTAB denied the motion for summary judgment filed by the opposer, Qualcomm, because Qualcomm had not served initial disclosures prior to filing the motion. The TTAB held that a motion for summary judgment is premature in such a case, unless the motion asserts a claim or issue preclusion or the TTAB's lack of jurisdiction.[2]

FLO filed an intent-to-use application for the mark FLO for use in connection with various goods and services. Qualcomm argued in its summary judgment motion that FLO

---

1.   93 U.S.P.Q.2d (BNA) 1768 (T.T.A.B. 2010).
2.   *Id.* at 1771.

lacked a bona fide intent to use the mark, as well as a likelihood of confusion with its marks, FLOR and MEDIAFLO, for data processing, telecommunications and audiovisual processing and services. Qualcomm based its motion on the allegation that the applicant, FLO, was no longer in business and had abandoned its mark and therefore could no longer have a bona fide intent to use it.[3]

FLO argued that Qualcomm's motion was groundless and frivolous because no discovery had been taken and no initial or expert disclosures had been made. Although FLO did not expressly allege that the motion was premature, the TTAB noted that the requirement that a party serve its initial disclosures prior to or concurrently with the filing of a motion for summary judgment cannot be waived.

The TTAB identified several other deficiencies in Qualcomm's motion. The TTAB found that Qualcomm's notice of opposition was deficient because it did not plead any of the grounds for opposition, and Qualcomm had not sought leave to file an amended notice of opposition with the pleaded grounds. The TTAB noted that summary judgment cannot be granted based on an unpleaded claim.

The TTAB rejected Qualcomm's alleged claim of abandonment, finding that it was not available in an opposition of an intent-to-use application, where use of a mark is not required until the applicant files a statement of use.

Finally, the TTAB criticized Qualcomm's allegation in its notice of opposition that FLO knew or should have known of opposer's prior use and, therefore could not have established the required good faith belief that its mark could be registered. The TTAB observed that Qualcomm's allegation that FLO "knew or should have known" of Qualcomm's prior use, to the extent this related to fraud by false averments, was legally insufficient. The TTAB explained that a claim of fraud requires the opposer to allege particular facts concerning the applicant's intent.

Untimely Initial Disclosures and Consolidation

In *Dating DNA, LLC v. Imagini Holdings, Ltd.,*[4] the TTAB considered Dating DNA's motions to reopen discovery, to compel discovery, and to consolidate proceedings involving multiple applications.

The TTAB denied the motion to reopen, holding that Dating DNA's claim of an "oversight" in failing to file its initial disclosures did not constitute "excusable neglect."[5] In analyzing excusable neglect, the TTAB applied the four-part test set out by the U.S. Supreme Court in *Pioneer Investment Services Co. v. Brunswick Associates Limited Partnership.*[6] That test focuses on: (1) the danger of prejudice to the nonmoving party; (2) the length of delay and its potential impact on judicial proceedings; (3) the reason for the delay, including whether it was within the reasonable control of the moving party; and (4) whether the moving party acted in good faith.[7]

The TTAB observed that two factors (length of delay and reasons for the delay) weighed heavily against Dating DNA, which failed to serve its initial disclosures before it served written discovery on Imagini Holdings.

---

3. *Qualcomm*, 93 U.S.P.Q.2d at 1769.
4. 94 U.S.P.Q.2d (BNA) 1889 (T.T.A.B. 2010).
5. *Id.* at 1892.
6. *Id.* (citing Pioneer Inv. Servs. Co. v. Brunswick Assocs. LP, 507 U.S. 380, 395 (1993)).
7. *Id.*

Imagini Holdings refused to respond to discovery, relying on Trademark Rule 2.120(a)(3), which requires that a party make initial disclosures prior to seeking discovery.[8] In response, Dating DNA moved to reopen discovery and compel Imagini Holdings to answer the discovery request. In analyzing Dating DNA's oversight, the TTAB highlighted the fact that Dating DNA failed to present any critical facts detailing the reason for its oversight. In addition, there was no evidence that Dating DNA was unaware of the discovery and trial deadlines, which might have excused the delay in filing its disclosures. The TTAB also noted that Dating DNA did not request an extension of the discovery period. For these reasons, the TTAB held the delay was within Dating DNA's reasonable control, and the length of the delay was meaningful.

As to the remaining factors, the TTAB found neither substantial prejudice to Imagini Holdings, nor bad faith on the part of Dating DNA.

Dating DNA argued that the TTAB should grant its motion to compel because Imagini Holdings did not disclose its intent to withhold discovery responses until two days after discovery had closed. The TTAB determined that Dating DNA chose to serve its discovery requests late, and Imagini Holding had no duty to inform Dating DNA that it would not respond to discovery. Thus, the motion to compel was denied.

The TTAB granted Dating DNA's motion to consolidate the oppositions in light of the fact that both proceedings involved identical parties, similar marks, and related or identical issues.[9] The TTAB ordered that each proceeding be treated separately. Discovery was therefore closed in the proceeding involving the motions to reopen and compel. The consolidated cases were set for trial at the closing of discovery in the second opposition.

Discussion of Settlement Does Not Obviate Required Discovery Conference

In *Promgirl, Inc. v. JPC Co.,*[10] the TTAB denied Opposer Promgirl's motion for sanctions but ordered a mandatory discovery conference before the TTAB. The TTAB held that the parties were required to engage in a full discovery conference, addressing not only settlement discussions but also the development of a disclosure and discovery plan, covering the timing, scope and sequence of discovery, supplementation of disclosures and discovery responses, signing of disclosures and discovery responses, and protective orders. The TTAB based its decision on Trademark Rule 2.120(a)(1), which adopted the disclosure requirement of Federal Rule of Procedure 26, and on a previous TTAB Order regarding the same. The TTAB adopted the Rule 26 mandatory discovery conference "to avoid needless disputes and motions and to facilitate either prompt and genuine settlement discussions or a smooth and timely transition to disclosures, discovery and trial."[11] The TTAB may also make any appropriate order where there is failure to participate in such a discovery conference or comply with a TTAB Order.[12] The TTAB noted that this requirement for parties to participate in a full discovery conference is applicable to all proceed-

---

8. *Id.* at 1893 (referring to 37 C.F.R. § 2.120).

9. *Id.*

10. 94 U.S.P.Q.2d (BNA) 1759 (T.T.A.B. 2009) (precedential decision of TTAB).

11. *Id.* at 1761; *see* Guthy-Render Corp. v. Boyd, 88 U.S.P.Q.2d (BNA) 1701 (T.T.A.B. 2008).

12. Trademark Rule 2.120(g)(1).

ings that commenced after November 1, 2007. Furthermore, the TTAB noted that this requirement is a mutual obligation, and the responsibility to schedule a discovery conference is shared between the parties in dispute.

The TTAB ordered Promgirl and Applicant JPC to conduct a discovery conference by a date certain. Promgirl and JPC instead engaged in settlement discussions that were unsuccessful. Afterward, Promgirl contended that JPC became unavailable to continue with the required discovery conference and moved for sanctions, or alternatively, to compel JPC's participation in a discovery conference.

The TTAB noted that a mere discussion of settlement did not replace a full discovery conference and that, although the parties may discuss any additional topics to those in the TTAB's Order, they are required minimally to engage in a discussion involving all of the topics specified in Rule 26 and the TTAB Order. Thus, in the absence of a successful settlement, the parties must "discuss their plans relating to disclosures, discovery, and trial evidence."[13]

The TTAB noted that the e-mail communications between the parties demonstrated that JPC made no efforts to schedule a discovery conference on its own, even though it shared that responsibility with Promgirl. The TTAB also noted that when it became clear that settlement would not be reached, Promgirl attempted to arrange for a discovery conference but JPC was not cooperative. However, the TTAB recognized that Promgirl is not without blame because it waited until nearly the deadline for the conference to attempt to schedule it. Moreover, it noted that neither party requested TTAB participation in the discovery conference ten days prior to the deadline or once it became clear that they could not settle.

Nevertheless, because the record demonstrated that Promgirl tried to schedule a discovery conference while JPC was not very cooperative, the TTAB ordered that JPC had the burden of arranging a time for the conference convenient for both Promgirl's counsel and the TTAB attorney by the new deadline determined by the TTAB.

Oppositions

TTAB May Refuse to Treat Pleadings as Amended by Agreement

In *Odom's Tennessee Pride Sausage, Inc. v. FF Acquisition LLC*,[14] the Federal Circuit affirmed the TTAB's grant of summary judgment to the applicant, dismissing Odom's opposition.

Odom's opposition had been premised solely on likelihood of confusion. Its notice of opposition mentioned several of Odom's registered marks, but its papers filed in opposition to FF Acquisition's (FFA) motion for summary judgment also mentioned an unregistered mark. Nevertheless, the TTAB granted summary judgment to the FFA without considering Odom's unregistered mark.

Each of the marks involved included a line drawing of a farm boy. In each, the farm boy was about the same age, smiling, and wearing overalls. Some of Odom's cited registered marks show the boy waving, as does the drawing of the boy in the mark depicted in the application.

---

13. *Promgirl*, 94 U.S.P.Q.2d at 1761.
14. 600 F.3d 1343 (Fed. Cir. 2010).

The Federal Circuit held that, although the TTAB had the power to consider Odom's pleadings to have been amended by agreement of the parties, it was not required to do so.[15] The court noted that Odom's unregistered mark created a different commercial impression from Odom's cited, registered marks, therefore implying that the TTAB's substantive decision might have been different if the unregistered mark had been considered. The court further found that the TTAB's decision not to consider the pleadings as being amended was discretionary, but it did not provide any insight into how it would approach an argument that the TTAB had abused its discretion.

Neither the Federal Circuit opinion nor the TTAB decision provided any representation of the unregistered mark or any analysis of why the TTAB had made the discretionary decision not to consider the unregistered mark.

The Federal Circuit also agreed with the TTAB's substantive conclusion that no reasonable trier of fact could have concluded that any of Odom's cited, registered marks were likely to cause confusion with the mark covered by the application. Each of the marks under consideration contained a drawing of a farm boy. The mark in the application, however, was different in many aspects from any of Odom's registered marks. Among the differences were: (1) the boys' hands and feet differed in size and shape; (2) one boy wore a cowboy hat while the other wore a tall pilgrim hat with a ribbon; (3) one boy was barefoot, while the other had heavy shoes; (4) only one of the boys carried a fishing pole; and (5) one boy faced forward, while the other is shown from the side. Even though the TTAB had found that some of the likelihood-of-confusion factors favored Odom, the court concluded that the TTAB correctly ruled that these factors were outweighed by the differences among the marks themselves.

Noncommercial Use Defense to Dilution Claim Not Available in Inter Partes Proceedings

In *American Express Marketing & Development Corp. v. Gilad Development Corp.*,[16] the TTAB held, as a matter of first impression, that the "noncommercial use" exception to a trademark dilution claim cannot be raised in TTAB proceedings involving an application to register a mark or a request for cancellation of a registration because the involved marks necessarily are used or intended to be used as indicators of source for goods or services.

The subject dispute arose after Gilad filed intent-to-use applications for registration of the word mark GRAND AMERICAN EXPRESS and a related design mark for use in connection with a working replica of a 19th Century "express" train. American Express filed notices of opposition, alleging ownership of a family of famous AMERICAN EXPRESS marks, priority of use, likelihood of confusion, and trademark dilution. Proceedings on the oppositions were consolidated.

Gilad denied the salient allegations of both oppositions and asserted two affirmative defenses: (1) failure to state a claim; and (2) third-party use and registration of marks incorporating the terms "American" and "Express" that precluded American Express' claim of exclusive rights. Gilad did not assert an affirmative defense of noncommercial use.

---

15. *Id.* at 2032 (citing Trademark Trial and Appeal Board Manual of Procedures § 528.07(b)).

16. 94 U.S.P.Q.2d (BNA) 1294 (T.T.A.B. 2010).

Both parties subsequently filed motions for summary judgment. Gilad asserted that it was entitled to judgment as to both of American Express' dilution claims based on the noncommercial use exception of the Trademark Dilution Revision Act of 2006 (TDRA), which provides that "[a]ny noncommercial use of a mark" is not actionable as dilution. Gilad asserted that because its intended use of the marks was based on a historic 19th Century Currier & Ives lithograph titled "American Express Train," it constituted a form of noncommercial artistic expression.

In addition to filing a cross-motion for summary judgment on its claims, American Express opposed Gilad's summary judgment motion on the ground that it was improper as a matter of law because it was based on an unpleaded defense. In response, Gilad moved for leave to amend its answers to assert noncommercial use as an affirmative defense.

The TTAB concluded that granting leave to amend would otherwise be proper because: (1) Gilad had not acted in bad faith in waiting ten months after filing its answers before seeking to amend; (2) American Express had not been prejudiced by the delay as the proceedings were still in the discovery stage; and (3) the TTAB's prior precedents permitted amendments to pleadings to assert unpleaded defenses in connection with summary judgment motions. The TTAB, nonetheless, denied the motion as futile. First, the TTAB reviewed the TDRA, concluding that it permitted a party to bring a dilution claim in inter partes proceedings and provided specific defenses to such a claim, including noncommercial use. The TTAB then noted that the question of whether the noncommercial use exception could be asserted as an affirmative defense to a dilution claim in an inter partes proceeding before the TTAB was "an issue of first impression."[17]

To resolve that issue, the TTAB first looked to the Trademark Act to determine whether its definition of "service mark" provided any insight into whether a noncommercial use defense could be asserted in response to a notice of opposition to an application to register a mark as a service mark. The TTAB concluded that the definition of "service mark" precludes the assertion of the noncommercial use defense in that context because, in order to obtain registration of a mark as a "service mark," the applicant "must demonstrate . . . use of its marks as service marks in commerce."[18] Permitting the noncommercial use defense in that context would "contradict the purpose of the Trademark Act."[19]

The TTAB also observed that permitting the proponent of the registration to assert the "noncommercial use" defense would result in an anomaly, as the proponent of the registration would have to argue that the same "use in commerce" that qualified the mark for registration under the Trademark Act also constituted a "noncommercial use" under the TDRA. Because both conditions could not exist simultaneously, the TTAB concluded that the commercial use requirement for registration, by definition, precludes an applicant or a registrant from relying on a "noncommercial use" defense in an inter partes proceeding.

The TTAB also concluded that, even if the noncommercial use exception provided in the TDRA were applicable in TTAB proceedings, Gilad's use or intended use of the marks would not qualify as noncommercial use, as the mere fact that Gilad chose the marks to evoke a historical era was not sufficient to create protected artistic expression or speech. Accordingly, the TTAB denied Gilad's motion for summary judgment.

---

17. *Id.* at 1298.
18. *Id.*
19. *Id.*

American Express' summary judgment motion, however, fared no better. The TTAB concluded that American Express had failed to meet its burden of showing sufficient similarity between its marks and Gilad's marks and between its goods and services and Gilad's goods and services and, therefore, denied American Express' motion.

Finally, the TTAB used this case to clarify its procedures with respect to cases in which a party moves for leave to amend a pleading to assert an unpleaded issue in connection with a summary judgment motion. After acknowledging that its prior precedents may have incorrectly suggested that a party could move for leave to amend to assert the unpleaded issue any time before the TTAB considered the summary judgment motion, the TTAB made clear that, in future cases, it "would not hesitate to deny" summary judgment motions based on unpleaded issues unless they are accompanied by an appropriate motion to amend the pleadings.[20]

Opposition Sustained Where Legal Use of Mark Would Be Impossible

In *John W. Carson Foundation v. Toilets.com, Inc.,*[21] the TTAB granted summary judgment sustaining an opposition filed by The John W. Carson Foundation (Foundation) against the intent-to-use application filed by Toilets.com, Inc. (Toilets) for "Here's Johnny" as a mark for "portable toilets." The TTAB relied upon res judicata and lack of a bona fide intent to use the mark in commerce.

Foundation was the successor in interest to the publicity rights of the late John W. Carson (Carson). A number of years before the current application, a different corporation, Here's Johnny Portable Toilets, Inc., had filed an application to register "Here's Johnny" as a trademark for portable toilets. Carson both filed an opposition to the application and sued in federal court. The federal litigation resulted in judgment for Carson on the basis of his right of publicity, but not on the basis of likelihood of confusion.[22] The U.S. District Court for the Eastern District of Michigan, therefore, instructed the USPTO to sustain Carson's opposition. The court also issued a permanent, national injunction against defendant's commercial use of the phrase "Here's Johnny."[23]

The TTAB first ruled that the application was barred by res judicata. Res judicata bars a law suit when three elements are met: (1) the parties (or their privies) are identical; (2) there has been an earlier final judgment on the merits of a claim; and (3) the second claim is based on the same set of transactional facts as the first.[24]

As to the first element, the required privity is not contractual, but operational. Although the corporation seeking to register "Here's Johnny" differed between the previous and the current litigation, both corporations were entirely owned by the same individual. Carson had transferred his right of publicity to Foundation, making it the successor-in-

---

20. *Id.* at 1296–97.

21. 94 U.S.P.Q.2d (BNA) 1942 (T.T.A.B. 2010) (precedential).

22. *See* Carson v. Here's Johnny Portable Toilets, Inc., 698 F.2d 831 (6th Cir. 1983) (affirming judgment for defendant on likelihood-of-confusion claim; reversing and remanding for judgment for plaintiff on right-of-publicity claim and for determination of proper remedy); *see also* Carson v. Here's Johnny Portable Toilets, Inc., 810 F.2d 104 (6th Cir. 1987) (affirming injunction granted on remand).

23. *Carson,* 94 U.S.P.Q.2d at 1947.

24. *Id.* at 1946 (quoting Jet, Inc. v. Sewage Am. Sys., 223 F.3d 1360 (Fed. Cir. 2000)).

interest to the right at issue in both litigations. The TTAB, therefore, held that the first prong had been met.

As to the second prong, Toilets attacked the identity of the "claim," not the finality of the judgment. Toilets' attack involved conflation of the right of publicity and trademark infringement. It argued that Foundation's essential objection to the currently pending application was likelihood of confusion, which had been ruled not to exist in the earlier litigation. The TTAB explained that Foundation had not pleaded likelihood of confusion in its opposition; rather, it had pleaded false suggestion of a connection under section 2(a) of the Trademark Act. False suggestion of connection with a natural person protected the right of publicity. Therefore, the claims were equivalent for the purposes of res judicata.

As to the third prong, the TTAB held that it was met because both disputes involved the same mark, HERE'S JOHNNY, for the same goods, portable toilets.

The TTAB also held that registration was barred for lack of a bona fide intent to use the mark in commerce. Given that a registration may issue from an intent-to-use application only after legal use of the mark in commerce, a registration could not issue from the currently pending application. The TTAB rejected Toilet's attempt to read the injunction as barring only corporate name or trade name use of the phrase "Here's Johnny."

Cancellations

Federal Circuit Rejects TTAB's Restrictive Interpretation of Standing

In *University of South Carolina v. University of Southern California*,[25] the Federal Circuit affirmed the TTAB's decision: (1) refusing the University of South Carolina's (South Carolina) application to register a baseball logo including the letters "SC" based on a likelihood of confusion with an "SC" logo previously registered by the University of Southern California (Southern California); and (2) granting summary judgment against South Carolina on its petition to cancel Southern California's cited registration.

In affirming the TTAB's decision that confusion between the parties' marks was likely, the court agreed that South Carolina's baseball hats would appear in the same trade channels as goods bearing Southern California's registered mark, but rejected the TTAB's finding regarding the degree of care exercised by some groups of purchasers. Nevertheless, the court found this error harmless because South Carolina had not appealed the TTAB's findings that the marks were legally identical and would appear on the same classes of goods. These factors, coupled with the finding that the goods would appear in the same channels of trade, "on their own" supported a finding that confusion was likely.

The Federal Circuit then considered the TTAB's grant of summary judgment on South Carolina's cancellation petition. The TTAB had concluded that South Carolina lacked standing because it apparently believed that South Carolina was not an agent of the State of South Carolina, and as a result, lacked standing based on a false association with the State of South Carolina. The court noted that there are two judicially created requirements for standing: that the petitioner has a real interest in the proceeding, and that there is a reasonable basis for the petitioner's belief that the challenged mark has caused or will cause damage. To show a real interest, the petitioner must have a direct and personal stake in the outcome of the cancellation.

---

25. 367 F. App'x 129 (Fed. Cir. 2010).

The Federal Circuit rejected the TTAB's restrictive interpretation of standing, with-out deciding whether the university was an agent of the State of South Carolina. The court explained that South Carolina needed to show only that it had a reasonable belief that it would be damaged by Southern California's registration and a direct and personal stake in the cancellation of that registration. Because South Carolina sold goods bearing the "SC" logo, it had a commercial interest in registering its mark and a reasonable belief that it would likely be damaged.

Although the court found that South Carolina did have standing, it affirmed the TTAB's grant of summary judgment because South Carolina failed to show that Southern California's registered sc mark was unmistakably associated with another person or institution. South Carolina asserted that the use of the sc mark falsely suggested an affiliation with the State of South Carolina. The court observed that, to avoid summary judgment, South Carolina needed to show there was a genuine issue for trial on whether the letters "SC" pointed uniquely to the State of South Carolina. The court agreed that these letters might refer to the state of South Carolina, but noted that there was evidence in the record showing that the letters referred to many other entities as well. For this reason, South Carolina failed to meet its burden in opposition to the summary judgment motion.

Cancellation Proceeding Automatically Includes Entire File History as Evidence

In *Cold War Museum, Inc. v. Cold War Air Museum, Inc.,*[26] the Federal Circuit held that the evidence of record in an inter partes trademark cancellation proceeding automati-cally included the entire registration file, overruling a portion of *British Seagull Ltd. v. Brunswick Corp.*[27] In 2003, the Cold War Museum registered the service mark THE COLD WAR MUSEUM pursuant to the acquired distinctiveness provision of section 2(f) of the Lanham Act, 15 U.S.C. § 1052(f). After an initial rejection based on a finding that the proposed registration was "merely descriptive" of museum services, the applicant submitted a large volume of information to illustrate that the mark had acquired distinctiveness pursuant to section 2(f). The USPTO ultimately issued a registration in 2004. Three years later, the Cold War Air Museum (Air Museum) petitioned to cancel the Cold War Museum's service mark with the TTAB on descriptiveness grounds. The TTAB, relying on its own prece-dent, held that it could not consider any evidence submitted by the Cold War Museum solely in connection with the underlying registration to prove distinctiveness, as this in-formation had not been resubmitted in the cancellation proceeding. As a result, the TTAB held that THE COLD WAR MUSEUM mark had not acquired distinctiveness and cancelled the registration.[28] The Cold War Museum then appealed the decision to the Federal Circuit.

On appeal, the Federal Circuit reversed the TTAB's decision and held that the regu-lation concerning inter partes cancellation proceedings, 37 C.F.R. § 2.122(b), was "clear and unambiguous" in that the entire registration file, including "any evidence submitted by the applicant during prosecution," automatically becomes part of the record in a cancellation action "without any action by the parties."[29] The Federal Circuit recognized

---

26. 586 F.3d 1352 (Fed. Cir. 2009).
27. 28 U.S.P.Q.2d (BNA) 1197 (T.T.A.B. 1990).
28. *Cold War Museum,* 586 F.3d at 1354–56.
29. *Id.* at 1356 (quoting 37 C.F.R. § 2.122(b)).

that the TTAB improperly refused to consider the Cold War Museum's evidence of distinctiveness, which was submitted during prosecution of the application before the USPTO. Specifically, the Federal Circuit held that it was plain error for the TTAB to refuse to consider evidence in the form of "documents and other things filed in connection with the [trademark] application" as such an approach conflicted with the plain language of 37 C.F.R. § 2.122(b).[30] As a result, the appellate court chose to overrule expressly the inconsistent portions of the TTAB's prior *British Seagull* opinion that pertained to evidentiary issues on descriptiveness. Thus, the Federal Circuit held that evidence of the mark's acquired distinctiveness submitted during prosecution of the application was "automatically part of the record before the TTAB."[31]

The Federal Circuit also determined that evidence from the application process should have been considered in order to determine whether Air Museum had properly met its burden of proving a lack of acquired distinctiveness. Initially, the Federal Circuit noted that registrations issued under the acquired distinctiveness provision of section 2(f) enjoy a presumption of validity with respect to the registration, including a presumption that the mark has acquired distinctiveness. In analyzing the proper burdens applicable to a party seeking cancellation of a section 2(f) registration, the appellate court clarified that the fact that the mark has not acquired distinctiveness must be proven by a preponderance of the evidence. The court further noted that "the party seeking cancellation [of a mark] bears the burden [of persuasion] to establish a prima facie case that the registration is [somehow] invalid" and, "in a section 2(f) case," as here, also bears the initial burden to "establish a prima facie case of no acquired distinctiveness."[32] In reversing the TTAB's ruling, the Federal Circuit held that it was error for the TTAB to hold that the mark had not acquired distinctiveness where the Air Museum failed to argue the issue of acquired distinctiveness in the cancellation proceeding. As a result, the Air Museum had not overcome the registration's presumption of validity. Additionally, the Federal Circuit held that the TTAB erred as a matter of law by improperly shifting the burden to the Cold War Museum to prove that the mark had acquired distinctiveness because the presumption of validity was not overcome by a preponderance of the evidence by the Air Museum. Thus, the Federal Circuit held that, because the burden of production in this case never shifted to the Cold War Museum, there was no requirement for it to present evidence of distinctiveness.[33]

Other Proceedings

Third-Party Registrations and Applications Entitled to Little Weight Absent Evidence of Use

In *In re Mighty Leaf Tea*,[34] the Federal Circuit affirmed the refusal of the TTAB to register the ML word mark for personal and skin care products due to a likelihood of confusion with the mark ML MARK LEES (in a stylized format) for an overlapping set of products. In affirming the refusal, the court considered, but ultimately rejected, the

---

30. *Id.* at 1357 (quoting *British Seagull*, 28 U.S.P.Q.2d at 1200).
31. *Id.*
32. *Id.* at 1358 (citing Yamaha Int'l Corp. v. Hoshino Gakki Co., 840 F.2d 1572, 1579 n.9).
33. *Id.* at 1358–59.
34. 601 F.3d 1342 (Fed. Cir. 2010).

applicant's arguments about the importance of third party registrations and applications for marks incorporating the letters "ML" in connection with similar products.

The Federal Circuit concentrated on the shortcomings of the applicant's submitted evidence of third party marks which, the applicant asserted, created a "crowded field" such that confusion was unlikely. The applicant cited registrations of the MLE, MLUXE, M'LIS, JML, and AMLAVI marks, as well as pending applications to register the MLAB, TMLA, FEMLOGIC, and SIMLINE marks, all for similar products. The Federal Circuit did not accord much weight to this evidence, instead explaining that registrations do not evidence the extent to which the marks are actually visible to the public or used in commerce. Therefore, mere evidence of existing registrations was insufficient to show that marks containing the "ML" element are so common in the marketplace that the public is not likely to assume that all marks with that element belong to related entities. The court furthermore noted that not all uses of the same element create the same commercial impression, distinguishing cases where the existence of a shared element was considered unimportant because the shared element had a recognizable meaning of its own, such as the name of a street. In this case, the applicant had not provided evidence that the marks at issue shared a common, publicly understood meaning of "ML."

Ultimately, the Federal Circuit determined that the applicant had not demonstrated that the TTAB erred in holding that the applicant's evidence of third party registrations did not prove the weakness of "ML" as a mark for personal and skin care products. The cited mark was registered for use in connection with the same types of products as those identified in the application and would, therefore, presumably be offered for sale to the same types of customers through the same types of trade channels. Given that the application covered only the "ML" word mark, without stylistic or design elements, the court concluded that applicant's mark was confusingly similar to the mark cited by the TTAB.

Application of Apparently Religious Term Refused Based on Disparagement

In *In re Lebanese Arak Corp.*,[35] the TTAB affirmed the examining attorney's refusal of the mark KHORAN for wine. The TTAB viewed the mark as the phonetic equivalent of "Koran," the name of the holy book of Islam, a religion which forbids the consumption of alcoholic beverages. The applicant asserted that "KHORAN" was an Armenian word for "altar."

The TTAB first considered the proper statutory basis for the refusal. Lanham Act section 2(a) contains several grounds for possible refusal of an application to register a mark. Earlier TTAB cases involving use of words with religious connotations for products officially disapproved of by the referenced religions had been discussed pursuant to the ban on "immoral" or "scandalous" marks. After these early cases, however, the Federal Circuit had held that this ground of refusal turns on the perceptions of the public as a whole. Because religious minorities were a small portion of the general public, the TTAB recognized that continued use of the "immoral" or "scandalous" ground would result in outcomes in disharmony with earlier refusals. Therefore, the TTAB held that the proper statutory reference was the ban on registering matter which "may disparage."[36] This ground

---

35. 94 U.S.P.Q.2d (BNA) 1215 (T.T.A.B. 2010).
36. *Id.* at 1216 (citing 15 U.S.C. § 1052(a)).

turned on the perceptions of a substantial portion of the group referenced, as opposed to the perceptions of the general public.

The TTAB then applied the proper standard to the mark at issue. A refusal based on disparagement of a recognizable social group has two prongs. The first inquiry is the meaning of the matter when used as a mark for the specified goods or services. If the meaning refers to a recognizable social group, the second inquiry is whether a substantial portion of the referenced group would consider the matter disparaging if used as mark for the specified goods or services. The examining attorney had submitted more than sufficient evidence on the second prong by demonstrating that Muslims consider the consumption of alcoholic beverages, including wine, to be unacceptable.

The more difficult question was whether KHORAN would be perceived as the name of the holy book of Islam. The TTAB based its conclusion that the public would perceive KHORAN as the phonetic equivalent of "Koran" on the large number of variant English spellings employed for this Arabic word and on the lack of evidence that the general public knew that KHORAN was an Armenian word.

Two members of the TTAB dissented on the ground that the meaning of allegedly defamatory matter should be judged by the perceptions of the public as a whole. Because the evidence was unclear regarding the probable perception of the general public, the dissenters would have erred on the side of publishing the mark, thus providing an opportunity for members of the allegedly disparaged class to oppose the registration in an inter partes proceeding. In response, the majority asserted that the matter at issue had been shown to mean the holy book of Islam to both the general public and to adherents of Islam. However, the majority also indicated in dictum that it would have affirmed a disparagement refusal if a term was understood as disparaging by a specific social group and the term was neither known nor understood by the general public.

LICENSING

NFL Not a "Single Entity" under Section 1 of the Sherman Act

In ***American Needle, Inc. v. National Football League***,[37] the U.S. Supreme Court unanimously held that the National Football League (NFL) was not a "single entity" exempt from antitrust liability under section 1 of the Sherman Antitrust Act[38] when it granted an exclusive license to Reebok International Ltd. to manufacture and sell headwear bearing NFL team colors, names, logos and trademarks.

The NFL is an unincorporated association of thirty-two separately owned and operated football teams. The thirty-two professional football teams cooperate to produce their games, but each team owns its own intellectual property, including its colors, logos, and name. Prior to 1963, each team handled the marketing of its team related merchandise on its own. In 1963, however, the teams formed a separate corporate entity, the National Football League Properties (NFLP), to manage and promote collectively the management and marketing of all of the teams' intellectual property rights. The NFLP was charged with developing, licensing, and marketing the intellectual property owned by the teams as

---

37. 130 S. Ct. 2201 (2010).
38. 15 U.S.C. §§ 1–2 (1890).

well as conducting and engaging in advertising campaigns and promotional ventures on behalf of the NFL and its teams.

From 1963 to 2000, the NFLP granted nonexclusive licenses to various private vendors to manufacture and sell jerseys, baseball caps, hats, and other team labeled apparel. American Needle, a Chicago company that manufactures sports hats and uniforms, among other things, was a licensee of NFLP. However, in December 2000, the teams authorized the NFLP to grant exclusive licenses to vendors. In 2001, the NFLP granted an exclusive ten-year license to Reebok International Ltd. (Reebok) to sell headwear for the thirty-two NFL teams. As a result, American Needle's license was not renewed.

Thereafter, American Needle filed an antitrust action in the Northern District of Illinois against the NFL, the NFLP, the thirty-two individual NFL teams (the NFL Defendants), and Reebok alleging that the agreement violated sections 1 and 2 of the Sherman Antitrust Act. The district court granted summary judgment to the NFL Defendants on the question of whether the NFL and its thirty-two teams were a "single entity" for the purposes of the intellectual property agreement. The district court agreed with the NFL that the thirty-two teams acted as a "single entity" (not a joint venture) through the NFLP for the purpose of licensing intellectual property and that therefore they were immune from the antitrust prohibitions of section 1. The Seventh Circuit affirmed the district court's ruling.

American Needle appealed to the U.S. Supreme Court for a determination of whether the NFL's grant of an exclusive license for intellectual property was subject to the antitrust limitations of section 1. The Court reversed the Seventh Circuit, holding that the NFL was not exempt from section 1 in the context of the exclusive license with Reebok. NFLP, the Court contended, formed a joint venture between independently owned teams that were not viewed as a "single entity" for purposes of section 1.

Section 1 of the Act applies to concerted action. It makes illegal every contract, combination in the form of trust or otherwise, or conspiracy, in restraint of trade or commerce. Section 2 of the Act applies to concerted and independent action only if it monopolizes, thus, making it illegal for any person to monopolize, or attempt to monopolize, or combine or conspire with any other person or persons, to monopolize any part of the trade or commerce. Violation of section 1 of the Act requires proof of concerted action among "separate entities" because an entity acting independently cannot conspire with itself. Concerted action is that which joins together separate decision makers. Two or more separate economic actors, with separate economic interests, acting as one to restrain trade, are prohibited by section 1. American Needle argued that the NFL teams are separate and that therefore, the collective agreement among the thirty-two teams authorizing the NFLP to grant an exclusive license to Reebok constituted a conspiracy to restrict trade in the NFL headwear market.

On the other hand, the NFL relied on the U.S. Supreme Court's decision in *Copperweld Corp. v. Independence Tube Corp.,*[39] which held that a parent corporation and its wholly owned subsidiary are a single entity for antitrust purposes. The NFL contended that just as it operated jointly as a "single entity" to produce NFL football on the field, it likewise operated as a "single economic enterprise" to market the NFL brands through the NFLP. The Court agreed that the NFL acted as one source of economic power in producing the game of football. However, the Court concluded that "[a]lthough NFL teams have com-

---

39. 467 U.S. 752 (1984).

mon interests such as promoting the NFL brand, they are still separate, profit-maximizing entities, and their interests in licensing team trademarks are not necessarily aligned."[40]

The Court relied on the decision in *Copperweld* holding that "[c]oncerted activity inherently is fraught with anticompetitive risk insofar as it deprives the marketplace of independent centers of decision making that competition assumes and demands."[41] "[T]he NFL teams do not possess either the unitary decision-making quality or the single aggregation of economic power characteristic of independent action. Each of the teams is a substantial, independently owned, and independently managed business, whose 'general corporate actions are guided or determined' by 'separate corporate consciousnesses,' and whose 'objectives are' not 'common.'"[42] The Court noted that the teams compete amongst themselves on the field and in addition they compete for fans, gate receipts, player and manager contracts, as well as in the intellectual property market.

The activities of the NFLP and the NFL constituted concerted action according to the Court because the teams collectively licensed their individually owned trademarks through the NFLP to one vendor, effectively creating an illegal restraint of trade.

> To a firm making hats, the Saints and the Colts are two potentially competing suppliers of valuable trademarks. When each NFL team licenses its intellectual property, it is not pursuing the "common interests of the whole" league but is instead pursuing interests of each "corporation itself," teams are acting as "separate economic actors pursuing separate economic interests," and each team therefore is a potential "independent cente[r] of decisionmaking." Decisions by NFL teams to license their separately owned trademarks collectively and to only one vendor are decisions that "depriv[e] the marketplace of independent centers of decisionmaking," and therefore of actual or potential competition.[43]

The NFLP was viewed by the Court as an instrumentality of the NFL and as such, the formation of this separate corporate entity could not shield the NFL from antitrust liability under section 1 because the thirty-two separately owned teams have their own intellectual property and profit separately from their team-labeled wear. In addition, the NFLP licensing decisions are made by the thirty-two competing teams that earn a share of the NFLP's profits in addition to the individual team profits from the marketing of their intellectual property. Given that the actions of the thirty-two teams are covered by section 1, the actions of the NFLP are covered by section 1 with respect to NFL intellectual property licensing decisions.

The Court looked not merely at the NFL and the NFLP as a legal entity, but how the entities operated with respect to the licensing of the intellectual property, noting that a legally single entity can violate section 1 if it is controlled by a group of competitors who use the entity for concerted activity. "If the fact that potential competitors shared in profits or losses from a venture meant that the venture was immune from section 1, then any cartel 'could evade the antitrust law simply by creating a "joint venture" to serve as the

---

40. *Am. Needle*, 130 S. Ct. at 2213.
41. *Id.* at 2208 (quoting *Copperweld*, 467 U.S. at 768–69) (internal citation omitted).
42. *Id.* at 2212 (quoting *Copperweld*, 467 U.S. at 771).
43. *Id.* at 2213 (citations omitted).

exclusive seller of their competing products.'"[44] The case was remanded back to the district court for a rehearing.

Bankruptcy Court's Rejection of Ten-Year-Old Trademark License Overturned by Third Circuit

In *In re Exide Technologies*,[45] the Third Circuit overturned decisions of the bankruptcy and district courts that permitted a debtor-in-possession to reject a ten-year-old trademark license. The bankruptcy and district courts agreed that a ten-year-old trademark license was an "executory" contract under 11 U.S.C. § 365(a), which permits a debtor to "reject any executory contract" with court approval. The Third Circuit disagreed, holding that the lower courts had applied the wrong test in deciding whether the license was executory and that, under the correct test, the trademark license was not "executory."

Exide sold its industrial battery business to EnerSys Delaware, Inc. (EnerSys) in 1991, granting EnerSys a "perpetual, exclusive, royalty-free license" to use the EXIDE trademark in the industrial battery business. Nearly ten years later, Exide decided to return to the industrial battery business and sought to regain the rights to the EXIDE trademark. However, EnerSys repeatedly refused to release those rights. The parties became direct competitors in the industrial battery market, with EnerSys selling its batteries under the EXIDE trademark.

In 2002, Exide filed a Chapter 11 bankruptcy petition and attempted to regain the rights to the EXIDE trademark by invoking section 365(a) of the Bankruptcy Code, which permits a debtor-in-possession to reject an "executory contract," subject to court approval. The bankruptcy court held that Exide's ten-year-old trademark license to EnerSys remained "executory" and granted Exide's motion to reject the license. The U.S. District Court for Delaware affirmed.

On appeal, the Third Circuit held that the license was not executory. According to the court, the lower courts should have applied a balancing test comparing the licensee's performance rendered to the licensee's performance remaining.[46] EnerSys had paid the full $135 million purchase price and had been selling batteries under the license for more than ten years. According to the court, this substantial performance outweighed any unperformed obligations.

Although Judge Ambro joined the panel's opinion in full, he wrote a separate concurring opinion to address the currently unresolved question of whether a trademark licensee retains any rights in the subject of the trademark license when the license is rejected under section 365(a).[47] His opinion provides an analytical framework under which to analyze that question, on which the courts are split.

The lower courts in this case concluded that "[r]ejection of the Agreement leaves EnerSys without the right to use the Exide mark." Judge Ambro wrote separately to refute that conclusion. First, he reviewed the history behind section 365(n) of the Bankruptcy Code, a companion to section 365(a) that Congress enacted in 1988 to overturn a Fourth

---

44. *Id.* at 2215 (quoting Major League Baseball Props., Inc. v. Salvino, Inc., 542 F.3d 290, 335 (2d Cir. 2008)) (Sotomayor, J., concurring in judgment).

45. 607 F.3d 957 (3d Cir. 2010).

46. *Id.* at 963.

47. *Id.* at 964–68.

Circuit decision holding that an intellectual property licensee whose license is rejected under section 365(a) can treat the rejection as a breach and sue for money damages but does not retain any rights in the property subject to the license. Section 365(n) was intended "to make clear that the rights of an intellectual property licensee to use the licensed property cannot be unilaterally cut off as a result of the rejection of the license pursuant to section 365 in the event of the licensor's bankruptcy." Accordingly, section 365(n) provided that, when a bankruptcy trustee rejects an executory contract under which the debtor has licensed an intellectual property right, the licensee could either treat the contract as terminated by breach and sue for damages, or "retain its licensed rights—along with its duties—absent any obligations owed by the debtor-licensor."[48]

However, section 365(n) does not resolve the question of what rights EnerSys would have retained if its license to the EXIDE mark had been rejected as executory, because Congress intentionally omitted trademarks from the definition of intellectual property subject to section 365(n). Several courts, including the bankruptcy court here, have reasoned by negative inference that Congress omitted trademarks from section 365(n) because it intended for licensees under rejected trademark licenses to lose all of their rights under the license. Judge Ambro expressly disputed both the validity of that negative inference and the conclusion that trademark licensees should lose their rights when a trademark license is rejected as executory.

Judge Ambro first pointed out that, when it enacted section 365(n), Congress explained that it had omitted executory trademark, trade name and service mark licenses from section 365(n), even though such licenses were "of concern," because such contracts raise issues beyond the scope of the legislation, such as control of the quality of the products or services sold by the licensee. Because such matters could not be addressed without more extensive study, congressional action was postponed to allow the development of equitable treatment of this situation by bankruptcy courts. This explanation made it clear that Congress did not intend that trademark licensees should automatically lose their rights if the licenses are rejected in bankruptcy.

Judge Ambrose then cited a Congressional statement cautioning that Congress did not intend that any inferences be drawn concerning the treatment of executory contracts unrelated to intellectual property. Judge Ambrose explained that this statement likely was included in the legislative history of section 365(n) because of a National Bankruptcy Conference recommendation that the legislative history for section 365(n) include a caveat making it clear that no negative inferences should be drawn by courts that, because Congress has legislated in a particular way a licensing agreement, those other agreements that are not within the parameters of the legislation are to be dealt with in any particular way. Based on these statements, Judge Ambro concluded that the negative inference relied on by some courts was invalid.

In light of these Congressional statements and analyses from several commentators, Judge Ambro reasoned that the rejection of a trademark license should be treated as a breach, rather than a rescission, of the license, thereby allowing the licensee to retain its rights in the mark with respect to third parties, but not as against the licensor. He concluded that stripping trademark licensees of their rights in rejected contracts was "putting debtor-licensors in a catbird seat they often do not deserve" and that the courts should, instead, use section 365 to free a bankrupt trademark licensor from any burdensome duties

---

48. 607 F.3d at 964–66.

that hindered its reorganization without letting the licensor take back rights that it bargained away prebankruptcy.

Japanese Legal Term Determines License Scope

In ***Sunstar, Inc. v. Alberto-Culver Co.,***[49] the Seventh Circuit vacated the judgment for Alberto-Culver finding that Sunstar, buyer/licensee of an exclusive-use license agreement known in Japanese as *senyoshiyoken*, is entitled to make minor alterations to the marks licensed under the agreement. The district court had entered judgment for Alberto-Culver, enjoining Sunstar from using variations of the licensed mark other than those listed in the license agreement, but refused to award damages. The district court had also ordered termination of the license agreement due to Sunstar's breach.

A threshold issue on appeal was whether the Japanese legal term *senyoshiyoken*, used in the agreement to describe the type of license granted to Sunstar, should be given its meaning under Japanese law or the more restricted meaning advocated by Alberto-Culver. Under Japanese law, the holder of a *senyoshiyoken* "not only has an exclusive right to use the licensed trademarks within the geographical scope of the license . . . but can sue infringers of the trademarks in its own name."[50] Alberto-Culver argue that the parties used the term *senyoshiyoken* to indicate that Sunstar could register the license with the Japanese trademark office, not to confer on Sunstar the rights that a *senyoshiyoken* confers on the holder under Japanese law. The district court agreed and refused to instruct the jury on the meaning of the term under Japanese law. The Seventh Circuit rejected this reasoning, finding that sophisticated parties using a technical term can be presumed to intend its technical meaning, especially here, where the parties did not assign an alternative meaning to the term in the contract.

The court then determined that under Japanese law, the holder of a *senyoshiyoken* could alter a licensed mark if it was so similar to the original that it should be deemed to have been included in the license. To address this issue, the court turned to the rules of material alteration and "tacking on," which are the same under U.S. and Japanese law, and considered the probability and likely necessity that the licensed marks would evolve over the ninety-nine-year term of the license agreement in this case. The court concluded that Sunstar had the right to make minute changes to the licensed marks as long as the variants "can be regarded as the same as the registered trademark in question . . . ."[51] Accordingly, the Seventh Circuit vacated the district court judgments and remanded the case to the district court.

---

49. 586 F.3d 487 (7th Cir. 2009).
50. *Id.*
51. *Id.* at 498.

PART III
UNFAIR COMPETITION

CHAPTER 14

UNFAIR COMPETITION AND
DECEPTIVE TRADE PRACTICES

Cases relating to unfair competition and deceptive trade practices covered a wide array of topics. Domain names and other Internet-related issues figured prominently into these actions, as did false advertising, the right of publicity, the functionality of trademarks, geographic·deceptiveness of a trademark, and various consumer protection issues.

In cases involving allegations of improper use of domain names, some trademark owners prevailed. In *Volvo Trademark Holding AB v. Volvospares.com*, the U.S. District Court for the Eastern District of Virginia, which had in rem jurisdiction over a Web site registrant located outside the United States, granted summary judgment in favor of the plaintiff, finding that the registrant was acting in bad faith with the intent to profit, and that the volvospares.com domain name was confusingly similar to the famous and distinctive VOLVO trademark. Similarly, in *Continental Airlines, Inc. v. Continentalair.com*, the same district court found that the plaintiff's marks were famous, that the continentalair.com domain name was registered and used by the registrant in bad faith with intent to profit, that the use was dilutive, and that transfer of the domain name to the plaintiff was proper.

Others who brought domain-name-related actions prevailed in smaller victories. In *Occidental Hoteles Management, S.L. v. Hargrave Arts, LLC*, the U.S. District Court for the Northern District of Oklahoma held that the decision of an arbitration panel issued pursuant to ICANN's UDRP procedure for domain name disputes did not constitute a valid affirmative defense to claims of trademark infringement or cybersquatting in federal court. In *Office Depot, Inc. v. Zuccarini*, the Ninth Circuit upheld the exercise of quasi in rem jurisdiction over a domain name in the district in which the domain name registry was located for purposes of executing a judgment against the owner of the domain name.

Additionally, in *Transamerica Corp. v. Moniker Online Services*, the U.S. District Court for the Southern District of Florida denied the defendants' motion to dismiss where the plaintiff sufficiently pleaded claims under the Lanham Act and the ACPA. The court determined that, where a registrar is alleged to be acting as both the registrar and the de facto registrant, and acting in concert with infringing domain name registrants to profit from the infringement, the ACPA's safe harbor cannot apply as a matter of law, and claims for contributory and direct infringement may proceed.

Not all trademark owners seeking relief in domain-related-actions fared as well, however. In *Career Agents Network, Inc. v. careeragentsnetwork.biz*, the U.S. District Court for the Eastern District of Michigan held that use of the plaintiff's business name and trademark as domain names for "gripe" Web sites both was not in bad faith under the ACPA and constituted noncommercial use protected by the First Amendment.

In *Lahoti v. Vericheck, Inc.*, the Ninth Circuit vacated and remanded the district court's bench trial judgment to the extent that it held that the disputed mark, VERICHECK, was inherently distinctive and, thus, protectable under the ACPA and the Lanham Act. The court's decision was based on a determination that the district court applied improper legal standards to its assessment of the mark.

Other Internet-related practices and Web sites also were the topic of a few notable cases, as well as the subject of a new state statute. In *Rosetta Stone Ltd. v. Google Inc.*, the U.S. District Court for the Eastern District of Virginia not only granted summary judgment to the defendant on claims that the defendant's practice of selling trademarks as advertising keywords constituted direct, contributory and vicarious trademark infringement and dilution, but also held that the defendant's use of trademarks as keywords was "functional" and therefore a noninfringing use as a matter of law.

In *Denise E. Finkel v. Facebook, Inc.*, the Supreme Court of New York held that the defendant was immune from liability for defamation under the Communications Decency Act where the alleged defamatory content was created by a third party, even though the social networking site's terms of use asserted rights in the allegedly defamatory content.

The U.S. District Court for the Southern District of New York confirmed that "hot news" is still protectable against misappropriation. In *Barclays Capital, Inc. v. Theflyonthewall.com, Inc.,* the court held that an Internet subscription news service that published equity research recommendations from various financial firms before such information was made public violated the rights of the financial firms. In so holding, the court emphasized the substantial resources devoted to the production of such information, the time-sensitive value of these recommendations, the attempts by the financial firms to limit distribution of the recommendations to certain clients, and the fact that the defendant was a direct competitor and free-rider.

There also was a fair amount of judicial activity relating to false advertising claims. In *Osmose, Inc. v. Viance, LLC*, the Eleventh Circuit found that the district court did not clearly err in finding the defendant's "tests prove" or "establishment" claims material and literally false. However, the court found that the broad terms of the district court's injunction violated the First Amendment because the injunction was not restricted to statements made in commercial advertising and promotion.

In *Weight Watchers International, Inc. v. Jenny Craig, Inc.*, the U.S. District Court for the Southern District of New York found the plaintiff likely to succeed on the merits of its false advertising and unfair competition claims in connection with the defendant's advertising campaign involving alleged clinical trials comparing the two companies' weight loss programs, and issued a temporary restraining order against the defendant.

In *POM Wonderful LLC v. Purely Juice, Inc.,* the Ninth Circuit found both the defendant and its president liable for false advertising under the Lanham Act where advertisements disseminated by the defendant were literally false and the president had participated in the unlawful activities.

Courts also considered procedural issues relating to false advertising claims. In *Schering-Plough Healthcare Products, Inc. v. Schwarz Pharma, Inc.*, the Seventh Circuit held that a false advertising lawsuit involving a pharmaceutical label is not yet ripe if the same label is under misbranding proceedings in the FDA because the changes requested in the false advertising lawsuit require preapproval by the FDA.

In *VP Racing Fuels, Inc. v. General Petroleum Corp.,* the U.S. District Court for the Eastern District of California held that a federal Lanham Act claim for false advertising relating to the octane levels of fuel was preempted by the Petroleum Marketing Practices Act (PMPA). The court found that several state law claims, one of which was for false advertising, were not preempted, but dismissed some of these claims without prejudice for failure to satisfy the heightened pleading standard applicable to such claims.

In *Zhang v. Superior Court*, a California Court of Appeal held that an insured's state law unfair competition claim against an insurer for false advertising was not barred by the state's unfair insurance practices statute, because the alleged false advertising was not covered by the insurance statute.

Additionally, the Children's Advertising Review Unit of the National Advertising Board determined that the sweepstakes portion of a commercial for Mrs. Butterworth's Syrup, which aired during children's programming, did not adequately disclose the likelihood of winning by a voiceover stating that there was only one grand prize. The Board concluded that, to convey the likelihood of winning, the advertiser should have used a disclosure such as the one that is suggested by its Guidelines: "Many will enter, one will win."

The right of publicity also arose as a topic of some interest. In *Hilton v. Hallmark Cards*, the Ninth Circuit found no error in the denial of Hallmark's motion to dismiss the misappropriation of publicity and Lanham Act claims brought by Paris Hilton regarding unauthorized use of her image and alleged catchphrase on a birthday card. The court also affirmed the lower court's denial of the defendant's motion to strike the plaintiff's right of publicity claim.

In *Keller v. Electronic Arts, Inc.*, the U.S. District Court for the Northern District of California held that use of a professional athlete's name and likeness in a video game was not sufficiently transformative under the First Amendment, nor was mere reporting of factual information about the athlete sufficient to come under the purview of California's public interest defense.

In *Yeager v. Bowlin*, the U.S. District Court for the Eastern District of California held that California's single publication rule applies to common law right of publicity and false endorsement claims under the Lanham Act. The court determined that, although merely continuing to sell items on a Web site does not result in a constant republication of the material on that Web site, altering information on a Web site to include new information about the plaintiff constitutes a republication of information so as to restart the statute of limitations.

The Seventh Circuit decided two companion cases affirming district court judgments finding trade dresses functional where the designs at issue were the subject of utility patents. In *Jay Franco & Sons, Inc. v. Franek*, the court found a round beach towel design to be functional and not protectable as a trademark. In so holding, the court explained the important role of utility patents in assessing whether a design feature is useful and, therefore, functional. In *Specialized Seating, Inc. v. Greenwich Industries, L.P.*, the court affirmed the district court's finding that the configuration of a folding chair, which was the subject of a trademark registration, was functional and thus incapable of trademark protection, relying in part on four expired utility patents that, collectively, covered most elements of the folding chair design.

In another trademark-related unfair competition case, *Pernod Ricard USA LLC v. Bacardi U.S.A., Inc.*, the U.S. District Court for the District of Delaware held that a trademark referencing a geographic location exemplifying the product's "heritage" as opposed to its "source of production" was not deceptive, where the source of the product's production also is stated.

Finally, courts considered consumer protection laws. In *FTC v. MoneyGram International, Inc.,* the U.S. District Court for the Northern District of Illinois required the defendant to pay $18 million to consumers and to implement an antifraud program to settle FTC charges that the defendant permitted its money transfer system to be used for fraud. In *Marilao v. McDonalds,* the U.S. District Court for the Southern District of California determined that California Civil Code § 1749.5(b)(1) grants the vendor, not the consumer, the choice to either: (1) redeem a gift card in cash for its cash value; or (2) replace a gift card with a new card at no cost to the holder, as only section 1749.5(b)(2) requires that "a gift certificate with a cash value of less than ten dollars is redeemable in cash for its cash value."

LANHAM ACT

False Representation of Nature of Goods or Services

Jenny Craig Ordered to Cease Advertising Campaign Based on False Advertising Claim by Weight Watchers

In *Weight Watchers International, Inc. v. Jenny Craig, Inc.,*[1] the Southern District of New York granted a temporary restraining order against Jenny Craig to prohibit its television and print advertisements regarding alleged clinical trials comparing the two companies' weight loss programs. The court entered an order to show cause why a preliminary injunction should not be granted to enjoin Jenny Craig from broadcasting, publishing or disseminating in any form or media: (1) the subject advertisements; (2) any advertisement comparing studies done by Weight Watchers and Jenny Craig or any similar studies in any context; and (3) any advertisements that alleged that:

    (a) Jenny Craig or its weight loss program is in any way superior to Weight Watchers, the Weight Watchers weight loss program or any leading weight loss company or program;

    (b) Jenny Craig clients "lost over twice as much weight" or "lost over twice as much weight as those on the largest weight loss program";

    (c) Scientific evidence or clinical trials or studies have shown that Jenny Craig clients "lost over twice as much weight" or "lost over twice as much weight as those on the largest weight loss program";

    (d) Weight Watchers or its weight loss program are inferior in any way to Jenny Craig or its weight loss program; or

    (e) People following the Weight Watchers weight loss program lost less weight than people who followed Jenny Craig's program.

Weight Watchers alleged that Jenny Craig launched a major advertising campaign during a popular diet season containing blatantly false statements regarding an alleged clinical trial comparing the two companies' weight loss programs. Specifically, Weight

---

1.   No. 1:10-cv-00392 (S.D.N.Y. Jan. 19, 2010).

Watchers' claim focused on a Jenny Craig television commercial featuring Valerie Bertinelli in a laboratory setting announcing that a "major clinical trial" showed that "Jenny Craig clients lost, on average, over twice as much weight as those on the largest weight loss program!" Weight Watchers took the position that "the largest weight loss program" was a "clear and intended reference" to the Weight Watchers weight loss program.[2]

Further, Weight Watchers showed that the "major clinical trial" referenced in the Jenny Craig advertisement was actually two separate studies conducted ten years apart that did not compare Jenny Craig's program with the Weight Watchers program, but rather compared Jenny Craig's program to self-help programs. As such, Weight Watchers argued that Jenny Craig's advertisements constituted false advertising under section 43(a) of the Lanham Act,[3] deceptive trade practices and false advertising under the New York General Business Law,[4] and common law unfair competition.

Weight Watchers argued that Jenny Craig's claims were literally false because the cited studies: (1) were irrelevant and did not provide a reliable basis for its claims; (2) did not use a head-to-head comparison of the two companies' weight loss programs; and (3) used different protocols that could not be compared. Weight Watchers further argued that the Jenny Craig advertisements falsely claimed that a head-to-head study of the two companies' current programs was performed, when it was not. Weight Watchers also objected to the disclaimer in Jenny Craig's advertisements that its claims were based on two separate studies with the same protocol design as adding to the deception because it was small, incomplete, and false.

Lastly, Weight Watchers argued that Jenny Craig's deceptive claims were material to customers and likely to influence purchasing decisions because they went to the heart of why a weight loss consumer chooses a particular weight loss program, i.e., its ability to help them lose weight.

After the entry of the temporary restraining order, the case settled out of court. Under the terms of the settlement, Jenny Craig agreed to permanently cease the subject advertising campaign.[5]

Ninth Circuit Affirms Liability for False Advertising and Unfair Competition Based on False "No Added Sugar" Claim

In *POM Wonderful LLC v. Purely Juice, Inc.,*[6] the Ninth Circuit affirmed the district court's decision that Purely Juice engaged in false advertising and unfair competition when it falsely advertised its pomegranate juice as being pure with no added sugar. The court also found Purely Juice's president and founder, Paul Hachigian, personally liable

---

2. Memorandum of Law in Support of Weight Watchers International, Inc.'s Motion for a Preliminary Injunction and a Temporary Restraining Order at 1, Weight Watchers Int'l, Inc. v. Jenny Craig, Inc., No. 10-00392 (S.D.N.Y. filed Jan. 19, 2010).

3. 15 U.S.C. § 1125(a) (West 2010).

4. N.Y. GEN. BUS. LAW §§ 349–350.

5. Kelsey Swanekamp, *Jenny Craig Buckles Under Weight Watchers*, Feb. 5, 2010, *available at* http://www.forbes.com/2010/02/05/jenny-craig-weight-markets-equities-nutrisystem.html.

6. 362 F. App'x 577 (9th Cir. 2009).

for false advertising and unfair competition, due to his control of the company when the false advertising occurred.

First, the court held that intent is not a required element of a Lanham Act false advertising claim. Section 43(a) of the Lanham Act prohibits any "false or misleading description of fact, or false or misleading representation of fact" concerning the nature, characteristics, qualities or geographic origin of goods.[7] Deception of the public is presumed where an advertisement is literally false. Thus, the district court did not err in holding that Purely Juice committed a Lanham Act violation because its advertisements of purity were literally false. The court found Hachigian personally liable under the Lanham Act because he was directly involved in the manufacturing of the product, including selection of suppliers; therefore, he "'authorized and directed' the acts constituting false advertising under the Lanham Act."[8]

Second, the court held that Purely Juice had knowledge of false advertising under section 17500 of the California Business and Professions Code.[9] A party is liable under section 17500 if it makes any statement about a product or service that it knows or should know is likely to deceive members of the public.[10] The court focused on two factors in finding that Purely Juice had knowledge that its advertisements were misleading. First, Purely Juice continued to sell its products as pure after testing revealed that they were not pure. Second, despite knowing that certain harvesting and supply conditions had affected the availability of pure pomegranate concentrate, Purely Juice did not subject its brokers or suppliers to any verification procedures and instead relied on the suppliers' word and unverified certificates of quality. Therefore, Purely Juice knew, or should have known, that products it was selling were falsely advertised.

The court also found Hachigian personally liable under section 17500 because he was in control of Purely Juice, and was directly involved with manufacturing, marketing, and selection of concentrate suppliers. Therefore, he knew or should have known of the false advertising.

Third, the court let stand, without discussion, the district court's ruling that Purely Juice engaged in unfair competition under section 17200 of the California Code.[11] Because section 17200 defines unfair competition to include any violation of the false advertising law,[12] any violation of section 17500 necessarily violates section 17200. Thus, the court also found Hachigian personally liable under section 17200 due to his control over the acts that constituted false advertising.

The court also rejected Hachigian's argument that personal liability could only be based on the alter ego doctrine, finding that liability outside the alter ego doctrine can be based upon a corporate officer personally committing a tort.

---

7.   15 U.S.C. § 1125(a)(1)(A)–(B).
8.   *POM*, 362 F. App'x at 581.
9.   CAL. BUS. & PROF. CODE § 17500.
10.   *Id.*
11.   *Id.* § 17200.
12.   *Id.*

ADVERTISING

False Advertising

Literally False "Tests Prove" or "Establishment" Claims Justify Injunction If Limited to Commercial Advertising and Promotion

In ***Osmose, Inc. v. Viance, LLC,***[13] the Eleventh Circuit affirmed-in-part and vacated one provision of a preliminary injunction entered by the district court with additional instructions to modify the injunction as a whole to remove any First Amendment concerns. The injunction arose from a false advertising claim where Viance released several advertising statements expressing serious safety concerns about use of Osmose's copper-based wood preservative called MCQ. Viance and Osmose were competitors in the wood preservative market that sold preservatives used to protect wood against rot, decay, and insect attack. Following Viance's advertisements, Osmose sued for false advertising under section 43(a) of the Lanham Act and various related false advertising claims under Georgia law. The district court granted Osmose's motion for a preliminary injunction and this appeal followed.

In order to establish likelihood of success on a false advertising claim, the district court found, and the Eleventh Circuit agreed, that Viance's various statements referring to "findings" were "tests prove" or "establishment" claims, placing the burden on Osmose to demonstrate that Viance's tests did not establish the propositions they espoused. Statements regarding serious safety concerns could be construed as more than general statements of opinion. The court concluded that Viance's tests did not assess the effect of alleged wood decay, thereby demonstrating that the tests did not support Viance's conclusions. The court also found that qualifying language in Viance's test results undermined the breadth of the overall conclusions. Based on the foregoing, the court concluded that the district court did not clearly err in determining that Viance's statements regarding MCQ were literally false.

Because the court found Viance's ads to be literally false, Osmose was not required to present evidence of consumer deception, only materiality. Materiality is demonstrated if the statements are likely to affect a purchasing decision or make misrepresentations about an inherent quality or characteristic of the product. Viance challenged materiality only with respect to statements found in the testing report of an independent company, Timber Products. The court found that heavy reliance on Timber Product's independence and reputation enhanced the likelihood that Viance's misrepresentations would influence purchasing decisions.

The court agreed that a likelihood of injury was shown with respect to the statements made based on the Timber Products report because the statements were about product safety. The court found reasonable the district court's inference that the serious nature of the advertisement claims would irreparably harm Osmose's goodwill and market position. With respect to the balance of hardships, the court found that stopping the advertisements

---

13.   612 F.3d 1298 (11th Cir. 2010).

did not disparage Viance's product or inappropriately bolster Osmose's product. The effect was only to prohibit Viance's advertisement of unsupported generalizations. Such an injunction did not disserve the public interest.

The court, however, agreed with Viance that the district court erred by enjoining advertising statements regarding environmental certifications, because it did not identify or analyze any statements made by Viance to that effect.

Lastly, the court turned to First Amendment concerns. Viance argued that the injunction was an unconstitutional prior restraint because it could apply to protected, noncommercial speech such as petitions to the government, scientific papers, arguments before certification organizations, and testimony in the litigation. The court agreed and remanded with instructions to limit the scope of the injunction to statements made in commercial advertising and promotion.

Mark That Depicts Product "Heritage" as Opposed to "Origin" Is Not Deceptive

In *Pernod Ricard USA LLC v. Bacardi U.S.A., Inc.,*[14] the U.S. District Court for the District of Delaware held that the defendant's use of the words "Havana Club" on packaging of a rum product that is manufactured in Puerto Rico, rather than Cuba, is not a false and misleading representation of geographic origin in violation of 15 U.S.C. § 1125(a), when the product has an established Cuban heritage and the packaging includes a "Puerto Rican Rum" statement on the front of the bottle and a statement that the rum is "crafted in Puerto Rico" on the back of the bottle.

The court refused to dismiss the case based on Defendant Bacardi's argument that Plaintiff Pernod lacked standing. The court held that a rum producer that sells its product in the United States can establish standing to challenge an allegedly false designation of origin when it can demonstrate a commercial injury.[15]

This matter was brought by Pernod with allegations of false and misleading misrepresentations about geographic origin and false advertising based on Bacardi's statements that it owned the rights to the HAVANA CLUB mark in the United States. The court dismissed that portion of the complaint referencing the rights to the mark, and a bench trial was held as to the geographic origin claim.[16]

Bacardi, having acquired the HAVANA CLUB mark from the Arechabala family of Cuba, did not dispute that it intentionally positioned its rum product as a product of Cuban heritage. Pernod alleged that the use of the mark for a rum not produced in Cuba and statements that it had been made in Cuba and sold in the United States prior to 1960 represented false and misleading misrepresentations in violation of the Lanham Act. Pernod's case was premised on its expert's testimony that a survey established that HAVANA CLUB deceived a significant number of likely rum purchasers into believing that the rum was made in Cuba. The survey, however, assessed consumer confusion as to Bacardi's rum bottle, not Bacardi's advertising, which the court found could not estab-

---

14. No. 06-cv-505, 2010 U.S. Dist. LEXIS 34424 (D. Del. Apr. 6, 2010) (not for publication).

15. *Id.* at *11–*12.

16. *Id.* at *2.

lish actual confusion with Barcardi's print advertisements, commercials, or other promotional advertisements.

The court acknowledged that the issue before it, whether geographic origin is more
like the source of production or its heritage, was a unique question. The court found there
could be no deception because the HAVANA CLUB label clearly and truthfully provided the
origin of Bacardi's rum as Puerto Rico. Additionally, it found that the record established
that HAVANA CLUB rum had a Cuban heritage in that Bacardi was originally a Cuban company and had acquired rights to HAVANA CLUB, as well as its rum recipe, from the Cuban
Arechabala family. The court also found that Barcardi's references to its Cuban heritage
are protected by the First Amendment.[17]

False Advertising Lawsuit Not Ripe If the Drug Label Is under FDA Misbranding Proceedings

In ***Schering-Plough Healthcare Products, Inc. v. Schwarz Pharma, Inc.,***[18] the Seventh Circuit found that when the FDA is conducting a misbranding proceeding to determine whether a company's drugs are misbranded, a false advertisement lawsuit based on
the same label is not yet ripe. The district court dismissed Schering's lawsuit without
prejudice with the suggestion that it re-file the lawsuit if and when the FDA decided in its
administrative proceeding whether the defendants' drugs are misbranded.

Schering appealed the district court's decision on the basis that the statement on Defendants' drug labels that the drugs are prescription only is "literally false" and, therefore,
violates the Lanham Act irrespective of the Food, Drug, and Cosmetic Act (the FD&C
Act), which governs the FDA misbranding proceeding. The defendants argued that once
the FDA makes a decision, defendants will either prevail, because their drugs are not
misbranded, or they will make whatever changes the FDA requires, and, therefore, the
suit should have been dismissed with prejudice. The defendants further argued that the
dismissal without prejudice by the district court was not appealable. The Seventh Circuit
found that dismissal without prejudice is appealable because it signals the end of the
involvement by the district court, and the district court is not waiting for some curable
defect to be addressed by the parties.

The Seventh Circuit, on the issue of ripeness, determined that even though the purposes of the Lanham Act and the FD&C Act are different, there can still be a conflict
between the statutes, which can provide an opportunity to delay a Lanham Act litigation
pending the outcome of the FDA agency proceeding. The Seventh Circuit found that the
courts need to wait for FDA's decision in the misbranding proceeding because under the
FD&C Act, the change requested by Schering is neither a minor nor moderate change, and
by default is a major change, which requires the FDA's preapproval.

The Seventh Circuit explained that proof of literal falsity allows the plaintiff to dispense with evidence that anyone was misled or likely to be misled, but only applies where
the statement is patently false and means what it says to any linguistically competent
person. The Seventh Circuit went on to discuss that it does not believe consumers of
defendants' or Schering's drugs are obviously misled because the patients taking the pre-

---

17.   *Id.* at *28.
18.   586 F.3d 500 (7th Cir. 2009).

scription medication would only do so at the direction of a physician, who presumably is aware of the over-the-counter version offered by Schering and still chose to prescribe the medication. As a result, Schering was not able to succeed on its claim of violation of the Lanham Act by claiming "literal falsity" in the defendants' advertisement.

Court Dismisses Lanham Act False Advertising Claim as Preempted by Petroleum Marketing Practices Act, but Allows State Law Claims

In *VP Racing Fuels, Inc. v. General Petroleum Corp.*,[19] the U.S. District Court for the Eastern District of California dismissed with prejudice a federal Lanham Act claim for false advertising as preempted by the Petroleum Marketing Practices Act (PMPA). The court found that the state law claims, one of which was for false advertising, were not preempted, but dismissed some of them without prejudice for failure to satisfy the heightened pleading standard applicable to those claims.

The PMPA regulates the testing, determination, certification, disclosure, and display of gasoline octane ratings. As originally enacted, the PMPA preempted state law dealing with any act or omission to which the PMPA applied, unless the provisions of the state law were the same as the applicable provisions of the PMPA. The PMPA was later amended to allow states broader authority to regulate labeling and posting of octane ratings. As a result of the amendment, state law is not preempted as to any act or omission covered by the PMPA so long as the state law is not different from or in addition to the requirements under the PMPA.

In this action, VP Racing alleged that General Petroleum sold or caused to be sold fuel that had a lower octane level than what was represented to consumers. VP Racing alleged false advertising under the Lanham Act, as well as false advertising and unfair competition under two California statutes. General Petroleum moved to dismiss the claims as preempted by the PMPA or, in the alternative, for failure to plead fraud with particularity, contending that all of the claims essentially sounded in fraud.

After reviewing general preemption principles and the preemption language of the PMPA, the court concluded that the Lanham Act claim for false advertising was preempted. The court explained that section 43(a) of the Lanham Act and the relevant provisions of the PMPA were not capable of coexistence; thus, the more specific provisions of the PMPA should prevail over the more general provisions of the Lanham Act. The provisions were inconsistent because a defendant could be in complete compliance with the PMPA's requirements and still be in violation of section 43(a). For these reasons, the court dismissed the federal false advertising claim with prejudice.

In contrast, the court held that the state claims were not preempted by the PMPA. One of the California statutes prohibited unlawful business practices, including unlawful acts for which there is no direct private right of action. The court concluded that the PMPA allows states to enforce PMPA's standards; therefore, this California state law adopted the PMPA as the predicate law for finding an unlawful act. The court further held that the PMPA did not preempt the California state law claim addressing false advertising, ex-

---

19. 673 F. Supp. 2d 1073 (E.D. Cal. 2009).

plaining that it was not the act of certifying or displaying the octane level that VP Racing complained about, but rather the act of intentionally misrepresenting the octane level.

Although the court refused to dismiss the state law claims based on preemption, it concluded some of the claims were not pleaded with sufficient particularity, including the claims alleging unlawful acts and false advertising. The court dismissed those claims without prejudice and granted VP Racing leave to file an amended complaint.

California State Law Unfair Competition Claim for False Advertising Is Not Barred by California Unfair Insurance Practices Statute

In *Zhang v. Superior Court*,[20] the California Court of Appeal, Fourth District, held that the trial court's order sustaining a demurrer to an insured's cause of action against an insurer for false advertising in violation of the state unfair competition statute was erroneous. The trial court had held that the insurer's fraudulent conduct, which was connected to conduct that would violate California's unfair insurance practices statute, could not also give rise to a private civil cause of action under the unfair competition statute. The Court of Appeal disagreed and reinstated the action.

Zhang sued her insurer, California Capital Insurance Co., over a dispute following a fire at her business. Among other things, she alleged that California Capital engaged in misleading advertising by promising insureds that it would timely pay covered claims when it actually had no intention of doing so. California Capital filed a demurrer on the ground that the alleged conduct was prohibited by the unfair insurance practices statute and, therefore, Zhang could not state a private cause of action under the unfair competition statute.

The court recognized that if an insured relies on conduct that violates the unfair insurance practices statute, but is not otherwise prohibited, controlling precedent of the California Supreme Court requires that a civil action under the unfair competition law would be barred.[21] For example, Zhang's claim might have been barred if she had alleged conduct covered by the unfair insurance practices statute, such as that California Capital had not attempted in good faith promptly and fairly to settle her insurance claim, or that it had failed, after paying a claim, to inform Zhang of the coverage under which payment was made.

In this case, however, Zhang made additional allegations that extended beyond the unfair insurance practices statute and were, instead, covered by the unfair competition statute. She alleged that California Capital made fraudulent misrepresentations and promulgated misleading advertising concerning its intentions to pay proper coverage in the event of a loss.

The court observed that conduct characterized as unfair solely because it is described in the insurance practices statute will not give rise to a claim under the unfair competition statute. However, if a plaintiff alleges conduct expressly prohibited by the unfair competition statute, such as the Zhang's false advertising allegations, the cause of action will not be barred. Accordingly, the court reinstated Zhang's claims against California Capital.

---

20. 100 Cal. Rptr. 3d 803 (Cal. Ct. App. 2009).

21. *Id.* at 807 (relying on Moradi-Shalal v. Fireman's Fund Ins. Cos., 46 Cal. 3d 287, 250 Cal. Rptr. 116 (1988)).

Online Advertising

Google Wins Summary Judgment on Claims Challenging Its Use of Trademarks as Advertising Keywords

In *Rosetta Stone Ltd. v. Google Inc.,*[22] the plaintiff asserted seven claims challenging Google's sale of plaintiff's federally registered trademarks as keywords in Google's AdWords Program, including direct, contributory and vicarious trademark infringement and dilution under federal law, and trademark infringement, unfair competition and unjust enrichment under state law. On August 2, 2010, the court granted Google's motion to dismiss the state law unjust enrichment claim.[23] The following day, the court not only granted Google's motion for summary judgment on the six remaining counts, but held that, because Google's use of trademarks as keyword triggers for Sponsored Links is functional, the functionality doctrine precludes a finding that this practice violates trademark law.

The functionality doctrine prevents trademark law from inhibiting competition by allowing one party to monopolize a useful product feature. A feature is functional under the doctrine if it is essential to the use or purpose of the article or if it affects the cost or quality of the article. Courts have previously recognized both that the use of trademarks in computer code is functional when necessary to achieve compatibility between devices and that trademarks play an important role in allowing search engines to serve their purpose as information providers. Here, the court held the keywords used by Google to identify the information in its databases that is relevant to a user's query, including trademarked keywords, serve "an essential indexing function" without which Google would be forced to create a more costly and less efficient system to generate paid advertisements.[24] The court also held that keywords serve an advertising function that benefits consumers by providing a highly useful means of searching the Internet for products and competitive prices.

Notwithstanding its holding under the functionality doctrine, the court separately addressed the merits of each of Rosetta's Stone's infringement, unfair competition, and dilution claims, concluding that: (1) Google's use of trademarked keywords was not intended to and did not cause either a likelihood of or actual confusion among the relatively sophisticated consumers who purchased Rosetta Stone products, and therefore did not violate infringement or unfair competition prohibitions under federal or state law; (2) Google's lack of control over third party advertisers—along with its use of a Trust and Safety Team to address problems with fraud and counterfeit goods—precluded claims for contributory and vicarious infringement; and (3) the fact that Google was not using Rosetta Stone's marks on its own goods precluded a finding for the plaintiff on the dilution claim. Moreover, rather than being harmed by Google's sale of its trademarks, public awareness of Rosetta Stone's brand had increased by 60 percent during the four years immediately following Google's institution of the sale of trademarks as keyword triggers, which also precluded success on a dilution claim.[25] Therefore, the court denied Rosetta Stone's summary judgment motion and granted summary judgment to Google.

---

22. No. 09-736, 2010 WL 3063152 (E.D. Va. Aug. 3, 2010).
23. *See* Rosetta Stone v. Google, Inc., 2010 WL 3063857 (E.D. Va. Aug. 2, 2010).
24. *See Rosetta Stone*, 2010 WL 3063152, at *12.
25. *Id.* at *17.

Telephone Consumer Protection Act

FTC Settles with MoneyGram International; Company to Refund $18 Million to Consumers

In *Federal Trade Commission v. MoneyGram International, Inc.,*[26] the Northern District of Illinois approved a stipulated order for permanent injunction and final judgment brought by the parties, under which MoneyGram International will pay $18 million to consumers as part of a settlement of FTC charges that the company allowed fraudulent telemarketers to use its money-transfer system to bilk U.S. consumers out of millions of dollars. The settlement comes as part of the FTC's continuing campaign to hold responsible companies such as payment processors and list brokers for helping to facilitate wrongdoing in telemarketing.

Under the Telemarketing Sales Rule, persons who provide goods or services to telemarketers have an affirmative obligation to use due diligence to assure that the promotion they are assisting is reasonably compliant. Otherwise, they can be held responsible for the underlying wrongdoing.

Here, MoneyGram was charged with knowing or avoidance of knowing that its facilities were used to have payments sent to Canada for allegedly phony lottery or prize schemes. Under such schemes, consumers were told that they had won thousands of dollars and just had to pay a fee for "taxes" "customs" or "insurance" to get their winnings. In other instances, consumers were told that they had been awarded loans and had to forward necessary fees, but received nothing in return.

The FTC charged that MoneyGram had been alerted to the fact that various frauds were being perpetrated, but ignored the warnings because proposals to deal with the problem were too costly or were not of their concern.

In addition to paying the $18 million under the settlement, MoneyGram is barred from knowingly providing substantial help or support to any sellers or telemarketers violating the Telemarketing Sales Rule. The court order requires the company to implement a comprehensive antifraud program. Under the antifraud program, MoneyGram must: (1) conduct background checks on prospective agents; (2) educate and train its employees about consumer fraud; institute agent monitoring; and (3) discipline agents who fail to comply with the rules. The order also requires MoneyGram to provide a clear and conspicuous fraud warning on the front of all its money-transfer forms.

The order's conduct provisions apply to all MoneyGram money transfers sent worldwide from either the United States or Canada. MoneyGram is also required to develop and maintain a system for receiving consumer complaints and data, and to provide that information to the FTC upon request. In addition, MoneyGram must take all reasonable steps to identify agents involved in fraud. It must review its transaction data to identify any unusual or suspicious activity by its agents and fire any agent who it believes may be participating in fraudulent activities. It also must fire or suspend any agent who has not taken appropriate steps to stop fraudulent money transfers.

---

26. No. 09-6576 (N.D. Ill. Oct. 19, 2009).

Children's Advertising

Children's Advertising Review Unit Finds That Certain Sweepstakes Disclosures Are Not Clear to Children

The Children's Advertising Review Unit (CARU) of the Council of Better Business Bureaus, Inc. issued a News Release with the results of its review of a television commercial for Mrs. Butterworth's Syrup, marketed by Pinnacle Foods Group, LLC.[27]

The commercial aired during children's programming and featured a young boy sitting at a breakfast table discussing the rich taste of Mrs. Butterworth's syrup with an animated bottle. A voiceover during the commercial announced that children may enter a sweepstakes at www.WheresMrsButterworth.com for a chance to win one grand prize of a Nickelodeon cruise. The commercial closed with a shot of the boy enthusiastically saying, "Sweet!"

The commercial came to CARU's attention through its routine monitoring of advertising directed to children. Its review of the commercial's sweepstakes component focused on whether the likelihood of winning was clear and understandable to children.

According to CARU's Self-Regulatory Guidelines for Children's Advertising (the Guidelines), advertisers "should recognize that their use of premiums, kids' clubs, contests and sweepstakes has the potential to enhance the appeal of their products to children."[28] For this reason, the Guidelines further provide that advertisers "should take special care in using these kinds of promotions to guard against exploiting children's immaturity."[29]

Although the voiceover in the commercial said children may enter the sweepstakes for a chance to win one grand prize, CARU was concerned that children would not understand from the disclosure how many children actually enter the sweepstakes to try and win the sole grand prize. The Guidelines thus caution that advertisers "should recognize that children may have unrealistic expectations about the chances of winning a sweepstakes or contest or inflated expectations of the prizes to be won."[30] Upon review of the Mrs. Butterworth's commercial, CARU concluded that the likelihood of winning was not clear and understandable to a child audience. To convey the likelihood of winning, CARU concluded that the advertiser should have used a disclosure such as the one that its Guidelines suggest: "Many will enter, one will win."

Sweepstakes and Promotions

Redeeming Gift Cards for Cash Not Required by Law

In *Marilao v. McDonald's Corp.*,[31] plaintiff Rey Marilao filed a putative class action against defendant McDonald's Corporation alleging that the fast food company's refusal

---

27. *See* News Release, *available at* http://www.caru.org/news/2009/5024PR.pdf.
28. CARU's Self-Regulatory Guidelines for Children's Advertising, § II.D.2(f)(1).
29. *Id.* § II.D.2(f)(2).
30. *Id.* § II.D.2(f)(2)(iii)(a).
31. 632 F. Supp. 2d 1008 (S.D. Cal. 2009).

to redeem gift certificates for cash value violated California's Unfair Competition Law (UCL)[32] and unjustly enriched McDonald's. The U.S. District Court for the Southern District of California disagreed and granted McDonald's motion to dismiss the case under Federal Rule of Civil Procedure 12(b)(6) for failure to state a claim.

Marilao alleged that McDonald's violated the UCL by violating California Civil Code § 1749.5(b)(1), which provides that "[a]ny gift certificate sold after January 1, 1997, is redeemable in cash for its cash value, or subject to replacement with a new gift certificate at no cost to the purchaser or holder."[33] The McDonald's gift cards at issue read that "[t]he value on this card may not be redeemed for cash . . . unless required by law."[34] According to Marilao, he desired to redeem his gift card for cash instead of dining at McDonald's. When he attempted to redeem his gift card for cash, he was told he could not receive cash. Marilao argued that this refusal violated section 1749.5(b)(1).

The district court disagreed. The court cited California Civil Code § 1448, entitled "Right of Selection," which provides that "[i]f an obligation requires the performance of one of two acts, in the alternative, the party required to perform has the right of selection, unless it is otherwise provided by the terms of the obligation."[35] The court then reasoned that McDonald's, the vendor of the gift card, was the party required to perform by *either*: (1) redeeming a gift card in cash for its cash value; or (2) by replacing a gift card with a new card at no cost to the purchaser or holder. Because section 1749.5 does not displace McDonald's right to select cash redemption or card replacement, no law was violated. Furthermore, the court noted, "Plaintiff cites no binding authority interpreting § 1749.5(b)(1) as entitling a gift card purchaser or holder to redeem a gift card in cash for its full cash value whenever it is presented."[36] The court's rationale was further bolstered by reference to Opinion 1488 of the Legislative Counsel of California, which provided that "'section 1749.5 allows the merchant or other issuer to choose one of the available options to meet his or her obligation' and 'does not require a merchant to redeem a gift certificate in cash whenever it is presented by a consumer.'"[37]

Finally, the court noted that, although section 1749.5(b)(1) does not require a merchant to redeem a gift card in cash for its cash value whenever presented by a purchaser or holder, section 1749.5(b)(2) does. Section 1749.5(b)(2) was added in 2007 and provides that "[n]otwithstanding paragraph (1), any gift certificate with a cash value of less than ten dollars ($10) is redeemable in cash for its cash value."[38] This section does not give the vendor or merchant a right of selection. Marilao, however, did not allege that McDonald's violated this provision or his gift card had a cash value of less than ten dollars.

In addition, the court dismissed Marilao's unfair competition claim for lack of standing because Marilao failed to plead facts alleging that he suffered an injury in fact as

---

32. CAL. BUS. & PROF. CODE § 17200 (West 2010).
33. *Marilao*, 632 F. Supp. 2d at 1011.
34. *Id.* at 1010.
35. *Id.* at 1011.
36. *Id.* at 1012.
37. *Id.*
38. *Id.*

required by the UCL[39] for a private action.[40] "A plaintiff suffers an injury in fact for purposes of standing under the UCL when he or she has: (1) expended money due to the defendant's acts of unfair competition; (2) lost money or property; or (3) been denied money to which he or she has a cognizable claim."[41] The court determined that Marilao did not expend money because he was given the card as a gift, the card still had value for purchasing McDonald's products, and Marilao had not been denied money because he failed to allege a cognizable claim under section 1749.5(b)(1).[42]

The court also dismissed Marilao's unjust enrichment action for failure to state a claim. To prevail on an unjust enrichment claim, a plaintiff must show "receipt of a benefit and [the] unjust retention of the benefit at the expense of another."[43] Marilao alleged that, because gift card users cannot redeem their partially used balances for cash, there is an increased probability that the remaining funds will go unused and "all revert to McDonald's."[44] However, the court determined that: (1) Marilao was free to use the gift card until all the funds were depleted; and (2) Marilao's unjust enrichment claim was based on his failed cause of action under section 1749.5(b)(1). As a result, Marilao failed "to sufficiently plead that McDonald's has been unjustly enriched as Plaintiff alleges no wrongful conduct by McDonald's."[45] "There is no equitable reason for invoking restitution when the plaintiff gets the exchange which he expected."[46]

INTERNET AND E-COMMERCE

CDA Immunity for Defamation Claim

In *Finkel v. Facebook, Inc.,*[47] the Supreme Court of New York granted defendant Facebook's motion to dismiss, holding that Facebook was immune from liability for alleged defamatory content posted on its Web site by a third party under the CDA. Finkel and four defendants were high school classmates and members of Facebook's social networking Internet Web site. Defendant classmates allegedly created a group on the Web site and posted defamatory statements about Finkel, who sued Facebook, the classmates, and their parents for defamation. Facebook filed a motion to dismiss under the CDA arguing its role as an interactive computer service entitled it to exemption from civil liability for defamation.

The court relied on the plain language of the CDA which provides "no provider or user of an interactive computer service shall be treated as the publisher or speaker of any information provided by another information content provider"[48] and that "no cause of action may be brought and no liability may be imposed under any State or local law that

---

39. CAL. BUS. & PROF. CODE § 17204.
40. *Marilao,* 632 F. Supp. 2d at 1012.
41. *Id.* (citing Hall v. Time Inc., 158 Cal. App. 4th 847, 854–55 (2008)).
42. *Id.* at 1013.
43. *Id.* (citing Lectrodryer v. Seoul-Bank, 77 Cal. App. 4th 723, 726 (2000)).
44. *Id.*
45. *Id.*
46. *Id.* (citing Comet Theatre Enters., Inc. v. Cartwright, 195 F.2d 80, 83 (9th Cir. 1952)).
47. No. 102578/09, 2009 N.Y. Misc. LEXIS 3021 (N.Y. Sup. Ct., Sept. 15, 2009).
48. 47 U.S.C. § 230(c)(1)(1996).

is inconsistent with this section."[49] The court also recognized settled case law on this subject holding ISPs immune from defamation and other, nonintellectual property, state law claims arising from third-party content. For example, *Barrett v. Rosenthal* held that "lawsuits seeking to hold a service provider liable for its exercise of a publisher's traditional editorial functions, such as deciding whether to publish, withdraw, postpone or alter content, are barred" by the CDA. [50]

The court rejected Finkel's argument that Facebook's terms of use granted it an ownership interest in the alleged defamatory content placed on its Web site. Although Facebook owned the content of its website, it was an undisputed fact that it did not publish the alleged defamatory content. Therefore, the court determined that Facebook, an interactive computer service, was not subject to liability for the alleged defamatory statements published on its Web site by the defendant classmates.

The court granted Facebook's motion to dismiss and ordered that the case caption be amended accordingly to delete Facebook as a party. The case will continue without Facebook: the remaining parties were ordered to appear at a preliminary conference.

Anticybersquatting Consumer Protection Act

Location of Registry Is Situs for Quasi In Rem Jurisdiction over Domain Names for Purposes of Executing ACPA Judgment

In *Office Depot, Inc. v. Zuccarini*,[51] the Ninth Circuit faced the somewhat novel question of where an intangible domain name owned by a judgment debtor is "located" for purposes of executing a judgment against the debtor under the ACPA under "type two" quasi in rem jurisdiction. Type two quasi in rem jurisdiction (sometimes called "attachment" jurisdiction) is used to exercise jurisdiction over property located within the jurisdiction of the court in a dispute unrelated to that property. Here, the underlying dispute between Office Depot and Zuccarini related to Zuccarini's registration of the domain name "offic-depot.com," but the assignee seeking to collect on Office Depot's judgment sought to take control of and auction off some of Zuccarini's "many" other domain names, not including the "offic-depot.com" domain name.

Federal Rule of Civil Procedure 69 permits federal district courts to exercise in rem jurisdiction over property in their districts by seizing the debtor's assets in compliance with state law, except that federal statutes govern to the extent they are applicable. Quasi in rem jurisdiction may be asserted over both tangible and intangible property, although "the situs of intangibles is often a matter of controversy."[52] Moreover, the situs of intangible property may be different for different purposes.

The court observed that if domain names are property subject to execution, and further, if they are located within a district, that district would be an appropriate location to execute judgment on them. The court then considered two questions: (1) whether, under

---

49. *Id.* § (e)(3).
50. *See Finkel*, 2009 N.Y. Misc. LEXIS at *2 (quoting Barrett v. Rosenthal, Inc., 146 P.3d 510, 518 n.9 (Cal. 2006)).
51. 596 F.3d 696 (9th Cir. 2010).
52. *Id.* at 700 (quoting Hanson v. Denckla, 357 U.S. 235, 246–47 (1958)).

state law, domain names are property subject to execution; and (2) if so, where domain names are located for purposes of execution.[53]

On the first question, the court noted that it already had held domain names are intangible property subject to a writ of execution under California law. The court then focused on the second question, the location of the domain names. California law says nothing specific about the location of domain names. Therefore, the court looked for applicable federal law, pursuant to Rule 69, and found the ACPA to be persuasive because the enforcement proceeding under review concerned enforcement of a judgment issued under the ACPA.

The ACPA provides that in rem jurisdiction over domain names can be asserted in the judicial district in which "the domain name registrar, registry, or other domain name authority that registered or assigned the domain name is located."[54] Therefore, the court upheld the district court's exercise of quasi in rem jurisdiction over domain names registered with a domain name registry located within that district for purposes of executing a judgment against the owner of the domain names.[55] The court added that, although the question was not before it, it saw no reason why, for the same purpose, domain names would not also be located in the district in which the domain name registrar was located.

Court's Application of Improper Legal Standards in Determining Mark Validity Leads to Remand on ACPA and Lanham Act Claims

In *Lahoti v. Vericheck, Inc.*,[56] the Ninth Circuit vacated and remanded the district court's judgment as a result of the district court's application of improper legal standards in deciding whether the disputed mark was an inherently distinctive, legally protectable mark under the ACPA and the Lanham Act. The court found no error, however, in the district court's conclusion that the registrant of the domain name had acted in bad faith.[57]

Plaintiff David Lahoti was a self-proclaimed Internet entrepreneur who registered the www.vericheck.com domain name in 2003, along with more than 400 other domain names that contained the trademarks of major companies, including nissan.org and ebays.com. Lahoti had been ordered in at least two previous cases to give up control of a domain name because the domain name infringed the associated trademark, and he was previously held to be a cybersquatter by the U.S. District Court for the Central District of California. Defendant Vericheck, Inc. was a corporation that provided electronic financial transaction processing services.

In 1999, Vericheck unsuccessfully attempted to register the www.vericheck.com domain name, learning that it had already been registered by a third party. In 2001, Vericheck

---

53. *Id.* at 701.
54. 15 U.S.C. § 1125(d)(2)(C)(i) (2006).
55. *Office Depot*, 596 F.3d at 702.
56. 586 F.3d 1190 (9th Cir. 2009). See discussion of district court decision at pp. 266–267 *supra*.
57. *Id.* at 1204.

received a Georgia state registration for the VERICHECK mark in connection with its check-verification and check-collection services. Vericheck was unable to obtain federal registration for its mark because an unrelated Arizona company had already registered the mark. In 2004, Vericheck received complaints about the www.vericheck.com Web site, which merely contained a few lines of code and links to Vericheck's competitors, generating income for Lahoti.

After negotiations to purchase the domain name registration broke down in 2006, Vericheck filed an arbitration complaint pursuant to the Uniform Domain Name Dispute Resolution Policy (UDRP). The UDRP arbitrator ordered Lahoti to transfer the domain. Instead of complying, Lahoti sought a declaratory judgment in the U.S. District Court for the Western District of Washington that he had not violated the cybersquatting or trademark infringement sections of the Lanham Act. Vericheck counterclaimed that, inter alia, Lahoti violated the ACPA. After an unsuccessful bench trial and summary judgment motion, Lahoti appealed, challenging the district court's finding that his use of Vericheck's Georgia state service mark was in bad faith and that he had violated the ACPA and the Lanham Act where the mark in question was found to be inherently distinctive. The district court also found that Vericheck had a valid trademark—a key element of both the ACPA and Lanham Act claims.

Initially, the Ninth Circuit clarified that the appropriate standard of review on appeal of the district court's factual determination of trademark strength was that of clear error. It then held the district court's analysis to be legally flawed with respect to the distinctiveness of the unregistered mark. Specifically, the district court improperly required that the mark describe all of Vericheck's services instead of the proper test of "whether, when the mark is seen on the goods or services, it immediately conveys information about their nature."[58] The Ninth Circuit also held that the district court improperly examined the mark in the abstract rather than in an appropriate industry context that related to Vericheck's actual business. Moreover, the court concluded that the district court erroneously analyzed the mark's component parts instead of considering the mark as a whole. Because of the improper legal standards applied by the district court, the court held that the district court's decision on the ACPA and Lanham Act claims could not stand as a matter of law. Accordingly, the prior judgment was vacated and remanded.

As to the district court's bad faith determination in connection with Lahoti's maintenance of the www.vericheck.com domain name, the Ninth Circuit held that the record supported the finding that Lahoti was motivated by an intent to profit from use of the mark. The court was especially persuaded by evidence that Lahoti was a repeat cybersquatter and held that he was not entitled to the safe harbor defense that was available under the statute. In reaching this conclusion, the Ninth Circuit explained that "a reasonable person who had previously been declared a cybersquatter in a judicial proceeding should have known that his actions might be unlawful."[59] Additionally, the Ninth Circuit noted that there was no evidence that Lahoti ever used the domain name in connection with any goods or services and affirmed the district court's summary judgment on the issue of Lahoti's bad faith.

---

58. *Id.* at 1201 (quoting *In re* Patent & Trademark Servs. Inc., 49 U.S.P.Q.2d (BNA) 1537, 1539 (T.T.A.B. 1998)).

59. *Id.* at 1203.

District Court Holds Use of Plaintiff's Mark in Domain Name on "Gripe" Web Site Does Not Violate the ACPA

In *Career Agents Network, Inc. v. careeragentsnetwork.biz,*[60] applying a balancing test previously used by the Sixth Circuit, the U.S. District Court for the Eastern District of Michigan concluded that defendant's registration of plaintiff's business name and trademark as domain names for use on Web sites criticizing plaintiff's business did not constitute cybersquatting as defined by the ACPA. The court granted summary judgment to defendant on ACPA and trademark infringement claims and further held that the First Amendment protected defendant's use of plaintiff's business name and trademark in connection with criticism of plaintiff's business.

After becoming dissatisfied with plaintiff's business dealings, and allegedly losing a $49,000 investment, defendant registered the plaintiff's business name and common law trademark as domain names, which it used on two Web sites criticizing the plaintiff's business methods. Each Web site consisted of a single page with the caption "WARNING" followed by a statement warning anyone who was considering investing in plaintiff's business opportunity that they probably would not recoup their investment, and stating that they had been "warned by those who know and have lost $20,000–$150,000 by trusting them and their plan."[61] Defendant also employed a search engine optimizer (SEO) to increase the visibility of its Web sites and a privacy protection service (PPS) to protect his contact information.

Plaintiff sued under the ACPA, as well as for trademark infringement, and ultimately moved for summary judgment, as did the defendant. After reviewing the statutory elements of a cybersquatting claim, the list of statutory violations, and the nonexclusive list of factors to be considered when determining whether a statutory violation has occurred, the court balanced the "bad faith intent" factors and concluded that "no reasonable jury could find a 'bad faith intent to profit' under the circumstances of this case."[62] The court also held that the use of an SEO or PPS did not constitute an attempt to provide "false or misleading" contact information or an attempt to divert customers from plaintiff's business in order to bolster defendant's business. Accordingly, the court denied plaintiff's motion for summary judgment, and entered judgment in favor of defendant, on plaintiff's ACPA claim, expressly finding that the defendant's "use of Plaintiff's alleged mark in the Domain Names registered to criticize Plaintiff's business" was neither "inconsistent with" nor "a violation of" the ACPA.[63]

The court then found that the use at issue was not commercial and did not create a likelihood of confusion, and therefore did not violate the Lanham Act. The court also denied plaintiff's summary judgment motion on the Lanham Act claim and entered judgment in favor of defendant, on the ground that the defendant had a First Amendment right to express his opinion about plaintiff's business practices.

---

60.   No. 09-12269, 2010 WL 743053 (E.D. Mich. Feb. 26, 2010).
61.   *Id.* at *2.
62.   *Id.* at *5.
63.   *Id.* at *8.

Judgment Granted in Favor of Trademark Owner Where Registrant Was Acting in Bad Faith with the Intent to Profit

In ***Volvo Trademark Holding AB v. Volvospares.com,***[64] the U.S. District Court for the Eastern District of Virginia granted plaintiffs' motion for summary judgment. Volvo Trademark Holding AB, along with various other Volvo entities (collectively, Volvo), filed a motion for summary judgment seeking transfer of the domain "volvospares.com" to Volvo, pursuant to the ACPA. In its complaint, Volvo alleged that the volvospares.com domain name is an unauthorized use of Volvo's mark that is likely to cause confusion, dilution, and tarnishment, and that the mark was being used in bad faith with the intent to profit. It was undisputed that volvospares.com was in direct competition with authorized Volvo dealers and service centers. The registrant of volvospares.com disclaimed any affiliation with Volvo.

The court found that it had in rem jurisdiction over defendant because: (1) Volvo could not obtain in personam jurisdiction over the registrant, who was outside the United States; and (2) the domain name registry was located within the court's district.[65]

The court concluded that no genuine issue of material fact existed as to Volvo's ACPA claim because: (1) the registrant had a bad faith intent to profit from the VOLVO mark; and (2) the registrant registered or used a domain name that is confusingly similar or dilutive to a famous mark.[66] Applying the facts of the case to the statutory bad faith factors,[67] the court concluded that the registrant was acting in bad faith with the intent to profit where he intended to divert sales from authorized Volvo dealers; the VOLVO mark was registered for decades before volvospares.com was registered; and the registrant should have known he was infringing based on the distinctiveness of the VOLVO mark. After concluding that the VOLVO mark was distinctive and famous, the court found that volvospares.com was confusingly similar to or dilutive of the VOLVO mark because "Volvo" was the dominant portion of volvospares.com. The court further found that the registrant's disclaimer did nothing to negate the confusion caused by its use of the VOLVO mark.

Lastly, although the registrant submitted a copy of a Uniform Domain Name Dispute Resolution Policy (UDRP) decision in its favor, which found that Volvo failed to prove bad faith before the administrative body, the court held that the UDRP decision did not preclude Volvo from seeking relief in federal court.[68] That the registrant registered his volvospares.com before certain other Volvo-owned domain names (e.g., Volvoparts.com) is irrelevant to whether the use of volvospares.com was actionable infringement. Thus, the court granted summary judgment in favor of Volvo and ordered that the domain be transferred.

---

64. No. 09-1247, 2010 WL 1404175 (E.D. Va. Apr. 1, 2010).
65. *Id.* at *2 (citing 15 U.S.C. § 1125(d)(2)(A)(ii)(1)).
66. *Id.* at *3 (citing 15 U.S.C. § 1125(d)(1)(A)).
67. *See* 15 U.S.C. § 1125 (d)(1)(B).
68. *Volvo*, 2010 WL 1404175, at *5.

District Court Transfers "continentalair.com" to Continental Airlines in Default Judgment

In *Continental Airlines, Inc. v. Continentalair.com,*[69] the U.S. District Court for the Eastern District of Virginia, adopting the Report and Recommendation of the Magistrate Judge, granted a motion for default judgment and ordered the continentalair.com domain name transferred to Continental Airlines pursuant to the ACPA.[70]

Continental Airlines took numerous steps to serve the registrant of continentalair.com, including mail, e-mail, fax, and Federal Express to contact both the registrant and his Korean counsel. As ordered by the court, Continental Airlines also published a notice in *The Washington Times* inviting anyone with an interest in the domain name to file an answer or response to the complaint. Defendant failed to appear and answer or otherwise plead and Continental Airlines moved for default judgment. Following Federal Rule of Civil Procedure 55, once default was entered by the clerk of the court, all factual allegations made by the plaintiff in the complaint were deemed admitted.

Under the ACPA, a court may have in rem jurisdiction over a domain name if the trademark owner is unable to obtain personal jurisdiction over the entity who would otherwise be the defendant. In this matter, the domain name in question appeared to be registered to a South Korean who lacked the minimum contacts necessary to establish personal jurisdiction in a United States court. Thus, in rem jurisdiction was proper.

An ACPA claim requires that the domain name: (1) have been registered or used with a bad faith intent to profit; and (2) that it is identical or confusingly similar to a distinctive or famous mark or dilutive of a famous mark.

Based on the facts alleged in the complaint, the court readily found the Continental Airlines trademarks both distinctive and famous for the purposes of the ACPA: there were numerous registrations (several of which were incontestable), a long history of exclusive use, global renown, and significant marketing campaigns. Because the dominant portion of the Continental Airlines trademarks and the disputed domain were identical, the court determined that registration and use of continentalair.com by the registrant was likely to cause confusion. The court also found as a matter of law that use of a famous trademark as a domain name was dilutive. Finally, the court concluded that the registrant had registered or used the domain name with bad faith intent to profit because the registrant had no intellectual property rights to the name, the domain name was not his legal name and did not identify him, and he had not put the domain to any bona fide use (commercial or otherwise). Instead, the registrant's intent was to divert Continental Airlines' customers to competitors and otherwise harm Continental Airlines, and the registrant had continued to offer to sell the domain, had registered the domain using false contact information, and had a pattern of registering domain names which were confusing similar to distinctive marks. Given these findings, the court ordered the domain name transferred.

The magistrate judge's report points out, in a footnote, that Continental Airlines' motion for default judgment included a request to make this case exceptional and award

---

69. No. 09-0770, 2009 WL 4884534 (E.D. Va. Dec. 17, 2009).
70. 15 U.S.C.A. § 1125(d)(2) (West 2010).

attorneys' fees. Because that request was not in the original complaint and was not in the published notice, Continental Airlines was given the option of filing and serving an amended complaint or proceeding without that request. Continental Airlines elected to proceed without that request.

Motion to Dismiss Denied Where Service Mark Owner Properly Stated Claims under the Lanham Act and the ACPA

In *Transamerica Corp. v. Moniker Online Services, LLC,*[71] the U.S. District Court for the Southern District of Florida denied the motion of Moniker Online Services, LLC (Moniker Online), Moniker Privacy Services, Inc. (Moniker Privacy), and Oversee.net (Oversee) (collectively, defendants) to dismiss Transamerica's complaint, which asserted numerous Lanham Act (e.g., direct and contributory service mark infringement, unfair competition), cybersquatting, and related state law claims. Moniker Online is accredited by the Internet Corporation for Assigned Names and Numbers (ICANN) to register Internet domain names on behalf of third parties. Moniker Online registered several domain names that are substantially similar to Transamerica's registered service marks.

The district court first reviewed defendants' claim that Transamerica failed to plead use of its marks in commerce. Defendants claimed that as a registrar, Moniker Online simply registers a domain on behalf of a third party and then its role ends. The district court concluded that "the use of a trademark to draw consumers to a particular Web site not belonging to the trademark holder constitutes use in commerce under the Lanham Act."[72] The court found that Transamerica's complaint sufficiently alleged use in commerce where it claimed that defendants, along with various anonymous John Doe defendants, registered domain names similar to "Transamerica" and actively monetized those domain names in order to profit from their infringing use.

Next, the court reviewed defendants' claims that Transamerica failed to plead inducement, knowledge, and control in support of its contributory service mark counterfeiting and infringement claims. To be liable for contributory trademark infringement, a defendant must have: (1) intentionally induced the primary infringer to infringe; or (2) continued to supply an infringing product to an infringer with knowledge that the infringer is mislabeling the product supplied.[73] The court found that Transamerica's allegations, that defendants were the authorized licensees and/or acting in concert with anonymous individuals who were monetizing the counterfeit domain names, and profiting with them jointly in the process, were sufficient to state a claim for contributory counterfeiting and infringement.

Although defendants claimed they were immune from liability under the ACPA because they were neither the registrants nor the registrants' official licensees, the court disagreed. The court held that because defendants are both the registrant *and* the alleged de facto registrar, they do not qualify for the safe harbor provision found under ACPA that exempts domain name registrars from liability.[74] Even if defendants were only acting as

---

71.   672 F. Supp. 2d 1353 (S.D. Fla. 2009).
72.   *Id.* at 1362.
73.   *Id.* (citing Perfect 10, Inc. v. Visa Int'l Serv. Ass'n, 494 F.3d 788, 807 (9th Cir. 2007)).
74.   *Id.* at 1365.

registrars, the court still could not grant immunity as a matter of law because the complaint alleged that defendants acted in bad faith and with reckless disregard of Transamerica's known trademark rights, as well as the trademark rights of countless other trademark owners. In alleging that defendants were part of a scheme by which they jointly profit from the misuse of others' trademarks and service marks, Transamerica had met its burden to state a claim under ACPA.

The court also concluded that Transamerica's federal and state unfair competition claims, premised on the alleged trademark infringement, were sufficient to survive the motion to dismiss. Next, the court denied the motion as to Florida's Deceptive and Unfair Trade Practices Act because the Act was amended in 2001 to cover even nonconsumer complaints. Finally, the court denied the motion to dismiss Transamerica's claim of false advertising under the Florida Statute § 817.06. The court reasoned that Transamerica's allegations that defendants used the well-known TRANSAMERICA mark to lead consumers to their own Web sites where consumers believed that they were accessing Transamerica products and services, when in fact they were not, were sufficient to state a false advertising claim under Florida's false and misleading advertising statutes.

Uniform Domain Name Dispute Resolution Policy

UDRP Decision Not Binding on Court

In *Occidental Hoteles Management, S.L. v. Hargrave Arts, LLC,*[75] a federal district court refused to strike affirmative defenses as barred by an earlier decision by an arbitration panel acting pursuant to the Uniform Dispute Resolution Policy (UDRP) of the Internet Corporation for Assigned Names and Numbers (ICANN).

Occidental sued Hargrave in federal court over Hargrave's use of the trade name "Occidental Hotels and Resorts" on three Web sites (www.occidentalhotels.net, www.occidentalhotels.us, and www.occidentalresorts.net). Occidental promotes its services on Web sites at www.occidental-hoteles.com and www.occidentalhotels.com. The suit included three claims under the Lanham Act (likelihood of confusion regarding a common-law mark; likelihood of dilution; and domain name piracy) and two claims under Oklahoma state statutes. Hargrave asserted a number of affirmative defenses, and Occidental filed a motion to strike all of them.

First, Hargrave asserted that an earlier arbitration proceeding barred Occidental's claims in the federal court case. The arbitration at issue was a UDRP proceeding brought in 2007 by Occidental against Hargrave over the domain name occidentalhotels.net. The arbitration panel dismissed the claim without prejudice because Occidental had not shown sufficient evidence that it had rights in the OCCIDENTAL mark. At the time of the arbitration, Occidental did not have either a state or federal registration for the OCCIDENTAL mark

The district court held that this UDRP arbitration decision did not bar Occidental's claims for several reasons. First, the ICANN rules specify that UDRP arbitrations do not foreclose judicial proceedings regarding the same dispute. Second, even if UDRP decisions in general had preclusive effect, the court found that the specific arbitration relied upon by Hargrave would not have had preclusive effect as to the current suit for several

---

75.   No. 09-526, 2010 WL 1490296 (N.D. Okla. Apr. 8, 2010).

reasons: (1) the arbitration had been decided without prejudice; (2) the arbitration did not involve all of the domain names at issue in the lawsuit; and (3) the arbitration did not include all of the defendants named in this lawsuit.

The court also rejected Hargrave's attempt to reserve not-yet-stated affirmative defenses, on the ground that the Federal Rules of Civil Procedure governed any later decisions as to whether Hargrave would be allowed to amend his answer at some future date. The court denied the motion to strike three other affirmative defenses because each required factual development of the record before the court could judge their applicability.

TRADE DRESS

Defenses

Seventh Circuit Finds Round Beach Towel Design to Be Functional

In *Jay Franco & Sons, Inc. v. Franek*,[76] the Seventh Circuit affirmed a summary judgment that a round beach towel was functional and not protectable as a trademark. The court explained the role of utility patents in determining whether the main features of a design were useful and, therefore, functional.

Clemens Franek designed a round beach towel and sold it through his company. Advertising for the towel described it as a radical beach fashion item. The advertising also proclaimed that the round shape eliminated the need for a sunbather to reposition the towel as the sun moved across the sky; the sunbather could simply shift his position on the round towel. Franek's company secured a trademark registration for the round beach towel configuration, and the right to use the registered mark became incontestable. The company later dissolved and assigned the mark and registration to Franek, who continued to sell round towels.

Franek discovered that Jay Franco & Sons (JF&S) were selling its own round beach towels. Franek sued two of JF&S's customers, Target and Walmart, for trademark infringement. JF&S had agreed to indemnify Target and Walmart, and filed its own suit to cancel Franek's registration and invalidate his mark. The two cases were consolidated, and the district court eventually granted summary judgment in favor of JF&S and dismissed the remaining claims and counterclaims.

The Seventh Circuit reviewed application of the functionality defense. The court observed that incontestable marks may be challenged on a number of grounds, one of which is functionality. Relying on the U.S. Supreme Court's *TrafFix* decision,[77] the court noted that a design is functional when it is essential to the use or purpose of product, or when it affects the cost or quality of the product. If the design enables a product to operate, or if it improves on a substitute design in some way, including an improvement that makes the product cheaper, then the design is functional and cannot be protected as a trademark. The court qualified that requirement by observing that any pleasure a customer gains from the design's identification of the product's source does not count as

---

76. 615 F.3d 855 (7th Cir. 2010).
77. TrafFix Devices, Inc. v. Mktg. Displays, Inc., 532 U.S. 23, 33 (2001).

functional. Functionality focuses on the benefit produced, and a design producing any benefit other than source identification is functional.

The court then considered how to determine whether a design meets those criteria for functionality. The court reasoned that utility patents help in the determination, because inventions claimed in a utility patent are supposed to be useful. The court reasoned that such patents provide strong evidence that features claimed in a patent are functional. In this case, the court focused on one patent for a nonrectangular towel that was issued to someone other than Franek. The patent included an independent claim covering elements other than a round shaped towel. However, a round-shaped towel was covered in a dependent claim that also covered all of the elements in the independent claim. The dependent claim described the benefit of the round shape, in a manner very similar to the advertising for Franek's towel. The round shape permitted a sunbather to reposition his or her body toward the changing angle of the sun while the towel remained stationary.

Franek attempted, unsuccessfully, to avoid the presumption of functionality arising from the cited patent. He argued there was no infringement of the cited patent, because Franek's design included only the round shape described in the dependent claim and did not include the elements described in the independent claim. Infringement of a dependent claim exists only if the independent claim is also infringed. Franek also argued that his towel did not infringe the cited patent because the patent application was two years after Franek started selling his round beach towel. In rejecting these arguments, the court observed that proving patent infringement might be sufficient to show that a design is useful and therefore functional, but it was not necessary to prove patent infringement in order to show that a feature was useful and functional. The court reasoned that the functionality of a design was determined by whether the features of the design were useful, not by whether the feature was patentable or whether infringement of a patent had occurred.

The court explained that nonpatentability of an invention does not necessarily mean that a feature of an invention is not useful or functional. An otherwise useful invention may be nonpatentable because the invention is obvious or it is taught by prior art. Applying those observations to Franek's towel design, the court found that, although his design may lack some of the elements of the patent's independent claim, thereby avoiding a patent infringement claim, the dependent claim's coverage of a round beach towel for sunbathing suggested that a round towel design was useful for sunbathing.

The Seventh Circuit also commented that granting a producer the exclusive use of a basic element of design, such as the shape of a circle, limited design options available to others. The more basic the design element, the more likely it is that restricting its use will impair competition. The court concluded that the round shape of Franek's towel design was just such a basic design element that should not be removed from competitors' design palettes.

Existence of Utility Patents Leads to Seventh Circuit's Affirmance of Judgment against Trade Dress Plaintiff

In *Specialized Seating, Inc. v. Greenwich Industries, L.P.,*[78] the Seventh Circuit affirmed the district court's judgment that the design of a folding chair covered by a

---

78.   616 F.3d 722 (7th Cir. 2010).

trademark registration was functional and therefore incapable of trademark protection.[79] The court relied heavily on the fact that the folding chair configuration, as described in the trademark registration, was largely covered by four expired utility patents.

Greenwich acquired a company, then called Clarin, that for many years sold a folding chair referred to as an "X-frame" chair. The X-frame designation is based on the appearance of the profile of the chair, which looks like an X. Greenwich, which has continued to sell the chair since the Clarin acquisition, secured a trademark registration covering the chair's design. The registration described the configuration as including, among other things, an X-frame profile, cross bars in specific locations, and a back support that slants inward on its outer sides.

After waiting for the period of a restrictive covenant to expire, the former general manager of Clarin joined Specialized, one of Greenwich's competitors. Specialized then started selling a folding chair that was similar but not identical to Greenwich's chair. After Greenwich complained about Specialized's sales of the folding chair, Specialized sought a declaratory judgment that its chair did not violate the Lanham Act, and Greenwich counterclaimed for an injunction preventing further sales of Specialized's folding chair.

Following a bench trial, the district court held that the X-frame construction of Greenwich's folding chair was functional, both with respect to individual elements of the chair described in the trademark registration and the overall chair design.

The district court also held that Greenwich defrauded the USPTO by failing to identify three expired utility patents. Greenwich did disclose one utility patent, but it told the PTO examiner that the patent did not include all of the features of the mark's design. The patents that Greenwich failed to disclose, together with the one patent it did disclose, collectively covered nearly every feature of the configuration described in the trademark registration.

The Seventh Circuit focused its decision on the functionality issue and noted that findings of fact made after a bench trial must stand unless they are clearly erroneous. The court observed that functionality is a fact-specific determination based upon the determination of whether aspects of the design are either essential to the product's use or purpose, or affect the product's cost or quality.

Here, the Seventh Circuit rejected Greenwich's argument that the district court made legal errors in finding that the design of the folding chair was functional. The court explained that, because inventions covered by utility patents pass into the public domain when the patent expires, trademark law should not be used to extend protection beyond the term of the patent.

In approving the district court's holding, the court commented that the availability of alternative designs that are also functional does not prevent Greenwich's design from being functional. A design is functional not because it is the only available design, but because it is one of many solutions to a problem. One of the other designs might be protectable through a utility or design patent, but none of the functional designs—including Greenwich's—can be protected indefinitely by applying trademark law. The court noted that one goal of the functionality doctrine is to ensure that trademark law will not be used to extend the term of a patent beyond its expiration. When a utility patent expires, competitors are free to copy the design to increase competition and reduce costs to the consumer, and the functionality doctrine serves to foster this competition.

---

79. *Id.* at 728.

The Seventh Circuit also addressed Greenwich's argument that the overall appearance of the chair was distinctive and could be protected as trade dress even though most of the component elements served some function. The court explained that trade dress protection is available only if the feature that makes the overall appearance distinctive is not functional. For example, a distinctive cutout or pattern on the chair's backrest could be the basis for claiming trade dress protection. In this case, however, none of the claimed features was added to create a distinctive appearance that would serve as a source identifier. Each of the features was functional and therefore could not be used as a basis for finding that the overall design was distinctive and protectable.

Having found Greenwich's design to be functional, and therefore invalid and unprotectable, the Seventh Circuit did not review the district court's finding of fraud on the PTO. The court observed that a finding of fraud would only affect the mark's registration and not its validity, as the mark could still be enforced without a registration.

RIGHTS OF PUBLICITY

Common Law

Motion to Strike Celebrity's Right-of-Publicity Claim Denied Where Likelihood of Success on the Merits Was Shown Despite Protected Nature of "Speech" Depicted on Subject Greeting Card

In *Hilton v. Hallmark Cards*,[80] the Ninth Circuit considered the issue of whether California law allowed a celebrity to sue a greeting card company for using her image and catchphrase in a commercial birthday card without her permission. At issue was a Hallmark greeting card that showed Paris Hilton's face attached to a cartoon body serving a plate of food to a customer with the language, "Don't touch that, it's hot." "What's hot?" "That's hot."[81] Hilton alleged that the card copied a scene that she made famous on her television show, *The Simple Life*.

In 2007, Paris Hilton filed a complaint against Hallmark Cards asserting claims of misappropriation of publicity under California common law, false designation under the Lanham Act, 15 U.S.C.S. § 1125(a), and infringement of a registered trademark. The U.S. District Court for the Central District of California denied Hallmark's motion to strike the right of publicity claim under California's "anti-SLAPP" law, California Code of Civil Procedure § 425.16, and denied two portions of Hallmark's separate Federal Rule of Civil Procedure 12(b)(6) motion to dismiss pertaining to the misappropriation of publicity and false designation claims under the Lanham Act. Hallmark appealed the denial of the motions to the Ninth Circuit.

On appeal, the Ninth Circuit held that the appellate court lacked jurisdiction to review Hallmark's 12(b)(6) motion to dismiss the right of publicity claim because it was "not inextricably intertwined with any properly appealable order," such as the decision on the anti-SLAPP motion to strike.[82] Accordingly, the appellate court dismissed the appeal of

---

80.   580 F.3d 874, 879 (9th Cir. 2009).
81.   *See id.*
82.   *Id.* at 882.

the denial of Hallmark's motion to dismiss the misappropriation of publicity claim and the Lanham Act claim.

The Ninth Circuit also affirmed the denial of Hallmark's motion to strike the right of publicity claim pursuant to the California anti-SLAPP statute. The Ninth Circuit first ruled as a threshold issue that Hallmark's card qualified as "speech" and fell within types of communications that California courts considered in furtherance of the exercise of free speech rights upon which to base anti-SLAPP motions to strike. The appellate court further recognized that Paris Hilton was a topic of widespread public interest, thus making Hallmark's card "in connection with an issue of public interest."[83] However, in light of these findings, the Ninth Circuit ultimately held that Hilton had stated a claim for misappropriation of the common law right of publicity, and Hallmark was not entitled as a matter of law to the transformative use or public interest defenses.[84] As a result, the appellate court held that Paris Hilton's suit would not be stricken under the anti-SLAPP suit, as she had a probability of prevailing on the merits of the case before a trier of fact. The case was remanded for further proceedings.

Permanent Injunction Issued to Restrain "Hot News" Misappropriation

In ***Barclays Capital, Inc. v. Theflyonthewall.com, Inc.,***[85] the United States District Court for the Southern District of New York issued a permanent injunction restraining the Internet subscription news service, Theflyonthewall.com, Inc. (Fly), from further copyright infringement and "hot news" misappropriation of the equity research recommendations of financial services firms Barclays Capital, Inc. (Barclays); Merrill Lynch, Pierce, Fenner & Smith, Inc. (Merrill Lynch); and Morgan Stanley & Co., Inc. (Morgan Stanley) (collectively, the Firms).

After a four-day bench trial, Judge D. Cote found the investment services the Firms offer their clients include equity research reports, financial analysis, and trading tools to support clients' investment decisions for the purpose of assisting with maximizing clients' returns on investments. The Firms' production of "equity research" was found to be a critical component of the Firms' business models, and each of the Firms devotes substantial resources to the production of its equity research reports. Only a small portion of the Firms' reports were found to be "actionable" reports or recommendations that are likely to cause any investor to immediately make a trade decision. Although some of these reports are distributed around the clock, a large majority of these actionable reports are issued to the Firms' clients between midnight and 7:00 a.m. Eastern Time, before the New York Stock Exchange opens for trading. The content of these reports includes the Firms' investment recommendations according to their rating systems.

The trial judge further found that the value of the Firms' research derives, in part, from its exclusivity and timeliness, and that the Firms' have made efforts to control access to their research. For example, the Firms limit full access to their research output to clients meeting certain thresholds of revenue generation and forbid their clients from redistribution or reprinting of the research without written consent. Similar restrictions are also inserted into third-party license agreements. The media and communications

---

83. *Id.* at 885–86, 888.
84. *Id.* at 889–92.
85. 700 F. Supp. 2d 310 (S.D.N.Y. 2010).

policies of all of the Firms purport to limit distribution of research information to the media. Judge Cote further found that the Firms sought to uncover instances of unauthorized redistribution of their research recommendations and acted to disable any unauthorized uses they found.

Although the Firms tried to limit distribution of their recommendations to entitled clients, they found that many of their recommendations "leak" and are posted online or reported as financial news in the media. In 2004, the Firms identified Fly as a major unauthorized publisher of their recommendations. Fly is engaged in the business of collecting Wall Street news, rumors, and other information and publishing the information on its online subscription newsfeed, www.theflyonthewall.com.

Fly characterizes itself as a "single source" Internet subscription news service that quickly reports relevant market-moving news and information on the Web. Fly's online newsfeed is continuously updated between 5:00 a.m. and 7:00 p.m. Eastern Time. The newsfeed presents a constant stream of headlines in various categories, including the category of "Recommendations." For its sources for those recommendations, Fly relies almost exclusively on employees at the Firms who e-mailed research reports to Fly soon after they were released. Those employees were not authorized to release reports to Fly.

In the first cause of action, Morgan Stanley and Barclays (the Copyright Plaintiffs) asserted a claim for copyright infringement. The Copyright Plaintiffs claim that these disseminations by Fly frequently occur before they have an opportunity to share the recommendations with their clients, for whom the research is intended. The Copyright Plaintiffs contend that their recommendations are "hot news" and that Fly's regular taking and redistribution of their recommendations constitutes misappropriation in violation of the New York common law of unfair competition and infringement of their copyrights in seventeen research reports released in February and March 2005.

Fly did not dispute the copyright infringement claim or the appropriateness of an injunction. To satisfy the claim for copyright infringement, the Firms proffered registration certificates for the seventeen reports which were copied verbatim by Fly. Fly initially asserted that its copying was a fair use of the Firms' reports under 17 U.S.C. § 107, but later did not dispute the copyright infringement claim.

With regard to the claim of misappropriation of time-sensitive recommendations contained in their equity research reports, Judge Cote cited *International News Service v. Associated Press*[86] in support of his decision that the Firms had "quasi-property" rights in the "hot news." In resolving this matter in favor of the Firms, the court conducted an analysis of the five elements established in *National Basketball Association v. Motorola* to determine whether the state law misappropriation claim survived preemption by the Federal Copyright Act.[87] The five elements are: (1) the plaintiff generates or gathers information at a cost; (2) the information is time-sensitive; (3) the defendant's use of the information constitutes free-riding on the plaintiff's efforts; (4) the defendant is in direct competition with the plaintiffs; and (5) the continued unauthorized use of the information would so reduce the incentive to create the product or service that its existence or quality would be substantially threatened.[88]

---

86. 248 U.S. 215 (1918).
87. Nat'l Basketball Ass'n v. Motorola, Inc. 105 F.3d 841 (2d Cir. 1997).
88. *Id.* at 845.

In the present case, the district court found the Firms collectively employ hundreds of analysts and spend hundreds of millions of dollars each year producing their equity research reports. According to the district court, these facts support a finding that the plaintiff "generates or collects information at some cost or expense." The court found that the rest of the *NBA* factors clearly weighed in the Firms' favor and, thus, warranted injunctive relief.

The injunction requires that Fly delay dissemination of the Firms' recommendations until one-half hour after the opening of the New York Stock Exchange, or 10:00 a.m. Eastern Time, whichever is later. For research recommendations issued while the market in New York is open for trading, Fly must delay publishing the recommendations for at least two hours. The Copyright Plaintiffs elected to pursue copyright statutory damages and were awarded minimum statutory damages as set out in 17 U.S.C. § 504(c)(1).

Defenses

Court Rejects Transformative Use and Public Interest Affirmative Defenses Asserted in a Publicity Rights Violation

In *Keller v. Electronic Arts, Inc.*,[89] the U.S. District Court for the Northern District of California denied the motion of Electronic Arts, Inc. (EA) to dismiss Keller's claim of a right of publicity violation under California law based on EA's incorporation of Keller's identity into an NCAA football-based video game. In its motion, EA did not contest Keller's allegation that it used Keller's identity within a video game; however, EA asserted that the allegations of publicity rights violations were specifically barred by the First Amendment, California's Public Interest Defense, and by the section 3344(d) exemption of the California Civil Code. The court rejected these affirmative defenses.

EA claimed that its use of Keller's image was transformative and thus protected by the First Amendment. With respect to this transformative use defense, the court evaluated EA's use of Keller's image to determine whether the challenged image contained a likeness of Keller so transformed that "it has become primarily the defendant's own expression rather than celebrity likeness."[90] The court performed the requisite balancing test between the right of publicity and the First Amendment and determined that the depiction of Keller's image alone, regardless of the transformative nature of the video game when taken as a whole, was not sufficiently transformative to bar a claim of right of publicity under California law. The court reasoned that the video game incorporated Keller's image as he was and in the same setting: a starting quarterback portrayed in his collegiate uniform (including jersey number) as well as other similar physical characteristics. Accordingly, the court rejected EA's transformative use defense.

EA also asserted two other affirmative defenses based on California law, one of which was based on the public interest defense, under which California courts have held that "no cause of action will lie for the publication of matters in the public interest, which rests on the right of the public to know and the freedom of the press to tell it."[91] The court rejected this defense and held that EA's video game did more than report or publish historical facts

---

89. No. 09-1967, 2010 WL 530108 (N.D. Cal. Feb. 8, 2010).

90. *Id.* at *4.

91. Hilton v. Hallmark Cards, 580 F.3d 874, 889 (9th Cir. 2009) (citing Montana v. San Jose Mercury News, Inc., 34 Cal. App. 4th 790, 793 (Cal. Ct. App. 1995)).

like rosters and statistics, and in fact, allowed consumers to assume the identity of Keller and other players and compete in simulated football games. Furthermore, the court distinguished the facts here from prior cases involving the use of the names and statistics in fantasy baseball and football games that depend on the use of player names and statistics.[92] The court noted, that in contrast, EA's game did not depend on current statistics regarding the players. Accordingly, the court denied EA's public interest defense.

The final defense asserted by EA was based on the California Civil Code § 3344(d) exemption, which provides a "public affairs exemption to the statutory right of publicity" and exempts from liability "a use of a name . . . or likeness in connection with any news, public affairs, or sports broadcast or account or any political campaign."[93] The court relied on the decision by the court in *Montana v. San Jose Mercury News, Inc.*[94] and construed section 3344(d) as exempting the factual reporting of matter that is considered as a "public affair." Neither EA nor Keller denied that college athletics are examples of public affairs; however, the court determined that EA's use of Keller's image and physical likeness in the video game extended beyond the factual reporting of information about him. Accordingly, the court rejected this defense.

California's Single-Publication Rule Applies to Common Law Right of Publicity and False Endorsement under the Lanham Act

In *Yeager v. Bowlin*,[95] retired General Charles "Chuck" Yeager—a well-known aviator—entered into an agreement with defendants Connie and Ed Bowlin, whereby defendants would sell certain Yeager memorabilia, including artwork signed by Yeager. Eventually, the parties disagreed over the number of prints Yeager was entitled to keep and Yeager demanded that his collection be returned and that any references to Yeager be removed from defendants' Web site. When defendants did not comply with Yeager's request, Yeager and his foundation filed suit for, *inter alia,* breach of contract, violation of California's statutory right of publicity, the common law right of privacy/right to control publicity and likeness, and false endorsement under the Lanham Act.

Defendants moved for summary judgment, arguing that Yeager's claims were time barred and Yeager failed to establish the existence of a written contract. Because there was no evidence of a written contract, the district court dismissed that claim. With respect to the statute of limitations argument, the district court found that the breach of oral contract claims under California law have a two-year statute of limitations and the breaches were known or should have been known to the plaintiffs between 2000 or at the latest in 2004. Because the complaint was not filed until 2008, the district court dismissed plaintiffs' breach of contract claims. The district court also dismissed plaintiffs' fraud and unjust enrichment claims because they have a three-year statute of limitations and plaintiffs knew about the alleged fraud in late 2003.

With regards to the remaining claims, the district court noted that the statute of limitations for Yeager's right to privacy claims is two years, the statute of limitations for Yeager's

---

92. *See, e.g.,* C.B.C. Distrib. & Mktg v. Major League Baseball Advanced Media, 505 F.3d 818, 820–21 (8th Cir. 2007).

93. *Keller*, 2010 WL 530108, at *7 (citing CAL. CIV. CODE § 3344(d)).

94. Montana v. San Jose Mercury News, Inc., 34 Cal. App. 4th 790, 793 (Cal. Ct. App. 1995).

95. No. 08-102, 2010 U.S. Dist. LEXIS 718 (E.D. Cal. Jan. 6, 2010).

statutory unfair competition claim is four years, and the statute of limitations for Yeager's false endorsement under the Lanham Act is either the two-year statute applicable to right of privacy claims or the three-year statute applicable to fraud claims.

Defendants argued that the privacy, statutory right of publicity, and false endorsement claims were barred based on the single publication rule. The single publication rule states that "[n]o person shall have more than one cause of action for damages for . . . invasion of privacy or any other tort founded upon any single publication or exhibition or utterance, such as any one issue of a newspaper or book or magazine or any one presentation to an audience or any one broadcast over radio or television or any one exhibition of a motion picture."[96] Furthermore, "[u]nder the single publication rule, with respect to the statute of limitations, publication generally is said to occur on the 'first general distribution of the publication to the public'"[97] and the statute of limitations begins to run regardless of whether plaintiffs had the publication or knew of its existence.

Yeager argued that the single publication rule is inapplicable because defendants, as Web site sellers, were continuously offering for sale and selling the products at issue in this litigation. Thus, the statute of limitations should restart for each sale. Yeager also argued that the statute of limitations should be equitably tolled due to defendants' improper conduct.

The district court rejected Yeager's equitable tolling argument because plaintiffs retained legal counsel in 2005 and "equitable tolling ceases once a claimant retains counsel because the claimant 'has gained the means of knowledge of her rights and can be charged with constructive knowledge of the law's requirements.'"[98] Equitable tolling was also not available to Yeager because he failed to demonstrate that defendants actively induced Yeager to delay suing before the statute of limitations period expired.

The district court also rejected Yeager's argument that the single-publication rule was inapplicable to the defendants' Web site. The court noted that such a position would effectively eliminate the single-publication rule because the statute of limitations would never run so long as the Web site remained operational with items for sale. The court further noted that California courts have explicitly found that the repeated sale of identical products is subject to the single-publication rule, and that the defendants' Web site displayed the identical content to all of its viewers.

The court concluded that the defendants' Web site constituted a "single integrated publication" for purposes of the rule,[99] that Yeager's claims were based on material that had been posted on the defendants' Web site since 2000, and that, accordingly, his claims, which were filed in 2008, were time barred.

The court noted that the single-publication rule may not apply when a party republishes information, but that the defendants' revisions to their site in 2003 to include new information about Yeager did not change the result because Yeager's claims were still time-barred by 2008.

Finally, the district court held that, even if the single-publication rule did not apply, the plaintiffs' privacy claims were time barred because more than two years passed between Yeager's notice of the alleged violations in 2005 and the 2008 filing of suit.

---

96. *Id.* (citing CAL. CIV. CODE § 3425.3).
97. *Id.* (citing Shively v. Bozanich, 31 Cal. 4th 1230, 1245 (2003)).
98. *Id.* (citing Leorna v. U.S. Dep't of State, 105 F.3d 548, 551 (9th Cir. 1997)).
99. *Id.*

PART IV
COPYRIGHTS

CHAPTER 15

SUBJECT MATTER OF COPYRIGHT

Copyright decisions discussing somewhat novel subject matter provided significant clarifications of subject matter properly protectable under the Copyright Act, including toys, derivative works, and medical forms.

The Fourth Circuit upheld a district court's determination that the design elements of a furniture collection were copyrightable and that the defendant had infringed upon these designs. In *Universal Furniture International, Inc. v. Collezione Europa USA, Inc.*, the court found that the furniture designs at issue were conceptually separable from the utilitarian aspects of the furniture collection and rejected the defendant's argument to the contrary.

On a related matter, in *Lanard Toys Limited v. Novelty, Inc.*, the Ninth Circuit found no error in a district court's determination that a toy helicopter and launcher handle were not useful articles and were therefore copyrightable. The defendant argued that the launch handle was "merely a functional or utilitarian slingshot" that propels other toys. The court disagreed.

In a case involving the copyrightability of derivative works, *Schrock v. Learning Curve International, LLC*, the Seventh Circuit found erroneous a district court's determination that authorized photographs of the defendant's "Thomas & Friends" toys could not be copyrighted by the plaintiff because the copyrights to a derivative work were owned by the defendant. In its opinion, the court made clear that the only requirement for a photographer—or any *authorized* creator of a derivative work—to retain copyright ownership in the derivative works was the authorization and an "incremental original expression"; additional permission to register the works with the Copyright Office was not required. The case was remanded to consider whether the defendant had an implied license to continue using the photographs at issue.

In a separate case discussing the originality requirement of copyright law, the Eleventh Circuit held that blank medical forms were not sufficiently original to merit copyright protection. In *Utopia Provider Systems, Inc. v. Pro-Med Clinical Systems, LLC*, the court held that, because the forms did not present a novel arrangement or selection of headings, and because the forms themselves do not provide information to the doctors conducting the exams regarding the questions they should ask the patient, but rather merely help to document the doctor's encounter with his or her patient, the forms were not sufficiently original.

ORIGINALITY AND FIXATION

Blank Forms Lack Sufficient Originality to Be Copyrightable and Related Contract Claims Not Preempted

In ***Utopia Provider Systems, Inc. v. Pro-Med Clinical Systems, LLC,***[1] the appellate court found that the district court correctly granted summary judgment to the defendant on the plaintiff's copyright infringement claim and dismissed without prejudice the plaintiff's related state law claims. The underlying dispute concerned Pro-Med's use of various paper templates and related materials that were based upon Utopia's copyrighted material. The lower court determined that Utopia's copyrighted material was not subject to a valid copyright, and it was inappropriate to exercise supplemental jurisdiction in federal court over the related state law claims.

The material claimed by Utopia to be subject to a copyright was originally developed by the company's principals, Dr. Michael S. McHale and Joshua Plummer. McHale and Plummer developed a system of templates for use in hospital emergency departments. They created Utopia to own and manage the rights, which then entered into a license agreement with Pro-Med to market and distribute such rights associated with the forms. The agreement called for Pro-Med to pay a royalty of 50 percent of the revenue it generated from sales of the products it created using the materials licensed from Utopia.

Pro-Med extensively copied Utopia's licensed material in creating their products, both with respect to the blank forms to be used by hospitals and an electronic system utilizing such forms. After the license agreement expired, Pro-Med continued to sell its products without paying royalties to Utopia.

The first issue the appellate court evaluated was Pro-Med's contention that it cannot be liable for copyright infringement because the materials provided under the license agreement were not copyrightable in the first place. This claim was based on the fact that the templates provided were essentially blank forms that Pro-Med did not believe conveyed information justifying copyrightability. The court noted that Utopia had received a certificate of registration, which provided it with prima facie validity on its claim. Nonetheless, the court found the certificate was not controlling when other evidence raised the issue of originality.

The court, relying on *John H. Harland Co. v. Clarke Checks, Inc.,*[2] recognized the well-established rule that blank forms generally are not copyrightable. The test for copyrightability was whether the blank forms conveyed information. The court held that the forms did not convey any information about emergency room patients before being completed. The court explained that the forms could convey information only if their wording and organization managed to convey information to the doctors about questions they should ask the patient. The court held that the forms only asked questions that any reasonable physician would already be asking. In addition, differences in the various forms were related only to the underlying illnesses for which treatment was being sought.

In essence, the forms at issue were similar to noncopyrightable forms that contain obvious headings rather than headings that convey information, such as baseball score cards and travel diaries. Even the original creator admitted that the forms did not realisti-

1.   596 F.3d 1313 (11th Cir. 2010).
2.   711 F.2d 966, 971 (11th Cir.1983).

cally instruct the physician on patient care, but merely prompted the physician as to how to record the information that would have been sought in any event. Under these circumstances, the court agreed with the lower court that there was not enough original material being provided in these forms to make them copyrightable. Therefore, the district court's granting of Pro-Med's motion for summary judgment on Utopia's copyright infringement claims was appropriate.

With respect to the second issue, the dismissal of the additional state law claims, both Pro-Med and Utopia objected and appealed. Pro-Med argued that the state law claims for breach of contract were within the federal court's exclusive jurisdiction and should have been found preempted by the Copyright Act of 1976. Utopia, on the other hand, claimed that the district court abused its discretion by not exercising supplemental jurisdiction and retaining the state law claims of breach of duty and breach of contract.

The court disagreed with Pro-Med's argument. Citing *Crow v. Wainwright,*[3] the appellate court noted that the standard two-part test for preemption under section 301 of the Copyright Act of 1976 required that the claims be both within the subject matter of copyright and equivalent to one of the exclusive rights of copyright. In this case, the contract rights allegedly breached by improper copying of the blank forms at issue clearly involved the subject matter of copyright; however, the rights being enforced were not equivalent under the second part of the test.

The appellate court found that this situation was essentially the same as that of *Lipscher v. LRP Publications, Inc.*[4] In that case, the court held that the breach of contract claim under state law required proof of the existence of a valid licensing agreement, which constituted an extra element and prevented the rights from being equivalent to the exclusive rights under the Copyright Act. Using that same reasoning in this case, the court held that the state law claims for breach of contract were not preempted.

Turning to Utopia's argument that the district court abused its discretion, the appellate court also upheld the lower court's decision. The district court held that resolution of Utopia's breach of contract claim would involve a serious inquiry into and application of state law better suited for a state court. The appellate court held that this determination was well within the district court's discretion and upheld the dismissal of the state law claims.

Works Subject to Protection

Pictorial, Graphic, and Sculptural Works

Flying and Launching Toys Are Copyrightable

In *Lanard Toys Ltd. v. Novelty, Inc.,*[5] a divided panel of the Ninth Circuit affirmed the finding of willful infringement of copyright and trade dress regarding flying toys. The court determined there was sufficient evidence for the jury to find that toys and launcher handles of toys were copyrightable. It also found sufficient evidence for a jury to deny the argument that they were uncopyrightable "useful articles," and it affirmed the district court's judgment.[6]

---

3. 720 F.2d 1224, 1225–26 (11th Cir. 1983).
4. 266 F.3d 1305, 1310 (11th Cir. 2001).
5. No. 08-55795, 2010 U.S. App. LEXIS 7585, at *1 (9th Cir. Apr. 13, 2010).
6. *Id.* at *6 (citing 17 U.S.C. §§ 101, 113(b)).

The panel rejected the claim that the "Drop Copter" toy and the launcher handle of the "Wild Copters" and "Stunt Plane" toys were uncopyrightable useful articles. The court agreed with cases recognizing that various types of toys may qualify for copyright protection as pictorial, graphic, or sculptural works even where there is some mechanical or functional element to the toy. In addition, pictorial, graphic, or sculptural works that have no other utilitarian function other than to portray real objects are copyrightable.

The appellate court found that the question was properly submitted to the jury because there was a genuine dispute regarding whether the toy and launcher handles were exempt uncopyrightable useful articles. The appellants argued that "Drop Copter" is merely a sling shot whose sole function is to propel other toys into the air. The court disagreed, citing *Gay Toys, Inc. v. Buddy L. Corp.*[7] The court explained that the toys do not actually fly or transport people like real helicopters, but are mere portrayals of the real objects. It further explained that "toy airplanes are not uncopyrightable useful articles because they have no intrinsic utilitarian function other than to portray real airplanes."[8]

With regard to the launcher handle of the Wild Copter and Stunt Plane toys, Lanard demonstrated that the Wild Copter toy was registered with the Copyright Office in 1994, within five years of the first publication of the work, which established the presumption of a valid copyright. A senior-level employee had also testified that he developed the Wild Copter design in the early 1990s. The court affirmed the district court's finding that sufficient evidence was presented for the jury to find that Lanard had met the burden of proving copyright validity.[9]

The Ninth Circuit disagreed with the contention that the jury's finding of willful copyright infringement by Novelty was not supported by substantial evidence. The panel noted that, viewed in its entirety, evidence presented at trial was sufficient to support both the jury's finding of willful copyright infringement by Novelty and the district court's decision to deny the appellants' motion for JMOL on this issue.

The court also found that there was sufficient evidence for the jury to infer that the defendants actually knew, or recklessly disregarded facts that would have caused a reasonable person to know, that they were infringing valid copyrights. The court found the jury's direct observation of the infringing toys was evidence of the "exactitude" in which Lanard's toys were copied and further supported a finding of willfulness.[10]

Finally, the appellants claimed that, because Lanard made a final and binding election of statutory damages, the district court abused its discretion by allowing evidence of actual damages. The Ninth Circuit found that Lanard's amendment made it clear that it sought statutory damages as to some of its copyright claims. The court noted that the defendants failed to seek additional discovery on the issue of actual damages for the remaining claims, although time was allowed for such inquiry. Thus, in these circumstances, the court held that the district court did not abuse its discretion by allowing evidence of actual damages.

---

7. *Id.* at *8 (citing Gay Toys, Inc. v. Buddy L. Corp., 703 F.2d 970, 973 (6th Cir. 1983)).
8. *Id.*
9. *Id.* at *7.
10. *Id.* at *14.

The dissenting opinion differed from the majority by primarily asserting that Lanard's toys are plainly useful articles and exempt from copyright according to 17 U.S.C. § 101. The dissent distinguished this case from *Gay Toys*, finding Lanard toys are more than portrayals. They actually propel objects into the air, called "portrayal" through flight, and are outside the copyright statute's definition of a "sculptural work."[11]

Furniture Decorations Protected by Copyright as Sculptural Works

In *Universal Furniture International, Inc. v. Collezione Europa USA, Inc.,*[12] the Fourth Circuit upheld the district court's finding of copyright ownership, copyright infringement in furniture design elements, and a damages award based on the infringer's gross revenues from selling the infringing furniture.

In 1994, Universal Furniture Industries (UFI) entered into a design agreement with the Hekler design firm. In 1998, UFI merged and became Universal Furniture Limited (UFL). In 2001, UFL entered into an asset purchase agreement with Universal, a business that designs, imports, and distributes furniture that is manufactured outside the United States. Universal thus acquired all of UFL's intellectual property rights, including the designs created under the 1994 service agreement with the Hekler design firm, which created the copyrighted designs at issue in 2001 and 2002.

As part of its defense, Collezione argued that Universal failed to establish valid copyright ownership in the furniture designs because it failed to prove a proper chain of title, as a result of the various intellectual property transfers. In evaluating this argument, the appellate court relied upon the prima facie effect accorded by a certificate of registration from the Copyright Office, which shifted the burden onto the defendant to prove that the claimed copyrights were not owned by the plaintiff.

Given that the terms of the 1994 service agreement were not time-limited, the appellate court found that the agreement could cover the 2001 and 2002 designs at issue, and that Universal's documentation linked Universal to the Hekler agreement. Thus, the designs at issue were made pursuant to the agreement in 2001 and 2002. Interestingly, the court commented that, although the Copyright Act generally requires a writing to transfer copyright ownership, the Act makes exceptions for transfers that occur "by operation of law."[13] Relying on opinions from other circuits that mergers transfer copyrights "by operation of law" and obviate the writing requirement,[14] the court found no error in the district court's conclusion that Universal established its ownership in the copyrights at issue.

The court next addressed whether the designs of Universal's furniture collections were sufficiently original to qualify for copyright protection. The court noted that submission of a valid certificate of copyright registration creates a presumption of originality for five years from the date of the registration, but that the presumption is easy to rebut. Nevertheless, the court concluded that the designs at issue satisfied the low threshold for originality. Although the ornamental designs originated in the public domain, the

---

11. *Id.* at *17.
12. 618 F.3d 417 (4th Cir. 2010).
13. *See* 17 U.S.C. § 204(a).
14. *See* Taylor Corp. v. Four Seasons Greetings, LLC, 403 F.3d 958, 963 (8th Cir. 2005); Lone Ranger Television, Inc. v. Program Radio Corp., 740 F.2d 718, 721 (9th Cir. 1984).

court determined that the author selected, coordinated, and arranged the individual elements in a unique way.

The court found the question of conceptual separability more vexing, however, because a sculptural work that is a useful article is protected by copyright only to the extent that the sculptural features can be identified separately from, and are capable of existing independently of, the utilitarian aspects of the article. In holding that the decorative design elements that are separable from the furniture itself are capable of copyright protection, the court distinguished the *Superior Form Builders*[15] case, which held that the industrial design of furniture cannot be separated from its utilitarian functions and, thus, cannot be the subject of a copyright.

Here, Universal's furniture collections were highly ornate and adorned with three-dimensional shells, acanthus leaves, columns, finials, rosettes, and other carvings. Universal presented testimony that the collections were "an ornamentation explosion" and "essentially vehicles for expressing ornament." Universal's design process reflected artistic judgment independent of functional influences. The designer's objective was not to improve the furniture's utility, but instead to give the furniture "a pretty face." Moreover, the shape of the furniture was developed prior to adding the ornamentation and, for many of the decorative elements on the furniture, such as carved shells and leaves, the purpose was entirely aesthetic. The ornamentation had little or nothing to do with the furniture's function. Universal therefore established that the decorative designs were superfluous, nonfunctional adornments for which the shape of the furniture served as a vehicle, rather than "industrial designs" of furniture.

Further supporting Universal's assertion of valid copyrights in the decorative designs, the House Committee that drafted the 1976 Copyright Act, while indicating in the House Report that only elements that could be identified separately from the useful article were copyrightable, also provided that the carving on the back of a chair could qualify for copyright protection. Here, the designs were wholly unnecessary to the furniture's utilitarian function and were capable of existing independently from the utilitarian aspects of the furniture. Therefore, the court held that the compilation of design elements on Universal's furniture was entitled to copyright protection.

After determining that Universal was the owner of valid copyrights in the designs at issue, the court affirmed the district court's finding of copyright infringement based upon substantial similarity between the protected elements of Universal's furniture collection and Collezione's collection.

The court also upheld the district court's damages award, which was equal to Collezione's gross revenues from sales of the infringing furniture collections, because Collezione did not meet its burden of proving deductible expenses as required by the Copyright Act. Collezione presented methods of calculating costs that the court found to be confusing, unreliable, and internally inconsistent and, furthermore, relied on testimony from its chief financial officer that was equivocal and unpersuasive.

---

15. *See* Superior Form Builders v. Dan Chase Taxidermy Supply Co., 74 F.3d 488 (4th Cir. 1996).

Derivative Works

Derivative Works Are Not Subject to a Higher Standard of Originality; Derivative-Work Authors Can Copyright Their Works without Permission from Owners of Underlying Works

In *Schrock v. Learning Curve International, Inc.,*[16] the Seventh Circuit reversed the judgment of the U.S. District Court for the Northern District of Illinois. The district court granted summary judgment for Defendants HIT Entertainment (HIT), the owner of the copyright to the popular "Thomas & Friends" train characters, and Learning Curve, HIT's licensee, which made toy figures of the characters.

Learning Curve had retained Schrock, a professional photographer, to take pictures of the toys for promotional materials. Learning Curve eventually stopped giving Schrock work, but continued to use some of his photos in its printed advertising, on packaging, and on the Internet. Schrock then registered his photos for copyright protection and sued Learning Curve and HIT for infringement. Learning Curve and HIT moved for summary judgment. The district court found that the photos were "derivative works" and held that Schrock had no copyright in the photos because Schrock needed permission not only to make the photographs, but also to copyright them.

The Seventh Circuit reversed. Although acknowledging deep disagreement among courts and commentators over whether photographs of a copyrighted work are derivative works, the Seventh Circuit found that the classification of the photos as derivative works does not affect the applicable legal standard for determining copyrightability, although it does determine the scope of copyright protection. Accordingly, the court assumed, without deciding, that the photos were derivative works within the meaning of the Copyright Act.

The Seventh Circuit noted that the Copyright Act specifically grants the author of a derivative work copyright protection in the incremental original expression the author contributes so long as the derivative work does not infringe the underlying work.[17] However, the copyright in the derivative work "extends only to the material contributed by the author of such work, as distinguished from the preexisting material employed in the work."[18] The Seventh Circuit addressed two related issues raised by the appeal: (1) the standard of originality required of a derivative work for copyright protection; and (2) whether the author of a derivative work must also have permission not only to make the derivative work but also to copyright it.

The Seventh Circuit found that, for a work to be copyrightable, the work—whether or not it is derivative—must be original—that is, it must be independently created by the author and possess at least some minimal degree of creativity, although a slight amount will suffice. Moreover, the Seventh Circuit noted that federal courts have applied a generous standard of originality in evaluating photographic works for copyright protection. They have found original expression in the staging and creation of the scene depicted in the photograph and in the rendition of the subject matter—that is, the effect created by the combination of perspective, angle, lighting, shading, focus, lens, and

---

16. 586 F.3d 513 (7th Cir. 2009).
17. 17 U.S.C. § 101; *see* § 103(a) and (b).
18. 17 U.S.C. § 103(b).

other such factors, which most photographs contain to some degree unless they are slavish copies of the underlying work. The Seventh Circuit found that Schrock's photographs did not fall into the narrow category of photographs that can be classified as slavish copies, which lack any independently created expression, based on Schrock's testimony of how he used various camera and lighting techniques. Thus, Schrock's photographs satisfied the minimal degree of creativity necessary to meet the requirement of originality.

In addition to finding that the photographs satisfied the generally accepted test for originality, the Seventh Circuit rejected two reasons why it should nonetheless conclude that Schrock's photographs were not original. First, the Seventh Circuit found that, even if the photographs were intended solely for a commercial function, the purpose of the photographs was irrelevant.

Additionally, the Seventh Circuit held that derivative works are not subject to a higher standard of originality than other works of authorship, noting that nothing in the Copyright Act suggests that derivative works are subject to a more exacting originality requirement. In explaining this holding, the Seventh Circuit clarified one of its earlier decisions upon which the district court had relied. In *Gracen v. Bradford Exchange*, the Seventh Circuit held that Gracen could not maintain her suit because her painting, a derivative work, was not "substantially different from the underlying work to be copyrightable."[19] In *Schrock*, the Seventh Circuit pointed out, however, that this statement should not be read to require a heightened originality requirement. The case upon which *Gracen* relied and a more recent Seventh Circuit case[20] explained the general principles that: "(1) the originality requirement for derivative works is not more demanding than the originality requirement for other works; and (2) the key inquiry is whether there is sufficient nontrivial expressive variation in the derivative work to make it distinguishable from the underlying work in some meaningful way."[21] The Seventh Circuit found that Schrock's photos of the "Thomas & Friends" toys possessed sufficient incremental original expression—that is, minimal sufficient variation in angle, perspective, lighting, and dimension—to be distinguishable from the underlying works and to qualify for the limited derivative-work copyright provided by section 103(b), which, although narrow, at least protects against the kind of outright copying that occurred.

Elaborating on the second issue, the Seventh Circuit held that, even if the photographs were derivative works, it does not follow that Schrock needed authorization from Learning Curve to copyright the photos. To be copyrightable, a derivative work must not infringe the underlying work. Because the owner of the copyright in the underlying work has the exclusive right to "prepare derivative works based upon the copyrighted work,"[22] the author of a derivative work must have permission to make that work from the owner of the copyright in the underlying work. The Seventh Circuit held that, so long as Schrock was authorized to make the photographs, which he was, he owned the copyright in the photos to the extent of their incremental original expression.

Once again, the Seventh Circuit clarified *Gracen*, upon which the district court relied when it held that Schrock needed permission not only to make the photographs but also to

---

19. 698 F.2d 300, 305 (7th Cir. 1983).
20. Bucklew v. Hawkins, Ash, Baptie & Co., 329 F.3d 923, 929 (7th Cir. 2003).
21. *Schrock*, 586 F.3d at 521.
22. 17 U.S.C. § 106(2).

copyright them. The Seventh Circuit found the suggestion in *Gracen* that the author of a derivative work must also have permission to copyright it was dicta. More importantly, the dicta was incorrect, as there is nothing in the Copyright Act that requires the author of a derivative work to obtain permission to copyright such work from the owner of the copyright in the underlying work. Rather, the Copyright Act provides that copyright in a derivative work, like any other work, arises by operation of law when the author's original expression is fixed in a tangible medium.[23] The Seventh Circuit also noted that a more recent Seventh Circuit case[24] had discussed this rule of law, along with the fact that the parties may alter this rule by agreement.

The Seventh Circuit explained that, because the owner of a copyrighted work has the exclusive right to control derivative works, the owner may limit the derivative work author's rights by contract, license, or agreement. Thus, if an agreement between the parties bars the licensee from obtaining copyright protection even in a licensed derivative work, that contractual provision would govern. The Seventh Circuit found that the evidence submitted with the summary judgment motion did not establish as a matter of law that Learning Curve and Schrock altered Schrock's rights by contract because the record did not include any written agreements, and the agreement between Learning Curve and Schrock appeared to consist of a series of oral agreements followed by invoices.

Accordingly, the Seventh Circuit reversed the judgment of the district court and remanded for further proceedings consistent with the opinion.

---

23. 17 U.S.C. § 102(a).
24. Liu v. Price Waterhouse LLP, 302 F.3d 749, 755 (7th Cir. 2002).

CHAPTER 16

COPYRIGHT EXCLUSIVE RIGHTS AND LIMITATIONS

Courts continue to wrestle with and further define the exclusive rights granted to copyright owners under the Copyright Act in the digital age, as well as limitations to those rights. Several courts, as well as the Library of Congress, sought to clarify both the rights established under the DMCA and the protections it provides ISPs. Other cases examined more traditional issues, such as proof of ownership, fair use, and public performance rights.

On July 26, 2010, the Library of Congress promulgated rules indicating that the DMCA prohibition against circumventing technical measures designed to prevent the un-authorized use of copyright-protected material shall not apply to six noninfringing uses, including cell phone jail breaking.

However, in *TracFone Wireless, Inc. v. Anadisk LLC,* the U.S. District Court for the Southern District of Florida awarded the DMCA's maximum statutory award of $12 million against a defaulting cell phone reflasher that circumvented access protection software on nearly 5,000 phones. Similarly, the U.S. District Court for the Northern District of California, in *Apple Inc. v. Psystar Corp.,* granted the plaintiff's motion for summary judgment under the DMCA's anticircumvention rules, finding that the defendant had circumvented the plaintiff's technical measures designed to protect its copyrighted material and trafficked in devices designed for circumvention.

Courts also clarified the protections afforded ISPs under the safe harbor provisions of the DMCA. In *Viacom International, Inc. v. YouTube, Inc.,* the U.S. District Court for the Southern District of New York discussed the limitations on such rights by ruling that the safe harbor protections afforded ISPs were not voided by a general knowledge that there are common and widespread infringements. According to the court, absent a showing of actual or constructive knowledge of specific and identifiable infringements, the safe harbor rules will protect an ISP that is otherwise compliant with the statute.

The U.S. District Court for the Central District of California, in *UMG Recordings Inc. v. Veoh Networks, Inc.,* held that a video-sharing Web site qualified as an ISP and was entitled to the safe harbor protections outlined in the DMCA. For this reason, an infringement action brought by an organization with rights to millions of sound recordings and compositions could not succeed because the Web site had complied with the take-down provisions of the DMCA.

In a copyright royalty proceeding, *In re Application of Cellco,* the U.S. District Court for the Southern District of New York limited the copyright holder's right to a license fee for the public performance of its copyrighted composition. The court held that the transmission of a ringtone to a customer's cellular phone was not a public performance; therefore, ASCAP was not entitled to a blanket license for such downloads. The court further rejected ASCAP's claims of secondary liability based on the end-users' use of the ringtones in public places, again holding that the ringing of a cell phone does not constitute a public performance.

On the other hand, despite being similarly positioned as an end-user who downloads music for personal, noncommercial use, the defendant's fair-use defense in *Sony BMG Music Entertainment v. Tenenbaum* was unsuccessful in the context of peer-to-peer downloading and the resulting infringement upon the copyright holder's right to reproduce its work. Although the U.S. District Court for the District of Massachusetts was sympathetic, even urging Congress to update the Copyright Act in light of these difficult cases, the court found the defendant's use to be infringing.

In an action brought under the Visual Artists Rights Act (VARA), the First Circuit held that VARA applies not only to finished works of art, but also to unfinished works. In *Massachusetts Museum of Contemporary Art Foundation v. Büchel,* the court held that an artist had the right, under VARA, to prevent a museum from displaying his unfinished work because, inter alia, there was sufficient evidence for a jury to find that such a display would harm the "honor and reputation" of the artist.

EXCLUSIVE RIGHTS

Public Performance

Publicly Played Ring Tones Do Not Violate the Copyright Act

In re Application of Cellco Partnership d/b/a Verizon Wireless; Related to United States of America v. American Society of Composers, Authors and Publishers[1] held that the transmission of a ringtone to a customer's cellular telephone did not constitute a performance of a musical work "publicly" within the meaning of 17 U.S.C. §§ 101 and 106(4).[2] Moreover, the court concluded that when a ring tones are played on a cellular telephone, users are exempt from copyright liability. It follows that Cellco was not liable, either secondarily or directly. Further still, the public use of ring tones by Cellco's customers satisfies the exemption requirements set forth under 17 U.S.C. § 110(4).

Cellco, doing business as Verizon Wireless (Verizon), sells downloadable digital files consisting of a portion of a musical composition. When these digital audio files are set to play to alert a Verizon customer of an incoming call, they are known as "ring tones." Ring tones cannot be played while being downloaded. They may only be played after they are purchased. The underlying audio file is stored on the telephone where the customer can select it as the alert for incoming calls or choose to play it at any time.[3] Verizon receives no money from the use of the ringtone after the initial sale and download. Verizon does not know if customers have selected the ringtone to activate when a call is received and sends the same signal to the customers' phones regardless of the alert ringtone selected.

---

1.   663 F. Supp. 2d 363 (S.D.N.Y. 2009).
2.   *Id.*
3.   *Id.* at 366 n.3. Pursuant to a previous ruling by the Copyright Royalty Judges, Verizon already pays songwriters and music publishers a royalty of twenty-four cents per each ringtone download for the reproduction and distribution of their musical works.

Verizon filed a motion for summary judgment on the question of whether it was required to pay public performance licensing fees for ring tones downloaded by its customers. Judge Denise Cote ruled that ring tones do not constitute a public performance of a musical work and, therefore, no license was needed. The motion for summary judgment was granted.

ASCAP, which licenses public performance rights for musical works in its catalog, argued that the subject ring tones are public performances, and as such require licensing for two reasons. First, the customer's act of downloading the ringtone constitutes a public performance itself. Second, Verizon is directly and secondarily liable for infringement of the public performance right whenever customers' phones play the downloaded ring tones. The court rejected both arguments.

Public performance is defined in section 106(4)[4] as either "to perform or display it at a place open to the public or at a place where a substantial number of persons outside of a normal circle of family and social acquaintances are gathered" or "to transmit or communicate a performance or display of the work to the public (or group outside family and friends) by means of any device or process whether the members of the public are capable of receiving the performance at the same place or different places at the same time or separate times." There is an exemption if there is no direct or indirect commercial advantage. Citing its recent decision in *Cartoon Network v. CSC,*[5] the court noted that the Transmission Clause speaks of those capable of receiving the performance rather than those capable of receiving the transmission. Thus, because only one subscriber is capable of receiving the download, the transmission is not to the public and not subject to the Transmission Clause.[6] Furthermore, refuting ASCAP's argument that the downloading process is but one link in a chain of transmission, the court ruled that there is no public performance even when ring tones are used to alert users to incoming calls. The court relied again on *Cartoon Network* as well as *United States v. ASCAP*[7] in concluding that songs that are not directly accessible to the public during download do not fall within the scope of section 106(4). The fact that Verizon could change its technology to allow contemporaneous listening during the download process did not alter the court's reasoning.

The court next addressed whether Verizon was liable, either directly or secondarily, for public performance licenses when downloaded ring tones are played. In order to be directly liable for infringement of the public performance right of a copyrighted work, the infringer must have direct control over that performance. In order to be secondarily liable, there must be direct infringement.

ASCAP argued that every time a customer's phone uses a ringtone alert, Verizon is secondarily liable for infringement of the right of public performance. Therefore Verizon owes appropriate license fees because consumers are liable for infringement whenever their cell phone plays the downloaded ringtone. The court denied this notion, noting that the Copyright Act exempts performances of musical works that occur within "the normal circle of family and its social acquaintances" or performances undertaken "without any purpose of direct or indirect commercial advantage."[8] Judge Cote found that the ring tones

---

4. Commonly referred to as the Transmission Clause.
5. 536 F.3d 121, 127 (2d Cir. 2008).
6. *In re Cellco,* 663 F. Supp. 2d at 370.
7. 485 F. Supp. 2d 438 (S.D.N.Y. 2007).
8. *Id.* at 374.

fit both these exemptions: they are normally played in the company of family and friends and, because the consumer gets no fees when the ring tones play, the ring tones do not carry any commercial benefit that could make the consumer liable for infringement. Given that the consumer cannot be liable, Verizon cannot be secondarily liable.

ASCAP also argued that Verizon has direct control of all the elements that trigger the performance (i.e., they make the ringtone commercially available, allow and encourage customers to download the tones, provide the cellular network that allows calls to be received and trigger the phone to ring by alerting the device that an incoming call was being transmitted) and is therefore directly liable for infringement. The court, however, noted a significant break in this chain as Verizon does not send the ring tone to the phone to indicate an incoming call, but rather sends a generic signal to the device. It is the customer who is in charge of setting the phone alert as he or she desires.

ASCAP further contended that subject works are performed publicly as defined by section 101 of the Copyright Act relying upon *Arista Records v. Usenet.com*[9] as precedent. In *Arista*, the court found a Web site that ran online bulletin boards, on which users posted downloadable sound recordings, guilty of infringement because the site "actively engaged" in the "exchange of content between users who upload infringing content and users who download such content."[10] However, Judge Cote differentiated the current case by pointing out that Usenet.com paid no royalties, whereas Verizon paid mechanical license fees to ASCAP members. Furthermore, although Verizon does sell the ring tones, it does not participate in how customers use the tones. Hence, its active participation is much more attenuated than that of Usenet.com. Judge Cote further wrote that although the marketing and transmission of ring tones implicates some rights protected under the Copyright Act, they do not implicate the public performance right.

Finally, ASCAP argued that services such as Napster, Aimster and Grokster relied on automated systems that "require no human intervention by the party enjoying the revenue."[11] Those services were nonetheless deemed to be secondarily liable for their customers' infringement. Here, the court again asserted that, because there is no direct liability, Verizon cannot be secondarily liable. After all, Verizon is not gaining revenue from the playing of the ring tones. The fact that Verizon uses an automated service to alert subscribers to incoming calls demonstrates that there is no sufficient nexus, between Verizon and the publicly ringing telephone, which justifies the need for a section 106(4) license. The court also noted that, although Verizon could avoid this controversy by simply not including ASCAP's catalogue in its ringtone offerings, there has been no evidence of infringement and, therefore, they do not need to take this extreme measure.

Rights to Attribution and Integrity

Visual Artists Rights Act Applies to Unfinished Works of Art

In ***Massachusetts Museum of Contemporary Art Foundation, Inc. v. Büchel***,[12] the First Circuit reversed in part the grant of summary judgment for the Massachusetts Mu-

---

9.   663 F. Supp. 2d 124 (S.D.N.Y. 2009).

10. *Id.* at 149.

11. In re *Cellco*, 663 F. Supp. 2d at 378.

12. 593 F.3d 38 (1st Cir. 2010).

seum of Contemporary Art (Mass MoCA) by the U.S. District Court for the District of Massachusetts and remanded the case for further proceedings. Mass MoCA commissioned Christoph Büchel to create an art installation, though the project was never completed. Mass MoCA sought a declaration that it was entitled to exhibit the partial installation, and Büchel counterclaimed under the Visual Artists Rights Act (VARA)[13] and the Copyright Act, seeking an injunction and damages. On cross-motions for summary judgment, the district court assumed that VARA applied to unfinished works of art, granted Mass MoCA's motion for summary judgment on its declaratory relief claim, and denied Büchel's five counterclaims. The First Circuit concluded that VARA applied to unfinished works and that Büchel asserted viable claims under VARA and the Copyright Act.

Swiss visual artist Büchel conceived an exhibit, entitled "Training Ground for Democracy" (Training Ground), which was essentially a village roughly the size of a football field, through which visitors would walk. Büchel prepared a basic schematic model of the project, and Mass MoCA agreed to acquire, at Büchel's direction but at MoCA's expense, the materials. The parties, however, never formalized the details of their relationship, their understanding as to the intellectual property rights at issue, or the project's financial scope and precise specifications by executing a written agreement, though they did apparently agree that once the installation was completed and after public exhibition, Mass MoCA would not contest Büchel's sole title to any copyright in the completed work. Despite spiraling costs and communications that became so strained that Büchel eventually refused to work, Mass MoCA continued putting together the installation. The parties disagreed as to whether in Büchel's absence Mass MoCA employees, who continued working, were executing Büchel's instructions or independent artistic judgment in direct contravention of Büchel's express wishes. The parties' key conflict involved Büchel's dissatisfaction with the way Mass MoCA implemented his instructions and procured materials, including major components, such as a movie theater, house, bar, mobile home, sea containers, bomb carousel, and aircraft fuselage, some but not all of which became part of the work.

One day after filing suit, Mass MoCA announced publicly that it had filed suit and was cancelling Training Ground; that Mass MoCA was opening a new exhibit, "Made at Mass MoCA," to explore issues raised during complex collaborative art projects; and that visitors to the new exhibit would walk past Training Ground materials, which Mass MoCA had taken steps to cover. The parties disagreed on whether the tarpaulins used to restrict view of the unfinished work, however, concealed Training Ground or invited visitors to peek behind the coverings and also whether Mass MoCA promoted and showed the unfinished work to numerous visitors, some of whom reacted unfavorably, without Büchel's consent. Several days after the district court ruled, Mass MoCA dismantled the Training Ground materials.

The First Circuit addressed two issues on appeal: (1) whether VARA applies to unfinished works of art, and, if so, whether summary judgment was improperly granted to Mass MoCA on Büchel's VARA claims; and (2) whether summary judgment was improperly granted to Mass MoCA on Büchel's copyright claims. VARA was a 1990 amendment to the Copyright Act to protect the "moral rights" of certain visual artists in the works they create, including: (1) the right of attribution, which protects the author's right to be identified as the author of his or her work and protects against the use of the author's name

---

13. 17 U.S.C. § 106A.

in connection with works created by others; and (2) the right of integrity, which allows the author to prevent deforming or mutilating changes to the author's work.

The First Circuit held that VARA protects the moral rights of artists who have created works of art within the meaning of the Copyright Act, even if such works are unfinished. The First Circuit found that, although VARA does not state when a project becomes a visual work of art, VARA is part of the Copyright Act, which states that a work is "created" when it "is fixed in a copy . . . for the first time" and that "where a work is prepared over a period of time, the portion of it that has been fixed at any particular time constitutes the work as of that time."[14] Moreover, a work becomes "fixed" when it has been formed "by or under the authority of the author," in a way that is "sufficiently permanent or stable to permit it to be perceived, reproduced, or otherwise communicated for a period of more than transitory duration."[15] The First Circuit found that, based upon the clear language of the statute, its history, and purpose, VARA's protections extend to unfinished works. Moral rights protect the artist's "personality and creative energy" in his or her work, and the "convergence between artist and artwork does not await the final brush stroke or the placement of the last element in a complex installation."[16]

The First Circuit held that Büchel's right of attribution claim was moot, as Training Ground no longer existed since Mass MoCA had dismantled it, and VARA does not provide for damages but only injunctive relief to protect the right to assert or disclaim authorship of a work. The First Circuit based this finding on the difference between the statutory language setting forth the rights of attribution and integrity. The First Circuit noted that the right of integrity confers the right to protect the work against intentional alterations that would be prejudicial to honor or reputation and the right to protect a work of "recognized stature" from destruction, which are framed as rights "to prevent."[17] The First Circuit further noted that both integrity rights also contain a clause, which states that the occurrence of such conduct constitutes, at least in certain circumstances, a "violation" of the right to prevent the conduct from happening.[18] These "violation" clauses, which the First Circuit concluded permit a damages remedy, are omitted from the sections codifying the right of attribution. Moreover, the First Circuit noted that the damages remedy for the destruction of a work of recognized stature is narrower than the right to prevent destruction of such works. Specifically, although an artist may seek an injunction to "prevent any destruction of a work of recognized stature," only an "intentional or grossly negligent destruction of that work is a violation" entitling the artist to damages.[19]

The First Circuit held that the right of integrity under VARA protects artists from distortions, mutilations, or modifications of their works that are prejudicial and found that prejudice must be shown for both injunctive relief and damages. The First Circuit concluded that summary judgment was improperly granted to Mass MoCA on the first of Büchel's integrity claims because based upon the evidence a jury issue existed at least as to whether Mass MoCA proceeded with the installation during Büchel's absence knowing that the construction would frustrate and likely contradict his artistic vision, resulting in

---

14. 17 U.S.C. § 101.
15. *Id.*
16. *Mass. MoCA*, 593 F.3d at 51.
17. 17 U.S.C. § 106A(a).
18. *Id.*
19. *Id.*

an intentional distortion or other modification of Training Ground. Moreover, a jury could conclude that Mass MoCA's alterations had a detrimental impact on Büchel's honor or reputation, as the record showed that some viewers of the unfinished installation reacted unfavorably to the work in its allegedly modified and distorted form.

The First Circuit agreed with the district court, however, with respect to Büchel's two other integrity claims. The First Circuit found that the mere covering of the installation could not reasonably be deemed an intentional act of distortion or modification. In addition, merely exhibiting the work of art in its unfinished state, without the artist's consent, did not constitute distortion, as a separate moral right of disclosure or divulgation protects an author's authority to prevent third parties from disclosing the artist's work to the public without the artist's consent, and this right is outside the scope of VARA.

The First Circuit, reversing the district court, held that the record revealed a genuine issue of material fact regarding whether Mass MoCA violated Büchel's exclusive right to display his work publicly, as there was significant evidence suggesting that the work was repeatedly and intentionally shown to numerous people. In addition, although Mass MoCA argued that it owned the physical copy of Training Ground and was permitted to display it under section 109(c),[20] there were disputed issues of fact regarding whether Mass MoCA's copy was lawfully made as required to obtain the benefit of section 109(c) because it may have been created in violation of Büchel's rights under VARA. However, the First Circuit held that Büchel failed to adequately develop his claim that Mass MoCA violated his exclusive right to prepare derivative works based upon Training Ground; therefore, the First Circuit deemed that claim to be waived.

LIMITATIONS ON COPYRIGHT

Fair Use

Personal, Noncommercial File Sharing of Copyrighted Music Is Not a Fair Use

In *Sony BMG Music Entertainment v. Tenenbaum,*[21] the court granted summary judgment rejecting Tenenbaum's argument that his file sharing of copyrighted songs was a fair use that precluded his liability for copyright infringement. The court's decision explains why Tenenbaum's personal, noncommercial use could not qualify as a fair use and suggests other circumstances in which a fair-use defense might be more successful.

In 2007, Joel Tenenbaum was sued by four record companies for downloading and distributing thirty of their copyrighted works via peer-to-peer, file-sharing software. Tenenbaum's music file sharing activities spanned four years, during which he made more

---

20. 17 U.S.C. § 109(c).

21. 672 F. Supp. 2d 217 (D. Mass. 2009). The jury verdict in the case is reported at 2009 WL 2390631 (D. Mass. July 31, 2009), and the entry of judgment including partial injunctive relief is reported at 2009 WL 4723397 (D. Mass. Dec. 7, 2009). As of February 10, 2010, a motion for new trial including a challenge to the constitutionality of the statutory damages provision of the Copyright Act was pending before the court.

than 800 songs available to other users. Tenenbaum sought to present an extremely broad fair-use defense to the jury at his copyright infringement trial, arguing that all file sharing for private enjoyment should be considered fair use. The plaintiff record companies moved for partial summary judgment on the fair-use defense. The court examined, but did not decide, the issue of whether fair use was an equitable issue for determination by the court, instead simply presuming that the question could go to the jury if it survived the summary judgment analysis. The court also noted that fair use had been decided at the summary judgment stage in hundreds of cases.

At the outset, the court noted that the imbalance of resources between the parties and the "upheaval of norms of behavior brought on by the internet" were serious concerns and the court therefore allowed Tenenbaum to present his fair-use defense, despite its presentation on the eve of trial.[22] The court also noted that it was prepared to consider novel and expansive fair-use arguments related to individual facts and rapid technological change. For example, the court considered arguments that file sharing was used for purposes of sampling music prior to purchase, space-shifting, storage purposes, or acquiring music in digital form online before digital music was offered legally in that format, but Tenenbaum presented no such or similar factual arguments. Instead, Tenenbaum argued that because he did not make money from his file sharing activities and his use was for private enjoyment and noncommercial, his use was presumptively fair. The court rejected that argument as inconsistent with precedent requiring the defendant asserting fair use to establish a factual basis for the defense.

The court then proceeded to analyze Tenenbaum's arguments under the traditional, statutory fair-use balancing factors, set out in 17 U.S.C. § 107. As to the purpose and character of Tenenbaum's use, the court determined that Tenenbaum's use fell somewhere in the middle of the spectrum, being neither a large-scale, profit-making enterprise, nor scholarly or educational in nature. More importantly, the court recognized that Tenenbaum's use had no transformative purpose and no public benefit. Therefore, this factor weighed against Tenenbaum.

As to the nature of the copyrighted work, music generally commands strong copyright protection. Therefore, this factor weighed against Tenenbaum.

As to the amount and substantiality of the portion used, Tenenbaum downloaded entire songs but argued that because he did not download entire albums, this factor should weigh in his favor. The court rejected this argument entirely, noting that Tenenbaum's argument would be compelling only if Tenenbaum had sampled individual songs in order to decide whether to purchase a full album. Instead, Tenenbaum obtained substitutes for complete works distributed exactly in the single-song format he downloaded. Because Tenenbaum downloaded entire songs for repeated listening, the court found this factor weighed against Tenenbaum.

The fourth factor concerns the impact of the defendant's use on the potential market for or value of the work. Although Tenenbaum's activity itself was noncommercial, the court noted that Tenenbaum's use essentially would eliminate any market for the works, as why would anyone pay for works that could be obtained for free? Therefore this factor also weighed against Tenenbaum.

---

22. 672 F. Supp. at 219.

Finally, the court considered a variety of nonstatutory factors that Tenenbaum somewhat creatively raised in defense of his fair-use argument. Tenenbaum argued that plaintiffs: (1) assumed the risk of copyright infringement; (2) acquiesced in the infringement; (3) failed to take measures to protect the works from authorized copying because they released the works in an environment in which unauthorized file sharing was rampant; (4) encouraged illegal file sharing by marketing the works; and (5) failed to provide authorized digital alternatives. Tenenbaum also argued that his downloading and file sharing should be considered a fair use because preventing illegal file sharing is difficult and expensive. Additionally, enforcing the copyright statute against him would be inequitable. The court evaluated but rejected each of those arguments as essentially irrelevant to the question of fair use, and, in some cases, unsupported by any facts.[23]

The court concluded in part by urging Congress to amend the Copyright Act to "reflect the realities of file sharing," noting that "[t]here is something wrong with a law that routinely threatens teenagers and students with astronomical penalties for an activity whose implications they may not have fully understood."[24] The court further noted, looking beyond the facts presented in this case, a defendant that shared files online before digital music was distributed commercially via the Internet, or that shared only a few files, with a few people, would present a strong case for fair use, as "[o]ne of equities in copyright is surely the disequilibrium produced by the advent of a novel, widely accessible technology."[25] Tenenbaum's widespread, unlimited file sharing presented no such case; therefore, summary judgment for the plaintiff recording companies on his affirmative fair-use defense was granted by the court.

Statutory Exemptions

Court Adopts Effectiveness Standard for Access Controls (DRM) under the DMCA

In *Apple Inc. v. Psystar Corp.*,[26] the Northern District of California granted Apple's motion for summary judgment finding that Psystar circumvented Apple's Digital Rights Management (DMR) technology and trafficked in devices designed for circumvention in violation of the DMCA.

Apple sells both hardware and software. Apple's software contains DMR technology to ensure that it is only ever used on Apple hardware. Section 1201(a) of the DMCA protects technology that "effectively controls access to a work."[27] Circumvention of DRM technology is, therefore, a violation of the DMCA. Nevertheless there are exemptions for certain users to bypass DRM technology for purposes of education, research or other fair use. A group called the OSx86 Project[28] provides an open forum for such persons seeking to bypass Apple's DRM technology. The Osx86 Project specifically forbids use of the provided tools for anything other than educational purposes.

---

23. *Id.* at 232–37.
24. *Id.* at 237.
25. *Id.* at 238.
26. 673 F. Supp. 2d 931 (N.D. Cal. 2009).
27. 17 U.S.C. § 1201(d) (2006).
28. Information about the Osx86 Project is available at http://www.osx86project.org.

In April of 2008, using tools and information clearly acquired from the OSx86 Project, Psystar began to sell machines running Apple software on non-Apple, Intel x86 hardware. These computers were the first commercially distributed "Hackintosh" computers. Psystar believed that purchasers of software had the right to use it on the hardware of their choice. Apple disagreed. In July 2008, Apple filed suit against Psystar alleging a variety of copyright and trademark violations, along with violations of Apple's End User License Agreements (EULAs) attached to the purchase of Apple software.

Psystar argued that the widespread availability of tools and information for bypassing Apple's DRM technology rendered it ineffective at controlling access to the underlying work. Because the language of the DMCA only refers to "effective controls," Psystar argued that its circumvention should not constitute a violation. The court rejected this interpretation of the DMCA. The court held that the widespread availability of circumvention tools does not render DRM technology ineffective for purposes of the DMCA. Rather, so long as the DRM technology worked out-of-the-box, and could not be circumvented absent outside information or tools, the court would deem it effective.

Accordingly, in November 2009, the court granted summary judgment in favor of Apple's claim that Psystar violated the DMCA by circumventing Apple's protection barrier and trafficking devices designed for circumvention. The court also, for reasons not discussed in this article, granted Apple's motion for summary judgment on its copyright infringement and breach of contract claims. Apple was awarded $2.7 million in damages and fees. The court also barred Psystar from further distributions of circumvention technology. Collections, along with Apple's claims relating to trademark and unfair completion, were deferred pending Psystar's appeal of the underlying copyright judgments.

DMCA SAFE HARBORS

Hosting of User Content

YouTube Sails into DMCA Safe Harbor

In *Viacom International Inc. v. YouTube, Inc.,*[29] the U.S. District Court for the Southern District of New York granted a motion for summary judgment for the defendants, on the grounds that they are entitled to the DMCA, 17 U.S.C. § 512(c), safe harbor protection against the plaintiffs' direct and secondary infringement claims.

YouTube operates a Web site onto which users may upload videos. The uploaded videos are copied and formatted by YouTube's computer systems, and then made available for viewing on the YouTube Web site. As a "provider of online services or network access, or the operator of facilities therefor," defined by section 512(k)(1)(B), YouTube is a service provider for the purposes of section 512(c).

The replication, transmittal, and display of videos on the YouTube Web site fall under the protection that section 512(c)(1) gives to "infringement of copyright by reason of the storage at the direction of a user of material" on a service provider's system or network.

Under the DMCA, if a service provider knows (from notice from the copyright owner or from a "red flag") of specific instances of infringement, the service provider must

---

29. 718 F. Supp. 2d 514 (S.D.N.Y. 2010).

promptly remove the infringing material. If not, the burden is on the copyright owner to identify the infringement. The service provider has no duty to monitor or search its service for infringement even though it may have general knowledge that infringement is "ubiquitous."

Here, the YouTube defendants designated an agent to receive notification of claimed infringements. When they received specific notice that a particular item infringed a copyright, they swiftly removed it.

YouTube did not take down other video clips that infringed the same works. Although works may be described representatively, the takedown notice must provide information reasonably sufficient to permit the service provider to locate them.[30] A notice that provided a copy or description of the allegedly infringing material with the uniform resource locator (URL, i.e., Web site address) containing the infringing material would be sufficient. Because the notices here did not give the location of the other video clips that infringed the same works, they were insufficient. YouTube had no obligation to search for them.

Because YouTube removed the identified material when it was given the proper notices, it was protected from liability for all monetary relief for direct, vicarious, and contributory infringement.

Video-Sharing Web Site Protected by Safe Harbor Provision of DMCA

In *UMG Recordings, Inc. v. Veoh Networks Inc.,*[31] the U.S. District Court for the Central District of California granted Veoh's motion for summary judgment that it qualified for protection from copyright infringement liability under the safe harbor provision of the DCMA.

UMG controls the copyrights to a vast library of sound recordings and musical compositions and Veoh operates a Web site that allows users to share videos with others. Alleging that Veoh permits users to upload allegedly infringing videos, UMG sued Veoh for direct, contributory, and vicarious copyright infringement, and for inducement of copyright infringement. The court evaluated the extent to which the DMCA obligates Internet-based services, which rely on content contributed by users, to police their systems to prevent copyright infringement.

The court first analyzed whether Veoh had knowledge of infringing material and whether Veoh expeditiously removed infringing material when it acquired knowledge of such material as required by section 512(c)(1)(A) of the DMCA. The court found that merely hosting user-contributed material capable of copyright protection, such as videos with music, was not enough to impute actual knowledge to a service provider because much of the content on the Internet is eligible for copyright protection. Further, the DMCA's notice-and-takedown provisions would be superfluous because any service provider that hosted copyrighted material would be disqualified from the safe harbor provision regardless of whether the copyright holder gave notice or whether the service provider otherwise acquired actual or constructive knowledge of specific infringements. Additionally, the court found that a list of artists is not information reasonably sufficient to permit

---

30. 17 U.S.C. § 512(c)(3)(A)(iii) (2006).
31. 665 F. Supp. 2d 1099 (C.D. Cal. 2009).

the service provider to locate infringing material because searching for a name would not necessarily result in only infringing material. Furthermore, requiring service providers to perform such searches would conflict with the principle articulated in *Perfect 10, Inc. v. CCBill LLC*[32] that the burden is on the copyright holder to provide notice of allegedly infringing material, and that it takes willful ignorance of readily apparent infringement to find a "red flag."

The court next rejected the argument that Veoh was aware of facts or circumstances from which infringing activity was apparent because its founders, employees, and investors knew that widespread infringement was occurring on the Veoh system. The court found that such general awareness is not enough to raise a "red flag" because it would defeat the DMCA's primary objective of encouraging the expansion of electronic communication, commerce, and education while balancing the respective interests of service providers, content owners, and content consumers. Explaining that the DMCA does not place the burden on ferreting out infringement on the service provider, the court also found that the DMCA does not require service providers to utilize filtering technology to detect infringing material. Finally, the court found that upon gaining actual knowledge of infringing videos, Veoh expeditiously removed them. Thus, the court held that Veoh fulfilled the requirements of section 512(c)(1)(A).

Next, the court reviewed whether Veoh had the "right and ability" to control the allegedly infringing activity of its users because Veoh did utilize filtering systems and had the ability both to remove the allegedly infringing material from its systems and to search its systems for potentially infringing content. Analyzing the statutory language, the court found that the capacity to control and remove material are features that an ISP that stores content must have in order to be eligible for the safe harbor provision. The court explained that "Congress could not have intended for courts to hold that a service provider loses immunity under the safe harbor provision of the DMCA because it engages in acts that are specifically required by the DMCA."[33]

The court also explained that Veoh's "right and ability" to utilize filtering technology cannot be the basis for excluding Veoh from the protection of the safe harbor provision because doing so would effectively require service providers to implement specific filtering technologies and perform regular searches of their content. Further, it would condition the applicability of section 512(c) on a service provider monitoring its service or affirmatively seeking facts indicating infringing activity.

Finally, the court evaluated whether Veoh adopted and reasonably implemented a policy of terminating repeat infringers as required by section 512(f). Citing the standards set forth in *Perfect 10, Inc. v. CCBill LLC*, the court found that Veoh's policy of not automatically terminating users who upload videos that are blocked by its filtering software is nonetheless adequate under the DMCA. The court explained that however beneficial filtering technology may be in helping to identify infringing material, it does not meet the standard of reliability and verifiability required to justify terminating a user's account, which is compiled by collecting information from copyright holders. The court concluded that Veoh had no way of verifying the accuracy of the database, and even if it did, it would be unreasonable to place that burden on Veoh. The court also found that

---

32. 488 F.3d 1102 (9th Cir. 2007).
33. *UMG Recordings*, 665 F. Supp. 2d at 1113.

nothing in the statute, legislative history, or case law established that Veoh's policy of terminating a user only after a second warning was unreasonable or inappropriate. Thus, the court held that Veoh is covered by the DMCA's safe harbor provision and granted Veoh's motion for summary judgment.

ANTICIRCUMVENTION

Cell Phone Jailbreaking Exempt from DMCA Prohibition against Circumvention of Access Controls

On July 20, 2010, the Library of Congress promulgated rules indicating that the prohibition against circumvention of technological measures that control access to copyrighted works shall not apply to persons who engage in noninfringing uses of six classes of copyrighted works.[34] The new exemptions allow wireless phone users to break access controls on their devices in order to switch wireless carriers, video game players to break technical protections to investigate or correct security flaws, certain educators and filmmakers to circumvent copy protection on DVDs for noncommercial purposes, computer owners to bypass security dongles if the dongle no longer works and cannot be replaced; and electronic book readers to break digital locks to access read-aloud software and similar aides. These exemptions took effect on July 27, 2010.

In conducting the rulemaking, the Librarian assessed whether the implementation of access control measures diminished the ability of individuals to use copyrighted works in ways that are not infringing. The Librarian examined several factors that required the Librarian to carefully balance the availability of works for use, the effect of the prohibition on particular uses, and the effect of circumvention on copyrighted works. Pursuant to the authority granted in 17 U.S.C. § 1201(a)(1)(C) and (D), and upon the recommendation of the Register of Copyrights, the Librarian designated six classes of works with respect to which users have been adversely affected in their ability to make noninfringing uses and determined that the prohibition against circumvention of technological measures that control access to copyrighted works set forth in section 1201(a)(1)(A) shall not apply to persons who engage in noninfringing uses of the six classes of copyrighted works.

The first class included motion pictures on DVDs that are protected by the Content Scrambling System (CSS) when circumvention is accomplished solely in order to accomplish the incorporation of short portions of motion pictures into new works for the purpose of criticism or comment, and where the person engaging in circumvention believes and has reasonable grounds for believing that circumvention is necessary to fulfill the purpose of the use in the following instances: (1) educational uses by college and university professors and by college and university film and media studies students; (2) documentary filmmaking; and (3) noncommercial videos. This exemption did not apply to K–12 teachers and students, or for college and university students other than film and media studies students. Additionally, the circumvention of access controls must be accomplished solely in order to enable incorporation of short portions of motion pictures into

---

34. Exemption to Prohibition on Circumvention of Copyright Protection Systems for Access Control Technologies, 75 Fed. Reg. 47,464 (Aug. 6, 2010) (to be codified at 37 C.F.R. § 201).

new works for purposes of criticism of comment. Similarly, in order to meet the requirements of the designated class, a new work must be created, whether that work is a compilation of clips for use in the classroom, or a documentary or video incorporating a clip or clips from a copyrighted motion picture. The final requirement of the class is that the person engaging in the circumvention must reasonably believe that the circumvention is necessary in order to fulfill the purpose of the use. The class was limited to include only motion pictures rather than all audiovisual works because there was no evidence presented that addressed any audiovisual works other than motion pictures.

Secondly, the Librarian exempted uses of computer programs that enable wireless telephone devices to execute software applications, where circumvention is accomplished for the sole purpose of enabling interoperability of such applications with computer programs on the telephone handset (also known as "jailbreaking"). The arguments here focused on Apple's iPhone. The Register found that the Second Circuit's decision in *Krause v. Titleserv, Inc.*,[35] did not provide clear guidance as to how to resolve the issue of jailbreaking. After reviewing arguments regarding fair use, the Register concluded that when a person jailbreaks a smartphone in order to make the operating system on that phone interoperable with an independently created application that has not been approved by the maker of the smartphone or the maker of its operating system, the modifications that are made purely for the purpose of such interoperability favored a finding of fair use. The Register also found that designating a class of works that would permit jailbreaking for purposes of interoperability will not adversely affect the market for or value of the copyrighted works to the copyright owner.

The third class included computer programs that enable used wireless telephone handsets to connect to a wireless telecommunications network, when circumvention is initiated by the owner of the copy of the computer program solely in order to connect to a wireless telecommunications network and access to the network is authorized by the operator of the network. This class was revised from a similar exemption approved in 2006.

Next, the fourth class included video games accessible on personal computers and protected by technological protection measures that control access to lawfully obtained works, when circumvention is accomplished solely for the purpose of good faith testing for, investigating, or correcting security flaws or vulnerabilities, if: (1) the information derived from the security testing is used primarily to promote the security of the owner or operator of a computer, computer system, or computer network; and (2) the information derived from the security testing is used or maintained in a manner that does not facilitate copyright infringement or a violation of applicable law.

The fifth class exempts users of computer programs protected by dongles that prevent access where the dongle no longer functions properly due to malfunction or damage and is obsolete. Finally, the last class included literary works distributed in e-book format when all existing e-book editions of the work contain access controls that prevent the enabling either of the book's read-aloud function or of screen readers that render the text into a specialized format.

---

35. 402 F.3d 119 (2d Cir. 2005).

Circumvention of Technological Measures Controlling Access Results in $12 Million Damages Award

In *TracFone Wireless, Inc. v. Anadisk LLC,*[36] the U.S. District Court for the Southern District of Florida entered a default final judgment and permanent injunction against the defendants for copyright infringement and violation of the anticircumvention provisions of the DMCA.

Plaintiff TracFone provides prepaid wireless telephone service in the United States. It subsidizes its customers' acquisition of its phones by selling them below its cost. It recoups this discount by selling prepaid phone service to customers who buy its phones. It protects its investment by installing proprietary software on the phones that prevent them from being used on other wireless systems. The phones are sold subject to terms and conditions, printed on the retail packaging and in packaging inserts, which restrict and limit the sale and use of the phones.

Defendants are engaged in the business of buying TracFone phones in bulk, unlocking or reflashing them, altering the phones' software and reselling them for a profit. Defendants purchased phones, removed them from their original packages, shipped them overseas and unlocked or "reflashed" the phones, thereby altering TracFone's copyrighted and proprietary software installed on the phones.

TracFone proved its ownership of a valid copyright by attaching to its complaint its U.S. copyright registration certificate. Defendants' modification of TracFone's software without TracFone's consent, created an unauthorized reproduction and derivative work of the TracFone software. The court therefore concluded that TracFone had established its copyright infringement claim. The court did not assess damages for copyright infringement because TracFone elected to collect only statutory damages under the DMCA.

The DMCA prohibits circumvention of a technological measure that effectively controls access to a copyrighted work and the trafficking in instruments and services used in such circumvention.[37] The court found that TracFone software contained access controls, which the defendants circumvented in order to sell the altered phones for a profit. The court therefore concluded that the defendants violated the anticircumvention provisions of the DMCA.

TracFone elected to receive statutory damages under the DMCA, which provides for an award of "not less than $200 or more than $2,500 per act of circumvention, device, product, component, offer, or performance of service, as the court considers just."[38]

The court found that defendants altered or sold as part of a conspiracy to alter, at a minimum, 4,990 TracFone prepaid phones. The sale of these altered phones caused substantial and irreparable harm to TracFone. The defendants' actions were willful. The court concluded that the defendants' actions necessitated an award at the maximum statutory amount. It therefore awarded TracFone judgment against the defendants, jointly and severally, in the amount of $12,375,000 ($2,500 for each of the 4,990 TracFone prepaid phones that the defendants had altered or sold as part of a conspiracy to alter), together with interest at the legal rate.

---

36. 685 F. Supp. 2d 1304 (S.D. Fla. 2010).
37. *See* 17 U.S.C. § 1201(a)(1) and (2).
38. 17 U.S.C. § 1203(c)(3)(A).

The court also entered a permanent injunction prohibiting the defendants from purchasing or selling TracFone wireless handsets, "rekitting," reflashing or unlocking any TracFone handset or accessing, altering, erasing, tampering with, or otherwise disabling TracFone proprietary prepaid cellular software. The court retained jurisdiction to enforce the permanent injunction, and included a provision that future violations would result in an additional damage award of $5,000 per phone or an award of $1,000,000, whichever is greater.

CHAPTER 17

COPYRIGHT OWNERSHIP, DURATION, AND TRANSFER

The relatively few cases involving actions to determine copyright ownership concerned the effect of transfers on copyright ownership, registration of individual photographs as part of a compilation, and rights in a work for hire.

The Sixth Circuit in *Cincom Systems, Inc. v. Novelis Corp.* affirmed the district court's grant of summary judgment for copyright infringement where a series of mergers that were part of an internal corporate restructuring resulted in a prohibited transfer of a software license granted to a former subsidiary. The plaintiff had granted a nonexclusive and nontransferable license that required the plaintiff's express written approval prior to any transfer. Because the corporate restructuring transferred the license without the plaintiff's approval, the court held that the plaintiff's copyright was infringed.

In another case involving copyright transfer, the Fifth Circuit in *Isbell v. DM Records, Inc.* held that a contract assigning a 50 percent interest in a copyrighted work, including all claims for infringement of copyright, did not extinguish the transferor's right to sue for infringement. And in *MOB Music Publishing v. Zanzibar on the Waterfront LLC*, the U.S. District Court for the District of Columbia held that the prima facie case for ownership established by the presentation of an original copyright registration was not sufficiently rebutted by a claim that the chain of title to the registration had not been properly established. In *Latin American Music Co. v. ASCAP*, the First Circuit determined that the validity of an oral termination of a prior transfer of a copyright was governed by New York contract law, and that the provisions of the Copyright Act were inapplicable.

Rights in individual photographs registered as part of a compilation were also at issue in two district court cases. In *Bean v. Houghton Mifflin Publishing Co.*, the U.S. District Court for the District of Arizona found that copyright registrations for compilations containing the plaintiff's photographs did not also include registrations of the individual photographs contained within the compilations. Without these individual copyright registration rights, the plaintiff could not sue for copyright infringement. Likewise, in *Muench Photography, Inc. v. Houghton Mifflin*, the U.S. District Court for the Southern District of New York found that the plaintiff failed to state a cause of action for copyright infringement of individual photographs that the plaintiff had contributed to an automated database because only the database as a whole was registered. The court held that the individual works at issue were not registered because the registration for the database did not include the authors' names.

Finally, in *JustMed, Inc. v. Byce*, the Ninth Circuit agreed with the district court's finding that the defendant was an employee of the plaintiff; thus, the work at issue constituted a work for hire.

OWNERSHIP

Summary Judgment Granted Where Plaintiffs Established Copyright Ownership through Copyright Registration and Assignment of Ownership

In *MOB Music Publishing v. Zanzibar on the Waterfront, LLC,*[1] the U.S. District Court for the District of Columbia granted the plaintiffs' motion for summary judgment, finding Zanzibar jointly and severally liable for infringing copyright behavior.[2] The court awarded the plaintiffs $40,000 in statutory damages.

MOB Music Publishing, Marley Marl Music, Inc., WB Music Corporation, Ain't Nothing But Funkin' Music, Music of Windswept, and Blotter Music (collectively, the plaintiffs) brought a copyright infringement action against Zanzibar, a nightclub in Washington, D.C., and Michael Daley, managing member of Zanzibar, alleging that Zanzibar played their copyrighted songs without authorization. The plaintiffs all had granted the American Society of Composers, Authors and Publishers (ASCAP) the nonexclusive right to license their songs to establishments who publicly performed their copyrighted music. On two separate occasions after Zanzibar refused to renew its expired ASCAP license to play hundreds of thousands of songs in ASCAP's repertory, ASCAP investigators observed several ASCAP songs played at Zanzibar.

The court ruled in favor of the plaintiffs, finding that the plaintiffs proved the elements essential to copyright infringement: (1) ownership of a valid copyright; and (2) "copying of constituent elements of work that are original."[3] The court found that the plaintiffs' presentation of original copyright registration forms listing themselves as copyright claimants established prima facie evidence of ownership of a valid copyright. In instances where the plaintiffs were not the original copyright claimants of the song, the court found that the presentation of an original copyright registration form along with certificates of assignments documenting the transfer of copyrights from the original copyright claimants to the plaintiffs was adequate to establish prima facie evidence of ownership of a valid copyright. The court determined that the defendants produced no actual evidence to controvert the plaintiffs' chains of title and, therefore, did not create a genuine issue of material facts necessary to overcome the plaintiff's prima facie evidence of ownership. As for the second element, the court found that affidavits from ASCAP investigators indicating that they had observed Zanzibar's playing of ASCAP songs without a license, in the absence of any affirmative proof from the defendants that the songs were not played, was adequate to establish proof of copyright infringement.

The court also found that Michael Daley and Zanzibar were jointly and severally liable for the copyright infringement. Daley was vicariously liable because he had control over the primary copyright infringers. Even though the songs in question were played by independent contractors and not employees of Zanzibar, Daley had the "right and ability" to supervise the type of music performed and had a "direct financial interest" in the type of music performed in the form of salary and dividends.

The court granted the plaintiffs $40,000 in damages pursuant to 17 U.S.C. § 504(c)(1), which included the total ASCAP license fee "saved" by the defendants and an amount to

---

1.   698 F. Supp. 2d. 197 (D.D.C. 2010).
2.   *Id.* at 206–07.
3.   *Id.* at 202.

deter future misconduct. The court determined that the damages to deter infringement were warranted, given that an ASCAP investigator had observed the playing of an ASCAP song even after ASCAP repeatedly efforts to make Zanzibar renew their license and this lawsuit had been filed. For the same reasons, the court granted a permanent injunction prohibiting defendants from publicly performing copyrighted songs from ASCAP's repertory and also granted an award of reasonable attorneys' fees.

Registration and Notice Formalities

Author of Works Included in Compilation Could Not Rely on Registration of Compilation for Infringement Suit

In *Bean v. Houghton Mifflin Publishing Co.,*[4] the U.S. District Court for the District of Arizona granted Houghton Mifflin's motion to dismiss Bean's copyright infringement suit. Although Bean's licensing agent had properly registered copyrights in compilations that contained Bean's photographs, the court held that those registrations did not extend to Bean's individual works. Without valid copyright registrations of his individual works, Bean could not bring suit for copyright infringement.

Between 2000 and 2009, Bean transferred interests in 150 of his photographs to his licensing agent, Corbis Corporation. In turn, Corbis included some of his photographs in each of six compilations of images. In total, the compilations included between 11,000 and 613,000 images created by many different photographers. Corbis registered copyrights in all six compilations. The registration documents identified Corbis as the author of the compilations and indicated that others created the individual photographs. The registration for one compilation listed Bean as one of the photographers; the other compilations did not. None of the registration documents indicated which images Bean created.

Corbis then sold to Houghton Mifflin limited licenses to use Bean's photographs, some of which were part of the compilations. Believing that Houghton Mifflin was exceeding the uses allowed under this license agreement, Bean filed suit against Houghton Mifflin for copyright infringement. Houghton Mifflin then moved to dismiss the suit under Federal Rule of Civil Procedure 12(b)(6), arguing that Bean did not have valid copyright registrations covering the works at issue.

The district court noted that, in deciding a Rule 12(b)(6) motion, it was to view the facts in the light most favorable to the nonmoving party. The court then reviewed the Copyright Act's provision discussing compilations, which provides that "an applicant may obtain copyright protection for the compilation itself—that is, the original work of compiling the various data or materials included in the compilation—even if the applicant does not actually own or have a copyright in the individual data or materials that make up the compilation."[5] The court also reiterated that "copyright in a compilation . . . extends only to the material contributed by the author of such work, as distinguished from the preexisting material employed in the work."[6]

The court therefore analyzed whether Corbis's registration of the six compilations also registered the copyrights in the individual works contained within the compilations.

---

4. No. 10-8034, 2010 WL 3168624 (D. Ariz. Aug. 10, 2010).
5. *Id.* at *2 (citing 17 U.S.C. §§ 101, 201(c)).
6. *Id.* (citing 17 U.S.C. § 103(a)).

To register an individual work, Section 409 of the Copyright Act requires naming the individual work's author and title. Registering a compilation requires naming the compilation's author and title. Given that Corbis's certificates of registration included only one title apiece—a compilation title—and did not provide titles for the individual photographs, and each certificate listed only a few of the photographers whose works were in the compilation, the court concluded that Corbis's compilation registrations did not serve to register copyrights in the individual photographs.

The court also rejected Bean's argument that section 411 of the Copyright Act could save copyright registrations not fully complying with section 409, finding that section 411 applied only when a copyright registration unintentionally contained inaccurate information. In contrast, Corbis's compilation registrations were valid registrations covering the compilations and required no saving. According to the court, allowing Corbis's compilation registrations to stand as registrations for the individual works "would eviscerate the requirements of § 409" for individual works.[7]

The court therefore concluded that Corbis's compilation registrations did not register copyrights in the individual works contained within the compilations. Given that valid copyright registration is a prerequisite to suing for copyright infringement, and because none of Bean's 150 photographs were registered as individual works, the court granted Houghton Mifflin's motion to dismiss Bean's infringement claim.

Automated Database Registration Must Include Names of All Authors to Protect Underlying Individual Works

In *Muench Photography, Inc. v. Houghton Mifflin Harcourt Publishing Co.,*[8] the U.S. District Court for the Southern District of New York held that a copyright registration in an automated database of photographs by a third-party assignee must contain all of the names of the individual photographers to allow the photographers to sue for copyright infringement. Corbis Corporation, a third-party assignee, registered, among others, approximately 180 of the plaintiff's images as part of several automated databases of photographs with the Copyright Office. Muench Photography, Inc. (MPI), through its agent, Corbis, licensed the images to the defendants, Houghton Mifflin Harcourt Publishing Company (HMH) and R.R. Donnelly & Sons Company, but MPI claimed that the defendants exceeded the scope and terms of those licenses, causing unauthorized reproductions of the images to be made and distributed.

When Corbis registered the images, the company used Form VA, which includes a request for information concerning the author(s) of the material to be registered. Corbis listed itself as one author, the names of three other individuals, and included the phrase "& others," or "and (number) other photographers." Corbis also listed itself as the copyright claimant on each registration form.

Corbis contacted the Copyright Office to ensure the validity of the copyright registration procedure used for the images. The Copyright Office's chief of the Examining Division confirmed that the Copyright Office preferred, but did not require, the registration application to include the names of all of the photographers on continuation sheets for the claim to extend to the individual author's works.

---

7. *Id.* at *4.
8. 712 F. Supp. 2d 84 (S.D.N.Y. 2010).

Section 411 of the Copyright Act provides that "no civil action for infringement of the copyright in any United States work shall be instituted until preregistration or registration of the copyright claim has been made in accordance with this title."[9] The Copyright Act also provides in section 409 that an application for copyright registration must include "the name and nationality or domicile of the author or authors."[10]

According to the court, the plaintiff did not register its photographs pursuant to section 202.3(b)(4) of the Code of Federal Regulations (setting forth the requirements to register a single application for multiple works) or section 202.3(b)(10) (listing the requirements to register a group of photographs). Instead, the plaintiff argued that the text of section 103 of the Copyright Act, coupled with the case law and the Copyright Office's own interpretation of the statute, provided that the registration of a collective work covers individual works even if the registration form omits individual authors' names.

The text of section 103 provides that "copyright in a compilation or derivative work extends only to the material contributed by the author."[11] The court explained that the registration of a collective work reaches the individual works only when the author of the collective work is also the author of each of the individual works contained within the collective work.

Regarding its case law argument, the plaintiff relied principally on the Arizona district court's holding in *Bean v. McDougal Littell*,[12] which also involved Corbis copyright registrations. Judge Preska distinguished the *Bean* case from the current case, finding that, unlike the defendants in the current case, the defendants in *Bean* did not focus on section 409; rather, the *Bean* defendants' focus was on an earlier case involving whether the copyright registration of a magazine reached the contributions of an individual author who did not transfer full ownership rights to the registrant.[13] The court in *Bean* found that the photographers made a valid transfer of their rights and thus were entitled to bring a claim for copyright infringement.

According to Judge Preska, the *Bean* court erroneously relied on the *Morris* court's decision because it never explained why the registration of an automated database should be governed by the same rules that apply to the registration of serials. The court then found that automated databases and serials are separate forms of copyrightable works and, thus, are subject to separate copyright regulations. Specifically, serials are governed by 37 C.F.R. § 202.3(b)(6) as well as Circular 62, whereas automated databases are governed by 37 C.F.R. § 202.3(b)(5) and Circular 65.

Regarding the plaintiff's reliance on the representations of the Copyright Office, the court held that Corbis was not entitled to rely on those representations because the interpretations of the Copyright Office, in this case, conflict with a plain reading of 17 U.S.C. § 409.

According to the court, a plain reading of section 409(2) of the Copyright Act mandates that the copyright registrations at issue contain the names of all the authors of the

---

9.   17 U.S.C. § 411(a) (2006).

10.   17 U.S.C. § 409(2).

11.   17 U.S.C. § 103(b).

12.   669 F. Supp. 2d 1031 (D. Ariz. 2008).

13.   Morris v. Bus. Concepts Inc., 283 F.3d 502, 506 (2d Cir. 2002) (holding that, "unless the copyright owner of a collective work also owns all the rights in a constituent part, a collective work registration will not extend to a constituent part.").

work. After noting that its task is to apply the text, not improve upon it, the court held that, because the Copyright Act is clear on its face, the copyright registration must include certain pieces of information, including the author's name.

The court held that MPI failed to comply with the precondition to suit, thereby failing to state a cause of action with respect to the inadequate registrations. The court also held that the "innocent error rule," which operates to save a copyright registration for technical defects, such as a misspelling or accidental omission of information, does not apply in this case. The court granted the defendants' summary judgment motion with respect to MPI's images that Corbis had attempted to register. However, the court pointed out that MPI could still register the photographs immediately, which would allow it to collect statutory damages against future infringers.

Works Made for Hire

Work-for-Hire Doctrine Requires Fact-Based, Holistic Analysis of Relationship

In *JustMed, Inc. v. Byce*,[14] the Ninth Circuit: (1) held that it had jurisdiction over Plaintiff JustMed's state law claims for conversion and misappropriation of trade secrets because those claims required JustMed to prove its ownership of copyright in the disputed software; (2) affirmed the district court's judgment, after a bench trial, holding that Defendant Michael Byce wrote the source code as an employee of JustMed and that, accordingly, JustMed owns the copyright to the software under the work-for-hire doctrine; and (3) reversed the district court's finding that Byce misappropriated the source code in violation of the Idaho Trade Secrets Act.

JustMed was a start-up technology company. Byce, who had no employment agreement, wrote substantially all the software for JustMed's product. Nearing the end of that work, he became concerned that JustMed's founder, Joel Just, did not view him as an equal in the company. Byce therefore removed JustMed's name from the copyright notice on the source code and inserted his own. He also deleted copies of the source code from JustMed's computers to gain leverage to acquire a greater share of the company.

JustMed filed suit in state court, asserting claims for conversion and misappropriation of trade secrets, as well as other state law claims. Byce removed the case to federal court. The district court found that JustMed owned the copyright to the disputed software, and that Byce had misappropriated the software in violation of Idaho's Trade Secrets Act.[15]

Applying the "well-pleaded complaint rule," the Ninth Circuit concluded that it had jurisdiction over the dispute. Although JustMed's state law claims required it to prove ownership of the source code, the complaint, which acknowledged that ownership of the source code was disputed, directly implicated the Copyright Act's work-for-hire doctrine.

The court next examined whether, for purposes of the work-for-hire doctrine, Byce was an employee of JustMed or an independent contractor. The court reviewed de novo the district court's conclusions of law, including the determination that the source code

---

14. 600 F.3d 1118 (9th Cir. 2010).
15 *See* IDAHO CODE ANN. §§ 48-801 to 807 (2010).

was a work made for hire. The district court's factual findings were subject to a review for clear error.

In a detailed, fact-specific analysis, the court affirmed the holding that the source code was a work made for hire. The court noted that "'all of the incidents of the relationship must be assessed and weighed with no one factor being decisive.'"[16] In reaching its conclusion, the court "[drew] some guidance . . . from JustMed's status as a technology start-up company"[17] and identified several facts that favored finding Byce to be an employee, including: (1) JustMed hired Byce to replace an employee and paid Byce the same salary (in the form of shares of stock) as the former employee; (2) Byce had a formal title (Director of Research and Development and Director of Engineering), which indicated that he had broad duties and a permanent relationship with the company; (3) Byce worked on tasks besides programming; and (4) Byce's work was the core of JustMed's regular business. As the court noted, "[i]t seems highly unlikely that JustMed would leave . . . an important, continuous responsibility [(i.e., future software updates)] to an independent contractor who would terminate his relationship with the company upon completing a working version of the software."[18]

Although other factors arguably favored a finding that Byce was an independent contractor, the court found them unpersuasive in light of the way JustMed conducted its business. The court discounted JustMed's lack of control over Byce's creation of the source code, finding that "[t]he business model and Byce's duties do not require that the project be completed in a particular manner or that Just continually oversee Byce's work, so long as JustMed eventually found itself with a marketable product."[19] Byce's hours and the fact that he worked from home also were not deemed particularly relevant. The court was not persuaded that Byce's skill as a computer programmer outweighed the other facts because JustMed's regular business required it to employ programmers. Finally, the court noted that JustMed's failure to pay employment-related taxes and to provide employee benefits and forms "is more likely attributable to the start-up nature of the business than to Byce's alleged status as an independent contractor. The indications are that other employees . . . were treated similarly."[20]

The court next found reversible error in the district court's holding that Byce had misappropriated a trade secret in violation of the Idaho statute, which is a slightly modified version of the Uniform Trade Secrets Act. The court held that Byce could not be liable for acquiring the source code through improper means because he created much of it and had access to it as JustMed's employee.

Although Byce acquired access to the source code under circumstances giving rise to a duty to maintain its confidentiality, the court held that he was not liable for "disclosing" or "using" the source code, as those terms are used in the statute. The court held that Byce's disclosure of a portion of the source code to the Copyright Office (in connection with registration of a copyright) was not necessarily inconsistent with maintaining the secrecy and value of the trade secret. Furthermore, Byce's "use" of the source code—

---

16. *JustMed*, 600 F.3d at 1125–26 (quoting Nationwide Mut. Ins. Co. v. Darden, 503 U.S. 318, 324 (1992)).

17. *Id.* at 1126.

18. *Id.* at 1127.

19. *Id.*

20. *Id.* at 1128.

filing a portion to register a copyright and threatening to withhold the source code from JustMed—was insufficient to hold him liable for misappropriation. The court noted that "[h]is possession of the source code for some period of time did not result in a loss of secrecy or loss in value, which is evident from the fact that the court did not award damages for lost value or unjust enrichment."[21]

Given that Byce had threatened misappropriation, however, the court remanded for the district court to determine whether to issue an injunction against the threatened use or disclosure of the source code.

TRANSFER

Transfer Formalities

Assignor of 50 Percent Interest in Work Retained Right to Sue for Infringement

In *Isbell Records, Inc. v. DM Records, Inc.,*[22] the Fifth Circuit held that, when Alvertis Isbell assigned 50 percent of his interest in two musical compositions to a third party, he did not extinguish his right, and thus standing, to sue for infringement of the copyright in those compositions.

In 1997, DM Records purchased the assets of Belmark Records, which had filed for bankruptcy. DM Records claimed that those assets included the sound recordings, "Dazzey Duks" and "Whoomp! (There It Is)." Alvertis Isbell, d/b/a Alvert Music, a publishing company that owned musical compositions, and DM Records disputed whether the assets DM Records purchased included the musical compositions contained in the sound recordings. Alvert Music maintained that DM Records' purchase did not include those compositions and that DM Records infringed Alvert Music's copyright in the two compositions at issue.

Alvert Music had transferred a partial interest in the two musical compositions to Bridgeport Music, Inc. in 2004. The Short Form Copyright Assignment document provided, in pertinent part:

> [T]he undersigned does hereby sell, assign, transfer, and set over to Bridgeport Music, Inc . . . fifty percent (50%) of his interest now owned or subsequently procured in the universe-wide copyright in and to the following musical composition(s) set forth in Exhibit A attached hereto, and all of the universe-wide right, title, and interest of the undersigned . . . *including all claims for infringement of the copyrights* . . . .[23]

DM Records asserted that Alvert Music did not hold valid rights in the copyrights and, thus, did not have valid infringement claims because of this assignment to Bridgeport Music, Inc. The U.S. District Court for the Eastern District of Texas agreed and granted DM Records' motion to dismiss, holding that the assignment instrument transferred all rights to bring suit for copyright infringement, and that Isbell lacked standing to sue.

---

21. *Id.* at 1131.
22. 586 F.3d 334 (5th Cir. 2009).
23. *Id.* at 336 (emphasis added).

The Fifth Circuit reviewed the district court's decision de novo. The court considered the two separate clauses in the assignment, the first providing that Alvert Music assigned to Bridgeport "fifty percent (50%) of [its] interest" and the second providing that Alvert Music assigned to Bridgeport "all claims for infringement of the copyrights . . . ."[24]

The Fifth Circuit determined that the district court failed to interpret the assigning sentence as a whole, which made the contract internally self-contradictory. An interpretation concluding that 100 percent of the rights were transferred contradicted "the clear language of the first clause,"[25] which provides that only 50 percent of Alvert Music's interest was being transferred. Consequently, the Fifth Circuit held that Alvert Music still had the right to bring a copyright claim and had standing to do so. The case was reversed and remanded to the district court for further proceedings.

Termination of Transfers

State Law Controls Termination Rights When Copyright Act Provisions Do Not Apply

In *Latin American Music Co. v. ASCAP,*[26] the First Circuit affirmed the district court's decision that the rights to a single song, "Cabello Viejo," belong to the American Society of Composers, Authors, and Publishers (ASCAP). The court found that ASCAP's predecessor-in-interest, West Side Music Publishing, Inc. (West Side) lawfully terminated a 1982 contract that had transferred West Side's rights in the song to Latin American Music Company (LAMCO) and Asociación de Compositores y Editores de Música Latino Americana (ACEMLA). LAMCO and ACEMLA claimed that the law governing the termination of the 1982 contract was the Copyright Act of 1976 and not New York state law.

Through the contract at issue, West Side had granted rights to "Cabello Viejo," a song by Simon Diaz, to ACEMLA, LAMCO's predecessor. The contract was formed in New York and was completely silent as to termination. It did not specify an end date or a method by which termination was to be effectuated. West Side's president testified in a videotaped deposition that he had verbally terminated the contract during a conversation with ACEMLA's president. Later, LAMCO claimed that the Copyright Act was applicable and that ASCAP did not properly terminate the contract because the termination was not in writing; therefore, it still owned the rights to the song.

The court rejected LAMCO's argument that the Copyright Act applies. Section 204 of the Copyright Act requires a writing to transfer or grant copyright ownership, but does not reference the termination of such a transfer or grant. LAMCO claimed that this meant that notice of termination also must be in writing because a termination, if valid, would have the legal effect of transferring back the ownership interest to the original transferor. The court disagreed, finding that the language of the statute clearly did not apply to terminations. Moreover, it noted that such an interpretation would allow the owner of the rights being terminated to refuse to convey back the ownership interest and thereby effectively block the termination. Additionally, LAMCO argued that section 203 of the Copyright Act applied and required a writing for a valid termination. However, section 203 of the

---

24. *Id.*
25. *Id.* at 337.
26. 593 F.3d 95 (1st Cir. 2010).

Copyright Act applies only where an author or an author's statutory heirs are terminating the grant of copyright ownership. Here, neither the author nor the author's statutory heirs were terminating the grant of copyright ownership; therefore, section 203 did not apply.

Given the fact that no provision of the Copyright Act was applicable, and given that, "unless a contract provides otherwise, it is governed by the law of the state in which it was formed,"[27] the court agreed with ASCAP that there was no preemption and that New York state law governed the termination of the 1982 contract. Relying on *Italian & French Wine Co. of Buffalo, Inc. v. Negociants U.S.A., Inc.*,[28] the court found that, under New York law, a contract of an unspecified duration can be terminated upon reasonable notice. Determination of what constitutes "reasonable notice" was a jury question. LAMCO did not present any real support for their argument that reasonable notice requires written notice under New York law. Therefore, the jury could decide that ASCAP's oral termination complied with New York law.

Internal Corporate Restructuring Terminates Copyright License, Leading to Infringement

In *Cincom System, Inc. v. Novelis Corp.*,[29] the Sixth Circuit affirmed the district court's summary judgment finding of copyright infringement where a series of mergers as part of an internal corporate restructuring resulted in a prohibited transfer of a software license granted to a former subsidiary.

Cincom developed, licensed, and serviced software for its corporate customers. Rather than sell the computer programs themselves, Cincom only sold licenses that allowed its customers to use programs for an annual fee. Cincom licensed the software to Alcan Rolled Products Division (Alcan Ohio). The license listed Alcan Rolled Products Division as the customer and granted to Alcan Ohio a nonexclusive and nontransferable license to use Cincom's software. The license agreement provided that Ohio law would govern its terms, and that Alcan Ohio could not transfer its rights or obligations under the agreement without Cincom's prior written approval.

As a result of corporate restructuring, Alcan Ohio merged into Alcan Texas, with Alcan Texas remaining as the surviving corporate entity. After further mergers and name changes, Novelis became the owner of a computer on which Cincom's software was stored. Alcan Ohio never sought or obtained Cincom's written approval to continue to use the licensed software before restructuring its rolled products division.

Under federal common law, a copyright license is presumed to be nonassignable and nontransferable in the absence of express provisions to the contrary. State contract law allowing the transfer of a license, absent express authorization, must yield to the federal common law prohibiting such unauthorized transfers.

Copyright law prevents the "free flow" of information without the author's permission. Although the primary reason for the federal common law rule prohibiting the transfer of a license without authorization is to prevent the license from coming into a competitor's possession, the rule upholds the federal policy allowing the copyright holder to control the use of his creation. The transferee need not be a competitor for the rule to apply.

---

27. *Id.* at 99.
28. 842 F. Supp. 693 (W.D.N.Y. 1993).
29. 581 F.3d 431 (6th Cir. 2009).

A transfer occurs any time an entity, other than the one to which the license was expressly granted, gains possession of the license. The vesting of the license in the surviving entity could not occur without being transferred by the old entity. With the merger and reorganization, Alcan Ohio ceased to exist as a legal entity under Ohio law. The license once held by Alcan Ohio automatically vested by operation of law in Novelis, Alcan Ohio's successor, after the completion of the corporate restructuring.

Cincom had granted a nonexclusive and nontransferable license, requiring Cincom's express written approval prior to any transfer of the license. Ohio law caused the license agreement to flow to Novelis following Alcan Ohio's merger, and the court held that this transfer without permission breached the license contract. Because Novelis did not abide by the express terms of Cincom's license and gain Cincom's prior written approval prior to the transfer, the court held that Novelis had infringed Cincom's copyright.

CHAPTER 18

COPYRIGHT LITIGATION

Over the past year, copyright litigation decisions involved discussion of the substantial similarity test, statutory damages, the first-sale doctrine, personal jurisdiction, attorneys' fees, fair use, and implied licenses, among others.

The Eleventh Circuit in *Baby Buddies, Inc. v. Toys "R" Us, Inc.* held that, when evaluating copyright infringement claims involving useful articles, the substantial similarity test is applied only to the copyrightable elements that are conceptually or physically separable from the utilitarian aspects of the article.

The Ninth Circuit considered the substantial similarity test in *Benay v. Warner Bros. Entertainment, Inc.*, with the court holding that the substantial similarity standard necessary to prove copyright infringement differs from the substantial similarity standard necessary to prove breach of an implied-in-fact contract in California. In *Mattel, Inc. v. MGA Entertainment, Inc.*, the Ninth Circuit explained that two different standards of infringement can apply depending on the range of possible expression of the relevant ideas—either substantially similar or virtually identical. In *Doody v. Penguin Group (USA), Inc.*, the U.S. District Court for the District of Hawaii decided that substantial similarity for infringement required a comparison to specific allegedly infringing works and not to a collection of different works.

Also addressing substantial similarity, the U.S. District Court for the Southern District of New York in *Lewinson v. Holt & Co.* granted summary judgment to the defendant where it found that a manuscript for a children's story and a children's book were not substantially similar after comparing the theme, plot, characters, sequence, setting, and total look and feel of the two works, even though the publisher of the children's book had access to the manuscript. Likewise, in *Frye v. YMCA Camp Kitaki*, the Eighth Circuit affirmed the district court's conclusions that two plays with medieval-themed *scènes à faire* were not substantially similar; thus, no copyright infringement occurred.

Conversely, in *Lombardi v. Whitehall*, probative similarities between architectural works sufficed for the U.S. District Court for the Southern District of New York to deny summary judgment against a copyright infringement claim. Yet in *Peter F. Gaito Architecture, LLC v. Simone Development Corp.*, the Second Circuit held that the district court properly considered the question of noninfringement and determined noninfringement as a matter of law in a copyright action on a Rule 12(b)(6) motion to dismiss, and that the district court did not err in concluding that the plaintiffs' amended complaint and the documents incorporated therein failed to allege substantial similarity between the defendants' work and the protectable elements of the plaintiff's work.

In *Art Attacks Ink, LLC v. MGA Entertainment Inc.*, the plaintiff alleged that the defendant had copied its "Spoiled Brats" designs in creating the defendant's line of "Bratz" dolls, but the Ninth Circuit held that the copyright holder failed to prove that its rights had been infringed. Lacking direct evidence of copying, the plaintiff was required to prove that the defendant had access to the copyrighted material. Having only disseminated the copyrighted designs via a booth display at a trade show and a rudimentary Web site, the court held that the plaintiff had failed to prove the defendant had such access.

In *Blackwell Publishing, Inc. v. Excel Research Group*, the U.S. District Court for the Eastern District of Michigan found a copy shop directly liable for copyright infringement due to its practice of lending coursepacks to students and providing them with photocopying equipment, even though the students performed the actual copying. Similarly, in *Columbia Pictures Industries, Inc. v. Fung*, the U.S. District Court for the Central District of California granted summary judgment on liability for inducement of infringement against an operator of several Web sites connected to a file-sharing network based on "Torrent" technology, which allowed users to download infringing copies of popular copyrighted works. In its decision, the district court rejected the defendant's DMCA and First Amendment defenses.

The Second Circuit, in *Bryant v. Media Right Productions, Inc.*, found that the district court did not err in concluding that an album constitutes a compilation of individual songs for purposes of awarding statutory damages under section 504(c) of the Copyright Act. Therefore, the plaintiffs were entitled only to an award of statutory damages based on each album infringed by the defendants, for a total of four awards, rather than one statutory award for each of the songs contained on the albums (which would have totaled forty awards). Additionally, in *MCS Music America, Inc. v. Yahoo! Inc.*, the U.S. District Court for the Middle District of Tennessee held that a musical composition, even where recorded multiple times by different musicians, constituted one work for determining the amount of copyright damages.

In *John Wiley & Sons, Inc. v. Kirtsaeng*, the U.S. District Court for the Southern District of New York held that importers of textbooks manufactured and sold abroad could not assert the first-sale doctrine as a defense to infringement of the publishers' distribution rights. The decision clarified that the Copyright Act's importation prohibition applies to goods lawfully made abroad. Likewise, in *Pearson Education, Inc. v. Liu*, the same district court held that the first-sale doctrine did not apply to the sale of foreign editions of copyrighted textbooks which were manufactured abroad because the copies were not "lawfully made under this title" as required by section 109(a) of the Copyright Act. In another first-sale decision, *Vernor v. Autodesk, Inc.*, an eBay reseller was protected by the first-sale doctrine after a court determined that he was the owner of software transferred under a license agreement. The court found that the transfer of software copies via the license was a transfer of ownership because there was no provision in the agreement for the copyright holder to regain possession of the copy.

Several decisions addressed procedural issues, including decisions regarding personal jurisdiction. The Ninth Circuit in *Brayton Purcell LLP v. Recordon & Recordon* held that personal jurisdiction was established over a law firm whose Web site contained copyrighted material taken verbatim from another law firm's Web site where the infringer's Web site put the two firms in direct competition for clients, despite the fact that the two firms practiced in different geographical areas of California. In another personal jurisdiction case, the Second Circuit in *Penguin Group (USA) Inc. v. American Buddha* certified a question to the New York Court of Appeals regarding the application of New York's long-arm statute to determine personal jurisdiction in a copyright infringement claim involving the Internet.

The Second Circuit also upheld a district court's decision to deny an anonymous defendant's motion to quash a subpoena served on his ISP in *Arista Records, LLC v. Doe*

3, requiring the defendant to disclose his identity and other information. In upholding the district court's ruling, the court held that the First Amendment privilege of anonymity does not provide a license for copyright infringement. In *Crispin v. Audigier,* the U.S. District Court for the Central District of California reversed and remanded an order compelling three social media sites to produce communications based on limitations on production under the Stored Communications Act.

In *R.C. Olmstead, Inc., v. CU Interface, LLC*, the Sixth Circuit affirmed the district court's grant of summary judgment in favor of the defendants on the plaintiff's claims of copyright and trade secret infringement, where the plaintiff claimed that several discovery rulings unfairly inhibited its ability to prove its claims. Among other rulings, the district court rejected the plaintiff's inadequate expert report and refused to draw adverse inferences based on a third party's destruction of evidence. After rejecting the report, the district court granted summary judgment for the defendant, determining that the plaintiff failed to raise a genuine issue of material fact as to whether the defendant copied the plaintiff's software.

The Second Circuit in *Salinger v. Colting* held that the U.S. Supreme Court's decision in *eBay, Inc. v. MercExchange, L.L.C.*, which articulated the four-factor test for evaluation of injunctions in the patent context, also applied to preliminary injunctions issued in copyright infringement cases. The court found that, although the district court applied the Second Circuit's longstanding standard for preliminary injunctions in copyright cases, which generally focused solely on whether the plaintiff had shown a likelihood of success on the merits and presumed that such a plaintiff was also likely to suffer irreparable harm, this standard had been abrogated by the U.S. Supreme Court's *eBay* decision. In a DMCA case addressing the propriety of a preliminary injunction, the U.S. District Court for the Central District of California in *Perfect 10, Inc. v. Google, Inc.* denied a preliminary injunction against the defendant, despite allegations of infringement relating to the defendant's Web and image search, related caching feature, blogger service, and the defendant's forwarding of the plaintiff's DMCA notices to chillingeffects.org, finding that the plaintiff was unlikely to succeed on the merits of its claims.

Courts addressed various other copyright issues as well. In *Airframe Systems, Inc. v. Raytheon Co.*, the First Circuit rejected a copyright infringement claim against the defendant because a prior copyright infringement action against the same business unit, although owned by a different corporation, had been dismissed for failure to state a claim. In *Dallal v. New York Times Co.*, the Second Circuit held that section 204(a) of the Copyright Act requires a written agreement to affect a transfer of copyright ownership.

The Fourth Circuit in *Thomas M. Gilbert Architects, P.C. v. Accent Builders & Developers, LLC* held that a developer did not have an implied license to modify an architect's copyrighted plans because express language in the parties' agreement clearly reflected a contrary intent. In contrast, in *Estate of Roberto Hevia-Acosta v. Portrio Corp.*, the First Circuit, evaluating intent under a totality of circumstances test, found that a deceased architectural designer had given his business partner an implied license to use his copyrighted designs.

In *Maverick Recording Co. v. Harper*, the Fifth Circuit rejected the defendant's innocent infringement defense because the plaintiffs provided proper notice of copyright on their published phonorecords, and the defendant did not dispute that she had access to the phonorecords.

The requirement of copyright registration featured prominently in several decisions. In *Moberg v. 33T LLC*, the U.S. District Court for the District of Delaware held that an owner who posted his foreign copyrighted work on a foreign Web site was not required to register his photographs before filing suit for copyright infringement in a U.S. court because posting a work created outside the United States by a foreign national on a Web site based outside the United States did not constitute publishing the work simultaneously in the United States and in the foreign country. In *Cosmetic Ideas, Inc. v. IAC/InteractiveCorp*, the Ninth Circuit held that the requirement of copyright registration as a precondition to filing an infringement lawsuit was satisfied by filing an application for copyright registration. Deciding a similar issue, the U.S. Supreme Court in *Reed Elsevier, Inc. v. Muchnick* held that the Copyright Act's registration requirement was not jurisdictional. Addressing the registration requirement in the context of damages, the U.S. District Court for the Southern District of New York in *Elsevier B.V. v. UnitedHealth Group, Inc.* determined that section 412 of the Copyright Act requires a registration in the United States prior to an award of statutory damages for copyright infringement of a foreign work. The court noted that, because the Berne Convention is not self-executing, it cannot be used to support a claim for preemption that would invalidate this requirement.

In other cases discussing damage awards, the U.S. District Court for the Northern District of California in *Lenz v. Universal Music Corp.* held that it is not necessary to show actual expenses or economic losses to recover damages under the DMCA.

Evaluating the issuance of attorneys' fees, the Sixth Circuit in *Bridgeport Music, Inc. v. Universal-MCA Music Publishing, Inc.* affirmed the district court's order granting motions to dismiss in twenty cases and directing each party to pay its own attorneys' fees and costs. The court considered each case individually and held that the district court did not abuse its discretion in finding that the defendants would not suffer prejudice and, thus, were not entitled to payment of a pro rata share of attorneys' fees as a condition for dismissal under Rule 41(a)(2).

In another case involving attorneys' fees, the U.S. District Court for the Southern District of New York in *Porto v. Guirgis* dismissed a copyright infringement claim involving a play and a novel based on a fictional trial of Judas Iscariot. The court held that the protectable elements of the works were different and awarded attorneys' fees and costs to the defendants, holding that the plaintiff brought the objectively unreasonable claim in bad faith. Additionally, in *Vargas v. Pfizer Inc.*, the Second Circuit upheld two district court opinions granting summary judgment and attorneys' fees to the defendant where, inter alia, the plaintiff failed to show substantial similarity between the works at issue.

Finally, in *Society of the Holy Transfiguration Monastery, Inc. v. Archbishop Gregory of Denver, Colorado*, the U.S. District Court for the District of Massachusetts awarded partial summary judgment to the plaintiff for breach of a settlement agreement reached in a prior copyright case and for copyright infringement of its English-language translation of an ancient Greek religious text, rejecting an argument of fair use. Likewise, in *Gaylord v. United States*, the Federal Circuit held that the fair-use defense was inapplicable where the government used a photograph of a sculpture it had previously commissioned on a postage stamp.

PROCEDURAL MATTERS

Formalities

Motion to Quash Subpoena Served on ISP to Disclose Identity of Anonymous Defendant Denied

In *Arista Records, LLC v. Doe 3,*[1] the Second Circuit affirmed a district court order denying the defendants' motion to quash a subpoena served on an ISP in an attempt to obtain the identities of various anonymous defendants.

Arista Records, LLC and other plaintiffs[2] brought a John Doe action against sixteen defendants who allegedly infringed the plaintiffs' copyrights by downloading and/or distributing the plaintiffs' copyrighted songs through an online "peer-to-peer" network without permission. The plaintiffs could identify the alleged infringers only through the Internet protocol (IP) addresses assigned to them by their ISP, the State University of New York at Albany (SUNYA). The plaintiffs' subpoena required SUNYA to disclose the defendants' names, addresses, and other identifying information. The subpoena request was supported by a declaration stating that a third-party investigator had found copyrighted music in each of the defendants' folders on the online file-sharing network and that the Recording Industry Association of America had verified that these files were infringing.

The defendants motioned to quash the subpoena or, alternatively, to require that the plaintiffs sue each defendant separately. Magistrate Judge Treece, utilizing then-District Judge Denny Chin's five-factor *Sony Music* test, considered the defendants' "expectation of privacy, the prima facie strength of plaintiffs' claims of injury, the specificity of the discovery request, plaintiffs' need for the information, and its availability through other means" and found that all five factors weighed against quashing the plaintiffs' subpoena.[3] Among other things, the magistrate judge found that the defendants' identities, which could only be obtained through the ISPs, were necessary for the plaintiffs to prosecute their copyright claims. The magistrate judge also found that the defendants' expectations of privacy were minimal because the defendants granted others electronic access to their information and data. Determining that the defendants' First Amendment rights did not outweigh these factors, the magistrate judge denied the plaintiffs' motion to quash the subpoena.

In response to the magistrate judge's decision, one defendant, Doe 3, objected in district court, arguing that the magistrate judge lacked jurisdiction over the motion; thus, the motion should be reviewed de novo. The district court rejected Doe 3's objections, finding that the motion to quash was a nondispositive motion over which the magistrate judge had authority. The district court used a clear error standard of review in upholding the magistrate judge's order.

---

1. 604 F.3d 110 (2d Cir. 2010).
2. The plaintiffs were Arista Records, LLC, Atlantic Recording Corporation, BMG Music, Capitol Records, LLC, Elektra Entertainment Group, Inc., Interscope Records, Maverick Recording Company, Motown Record Company, L.P., Sony BMG Music Entertainment, UMG Recordings, Inc., Virgin Records America, Inc., Warner Bros. Records Inc., and Zomba Recording LLC.
3. 604 F.3d at 114.

On appeal, the Second Circuit agreed that the magistrate judge had jurisdiction over the motion to quash. The Second Circuit reviewed the district court's decision for abuse of discretion and found that the decision was not based on "an error of law or on a clearly erroneous factual finding."[4] Although noting that the U.S. Supreme Court has recognized that the First Amendment protects anonymity and that "the Internet is a valuable forum for the exchange of ideas," the Second Circuit noted that the First Amendment does not protect anonymity if it is used to mask or facilitate copyright infringement.[5]

In addition, the Second Circuit rejected Doe 3's contention that the plaintiffs did not make a "particularized showing" sufficient to overcome his First Amendment privilege of anonymity because *Bell Atlantic Corp. v. Twombly*[6] and *Ashcroft v. Iqbal*[7] do not require more than a showing of specific evidence or facts beyond those necessary to state a claim, and the plaintiffs had met this burden. The plaintiffs' allegation that each defendant downloaded and distributed the plaintiffs' music on a file-sharing network was adequately supported by the plaintiffs' presentation of the IP addresses of each defendant, along with a list of each of the infringing recordings that had been downloaded and/or distributed, the date the copyrighted recordings were found in their folders, and the file-sharing network on which each recording was found. The plaintiffs' allegation that the defendants downloaded and/or distributed their music continuously was adequately supported by the improbability that the defendants had only the plaintiffs' music in their file-sharing folders at the precise moment investigators were looking at the folders and the fact that the defendants' attorneys had represented that some of the Doe defendants were, in fact, the same person. The plaintiffs did not need factual support to show that the defendants' downloading and/or distributing was without permission because such factual support did not seem possible so long as the defendants remained anonymous.[8]

The Second Circuit next considered and rejected Doe 3's fair-use argument using a standard set forth by the U.S. Supreme Court in *Harper & Row, Publishers, Inc. v. Nation Enterprises*: "(1) the purpose and character of the use; (2) the nature of the copyrighted work; (3) the substantiality of the portion used in relation to the copyrighted work as a whole; and (4) the effect on the potential market for or value of the copyrighted work."[9] As for the first element, even though Doe 3 asserted he could show a purpose and character of use that was permissible, the assertion could not be verified if Doe 3 remained anonymous and avoided suit. The court found that the second through fourth elements clearly weighed against finding that Doe 3's use constituted fair use. Moreover, detriment to the potential market was likely, given that over one million copies of the file-sharing software had been downloaded, billions of files had been shared across the networks in question, and the evidence supported that the vast majority of downloads were infringing.

Finally, the court questioned the magistrate judge's assertion that allowing others to access computer information and data renders an Internet user's expectation of privacy void where the information sought was the identity of the computer owner and not the

---

4.   *Id.* at 117.
5.   *Id.* at 118.
6.   550 U.S. 544 (2007).
7.   556 U.S. ___, 129 S. Ct. 1937 (2009).
8.   604 F.3d at 120.
9.   *Id.* at 124 (quoting Harper & Row, Publishers, Inc. v. Nation Enters., 471 U.S. 539, 560 (1985)).

information shared with others. Instead, the court found that Doe 3's expectation of privacy was not enough to allow Doe 3 to avoid defending a copyright infringement claim.[10]

Copyright Act Registration Requirement Is Satisfied by Application

In *Cosmetic Ideas, Inc. v. IAC/InteractiveCorp,*[11] the Ninth Circuit reversed a district court dismissal of a copyright infringement claim based on Cosmetic Ideas' failure to obtain a copyright registration prior to filing the infringement action. Cosmetic Ideas created a piece of costume jewelry that it alleged was copied by the Home Shopping Network (HSN). Cosmetic Ideas sought copyright registration of the necklace on March 6, 2008, and received confirmation of the application on March 12, 2008. On March 27, 2008, Cosmetic Ideas filed suit against IAC, HSN, and other related parties. The district court granted the defendants' motion to dismiss the infringement action for lack of subject matter jurisdiction based on the court's interpretation of section 411 of the Copyright Act of 1976, requiring that a registration be completed with the Copyright Office before an infringement suit is brought.

The court first recognized the U.S. Supreme Court's recent holding in *Reed Elsevier Inc. v. Muchnick,*[12] which found that "[s]ection 411(a)'s registration requirement is a precondition to filing a claim"; it "does not restrict a federal court's subject-matter jurisdiction."[13] Accordingly, this case could not be dismissed for lack of subject matter jurisdiction; however, the court noted that was not the only basis that could support the dismissal.

Because HSN had also filed a 12(b)(6) motion to dismiss for failure to state a claim, the court was required to look further at section 411 and define exactly what "registration" meant in regard to it functioning as a precondition of filing an infringement action. After determining that the plain language of the statute was inconclusive (with some sections pointing toward an application satisfying the registration requirement and others indicating that an accepted registration is required) and noting that the other circuits had split on this particular issue, the court looked to the history and purpose of the Copyright Act of 1976 for an answer.

After reviewing the legislative history, the court decided that the application approach more closely reflected Congress's intent in enacting the Copyright Act. According to the court, the approach of allowing an infringement suit to be filed after an application is filed with the Copyright Office removes unnecessary delays in litigation, assists the goal of removing unnecessary formality in the copyright process, and removes the undesirable scenario of a copyright applicant losing the ability to sue due to an attempt to register right before the statute of limitations would run.

The court ultimately held that a copyright application must be properly filed, but that a decision on that application is not a necessary precondition to filing an infringement suit. The court noted that this holding affords broad copyright protection while also avoiding unfairness and waste of judicial resources. Thus, the district court's judgment dismissing Cosmetic Ideas' action was vacated and reversed.

---

10. *Id.*
11. 606 F.3d 612 (8th Cir. 2010).
12. 559 U.S. ___, 130 S. Ct. 1237 (2010).
13. 130 S. Ct. at 1241.

Communications on Social Media Sites May Be Protected from Discovery under the Stored Communications Act

In *Crispin v. Audigier,*[14] the U.S. District Court for the Central District of California vacated an order of a magistrate judge and reconsidered the decision insofar as it concluded that nonpublic conversations on certain social media sites, including Facebook and MySpace, were not subject to the Stored Communications Act (SCA).

In December 2009, Buckley Crispin filed a lawsuit against Christian Audigier, Christian Audiger, Inc., and other sublicensees, pleading five causes of action, including copyright infringement and breach of an oral contract for the use of Crispin's works of art on garments produced by Audigier. During discovery, the defendants subpoenaed Media Temple, Facebook, and MySpace requesting "Crispin's basic subscriber information, as well as all communications between Crispin and [a tattoo artist], and all communications that referred or related to [the defendants]."[15] Crispin filed an ex parte motion to quash the subpoenas, alleging, among other things, that the subpoenas "sought electronic communications that third-party Internet Service Providers ('ISPs') are prohibited from disclosing under the Stored Communications Act ('SCA')."[16] The magistrate judge concluded that the SCA: (1) applies only to electronic communication services (ECSs); (2) prohibits only voluntary disclosure of information maintained by an ECS; (3) prohibits only disclosure of communications held in electronic storage; and (4) did not apply to Media Temple, Facebook, and MySpace because they were not ESCs, and the subpoenaed materials were not held in electronic storage. Crispin moved to reconsider the magistrate judge's decision as it related to this final point and appealed to the district court.

After establishing the magistrate judge's authority to rule on the motions and the court's authority to "act as an appellate court . . . to 'affirm, modify, vacate, set aside or reverse' the magistrate judge's order,"[17] the court addressed the scope and purpose of the SCA. "The SCA prevents 'providers' of communication services from divulging private communications to certain entities and individuals . . . [and] creates a set of Fourth Amendment-like privacy protections by statute, regulating the relationship between government investigators and service providers in possession of user's private information."[18] It does this through defining different standards of care for an ECS, which is defined as "any service which provides to users thereof the ability to send or receive wire or electronic communications,"[19] and a remote computing service (RCS), which is defined as "the provision to the public of computer storage and processing services by means of an electronic communication system."[20] ECS providers are "prohibited from divulging only 'the contents of a communication while in electronic storage by that service'"; RCS providers may divulge only the contents of the communication if the provider is "authorized to access the

---

14.   No. 09-09509, 2010 WL 2293238 (C.D. Cal. May 26, 2010).
15.   *Id.* at *1.
16.   *Id.*; *see also* Stored Communications Act, 18 U.S.C. §§ 2701–2712 (2010).
17.   *Crispin,* 2010 WL 2293238, at *3 (quoting 28 U.S.C. § 2106).
18.   *Id.* (quoting Quon v. Arch Wireless Operating Co., Inc., 529 F.3d 892 (9th Cir. 2008)).
19.   *Id.* at *4 (citing 18 U.S.C. § 2510 (15) (2002)).
20.   *Id.* (citing 18 U.S.C. § 2711 (2) (2009)). *See also* the use of "electronic communication system" in the definition for RCS (18 U.S.C. § 2510 (2002)).

contents of [the] communications for purposes of providing . . . services other than storage or computer processing."[21]

The court next addressed the issue of whether a party has the right to move to quash the subpoena under the SCA. Noting that a party typically does not have the right to move to quash a third-party subpoena absent a "right or privilege," the court further noted that other courts "have concluded that individuals have standing to move to quash a subpoena seeking personal information protected by the SCA,"[22] and that concluding otherwise might lead to anomalous results. The court further articulated that the SCA has implied privacy protections built into it by Congress without which "a user's entire portfolio of stored communications and data might be fair game for an adversary."[23] Further, the service provider immunity for providing information under the SCA is limited to subpoenas issued under Chapter 121, which includes § 2703.The court concluded that "[g]iven the fact that § 2703(e)'s reference to subpoena is modified by the phrase 'under this chapter,' given the overall structure and purpose of the statute, as well as § 2703(e)'s place in it, and given the supporting case law . . . [Crispin] has standing to move to quash the subpoenas that were issued under the SCA."[24]

The court then addressed the issue of whether to grant Crispin's motion to quash the subpoenas requested by the defendants. The court first noted that the magistrate judge's finding that Media Temple, Facebook, and MySpace were not ECSs is contrary to the law. The magistrate judge narrowly interpreted the definition of an ECS and ignored the private communications features (e.g., private messaging or Web mail) of the site, treating the communications as a public computer bulletin board. Whereas public bulletin boards would not fall under the definition of an ECS, bulletin boards or messaging that is restricted in some fashion would merit protection under the SCA. Citing to various cases, the court found that the communications features of the three sites were adequately restrictive and concluded that each of them was an ECS.

Lastly, the court addressed the nature of the communications. After a thorough analysis, it concluded that "Media Temple's webmail service and Facebook's and MySpace's private messaging" are protected, noting that:

> As respects messages that have not yet been opened, those entities operate as ECS providers and the messages are in electronic storage because they fall within the definition of "temporary, intermediate storage" under § 2510(17)(A). As respects messages that have been opened and retained by Crispin, under the reasoning of *Weaver* and *Flagg*, and the dicta in *Theofel*, the three entities operate as RCS providers providing storage services under § 2702(a)(2).[25]

Both are protectable under the SCA. However, the court found the bulletin-board-like features of two of the services (Facebook wall and MySpace comments) to present a more difficult question. The court ultimately concluded that the legislative history supports the

---

21. *Id.* at *4 (citing 18 U.S.C. § 2702(a)(1)–(2)).
22. *Id.* at *5.
23. *Id.* at *7 (citing William Jeremy Robison, *Free at What Cost? Cloud Computing Privacy Under the Stored Communications Act*, 98 Geo. L.J. 1195, 1208–09 (2010)).
24. *Id.*
25. *Id.* at *13.

protection of such communications and that utilization of the access/privacy settings, even if available to hundreds or thousands of approved users, would indicate that the communications should be treated as sufficiently restricted as required under the SCA.

The court concluded that: (1) as relating to the Web mail and private messaging features provided by Media Temple, Facebook, and MySpace, Crispin's motion to quash the subpoena should be granted; and (2) as relating to the Facebook wall and MySpace comments postings, the magistrate judge should determine whether the general public had access, or whether access was limited to few.

Owner of Foreign Copyrighted Work Not Required to Register Work Prior to Filing U.S. Suit for Infringement

In *Moberg v. 33T LLC*,[26] the U.S. District Court for the District of Delaware held that posting a work created outside the United States by a foreign national on a Web site based outside the United States does not constitute publishing the work simultaneously in the United States and in the foreign country. Noting that this was a case of first impression, the court considered the correlation between the posting of foreign copyrighted works on a foreign Web site and the copyright holder's ability to file suit for infringement in the United States, ultimately concluding that Moberg was not required to register his photographs before filing suit for copyright infringement in a United States court.

Moberg, a citizen of Sweden, was the copyright holder of photographs that were first published on a German Web site that sells art, with the Web site attributing the photograph authorship to Moberg. In filing suit, and without prior registration of his photographs, Moberg alleged that five of his photographs were posted without his authorization on three separate Web sites that sell Web site design templates. The three Web sites were owned by 33T LLC, a Delaware limited liability company, and two French individuals.

Under U.S. copyright law, a "United States work" must be registered for the court to have subject matter jurisdiction over a claim for copyright infringement.[27] In this case, the court first determined whether Moberg's photographs were United States works, considering whether the photographs could be United States works because they were "published" simultaneously in Germany and in the United States when they were posted on the German art Web site. In making this determination, the court evaluated: (1) whether posting the photographs on the Internet was considered "publication," and, if so; (2) whether "publication" on the Internet caused the photographs to be published only in the country where the Internet Web site is located or in every country around the world simultaneously.

In considering how the posting of foreign copyrighted works on a foreign Web site affects the copyright holder's ability to file suit for infringement in the United States under the Copyright Act, the court reviewed the public policy considerations outlined in a law review article discussing the interrelation between the Copyright Act, the Berne Convention, the Internet, and what constitutes "publication."[28] Ultimately, the court held that, even assuming that posting Moberg's photographs on the German Web site constituted

---

26.   666 F. Supp. 2d 415 (D. Del. 2009).

27.   17 U.S.C § 411(a).

28.   *See* Thomas Cotter, *Toward a Functional Definition of Publication in Copyright Law*, 92 MINN. L. REV. 1724, 1749 (2008).

"publication," the photographs were not published simultaneously in the United States as a matter of law.

The district court found that, if publication of a work on a Web site caused that work to be simultaneously published around in the world, such treatment would subject the copyright holder to the formalities existing in the copyright laws of every country that has copyright laws, requiring the author to survey these laws, determine what requirements exist as preconditions to enforcement, and comply with those requirements prior to posting any copyrighted works on the Internet. According to the court, such a result would be contrary to the purposes of the Berne Convention.

Additionally, the court reasoned that transforming foreign copyrighted works into United States works simply by posting them on the Internet would allow American citizens to infringe these works without fear of legal retribution because the majority of foreign works are never registered in the United States. Finally, the court explained that the Copyright Act, in accord with the Berne Convention, provides for protection of foreign works in the United States without requiring the authors to assume any formalities. Finding that Moberg's photographs were not United States works, the court dismissed the motion to dismiss the claim for lack of subject matter jurisdiction and allowed Moberg's copyright infringement claims to stand without registration of the photographs. However, the court left unresolved the issue of whether posting the photographs on the Internet was considered "publication."

The court also denied a motion to dismiss for lack of personal jurisdiction, holding that 33T LLC's Web site targeted American citizens because it was in English, its Web site address ended in the domain name ".us," and it allowed customers to pay using U.S. currency. The court also directed the parties to undertake discovery limited to determining the Web site's contacts with the State of Delaware. However, the court found that Moberg failed to properly effect service upon the individual French defendants when he undertook service by certified mail. The court quashed Moberg's prior attempts at service and directed that he accomplish service pursuant to the other avenues available to him, such as those outlined in the U.S. Department of State circular on the preferred methods of serving an individual in France.

Jurisdiction

Copyright Registration Requirement Not Jurisdictional

In *Reed Elsevier, Inc. v. Muchnick,*[29] the U.S. Supreme Court held that the copyright statute's registration requirement is not jurisdictional. The Court held, "Section 411(a)'s registration requirement is a precondition to filing a claim that does not restrict a federal court's subject-matter jurisdiction."[30] Section 411 of the copyright statute states, "no civil action for infringement of the copyright in any United States work shall be instituted until preregistration or registration of the copyright claim has been made . . . ."[31]

This case originated when the Court was deciding *New York Times Co. v. Tasini,*[32] where six freelance authors sued certain online database owners and print publishers for

---

29.   559 U.S. ___, 130 S. Ct. 1237 (2010).
30.   *Id.* 130 S. Ct. at 1241.
31.   17 U.S.C. § 411(a).
32.   533 U.S. 483 (2001).

copyright infringement because they reproduced the authors' work electronically without permission. Several similar cases were stayed pending the Court's review of the *Tasini* decision by the Second Circuit. When the Court issued its opinion in *Tasini* in 2001, the other cases resumed and were consolidated into this case in the U.S. District Court for the Southern District of New York.

The plaintiffs in this case were also authors of freelance newspaper or magazine articles. Some of the authors had registered their works with the Copyright Office, while others had not. The trial court referred the parties to mediation, and the authors, publishers, electronic database owners, and their insurers negotiated their dispute. More than three years later, they requested that the court certify a class for settlement and approve a settlement agreement. Although lead plaintiff Muchnick and nine other authors objected on various procedural and substantive law grounds, the court granted the motion in an effort "to achieve a global peace in the publishing industry."[33] Muchnick and the nine other authors appealed.

On appeal, the Second Circuit sua sponte asked the parties whether section 411 deprives federal courts of subject matter jurisdiction over copyright infringement claims for unregistered works. The parties asserted that the district court had subject matter jurisdiction to approve the settlement agreement, despite the inclusion of some unregistered works. Nonetheless, the appellate court held that the lower court lacked jurisdiction to certify the class and approve the settlement because some of the claims arose from unregistered works. The panel relied on the assumption that section 411 was jurisdictional.

The parties on both sides disagreed with the Second Circuit. When the U.S. Supreme Court granted certiorari, it appointed an amicus curiae to defend the appellate court's position. Justice Thomas, writing for the majority, noted, "Courts—including this Court—have sometimes mischaracterized claim-processing rules or elements of a cause of action as jurisdictional limitations, particularly when that characterization was not central to the case, and thus did not require close analysis."[34] Recent cases "evince a marked desire to curtail such 'drive-by jurisdictional rulings,' which too easily can miss the 'critical difference[s]' between true jurisdictional conditions and nonjurisdictional limitations on causes of action."[35]

The majority analyzed three main features of section 411. First, the Court examined whether section 411 clearly states that the copyright registration requirement is jurisdictional. The Court concluded it does not. Although the final sentence of section 411 refers to "the court of jurisdiction," it does so only in the context of allowing a federal court to determine the narrow issue of the registrability of a copyright in cases where the Register of Copyrights does not appear. In this way, the statute is explicit that a federal court has jurisdiction to determine registrability, but does not directly speak in section 411 to more general subject matter jurisdiction.

Second, the majority found that subject matter jurisdiction over copyright claims is granted in 28 U.S.C. §§ 1331 and 1338. Neither of those statutory sections contains a registration requirement. Finally, the majority noted that the copyright registration section of the statute contains exceptions. Registration is not required for non-U.S. works,

---

33. *Muchnick*, 130 S. Ct. at 1242 (quoting *In re* Literary Works in Elec. Databases Copyright Litig., 509 F.3d 116, 119 (2d Cir. 2007)).

34. *Id.* at 1243–44.

35. *Id.* at 1244 (internal citation omitted).

for section 106A claims, and for works where registration was refused. Requirements that have such exceptions usually are not ones to which the Court "ascribes jurisdictional significance."[36] In summing up this analysis, Justice Thomas wrote, "Section 411(a) imposes a precondition to filing a claim that is not clearly labeled jurisdictional, is not located in a jurisdiction-granting provision, and admits of congressionally authorized exceptions."[37]

The Court was also dismissive of the amicus arguments. It found that "[a]lthough § 411(a)'s historical treatment as 'jurisdictional' is a factor in the analysis, it is not dispositive" because context is relevant to whether a statute qualifies a requirement as jurisdictional.[38] The Court also declined to apply judicial estoppel, even though some of the petitioners contradicted themselves in their arguments at different procedural stages. There were no "inconsistent court determinations" requiring judicial estoppel because the district court did not rely on the petitioners' view of section 411, and the Court of Appeals also rejected it outright.[39]

The Court concluded that the district court had authority to consider the parties' request to approve their settlement, even though some of the underlying infringement claims were for unregistered works. The Court reversed the Second Circuit and remanded the case.

In the concurring opinion, Justice Ginsburg aimed "to stave off continuing controversy over what qualifies as 'jurisdictional,' and what does not . . . ."[40] Justice Ginsburg reconciled the main precedents relied on by the majority, opining in her view that either Congress must state that a statutory limitation is jurisdictional, or a presiding court must rely on the interpretation of the U.S. Supreme Court itself, not the lower courts, as to whether a requirement has been treated historically as jurisdictional.

Personal Jurisdiction in Copyright Claim Certified to State Court to Decide

In *Penguin Group (USA) Inc. v. American Buddha,*[41] the Second Circuit certified to the New York Court of Appeals the question of whether, in a copyright infringement case, the situs of the injury to determine long-arm jurisdiction was the location of the infringing action, or whether it was the location of the copyright owner's business.

Penguin, a major book publisher, had its principal place of business in New York City. American Buddha was incorporated as an Oregon nonprofit organization, operating an online "library" with 50,000 members. American Buddha made books available to its members online, including four works for which Penguin claimed copyright ownership. American Buddha's Web sites were hosted on servers located in Arizona and Oregon. It told its members that they could download works in its library without infringing any copyrights due to the fair-use and libraries provisions in the Copyright Act.

The U.S. District Court for the Southern District of New York granted American Buddha's motion to dismiss the case under Federal Rule of Civil Procedure 12(b)(2) for

---

36. *Id.* at 1246.
37. *Id.* at 1247.
38. *Id.* at 1248.
39. *Id.* at 1249.
40. *Id.* at 1250.
41. 609 F.3d 30 (2d Cir. 2010).

lack of personal jurisdiction. The only issue on appeal was "whether there is a basis for personal jurisdiction over American Buddha in New York enabling the district court to decide this dispute."[42] The Second Circuit explained: "In litigation arising under federal statutes that do not contain their own jurisdictional provision, such as the Copyright Act[,] . . . federal courts are to apply the personal jurisdiction rules of the forum state . . . provided that those rules are consistent with the requirements of Due Process."[43] There was no need to analyze due process considerations before determining whether there was personal jurisdiction.

The New York long-arm statute allows jurisdiction over an out-of-state defendant whose tortious act outside the state injures a person or property in the state, "'if he . . . expects or should reasonably expect the act to have consequences in the state and derives substantial revenue from interstate or international commerce . . . .'"[44] Both the district court and the Second Circuit recognized that the federal district courts have applied this statute in differing ways in intellectual property cases. Some precedents placed the situs of injury where a plaintiff lost sales; some placed it where a defendant's business was located; and some placed it where the infringing conduct took place. Neither the Second Circuit nor the New York Court of Appeals has previously decided where the situs of injury is in an intellectual property case.

The district court relied on the cases placing the situs of injury at a defendant's place of business because Penguin brought its claim against only American Buddha, not against any members who may have downloaded books from American Buddha's Web site. The district court found that Penguin lost business when American Buddha copied the works in question, an act that took place at the business locations in Arizona and Oregon. Thus, the district court concluded that it lacked personal jurisdiction to hear the matter.

The Second Circuit determined that the legislative history of the New York long-arm statute showed that the intent of the state legislature was to protect New York residents without unduly burdening nonresidents who had only remote connections to the state. The Second Circuit did not find the legislative history helpful, however, because it did not mention commercial tort cases or copyright cases. Thus, the Second Circuit concluded that how the legislature intended the balance to be struck in this context was a question best answered by the New York Court of Appeals.

Both the district court and the Second Circuit acknowledged that the Internet complicated its own analysis, and the Second Circuit suggested the Internet would be a factor in the New York Court of Appeals' analysis. In dicta, the Second Circuit also questioned "whether a copyright—in and of itself an intangible thing—has a physical location for jurisdictional purposes and, if so, what that location is."[45]

The exact question the Second Circuit certified to the New York Court of Appeals was: "In copyright infringement cases, is the situs of injury for purposes of determining long-arm jurisdiction under N.Y. C.P.L.R. § 302(a)(3)(ii) the location of the infringing action or the residence or location of the principal place of business of the copyright holder?"[46]

---

42. *Id.* at 32.
43. *Id.* at 35.
44. *Id.* at 35 (quoting N.Y. C.P.L.R. 302(a)(3)(ii) (McKinney 2010)) (omissions in original).
45. *Id.* at 36 n.4.
46. *Id.* at 42.

The Second Circuit made clear, however, that it did not intend to limit the Court of Appeals by the way in which the question was worded.

Venue

Personal Jurisdiction Established in a Copyright Infringement Action Based on Infringing Web Site Text

In ***Brayton Purcell LLP v. Recordon & Recordon,***[47] the Ninth Circuit upheld a decision by the U.S. District Court for the Northern District of California denying the defendant's motion to dismiss for, inter alia, improper venue. The Ninth Circuit found that the appellant-defendant was subject to personal jurisdiction in the northern district of California where the action was pending; therefore, venue was proper and the district court decision was affirmed.

In July 2004, Recordon, a San Diego-based law firm, contracted with a Web-design company to update its Web site and add an elder law practice section. After the Recordon Web site was updated, Brayton, with the help of "Copyscape," a tool that finds unauthorized use of copyrighted material on the Internet, learned that Recordon's elder law practice section "consisted entirely of material copied verbatim from, and without attribution to, material found in the Brayton Web site's elder law section."[48]

Brayton filed suit against Recordon in the U.S. District Court for the Northern District of California, alleging copyright infringement, unfair competition, false advertising, and common law misrepresentation. Recordon, whose practice was limited to Southern California, filed a motion for dismissal pursuant to Federal Rule of Civil Procedure 12(b)(2) for lack of personal jurisdiction and Federal Rule of Civil Procedure 12(b)(3) for improper venue, and, alternatively, requested a transfer of venue from the northern district to the southern district pursuant to 28 U.S.C. § 1404(a). The district court denied Recordon's motion, and the matter proceeded to arbitration where judgment was awarded in favor of Brayton. Recordon appealed the district court's denial of its motion to dismiss for improper venue but not the entry of judgment of the arbitration award.

Pursuant to 28 U.S.C. § 1400(a), venue in copyright infringement actions is proper "in the district in which the defendant or his agent resides or may be found." The Ninth Circuit interprets this statute to allow venue in any jurisdiction where a defendant "would be amenable to personal jurisdiction if the district were a separate state."[49] The determination regarding whether personal jurisdiction lies is established through a three-prong test aimed establishing minimum contacts between the infringing party and the forum:

(1) The nonresident defendant must purposefully direct his or her activities or consummate some transaction with the forum or resident thereof; or perform some act by which he or she purposefully avails him- or herself of the privilege of conducting activities in the forum, thereby invoking the benefits and protections of its laws;

---

47. 606 F.3d 1124 (9th Cir. 2010).
48. *Id.* at 1127.
49. *Id.* at 1128.

(2) The claim must be one which arises out of or relates to the defendant's forum-related activities; and

(3) The exercise of jurisdiction must comport with fair play and substantial justice, i.e., must be reasonable.[50]

Only the first prong was at issue in the appeal, which is satisfied by either purposeful availment, most often applied in contract suits, or purposeful direction, most often applied in tort suits. Because a copyright infringement action often is characterized as a tort, the court evaluated purposeful direction by applying a three-part test to determine whether Recordon: "(1) committed an intentional act, (2) expressly aimed at the [northern district of California], (3) causing harm that the defendant knows is likely to be suffered in the [northern district of California]."[51]

The court found that the "intentional act" requirement was easily satisfied because Recordon had committed an intentional act when it copied Brayton's elder law section on its Web site that infringed Brayton's copyright. Although maintenance of a passive Web site alone cannot satisfy the second requirement—express aiming toward the northern district—the court found that Recordon's actions satisfied this requirement because it "individually targeted [Brayton] by making commercial use of [Brayton's] copyrighted materials for the purpose of competing with [Brayton] for elder abuse clients."[52] Finally, the court found that the third requirement, "foreseeable harm," was satisfied because it was foreseeable that Brayton would be harmed by Recordon's infringement of its copyrighted Web site text, including harm to its business reputation and goodwill, and decreased business and profits.[53] Further, it was foreseeable that some of this harm would occur in the northern district, where Brayton did business. The court concluded that Recordon satisfied the "purposeful direction" prong for specific personal jurisdiction and held that Recordon was subject to personal jurisdiction in the northern district of California.

The dissent argued that Recordon's conduct was not "expressly aimed" at the northern district of California. Instead, the dissent argued that the evidence showed that Recordon's elder law Web site was aimed only at the southern district:

> The firm operated exclusively out of Southern California, practiced entirely in Southern California, and had never had any clients or legal work in the Northern District. Accordingly, it is beyond dispute that the 'elder law' material on Recordon & Recordon's website was directed toward clients or prospective clients in Southern California exclusively.[54]

The dissent found that these facts precluded a finding of express aiming for jurisdiction purposes.

---

50. *Id.*

51. *Id.*

52. *Id.* at 1129. The court further stated that "[w]hile Recordon claims its practice is limited to Southern California, nothing on its website indicates to potential clients that Recordon's practice is so limited. In addition, Kathy and Stephen Recordon are licensed to practice throughout the state of California, enabling them to compete with Brayton within the Forum." *Id.* at 1130.

53. *Id.* at 1131.

54. *Id.* at 1132.

INFRINGEMENT

Actionable Conduct

District Court May Consider the Question of Noninfringement in a Copyright Action on a Rule 12(b)(6) Motion

In **Peter F. Gaito Architecture, LLC v. Simone Development Corp.,**[55] the Second Circuit held that "a district court may consider the question of non-infringement in a copyright action on a Rule 12(b)(6) motion to dismiss," that "the district court properly determined non-infringement as a matter of law, and did not err in concluding that plaintiffs' Amended Complaint," and that the documents incorporated therein failed to allege substantial similarity between the defendants' work and the protectable elements of the plaintiff's work.[56]

In August 2004, the City of New Rochelle issued a Request for Development Proposals to identify a real estate development team for a mixed-use development project (the Church Street Project). On November 1, 2004, the plaintiffs together with certain of the defendants submitted a joint proposal. On March 11, 2005, New Rochelle awarded them the Church Street Project for an estimated price of $175 million. Thereafter, the plaintiffs prepared certain schematics for the Church Street Project, and, on April 5, 2005, Gaito registered the designs with the U.S. Copyright Office. Based on those designs, the defendant, Simone Church Street LLC, "entered into a Memorandum of Understanding with [New Rochelle] as the developer for the [Church Street] Project."[57] In about June 2005, a dispute arose between the plaintiffs and certain of the defendants, and the defendants Joseph Simone, Simone Development Corp., Simone Church Street LLC, Thomas Metallo, and TNS Development Group Ltd. terminated their relationship with the plaintiffs and retained the defendants, SLCE Architects, LLP (SLCE), an architectural and planning firm, and Saccardi & Schiff, Inc., a planning firm, to work on the Church Street Project.

The amended complaint alleged that the defendants unlawfully used the plaintiffs' copyrighted designs for the Church Street Project without the plaintiffs' permission, and that SLCE developed a redesign of the project largely based on the plaintiffs' designs. The Amended Complaint asserted violations of the Copyright Act, 17 U.S.C. § 101 *et seq.*, and claims for quantum meruit and unjust enrichment under New York state law. The plaintiffs attached to the Amended Complaint as exhibits both the plaintiffs' designs and SLCE's redesigns. On November 19, 2008, the defendants moved to dismiss the action pursuant to Federal Rule of Civil Procedure 12(b)(6) on the grounds that, even if the defendants had access to the plaintiffs' designs, there was no substantial similarity between the protectable elements of the designs and SLCE's redesigns.

On May 22, 2009, the district court granted the motion to dismiss. The district court assumed actual copying by the defendants for purposes of the motion and concluded that there was no substantial similarity between the protectable elements of the plaintiffs' design and SLCE's redesign. The district court declined to exercise supplemental jurisdiction over the plaintiffs' remaining state law claims and dismissed those claims without prejudice.

---

55. 602 F.3d 57 (2d Cir. 2010).
56. *Id.* at 59.
57. *Id.* at 60 (internal quotation marks omitted).

The Second Circuit reviewed de novo the district court's dismissal of the Amended Complaint for failure to state a claim upon which relief may be granted. The Second Circuit noted that, to establish copyright infringement, a plaintiff must show that: (1) the defendant copied the plaintiff's work; and (2) the copying was illegal because a substantial similarity existed between the protectable elements of the plaintiff's work and the defendant's work. Like the district court, the Second Circuit assumed for purposes of the motion to dismiss that actual copying by the defendants occurred.

The Second Circuit first considered a question it had not directly addressed before: whether a district court may decide the issue of substantial similarity on a motion to dismiss. The Second Circuit noted that the test for infringement of a copyright is vague by necessity and is traditionally reserved for the trier of fact, and that the question of substantial similarity is one of the most difficult to answer in copyright law and generally presents a very close question of fact. However, the Second Circuit found that the issue of substantial similarity is not exclusively reserved for the jury, and that it had recognized, in certain circumstances, that it is appropriate for the district court to decide the question as a matter of law. The Second Circuit noted that it had repeatedly recognized that a district court may decide the issue of noninfringement as a matter of law "'either because the similarity between the two works concerns only non-copyrightable elements of the plaintiff's work, or because no reasonable jury, properly instructed, could find that the two works are substantially similar.'"[58]

The Second Circuit held that the same principles govern when the question of substantial similarity is raised on a motion to dismiss at the pleadings stage. Although certain cases may require the aid of discovery or expert testimony to resolve the question of substantial similarity, generally, when a court decides whether two works are substantially similar in copyright actions, no discovery or fact-finding is necessary because the works supersede and control any contrary description of them, and a court need only compare the two works. Therefore, when the works at issue are attached to the complaint, as they were in this case, it is appropriate for the district court to examine the similarity between the two works on a motion to dismiss because the court has all the evidence necessary to decide the issue. The Second Circuit noted that this approach was consistent with its previous precedents, the position of many of the district courts in the second circuit, and other circuits.

Having determined that the district court could consider the question of substantial similarity on a motion to dismiss, the Second Circuit examined de novo the issue of whether the district court erred in finding no substantial similarity. The Second Circuit stated that, under the "standard test for substantial similarity" or "'ordinary observer test,' we ask whether 'an average lay observer would recognize the alleged copy as having been appropriated from the copyrighted work.'"[59] However, the similarity between the two works must involve the expression of ideas, not only the ideas themselves, and, where there are both protectable and unprotectable elements of a work, only the protectable elements should be compared. Moreover, the comparison should focus on the "'total concept and overall feel'" and "on whether the alleged infringer has misappropriated 'the

---

58. *Id.* at 63 (quoting Warner Bros. Inc. v. Am. Broad. Cos., 720 F.2d 231, 240 (2d Cir. 1983) (internal quotation marks and emphasis omitted)).
59. *Id.* at 66 (quoting Knitwaves, Inc. v. Lollytogs Ltd., 71 F.3d 996, 1002 (2d Cir. 1995) (internal quotation marks omitted)).

original way in which the author has "selected, coordinated, and arranged" the elements of his or her work."[60]

Based on these principles, the Second Circuit found "an utter lack of similarity between the two designs": (1) whereas the plaintiffs' overall design of the Church Street Project consisted of three structures and included a series of townhouses, the defendants' redesign consisted of one structure and no townhouses; (2) whereas both designs incorporated pedestrian plazas, the location of the plazas, connection between the plazas and other elements of the design, and shape of the plazas were different; and (3) "critically," it was "patent that the overall visual impressions of the two designs [were] entirely different."[61]

The Second Circuit also rejected the thirty-five alleged similarities set forth in the Amended Complaint as ideas and concepts that were not copyrightable as protectable expression of ideas. These unprotectable ideas included the placement and inclusion of certain features in the Church Street Project as well as the orientation of the project, specific parameters, and specifications for the project. The Second Circuit found that the components and features that the plaintiffs alleged the defendants had misappropriated, such as "'architecture that was light, airy, transparent, [and] made of glass with hints of traditional materials'" were "generalized concepts . . . 'common to countless other urban high-rise residential developments.'"[62] As to the copying of the placement of certain elements and features, this constituted no more than "'generalized notions of where to place functional elements,'" which was not protectable.[63] In addition, the alleged infringement of various design parameters, even in the aggregate, constituted ideas that were not protectable expression, and the inclusion of such parameters in the Memorandum of Understanding did not transform such ideas into protectable expression.

The Second Circuit concluded that the key question was not whether the plaintiffs' designs as a whole were entitled to protection, but rather whether the defendants misappropriated the protectable elements of those designs. The Second Circuit affirmed the district court's dismissal of the federal copyright claim because no substantial similarity existed between the defendants' work and protectable elements of the plaintiffs' work; therefore, the Amended Complaint failed to "state a claim to relief that is plausible on its face."[64] In addition, there was no error in the district court's decision not to exercise supplemental jurisdiction over the plaintiffs' state law claims.

Evidence of Web Site and Booth Display Does Not Prove That Defendant Had Access to the Copyrighted Work

In *Art Attacks Ink, LLC v. MGA Entertainment Inc.,*[65] the Ninth Circuit affirmed the district court's grant of judgment for MGA. Art Attacks filed suit for copyright, trade dress, and trademark infringement. A jury found for MGA on the trademark claim but could not reach a verdict on the remaining claims. Thereafter, the district court granted MGA's Federal Rules of Civil Procedure § 50(b) motion for JMOL. The Ninth Circuit

---

60. *Id.* (citations omitted).
61. *Id.* at 66–67.
62. *Id.* at 68.
63. *Id.* (quoting Attia v. Soc'y of the N.Y. Hosp., 201 F.3d 50, 55 (2d Cir. 1999)).
64. *Id.* at 61 (citation omitted).
65. 581 F.3d 1138 (9th Cir. 2009).

found that no reasonable jury could have concluded that there was more than a "bare possibility" that MGA had access to Art Attacks' Spoiled Brats designs.

Art Attacks is a small family business that developed a Spoiled Brats collection featuring cartoonish, predominantly female characters with oversized eyes, disproportionately large heads and feet, makeup, and bare midriffs. Art Attacks copyrighted the Spoiled Brats characters in 1996. It displayed its designs on its Web site and in booths at county fairs, Wal-Mart stores in Arizona and California, the Camp Pendleton Exchange, conventions, amusement centers, and other malls. Art Attacks did not advertize in broadcast or print media. In 2001, MGA began selling "Bratz" dolls, which, like Art Attacks' copyrighted designs, featured large eyes, heavy makeup, bare midriffs, and oversized eyes, heads, and feet.

Because there was no direct evidence of copying, Art Attacks had the burden of showing that MGA had "access" to its work.[66] To prove access, Art Attacks had to show that there was a reasonable possibility, not just a bare possibility, that MGA had a chance to view the copyrighted work. Access is a fact-based showing and may be proven either: (1) by circumstantial evidence establishing a chain of events linking the copyrighted work and alleged infringer's access; or (2) by showing that the work had been widely disseminated.

Art Attacks produced evidence that it displayed the Spoiled Brats designs at the Los Angeles County Fair before MGA began marketing the Bratz dolls, and that an MGA employee who designed the text of the Bratz mark used on doll packaging attended the Los Angeles County Fair. However, there was no evidence that the MGA employee saw the Art Attacks booth or even visited the fair before MGA began to market its doll. Air Attacks did not attend the Los Angeles County Fair until 1998, and MGA began marketing the Bratz dolls in 2002, making the relevant period from only 1998–2001. The court concluded that Art Attacks did not show a chain of events sufficient to demonstrate that MGA had access to copyrighted material.[67]

The court was similarly unpersuaded that Art Attacks had widely disseminated its copyrighted work.[68] Art Attacks argued that its work was widely disseminated in three ways: (1) on the Art Attacks booth itself; (2) on Spoiled Brats T-shirts that served as "walking billboards;" and (3) via the Internet. Although Art Attacks displayed Spoiled Brats images in its fair booths and store kiosks, and millions of people attended the relevant county fairs, there was no evidence showing how many people noticed the booth and viewed the Spoiled Brats displays. The Spoiled Brats design was not the only design displayed at the booth and appeared in a binder and on the walls. Additionally, testimony of Art Attacks' owner that she saw one person wearing a Spoiled Brats shirt in public did not create more than a "bare possibility" that MGA had access to the designs. Finally, the company's image-heavy Web site took two full minutes to fully load. To see the Spoiled Brats designs, one of several images on the page, a viewer had to scroll down on the page or click through the main Web site to a Spoiled Brats-specific page to obtain a mail-in order form. The Web site also lacked "metatags" that would have identified the Web site to search engines, making it unlikely that someone searching for Spoiled Brats would find

66. *Id.*at 1143.
67. *Id.* at 1144.
68. *Id.* at 1144–45.

the Web page. The court concluded such a limited Web site could not have widely disseminated the copyrighted Spoiled Brats material.[69]

Copy Shop Directly Liable for Copyright Infringement of Coursepacks Copied by Students

In ***Blackwell Publishing, Inc. v. Excel Research Group,***[70] the U.S. District Court for the Eastern District of Michigan granted a motion for partial summary judgment on copyright infringement brought by several publishers, agreeing that the defendant copy shop's practice of lending coursepacks to students and providing them with photocopying equipment constituted copyright infringement. Rather than finding the copy shop (Excel) liable for contributory infringement, the court determined that Excel was directly liable for copyright infringement of the thirty-three coursepacks at issue, even though the students performed the actual copying of the coursepacks.

The court began its analysis with a review of the coursepack copying process. In summary, professors at the University of Michigan submitted the contents of the coursepacks to Excel, which maintained master copies of each coursepack. Excel numbered the pages by hand and took steps to ensure good copy quality, which sometimes required recopying the original source. Upon request from a student, an Excel staff member would provide the master copy to the student, who then would make a copy using Excel's copy machines and return the coursepack once done. In addition to paying Excel a fee, each student would sign a form stating that the student was enrolled in the class and that the student was making the copy for educational purposes. However, no copyright permission was obtained from the publishers, and Excel paid no copyright fees to them. As a result, the publishers sued, claiming that Excel violated their right of reproduction and distribution under section 106 of the Copyright Act.

In evaluating the facts of the case, the court found that four of the thirty-three works at issue were subject to a license agreement that authorized students and other members of the University community to print and download materials. However, the court explained that the license agreement did not authorize the copying of copyrighted material by Excel and did not provide the students with the ability to make copies at a commercial establishment where a third party profited from the copying. The remaining twenty-nine works were not covered by any license agreement; thus, Excel was not permitted to make copies of these works either. Rejecting the argument that Excel merely sells access to a copy machine, the court therefore held that Excel was not authorized to make copies of the coursepacks and was liable for infringement.

The court also rejected the argument that the students were the purported infringers because they performed the actual copying. Instead, the court found that Excel was the source of reproduction because it controlled the entire copying process. Specifically, Excel maintained an inventory of copyrighted materials given to it by professors, and students wishing to access the copyrighted material had to visit Excel to obtain it. As part of the process, Excel gave the coursepacks to the students to copy and accepted payment for the transaction. Additionally, Excel owned and supplied all of the tools of reproduction—the venue, the copy machines, the paper, and the utilities. Excel staff members also were

---

69. *Id.* at 1145.
70. 661 F. Supp. 2d 786 (E.D. Mich. 2009).

available to assist students in the copying process and provided binding services if requested by the students. Notably, the court distinguished this process from a scenario in which a student obtains a coursepack from a friend (or another third party) and makes a copy on Excel premises as not mere student copying. As a result, the court held that Excel engaged in the unauthorized distribution of the publishers' works when: (1) it gave the coursepacks to the students for copying; and (2) when the students paid for the copying of the coursepacks.

In evaluating Excel's fair-use defense, the court noted that this case was not seriously distinguishable from *Princeton University Press v. Michigan Document Services, Inc.*[71] In that case, the Sixth Circuit found that a copy shop's sale of coursepacks to students at the University of Michigan without permission from the copyright holders did not constitute a fair use. Reasoning that "copyright law should not turn on who presses the start button on a copier,"[72] the court in this case evaluated Excel's fair-use defense and found that all four factors favored the publishers. First, the court found that Excel's use was for-profit and commercial because, even though students were performing the actual copying, they paid Excel for the privilege of making the copy. Second, the court noted that there was no dispute as to the creative nature of the material. Next, the court, like the *Michigan Document Services* court, held that the substantiality of the material taken from the copyrighted works was presumptively high, based on the professors' selection and use of the excerpts in their required course materials. In analyzing the fourth factor, the court found that Excel adversely impacted the marketplace by charging less than competitors for coursepacks because it did not have to pay royalty fees to the publishers. Finally, the court declined to examine other nonstatutory factors, explaining that the issue was whether Excel violated copyright law and not whether free distribution of educational works has social benefits. Thus, the court held that Excel was directly liable for copyright infringement and granted partial summary judgment in favor of the publishers.

First-Sale Doctrine Not Applicable to Defend Copyright Infringement

In *John Wiley & Sons, Inc. v. Kirtsaeng*,[73] the U.S. District Court for the Southern District of New York held that importers of textbooks manufactured and sold abroad could not assert the first-sale doctrine as a defense to infringement of the publishers' distribution rights. Wiley alleged that Kirtsaeng and his associates purchased foreign editions of Wiley textbooks abroad and resold them in the United States over the Internet without Wiley's authorization. The court found that the importation prohibition in section 602(a)(1) of the Copyright Act applied, despite a first sale abroad, where the goods were lawfully made abroad rather than in the United States.

The court first looked to the language in section 109(a) of the Copyright Act, which applies to copies "lawfully made under this title." Using the dictionary definition of "under," the court reasoned that the imported goods must be manufactured "subject to" or "with the authorization of" the Copyright Act in order for section 109(a) to apply. How-

---

71.   99 F.3d 1381 (6th Cir. 1996) (en banc) (determining that it was not a fair use when a copy shop sold coursepacks to students at the University of Michigan without permission of the copyright holders).

72.   *Blackwell,* 661 F. Supp. 2d at 794.

73.   No. 08 Civ. 7834, 2009 WL 3364037 (S.D.N.Y. Oct. 19, 2009).

ever, the court found that there was still some ambiguity as to the relationship between "made" and "under this title." Thus, the court turned to statutory context, legislative history, and public policy considerations to resolve the issue.

Ultimately, the court was persuaded by the U.S. Supreme Court's dicta in *Quality King Distributors v. L'Anza Research International*.[74] In *Quality King*, the Court held that the importation of goods subject to U.S. copyright cannot constitute copyright infringement when the goods are manufactured in the United States, sold by the U.S. copyright owner to an entity abroad, and subsequently reimported into the United States. As such, once the U.S. copyright owner sold its goods, whether in the United States or otherwise, the first-sale doctrine protected the subsequent owner of the goods from liability under the Act. The Court then suggested that it would limit section 109(a)'s coverage to U.S. manufactured goods.[75] Despite opining that this limitation may be an imperfect solution, the district court held that section 109(a) does not cover foreign-manufactured goods, and the first-sale doctrine could not be applied should Wiley establish its case.

The court also considered the defenses of waiver and lack of standing. The court found that Wiley did not waive its rights to exclusive distribution in the United States when it assigned the Asian copyright in an agreement that did not prohibit importation into the United States, and that the assignment did not constitute a "first sale" pursuant to section 109(a). Rejecting the argument that Wiley lacked standing to bring the lawsuit, the court explained that Wiley is still the owner of the U.S. copyright and has standing to sue Kirtsaeng for infringement, despite its assignment of Asian copyrights to Wiley Asia.

First-Sale Doctrine Not Applicable to Copies of Copyrighted Work Manufactured Abroad

In ***Pearson Education, Inc. v. Liu***,[76] the U.S. District Court for the Southern District of New York denied the defendants' motion to dismiss a copyright infringement lawsuit. Pearson, along with other publishers of copyrighted textbooks, brought an action against the defendants seeking a permanent injunction to stop the defendants from selling foreign editions of copyrighted textbooks in the United States. In response to the suit, the defendants filed a motion to dismiss, arguing that the first-sale doctrine shielded them from liability. Although the court read section 109(a) of the Copyright Act as equally applicable to U.S.- and foreign-manufactured goods, it nonetheless refused to allow a first-sale defense in light of the U.S. Supreme Court's dicta in *Quality King Distributors v. L'Anza Research International*.[77]

In undertaking its analysis, the district court noted that two conditions must be satisfied for the first-sale doctrine to apply under section 109(a). First, the person claiming the doctrine's protection must be the owner of the copy of the work. Second, the copy must have been "lawfully made under this title." The interpretation of this phrase, however, is divided among courts. On one hand, some courts have held that, because a U.S. copyright holder cannot sue a foreign manufacturer for violating his or her exclusive right to reproduce a copyrighted work, a copyrighted work is not "lawfully made under this title"

---

74. 523 U.S. 135 (1998).
75. *Id.* at 145 n.14.
76. 656 F. Supp. 2d 407 (S.D.N.Y. 2009).
77. 523 U.S. 135 (1998).

unless it is also legally manufactured in the United States. On the other hand, other courts have implicitly suggested that "lawfully made under this title" does not refer to the place a copy is manufactured, but rather to the lawfulness of manufacturing the work under U.S. copyright law. Here, the court found that nothing in the language of section 109(a) or "the history, purposes, and policies of the first-sale doctrine limits the doctrine to copies of a work manufactured in the United States."[78]

Although it did not directly resolve the question, the U.S. Supreme Court had previously suggested, in dicta, that the first-sale doctrine does not apply to copies of a copyrighted work manufactured abroad. In *Quality King*, the Court specifically considered facts highly similar to those presented in this case—that is, a situation in which books manufactured by a foreign publisher for sale abroad are imported into, and distributed within, the United States without the consent of the U.S. copyright holder. In these circumstances, the Court expressed the view that the U.S. copyright holder is entitled to maintain an infringement action against the importer and that the first-sale doctrine does not apply.[79]

Here, the district court, in deference to the U.S. Supreme Court, held that the first-sale doctrine does not apply to copies of a copyrighted work manufactured abroad. Therefore, because the foreign editions were manufactured abroad, Liu did not acquire ownership of copies "lawfully made under this title," and the first-sale doctrine defense did not apply to shield the defendants from liability in this case.

Substantial Similarity

No Substantial Similarity between Pacifier Holders from Baby Buddies and Toys "R" Us

In **Baby Buddies, Inc. v. Toys "R" Us, Inc.,**[80] Baby Buddies claimed that Toys "R" Us infringed Baby Buddies' copyrighted pacifier holder. Toys "R" Us moved for summary judgment on the copyright claim, and the district court granted the motion.

The Eleventh Circuit affirmed summary judgment for Toys "R" Us on the copyright claim. By way of background, Baby Buddies sold a pacifier holder with a design that was registered with the Copyright Office. The pacifier holder included a molded plastic bear with a metal clip and ribbon bow attached to its back. A piece of ribbon, several inches long, connected the bear with a snap that could be looped through a hole in a pacifier. Toys "R" Us sold Baby Buddies' pacifier holder for some time, but then decided to produce and market its own pacifier holder. Toys "R" Us sold both products for a time, but ultimately phased out Baby Buddies' product.

The court stated that for Baby Buddies to prevail on its claim for copyright infringement, it must establish: (1) ownership of a valid copyright; and (2) copying of constituent

---

78.   *Liu,* 656 F. Supp. 2d at 415.

79.   *Quality King,* 523 U.S. at 148 (although the case involved the first-sale doctrine in a "round trip" transaction—in which the product was manufactured in the United States, sold in a foreign country, and then imported back into the United States—the U.S. Supreme Court, as an example, discussed the application of the first-sale doctrine to copies of a copyrighted work that are manufactured in a foreign country).

80.   611 F.3d 1308 (11th Cir. 2010).

elements of the work that are original. Toys "R" Us conceded the first element for purposes of its summary judgment motion. For the second element, a plaintiff must prove either direct or indirect copying. When attempting to establish indirect copying, a plaintiff must show a "striking similarity" between the copyrighted work and the accused work, unless the defendant had direct access to the copyrighted work, in which case the plaintiff's burden is reduced to showing the works are "substantially similar."

Toys "R" Us conceded that it had access to Baby Buddies' copyrighted pacifier holder; therefore, the court applied the "substantially similar" test where the court asks whether an average lay observer would recognize the alleged copy as having been appropriated from the copyrighted work. The Eleventh Circuit then turned to the question of determining which elements of the Baby Buddies pacifier holder are protected under its copyright. Looking to the Copyright Act, the court found that, although copyright protection extends to pictorial, graphic, and sculptural works, protection extends to works of artistic craftsmanship insofar as their form, but not their mechanical or utilitarian aspects, is concerned. Furthermore, "the design of a useful article . . . shall be considered a pictorial, graphic, or sculptural work only if, and only to the extent that, such design incorporates pictorial, graphic, or sculptural features that can be identified separately from, and are capable of existing independently of, the utilitarian aspects of the article."[81]

The court then noted that, as defined in the statute, a useful article, as a whole, does not receive copyright protection, but any constituent design elements that can be physically or conceptually separated from the underlying article can receive copyright protection. Additionally, the court stated that copyright protection extends only to the original elements of expression in a work.

After finding that the copyrighted pacifier holder is a useful article, the court assessed whether any potentially copyrightable elements are conceptually or physically separable from the utilitarian aspects of the pacifier holder. The court determined that the bear and bow were physically separable from the rest of the pacifier holder, which is not eligible for copyright protection. These noncopyrightable elements include, together, the ribbon tether, clip, and snap.

The court then applied the substantial similarity test separately to each copyrighted element of the Baby Buddies pacifier holder (i.e., the bear and bow). The Eleventh Circuit prefaced this portion of its analysis by acknowledging that, at the most narrow, focused level, two works will almost always be distinguishable and, at the broadest level of abstraction, they will almost always appear identical. The court also stressed that, although its analysis included identifying and comparing the protected expressive features of the two works, the purpose of the analysis was to determine whether the work's protected expression has been copied, not simply to count the number of similarities and differences. The court noted that copyright protection does not extend to the idea of a sculpted teddy bear.

After examining the color, shape, and arrangement of the bear and ribbon bow, the court concluded that there are almost no similarities between the two pacifier holders beyond the general ideas of including a teddy bear, a ribbon bow, and a pastel-based color scheme on a baby's pacifier holder. Consequently, the court affirmed summary judgment against Baby Buddies on the copyright infringement claim, holding that no reasonable jury could conclude that the pacifier holders are substantially similar at the protected

---

81. *Id.* at 1315–16 (quoting 17 U.S.C. § 101).

level. The court further held that, although Baby Buddies has the right to prevent others from copying its creative expression, it cannot prevent others from expressing similar ideas differently. The court noted that, if Baby Buddies has found the most appealing way to express an idea, the marketplace will reward it accordingly.

Different Substantial Similarity Standards for Federal Copyright and California Implied-in-Fact Contracts

In *Benay v. Warner Bros. Entertainment, Inc.*,[82] the plaintiff brothers claimed, among other things, copyright infringement and breach of an implied-in-fact contract relating to a screenplay. They had pitched and provided the screenplay to the defendants, who later released a movie with the same title as the screenplay, *The Last Samurai*. The U.S. District Court for the Central District of California granted the motion for summary judgment on both claims subsequently filed by the defendants. The Ninth Circuit affirmed the grant of summary judgment on the copyright claim, but reversed and remanded the summary judgment grant on the claim for breach of implied-in-fact contract.[83]

The appellate panel reviewed the Benays' copyright claim de novo, viewing the evidence in the light most favorable to the plaintiffs. To prevail on their copyright claim, the Benays had the burden of demonstrating: (1) ownership of a valid copyright; and (2) copying of constituent elements of the work that are original. Warner Bros. did not deny that the Benays had a valid copyright; rather, the focus of the copyright claim in the summary judgment motion involved the second element.

The panel explained that summary judgment was appropriate if no reasonable juror could find "substantial similarity" of ideas and expression.[84] Absent evidence of direct copying, the plaintiffs have the burden of proving substantial similarity under both an extrinsic test and an intrinsic test. The panel further explained that the extrinsic test is an objective comparison of specific expressive elements. The intrinsic test is a subjective comparison that focuses on whether an ordinary, reasonable audience would find the works substantially similar in the total concept and feel of the works. In its review, the panel examined only the extrinsic test because the intrinsic test is left to the trier of fact.

According to the court, a plaintiff's burden of proof is lowered if the defendant had access to the copyrighted work. This is called the "inverse ratio" rule.[85] The Ninth Circuit assumed this rule without deciding whether it applied.

Turning to its substantial similarity analysis, the court held that the most important similarities between the screenplay and film involved unprotectable elements, such as historical facts, familiar stock scenes, and characteristics that flow naturally from the basic plot premise of the two works. An examination of the protectable elements—including plot themes, dialogue, mood, setting, pace, characters, and sequence of events—exposed many more differences than similarities. Based on this analysis, the Ninth Circuit concluded that the protected elements of the screenplay, standing alone, were not sufficiently similar to satisfy the extrinsic test.

---

82.   607 F.3d 620 (9th Cir. 2010).
83.   *Id.* at 622.
84.   *Id.* at 624 (quoting Kouf v. Walt Disney Pictures & Television, 16 F.3d 1042, 1045 (9th Cir. 1994)).
85.   *Id.* at 625.

The court then addressed the Benays' claim of breach of an implied-in-fact contract under California law, noting that "contract law, whether through express or implied-in-fact contracts, is the most significant remaining state-law protection for literary or artistic ideas."[86]

According to the court, contract law claims for the protection of ideas are not preempted by federal copyright law because they allege an extra element that changes the nature of the action. That extra element is the agreement between the parties that the defendant will pay for the use of the plaintiff's ideas, independent of any protection offered by federal copyright law.[87]

To prevail on a breach of an implied-in-fact contract claim, the Benays had the burden of establishing that: (1) they submitted the screenplay for sale to the defendants; (2) they conditioned the use of the screenplay on payment; (3) the defendants knew or should have known of the condition; (4) the defendants voluntarily accepted the screenplay; (5) the defendants actually used the screenplay; and (6) the screenplay had value.[88]

Warner Bros. argued three alternative grounds for affirming the district court's grant of summary judgment, including the claims that: (1) the Benays could not establish that Warner Bros. actually used the screenplay; (2) the California two-year statute of limitations had passed; and (3) there was no privity of contract between all but one co-defendant.

Regarding Warner Bros.' first challenge, the court noted that, in the case of implied-in-fact contracts (as opposed to explicit contracts with the terms spelled out), "the weight of California authority is that there must be 'substantial similarity' between plaintiff's idea and defendant's production to render defendant liable."[89]

The standard for evaluating substantial similarity under California contract law, however, differs from the substantial similarity standard in federal copyright law. The court stated that, although the requirement of substantial similarity in both copyright law and implied-in-fact contract claims means that "copying less than substantial material is non-actionable," "it does not follow that plaintiffs in idea-submission cases must prove substantial similarity of *copyright-protected* elements."[90] Therefore, a holding that the screenplay and movie are not substantially similar for copyright infringement does not preclude a finding of substantially similarity for purposes of implied-in-fact contract under California law.[91]

Analyzing the Benays' screenplay and Warner Bros.' movie, the court noted a number of similarities, but declined to decide whether, and to what degree, the similarities were due to the use of the screenplay. The court concluded that there might be evidence from which a reasonable fact finder could find unauthorized use and remanded the implied-in-fact contract claim to the district court.

---

86. *Id.* at 629 (noting that other state-law protections, such as those against plagiarism, have been preempted by federal law).

87. *Id.*

88. *Id.*

89. *Id.* at 631 (quoting 4 Nimmer § 19D.08[A] (citing Kurlan v. Columbia Broad. Sys., Inc., 40 Cal. 2d 799, 809, 256 P.2d 962 (1953); Sutton v. Walt Disney Prods., 118 Cal. App. 2d 598, 603, 258 P.2d 519 (1953); Whitfield v. Lear, 751 F.2d 90, 93 (2d Cir.1984))).

90. *Id.*

91. *Id.*

In Warner Bros.' second challenge regarding the tolling of the statute of limitations, the defendants argued that the date of accrual began earlier than two years from the release of the film, the date that the Benays filed suit. The court noted that the date of accrual depends on the nature of a defendant's obligation, if any, to the plaintiff. It held that in implied-in-fact contact cases, California courts generally assume that the accrual date is the date on which the work is released to the general public.

The Ninth Circuit declined to address the question of whether the required privity of contract between the Benays and Warner Bros. existed and noted that the Benays did not have the opportunity to respond to this claim in the lower court. Thus, the court affirmed the district court's summary judgment grant for the defendants on the copyright infringement claim and reversed the district court's summary judgment grant for the defendants on the breach of implied-in-fact contract claim.

Stock Scènes à Faire *Did Not Prove Substantial Similarity*

In *Frye v. YMCA Camp Kitaki*,[92] the Eighth Circuit affirmed the U.S. District Court of Nebraska's conclusion that the YMCA did not infringe Frye's copyright. In particular, the Eighth Circuit held that the district court's finding that the parties' two plays were not substantially similar was not clearly erroneous.

In 1986, Frye developed a play into an adventure trail activity called *Kastleland* for the YMCA's Camp Kitaki. It was performed there from 1987 through 1998, with variations in the production over time. The play started and ended at a campfire. It included stock medieval characters, such as a bard and a knight. The young campers also participated in a quest in which they undertook seven challenges (swordplay, target shooting, etc.) to earn power words ("courage," "self-control," etc.) and defeat seven dragons.

In 1998, Frye ended his association with the YMCA, and they arrived at a settlement agreement and stipulated judgment in federal court. The YMCA agreed not to infringe on Frye's copyright in *Kastleland*; Frye agreed in return not to enter YMCA property without permission.

In 2005, Camp Kitaki's new director, Russ Koos, wrote a medieval-themed adventure trail play called *KnightQuest*, which was first used at the camp in 2007. *KnightQuest* also started and ended at a campfire. Its characters included a wizard and four "shadow lords." The wizard involved the campers in a quest in which the campers undertook four trials (swordplay, target shooting, etc.) to learn YMCA core values (truthfulness, respect, etc.), become knights, and reform the shadow lords.

In 2008, Frye filed a complaint in the district court, which included a motion to hold the YMCA in contempt for violating the 1998 stipulated judgment. The district court denied the motion for contempt and dismissed Frye's lawsuit.

On appeal, the Eighth Circuit limited its review to the district court's finding that *Kastleland* and *KnightQuest* were not substantially similar. Determining substantial similarity involved a two-part test: (1) an extrinsic test, focused on "objective similarities in the details of the work";[93] and (2) an intrinsic test, focused on "similarities of expression," gauged by the way an "ordinary, reasonable person" responded to the expression.[94]

---

92. No. 09-3010, 2010 U.S. App. LEXIS 17389 (8th Cir. Aug. 20, 2010).

93. *Id.* at *2.

94. *Id.*

The Eighth Circuit reiterated that the Copyright Act does not protect ideas; it only protects the expression of ideas. In addition, it found that *scènes à faire*—standard characters, settings, and events—"cannot amount to infringing conduct."[95] In this case, unprotected ideas, the *scènes à faire*, and any insubstantial similarities did not add up to substantial similarity. As a result, the Eighth Circuit affirmed the district court's decision.

Applicable Copyright Infringement Test Depends on Range of Possible Expression of Ideas

In *Mattel, Inc. v. MGA Entertainment, Inc.,*[96] the Ninth Circuit held that the U.S. District Court for the Central District of California erred in granting Mattel summary judgment on its copyright infringement claim and found that, to establish infringement, sculpts[97] of Mattel's "Barbies" and MGA's "Bratz" had to be virtually identical, and sketches of the dolls had to be substantially similar, disregarding similarities in unprotectable ideas.

While employed by Mattel, Bryant brought to MGA, one of Mattel's competitors, some preliminary sketches for Bratz dolls and began working with MGA to develop Bratz, producing sketches and creating a preliminary Bratz sculpt. Mattel argued that Mattel owned both the sketches and the sculpt by virtue of Bryant's employment agreement with Mattel. In pertinent part, the employment agreement provided:

> I agree to communicate to the Company as promptly and fully as practicable all *inventions* (as defined below) conceived or reduced to practice by me (alone or jointly by others) at any time during my employment by the Company. I hereby assign to the Company . . . all my right, title and interest in such *inventions*, and all my right, title and interest in any . . . copyrights . . . based thereon.[98]

In granting Mattel's motion for summary judgment, the district court held that the employment agreement assigned to Mattel ownership of any doll or doll fashions that Bryant designed during his period of employment, whether they were created on his own time or during his Mattel working hours. However, the Ninth Circuit found that the phrase "at any time during my employment" was ambiguous, and because there was conflicting evidence about its meaning, the Ninth Circuit concluded that the district court erred in its summary judgment ruling.

Because the district court's erroneous ruling underlay the finding of copyright infringement, the Ninth Circuit vacated the copyright injunction granted by the district court. Anticipating that the jury might find that the employment agreement assigns ownership of the sketches and sculpt to Mattel, the Ninth Circuit went on to address the proper standards for copyright infringement in the event Mattel is found to be the owner of the sketches or the sculpt.

The Ninth Circuit explained that two different standards for infringement can apply depending on the range of possible of expression of the relevant ideas—either substan-

---

95. *Id.*
96. No. 09-55673, No. 09-55812, 2010 U.S. App. LEXIS 24150 (9th Cir. 2010).
97. A sculpt is a mannequin-like plastic doll body without skin coloring, face paint, hair, or clothing. *Id.* at *3.
98. *Id.* at *7.

tially similar or virtually identical. The court explained that ideas, *scenes a faire* (standard features), and unoriginal components are not protectable and may be freely copied. To determine the scope of protection, one must first filter out any unprotectable elements. Copyright protection is "broad,"[99] and a work will infringe if it is substantially similar where there is a wide range of the possible expression of those ideas. Copyright protection is "thin," and a work must be "virtually identical"[100] to infringe where there is only a narrow range of expression of those ideas.

Applying these standards, the Ninth Circuit distinguished between the sculpts and sketches, finding that, in order to justify a copyright injunction, Mattel will have to show that the Bratz sculpts are virtually identical to Bryant's preliminary sculpt or that the Bratz dolls are substantially similar to Bryant's sketches, disregarding similarities in unprotectable ideas. The Ninth Circuit ultimately concluded that the district court erred in applying a substantially similar standard to the Bratz doll sculpt. Reasoning that depicting a young, fashion-forward female with exaggerated features, including an oversized head and feet, is an unoriginal, unprotectable idea, the court found that the preliminary sculpt is entitled to only thin copyright protection against virtually identical copying.

However, the Ninth Circuit found that the district court correctly applied the substantially similar standard to the sketches of the Bratz doll because there are many ways that dolls can be depicted in sketches, with differing colors, clothing styles, hairstyles, jewelry, and accessories. Nevertheless, the Ninth Circuit concluded that the district court erred in applying the substantially similar test because the district court failed to filter out all the unprotectable elements in the sketches. The court explained that fashion dolls with a bratty look or attitude, or dolls sporting trendy clothing, are unprotectable ideas.

Summary Judgment Granted for Inadequate Support of Copyright and Trade Secret Infringement Claims

In *R.C. Olmstead, Inc., v. CU Interface, LLC*,[101] the Sixth Circuit affirmed the district court's grant of summary judgment in favor of the defendants on the plaintiff's claims of copyright and trade secret infringement. The court also declined to impose sanctions based on spoliation of evidence.

R.C. Olmstead, Inc. develops and sells data processing software, hardware, and related services to credit unions. In 1999, Olmstead licensed for a term of five years the use of its hardware and RCO-1 software to Canton School Employees Federal Credit Union (CSE). Pursuant to the agreement, Olmstead provided hardware to CSE, including the server on which the RCO-1 software was to run. The server contained the executable version of Olmstead's code, which used emulators to run the software. Their agreement did not expressly or otherwise limit access to the software or the emulators. As permitted by the license agreement, CSE engaged CU Interface, LLC, and its independent contractor, Thomas Burkhart (collectively, CUI) to provide maintenance and support. CUI had developed a terminal emulation program that enabled older terminal applications, such as RCO-1, to run on personal computers.

---

99. *Id.* at *21.
100. *Id.*
101. 606 F.3d 262 (6th Cir. 2010).

In 2003, CUI and CSE entered into their own agreement to develop a credit union data software processing system. To assess CSE needs, CUI programmer Jason Akin interviewed CSE employees. Akin asked at least one employee about the Olmstead software at the CSE facility. He was provided with a username and password to Olmstead software that allowed him access to the Olmstead RCO-1 software.

When Olmstead discovered that CSE was developing its own software, it exercised its option to terminate the license agreement. Olmstead informed CSE that it would be collecting the hardware and software leased to CSE under the terms of the agreement. When CSE learned that the representative sent by Olmsted to collect the hardware was accompanied by a third-party computer forensic analyst, CSE refused to allow Olmstead to remove the software and inspect the servers to determine whether and when CUI employees had access to the literal elements of Olmstead's software. Eventually, CSE's chief executive officer destroyed the servers by drilling holes through them.

Olmstead filed a lawsuit in federal court against CUI and CSE alleging several causes of action, including misappropriation of trade secrets, tortious interference with contractual and business relationships, copyright infringement, violations of the DMCA, unjust enrichment, breach of contract, and spoliation. The parties filed cross motions for summary judgment, but before the district court ruled on the motions, CSE and Olmstead reached a settlement. CSE was dismissed as a party to the case.

Olmstead claimed that several discovery rulings unfairly inhibited its ability to prove its claims, including the lower court's rejection of Olmstead's inadequate expert report under Rule 26(a)(2)(B) of the Federal Rules of Civil Procedure and refusal to draw adverse inferences based on a third party's destruction of evidence. After rejecting the report, the U.S. District Court for the Northern District of Ohio granted summary judgment for CUI. The district court determined that Olmstead failed to raise a genuine issue of material fact as to whether CUI copied Olmstead's software. It also held that Olmstead's end-use product, the RCO-1 interface, was not a trade secret.

The Sixth Circuit found that the district court did not abuse its discretion with respect to its subsidiary rulings. In addition, because Olmstead did not raise a genuine issue of material fact on either the copyright claim or the trade secret claim, the district court properly granted summary judgment. The Sixth Circuit noted that exclusion under Rule 37(c)(1) of the Federal Rules of Civil Procedure was proper due to the fact that Olmstead's expert's report was insufficient because it did not discuss the basis of the conclusion that similarities in CUI's software were the result of copying. Absent evidence of copying, summary judgment on the copyright infringement claim was affirmed.

The Sixth Circuit also held that the district court did not abuse its discretion in denying Olmstead employees access to the CUI end-use product. It held the district court's decision to grant Olmstead's experts access to the software properly balanced the need for Olmstead to have access to relevant and necessary information with CUI's interest in preventing a potential competitor from having access to its software. It noted that the district court reasoned that, during discovery, the parties agreed to a protective order under which material classified as "highly confidential" could only be viewed by experts and counsel. In addition, Olmsted had not contested CUI's claim that its end-use product contained trade secrets.

The district court determined that Olmstead was not entitled to any adverse evidentiary inference against CUI for CSE's alleged spoliation of evidence because Olmstead had not alleged any fault on CUI's part. The court also determined that there was no evidence in the record to indicate that CUI had accessed Olmstead's source code. Although CUI had access to Olmstead's end-use product based on the teller-level access to CSE Credit Union's programs, the RCO-1 interface was not a trade secret protected under Ohio law, and CUI had not engaged in any misappropriation as defined by Ohio law. The Sixth Circuit noted that, although the district court limited access to CUI's software to Olmstead's expert and counsel, Olmsted also had opportunities during discovery to depose CUI employees who had worked with both Olmstead and CUI software.

The Sixth Circuit also determined that the district court did not abuse its discretion in declining to sanction CUI for CSE's destruction of Olmstead's hard drives. It explained that the lower court's decision balanced the lack of any assertion of wrongdoing by CUI against the harm caused to Olmstead's claims. Ohio law also provides a remedy for a party injured by another party's spoliation of evidence.

With regard to Olmstead's copyright infringement claims, the Sixth Circuit determined that CUI was entitled to summary judgment on the merits because Olmstead presented no direct evidence of copying. In addition, Olmstead's indirect evidence was not sufficient to create a fact question as to whether copying occurred. The Sixth Circuit stated that, to prevail in a copyright infringement action, "a plaintiff must establish ownership of the copyright work, and that the defendant copied it."[102]

In affirming the district court's holding that Olmstead's end-user product was not a trade secret under Ohio state law, the Sixth Circuit pointed to several facts. First, Olmstead did not take reasonable steps to maintain its secrecy. In addition, its contract with CSE did not contain confidentiality provisions preventing third parties from viewing the interface. The agreement also expressly contemplated that CSE would use a third-party support firm to provide the terminal emulation software. These facts amply supported the district court's determination that Olmstead's user interface was not a trade secret.

Probative Similarities in Architectural Works Was Enough Evidence of Actual Copying to Defend against Motion for Summary Judgment

In *Lombardi v. Whitehall*,[103] the U.S. District Court for the Southern District of New York found that "probative similarities" between architectural works sufficed for a plaintiff to prove actual copying,[104] and that the common sense of an ordinary observer could gauge the gestalt of an architectural work to determine whether substantial similarities showed illegal copying.[105]

Lombardi was an architect, hired by site owner Stanley Scott, to design a building for a site at 137 Hudson Street in New York City and to obtain approval from the city's Landmarks Preservation Commission (LPC) and other regulatory boards. He did not sign a formal written contract with Scott, and they never discussed who would own the building plans or related copyrights. After creating the plans, Lombardi received approval from the LPC, which noted approvingly the proposed building's visual relationship with the adjacent historic building, which Scott also owned. Scott paid Lombardi for the plans.

---

102. *Id.* at 274 (citing Kohus v. Mariol, 328 F.3d 848, 853 (6th Cir. 2003)).
103. No. 04 6752, 2010 WL 742615 (S.D.N.Y. Mar. 3, 2010).
104. *Id.* at *14.
105. *Id.* at *15.

Scott then tried to sell 137 Hudson Street to another party, and, during the negotiations, Scott's lawyer asked Lombardi to review a set of plans to make sure they were essentially the same as those being reviewed by the regulatory boards. Lombardi did review the plans and was paid to do so, but the sale did not take place.

Next, Lombardi became part of a group that tried to buy the property. They received a letter of intent, which read that the closing documents would transfer to the buyer all of Scott's interest in and rights to the plans. But this sale did not take place either.

Finally, Whitehall bought the property. Lombardi provided consultation services and helped Scott during negotiations with Whitehall to ensure that the new construction would not limit the light and sight lines of the adjacent historic building. Lombardi billed Scott for his services. The sales contract asserted that Scott had the right to assign the existing plans free and clear of the rights of any other person, including Lombardi.

Whitehall hired another architectural firm, BKSK, "to create a fresh design."[106] He also gave copies of Lombardi's plans to BKSK, which reviewed these plans. The LPC rejected the new design because it wanted the building design to relate more to the adjacent historic building and expressed a preference for Lombardi's design. BKSK created new plans and came up with a design that related more to the adjacent building, more like Lombardi's original design. The LPC approved BKSK's revised design, and the Hubert building was constructed. In the meantime, Lombardi registered copyrights for his own plans and technical drawings.

In an amended complaint, Lombardi claimed that both BKSK's plans and the building itself infringed on his registered copyrights. He sought damages, equitable relief, and attorneys' fees. Whitehall moved for summary judgment in three separate motions, arguing that Lombardi: (1) was equitably estopped from claiming copyright infringement; (2) failed to show sufficient evidence of copyright infringement; and (3) was not entitled to attorneys' fees.

Lombardi conceded that he was not entitled to attorneys' fees, so the court granted Whitehall's motion for summary judgment on that point without discussion. As for equitable estoppel, the court viewed it as "a drastic remedy" that should be used sparingly.[107] Whitehall needed to show that Lombardi knew of the allegedly infringing behavior at the same time he acted in a way that could have caused Whitehall and others involved to think Lombardi was not concerned about the copyright. Each fact to which Whitehall pointed was contested, however, and therefore could not support equitable estoppel at the summary judgment stage. Even the look of the building itself was arguably unknown to Lombardi until the construction was complete because the building was covered by scaffolding and netting during construction.

The court reiterated that, "physical[ly] possess[ing] . . . a copyrighted work does not result in a grant of any of the rights protected by copyright law."[108] The court concluded that, "Whitehall's failure to determine the true owner of the Lombardi Plans can not [sic] estop Plaintiff from asserting his copyright claims."[109] Therefore, the court denied Whitehall's motion for summary judgment that raised equitable estoppel as an affirmative defense.

---

106. *Id.* at *10.
107. *Id.* at *8 (citation omitted).
108. *Id.* at *10 (citation omitted).
109. *Id.* at *11.

Turning to the motion based on insufficient evidence of copyright infringement, the court explained that a copyright plaintiff must show both: (1) actual copying of his or her work; and (2) substantial similarity between the works. To prove actual copying, a plaintiff must show both: (1) access to the copyrighted work; and (2) similarities between the two works. For the initial question of actual copying, the similarity need not be "substantial"; it must be only "probative." "Substantial" similarity becomes relevant if actual copying is found and the question then arises as to whether it was illegal copying. Circumstantial evidence may show the actual copying.

Here, both Lombardi and Whitehall claimed that they drew inspiration from the same adjacent historic building, and the court found that the design elements of the historic building were already in the public domain. No one had an exclusive right to the pre-existing material, but copyright can protect an original combination of unoriginal pre-existing elements. The court found that there were still questions of fact as to whether Whitehall copied the historic building or Lombardi's plans. Because a jury could possibly find for Lombardi on the issue of probative similarity, the court found that Lombardi met his initial burden of proving actual copying and denied this motion for summary judgment, too.

The Second Circuit has not decided a case on the substantial similarity standard as it would apply to an architectural work. Therefore, the southern district followed other trial courts in the circuit by applying the "total concept and feel" standard. The court found that common sense and the perspective of an "ordinary observer" could determine the total concept and feel of a work. Given that questions of fact remained as to substantial similarity, the court denied the motion for summary judgment on the question of copyright infringement.

Summary Judgment and Attorneys' Fees Affirmed Where Expert Opinions Insufficient to Prove Striking Similarity

In *Vargas v. Pfizer Inc.,*[110] the Second Circuit upheld two district court opinions: one granting summary judgment in a copyright infringement action and a second awarding attorneys' fees. The Second Circuit agreed with the district court and held that summary judgment on a claim that two copyrighted works are "strikingly similar" cannot be avoided by submitting inconsistent expert evidence.[111] The court found no error in the district court's later grant of $175,000 in attorneys' fees.

Ralph Vargas and Bland-Ricky Roberts (collectively, Plaintiffs) brought a copyright infringement action against East West Communications, Inc. and Brian Transeau (collectively, Defendants) alleging that Defendants' sound recording "Aparthenonia" infringed Plaintiffs' musical composition and recording titled "Bust Dat Groove Without Ride."

In moving for summary judgment, Plaintiffs relied on reports and testimony from three experts to prove copyright infringement by a showing that the two songs were "strikingly similar." Striking similarity exists when two works are so nearly alike that the only reasonable explanation for such a great degree of similarity is that the later . . . was copied from the first."[112]

---

110. 352 F. App'x 458 (2d Cir. 2009).
111. *Id.* at 460.
112. Vargas v. Transeau, 514 F. Supp. 2d 439, 443 (S.D.N.Y. 2007).

The district court granted summary judgment in the Defendants' favor and found that the expert reports were insufficient to create a genuine issue of material fact because, among other things, the experts provided inconsistent opinions. For example, one of Plaintiffs' experts proffered an opinion that directly undermined Plaintiff's case: the expert opined that the allegedly infringed work was not a digital copy of the original work.[113] Plaintiffs' two other experts, although contradicting the third expert and supporting plaintiff's claim of infringement, failed to provide more than conclusory statements to support their opinions.

The Second Circuit affirmed the grant of summary judgment and found that the "Plaintiffs [could not] avoid summary judgment simply by submitting any expert evidence, particularly where that evidence is both internally and externally inconsistent."[114] Further, the court found that the Plaintiffs failed to sufficiently rebut "ample evidence" presented by the defendants that established "a reasonable possibility of independent creation" of the allegedly infringed work, thereby making a finding of striking similarity unsupported.[115]

The Second Circuit went on to affirm the district court's awarding of $175,000 in attorneys' fees. In evaluating whether the fee award was warranted, the district court found that Plaintiffs' claims were not objectively reasonable. On appeal, Plaintiffs argued that it was "difficult, if not impossible" to agree with the district court decision because: (1) the court had to ask for more evidence from Defendants before granting summary judgment; (2) Plaintiffs had prevailed on Defendants' first summary judgment motion; (3) Plaintiffs successfully settled with three of the five defendants; and (4) Plaintiffs "initial[ly] survived Defendants' second motion for summary judgment."[116] The Second Circuit disagreed and found that the district court did not abuse its discretion in awarding attorneys' fees in the sum of $175,000.

Summary Judgment Is Appropriate When Objective Evidence of Substantial Similarity Is Absent

In ***Doody v. Penguin Group (USA), Inc.,***[117] the court granted summary judgment in favor of the defendant, Penguin Group, as to copyright infringement and various state law claims brought by the plaintiff, Louis Doody, the author of a copyrighted novel entitled *Gold of the Khan.* Doody claimed that his novel was infringed by a number of works authored by Clive Cussler and Dirk Cussler for publication by Penguin Group.

In analyzing Doody's copyright infringement claim, the court applied its extrinsic test to determine whether the works were substantially similar. This test requires finding objective evidence of substantial similarity of expression by looking only at the protected elements in the copyrighted works. Doody argued that the court should compare his novel to a group of the defendants' work to determine substantial similarity. The court rejected this argument entirely. The court then analyzed only the similarities between Doody's *Gold of the Khan* and the Cussler novel *Treasure of Khan* after Doody

---

113. *Id.* at 443.
114. 352 F. App'x at 460.
115. *Id.*
116. *Id.*
117. 673 F. Supp. 2d 1144 (D. Haw. 2009).

conceded that none of the other works by the Cusslers' would be infringing if considered individually. The court looked at potential similarities in plot, characters, theme, settings, and dialogue between the two novels. In doing so, the court identified a number of similar aspects; however, all were determined either to be similarities of nonprotectable ideas or broad themes, similarities of nonprotectable *scenes a faire*, or similarities between isolated and minor points that no reasonable jury could find significant on the issue of substantial similarity. The court refused to attach any special significance to use of the word "Khan" in the title of both novels, noting that each work involved the ancient treasure of Kublai Khan.

The court also rejected Doody's assertion of the inverse ratio rule, which suggests that less evidence of substantial similarity may be needed in cases where great evidence of access is present. The court determined that Doody's evidence of access, which consisted of a prior submission to the same publisher without any indication of editorial overlap with the defendants, was not sufficient to warrant application of the inverse ratio rule.

Finally, in resolving the various state law claims brought by Doody, the court determined that his claims for conversion and deceptive trade practices were preempted by the federal Copyright Act of 1976, whereas the state claim for breach of implied contract was not. The court determined that the presence of an extra element—the existence and breach of a contract—made the state claim distinct from claims preempted by the Copyright Act. Nonetheless, the court ultimately rejected the claim because any breach of contract would have required evidence of substantial similarity.

Summary Judgment Granted Where Children's Book Not Substantially Similar to Manuscript Submitted to Publisher

In *Lewinson v. Holt & Co.*,[118] the U.S. District Court for the Southern District of New York granted summary judgment where it found that a manuscript for a children's story and a children's book were not substantially similar after comparing the theme, plot, characters, sequence, setting, and total look and feel of the two works, even though the publisher of the children's book had access to the manuscript.

Before analyzing the merits of the claim, the court summarized the content of the two works. Lewinson submitted a manuscript to Holt for a children's story depicting children around the world saying "pacifier" in different languages. The manuscript, titled "What Do You Call It?," featured illustrations of children from different countries sucking on a pacifier with text providing the word "pacifier" in different languages. The manuscript ended with a picture of the children standing all over the planet with their flags, a dove, and a final message: "Paci on Earth." Lewinson obtained a copyright registration for this manuscript. Holt rejected Lewinson's manuscript, and Lewinson later revised the manuscript by adding more descriptions, creating a derivative work for which he did not obtain a copyright registration.

Holt later published a children's book titled *Can You Say Peace?*, which depicted children around the world saying "peace" in different languages. The book began with a description of International Peace Day followed by pictures of children from different countries and the word "peace" in different languages. The last page featured a picture of a globe with children standing on it and a dove with an olive branch.

---

118. 659 F. Supp. 2d 547 (S.D.N.Y. 2009).

The court first held that section 411(a) of the Copyright Act, which requires registration to bring an action for infringement, does not bar a plaintiff from suing for infringement of elements contained in a registered work from which an unregistered work was derived. However, a court must compare the allegedly infringing work with the registered work, not with the unregistered derivative work. Thus, the court examined whether the original elements of Lewinson's registered manuscript were infringed without reference to the unregistered version.

The court first explained that titles and phrases are not copyrightable; therefore, Lewinson could not base his copyright infringement claim on the alleged similarity between the title-questions of the works at issue (i.e., *How Do You Say It?* and *Can You Say Peace?*), based either on the use of these questions in the works' titles or in their text. In determining whether the works are substantially similar, the court examined the similarities in aspects of the theme, plot, characters, sequence, setting, and total concept and feel[119] of the two works. Noting that copyright law protects the expression of ideas, the court compared the theme, plot, characters, sequence, setting, and total look and feel of the two works. Finding many differences between the two, the court held that no reasonable observer could find that the works are substantially similar.

Attorneys' Fees Awarded Where Objectively Unreasonable Copyright Infringement Claim Brought in Bad Faith

In **Porto v. Guirgis,**[120] the U.S. District Court for the Southern District of New York dismissed a copyright infringement claim and ordered the plaintiff to pay attorneys' fees and costs to the defendants for bringing the objectively unreasonable claim in bad faith.

Porto alleged that Guirgis's play *The Last Days of Judas Iscariot* violates the copyrights for Porto's novel *Judas on Appeal*. Both works involve a fictional trial of Judas Iscariot in which the issue is whether Judas should be admitted to paradise. The novel depicted the trial before a fictional World Court of Religion held in the federal courthouse in New York City's Foley Square, while the play depicted the trial before a fictional judge in purgatory. Finding that the biblical characters and biblical story were unprotectable elements, the court compared the two works on protectable elements. The court found that the trials depicted in the two works were dramatically different in substance, setting, plot, theme, language, and the overall thrust and feel of the works. Without the unprotectable elements, the court held that no reasonable observer could regard these works as substantially similar and dismissed the copyright infringement claim.

The court further analyzed whether it should invoke its discretion to award attorneys' fees to the prevailing party under section 505 of the Copyright Act. In determining whether an award of attorneys' fees is appropriate, the court considered the factors presented in *Fogerty v. Fantasy, Inc.*: frivolousness, motivation, objective unreasonableness (both in the factual and in the legal components of the case), and the need in particular circumstances to advance considerations of compensation and deterrence so long as these factors further the purposes of the Copyright Act.[121]

---

119. The court explained that consideration of the total concept and feel of a work is especially appropriate in an infringement action involving children's works.

120. 659 F. Supp. 2d 597 (S.D.N.Y. 2009).

121. 510 U.S. 517, 534 n.19 (1994).

First, the court found indicia of bad faith because Porto's first counsel was warned that there was no colorable copyright infringement claim before any action had been filed. Next, the court found that the copyright infringement claim was objectively unreasonable because Porto could not point to a single similarity that relates to a protectable element of his novel. Having weighed the *Fogerty* factors, the court found that an award of reasonable costs and attorneys' fees was appropriate in this case to compensate Guirgis for the costs in litigating this matter and to deter future potential plaintiffs from filing objectively unreasonable claims.

Defenses

Fair Use

Government's Use of Photograph Depicting Sculpture It Commissioned Does Not Constitute Fair Use

In *Gaylord v. United States,*[122] the Federal Circuit held that the U.S. government's use of a photograph depicting a sculpture it commissioned did not constitute fair use. The United States, through the Department of the Army, entered into a contract with Cooper-Lecky Architects, P.C. wherein Cooper-Lecky would serve as the prime contractor for the building of the Korean War Veterans Memorial in Washington D.C. Cooper-Lecky held a competition to select the sculptor, and Frank Gaylord won the contest. After several years, Gaylord completed the sculpture, which consists of nineteen stainless-steel statues of staggered soldiers, and called it *The Column.* Gaylord secured five copyright registrations related to The Column. The memorial was dedicated in 1995.

In 1996, after a snowstorm, John Alli photographed The Column and decided to sell reprints of one of the photographs entitled "Real Life." Alli sought permission from Mr. Lecky of Cooper-Lecky, who held himself out as the sole owner of the underlying work. Alli entered into a license agreement with Mr. Lecky, but Mr. Lecky never notified Gaylord about the license agreement. When Gaylord sued Alli for copyright infringement in 2006, the parties settled their dispute.

Prior to the Gaylord and Alli settlement, the U.S. Postal Service decided in 2002 to issue a stamp commemorating the Korean War and selected Alli's photograph, "Real Life," for the stamp. Alli notified the Postal Service that it would need permission from the copyright owner and referred the Postal Service to Mr. Lecky.

The Postal Service did not obtain permission from Gaylord to use the sculptures on its stamps or any related retail goods. The Postal Service received more than $17 million from the sale of the stamp and received additional revenue from the sale of retail goods featuring images of the stamp.

Thus, in 2006, Gaylord filed suit against the United States for copyright infringement in the Court of Federal Claims. After a trial, the Court of Federal Claims found that the government's use of the sculpture on the stamp constituted fair use. Gaylord appealed to the Federal Circuit.

On appeal, the Federal Circuit reversed the lower court's finding of fair use. In considering the four fair-use factors, the Federal Circuit disagreed with the lower court's

---

122. 595 F.3d 1364 (Fed. Cir. 2010).

determination that the government's use was transformative. Although the stamp altered the appearance of the copyrighted work by changing the color and adding snow to the scene, the Federal Circuit found that these changes did not alter the purpose of the work or provide a different character to the work. The Federal Circuit noted that the stamp did not use the copyrighted work as part of an overall commentary or criticism. Therefore, the stamp was not transformative and, because it was used for a commercial purpose, the first factor weighed strongly against fair use.

The Federal Circuit also found that Gaylord's copyrighted work was expressive and creative, which weighed against fair use. With respect to the amount and substantiality copied, the Federal Circuit found that the government copied fourteen of the nineteen soldier sculptures, and the copied portion constituted the entire subject matter of the stamp. Accordingly, this factor weighed against fair use.

The Federal Circuit did find that the last factor favored fair use because the stamp did not adversely impact Gaylord's efforts to market derivative works. Weighing the four factors, the Federal Circuit found that three of the four factors militated against fair use; thus, the Federal Circuit held that the fair-use defense did not apply to the government's use of the copyrighted work.

After finding that the fair-use defense did not apply, the Federal Circuit considered the other defenses raised by the government, namely, joint authorship and whether Gaylord's sculptures were exempt from copyright protection under the Architectural Works Copyright Protection Act (AWCPA). The Federal Circuit held that the lower court's finding that the government was not a co-author was not clearly erroneous. In making this determination, the Federal Circuit agreed with the lower court's finding that the contributions of Cooper-Lecky and other third parties amounted to suggestions and criticisms and did not constitute independent copyrightable contributions. Furthermore, a 1994 agreement between Gaylord and Cooper-Lecky stated that Gaylord was the sole author of *The Column*; therefore, it was not the intent of the parties to create a joint work. Consequently, the Federal Circuit remanded for a determination of Gaylord's damages. Additionally, the Federal Circuit held that the lower court's determination that *The Column* was not an architectural work under the AWCPA was not clearly erroneous because the sculpture was not intended for human occupancy and, therefore, is not a building covered by the AWCPA.

Judge Newman argued in his dissent that the government should not be liable for copyright infringement: (1) because the terms of the contract the government had with Cooper-Lecky granted the government all rights in the memorial; and (2) because of the exemption provided in 28 U.S.C. § 1498, which prohibits any right of action by a copyright holder against the United States with respect to any work created by a person while in the service of the United States.[123] The majority acknowledged the dissent's arguments, which it claimed were raised sua sponte, and found that the government could not escape liability under the contract because Gaylord was not a party to the contract. Moreover, the government could not escape liability under section 1498 because Gaylord was not "in the service of the United States" nor was he using government "time, material or facilities" during his creation of *The Column*.[124]

---

123. *Id.* at 1381–83 (Newman, J., dissenting).
124. *Id.* at 1380 (majority opinion) (quoting 28 U.S.C. § 1498(b) (2006)).

Preliminary Injunction against Google Denied

In *Perfect 10, Inc. v. Google, Inc.,*[125] the court denied Perfect 10, Inc.'s (P10) motion for a preliminary injunction relating to Google's Web and image search and its related caching feature, Google's blogger service, and Google's forwarding of P10's DMCA takedown notices to chillingeffects.org (Chilling Effects) for publication. P10 also claimed that Google violated its rights of publicity. For each claim, P10 alleged direct infringement, contributory infringement, and vicarious infringement. Google claimed the fair-use defense and the DMCA safe harbor.

Applying the "serious questions" version of the sliding-scale test for preliminary injunctions, the court analyzed whether P10 would likely be able to establish a prima facie case for infringement for each type of conduct, and whether Google would likely be able to establish the applicability of an affirmative defense.

According to the U.S. Supreme Court, a preliminary injunction is appropriate when a plaintiff demonstrates that serious questions going to the merits are raised and the balance of hardships tips sharply in favor of the plaintiff.[126] The four preliminary injunction factors that a plaintiff is required to establish are as follows:

(1) He or she is likely to succeed on the merits;
(2) He or she is likely to suffer irreparable harm in the absence of preliminary relief;
(3) The balance of equities tips in his or her favor; and
(4) An injunction is in the public interest.

Regarding Google's Web and image search and its related caching feature, the Ninth Circuit previously concluded that P10 was not likely to succeed on the merits of its direct and vicarious infringement claims because Google was likely to prevail on its fair-use defense with respect to thumbnails. P10 argued that that the court should reach a different result now that Google hosts 22,000 thumbnails (up from the 2,500 when considered on appeal); however, the court disagreed and stated that the Ninth Circuit's fair-use analysis was based on the character, not the quantity, of the thumbnails.

P10 also failed to establish that it is likely to succeed on the merits of its contributory infringement claim as to Google's in-line linking in its Web and image search, its cache, and Google's Blogger service because: (1) many of P10's notices of infringement were inadequate; (2) P10 did not offer evidence that Google had not processed the notices that were adequate; and (3) P10's proposed relief was not tailored enough.[127] The court further stated that, even if Google were put on constructive notice, P10's proposed solutions to prevent further damage to the copyrighted works ran the risk of being dramatically overinclusive "because neither can identify images that are properly licensed or fair use as opposed to infringing."[128]

---

125. No. 04-9484 (C.D. Cal. July 30, 2010).
126. *Id.* at *3 (citing Winter v. Natural Res. Def. Council, Inc., 129 S. Ct. 365, 374 (2008)).
127. The court, quoting the Ninth Circuit, noted that "Google could be held contributorily liable if it had knowledge that infringing Perfect 10 images were available using its search engine, could take simple measures to prevent further damage to Perfect 10's copyrighted works, and failed to take such steps." *Id.* at *6 (quoting Perfect 10, Inc. v. Amazon.com, Inc., 508 F.3d 1146, 1172 (9th Cir. 2007)).
128. *Id.* at *11.

Regarding Google's blogger service, which is free to bloggers, the court held that P10 is unlikely to establish that Google directly infringed its copyrights because Google passively processes users' uploads. Moreover, the court found that P10 is also unlikely to be able to prove contributory infringement because the only blogger URLs that Google failed to remove were those associated with defective notices.

Concerning P10's blogger service vicarious infringement claim, P10 claimed that Google benefits from blogger infringements through clicks on ads placed next to infringing P10 images. The court found P10's evidence, which included example Web pages with ads placed next to infringing images and a disc with hundreds if not thousands of files, insufficient. According to the court, none of the example Web pages with ads placed next to infringing images is a blogger Web page, and P10 provided no explanation of how to locate the subject blogger Web pages containing advertisements on the disc.

The court further concluded that, even if P10 had provided sufficient evidence of Google advertising on blogger pages, P10 did not show a "direct" financial benefit to Google. Accordingly, the court concluded that P10 is unlikely to be able to establish vicarious liability for Google's blogger service. In addition, the court held that Google established that it is entitled to the DMCA safe harbor for its blogger service.

The court then addressed Google's forwarding of Adobe PDF "screenshot-style" DMCA notices depicting P10's images to Chilling Effects and stated that, if section 106 were construed literally, then this practice probably would constitute direct infringement because it involves "actual dissemination" of copies of P10's claimed copyrighted work with an intent that they be made available to the public.[129]

The court applied the four factors in 17 U.S.C. § 107 to address Google's fair-use defense. The first fair-use factor, which favored a finding of fair use, involves the determination of whether and to what extent the new work is transformative. The court found that Chilling Effect's publication of annotated versions of the notices with scholarly commentary is a transformative, noncommercial use. According to the court, Google assists Chilling Effects by substituting the image it has removed with a statement and a link to Chilling Effects. Google also makes it clear that its purpose in forwarding the notices is to aid in that nonprofit organization's mission of providing analysis and commentary on uses of the DMCA.

The second fair-use factor, which slightly favored P10, involves an analysis of the nature of the copyrighted work. The court previously found, and the Ninth Circuit affirmed, that P10's images are creative, but also previously published.

The third fair-use factor, which favored neither party, asks whether the amount and substantiality of the portion used in relation to the copyrighted work as a whole are reasonable in relation to the purpose of the copying. According to the court, although Google forwards the notices to Chilling Effects, this allows Chilling Effects to conduct and publish research and commentary on the notices.

The fourth fair-use factor, which favored Google, involves the effect of the use upon the potential market for or value of the copyrighted work. According to the court, P10 offered no evidence that visitors to Chilling Effects use these notices as substitutes for viewing the images on perfect10.com, nor could Chilling Effects be considered a potential customer of P10.

---

129. *Id.* at *18.

After weighing the fair-use factors together, the court found that Google's practice of forwarding and linking to the DMCA notices on Chilling Effects likely constituted fair use.

Addressing P10's right-of-publicity claim, the court held that P10 failed to establish that it was likely to prevail on this point because P10 never explained how its models were harmed, and P10 did not shown that Google inappropriately used the models' likenesses.[130]

Regarding the second preliminary injunction factor, the court held that P10 did not establish irreparable harm in the absence of preliminary relief. Although P10 offered evidence of its financial woes, the company failed to tie those financial difficulties to Google's conduct in any meaningful way. Moreover, the court held that nothing indicated that injunctive relief would help alleviate P10's financial concerns.

Regarding the remaining two preliminary injunction factors, after noting that P10 did not address whether the balance of equities or the public interest weighed in its favor, the court held that the balance of the equities and the public interest weighed in favor of Google.

The court concluded that P10 did not shown that the balance of hardships tipped sharply in its favor and denied P10's motion for a preliminary injunction.

District Court Grants Partial Summary Judgment for Breach of Contract and Copyright Infringement for Reproduction of Religious Text Translation

In *Society of the Holy Transfiguration Monastery, Inc. v. Archbishop Gregory of Denver, Colorado,*[131] the U.S. District Court for the District of Massachusetts awarded partial summary judgment to the Monastery for breach of a settlement agreement reached in a prior copyright case and for copyright infringement of its English-language translation of an ancient Greek religious text.

The Monastery published the Ascetical Homilies of St. Isaac the Syrian (St. Isaac Work) on November 25, 1985, and registered it on January 3, 1986. In 2006, it filed suit against the Archbishop for infringement of another work. In July 2006, the parties entered into a settlement agreement, which provided that the Archbishop would not challenge the validity of the Monastery's copyright and/or registrations in and to the St. Isaac Work at any time in the future. In the settlement agreement, the Archbishop further warranted and represented that: (1) he, either personally or through his associates and agents, had not copied, duplicated, transcribed, reproduced, or made a replica of the St. Isaac Works and would not print or publish it in the future; (2) he did not know of any copy, duplicate, transcript, reproduction, or replica of the work; and (3) he would not assist in the creation of any copy or replica of the work in the future. "No later than August 2007, the Archbishop posted (or caused to be posted) Homily 26 from the St. Isaac Work on his website."[132]

The Archbishop admitted violating the settlement agreement but argued that the settlement agreement should be voided on grounds of mutual mistake, material misrepresentation, economic distress, and restraint of trade. The court rejected these defenses.

The Archbishop claimed that he had not violated the settlement agreement due to mutual mistake. Specifically, he claimed that neither party knew at the time of the settle-

---

130. *Id.* at *22.
131. 685 F. Supp. 2d 217 (D. Mass. 2010).
132. *Id.* at 222.

ment that the work had already been posted on his Web site. Because only the Monastery was disadvantaged by this representation, and the Monastery had fully performed its promise under the settlement agreement, the court held that it would neither be just nor reasonable to allow the Archbishop to escape his contractual obligations while depriving the Monastery of the benefit of its bargain.

The Archbishop also claimed that the settlement agreement should be voided because the Monastery misrepresented that it owned the copyright, but produced no evidence to rebut the Monastery's evidence, which included a copyright registration certificate.

The Archbishop alleged that he entered the agreement under economic duress. Although a contract entered into under duress may be voidable, merely taking advantage of another's financial difficulty does not constitute duress. The person claiming duress must show that it was a result of the other party's wrongful and oppressive conduct. Such proof was lacking here. Moreover, a person may ratify an agreement entered under duress by accepting its benefits, remaining silent for a period of time after having the opportunity to avoid it, or acting on it. The court concluded that the Archbishop had ratified the settlement agreement.

Furthermore, the court held that the settlement agreement did not violate public policy as a restraint of trade or vocation. The agreement did not prevent the Archbishop from making his own translation of the religious text. The agreement only bound the Archbishop to respect the copyright of another. The Archbishop remained free to practice his vocation and to compete with the Monastery. The court therefore granted summary judgment to the Monastery on its claim for breach of the settlement agreement.

The Archbishop defended the infringement action by asserting fair use. The court placed the burden of proving fair use on the Archbishop and engaged in a balancing test. The Archbishop claimed that his use of Homily 46 was transformative because he placed a portion of the St. Isaac Work in a new media context (i.e., the Internet) for the instruction of Orthodox believers. The court, however, held that "[a] simple repackaging of a work in a new format, whether on the Internet or on a CD-ROM or on a flash drive, [wa]s not transformative when the result [wa]s simply a mirror image reflected on a new mirror."[133] The Archbishop argued that the nature of the work was factual, as part of the readers' religion. However, the court found that a religious contemplation in the form of a Homily (an admonitory sermon or discourse) was not a factual work but rather fell more appropriately within the category of imagination and creativity. Although only one of sixty-seven homilies was copied (three out of 383 pages of text), the court adopted Judge Learned Hand's cogent remark that "'no plagiarist can excuse the wrong by showing how much of his work he did not pirate."[134] Although the Monastery did not allege lost sales or profits as a result of the infringement, the Monastery had to spend time and resources to enforce its copyright. Weighing the four fair-use factors, the court concluded that they favored the Monastery.

Consequently, the court granted the Monestary's motion for partial summary judgment as to the breach of contract and copyright infringement claims.

---

133. *Id.* at 227.
134. *Id.* at 228 (quoting Sheldon v. Metro-Goldwyn Pictures Corp., 81 F.2d 49, 56 (2d Cir. 1936)).

Misuse

Partial Summary Judgment Granted to Plaintiff on "No Damages," Bad Faith, and Unclean Hands Affirmative Defenses under the DMCA

In *Lenz v. Universal Music Corp.,*[135] the U.S. District Court for the Northern District of California granted Plaintiff Stephanie Lenz's motion for partial summary judgment regarding several affirmative defenses asserted by Universal, including no damages, bad faith, and unclean hands. In an issue of first impression, the court granted Lenz's motion for summary judgment as to Universal's no-damages defense, holding that actual expenses or economic losses are not necessary for plaintiffs to recover under the DMCA, 17 U.S.C. § 512(f).[136] The court also found that Universal's various allegations of bad faith and unclean hands were not supported by evidence sufficient to demonstrate that Lenz's actions leading up to and during litigation were done in bad faith or constituted "unconscionable acts" under the unclean hands doctrine.

On February 7, 2007, Lenz videotaped her children dancing to Prince's "Let's Go Crazy" and posted the video on YouTube.com for the alleged purpose of sharing the video with her friends and family. On June 4, 2007, the owner to the rights of the song, Universal, sent a takedown notice to YouTube pursuant to the DMCA. YouTube took down Lenz's video in compliance with the notice and informed Lenz of the DMCA's counter-notification procedure. After obtaining legal advice, Lenz sent YouTube a counter-notification pursuant to section 512(g) of the DMCA, asserting that her video constituted fair use of "Let's Go Crazy" and, therefore, did not infringe on Universal's copyright. In addition, on July 24, 2007, Lenz filed a misrepresentation claim against Universal pursuant to section 512(f). In its answer, Universal asserted several affirmative defenses to which Lenz filed the motion for summary judgment discussed here.

In determining whether Universal's no-damages affirmative defense could survive summary judgment, the court first considered the language of section 512(f). The statute reads:

> [a]ny person who knowingly materially misrepresents under this section that material or activity is infringing . . . shall be liable for any damages, including costs and attorneys' fees, incurred by the alleged infringer (or other parties) . . . who is injured by such misrepresentation, as the result of the service provider relying upon such misrepresentation in removing or disabling access to the material or activity claimed to be infringing, or in replacing removed material or ceasing to disable access to it.[137]

After considering the plain language and legislative history of the statute, the court concluded that recovery under section 512(f) was available even for damages that are not economically substantial. The court found that Congress's choice to use the term "any damages" rather than "actual damages," coupled with a Senate Report's statement that the purpose of section 512(f) is to deter knowingly false allegations, supported Lenz's assertion of a broad interpretation of the "any damages" language.

---

135. No. 07-3783, 2010 WL 702466 (N.D. Cal. Feb. 25, 2010).

136. *Id.* at *10.

137. 17 U.S.C. § 512(f) (2006).

However, the court sided with Universal in its interpretation of the "as a result of" language, determining that, in order to recover under section 512(f), the misrepresentation must be a proximate cause rather than a "but for" cause of costs incurred by the alleged infringer. In addition to looking at the language and legislative history of the statute, the court found persuasive Universal's argument that a lower "but for" requirement would allow plaintiffs to satisfy the damages element by simply hiring attorneys and filing suit.

The court further limited recoverable damages under section 512(f), interpreting the phrase "including costs and attorneys' fees" as referring only to costs and fees incurred in response to takedown notices and prior to the institution of a section 512(f) suit. The court reasoned that Congress was fully aware of statutory fee-shifting provisions but still chose not to include such a provision in section 512(f). Thus, all other costs and fees were still subject to section 505, which provides that courts may allow recovery of full costs and reasonable attorneys' fees at their discretion.

The court's interpretation of section 512(f) led it to determine that Universal had failed to demonstrate that there was a genuine issue of material fact as to whether Lenz suffered *any* damages as defined by section 512(f).[138] As a result, the court granted Lenz's motion of summary judgment as to Universal's no-damages affirmative defense.

The court also granted Lenz's motion of summary judgment as to Universal's bad-faith and unclean hands affirmative defense, finding that Universal had not shown evidence from which a reasonable jury might find that any of Lenz's actions leading up to and during the suit were made in bad faith. For example, the court stated that Lenz's pleading of fair use was not an admission of copyright infringement that would render her claim to be made in bad faith because fair use of a work does not constitute copyright infringement.

The court also rejected Universal's argument that the large number of viewings of Lenz's video after the suit was filed was relevant to her allegation that she originally intended the video to be for friends and family. Thus, the large number of viewings was not evidence that she had made that allegation in bad faith. Also unconvincing to the court was Universal's claim that Lenz acted in bad faith when, in response to her friend's statement in an e-mail that she loved that Lenz had been "injured substantially and irreparably;-)," Lenz wrote, "I have ;-)."[139] The court, referencing Lenz's claim that her friend first used the "winky" face emoticon in reference to the stilted language that attorneys use, to which Lenz replied in kind, found that the evidence was not sufficient to establish that Lenz had acted in bad faith in claiming "substantial" and "irreparable" injury.

In addition, other affirmative defenses asserted by Universal, including estoppels, failure to state a claim, and waiver, were rejected by the court.

Estoppel

Claim Preclusion Bars Copyright Infringement Action

In *Airframe Systems, Inc. v. Raytheon Co.,*[140] the First Circuit affirmed the lower court's dismissal of a copyright infringement action on preclusion grounds. The appellate

---

138. *Lenz,* 2010 WL 702466, at *12.
139. *Id.* at *4.
140. 601 F.3d 9 (1st Cir. 2010).

court held that the doctrine of claim preclusion barred the plaintiff from pursuing a copyright infringement action in Massachusetts when Airframe did not appeal the dismissal of its earlier copyright action concerning the same series of events in New York.

Airframe's claims were about the actions of a single business unit, AIS. AIS performs systems integration for which it uses software. AIS purchased and renewed an annual license for Airframe's software suite. Around 1997 or 1998, John Stolarz, an Airframe employee, allegedly downloaded Airframe's source code onto an AIS computer and used it to modify Airframe's licensed software so that Airframe's software would run on newer AIS computers. AIS was, at the time, an unincorporated business division of Raytheon.

Airframe's source code remained on the AIS system until 2002, when AIS was purchased by L-3. AIS stopped using the modified program sometime prior to the transfer of its ownership from Raytheon to L-3. L-3 became the successor licensee of the Airframe software.

In 2003, Airframe discovered that its source code was on the AIS computer network. In 2005, Airframe sued L-3 and Stolarz for conspiracy to obtain its source code, possession of its source code, and the ability to use its source code without paying for license renewals or software updates, although it made no claim that such use had occurred. L-3 filed a motion to dismiss for failure to state a claim, which the district court granted in response. The district court held that, because Airframe's complaint had not alleged that L-3 actually used the source code, only that it could have done so, Airframe could not show infringement under the Copyright Act. Airframe did not appeal the merits of this decision or the court's failure to act on Airframe's stated intention to amend the complaint to allege infringing use.

Airframe then filed suit against L-3, Stolarz, and Raytheon in federal district court in Massachusetts. It alleged that AIS, under Raytheon's ownership, had conspired with Stolarz to obtain Airframe's source code. It also claimed that Raytheon, through AIS, infringed on Airframe's copyright by possessing and using the source code. In addition, it alleged L-3 continued to infringe. L-3 and Raytheon filed a motion to dismiss on the basis of claim preclusion.

The appellate court held that Airframe should have brought its use claim in the New York action, either in its initial complaint or in an amended one, because its claims of infringing possession and use were so closely related. It further held that Airframe should have named Raytheon as a defendant in the New York action because of Raytheon's close relationship with L-3 as to AIS operations during the relevant time period. It found no unfairness to Airframe in applying claim preclusion.

The panel used a transactional approach to determine that the asserted causes of action were sufficiently identical or related for claim preclusion purposes. It determined that the causes of action arose out of a common nucleus of operative facts. The claims of infringement through possession and use of Airframe's source code arose from the same common core of acts in the same timeframe. The causes of action formed a convenient trial unit: the infringement claims of possession and use would have been based on the same witnesses and evidence. In addition, Airframe's letter to the New York trial judge about amending its complaint to include a claim of infringing use established that treating the claims as a unit conformed to the parties' expectations.

The panel held that Raytheon did not need to show it was in privity with the original defendants to invoke a claim preclusion defense. It was reasonable to treat the two corporations as closely related for the purpose of claim preclusion. Although Raytheon was not a party to the original action, it was a predecessor corporation. All of Airframe's claims of infringement against L-3 and Raytheon in the present suit could have been brought against L-3 in the original suit. All the complained-of actions were done by the AIS business unit. The corporation was named only because it was the superior organization that included AIS. The corporations were interchangeable proxies for reaching the actions of AIS. In fact, the earlier suit included claims against L-3 for infringement during Raytheon's period of ownership of AIS.

The court explained that Raytheon showed good reasons why it should have been joined in the first action, and Airframe did not show any good reasons to justify a second chance. Therefore, the court affirmed the dismissal of the suit.

17 U.S.C. § 204(a) Requires Written Agreement to Effect Transfer of Ownership

In *Dallal v. New York Times Co.,*[141] the Second Circuit affirmed the judgment of the U.S. District Court for the Southern District of New York, which had denied Thomas Dallal's motion for judgment as a matter of law pursuant to Federal Rule of Civil Procedure 50(a). Dallal, a photographer, contended: (1) that he was entitled to JMOL on the New York Times Company's (the Times) defenses of oral agreement, implied license, and equitable estoppel because he had authorized the exclusive use of his photographs, effecting a "transfer of copyright ownership" within the meaning of 17 U.S.C. § 204(a);[142] and (2) that the writings that governed that transfer of ownership were his invoices, which contained language that he argued precluded Internet publication by the Times.

The Second Circuit found that "[s]ection 204(a) requires a written contract where there is a transfer of copyright ownership, including the grant of an exclusive license," but that a question of fact existed as to whether the parties had entered into a written contract for an exclusive license with respect to the photographs.[143]

The Second Circuit noted that, although Dallal relied on the language of his invoice, which he contended precluded Internet publication, and the testimony of a Times editor that the Times generally requires "first exclusive use" of photographs, the record contained no other evidence that the Times sought an exclusive license, such as evidence that the Times tried to prevent Dallal or others from republishing the photographs. As further support for denial of the Rule 50 motion, the Second Circuit also cited additional evidence that: (1) although Times editors signed Dallal's invoices, they did not return the invoices to Dallal; (2) the signatures denoted compliance with in-house accounting rather than an agreement to be bound; (3) Times employees informed Dallal that the Times did not intend to be bound by the invoices; (4) Dallal knew the photos would be published on the Internet; and (5) Dallal went ahead and accepted more than 1,000 assignments. Based upon such evidence, the Second Circuit held that the district court properly denied the Rule 50 motion and properly allowed the jury to consider whether an oral agreement existed for a nonexclusive license that permitted the Times to publish Dallal's work on the Internet.

---

141. 352 F. App'x 508 (2d Cir. 2009).

142. 17 U.S.C. § 204(a) provides: "A transfer of copyright ownership, other than by operation of law, is not valid unless an instrument of conveyance, or a note or memorandum of the transfer, is in writing and signed by the owner of the rights conveyed or such owner's duly authorized agent."

143. *Dallal*, 352 F. App'x at 511.

The Second Circuit also rejected Dallal's argument that he was entitled to JMOL on the Times' revision privilege defense under 17 U.S.C. § 201(c). Section "201(c) permits revisions by copyright holders in collective works, even where individual authors retain their copyrights, '[i]n the absence of an express transfer of the copyright or of any rights under it.'"[144] Based on the Second Circuit's determination that a question of fact existed as to whether the transactions were governed by an oral agreement rather than Dallal's invoices, which he had argued effected an "express transfer" of an ownership interest, the Second Circuit concluded that the revision privilege defense was not barred as a matter of law.

The Second Circuit found that the district court properly instructed the jury that an exclusive transfer of copyright cannot occur without a writing, and that the omission of the requirement that the author sign such a writing was immaterial because it was undisputed that Dallal signed the invoices. The Second Circuit also found no reversible error in the district court's charge to the jury that the parties disputed whether their agreement was established by the invoices, by oral statements, or by the parties' conduct and rejected Dallal's contention that the district court instructed the jury that the invoices were irrelevant.

Implied License

Ongoing Business Relationship Supports Finding of an Implied License to Copyrighted Designs

In *Estate of Hevia-Acosta v. Portrio Corp.*,[145] the First Circuit affirmed a district court holding that a deceased architectural designer had given his business partner an implied license to use his copyrighted design plans. Roberto Hevia-Acosta and Francisco Valcarce partnered on several real estate ventures, ultimately forming three companies together. One of the companies, Rio Grande Development Corporation (RG Development), owned Río Grande Village, a planned residential community in Río Grande, Puerto Rico. Hevia-Acosta worked on the architectural plans for the community (the Hevia Plans), but later died. His interests in the three companies were sold to Valcarce, and the Hevia Plans ultimately were used for the development of two residential complexes on the Río Grande Village site.

Hevia-Acosta's estate (the Estate) sued Valcarce and several other defendants, alleging that the defendants infringed a copyright on architectural plans created by Hevia-Acosta. The defendants denied the allegations and counterclaimed, alleging that the action was both frivolous and maliciously prosecuted. The district court dismissed the defendants' counterclaims and entered judgment in favor of the defendants on the copyright claim and in favor of the plaintiffs on the counterclaims. The district court entered judgment without imposing any attorneys' fees or costs on either party. Both sides appealed.

The appellate court analyzed whether the district court erred when it held that Hevia-Acosta granted the defendants an implied license to use the Hevia Plans. Using the approach discussed in *Nelson-Salabes, Inc. v. Morningside Development, LLC*,[146] the court

---

144. *Id.* (quoting 17 U.S.C. § 201(c)).
145. 602 F.3d 34 (1st Cir. 2010).
146. 284 F.3d 505, 514 (4th Cir. 2002).

began by explaining that determining whether an implied license has been granted involves evaluating "whether the licensee requested the work, whether the creator made and delivered that work, and whether the creator intended that the licensee would copy and make use of the work."[147] Noting that most courts generally pass over the request and delivery factors in cases involving whether an architect has granted an implied license, the court explained that intent is the touchstone for determining whether an implied license has been granted.

In determining intent, the court considered three factors set out in *Nelson-Salabes*:

(1) whether the parties were engaged in a short-term, discrete transaction as opposed to an ongoing relationship; (2) whether the creator utilized written contracts providing that copyrighted materials could only be used with the creator's future involvement or express permission; and (3) whether the creator's conduct during the creation or delivery of the copyrighted material indicated that use of the material without the creator's involvement or consent was permissible.[148]

Here, the court found that the undisputed facts and all three *Nelson-Salabes* factors supported the holding that Hevia-Acosta granted an implied, nonexclusive license to RG Development to use his plans to develop Río Grande Village.

First, the court explained that Hevia-Acosta's seven-year partnership with Valcarce constituted an ongoing relationship, and courts sometimes treat the existence of an ongoing relationship as a factor weighing against the implication of a license. However, the court found that, in this case, the relationship between Hevia-Acosta and Valcarce weighed in favor of finding an intent on Hevia-Acosta's part to grant a license to RG Development because the very essence of Hevia-Acosta's ongoing relationship with Valcarce and RG Development was founded on the successful completion of the project, which required RG Development's use of the Hevia Plans.

As for the second factor, the court noted that the Estate conceded that there was no evidence of an agreement limiting the use of the Hevia Plans to instances in which Hevia-Acosta either gave express permission or remained personally involved in the work; thus, this factor favored a finding of an implied license.

Next, the court found that the third *Nelson-Salabes* factor also supported a finding of an implied license because the evidence as to how the defendants obtained the plans reinforced the notion that Hevia-Acosta intended to grant a license. The Hevia Plans did not come from a third party. Instead, the plans went directly from Hevia-Acosta to Valcarce and the engineer working with them.

In addition to evaluating intent under the *Nelson-Salabes* factors, the court reviewed Hevia-Acosta's overall conduct and found that it spoke directly to the intent that the Hevia Plans be used to develop Río Grande Village. The court explained that Hevia-Acosta created the plans for that purpose and gave permission to an engineer to incorporate them into more elaborate blueprints for the project. The completed blueprints, which did incorporate the plans, were signed, sealed, and submitted by Río Grande Village to the appropriate governmental agency. The court found that those actions, taken in conjunction with the three *Nelson-Salabes* factors, established that Hevia-Acosta intended the Hevia Plans

---

147. *Portrio,* 602 F.3d at 41.
148. *Id.*

to be used for the development of Río Grande Village. Thus, the appellate court affirmed the district court's ruling that Hevia-Acosta granted RG Development an implied license to use the Hevia Plans.

The court then rejected the argument that the Estate revoked the implied license through letters written from the Estate to RG Development because the court found the letters related to an effort to prohibit the use of the Hevia Plans for a different development, not Rio Grande Village. The court also found that the defendants did not exceed the scope of the implied license by using third parties to implement the license because the work undertaken by the defendants and their agents was limited to the development of Río Grande Village. Finally, the court rejected the defendants' claims for attorneys' fees and costs, finding that the district court did not abuse its discretion in refusing to assess attorneys' fees against the Estate and holding that the parties should bear their own costs because both parties prevailed.

Implied Copyright Licenses Are Limited by Express Language in Contract

In *Thomas M. Gilbert Architects, P.C. v. Accent Builders & Developers, LLC,*[149] the court affirmed a grant of summary judgment in favor of the Gilbert architectural firm for actual damages and lost profits. Gilbert developed architectural plans for townhomes through a written agreement with Aspect Properties, which later formed Accent Builders and Developers to construct the buildings. The plans were designed in two phases and contained a written notice that the plans were the property of Gilbert under common law. The language further stated that the plans could be reused for a fee of $250, and changes could be made at an hourly rate set by Gilbert.

After construction began, Accent Builders owner Michael Tummillo asked Gilbert to make changes to the plans, but then believed Gilbert's price quote for the changes was too high. Tummillo then made the changes himself, removing the notice and any references to Gilbert. Tummillo subsequently received building approval without further contact with Gilbert. Shortly after Gilbert learned of Tummillo's changes, it registered the original plans with the U.S. Copyright Office and sued for infringement. The district court granted summary judgment for Gilbert on infringement, rejecting Accent's affirmative defense of an implied license to use.

Accent argued that Gilbert had granted it an implied, nonexclusive license to use, modify, copy, and distribute the plans. The court noted that the test established in *Nelson-Salabes, Inc. v. Morningside Development, LLC*[150] for such a defense was: (1) a person (the licensee) requests the creation of a work; (2) the creator (the licensor) makes that particular work and delivers it to the licensee who requested it; and (3) the licensor intends that the licensee copy and distribute his work. The parties only disputed the third prong of the *Nelson-Salabes* test as to whether Gilbert intended to grant such a license to use. The court noted there was an implied license granted between Gilbert and Aspect; however, language within the agreement made it a limited license rather than a general nonexclusive license.

---

149. No. 08-2103, 2010 WL 1804135 (4th Cir. May 6, 2010) (per curiam).

150. *Id.* at *3 (citing Nelson-Salabes, Inc. v. Morningside Dev., LLC, 284 F.3d 505, 514 (4th Cir. 2002)).

Accent argued that the totality of the circumstances, rather than the specific language in the contract, should be used to determine Gilbert's intent. The court found that, because Gilbert's intent was clear in the written agreement, there was no need to interpret contractual intent from the totality of the circumstances. Therefore, summary judgment was proper.

Accent also raised affirmative defenses of fair use and copyright misuse. The court rejected both defenses, concluding that there was no evidence in the record to show the changes made were minor enough to be insignificant. In addition, the doctrine of copyright misuse did not provide for a defense based on an allegedly high price alone.

Contributory

Operator of File-Sharing Service Found Liable for Copyright Infringement

In ***Columbia Pictures Industries, Inc. v. Fung,***[151] the U.S. District Court for the Central District of California granted the motion for summary judgment as to liability for inducement of infringement[152] filed by Columbia and other plaintiffs.[153] Columbia sued Gary Fung, the operator of several Web sites involved in a file-sharing network that allow users to download, free of charge, infringing copies of popular movies, television shows, sound recordings, software, and video games. In reaching its decision, the court relied heavily on the various decisions in the line of cases involving *Metro-Goldwyn-Mayer Studios, Inc. v. Grokster, Ltd.*[154]

Although the technology utilized by Fung was different, and arguably more advanced, than that prohibited by *Grokster,* the court extended the *Grokster* rationale to also apply to Fung's Web sites. In *Grokster*, the court analyzed basic "peer-to-peer" sharing sites which enabled individuals on a particular network, i.e., peers, to share files on their individual computers. These types of networks do not contain a central server that hosts all the potentially downloadable files; rather, the *Grokster* network involved a process whereby a user entered a search term into the software which triggered a "supernode," a computer that had indexed a multitude of other computers to contact those computers in search of matching files. Upon locating a match, the searching party would be sent the IP address and other identifying information so that it could download the requested file directly from that particular computer.

The Web sites operated, maintained, and promoted by Fung also involved a peer-to-peer exchange. However, rather than downloading content directly from one identified source, the Fung Web sites utilized "BitTorrent" or "Torrent" technology, which facili-

---

151. No. CV 06-5578, 2009 WL 6355911 (C.D. Cal. Dec. 21, 2009).

152. Although the motion for summary judgment was made on three separate grounds, the court addressed only the first theory because it covered the central question at issue, "defendants' secondary liability for its users' copyright infringement," and because the "inducement liability is overwhelmingly clear." *Id.* at *6.

153. Throughout this summary, Columbia will be used as the representative entity for all plaintiffs. In reality, plaintiffs in this action include multiple entities involved in the motion picture industry, including, among others, Disney Enterprises, Inc., Paramount Pictures Corp., and Tristar Pictures, Inc. *Id.* at *1 n.1.

154. 545 U.S. 913 (2005).

tates a much more efficient download of material as it enables the simultaneous access and download of content from all of the computers within the particular network that have the requested files. There are several steps involved in downloading files in a BitTorrent system. First, a user must install a BitTorrent client application. Once installed, a user who accesses a publicly available Torrent Web site can search an index to locate the Torrent files containing content they wish to download. These Torrent files do not contain the actual content searched for, but rather the information needed to retrieve the content through a peer-to-peer transfer. The next step requires the user to click on the desired Torrent file, which automatically triggers the identification and download of the requested content file from as many users as are available at the time of the request. Thus, technically speaking, the Torrent files do not link directly to copyrighted content but merely trigger a computer process whereby such content would automatically be downloaded.

On summary judgment, the court determined that there were no material issues of disputed fact regarding the evidence supporting the basic elements of the claim asserted. As set forth in *Grokster*, in order to establish a claim for inducement of copyright infringement, a defendant must have "taken purposeful acts aimed at assisting and encouraging others to infringe copyright."[155] By definition, this requires a showing by the plaintiff that there has been direct infringement of its copyrights by third parties. Under the relevant statute,[156] the plaintiff must establish that: (1) it owns the copyrights that have been infringed; (2) third parties have made unauthorized copies, downloads, or transfers of the copyrighted material; and (3) the infringement occurred within the United States.

The court found that Columbia owned, controlled, or had exclusive rights to the copyrights for the works at issue in this case, and that neither Fung nor his users were authorized to distribute these copyrighted materials.[157] Although Fung argued otherwise, the court held that both the transferor and transferee of copyrighted material are not required to be located in the United States. As reasoned by the court, the act of uploading copyrighted files for the use of others violates a copyright holder's distribution rights, and the act of downloading such copyrighted material violates a copyright holder's reproduction rights; either violation, if conducted in the United States, would create an independent ground for liability.

The plaintiffs presented, through expert testimony, evidence to show that more than 95 percent of the files available through Fung's Web sites were copyrighted and that, undisputedly, the Web sites were used in specific instances to download those copyrighted works. Furthermore, based on evidence Fung produced of IP addresses, which identify a particular computer connected to the Internet and the corresponding ISP, it was possible to identify the location of various users. This information was coupled with usage-summary data to determine that infringing downloads took place in the United States.

Having established the direct infringement by third parties, the court looked at various factors that could establish that Fung had induced such infringement. In *Grokster*, both the U.S. Supreme Court and the district court in its subsequent ruling on remand posited several "facts from which a reasonable fact-finder could infer intent to foster infringement."[158] Examples of such facts include using advertisements that target known infring-

---

155. *Fung*, 2009 WL 6355911, at *7 (citing *Grokster*, 545 U.S. at 936–37).

156. 17 U.S.C. § 106(1), (3).

157. *Fung*, 2009 WL 6355911, at *8.

158. *Grokster*, 545 U.S. at 938–40.

ers, failing to develop and implement filtering tools to protect copyrighted materials, relying on a business model dependent on high-volume use of software that was predominantly infringing, providing technical assistance to users to enable infringing use, and the "staggering scale of the infringement."[159]

Undisputed evidence of many of these factors was introduced against Fung, and the court found the evidence of Fung's intent to induce infringement "overwhelming and beyond reasonable dispute."[160] For example, not only did Fung structure and maintain the Web sites at issue, but he was personally aware that many of the works on his sites were copyrighted. Further, Fung stated that he knew that a major appeal of his Web sites was that they made available for download recent copyrighted blockbuster films such as *The DaVinci Code*. Users and advertisers, who drove Fung's revenue, were attracted by the availability of such blockbusters. Additionally, the court found Fung's Isohunt Web site had: (1) solicited infringement via the inclusion of a "Box Office Movies" feature that involved the periodic posting of lists of the top twenty grossing films in the United States, all of which were presumptively copyrighted; (2) provided links to information about the films; and (3) contained a mechanism whereby users could upload Torrents of these films. In addition, the technical processes embedded in Fung's Web sites, which enabled quicker downloads and included a "spider" program that could obtain files from other well-known infringing Web sites, suggest Fung's intent to promote infringement. Furthermore, Fung personally posted tips within the forum discussions on his Web sites that were meant to assist his users with their infringing uses.

The court rejected Fung's affirmative defense based on the safe harbor provisions in the DMCA.[161] To establish this defense, the following requirements must be satisfied: (1) a defendant does not know or have reason to know of infringing activities; (2) a defendant does not profit from infringement that it can control; and (3) upon receiving statutory notice from the copyright holder, the infringing material is removed.[162] Although, arguably, Columbia did not provide the appropriate statutory notice, the court held that Fung could not assert this defense because Fung had not provided evidence that he was unaware of infringing activity where the overwhelming statistical evidence indicated that millions of users in the United States were accessing material, an overwhelming percentage of which was copyrighted. Further, Fung provided no evidence that he had ever acted "to remove, or disable access to, the [infringing] material."[163] The court explained that the statutory safe harbors are not meant to protect individuals, such as Fung, who are clearly liable for inducement based on their "active bad faith conduct aimed at promoting infringement."[164]

The court also rejected Fung's position that the "First Amendment immunizes any and all activity on the internet";[165] thus, any statements made by him or his agents on his Web sites or Internet forums were protected. In fact, as in *Grokster* and *Napster*, the court found

---

159. Metro-Goldwyn-Mayer Studios, Inc. v. Grokster, Ltd., 454 F. Supp. 2d 966, 985–92 (C.D. Cal. 2006).
160. *Fung*, 2009 WL 6355911, at *11.
161. 17 U.S.C. § 512(d).
162. *Id.*
163. *Fung*, 2009 WL 6355911, at *16.
164. *Id.* at *18.
165. *Id.* at *16 n.22.

that the statements themselves are not the activity prohibited by the doctrine regarding the inducement of infringement, but rather are "probative of an intent to induce infringement . . . [and] often form the most substantial form of proof in inducement . . . ."[166] Further, the court explained that, because inducement involves "*conduct* not *expression*, and to the extent that Defendants' expression is being curtailed, they should recall that they 'could have expressed their theme without copying [Plaintiffs'] protected expression.'"[167]

REMEDIES

Injunctive Relief

Courts Must Apply eBay *Test When Issuing Preliminary Injunction for Alleged Copyright Infringement*

In *Salinger v. Colting,*[168] the Second Circuit held that the U.S. Supreme Court's decision in *eBay, Inc. v. MercExchange, L.L.C.,*[169] which articulated how to apply the traditional four-factor test as to when an injunction may issue in a patent case, applies with equal force to preliminary injunctions issued on the basis of alleged copyright infringement. Plaintiff-Appellee J.D. Salinger sued Defendant-Appellant Frederik Colting and others, claiming copyright infringement and unfair competition and alleging that Colting's novel *60 Years Later Coming Through the Rye* (*60 Years Later*) was derivative of Salinger's novel *The Catcher in the Rye* (*Catcher*). The U.S. District Court for the Southern District of New York granted Salinger's motion for a preliminary injunction. Although the Second Circuit concluded that the district court properly found that Salinger had a likelihood of success on the merits, the Second Circuit vacated the district court's order and remanded the case to the district court to apply the four-part *eBay* standard.

Salinger published *Catcher* in 1951 and registered and duly renewed his copyright in *Catcher*. *Catcher* has sold over thirty-five million copies. The central character, Holden Caulfield, "has become a cultural icon of 'adolescent alienation and rebellion,' . . . 'who refuses to be socialized,'" and "Salinger has conceded that *Catcher* is 'sort of' autobiographical."[170] Salinger never authorized any new narrative involving Holden or any work derivative of *Catcher*. Other than a 1949 film adaptation of an earlier short story, Salinger never permitted, and explicitly instructed his lawyers not to allow, adaptations of his works, and he has brought a series of legal actions to protect his intellectual property.

On May 9, 2009, without having sought Salinger's permission, Colting published *60 Years Later*, which tells the story of "Mr. C," a 76-year-old Holden, and Mr. C's 90-year-old author, a "fictionalized Salinger" who is haunted by his creation and wishes to bring him back to life and kill him, but ultimately sets him free, after which Mr. C reunites with his younger sister, Phoebe, and his estranged son.[171] The defendants marketed *60 Years*

---

166. *Grokster,* 545 U.S. 913; A&M Records, Inc. v. Napster, Inc., 239 F.3d 1004 (9th Cir. 2001).

167. *Fung,* 2009 WL 6355911, at *16 n.22 (citation omitted; emphasis in original).

168. 607 F.3d 68 (2d Cir. 2010).

169. 547 U.S. 388 (2006).

170. *Salinger,* 607 F.3d at 71 & n.3 (citations omitted).

171. *Id.* at 71–72.

Later as a sequel to *Catcher*. The Second Circuit noted that Salinger had pointed out the following "extensive similarities" between *Catcher* and *60 Years Later*: Mr. C is Holden; Mr. C narrates like Holden, references events from *Catcher*, and has eccentricities of Holden; the plot structures involving Mr. C and Holden are similar, including leaving an institution, wandering around New York, reconnecting with old friends, finding happiness with Phoebe, and returning to a different institution; and both works include similar scenes, including a "climatic carousel scene."[172]

On July 1, 2009, the district court granted Salinger's motion for a preliminary injunction, finding that: (1) Salinger had a valid copyright in *Catcher* and the Holden character; (2) absent a fair-use defense, the defendants infringed these copyrights; (3) a fair-use defense was likely to fail; and (4) a preliminary injunction should, therefore, issue. The district court found a valid copyright in both *Catcher* and the Holden character because the defendants did not contest the copyright in *Catcher*, and the Holder character was sufficiently delineated and inseparable from the book. The district court found substantial similarities between *Catcher* and *60 Years Later* and between Holden and Mr. C. to support the claim of unauthorized copyright infringement. The district court also found that defendants' fair-use defense was likely to fail; therefore, Salinger established a prima facie case of copyright infringement.

The Second Circuit held that, although the district court had applied the circuit's "longstanding standard for preliminary injunctions in copyright cases, [the Second] Circuit's standard is inconsistent with the 'test historically employed by courts of equity' and has, therefore, been abrogated by *eBay* . . . ."[173] The Second Circuit found that, in issuing the preliminary injunction, the district court presumed irreparable harm without discussion, based on the majority of decisions in the circuit that "presumed that a plaintiff likely to prevail on the merits of a copyright claim is also likely to suffer irreparable harm if an injunction does not issue."[174] That presumption had been applied in several ways, including: (1) a finding that a plaintiff likely to prevail on the merits need not make a detailed showing of irreparable harm; (2) a finding that the presumption was automatic and irrebuttable; or (3) a finding that the presumption was rebuttable where the plaintiff delayed in moving for an injunction.

The Second Circuit held "that *eBay* abrogated parts of this Court's preliminary injunction standard in copyright cases . . . ."[175] In *eBay*, the U.S. Supreme Court held that neither the district court nor the Federal Circuit correctly applied the four-part test of equitable factors when ruling on the propriety of a permanent injunction after finding patent infringement. The Court found that the district court and the Federal Circuit correctly articulated the four-factor test that must be satisfied for the court to issue a permanent injunction, but that, in applying the four-part test, both courts had applied general principles that were inconsistent with traditional equitable considerations. The Second Circuit noted that the district court in *eBay* appeared to apply principles suggesting that injunctive relief could not issue in a broad group of cases, and the Federal Circuit applied a "'general rule . . . that a permanent injunction will issue once infringement and validity

---

172. *Id.* at 72 (quoting eBay, Inc. v. MercExchange, L.L.C., 547 U.S. 388, 390 (2006)).
173. *Id.* at 74–75.
174. *Id.* at 75.
175. *Id.* at 76.

have been adjudged.'"[176] The U.S. Supreme Court in *eBay* held that the application of such broad classifications were inconsistent with traditional equitable principles.

The Second Circuit noted that it had not previously addressed the scope of *eBay*, that district courts within the circuit were split on its reach, and that other circuits were split on the application of *eBay* to cases that were not patent cases, including trademark and copyright cases. The Second Circuit concluded that *eBay* applies to preliminary injunctions issued for alleged copyright infringement.

First, the Second Circuit noted that the text and the logic of *eBay* suggest that traditional principles of equity are the standard for injunctions in all cases, not just patent cases, and that, in fact, *eBay* cited to two cases involving injunctions that were not patent cases. In addition, the *eBay* Court expressly relied on copyright cases and pointed out certain similarities in language regarding the grant of injunctive relief in both the Patent Act and the Copyright Act.

Second, the Second Circuit found that the standard for a preliminary injunction is not easier than the standard for a permanent injunction. One of the two cases upon which *eBay* relied in articulating the equitable test involved a preliminary injunction. In addition, in a recent U.S. Supreme Court decision, *Winter v. Natural Resources Defense Council*,[177] the U.S. Supreme Court applied *eBay* in a case involving a preliminary injunction.

Concluding that its pre-*eBay* standard for issuance of a preliminary injunction in copyright cases was inconsistent with the principle of equity set forth in *eBay* and the minimum considerations set forth in *Winter*, the Second Circuit held that a district court must undertake the following analysis in deciding whether to issue a preliminary injunction in a copyright case. First, in analyzing the initial factor, a probability of success on the merits, courts should be especially aware of the difficulty in predicting the merits of a copyright claim at a preliminary injunction hearing, given the time constraints involved, the complexities of the facts and arguments concerning substantial similarity and fair use, and the difficulty in predicting the outcome of such complex judgments.

Next, the court must weigh two related factors: whether irreparable injury to the plaintiff is likely in the absence of an injunction and the balance of hardships between the parties. After *eBay*, courts may not simply presume irreparable harm or adopt a categorical or general rule that the plaintiff will suffer irreparable harm, and courts may issue the injunction only if the balance of hardships tips in the plaintiff's favor. The Second Circuit found that the relevant harm is harm that occurs to the parties' legal interests when the harm cannot be remedied by damages or a permanent injunction. For the copyright holder, such legal interests include the property interest in the copyrighted work as well as, in certain instances, "a First Amendment interest in not speaking," and, for the defendant, the interest is a First Amendment interest of expression, so long as the expression does not infringe another's copyright. Harm may be irreparable for many reasons, including that a loss is hard to replace or measure or that one should not be expected to suffer it.

Finally, courts must examine the public interest in both copyright law (to promote the store of knowledge) and in free expression, recognizing that some uses will so patently infringe a copyright that the First Amendment value is virtually nonexistent.

The Second Circuit vacated and remanded the case because the district court only examined the first of the four factors, but noted that the district court's findings on the

---

176. *Id.* (quoting MercExchange, L.L.C. v. eBay, Inc., 401 F.3d 1323, 1338 (Fed. Cir. 2005)).
177. 129 S. Ct. 365, 375–76 (2008).

first factor, that Salinger is likely to succeed on the merits, should not be disturbed. The Second Circuit affirmed the findings that *Catcher* and *60 Years Later* are substantially similar[178] and that the defendants were not likely to prevail on their fair-use defense.

eBay Reseller Protected by First-Sale Doctrine Despite License Agreement Restricting Transfer of Ownership

In *Vernor v. Autodesk, Inc.,*[179] the U.S. District Court for the Western District of Washington held that an eBay reseller was the owner of software transferred under a license agreement and, thus, protected by the first-sale doctrine. Vernor, a frequent reseller of merchandise on eBay, attempted to sell two packages of AutoCAD design software in which Autodesk owned the copyright. Upon discovering Vernor's attempted eBay sale of this software, Autodesk invoked the takedown provisions of the DMCA. In response, Vernor sought a declaratory judgment that his sales of two other AutoCAD packages, and any other AutoCAD packages that he might acquire in the future, would not violate the Copyright Act. On cross-motions for summary judgment, the court held that the first-sale doctrine permitted Vernor to sell the AutoCAD packages without liability.

In granting the motion for summary judgment in Vernor's favor, the court evaluated whether Vernor had a first-sale right to resell the AutoCAD packages at issue. This issue required the court to determine whether Vernor was the owner of the AutoCAD packages containing the copyrighted material. In making this determination, the court noted that Autodesk unquestionably transferred possession of ten AutoCAD packages to an architectural firm, Cardwell/Thomas Associates (CTA), in settlement of a dispute. The settlement agreement stipulated that CTA agreed to adhere to all terms of the software license agreement, which, among other things, granted a nonexclusive, nontransferable license to use the enclosed program. With this background, the court analyzed the issue of whether Autodesk transferred ownership of the AutoCAD packages to CTA or whether CTA was a mere licensee who had no ownership interest to transfer to Vernor.

The court explained that Ninth Circuit precedent provided two different answers to the question of what distinguishes an owner from a mere licensee. In *United States v. Wise,*[180] the Ninth Circuit found that the distinction between a transfer of ownership and a mere license turned on the terms of the transfer agreement. That court found an ownership transfer in each instance in which the transferee could, at his election, retain possession of the transferred copy indefinitely, and the copyright holder had no right to regain possession. By contrast, the copyright holder's right to regain possession of the transferred copy was characteristic of a mere license. Three later cases from the Ninth Circuit, however, took more deferential views of the characterization of a transfer of copyrighted material as a license by suggesting that the mere labeling of a transfer agreement as a license was sufficient to ensure that the licensee did not have ownership of the copy of the software.[181]

The court ultimately agreed with the *Wise* court and concluded that the transfer of

---

178. The Second Circuit found it unnecessary to decide whether Salinger owned a valid copyright in the character Holden. *Salinger,* 607 F.3d at 83 n.11.

179. No. 07-1189, 2009 WL 3187613 (W.D. Wash. Sept. 30, 2009).

180. 550 F.2d 1180 (9th Cir. 1977).

181. *See* Wall Data Inc. v. Los Angeles County Sheriff's Dep't, 447 F.3d 769 (9th Cir. 2006); Triad Sys. Corp. v. S.E. Express Co., 64 F.3d 1330 (9th Cir. 1995); MAI Sys. Corp. v. Peak Computer, Inc., 991 F.2d 511 (9th Cir. 1993).

AutoCAD copies via the license was a transfer of ownership because there was no provision in the license agreement for the copyright holder to regain possession of the copy. The court viewed retaining title in a copy as meaningless unless the copyright holder had some means to regain possession of the copy. The court also reasoned that the license agreement severely restricted the use and transfer of the copy and that the licensees paid a single price to the copyright holder at the outset of the transaction. Thus, the court could not characterize Autodesk's decision to let its licensees retain possession of the software forever as something other than a transfer of ownership, despite the numerous restrictions on that ownership. Finding CTA (and, consequently, Vernor) to be the owner of the AutoCAD packages, the court held that Autodesk's copyright did not prevent Vernor from reselling the software.

The court also held that, because persons to whom Vernor would sell the packages would use the software in accordance with 17 U.S.C. § 117, Vernor would not be liable for contributory copyright infringement.

Damages

Actual

Innocent-Infringement Defense Rejected Based on Notice of Copyright and Defendant's Undisputed Access

In *Maverick Recording Co. v. Harper,*[182] the Fifth Circuit held that, as a matter of law, the innocent-infringement defense (to mitigate a damages award) was not available to the defendant, Whitney Harper, because: (1) the plaintiffs (a consortium of record companies) had provided proper notice of copyright on their published phonorecords; and (2) Harper did not dispute that she had "access" to those phonorecords within the meaning of 17 U.S.C. § 402(d). The court also affirmed a grant of summary judgment to the plaintiffs on their copyright infringement claim arising from Harper's downloading of thirty-seven sound recordings via the Internet.

The court directed entry of summary judgment for the plaintiffs on the innocent-infringer defense after rejecting Harper's assertion that a genuine issue of material fact existed concerning her claims of naiveté and lack of understanding of copyright law. Section 402(d) limits the application of the innocent-infringer defense "when a proper copyright notice 'appears on the published . . . phonorecords to which a defendant . . . had access, [in which case] no weight shall be given to such a defendant's interposition of a defense based on innocent infringement in mitigation of actual or statutory damages.'"[183] It was undisputed that the plaintiffs had provided proper copyright notice on each of the published phonorecords from which the audio files had been taken, and Harper did not contest that she had "access" to those phonorecords. Instead, Harper asserted that she did not understand the import of the copyrights. The court concluded that Harper's subjective understanding of copyright law is irrelevant in the context of section 402(d).

---

182. 598 F.3d 193 (5th Cir. 2010).
183. *Id.* at 198 (citing 17 U.S.C. § 402(d) (2006)) (alteration in original).

The court also found that there was sufficient evidence of copying by Harper to sustain the district court's grant of summary judgment of copyright infringement. Harper had not disputed that she downloaded the plaintiffs' audio files, but challenged the sufficiency of the plaintiffs' evidence (including expert witness testimony) that thirty-one of the thirty-seven audio files at issue existed on her computer. As to fifteen of those files, the court stated that the evidence showed that those files existed in a cache of approximately 700 songs discovered on Harper's hard drive. Regarding the remaining sixteen files, the court rejected Harper's argument that the evidence was insufficient because the plaintiffs' computer forensic expert was unable to recover complete copies of those audio files from Harper's computer. The court stated that there was "voluminous and undisputed evidence that [Harper] downloaded and shared the sixteen contested audio files."[184] The court concluded that the "uncontroverted evidence is more than sufficient to compel a finding that Harper had downloaded the files: there was no evidence from which a fact-finder could draw a reasonable inference that Harper had *not* downloaded them or that they were something other than audio files."[185]

The court brushed aside as irrelevant Harper's argument that the evidence did not show that she had "distributed" the thirty-seven audio files. Harper had not appealed the district court's finding that she had infringed the plaintiffs' copyrights by downloading—in other words copying—the audio files without authorization. Given that Harper was liable for copyright infringement regardless of whether the plaintiffs could show that she also distributed the files, the court need not consider her distribution argument.[186]

The court rejected Harper's due process argument, which had not been raised below and, therefore, had been waived.

Statutory

Second Circuit Upholds One Statutory Damage Award Per Album Rather Than Per Song Pursuant to 17 U.S.C. § 504

In ***Bryant v. Media Right Productions, Inc.,***[187] the plaintiffs recorded two copyrighted albums of music, each of which was composed of ten songs. The plaintiffs alleged that the defendants had copied the albums and sold them collectively and the songs individually in digital form without authorization and asserted that a statutory damage award should be based on the number of infringed songs, rather than the number of infringed albums. In other words, the plaintiffs argued that the albums should not be treated as compilations for purposes of applying the statutory damages provisions of 17 U.S.C. § 504. The Second Circuit rejected the plaintiffs' arguments and found that the district court did not err in determining that the plaintiffs were entitled to one statutory damage award for each album infringed by the defendants, a total of four awards, rather than one statutory damage award per each of the songs on the albums, which would have totaled forty awards. The Second Circuit also upheld the district court's finding that the infringe-

---

184. *Id.* at 196.
185. *Id.*
186. *Id.* at 199.
187. 603 F.3d 135 (2010).

ment was not willful and, given that the profits from infringing sales were less than $600, the district court did not abuse its discretion in awarding the plaintiffs $2,400 in statutory damages rather than the plaintiffs' claim for over $1 million.

Pursuant to section 504(c), a plaintiff is entitled to an award of statutory damages for all infringements with respect to one work, and all parts of a "compilation" constitute one work. A "compilation" is defined as "a work formed by the collection and assembling of preexisting materials or of data that are selected, coordinated, or arranged in such a way that the resulting work as a whole constitutes an original work of authorship."[188] The plaintiffs argued that each song on each of the albums qualifies as a separate work because each song is separately copyrighted and because one of the defendants sold the songs individually through Internet-based music retailers. The Second Circuit rejected this argument and held that an album falls within the Copyright Act's expansive definition of a compilation, noting that, "[a]n album is a collection of preexisting materials—songs—that are selected and arranged by the author in a way that results in an original work of authorship—the album. Based on a plain reading of the statute, therefore, infringement of an album should result in only one statutory damage award. The fact that each song may have received a separate copyright is irrelevant to this analysis."[189] In support of this conclusion, the Second Circuit cited the legislative history[190] and noted that, in two previous decisions, the Second Circuit focused on whether the copyright holder issued its works separately or together as a unit.[191]

The Second Circuit also rejected the plaintiffs' argument that, because one of the defendants had sold the songs individually in digital form, the court should adopt an "independent economic value" test. This test focuses on whether the works constituting the compilation (in this case, the songs) were sold individually. In denying this claim, the court noted that, although at least three circuits have adopted such a test, none of them have applied it to an album of music.[192] The court stated that the language of the Copyright Act provides no exceptions for "a part of a compilation that has independent economic value" and it "cannot disregard the statutory language simply because digital music has made it easier for infringers to make parts of an album available separately."[193]

The Second Circuit also found that the district court did not abuse its discretion in awarding only $2,400 in statutory damages because the defendants' profits from the infringing sales were meager, and deterrence was effectuated by requiring the defendants to pay their own attorneys' fees. Finally, the Second Circuit held that the district court did not abuse its discretion in denying attorneys' fees to the plaintiffs noting, among other things, that the plaintiffs had rejected an Offer of Judgment in the amount of $3,000 in favor of continuing to demand over $1 million in damages, notwithstanding the evidence that the defendants had received less than $600 in revenue from the infringing sales.

---

188. 17 U.S.C § 101.

189. *Bryant,* 603 F.3d at 140.

190. H.R. Rep. No. 1476 (1976), *as reprinted in* 1976 U.S.C.C.A.N. 5659.

191. *See* Twin Peaks Prods., Inc. v. Publ'ns Int'l Ltd., 996 F.2d 1366, 1381 (2d Cir. 1993); WB Music Corp. v. RTV Comm. Group. Inc., 445 F.3d 538, 541 (2d Cir. 2006).

192. *See* MCA Television Ltd. v. Feltner, 89 F.3d 766 (11th Cir. 1996); Columbia Pictures Television v. Krypton Bd. of Birmingham, Inc., 106 F.3d 284 (9th Cir. 1997), *rev'd on other grounds,* 523 U.S. 340 (1998); Walt Disney Co. v. Powell, 897 F.2d 565 (D.C. Cir. 1990).

193. *Bryant,* 603 F.3d at 142.

Court Orders Remittitur of Jury Award for Copyright Infringement

In *Capitol Records Inc. v. Thomas-Rasset*,[194] the U.S. District Court of Minnesota held that the jury's award of $1,920,000 as statutory damages for copyright infringement to be excessive, making remittitur of the judgment appropriate. The jury determined that Thomas-Rasset had illegally downloaded and distributed twenty-four sound recordings via an online peer-to-peer file-sharing application; however, the court determined that the jury's award was excessive and shocking and, accordingly, ordered a remittitur to three times the statutory minimum for each recording under the Copyright Act.

The court concluded that remittitur should be ordered only "when the verdict is so grossly excessive as to shock the conscience of the court."[195] In addition, in determining a verdict to be excessive, there must be "plain injustice or a monstrous or shocking result."[196] The court held that there is no authority supporting the plaintiffs' argument that a jury alone has the authority to determine the amount of the statutory damages awarded if within the statutory range. However, the court noted that, under the Seventh Amendment, the plaintiffs would have the right to reject the remittitur and request a new jury trial strictly on the issue of damages.

The court stated that statutory damages under the Copyright Act encompass both deterrent and compensatory components and are often chosen by the plaintiffs when actual damages are difficult to calculate. Thomas-Rasset's infringement was for personal use and for illegally distributing recordings for the purposes of obtaining free music. Because Thomas-Rasset was not a commercial actor and did not receive revenue from the infringing activity, the court determined that the award of nearly $2 million for the infringement of twenty-four songs was not necessary to serve as a deterrent and was, in fact, "simply shocking."[197]

Even so, the court acknowledged the impact of unauthorized peer-to-peer sharing and that such illegal activity has caused widespread harm to the recording industry. For this reason, the court held that an award of statutory damages in many multiples higher than the cost of purchasing a recording either online or buying a CD were justified. The court followed the "maximum recovery rule," which allows a court to reduce the award of statutory damages to an amount "sustainable by the record, so that the statutory damages award is no longer shocking or monstrous."[198] Based on this standard, the court determined that a remittitur in an amount three times the statutory minimum for damages under the Copyright Act—three times $750 per infringed recording—represented a maximum amount that the jury could reasonably award to compensate the plaintiffs and that would also address the deterrence aspect of the statutory award. In arriving at the remittitur, the court concluded that the practice of awarding treble damages in cases of willful statutory viola-

---

194. 680 F. Supp. 2d 1045 (D. Minn. 2010). In addition to Capitol Records, the other plaintiffs are Sony BMG Music Entertainment, Arista Records, LLC, Interscope Records, Warner Bros. Records, Inc., and UMG Recordings, which either own or control the exclusive rights in the infringed recordings.

195. *Id.* at 1050 (citing Eich v. Bd. of Regents for Cent. Mo. State Univ., 350 F.3d 752, 763 (8th Cir. 2003)).

196. *Id.*

197. *Id.* at 1054.

198. *Id.* at 1055.

tions was extensive; thus, limiting the plaintiffs' award to three times the minimum statutory damages was the "most reasoned solution."[199]

Berne Convention Does Not Preempt Registration Requirement for Statutory Damages

In *Elsevier B.V. v. UnitedHealth Group, Inc.,*[200] the U.S. District Court for the Southern District of New York denied Plaintiff Elsevier's request for declaratory judgment. Elsevier owns or exclusively licenses copyrights in scientific books and journals that it offers to subscribers on its on-line database. In this case, it claimed that the defendants had allowed improper access to Elsevier's database and violated its copyrights, including those to foreign works that have not been registered in the United States. Elsevier wanted to pursue statutory damages for the alleged infringements but could not do so with respect to unregistered works under the terms of section 412 of the Copyright Act of 1976. Elsevier argued that the statutory damages and attorneys' fees provisions of section 412 violate the Supremacy Clause of Article VI of the U.S. Constitution when applied to foreign copyrights that are unregistered. Elsevier claimed that Article Five of the Berne Convention for the Protection of Literary and Artistic Works (Berne Convention), which has been signed by the United States, supersedes section 412 to the extent that it conditions awards of statutory damages and attorneys' fees for infringement of a Berne Convention copyright on the registration of that copyright in the United States.

The court rejected Elsevier's argument that the Berne Convention is a self-executing treaty that would automatically be effective as domestic law and, therefore, supersedes section 412. The court, citing *Medellin v. Texas,*[201] noted that treaties are not effective as domestic law unless specifically ratified with that intent by Congress. When Congress adopted the Berne Convention Implementation Act of 1988, it declared that the obligations of the United States under the Berne Convention may only be performed pursuant to appropriate domestic law. The legislative history of the Implementation Act clearly indicated Congress's intent to keep the Berne Convention from being self-executing. Congress specifically noted the potential effect of the Berne Convention on section 412, but chose not to amend it. In fact, although deciding to amend section 411 due to inconsistencies with the Berne Convention, Congress stated that the incentives to register copyrighted works included in section 412 were not inconsistent with the Berne Convention.

The court continued its analysis by pointing out that every judge in its district that has faced this issue has come to the same conclusion that the Berne Convention is not self-executing. In fact, the very text of the Berne Convention indicates that it is not self-executing because it requires countries signing the Berne Convention to adopt legislation to implement it. Finally, the court rejected Elsevier's attempt to rely on *Bacardi Corp. of America v. Domenech,*[202] in which the U.S. Supreme Court concluded that the General Inter-American Convention for Trademark and Commercial Protection was self-executing because Article 35 provided that "it shall have the force of law in those States." The Berne Convention contains no similar language indicating an intent to have it be self-executing.

---

199. *Id.* at 1057.
200. No. 09-2124, 2010 WL 150167 (S.D.N.Y. Jan. 14, 2010).
201. 552 U.S. 491 (2008).
202. 311 U.S. 150 (1940).

Because the Berne Convention is not self-executing, the court concluded, Elsevier could not possibly use it to support a claim of preemption under Article VI of the U.S. Constitution. Accordingly, the court decided that it did not need to discuss any possible substantive conflict between section 412 of the Copyright Act and Article Five of the Berne Convention.

Music Composition Counts as One Work for Copyright Damages Determination

In *MCS Music America, Inc. v. Yahoo! Inc.,*[203] the U.S. District Court for the Middle District of Tennessee held that "the use of a single musical composition embodied in multiple sound recordings" constituted one work for purposes of determining statutory damages for copyright infringement.[204]

MCS claimed copyright ownership in 215 musical compositions and alleged that Yahoo digitally transmitted 308 separate sound recordings embodying those compositions. For example, in its complaint, MCS described how eight different versions of John McCutcheon's copyrighted composition *Christmas in the Trenches* were performed by different musicians, produced by different producers, and distributed by different record labels before being copied and distributed by Yahoo without permission.

While still in the pleadings stage, Yahoo moved for judgment on the pleadings under Rule 12(c) of the Federal Rules of Civil Procedure. In its analysis, the court applied the Rule 12(b)(6) standard, taking as true all well-pled allegations of the nonmoving party.

The parties agreed that MCS was entitled to one statutory damages award per infringed work, but they disagreed on what constituted a "work." MCS argued that each of the 308 sound recordings embodying the musical compositions constituted a separate "work" for which MCS could sue for infringement. In contrast, Yahoo argued that MCS could sue only for infringement of each of the 215 musical compositions at issue.

The court noted that the Copyright Act does not define what constitutes a "work." It does, however, provide that "a single statutory damage award may be recovered per *work* infringed."[205] After noting that ownership of sound recordings and musical compositions provides separate sets of rights, the court noted that "[t]he touchstone for recovery of statutory damages is registration."[206] The court compared this case to *Walt Disney Co. v. Powell*, in which sales of shirts with different depictions of Mickey and Minnie Mouse were held to infringe only two Disney works, despite copyrights in the two characters in six different poses.[207] Here, the court found that all variations of a single musical composition constituted one "work" for determining statutory damages. Thus, to recover statutory damages for each of the 308 recordings distributed by Yahoo, MCS would have had to own the copyright in each of the sound recordings.

The court therefore granted Yahoo's motion for judgment on the pleadings on this narrow issue of statutory damages only. The decision did not address actual damages.

---

203. No. 3:09-CV-00597, 2010 WL 500430 (M.D. Tenn. Feb. 5, 2010).
204. *Id.* at *1.
205. *Id.* at *2 (emphasis added) (citing 17 U.S.C. § 504(c)).
206. *Id.*
207. *Id.* at *3 (citing Walt Disney Co. v. Powell, 897 F.2d 565 (D.C. Cir. 1990)).

Costs and Attorneys' Fees

Case Dismissed; Payment of Defense Costs Not Required for Dismissal under Rule 41(a)(2)

In *Bridgeport Music, Inc. v. Universal-MCA Music Publishing, Inc.*,[208] the Sixth Circuit affirmed the district court's decision in granting motions to dismiss, ordering each party to pay their own attorneys' fees and costs.

Having unsuccessfully sought a stipulation of dismissal without prejudice, the Bridgeport plaintiffs filed motions to dismiss each of the twenty cases without prejudice pursuant to Federal Rule of Civil Procedure 41(a)(2), with the parties bearing their own costs and fees. The district court granted the request. The Universal defendants appealed, and the case was remanded because the decision had been inadequate for appellate review.[209]

Upon remand, Universal filed a motion seeking attorneys' fees as a condition of dismissal under Rule 41(a)(2). The consolidated matter was assigned to a magistrate judge, who was familiar with the underlying litigation. After briefing with case-by-case analysis and a full hearing, the magistrate judge recommended denial of Universal's motions for attorneys' fees. The district court adopted the magistrate judge's detailed recommendation. The Sixth Circuit reviewed the decision for abuse of discretion.

The Copyright Act contains fee-shifting provisions that allow an award of fees to prevailing defendants on equal footing with prevailing plaintiffs.[210] In deciding whether to award attorneys' fees, the court must weigh multiple factors, including frivolousness, motivation, objective unreasonableness, and the need in particular circumstances to advance considerations of compensation and deterrence.

Dismissal without consent of the nonmoving party requires court approval. The purpose of Rule 41(a)(2) is to protect the nonmoving party from unfair treatment. The court may condition an involuntary dismissal on whatever terms it deems necessary to offset the prejudice the nonmoving party may suffer from a dismissal without prejudice. Courts typically consider the effort and expense of preparation undertaken by the nonmoving party, the moving party's delay or lack of diligence, the reasons given for the dismissal, and whether a motion for summary judgment has been filed by the nonmoving party. Although dismissal orders under Rule 41(a)(2) are commonly accompanied with orders to pay defense costs, such payment is not required.

The district court specifically concluded that: (1) the delay in these cases could not clearly be attributed to the Bridgeport plaintiffs alone; (2) the Bridgeport plaintiffs' failed royalty-receipt theory had been objectively reasonable; and (3) the Bridgeport plaintiffs' cost-benefit analysis provided a reasonable explanation for seeking their dismissal. The court considered each case individually and held that the district court did not abuse its discretion in finding that the Universal defendants would not suffer prejudice and, thus, were not entitled to payment of a pro rata share of attorneys' fees as a condition for dismissal under Rule 41(a)(2).

---

208. 583 F.3d 948 (6th Cir. 2009).

209. Bridgeport Music, Inc. v. Universal-MCA Music Publ'g, Inc., 481 F.3d 926, 931 (6th Cir. 2007) (remanding case "for a more detailed order . . . relating to the dismissal.").

210. 17 U.S.C. § 505 (2006).

CHAPTER 19

OTHER COPYRIGHT MATTERS

Beyond the numerous copyright matters discussed in the previous chapters, copyright actions involving use of copyrighted works subject to a license or assignment, protection of foreign works, the application of the first-sale doctrine, and royalty rates were before the courts this year. In addition, a fair amount of new legislation that could potentially have great impact on the interpretation of copyright law was signed into law or introduced.

The U.S. District Court for the Eastern District of Wisconsin in *Edgenet, Inc. v. Home Depot USA, Inc.* granted the defendant's motion to dismiss the plaintiff's copyright infringement claim. Applying the three-part test used to determine if an implied license was created, the court held that the plaintiff intended to grant a nonexclusive license to the defendant. In addition, the court held that the defendant did not rescind the license based on a material breach and that the plaintiff did not exceed the scope of the license.

Applying the same three-part test, the Eleventh Circuit reversed the district court's finding of summary judgment in favor of the defendant in *Latimer v. Roaring Toyz, Inc.,* which had determined that the plaintiff granted an implied license to the defendant to use his photographs of customized motorcycles. The court instead held that a question of fact remained concerning the scope of the implied license given by the plaintiff. The court also held that the district court's sua sponte grant of summary judgment based on the fair-use defense was reversible error because the defendant had failed to plead that affirmative defense.

In *Thomsen v. Famous Dave's of America, Inc.,* the Eighth Circuit held that a settlement agreement between the plaintiff and the defendant unambiguously assigned ownership of certain copyrights relating to the décor and design of fast food restaurants to the defendant. As a result, the court held the plaintiff's copyright infringement and beach of settlement agreement claims failed as a matter of law.

The protection of foreign works also was the topic of a notable decision. The Tenth Circuit, in *Golan v. Holder,* held that section 514 of the Uruguay Round Agreements Act, which granted copyright protection to foreign works that were previously in the public domain in the United States, did not violate the First Amendment to the U.S. Constitution.

The Supreme Court granted certiorari in a case involving the application of the first-sale doctrine. The Court in *Omega S.A. v. Costco Wholesale Corp.* will be determining whether a copy of a work made and distributed abroad is subject to the first-sale doctrine when imported and sold in the United States without the authorization of the copyright owner.

Royalty rates paid to copyright owners also received a considerable amount of attention. In *Recording Industry Ass'n of America, Inc. v. Librarian of Congress,* the Court of Appeals for the District of Columbia affirmed the final determination of the Copyright Royalty Board, imposing a 1.5-percent-per-month late fee for late royalty payments and a

24¢ royalty rate for ringtones. In addition, the Copyright Royalty Judges set final regulations governing the statutory minimum fees to be paid by Commercial Webcasters under statutory licenses granted under sections 112(e) and 114 of the Copyright Act.

In addition to cases applying existing copyright law, new legislation was signed into law or introduced this year. In particular, on May 27, 2010, President Obama signed into law the Satellite Television Extension and Localism Act of 2010. This Act updates and reauthorizes the satellite carrier distant broadcast signal license found in section 119 of the Copyright Act for another five years. The Act also amends, in several respects, the cable statutory license found in section 111 of the Copyright Act. The effective date of this Act was February 27, 2010.

The United States Senate also passed the Copyright Cleanup, Clarification, and Corrections Act of 2010, a bill designed to facilitate a shift to electronic filing at the Copyright Office, clarify ambiguous copyright issues, and correct technical errors in the Copyright Act. The Copyright Cleanup, Clarification, and Corrections Act was unanimously approved on August 2, 2010 and was sent to the House of Representatives for consideration.

Two additional bills also were introduced this year. First, the Senate Judiciary Committee sent to the Senate floor an amended version of the proposed Performance Rights Act, which establishes a right for performers of sound recordings to be compensated for the public performance of their works by broadcast radio stations. Second, on August 5, 2010, Senator Charles E. Schumer introduced a bill in Congress entitled the Innovative Design Protection and Piracy Prevention Act (IDPPPA). The new bill, if enacted, would provide a three-year term of protection for a variety of fashion designs, accessories and eyeglass frames. As drafted, the IDPPPA incorporates carve outs that would insulate from liability consumers who inadvertently offer for sale, advertise, or distribute any article embodying a design protected by the new law.

The Copyright Office also amended its rules this year. Specifically, the Office adopted an interim rule to exempt online-only works from the mandatory deposit requirement of section 407 of the Copyright Act.

Internationally, ten nations and the European Union released a draft of the Anti-Counterfeiting Trade Agreement, which outlines a possible international agreement regarding copyright laws. The agreement includes various provisions on statutory damages, injunctions, anticircumvention rules, and safe harbors for ISPs.

COPYRIGHT OFFICE MATTERS

Interim Rule Exempts Online-Only Works from Mandatory Deposit Requirement; Electronic Serials Subject to Demand for Deposit

In a regulation that became effective on February 24, 2010, the Copyright Office adopted an interim rule governing mandatory deposit of published electronic works available only online (the Interim Rule).[1] The Interim Rule exempts online-only works from the mandatory deposit requirement established by 17 U.S.C. § 407.

The Interim Rule amends 37 C.F.R. § 202.19 to exempt online-only works from the mandatory deposit requirement of section 407, and to provide, initially, that online serials

---

1. Mandatory Deposit of Published Electronic Works Available Only Online, 75 Fed. Reg. 3863 (Jan. 25, 2010).

are subject to demands by the Copyright Office for mandatory deposit. The Interim Rule also adds 37 C.F.R. § 202.24, which identifies the conditions for the Copyright Office's demands for deposit, and amends Part 202, Appendix B, to add new "best edition" criteria for electronic serials available only online.

As amended, section 202.19 provides that works published in the U.S. and available only online are exempt from the mandatory deposit requirement until the Copyright Office issues a demand for deposit of copies. As provided in new section 202.24, the Register of Copyrights can make a demand only for the categories identified in section 202.19(c)(5) for works published on or after February 24, 2010. The Register may demand only one copy of such works. Electronic serials are the first category of online-only works for which demands will issue.[2]

Once a demand for deposit has been made, the "owner of copyright or of the exclusive right of publication must deposit the demanded work within three months of the date the demand notice is received."[3] Each copy deposited in response to a demand "must be able to be accessed and reviewed by the Copyright Office, Library of Congress, and the Library's authorized users on an ongoing basis."[4] For purposes of deposit, a copy is "'complete' if it includes all elements constituting the work in its published form, i.e., the complete work as published, including metadata and formatting codes otherwise exempt from mandatory deposit."[5]

The Register of Copyrights has the discretion to extend the period of time for making a deposit, to permit the deposit of incomplete copies, and to permit the deposit of copies other than those normally comprising the best edition.[6] Any request for such relief must be made in writing to the Copyright Acquisitions Division and must state the specific reasons why the request should be granted.[7]

PROCEEDINGS OF COPYRIGHT ROYALTY JUDGES

Copyright Royalty Board Sets Royalties for Commercial Webcasters

On February 8, 2010, the Copyright Royalty Judges (Judges) published in the Federal Register final regulations governing the statutory minimum fees to be paid by commercial Webcasters under the statutory licenses granted under sections 112(e) and 114 of the Copyright Act.[8] The regulations took effect on March 10, 2010, and permit certain digital performances of sound recordings and the making of ephemeral recordings from January 1, 2006, through December 31, 2010. Commercial Webcasters will pay a nonrefundable, minimum fee of $500 for each calendar year.

In 2007, the Judges had published their determination of royalty rates and terms for a digital public performance of sound recordings by means of either eligible nonsubscription

---

2. *See* 37 C.F.R. § 202.19(c)(5).
3. *Id.* § 202.24(a)(3)).
4. *Id.* § 202.24(a)(4).
5. *Id.* § 202.19(b)(2).
6. *Id.* § 202.24(d).
7. *Id.* § 202.24(d)(3).
8. 75 Fed. Reg. 6097 (Feb. 8, 2010).

transmission or a transmission by a new subscription service for the period of 2006–2010. However, Webcasters raised several objections to the Judges' determination, including an objection to the lack of a cap on the minimum fees payable by commercial Webcasters. In *Intercollegiate Broadcast System, Inc. v. Copyright Royalty Board,*[9] the D.C. Circuit affirmed the Judges' determination, but remanded the matter of setting the minimum fee to be paid by both commercial and noncommercial Webcasters under sections 112(e) and 114. Subsequently, the Judges published for comment the proposed change in the rule, influenced by a settlement agreement between copyright owners and commercial Webcasters.

The Judges adopted the change as final and amended part 380 of title 37 of the Code of Federal Regulations to include the statutory minimum fee of $500 to be paid by commercial Webcasters for each calendar year or part of a calendar year of the period 2006–2010 during which it is a licensee pursuant to 17 U.S.C. §§ 112(e) or 114. This minimum fee is payable for each individual channel and each individual station maintained by commercial Webcasters. It is also payable for each individual side channel maintained by broadcasters who are commercial Webcasters, provided that a commercial Webcaster shall not be required to pay more than $50,000 per calendar year in minimum fees in the aggregate. The minimum fee payable under section 112 is to be included within the minimum fee payable under section 114. Upon payment of the minimum fee, the commercial Webcaster will receive a credit in the amount of the minimum fee against any royalty fees payable in the same calendar year.

TREATIES AND INTERNATIONAL MATTERS

Statute Restoring Copyright Protection to Foreign Works Previously in the Public Domain Is Constitutional

In *Golan v. Holder,*[10] the Tenth Circuit reversed an award of summary judgment for the plaintiffs and remanded with instructions to grant summary judgment in favor of the government. The court held that Congress acted within its authority under the Copyright Clause of the Constitution in enacting section 514 of the Uruguay Round Agreements Act (URAA) (codified as amended at 17 U.S.C. §§ 104A, 109), which granted copyright protection to various foreign works that were previously in the public domain in the United States.[11] The court further held that section 514 of the URAA does not violate plaintiffs' freedom of speech under the First Amendment because it advances an important governmental interest and it is not substantially broader than necessary to advance that interest.[12]

In order to comply with Article 18 of the Berne Convention, Congress enacted section 514 of the URAA. Under section 514, foreign works that were not previously protected by copyright because of a failure to comply with formalities, lack of subject matter protection, or lack of national eligibility were granted copyright protection as "restored"

---

9.   574 F.3d 748, 762, 767 (D.C. Cir. 2009).
10. 609 F.3d 1076 (10th Cir. 2010).
11. *Id.* at 1095.
12. *Id.*

works.[13] Additionally, section 514 provides some protection for parties who had relied on the lack of copyright protection in exploiting the works, or in creating derivative works based upon the restored works, prior to their restoration.

The plaintiffs perform, distribute, and sell works that were removed from the public domain by this legislation. They are either prevented from using the works or are required to pay licensing fees to the copyright holders that are often cost-prohibitive. As such, they filed suit against the government, namely Eric Holder in his capacity as Attorney General of the United States and Marybeth Peters in her capacity as the Register of Copyrights. They lost in the lower court. In the first appeal, the Tenth Circuit had held that the legislation had "not exceeded the limitations inherent in the Copyright Clause" of the U.S. Constitution, and remanded the case to the district court to assess whether the legislation was content-based or content-neutral and to apply the appropriate level of First Amendment scrutiny.[14]

On remand, the parties agreed that the legislation is a content neutral regulation of speech, subject to intermediate scrutiny. The Tenth Circuit concurred.

In order for a statute to survive intermediate scrutiny, the statute must be directed at an important or substantial governmental interest unrelated to the suppression of free expression. The court found that securing protections abroad for American copyright holders is an important or substantial governmental interest.

Not all First Amendment interests are equal. In *Eldred v. Ashcroft,* the court held: "The First Amendment securely protects the freedom to make—or decline to make—one's own speech; it bears less heavily when speakers assert the right to make other people's speeches."[15] Here the plaintiffs were asserting a First Amendment right to use the copyrighted works of others. The court therefore concluded that section 514 of the URAA advances an important or substantial governmental interest unrelated to the suppression of free expression.

The court deferred to the Congressional judgment that American authors were being harmed abroad and needed section 514's protection. Because Congress had substantial evidence from which it could reasonably conclude that the ongoing harms to American authors were real and not conjectural, the court held that there was a substantial basis to support Congress' conclusion that section 514 addresses a real harm. Substantial evidence also supported Congress's conclusion that section 514 would alleviate these harms.

Furthermore, Congress balanced the interests of American copyright holders and the reliance parties who, prior to restoration, created a derivative work that was based on a restored work. Section 514 provides that a reliance party may continue to exploit the derivative work for the duration of the restored copyright upon payment of reasonable compensation.

Although there was evidence in the Congressional record that would have supported a different result, the court deferred to Congressional judgment that section 514's restoration of foreign copyrights with limited protection for reliance parties genuinely advanced the U.S.'s ability to protect American works abroad.

The court also found that section 514 does not burden substantially more speech than necessary. The court applied intermediate scrutiny and determined that section 514 is narrowly tailored to further the government's interest in securing protections for Ameri-

---

13. 17 U.S.C. § 104A(a), (h)(6)(C).
14. *Golan*, 609 F.3d at 1082.
15. *Id.* at 1084 (quoting Eldred v. Ashcroft, 537 U.S. 186, 221 (2003)).

can works in foreign countries, because the burdens on speech, which the U.S. imposed on both American and foreign reliance parties, directly addressed the harms that the government sought to alleviate.

Although the government could have complied with the Berne Convention and provided greater protection to American reliance parties, the existence of these alternatives does not undermine the narrow tailoring of section 514, as Congress is not required to adopt the least restrictive means of serving the government's legitimate content neutral interests.

The United Kingdom's approach to this problem, although different, is not substantially less restrictive of speech than section 514. In the United Kingdom, a copyright owner can buy out a reliance party; in the U.S., the copyright owner files notice and the reliance party has a twelve month grace period to continue exploiting the work. In the United States, a reliance party may also continue to use a derivative work upon payment of reasonable compensation, whereas, in the United Kingdom, creators of derivative works are unprotected.

In crafting the provisions of section 514, Congress appropriately balanced the interests of American copyright holders and American reliance parties. It is not the court's role to opine on the best method for striking the balance between competing interests, and so long as the government has not burdened substantially more speech than is necessary to further an important interest, the First Amendment does not permit the court to second guess Congress's legislative choice.

Under Article I of the U.S. Constitution, Congress has the authority to extend copyright protection to works that are in the public domain. The First Amendment does not draw absolute bright lines around the public domain, or make removal of works from the public domain of copyright unconstitutional per se. Because section 514 advances an important governmental interest and is not substantially broader than necessary to advance that interest, the court found that it does not violate plaintiff's freedom of speech under the First Amendment.

Draft of Anticounterfeiting Trade Agreement Released

A possible international agreement to strengthen intellectual property protection in the European Union, United States, and nine countries was released on April 21, 2010.[16] The draft text of the Anti-Counterfeiting Trade Agreement (ACTA) focuses on copyright protection within the EU, U.S., Australia, Canada, Japan, Korea, Mexico, Morocco, New Zealand, Singapore, and Switzerland. Parties to the agreement will give holders of intellectual property rights access to judicial or administrative systems to pursue enforcements of their IP right. The parties, however, disagree on the scope of the agreement, particularly whether it should be extended to all IP rights or limited to copyright and trademark rights.

The agreement's proposed language with respect to civil enforcement includes broad injunction powers and requires the establishment of statutory damages. Several sections of the draft ACTA allow right-holders to obtain an injunction by showing that infringement is imminent. In addition, a criminal enforcement chapter targets both commercial and

---

16. Consolidated Text Prepared for Public Release, Anti-Counterfeiting Trade Agreement, PUBLIC Predecisional/Deliberative Draft (Apr. 2010).

noncommercial infringement and has a proposal to include "inciting, aiding, and abetting" as an offense.[17] Other proposals for criminal enforcement center on labeling and unauthorized recording of movies in theaters. The draft ACTA also contains several options that allows customs officials and border agents to act upon their own initiative and hold suspected infringing shipments of goods without needing a right holder to complain first. However, the de minimis provision excludes "small quantities of goods of a noncommercial nature contained in travelers' personal luggage [or sent in small consignments]" from searches.[18]

Under the draft agreement's section entitled Special Measures Related to Technological Enforcement of Intellectual Property in the Digital Environment, ISPs are protected from liability as long as they have no direct responsibility for infringement. There are two options concerning the limitation of liability for ISPs. The first option focuses on whether the provider does not have actual knowledge of the infringement. The second option contains a notice-and-takedown requirement for ISPs to qualify for a safe harbor. Another proposal suggests conditioning the ISP safe harbor provision on the provider adopting and implementing a policy to address the unauthorized storage or transmission of materials protected by copyright and expeditiously removing or disabling access to the materials.

Alternatively, another option allows parties to require ISPs to "terminate or prevent an infringement" and parties can pass laws "governing the removal or disabling of access to information."[19] The option also allows right-holders to obtain information on the identity of the relevant subscriber from ISPs, and encourages countries to "promote the development of mutually supportive relationships between online service providers and right holders."[20]

The anticircumvention provisions provide for adequate and effective legal protection for technological protection measures, but also include provisions against devices that can be used to get around even those with a limited, commercially significant purpose. Countries can set limits to the ban, but only if those limits do not "impair the adequacy of legal protection of those measures."[21] Other chapters in the draft ACTA discuss international cooperation, enforcement practices, and institutional arrangements.

U.S. Supreme Court Grants Certiorari to Decide Issue of Whether the First-Sale Doctrine Applies to Copies Made Overseas

In *Omega S.A. v. Costco Wholesale Corp.,*[22] the Ninth Circuit held that a copy made and sold outside the United States does not fall within the first-sale exception under section 109(a) of the Copyright Act. On April 19, 2010, the U.S. Supreme Court granted certiorari to consider whether the first-sale doctrine applies to imported goods made and sold outside of the United States.

Section 602(a)(1) of the Copyright Act prohibits the "[i]mportation into the United States, without the authority of the owner of copyright under this title, of copies or

---

17. *See id.* at 16.
18. *Id.* at 10.
19. *Id.* at 21.
20. *Id.* at 22.
21. *Id.* at 23.
22. 541 F.3d 982 (9th Cir. 2008), *cert. granted,* 130 S. Ct. 2089 (2010).

phonorecords of a work that have been acquired outside the United States."[23] Section 109(a), however, which embodies the so-called first-sale doctrine, provides an exception to the general prohibition, such that "the owner of a particular copy or phonorecord lawfully *made under this title*, or any person authorized by such owner, is entitled, without the authority of the copyright owner, to sell or otherwise dispose of the possession of that copy or phonorecord."[24] The question for the Court was whether a copy made and sold overseas is "made under this title" and, thus, falls within the exception of section 109(a).

The Ninth Circuit held that the section 109(a) exception can only provide a defense when the claim involves domestically made copies of U.S.-copyrighted works.[25] In reaching this decision, the Ninth Circuit followed its own precedents and reversed the district court holding, which had relied on the first-sale doctrine as interpreted in *Quality King Distributors, Inc. v. L'anza Research International, Inc.,*[26] in which the U.S. Supreme Court held that the first-sale doctrine applies to imported copies. However, the Ninth Circuit here distinguished *Quality King*, finding that the holding is inapplicable to copies that originate outside of the United States. The Ninth Circuit reasoned that to hold otherwise would impermissibly apply the Copyright Act extraterritorially.

Following the Ninth Circuit's decision, Costco filed a petition for a writ of certiorari on the grounds that the Ninth Circuit's opinion was inconsistent with the Copyright Act and the Supreme Court's decision in *Quality King*. Certiorari was granted on April 19, 2010. A number of parties have filed amicus briefs, including major retail companies arguing for the reversal of the Ninth Circuit's decision and the American Bar Association arguing in support of the Ninth Circuit's decision.

LICENSING

Motion to Dismiss Copyright Infringement Claim Granted Where Licensor Did Not Rescind the License, and Licensee Did Not Exceed Scope of the License

In *Edgenet, Inc. v. Home Depot USA, Inc.,*[27] the U.S. District Court for the Eastern District of Wisconsin granted Home Depot's motion to dismiss for failure to state a claim under Federal Rule of Civil Procedure 12(b)(6), dismissing Edgenet's copyright infringement claim with prejudice and dismissing its various state law claims without prejudice. The court held that Edgenet's claim for copyright infringement could not stand because Home Depot obtained a legally valid license to the copyright, Edgenet did not rescind the license based on a material breach, and Home Depot did not exceed the scope of the license.

To state a claim for copyright infringement, Edgenet needed to sufficiently plead ownership of a valid copyright and Home Depot's unauthorized copying of protected elements of the copyrighted work. It was undisputed that Edgenet held a valid copyright.

---

23. 17 U.S.C. § 602(a)(1).
24. *Id.* § 109(a) (emphasis added).
25. 541 F.3d at 985.
26. 523 U.S. 135 (1998).
27. No. 09-CV-747, 2010 WL 148389 (E.D. Wis. Jan. 12, 2010), *appeal docketed*, No. 10-1335 (7th Cir. Feb. 11, 2010).

Therefore, the issue before the court in deciding the motion to dismiss was whether Edgenet had granted Home Depot a nonexclusive license to its product collection taxonomy and, if so, whether Home Depot's use of the copyrighted work exceeded the scope of the license.

The court determined Edgenet granted a nonexclusive license to its product collection taxonomy. Edgenet created the taxonomy at Home Depot's request, provided access to the taxonomy, intended that Home Depot copy and distribute the copyrighted work, and no material breach or rescission of the license occurred.

The court concluded Edgenet intended to grant the nonexclusive license based upon the parties' prior contractual dealings. Home Depot's alleged breaches of the May 2004 Content Services Agreement and failure to pay Edgenet upon termination of their working relationship constituted breach of a covenant between the two parties, but did not constitute a failure to meet a condition necessary to trigger the existence of the license grant contained in the December 2006 Statement of Work. The court based its finding on the fact that the May 2006 Statement of Work between the parties contained a license grant and covenants with which Home Depot had to comply upon the license grant but did not contain conditions precedent to the license being granted.

The court further concluded Edgenet did not rescind the license as the result of a material breach. The court found Edgenet did not allege sufficient factual matter to show a material breach of the license for at least two reasons. One, Edgenet alleged only that Home Depot Canada notified its suppliers it would no longer use Edgenet's services, but it did not state that the relationship had ceased, which would trigger an offer to pay the $100,000 license. Two, the court found Home Depot's belated offer to pay the $100,000 license fee was not a failure of performance rising to the level of material breach. In addition, the court noted that even if a material breach were assumed, Edgenet failed to exercise its right to cancel the contract within a reasonable period of time and continued to provide Home Depot with access to its taxonomies. Therefore, no rescission of the license occurred to support a claim for copyright infringement.[28]

The court next addressed whether Home Depot infringed Edgenet's copyright by exceeding the scope of the license. The court found the license grant to Edgenet's taxonomies extended to the questions and answers crafted regarding data submitted to Home Depot's suppliers. It also found the license grant was not limited to the 2006 version of the product collection taxonomy, nor was it limited to a single project. Therefore, Home Depot stayed within the scope of the license.[29]

Because the court concluded there were no facts Edgenet could plead to support a complaint that would survive a motion to dismiss, it dismissed Edgenet's copyright infringement claim with prejudice. However, the court dismissed without prejudice the pendent state law claims to enable Edgenet to pursue such claims in state court.

Photos Taken for Display at Bike Show Are Subject to Implied License

In *Latimer v. Roaring Toyz, Inc.,*[30] the Eleventh Circuit: (1) affirmed the district court's grant of summary judgment, finding that photographs of customized motorcycles were made pursuant to an implied license and, therefore, entitled to copyright protection;

---

28. *Id.* at *11.
29. *Id.* at *14.
30. 601 F.3d 1224 (11th Cir. 2010).

but (2) reversed the holdings that (i) the distribution of those photographs by defendant Kawasaki Motors Corp., USA (Kawasaki) was covered by an implied license and (ii) the publication of those photographs in *Cycle World* by defendant Hachette Filipacchi Media U.S., Inc. (Hachette) was a fair use.

At Kawasaki's request, Defendant Roaring Toyz customized two motorcycles and commissioned Ryan Hathaway to apply custom paint and graphics to the motorcycles. Hathaway knew that the motorcycles would be publicly displayed and photographed by the media, and that Kawasaki intended to promote the customized motorcycles as widely as possible.

Roaring Toyz asked Plaintiff Todd Latimer to photograph the customized motorcycles. Latimer understood that his photographs would be displayed by Kawasaki during Daytona Bike Week and during the "World Press Introduction" of the motorcycles in Las Vegas. (The court of appeals concluded that there was a genuine issue of fact regarding whether Latimer understood that Kawasaki would make other uses of his images.) During the press event in Las Vegas, Kawasaki distributed a press kit containing Latimer's digital images on a compact disc. *Cycle World* magazine later published three of Latimer's images from the press kit. Latimer sued Kawasaki, Hachette, and others for copyright infringement.

The district court granted summary judgment in favor of defendants Kawasaki and Hachette, finding that, although Latimer's photographs were not derivative works of Hathaway's custom paint and graphics (and therefore were copyrightable), Latimer had granted to Kawasaki an implied license to use his photographs. The district court also held that Hachette's publication of the photographs in *Cycle World* was fair use.

The court of appeals first addressed whether Latimer's photographs were unauthorized derivative works based on Hathaway's work and, according to the appellants, entitled to no copyright protection. The court noted that, under 17 U.S.C. § 103(a), "protection for a work employing preexisting material in which copyright subsists does not extend to any part of the work in which such material has been used unlawfully."[31] The court's decision did not analyze whether Latimer's photographs contained original elements that would be entitled to copyright protection as provided in section 103(b), but noted that "Latimer's photographs do not qualify for copyright protection if they are derivative works made without Ryan Hathaway's authorization."[32]

The court held that Latimer's photographs were entitled to copyright protection because they were not *unauthorized* derivative works. The court did not decide whether the photographs were derivative works. The objective evidence showed that Latimer's photography of the motorcycles was a use contemplated by an implied license granted to Kawasaki by Hathaway. Given that Latimer's works were not an unlawful use, the court found that section 103(a) did not limit Latimer's copyright in his photographs.

In finding that Hathaway had granted an implied license to Kawasaki to photograph the motorcycles, the court applied a three-part test: "[a]n implied license is created when one party (1) creates a work at another person's request; (2) delivers the work to that person; and (3) intends that the person copy and distribute the work."[33] And the court held that unless the party expressly limits the scope of the implied license upon delivery of the work, the license extends to all uses.

---

31. *Id.* at 1233–34.
32. *Id.* at 1234.
33. *Id.* at 1235.

The objective evidence showed that Hathaway created the original artwork at Kawasaki's request and knew that the customized motorcycles would be publicly displayed and photographed by the media. Hathaway also knew that Kawasaki sought as much media exposure as possible for the project and intended to promote the customized motorcycles as widely as possible. The court concluded that "it is reasonable to infer that Hathaway intended that his artwork be photographed and distributed by Kawasaki . . . ."[34] The court also found that "Hathaway did not expressly restrict the scope of the license when he delivered the work."[35] Thus, the court concluded, Latimer's photography of the motorcycles was a use contemplated by Hathaway's implied license to Kawasaki.

The court reversed the grant of summary judgment to Kawasaki, finding that there were genuine issues of fact concerning the scope of implied license given by Latimer to Kawasaki. The principal question was "whether Latimer delivered a warning adequate to put Kawasaki on notice that certain uses of Latimer's photos would constitute copyright infringement."[36] The pertinent facts were disputed.

The court also reversed the district court's grant of summary judgment to Hachette on its fair use defense. The court confirmed that fair use is an affirmative defense and should be pleaded as such a defense. Given that Hachette did not plead the defense in its answer or motion for summary judgment and offered no justification for its failure to plead fair use, the district court erred by raising the defense sua sponte. The court of appeals did not rule that the defense of fair use had been waived, but left open the possibility that Hachette could file a motion to amend its answer to assert the fair use defense, at which time the district court could consider whether the defense had been waived.

ASSIGNMENT

Settlement Agreement Unambiguously Transferred Ownership in Copyrights Relating to the Design and Décor of Fast Food Restaurants

In ***Thomsen v. Famous Dave's of America, Inc.,***[37] the Eighth Circuit held that a settlement agreement between the plaintiff and the defendant unambiguously assigned ownership of certain copyrights relating to the décor and design of fast food restaurants to the defendant, Famous Dave's.

Famous Dave's is a chain of barbeque restaurants. In 1995, the cofounder of the restaurant chain hired Thomsen, an independent contractor, to design and manufacture signs and décor for the first of what was to become thirty-six restaurants. None of the drawings and designs submitted by Thomsen to Famous Dave's were registered with the Copyright Office and only a small number of them were signed and marked "not for reproduction." Thomsen believed he was the only contractor working for Famous Dave's but later learned that Famous Dave's had hired another contractor to incorporate his designs into a new restaurant it was building. Thomsen sent Famous Dave's a cease and desist letter and demanded to be paid $600,000 for copyright infringement. The parties

---

34. *Id.* at 1236.
35. *Id.*
36. *Id.* at 1238.
37. 606 F.3d 905 (8th Cir. 2010).

then drafted and entered into a settlement agreement without the assistance of lawyers. In 2007, Thomsen brought suit against Famous Dave's for copyright infringement for the designs of the twenty restaurants he had created between 1995 and 2000 and breach of the settlement agreement. The district court granted summary judgment in favor of Famous Dave's.

On appeal, Thomsen asserted that in interpreting the relevant sections of the agreement, the court should place itself "'in the position of the parties at the time the agreement was negotiated' and take into account the surrounding circumstances in deciding whether he conveyed any copyrights to Famous Dave's."[38] The court rejected this approach on the ground that under Minnesota law, a court may consider parol evidence "'only if the contract is ambiguous on its face'"[39] and here the settlement agreement signed by the parties unambiguously assigned ownership of certain copyrights to Famous Dave's. In particular, the court found that paragraph 9 of the agreement, which states that "[Thomsen] is releasing all copyright, proprietary design and sign work to [Famous Dave's] in all other restaurants that he has worked on with [certain exceptions]" "is a clear conveyance '(releasing . . . to)' of the sum total of Thomsen's previous work for Famous Dave's '(all other restaurants that he has worked on)' with the explicit exception of [certain restaurants explicitly listed in the agreement]."[40]

In asking the court to rely on extrinsic evidence, Thomsen argued that, based on the dictionary definition of "release," paragraph 9 can reasonably be interpreted to mean he was liberating Famous Dave's from liability. The court rejected this argument, noting that, because the language of paragraph 9 uses the term "releasing . . . to," not "releasing . . . from," paragraph 9 is "susceptible to only one interpretation, and that is that Thomsen was giving up a right or claim *to* Famous Dave's, rather than liberating Famous Dave's *from* an obligation."[41]

The court further observed that although a word may have more than one meaning, "Thomsen's strained reading of the first sentence of paragraph 9 would make little sense for it would be saying that he 'liberating from an obligation all copyright, proprietary design and sign work to Famous Dave's.'"[42]

Finally, the court rejected Thomsen's argument that because he received no money for the copyright transfer, Famous Dave's interpretation of the agreement would lead to an absurd result, noting that Thomsen did receive up to $23,000 in the parties' settlement and that Famous Dave's also agreed not to sue Thomsen and to provide him with potential future work. Thus, the "agreement was an exchange of mutual promises and concessions that mended the parties relationship. Whether Thomsen made a wise bargain is irrelevant, as unambiguous contract language 'shall be enforced by courts even if the result is harsh.'"[43] Accordingly, the court concluded that Thomsen unambiguously transferred copyright

---

38. *Id.* at 908 (citing Midway Ctr. Assocs. v. Midway Ctr., Inc., 237 N.W.2d 76, 78 (Minn. 1975)).

39. *Id.* at 5 (citing Hous. & Redev. Auth. of Chisholm v. Norman, 696 N.W.2d 329, 337 (Minn. 2005)).

40. *Id.* at 908.

41. *Id.* at 909 (emphasis in original).

42. *Id.*

43. *Id.* at 911 (citing Denelsbeck v. Wells Fargo & Co., 666 N.W.2d 329, 347 (Minn. 2003)).

ownership of the restaurant designs to the company and Thomsen's copyright claims failed as a matter of law.

LEGISLATION

Senate Bill to Clean, Clarify, and Correct Copyright Act

On August 2, 2010, the U.S. Senate passed the **Copyright Cleanup, Clarification, and Corrections Act of 2010.**[44] The provisions of the law fall into three categories: those designed to make the Copyright Office's operations more efficient; those designed to clarify issues of copyright law made unclear either by recent court decisions or by ambiguities in the statute; and those that are technical.

First, the law includes statutory changes that will facilitate the Copyright Office's transition to digital files and record keeping, including a provision designed to make it easier for filers to submit documents electronically. As such, the law removes the text "in both electronic and hard copy formats" from the text following 17 U.S.C. § 512(c)(2), which addresses the registration of agents for purposes of DMCA notice and takedown procedures. The law also alters section 205(a), which regulates the way in which transfers of copyright are recorded at the Copyright Office, by including the following: "A sworn or official certification may be submitted to the Copyright Office electronically, pursuant to the regulations established by the Register of Copyrights."

Next, the law repeals 17 U.S.C. § 601, which prohibits the manufacture, importation, and public distribution of copies of certain works. In addition, the law changes the title of Chapter 6 from "Manufacturing Requirements, Importation, and Exportation" to "Importation and Exportation." To conform to this amendment, the law also repeals referring subsection 409(10), redesignates subsection 409(11) as 409(10), and strikes "unless the provisions of section 601 are applicable" from the first sentence of section 602(b).

The law also clarifies several copyright issues concerning sublicenses, phonorecord publication, judicial review of Copyright Royalty Judges, and sound recording licenses. In particular, the law modifies section 201(d)(2) so that sublicensing is expressly allowed in the absence of a written agreement to the contrary. Section 303(b) is revised so that the phonorecord publication exemption not only includes musical work, but also includes any dramatic work or literary work. Section 803(b)(6)(A) is revised to include a provision that regulations issued by the Copyright Royalty Judges are subject to judicial review. Finally, the Act amends section 114(f)(2)(C), which governs sound recording licenses, by striking "preexisting subscription digital audio transmission services or preexisting satellite digital radio audio services" and inserting "eligible nonsubscription services and new subscription services."

The remainder of the law addresses technical corrections such as rearrangements to reflect these changes and typographical consistency in the Copyright Act.

---

44. Pub. L. No. 111-295, 124 Stat. 3180 (2010). President Obama signed it into law December 9, 2010.

Senate to Consider Legislation That Would Increase or Alter Protection for New and Original Fashion Designs

On August 5, 2010, Senator Charles E. Schumer introduced a bill in Congress entitled the ***Innovative Design Protection and Piracy Prevention Act***[45] (IDPPPA). The new bill, if enacted, would provide a three-year term of protection for a variety of new and original fashion designs of articles of apparel, accessories and eyeglass frames. The IDPPPA would insulate from infringement liability consumers who inadvertently "offer for sale, advertise" or distribute any article embodying a design protected by the new law.

In particular, the IDPPPA would amend section 1301(a) of the Copyright Act to extend protection for design protection for an original article of apparel and would amend section 1302(b) to specify that the term apparel means "men's, women's or children's clothing, including undergarments, outerwear, gloves, footwear, and headgear; handbags, purses, wallets, duffel bags, suitcases, tote bags, belts; and eyeglass frames."[46]

The IDPPPA would add a new subsection, section 1301(c), that reads: "(c) RULE OF CONSTRUCTION.—In the case of a fashion design under this chapter, those differences or variations which are considered non-trivial for the purposes of establishing that a design is subject to protection under subsection (b)(7) shall be considered non-trivial for the purposes of establishing that a defendant's design is not substantially identical under subsection (b)(10) and section 1309(e)."[47] Therefore, under the proposed law, the owner of a fashion design-plaintiff would have the burden to establish that the design of defendant is substantially identical.

If enacted, the IDPPPA would amend section 1302(5) of the Copyright Act to specify that the design of a vessel hull is not subject to protection under this section of the Copyright Act and to add at the end of the "Designs Not Subject to Protection" the following: "(B) in the case of a fashion design, embodied in a useful article that was made public by the designer or owner in the United States or a foreign country before the date of enactment of this chapter or more than three years before the date upon which protection of the design is asserted under this chapter."[48]

The IDPPPA would amend the end of section 1303 of the Copyright Act, "Revisions, Adaptations, and Rearrangements" to include the following: "[t]he presence or absence of a particular color or colors or of a pictorial or graphic work imprinted on fabric shall not be considered in determining the protection of a fashion design under section 1301 or 1302 or in determining infringement under section 1309."[49] Therefore, the presence of or absence of any particular color or colors would be irrelevant in determining whether a fashion design is protectable or in determining whether a design has been infringed.

The proposed law would also amend the "Term of Protection," found at section 1305(a)(2) of the Copyright Act, to read as follows: "(2) for a fashion design, shall continue for a term of three years beginning on the date of the commencement of protection under section 1304."[50] The IDPPPA would thus provide for a three-year term of

45. S. 3728, 111th Cong. (2010).
46. *Id.* § 2(a)(2).
47. *Id.* § 2(a)(3).
48. *Id.* § 2(b)(3).
49. *Id.* § 2(c).
50. *Id.* § 2(d).

protection for original fashion designs. But, fashion designs created before the enactment of IDPPPA would have no protection under the proposed law.

The IDPPPA would amend section 1309(c) of the Copyright Act, to specify that it shall not be an act of infringement to offer for sale or advertise any article embodying a design created without knowledge that the design was protected. The proposed law would thus protect consumers and retailers from infringement liability for purchasing, selling, offering for sale, or advertising articles embodying protected designs.

Additionally, the IDPPPA would amend subsection (e) of section 1309 of the Copyright Act to read in part as follows: "(3) FASHION DESIGN.—In the case of a fashion design, a design shall not be deemed to have been copied from a protected design if that design—(A) is not substantially identical in overall visual appearance to and as to the original elements of a protected design; or (B) is the result of independent creation."[51] Therefore, the proposed law would require the owner of a fashion design to establish that the accused design is "substantially identical" as the standard for infringement liability. Independent creation would prevent any liability for infringement. The IDPPPA would also amend section 1309 of the Copyright Act to add subsection (i) to read: "HOME SEWING EXCEPTION.—(1) IN GENERAL.—It is not an infringement of the exclusive rights of a design owner for a person to produce a single copy of a protected design for personal use or for the use of an immediate family member, if that copy is not offered for sale or use in trade during the period of protection."[52] Therefore, the proposed law would provide a single copy exception for individuals who sew for personal noncommercial purposes.

Finally, the IDPPPA would amend section 1310(a) of the Copyright Act to state that the registration process shall not apply to fashion designs. The proposed law would also amend section 1327 of the Copyright Act, entitled "Penalty for False Representation," to provide for a minimum fine of $5,000 and a maximum fine of not more than $10,000.

Copyright Royalty Board's New Royalty Rates Affirmed

In *Recording Industry Ass'n of America, Inc. v. Librarian of Congress*,[53] the Court of Appeals for the District of Columbia affirmed the final determination of the Copyright Royalty Board (Board) imposing a new term and two new royalty rates. The Board, by law, sets the terms and rates for copyright royalties when copyright owners and licensees fail to do so themselves. Appellant, RIAA, participated as a party in the 17 U.S.C. § 115 statutory licensing proceeding before the Board to set section 115 license terms and rates. After the Board issued its final determination, in which the Board announced its decision to institute a 1.5-percent-per-month late fee for late royalty payments and a 24¢ royalty rate for ringtone sold, RIAA filed a motion for rehearing. The Board denied the motion. RIAA appealed, arguing that those two aspects of the Board's decision were arbitrary and capricious for purposes of the Administrative Procedure Act.

The D.C. Circuit found that the Board is authorized by the Copyright Act to impose a late fee for section 115 royalty payments. The court determined that the Board's decision to impose a late fee, as well as the amount of that fee, was informed by the criteria in

---

51. *Id.* § 2(e)(2).
52. *Id.* § 2(e)(3).
53. 608 F.3d 861 (D.C. Cir. 2010) (hereinafter *RIAA 2010*).

section 801(b)(1) of the Copyright Act: (1) maximizing the availability of creative works to the public; (2) providing copyright owners a fair return for their creative works and copyright users a fair income; (3) recognizing the relative roles of the copyright owners and users; and (4) minimizing any disruptive impact on the industries involved.

With regard to the late fee, the D.C. Circuit noted that the Copyright Act provides that the Board "may consider rates and terms under voluntary license agreements," in addition to mandatory objectives set forth in section 801(b)(1) when setting terms of the section 115 license.[54] The court noted that, in accordance with *Recording Industry Ass'n of America v. Librarian of Congress*,[55] the Librarian has interpreted "precedent to mean that marketplace analogies, along with other evidence, must be considered."[56] The D.C. Circuit explained that this means that the Board must take into account existing market for voluntary licenses and that the Board did so here.

The court explained that a late fee corresponds with the practices in other similar markets, such as Webcasting and satellite digital radio industries. The court noted that the Board considered other evidence presented by copyright owners during the proceedings and concluded that, although the Board *considers* market conditions when setting terms and rates, they are not required to choose a late fee that exactly matches a market rate. The court concluded that the Board appropriately took into account market evidence when imposing the late fee. The court also found that copyright owner's right of termination under regulations for the section 115 license did not negate the Board's authority to institute a late fee because the congressional scheme contemplates both a late fee and a termination right.

The D.C. Circuit disagreed with RIAA's contention that a late fee is inappropriate because the lateness of payments is purportedly due to uncertainty about how to divide royalties among multiple copyright owners. The court noted that, even if it were true that divided interests in a copyright made it difficult to make timely payments to each copyright owner, that fact would in no way prevent the imposition of a late fee. The court found that under regulations governing the operation of the section 115 license, a licensee can satisfy its obligation to pay a royalty by paying any *one* copyright owner—even when many individuals have a stake in a copyright.

The D.C. Circuit noted that the Board took into account the section 801(b)(1) criteria in making its decision to establish a penny-rate royalty structure for ringtones. The court found that the Board had considered criterion of maximizing the availability of creative work and concluded that a "nominal rate for ringtones" supports that objective. With regard to the criterion of affording the copyright owner a fair return, the court determined that the Board found that the new rates did not deprive copyright owners of a fair return on their creative works. The court concluded that the Board found that the penny rate met the statutory criterion of respecting the relative roles of the copyright owner and user. The court determined that under the criterion of minimizing disruptive impact on the industry, the Board found that the rate structure selected was reasonable and already in place in many markets, thus, minimizing any disruptive impact.

---

54. *Id.* at 366; *see* 17 U.S.C. § 115(c)(3)(D) (2006).

55. Recording Indus. Ass'n of Am., Inc. v. Librarian of Congress, 176 F.3d 528 (D.C. Cir. 1999) (hereinafter *RIAA 1999*).

56. *RIAA*, 608 F. 3d at 866 (quoting *RIAA 1999*, 176 F.3d at 534).

RIAA further challenged the fact that the structure of the ringtone royalty rate imposed by the Board is a penny rate rather than a percentage-of-revenue rate. RIAA argues that the penny-rate royalty structure inappropriately departs from market analogies for voluntary licenses. The D.C. Circuit noted that although existing market rates for voluntary licenses do not bind the Board when making its determinations, the Board considered those rates when selecting the penny-rate royalty structure. The court noted that, after weighing the costs and benefits of the parties' proposals and taking into account relevant market practices, the Board concluded that a penny rate was superior to those proposals. The court explained that, in the Board's view, the penny rate provided "the most efficient mechanism for capturing the value of the reproduction and distribution rights at issue" and concluded that the Board's preference for a penny-rate royalty structure was reasonable.[57]

With regard to RIAA's argument that plummeting ringtone prices render the penny rate inherently unreasonable, the D.C. Circuit found that the Board considered and rejected this contention, stating "[the claim] . . . is not supported by the record of evidence in this proceeding . . . RIAA [does not] offer any persuasive evidence that would in any way quantify any claimed adverse impact on projected future revenues stemming from the continued application of a penny-rate structure . . . ."[58]

Satellite Television Extension and Localism Act of 2010 Reauthorizes, Updates, and Modernizes the Satellite Carrier Distant Broadcast Signal License

On May 27, 2010, President Obama signed into law the **Satellite Television Extension and Localism Act of 2010 (the Act).**[59] The Act makes a number of changes to the "statutory licenses" laws, including the following: makes applicable various existing provisions to digital transmissions by removing the word "analog";[60] requires a satellite carrier, whose secondary transmissions are subject to statutory licensing, to deposit filing fees semiannually with the Register of Copyrights; revises requirements regarding local-into-satellite retransmissions; shifts certain tasks from the Librarian of Congress to the Copyright Royalty Judge; and redesignates superstations as non-network stations.[61]

The Act extends through December 31, 2014, the copyright liability moratorium allowing subscribers that do not receive a signal Grade A intensity of a local network broadcast station to receive signals of affiliated networks in certain specified instances. Additionally, the Act increases the maximum statutory damages for violation of territorial restrictions for willful or repeated individual violations from $5 to $250 per month, and for a pattern of violations, from $250,000 to $2.5 million for each three-month period.

The Act modifies requirements regarding statutory licenses for secondary transmissions into stations within local markets if the secondary transmission is made by a satellite carrier to the public and the satellite carrier is in compliance with rules and regulations of the

---

57. *RIAA*, 608 F.3d at 870 (quoting Mechanical & Digital Phonorecord Delivery Rate Determination Proceeding, 74 Fed. Reg. 4510, 4515 (Jan. 26, 2009)).

58. *Id.* at 870 (omission in original) (quoting Rate Determination Proceeding, 74 Fed. Reg. at 4516).

59. Pub. L. No. 111-175, 124 Stat. 1218 (2010).

60. *Id.,* 124 Stat. at 1219–23.

61. *Id.*

Federal Communications Commission (FCC). The Act also sets forth secondary transmission licensing provisions with respect to: states with a single full-power network station; states with all network stations and non-network stations in the same local market; certain additional stations; and networks of noncommercial educational broadcast stations.

Section 104 of the Act modifies various definitions, including defining a primary transmission as a transmission made to the public by a transmitting facility whose signals are being received and further transmitted by a secondary service, and specifies that, in the case of a television broadcast station, the primary stream and any multicast streams transmitted by the station constitute primary transmissions.

Under section 105 of the Act, whenever an injunction was imposed on a carrier because of certain willful or repeated pattern or other practice, before enactment of this subsection, the court that issued the injunction must waive the injunction if the court recognizes the entity as a qualified carrier under the Act that provides local-into-local service to all Designated Marketing Areas (DMAs). The Act imposes penalties on a qualified carrier if the court determines that the qualified entity has failed to provide local-into-local service to all DMAs.

Section 106 of the Act requires a fee to be paid upon filing a statement of account based on certain secondary transmissions of primary transmissions to cover reasonable expenses incurred by the Copyright Office. Section 107 terminates the effectiveness of provisions relating to limitations on exclusive rights regarding secondary transmissions of distant television programming by satellite on December 31, 2014.

The communications provision of the Act amends the Communication Act of 1934 to extend to: (1) December 31, 2014, termination of provisions allowing satellite transmission of network station signals; and (2) January 01, 2015, termination of provisions that prohibit certain television broadcast stations from engaging in exclusive contracts for carriage or failing to negotiate in good faith, and the termination of provisions prohibiting multichannel video programming distributors from failing to negotiate in good faith for retransmission consent. The Act also allows a satellite carrier to retransmit a significantly viewed signal of a station located outside the local market which a subscriber is located, only for subscribers currently receiving analog local-into-local service, or with regard to high-definition signals, only if the carrier also retransmits in high-definition format the signal of a station in the local market of the subscriber and affiliated with the same network; and allows a satellite carrier that retransmits high-definition signals in a local market to receive high-definition signals via a reception antenna.

The Act authorizes the FCC to require, as a condition of any provision, initial authorization, or authorization renewal that a provider of direct broadcast satellite service providing video programming or a qualified satellite provider providing such programming, reserve a specified portion of its channel capacity for noncommercial programming of an educational or informational nature; requires the Register of Copyrights to report to Congress on methods of phasing out of the statutory licensing requirements in specified provisions by making those provisions inapplicable to the secondary transmission of a primary transmission of a broadcast station that is authorized to license the secondary transmission; and requires the Comptroller General to study and report to Congress on changes to the carriage requirements currently imposed on multichannel video programming distributors under the Communications Act of 1934 and FCC regulations that would be of interest to consumers if Congress implemented such a phase-out.

The Act requires the FCC to report to Congress on the number of households in a state that receive local broadcast stations from a station located in a different state; the extent to which consumers have access to in-state broadcast programming; and whether there are alternatives to use of DMAs to define local markets that would provide more consumers with in-state broadcast programming. The Act requires the FCC to study and report concerning incentives that would induce a satellite carrier to provide television in certain local markets in which the carrier does not provide service.

Section 307 of the Act provides that, unless specifically provided otherwise, this Act shall take effect on February 27, 2010 and the secondary transmission of a performance or display of a work embodied in a primary transmission is not an infringement of copyright if it was made by a satellite carrier on or after February 27, 2010, prior to enactment of this Act, and was in compliance with the law as in existence on February 27, 2010.

The Act provides that the budgetary effects of this Act for the purpose of complying with the statutory Pay-As-You-Go Act of 2010 shall be determined by reference to the latest statement titled "Budgetary Effects of PAYGO Legislation" for this Act, provided that such statement has been submitted prior to the vote on passage.

Performance Rights Bill Amended by Senate Judiciary Committee

On October 16, 2009, the Senate Judiciary Committee approved and sent to the Senate floor an amended version of Senate Bill 379,[62] the *Performance Rights Act,* which would amend the Copyright Act of 1976 by adding a public performance right for sound recordings applicable to broadcast radio stations. Currently broadcast radio stations are required to pay licensing fees to the composer of a song that is broadcast, but not to the recording artist who performs it.

The amendments to the original version of S. 379 focused first on fees. The original bill provided for a single statutory license fee that could be paid by broadcast radio stations below a certain size in lieu of the payment of royalties to recording artists. This basic fee structure was amended to establish a system of flat annual license fees at multiple levels based upon revenues. Individual commercial broadcast stations with gross revenues of less than $1.25 million would be subject to four levels of flat fees ranging from a high of $5,000 to a low of only $100. Only commercial stations earning gross revenues of more than $1.25 million per year would be subject to payment of royalties to sound recording artists. All noncommercial public broadcast stations would be subject only to three levels of flat fees, ranging from a high of $1,000 per year for stations with gross revenues over $100,000 to a low of only $100 per year.

The amendments also contain language prohibiting anything in the Act from interfering in any fashion with the public performance rights or royalties that would be payable to songwriters or copyright owners of musical works. Sound recording licensees are specifically prohibited from publicly performing the sound recording unless they also have a license to publicly perform any included musical work. Additionally, the amendments prohibit the use of these statutory annual fees in any proceeding before the Copyright Royalty Board that involves setting rates. License fees for the public performance of copyrighted musical works cannot be adversely affected by the amount of the statutory fees for the public performance of sound recordings.

---

62. Performance Rights Act of 2009, S. 379, 111th Cong. (2009).

Finally, the amendments provide that the recipient of the license fee for the public performance of a sound recording by audio transmission is still responsible for any payments owed to a particular recording artist pursuant to that artist's contract. The amendments further require that such a licensor pay 1 percent of the license fee received into a fund to be distributed equally between the nonfeatured musicians and the nonfeatured vocalists on the sound recording that is being licensed for public performance.

PART V
TRADE SECRETS

CHAPTER 20

TRADE SECRETS

This past year, court decisions addressed various issues related to the protection of trade secrets, misappropriation claims, breach of nondisclosure agreements, and procedural, discovery, and evidentiary questions, including those involving res judicata, subpoenas, and expert witnesses.

Several noteworthy decisions addressed whether or not claimed trade secrets qualified for such protection. In *State ex rel. Perrea v. Cincinnati Public School,* the Supreme Court of Ohio held that high school semester exams developed by an Ohio school district were protected from public disclosure as trade secrets. By contrast, in *Keystone Fruit Marketing, Inc. v. Brownfield,* the Ninth Circuit upheld the dismissal of a trade secrets claim as a matter of law, finding that all the information contained in a spreadsheet was publicly available in well-known publications. Similarly, in *McKay Consulting v. Rockingham Memorial Hospital,* the U.S. District Court for the Western District of Virginia held that the plaintiff was foreclosed from seeking trade secret protection for his idea for increasing the reimbursement rates for certain hospitals because the idea was readily ascertainable and could have been independently formulated by other customers or competitors.

In other decisions, courts found that trade secret protection was not available because the information had not been treated as a secret. For example, in *Kema, Inc. v. Koperwhats,* the U.S. District Court for the Northern District of California held that the defendant had forfeited trade secret protection for the source code of his computer software as a matter of law by submitting it to the Copyright Office without redaction. Likewise, in *Southwest Stainless LP v. Sappington,* the Tenth Circuit held that the plaintiff's price quote was not subject to protection as a trade secret due to the plaintiff's disclosure of the quote to a prospective customer without a promise of confidentiality.

In determining what a plaintiff must show to prove a trade secret misappropriation claim, the First Circuit in *Astro-Med, Inc. v. Nihon Kohden America, Inc.* held that the plaintiff was not required to show the defendant's use of the trade secret; proof of acquisition or disclosure of a trade secret acquired by improper means was sufficient to establish misappropriation. In *Arizant Holdings Inc. v. Gust,* the U.S. District Court for the District of Minnesota held that forwarding e-mails from a corporate e-mail account to a personal e-mail account did not constitute acquisition by improper means, as required to prove misappropriation, where no company policy prohibiting such actions was in existence.

In *Kara Technology Inc. v. Stamps.com Inc.,* the Federal Circuit affirmed-in-part and reversed-in-part the district court's summary judgment in the defendant's favor, dismissing the plaintiff's claim for breach of a nondisclosure agreement as barred by Texas's four-year statute of limitations for such claims. The court upheld the district court's decision regarding the plaintiff's claim based on note-taking by the defendant's employees at a meeting more than four years before the complaint was filed, but found disputes of fact to exist regarding breach of the nondisclosure agreement not addressed by the district court's summary judgment order.

Two trade secret decisions involved sanctions issues. In *Flir Systems, Inc. v. Parrish*, the California Court of Appeal affirmed an award sanctioning the plaintiff for bringing and maintaining a trade secret action in bad faith. The court found that the plaintiff's claim for threatened misappropriation of trade secrets was objectively specious and that the plaintiff acted with subjective bad faith, as the claims were premised on the theory of inevitable disclosure (which had been conclusively rejected by California courts), the plaintiff had an anticompetitive motive in filing suit, and the plaintiff proceeded to trial with full knowledge that the claims lacked legal and factual support. In *Rimkus Consulting Group, Inc. v. Cammarata,* the U.S. District Court for the Southern District of Texas confronted a spoliation of evidence claim based on the defendant's destruction of e-mails. Although the elements of res judicata otherwise were present, the court held that a prior state court proceeding did not preclude the issues to which the deleted e-mails were relevant, including the misappropriation of trade secrets claims.

In another res judicata case, *Gillig v. Nike, Inc.,* the Federal Circuit upheld the district court's holding that the plaintiff's trade secrets claim was barred by the applicable statute of limitations, but found improper the district court's dismissal of the inventorship correction claims based on res judicata, to the extent the claims were based on an assignment that occurred after the filing of the complaint in the prior action.

In notable decisions addressing discovery and evidentiary matters in trade secret cases, courts considered issues involving third-party subpoenas and expert testimony. In *Premier Election Solutions, Inc. v. Systest Labs, Inc.,* the U.S. District Court for the District of Colorado quashed a third-party subpoena served by the defendant on the grounds that the information sought was protected as trade secrets and the defendant failed to show that disclosure of the trade secrets was relevant and necessary. In *U.S. Gypsum Co. v. LaFarge North America, Inc.,* the U.S. District Court for the Northern District of Illinois denied both parties' cross-motions to exclude expert testimony regarding the plaintiff's claimed trade secrets, finding both experts' opinions to be relevant and reliable.

DEFINITION

Copyright Office Submission Forfeits Trade Secrets Protection

In ***Kema, Inc. v. Koperwhats,***[1] the Northern District of California granted Kema's motion to dismiss Koperwhats's trade secret misappropriation claim. Koperwhats alleged violation of the California Uniform Trade Secrets Act based on a dispute with his former employer, Kema, over rights to computer software used by utility companies to analyze energy data. According to Koperwhats, Kema stole his software, improperly transferred it to a third party, and sold or otherwise distributed software programs utilizing his trade secrets. Kema moved to dismiss Koperwhats' claims under Federal Rule of Civil Procedure 12(b)(6).

Under California Civil Code § 3426.1, "a 'trade secret' must (1) '[d]erive independent economic value, actual or potential, from not being generally known to the public or

---

1.   658 F. Supp. 2d 1022 (N.D. Cal. 2009).

to other persons who can obtain economic value from its disclosure or use,' and must be (2) 'subject to efforts that are reasonable under the circumstances to maintain its secrecy.'"[2] Kema argued that Koperwhats could not meet this statutory definition of "trade secret" because he had disclosed the software at issue without attempting to maintain its secrecy. In support of its argument, Kema highlighted Koperwhats' own allegation that, in seeking a copyright registration, he had submitted the source code for the software to the Copyright Office. This source code submission was publicly accessible.

In response, Koperwhats claimed that his submission was accompanied by a notice that it contained trade secrets. The court noted, however, that this "notice" was, in fact, an e-mail that was sent to the Copyright Office ten months *after* Koperwhats applied for registration. Further, Koperwhats did not allege that his submission to the Copyright Office was redacted or otherwise complied with the procedure set forth in the applicable regulation for the submission of software containing trade secrets. Instead, the entirety of the Koperwhats submission—including the alleged trade secrets—was available to the public. As a result, the court dismissed Koperwhats' trade secret claim.

High School Exams Protected as Trade Secrets by Ohio Supreme Court

In *State ex rel. Perrea v. Cincinnati Public Schools,*[3] the Supreme Court of Ohio denied a writ of mandamus to compel disclosure of high school semester exams, finding the exams were exempt from disclosure under the Ohio Public Records Act because they constitute trade secrets under the Ohio Uniform Trade Secrets Act (OUTSA).[4]

Paul Perrea, a high school teacher in the Cincinnati Public Schools (CPS) district, filed a request under the Ohio Public Records Act for copies of the ninth-grade semester exams administered in January 2007. Perrea's request indicated that he intended to use the exams for the noncommercial purposes of "criticism, research, comment and/or education."[5] Perrea filed a writ of mandamus to compel the production of the exams under the Ohio Public Records Act after CPS refused his disclosure request.

CPS did not contest that the semester exams were "records" under the Ohio Public Records Act.[6] Rather, it relied on two exceptions to disclosure under the Act: that they were trade secrets and copyrighted material.

The court considered the following six factors to determine whether the semester exams met the statutory definition of a trade secret: "(1) The extent to which the information is known outside the business; (2) the extent to which it is known inside the business, i.e., by the employees; (3) the precautions taken by the holder of the trade secret to guard the secrecy of the information; (4) the savings effected and the value to the holder in having the information as against competitors; (5) the amount of effort or money expended in obtaining and developing the information; and (6) the amount of time and expense it would take for others to acquire and duplicate the information."[7]

---

2. *Id.* at 1030 (quoting CAL. CIV. CODE § 3426.1(d)(1)–(2) (West 1997)).
3. 916 N.E.2d 1049 (Ohio 2009).
4. OHIO REV. CODE ANN. §§ 1333.61–1333.69 (West 2004).
5. *Perrea*, 916 N.E.2d at 1051.
6. OHIO REV. CODE ANN. § 149.43 (West 2002).
7. *Perrea*, 916 N.E.2d at 1053 (quoting State ex rel. Plain Dealer v. Ohio Dept. of Ins., 687 N.E.2d 661, 672 (Ohio 1997)).

The court found that CPS had taken steps to maintain the secrecy of the semester exams because it prohibited copying, allowed teachers only limited access to exams, kept the exams in a secure location and required the return of all exams within a week after they were administered. The court rejected Perrea's argument that CPS had disclosed publicly the semester exams by placing the scoring guidelines on a teacher-accessible intranet Web site. The court noted that this disclosure did not reveal the actual questions asked and, even if a limited number of exam questions could be reconstructed based on the guidelines, this partial disclosure would not foreclose the possibility of a trade secret.

The court also found that CPS derived economic value from the secrecy of the exams. CPS spent over $750,000 developing the semester exams, the exams would have no or minimal value if they were made public before they were administered, CPS would have to spend over $270,000 to recreate the tests every year, and CPS would no longer be able to administer the exams if the tests were made public.

Persuaded by CPS's evidence, the court held that the semester exams were trade secrets and, thus, not public records subject to disclosure under the Ohio Public Records Act. Having reached this conclusion, the court declined to address the copyright exception to disclosure under the Act.

Not Generally Known or Readily Ascertainable

Idea Submission Not Protectable as Trade Secret

In *McKay Consulting, Inc. v. Rockingham Memorial Hospital,*[8] the Western District of Virginia granted Defendant Rockingham's motion to dismiss plaintiff's trade secret misappropriation claim. Plaintiff McKay alleged that it spent a significant amount of time and money formulating an "idea" to increase the reimbursement rates for certain hospitals, and that Defendant Rockingham disclosed that idea to another consultant in violation of its contractual obligations to McKay. Based on Rockingham's alleged conduct, McKay filed a complaint against Rockingham claiming, inter alia, misappropriation of trade secrets under the Virginia Uniform Trade Secrets Act.

On Rockingham's motion to dismiss, the court held that McKay's complaint did not contain sufficient allegations to state a claim for misappropriation of trade secrets. The court defined a trade secret as "information that '[d]erives independent economic value, actual or potential, from not being generally known to, and not being readily ascertainable by proper means by, other persons who can obtain economic value from its disclosure or use . . . .'"[9] It also noted that the "'crucial characteristic of a trade secret is secrecy rather than novelty,'"[10] and that "[i]n order to be protected as a trade secret, the information in question 'must be secret, and must not be of public knowledge or of a general knowledge in the trade or business.'"[11]

---

8.   665 F. Supp. 2d 626 (W.D. Va. 2009).

9.   *Id.* at 634 (quoting Va. Code Ann. § 53.1-336 (2006)).

10. *Id.* (quoting Dionne v. Se. Foam Converting & Packaging, Inc., 397 S.E.2d 110, 113 (Va. 1990)).

11. *Id.* (quoting Hoechst Diafoil Co. v. Nan Ya Plastics Corp., 174 F.3d 411, 418 (4th Cir. 1999)).

In its complaint, McKay alleged that it analyzed "statutes and regulations" and "data published by the Center for Medicare and Medicaid Services" in developing its idea to increase reimbursement rates.[12] According to the court, such information was "widely disseminated" and "readily ascertainable by proper means—namely, by reference to the widely known and published laws and regulations of the United States—and as such was 'generally known' to other persons who could obtain economic value from its disclosure or use—namely, other consulting groups like McKay or hospitals like [Rockingham]."[13]

The court acknowledged that the Virginia Uniform Trade Secrets Act permits "combination" trade secrets, but it found that McKay's information, "advice based on an understanding of various published laws and regulations," was "qualitatively different from, for example, a unique combination of utility programs which interact to create a software program."[14] Having concluded that McKay's idea was "'readily ascertainable' and could have been independently formulated by any of the hospitals it approached or by a competitor," the court held that McKay was foreclosed from seeking trade secret protection, and it granted Rockingham's motion to dismiss.[15]

Reasonable Efforts to Maintain Secrecy

Disclosure of Price Quote to Prospective Customer without Obligation of Confidentiality Extinguishes Trade Secret as a Matter of Law

In *Southwest Stainless LP v. Sappington,*[16] the Tenth Circuit held that the Northern District of Oklahoma erred in finding that Southwest Stainless's pricing information constituted a trade secret and reversed the district court's judgment of trade secret misappropriation in favor of Southwest Stainless.

Defendant John Sappington was at one time employed by plaintiff as a senior sales person, which gave him access to pricing information. Prior to leaving this position, Sappington assisted Southwest Stainless in developing a bid for services to provide to Hughes Anderson. Later that same week, Sappington started working for defendant Rolled Alloy, a direct competitor of Southwest Stainless. Rolled Alloy also submitted a bid to Hughes Anderson, which was ultimately selected despite being only slightly less than that the amount quoted by Southwest Stainless. Southwest Stainless later sued Sappington and Rolled Alloy, asserting that its Hughes Anderson bid constituted a trade secret that Sappington disclosed to Rolled Alloy and Rolled Alloy used this information to undercut its bid to Hughes Anderson.

Oklahoma has adopted six factors from the Restatement of Torts that may be used by courts in determining whether information is a trade secret. These factors include "'(1) the extent to which the information is known outside of the business; (2) the extent to which the information is known by employees and others involved in the business; (3) the

---

12. *Id.* at 634–35 (internal quotation omitted).

13. *Id.* at 635 (citing Religious Tech. Ctr. v. Netcom On-Line Commc'n Servs., 923 F. Supp. 1231, 1256 (N.D. Cal. 1995)).

14. *Id.* (citing Integrated Cash Mgmt. Servs., Inc. v. Digital Transactions, Inc., 920 F.2d 171, 174 (2d Cir. 1990)).

15. *Id.*

16. 582 F.3d 1176 (10th Cir. 2009).

extent of measures taken by the business to guard the secrecy of the information; (4) the value of the information to the business and to competitors; (5) the amount of effort or money expended by the business in developing the information; and (6) the ease or difficulty with which the information could be properly acquired or duplicated by others.'"[17]

The Tenth Circuit noted that although Southwest Stainless had shown it made general efforts to keep company information confidential, it was undisputed that Southwest Stainless disclosed its quote to Hughes Anderson and admitted that Hughes Anderson was under no obligation to keep the information confidential. Because the bid was therefore known outside of the company, Southwest Stainless failed to take appropriate measures to prevent Hughes Anderson from disseminating the information, and the competitor could have properly acquired the information simply by requesting it from Hughes Anderson. Accordingly, the bid was not a trade secret. As a result, the Tenth Circuit held that the district court erred in determining the Hughes Anderson quote constituted a trade secret and, thus, reversed the judgment on the trade secret misappropriation claim.

EMPLOYMENT RELATIONSHIP

Use Restrictions

Attorneys' Fees and Costs Award Affirmed Because Trade Secret Action Was Brought and Maintained in Bad Faith

In *Flir Systems, Inc. v. Parrish,*[18] California's Court of Appeal upheld a $1,641,216.78 attorneys' fees and costs award as a sanction for bringing and maintaining a trade secret action in bad faith. The plaintiffs, FLIR Systems, Inc. and Indigo Systems Corporation (collectively, Indigo), manufactured and sold devices known as "microbolometers," which are used with infrared cameras, night vision, and thermal imaging. Indigo sued former employees William Parrish and Timothy Fitzgibbons after they left Indigo and communicated their intent to start a new company that would mass produce bolometers.

After trial, the court found no misappropriation or threatened misappropriation of trade secrets. Instead, the court concluded that the action was brought in bad faith because it was brought without evidentiary support and was premised on a theory of "inevitable disclosure," a doctrine not recognized by California courts.[19]

Under the doctrine of inevitable disclosure, "a plaintiff may prove threatened misappropriation by showing that a former employee's new employment will inevitably lead that employee to rely on the plaintiff's trade secrets."[20] Furthermore, the "doctrine of inevitable disclosure permits a trade secret owner to prevent a former employee from working for a competitor [or in the same field] despite the owner's failure to prove the employee has taken or threatens to use trade secrets."[21]

---

17. *Id.* at 1189 (quoting Australian Gold, Inc. v. Hatfield, 436 F.3d 1228, 1245 (10th Cir.2006)).

18. 95 Cal. Rptr. 3d 307 (Cal. App. 2d Dist. 2009).

19. *Id.* at 316.

20. Clorox Co. v. SC Johnson & Son, Inc., 627 F. Supp. 2d 954, 969 (E.D. Wis. 2009).

21. *Whyte*, 125 Cal. Rptr. 2d at 281.

California courts have rejected the inevitable disclosure doctrine as "contrary to California law and policy because it creates an after-the-fact covenant not to compete,"[22] which restricts "employee mobility."[23] As far back as 1944, the California Supreme Court expressed its disapproval of the doctrine, finding the mere fact that someone was employed by the plaintiff, knew the plaintiff's trade secrets, and now works for a competitor, insufficient evidence "from which an inference could be drawn that he was using or intended to use" the plaintiff's trade secrets.[24] In 2002 the *Whyte* court expressly rejected the inevitable disclosure doctrine;[25] and since then, California courts continue to adhere to that holding.

Section 3426.4 of California's Uniform Trade Secrets Act provides that a trial court may award reasonable attorneys' fees and costs to the prevailing party if the claim of misappropriation was made in "bad faith." Courts have defined the test for "bad faith" as follows: (1) objective speciousness of the claim; and (2) subjective bad faith in bringing or maintaining the action.[26]

"Objective speciousness exists where the action superficially appears to have merit but there is a complete lack of evidence to support the claim."[27] For instance, in *Gemini Aluminum Corp. v. California Custom Shapes, Inc.,* the court found the plaintiff's case for misappropriation of a trade secret and interference with prospective economic advantage objectively specious because both the defendant's actions and the plaintiff's filing occurred after the trade secret or customer's identity "arguably held any economic value, actual or potential," to the plaintiff.[28] Objective speciousness is not the same as frivolousness; according to the *Flir* court, a nonfrivolous claim may still be objectively specious if the plaintiff alleges a valid claim but then fails to produce evidence in support of the claim.[29]

The trial court in *Flir* concluded that the claim was objectively specious because Indigo suffered no economic harm and failed to produce any evidence of either misappropriation or threatened misappropriation of trade secrets. Indigo alleged that it suffered actual damages and that the respondents had willfully misappropriated its trade secrets, but did not produce any evidence of actual damages, misappropriation, or threatened misappropriation. Also, objective speciousness was established by evidence that Indigo filed the lawsuit for anticompetitive reasons. Specifically, Indigo's CEO testified that the action was filed because the company could not "tolerate a direct competitive threat" from the Respondents.

Subjective bad faith means "that the action or tactic [was] pursued for an improper motive."[30] Courts answer this question through a "factual inquiry into the plaintiff's sub-

---

22. Metro Traffic Control, Inc. v. Shadow Traffic Network, 27 Cal. Rptr. 2d 573, 577 (Cal. App. 2d Dist. 1994).

23. *Whyte*, 125 Cal. Rptr. 2d at 281.

24. Continental Car-Na-Var Corp. v. Moseley, 148 P.2d 9, 11 (Cal. 1944).

25. *Whyte*, 125 Cal. Rptr. 2d at 281.

26. Flir Sys., Inc. v. Parrish, 95 Cal. Rptr. 3d 307, 313 (citing Gemini Aluminum Corp. v. California Custom Shapes, Inc. 116 Cal. Rptr. 2d 358 (Cal. App. 4th Dist. 2002)).

27. *Flir*, 95 Cal. Rptr. 3d at 313.

28. *Gemini Aluminum,* 16 Cal. Rptr. 2d at 36.

29. *Flir*, 95 Cal. Rptr. 3d at 314.

30. Yield Dynamics, Inc. v. Tea Sys. Corp., 66 Cal. Rptr. 3d 1, 29 (Cal. App. 6th Dist. 2007).

jective state of mind . . . [d]id he or she believe the action was valid? What was his or her intent or purpose in pursuing it?"[31] Courts have also found subjective bad faith where there was "evidence that appellants intended to cause unnecessary delay" or filed the action to harass respondents."[32]

In *Flir*, subjective bad faith was established because, even after the action's shortcomings were revealed to Indigo and its counsel, Indigo proceeded to trial without factual or legal support. Indigo's claims lacked legal support because they were premised on a theory of "inevitable disclosure"—a doctrine rejected by California courts—and because they sought a prohibitory injunction where the California Uniform Trade Secrets Act only authorizes mandatory injunctions. Other indicators of subjective bad faith included Indigo's use of expert testimony that lacked a scientific basis, Indigo's use of bad faith settlement tactics, and the refusal of Indigo executives to take responsibility for initiating and maintaining the action. On these facts, Indigo could not rely on its contention that it initially had a "reasonable suspicion" of actual or threatened misappropriation to refute a finding of subjective bad faith.

The California Court of Appeal rejected Indigo's argument that the trial court was estopped from finding bad faith because it denied a number of pretrial motions. The trial court had refused to grant the respondents' motion for summary judgment because Indigo had submitted expert declarations suggesting that there was a scientific methodology to predict the likelihood of trade secret misuse. However, Indigo's experts later admitted that no such methodology existed.

Finally, the court held that Indigo had no due process right to a post-trial bad faith hearing because the voluminous briefing, pleadings, discovery, settlement discussions, pretrial motions, and trial evidence which established bad faith obviated any need for a hearing. In the end, Indigo was unable to conquer the "uphill battle" of overcoming both the "sufficiency of evidence" and the "abuse of discretion" rules, and the court affirmed the award.

CONFIDENTIALITY AGREEMENTS

Confidential Information

Disputed Issues of Fact as to Alleged Misuse of Confidential Information Preclude Summary Judgment on Breach of Nondisclosure Agreement

In *Kara Technology Inc. v. Stamps.com Inc.*,[33] the Federal Circuit reversed the district court's summary judgment dismissing Kara's claim for breach of a Nondisclosure Agreement (NDA) as barred by Texas's four-year statute of limitations for such claims. The court also vacated the lower court's summary judgment of noninfringement in favor of Stamps.com, finding that the ruling was based on an incorrect reading of a claim term in the patents that was directed to verifying the authenticity of printed documents.[34]

---

31. *Gemini*, 116 Cal. Rptr. 2d at 369.
32. *Flir*, 95 Cal. Rptr. 3d at 315.
33. 582 F.3d 1341 (Fed. Cir. 2009).
34. *Id.* at 1350.

Stamps.com provides its customers with Web-based shipping and postage services. In May 2000, Stamps.com and Kara began to explore a collaborative business relationship. The parties signed an NDA prohibiting Stamps.com from disclosing any confidential information learned during its discussions with Kara. The NDA expressly prohibited Stamps.com from making copies of any written confidential information without the prior consent of Kara.

In July 2000, Stamps.com expressed to Kara that it was no longer interested in pursuing the collaboration. Two years later, Stamps.com released a PC-based postage product that Kara later contended was based on Kara's proprietary technology. As a result, Kara brought suit against Stamps.com, alleging patent infringement and breach of the NDA.

On appeal, the Federal Circuit first considered the lower court's claim construction. The district court construed "security indicia" to mean that the indicia must "be created under control of a key" and found that the "information contained in" the preestablished data must be a "key."[35] The Federal Circuit, however, agreed with Kara's arguments that the preestablished data need not contain a key and that the security indicia need not be created or validated by a key contained in that data.[36] Because the district court erred in construing these claim terms, the Federal Circuit vacated the judgment of noninfringement and remanded for a new infringement determination based on the proper constructions of these terms.

Regarding the breach of contract claim, the Federal Circuit agreed that the statute of limitations barred Kara's claim for breach of the NDA based on note-taking by Stamps.com employees at a meeting held more than four years before Kara's complaint was filed.[37] Nonetheless, the court found disputes of material fact regarding a second alleged breach of the NDA that was not addressed in the district court's summary judgment order.[38] Accordingly, the Federal Circuit reversed and remanded for further determination, ruling that a jury should decide whether Kara's claim was barred by the statute of limitations and whether Stamps.com breached the NDA in copying Kara's confidential information or using such information in developing its own product.

MISAPPROPRIATION

Res Judicata Will Not Bar a Plaintiff from Exercising the Right to Refrain from Adding an After-Acquired Claim

In *Gillig v. Nike, Inc.,*[39] John P. Gillig, Triple Tee's principal, met with John Thomas Stites III to discuss Gillig's unique design for golf clubs. Stites agreed to maintain these conversations in the strictest confidence. Gillig and Triple Tee alleged that Stites, who subsequently joined Nike, disclosed these trade secrets to Nike and that they were then used to develop a new type of golf club. Consequently, Triple Tee filed suit against Nike in 2004 alleging that Gillig assigned his trade secrets to Triple Tee in 2000, which were then misappropriated by Nike.

---

35. *Id.* at 1346.
36. *Id.* at 1348.
37. *Id.* at 1350.
38. *Id.*
39. 602 F.3d 1354 (Fed. Cir. 2010).

On summary judgment, the district court dismissed Triple Tee's trade secrets claim because Triple Tee did not have standing to assert a trade secrets claim and failed to meet one of the essential elements of its claim—ownership of the alleged trade secret. The district court found no evidence to support the purported assignment from Gillig to Triple Tee in 2000 and also held that the alleged assignment from Gillig to Triple Tee in 2005— after the Complaint was filed—would not cure the defect in standing. The court further refused to allow Triple Tee to substitute Gillig as the plaintiff. The decision was appealed to the Fifth Circuit and affirmed.

Several years later, Triple Tee filed a second action with Gillig as its co-plaintiff. In addition to bringing a misappropriation of trade secrets claim, they also alleged correction of inventorship claims under 35 U.S.C. § 256. Nike moved to dismiss Plaintiffs' complaint under Federal Rule of Civil Procedure 12(b)(6) arguing that Plaintiffs' trade secrets claim was barred by the statute of limitations and Plaintiffs' inventorship claims were barred by res judicata.

The district court granted Nike's motion to dismiss and held that Gillig's trade secret claim was barred by the statute of limitations and Gillig and Triple Tee's inventorship claims were barred by the doctrine of res judicata. Plaintiffs appealed to the Federal Circuit.

The parties agreed that Texas law applied to the misappropriation of trade secrets claim, which requires that it be brought "not later than three years after the misappropriation is discovered or by the exercise of reasonable diligence should have been discovered."[40] The doctrine of res judicata precludes relitigation of claims that have already been adjudicated or that could have been adjudicated. In order for the doctrine to apply, four prerequisites must be satisfied: "(1) the parties [in both actions] are identical or in privity; (2) the judgment in the prior action was rendered by a court of competent jurisdiction; (3) the prior action was concluded by a final judgment on the merits; and (4) the same claim or cause of action was involved in both actions."[41]

On appeal, the Federal Circuit, under de novo review, upheld the district court's holding that the trade secrets claim was barred by the statute of limitations but found error in the district court's dismissal of Gillig's inventorship claims based on res judicata to the extent Triple Tee is asserting an inventorship correction claim based on the 2005 assignment from Gillig.

In reaching this decision, the Federal Circuit noted that the misappropriation was first discovered in 2003 but the Complaint brought by Gillig and Triple Tee was not filed until 2008. The Federal Circuit found Plaintiffs' tolling arguments unconvincing.

With respect to the res judicata argument, the Federal Circuit found that Gillig was not in privity with Triple Tee solely because he was an officer and the principal owner. Absent a showing that the corporate form has been abused, stock ownership or being a corporate officer is insufficient to establish privity. Moreover, the Federal Circuit found that the "control of litigation" exception to privity does not apply because it is only applicable to issue preclusion or collateral estoppel, which was not at issue in this case.

The Federal Circuit also noted that the only issue decided by the previous litigation was that there was no assignment of any trade secret rights in 2000 from Gillig to Triple

---

40. *Id.* at 1358 (citing TEX. CIV. PRAC. & REM. CODE ANN. § 16.010(a)).

41. *Id.* at 1361 (citing Test Masters Educ. Servs., Inc. v. Singh, 428 F.3d 559, 571 (5th Cir. 2005).

Tee and that decision had no bearing on Gillig's inventorship claims or Triple Tee's inventorship claims if they are based on the later 2005 assignment. Furthermore, although the inventorship claims arose from the same nucleus of operative facts as the trade secrets claim, they were not barred by res judicata because the doctrine "does not apply to new rights acquired during the action which might have been, but which were not, litigated."[42] Indeed, "res judicata does not punish a plaintiff for exercising the option not to supplement the pleading with an after-acquired claim."[43] The Federal Circuit also noted that most of the inventorship claims could not have been brought during the first litigation because seven of the eight patents listed in Gillig's 2008 complaint were not yet issued.

Disclosure or Acquisition Is Sufficient to Constitute Misappropriation under UTSA

In *Astro-Med, Inc. v. Nihon Kohden America, Inc.*,[44] the First Circuit affirmed the district court's post-trial judgment upholding a jury verdict in favor of plaintiff Astro-Med, Inc., a sleep and neurological research product manufacturer. Astro-Med had obtained a jury verdict against its former employee Kevin Plant and his new employer Nihon Kohden for trade secret misappropriation, among other things.

On appeal, defendants contended that there was no evidence that either Plant or Nihon Kohden ever "used" any of Astro-Med's confidential information. Absent evidence of misuse, defendants argued, there could be no valid claim for trade secret misappropriation. The court rejected defendants' contention, explaining that under the Rhode Island Uniform Trade Secrets Act, Astro-Med was not required to show "use" of a trade secret, but instead could show "acquisition" or "disclosure" of a trade secret that had been acquired by "improper means." The Act defines "improper means" as "breach or inducement of a breach of a duty to maintain secrecy . . . ."[45]

The court found that Astro-Med had introduced evidence sufficient to show that Nihon Kohden's reason for hiring Plant was to get inside information from him about Astro-Med. The court further found that, viewing this evidence in the light most favorable to the jury verdict, the evidence provided a basis for the reasonable inference that Plant revealed and used the information, which Nihon Kohden then used to compete with Astro-Med.

According to the court, Astro-Med had made the requisite showing for trade secret misappropriation because "[m]isappropriation . . . includes disclosure of a trade secret by one who acquired it while under a duty to maintain its secrecy and the acquisition of a trade secret by one who knows that it was acquired by breach of a duty to maintain secrecy."[46] Accordingly, defendants properly had been subjected to liability for actual loss and unjust enrichment caused by the misappropriation.

---

42. *Id.* at 1363 (citing Computer Assocs. Int'l, Inc. v. Altai, Inc., 126 F.3d 365, 370 (2d Cir. 1997)).

43. *Id.* (citing Fla. Power & Light Co. v. United States, 198 F.3d 1358, 1360 (Fed. Cir. 1999)).

44. 591 F.3d 1 (1st Cir. 2009).

45. R.I. GEN. LAWS § 6-41-1(1) (2001).

46. *Astro-Med,* 591 F.3d at 18.

Wrongful Acquisition

Customer List Containing Publicly Available Information Not Protected by Washington Trade Secret Law

In ***Keystone Fruit Marketing, Inc. v. Brownfield,***[47] the Ninth Circuit affirmed the district court's summary judgment, finding that no genuine issue of material fact existed regarding whether certain customer information was publicly available and, thus, not protected by trade secret.

The district court held that William Brownfield breached his duty of loyalty to his former employer, Keystone Fruit Marketing (KFM) and that Brownfield tortiously interfered with an exclusive marketing contract between KFM and one of its clients. However, the district court also granted summary judgment to Brownfield earlier in the case on KFM's claims that Brownfield's accessing of his KFM electronic customer list, which was in the form of a spreadsheet entitled "Billscustomerlist.xls," after termination of his employment was not a violation of either the Computer Fraud and Abuse Act (CFFA)[48] or the Uniform Trade Secrets Act (UTSA).

On the CFAA issue, the district court ruled that because the spreadsheet was already on Brownfield's home computer, which was not a "protected computer" under the statute and that his accessing of the spreadsheet was not a violation. KFM did not appeal this ruling. As for the UTSA, the district court ruled that the spreadsheet was not a trade secret as a matter of law because the names and other information contained in it were publicly available. The district court noted that "[a] former employee, even in the absence of an enforceable covenant not to compete, remains under a duty not to misappropriate trade secrets acquired in the course of previous employment,"[49] but further noted that under Washington law "[t]o be a trade secret, information must be 'novel' in the sense that the information must not be readily ascertainable from another source."[50] The district court found no issue of fact, for purposes of summary judgment, that "the identities of and information about customers of Walla Walla sweet onions are readily available in the Blue Book and are well known in the produce industry" and that "the vast majority of onions are sold to a handful of major customers."[51]

On appeal to the Ninth Circuit, KFM argued that the district court erred in finding that the spreadsheet was not a trade secret as a matter of law. The parties agreed that the document contained "names, addresses, telephone numbers, e-mail addresses, buyer information, assistant buyer information, transportation personnel, inspectors, receiver information, and other contact information"[52] for both existing and prospective customers for KFM's onions. KFM asserted that the information compiled is not available to the public and was password protected within KFM's organization, while Brownfield argued that it was available to the public through a trade publication called the "Blue Book."

---

47. 352 F. App'x 169 (9th Cir. 2009).

48. 18 U.S.C. § 1030 (2008).

49. Keystone Fruit Mktg. v. Brownfield, No. 05-5087, 2006 WL 1873800, at *7 (E.D. Wash. July 6, 2006).

50. *Id.*

51. *Id.*

52. *Id.* at *3.

The Ninth Circuit upheld the ruling of the district court that the spreadsheet was not a trade secret under Washington's UTSA as a matter of law. Under Washington law, information cannot qualify as a trade secret if the information is readily ascertainable by proper means. Brownfield submitted evidence that all the information contained in the document was publicly available in well-known trade publications (such as the Blue Book), and KFM did not submit any evidence to contradict this assertion. Therefore, there was no genuine issue of material fact as to whether the information in the customer list file was readily ascertainable by proper means, and summary judgment was appropriate.

Forwarding E-mails from Corporate E-mail Account to Personal Account Does Not Violate UTSA Where No Company Policy Prohibits Such Action

In *Arizant Holdings Inc. v. Gust,*[53] the U.S. District Court of Minnesota held that there was no evidence that Gust violated any Arizant policy or directive or otherwise acted improperly when he forwarded the e-mails from his Arizant account to his personal account. Without such evidence, a fact-finder could not conclude that Gust's act of forwarding the e-mails to himself constituted improper acquisition of the trade secrets under the Minnesota Uniform Trade Secrets Act (UTSA).

Arizant sells patient-warming systems that are used, for example, during surgeries and in hospital gowns. Gregory Gust was a regional sales manager for Arizant from 1994 to 2007. By the end of this period, Gust's performance had declined, and Arizant eventually gave Gust the option to implement a performance-improvement plan or accept a severance package. Gust chose the severance package and resigned, effective on December 31, 2007. A competitor for patient-warming technologies employed Gust, and Arizant sued Gust for damages and return of money paid to Gust as part of the severance package.

Arizant alleged that Gust violated an employee confidentiality agreement and misappropriated trade secrets in violation of the Minnesota UTSA. Arizant's trade secret claim was based entirely on e-mails that Gust forwarded to his personal e-mail account from his Arizant e-mail account after he resigned from Arizant on December 31, 2007. The court granted Gust's motion for summary judgment on both claims.

The court dismissed Arizant's claim premised on Gust's confidentiality agreement after finding that Arizant had entered into a severance agreement with Gust which contained a merger clause, thereby rendering the confidentiality agreement null and void. The court also noted that Arizant alleged no damages resulting from the alleged breach. Gust's new employer made only two sales following his hiring, and neither sale involved Gust or was in his former Arizant sales territory.

The Minnesota UTSA forbids the improper acquisition, disclosure, or use of a trade secret. Arizant presented no evidence that Gust improperly "used" or "disclosed" any of the e-mails sent to his personal account. Likewise, the court found no improper acquisition because Arizant had no policy against forwarding company e-mails to personal e-mail accounts. The court discounted the fact that Gust was no longer an employee at the time that the e-mails were forwarded to Gust's personal account because it was undisputed that Arizant permitted Gust to continue to use his corporate e-mail account for several weeks after he resigned. Even though Gust had requested this privilege in order to notify his sales staff of his departure, the court noted that there was no evidence that Arizant had

---

53. 668 F. Supp. 2d 1194 (D. Minn. 2009).

limited him to use of the corporate e-mail account for that purpose. One e-mail, which Gust had forwarded from his personal account to his new employer, contained no trade secrets, but only a list of links to Web sites related to new health care initiatives. The court explained that "anyone who uses Google or another popular search engine to seek information about these initiatives could easily find the listed websites."[54]

LITIGATION

Third-Party Rule 45 Subpoena for Trade Secret Information Quashed

In ***Premier Election Solutions, Inc. v. SysTest Labs Inc.,***[55] the District Court of Colorado denied defendant SysTest Labs Inc.'s motion to compel compliance with a Rule 45 subpoena. The subpoena sought information from iBeta, a nonparty competitor, concerning certain "test cases" and "trusted builds" related to the election equipment/voting systems certification procedures at issue in the case. SysTest claimed the information was related to its damages arguments, because iBeta took over the certification procedures for the plaintiff after SysTest, who the plaintiff originally hired, lost its certification. iBeta objected, countering that the subpoena was burdensome and would require the production of trade secret information.

The district court first reviewed the relevant legal standards, noting that Federal Rule of Civil Procedure 26(b)(1) allows broad discovery of "any matter, not privileged, which is relevant to the claim or defense of any party," but that Rule 26(c) limits discovery by allowing the court, for good cause, "to protect a party or person from annoyance, embarrassment, oppression, or undue burden or expense." Furthermore, pursuant to Rule 26(c)(1)(G), a court may enter a protective order "requiring that a trade secret or other confidential research, development, or commercial information not be revealed or be revealed only in a specified way."

The court considered three arguments regarding the subpoena. First, iBeta argued that pursuant to Federal Rule of Civil Procedure 45(c)(3)(A)(ii), courts are required to "quash or modify a subpoena that . . . requires a person who is neither a party nor a party's officer to travel more than 100 miles from where that person resides, is employed, or regularly transacts business in person." The court found that this rule does not apply to a subpoena for documents alone, but only a subpoena that requires a nonparty to actually travel; even if the rule did apply, the court found that under the "straight line" method of calculating the distance, it was less than 100 miles.

Second, SysTest argued that iBeta's objections to the subpoena were untimely, as they were filed a day late. The court found that untimely objections can be considered where unusual circumstances exist, and that because of the overwhelming prejudice which would accrue to iBeta as a result of a strict application of the timing provision in Rule 45, unusual circumstances did exist and failure of the court to consider iBeta's objections filed one day out of time would result in manifest injustice. The unusual circumstances included the court's designation of the information at issue as highly confidential trade secret information; iBeta's status as a nonparty; and iBeta's good

---

54. *Id.* at 1204.
55. No. 09-01822, 2009 WL 3075597 (D. Colo. Sept. 22, 2009).

faith, the evidence of which included the absence of any showing of intentional failure to disclose or bad faith, the reported probability of settlement of the underlying case, an intervening holiday with no "received" stamp or other document indicating the date of receipt of the subpoena for guidance to iBeta's attorney, and iBeta's (albeit untimely) partial production of documents.

Finally, the court turned to iBeta's argument that the information at issue should be protected as trade secrets. As the objecting party, iBeta carried the burden to establish that the information for which it sought protection was a trade secret or other confidential research, development, or commercial information and then demonstrate that its disclosure might be harmful. iBeta submitted that it was the only company that had been able to lead a voter system manufacturer through successful U.S. Election Assistance Commission certification, and that it did so by application of its "test cases" and "trusted builds" methodology, among other things, which were developed over a one year period at a cost of $100,000.00 and approximately 1,400 hours of employee labor. Finding that iBeta had demonstrated that only iBeta was privy to the exact parameters of this methodology to help a manufacturer meet the requirements for certification, including the "test cases and trusted builds"; that the information was not known outside of iBeta itself, except as necessary to its relationships with the voter system manufacturers; and that iBeta had taken precautions to ensure that its processes were not revealed, the court concluded that all information and documentation which could reveal the data contained in the "test cases" and "trusted builds" was trade secret information belonging to iBeta and entitled to protection.

The burden then shifted to SysTest to establish that disclosure of the trade secrets was both relevant and necessary. SysTest claimed the trade secret information was relevant and necessary because iBeta had engaged in a "re-do" of the work performed previously by SysTest, which SysTest claimed would reduce the plaintiff's damages. The court found the relevance of Beta's "test cases" and "trusted builds" to the underlying case to be marginal, at best, and further stated its suspicion that SysTest sought discovery from iBeta for purposes unrelated to the litigation. Accordingly, the court denied the motion to compel with regard to documents or "electronically stored information, correspondence and invoices" or other data revealing the contents of iBeta's "test cases" or "trusted builds."

Discovery

Trade Secret Suits

Intentional Destruction of Electronic Evidence, in the Absence of Prejudice, Does Not Merit Terminal Sanction

In **Rimkus Consulting Group, Inc. v. Cammarata**,[56] the U.S. District Court for the Southern District of Texas examined a collection of motions and cross-motions pertaining to the defendants' establishment, during the time of their employment by Rimkus, of a competitor to Rimkus. The court focused primarily on the destruction of e-mail evidence by the defendants, as well as on the effects of an earlier proceeding in Louisiana state court.

---

56. 688 F. Supp.2d 598 (S.D. Tex. 2010).

Several Rimkus employees, while still working for Rimkus and allegedly violating noncompete clauses in their contracts, established a competitor company and, several months later, left to join that company. Rimkus further alleged that the employees took with them and used customer lists, pricing documents, strategy documents, and other confidential information. During the period of discovery, Rimkus eventually discovered that the defendants had destroyed e-mails, a contention that the defendants did not deny. Before the court were Rimkus' motions for monetary sanction and requests for terminal sanctions (striking of the pleadings, default judgment) or at least adverse jury instructions. Also before the court were motions by the defendants for summary judgment based on the preclusive effects of the results of Louisiana state court decisions. Not all of the motions and issues before the court are discussed in this summary.

The court reviewed the destruction of evidence issue first. Ultimately, the court decided that it would send to the jury the question of whether the destruction of e-mails was intentional and allow the jury to make an adverse inference if it was. The court's decision was made in light of, although without total deference to, Judge Scheindlin's opinion in *Pension Committee*.[57] The earlier case focused on negligent destruction of evidence, whereas the issue here was intentional destruction. Also, Fifth Circuit law does not allow for terminal sanctions or an adverse inference instruction unless there is a bad faith intentional action—gross negligence is not sufficient. Citing *Zubulake IV*,[58] the court noted that to obtain an adverse inference instruction sanction for spoliation, the movant must show that: (1) the party with control of the evidence had an obligation to preserve it; (2) it was destroyed with intent ("a culpable state of mind"); and (3) it was relevant to a claim or defense. Finally, the court found that the law did not allow for the imposition of terminal sanctions in the absence of irreparable harm from the spoliation, but that adverse inference instructions could be quite severe and that, in this instance, the monetary sanctions might also be considerable.

The court found conflicting evidence about the nature of the spoliation. For example, the defendants claimed that some e-mails were deleted according to a 'policy,' but there was significant evidence that no such formal policy existed. However, there was ample evidence for a reasonable jury to conclude that the spoliation was intentional and in bad faith. Thus, the court decided to allow the jury to hear the evidence relating to spoliation and to decide if the e-mails were intentionally destroyed to prevent their use by Rimkus. The jury would then be allowed to infer that such evidence was unfavorable to the defendants. Because the destroyed evidence was not all favorable to Rimkus and because much of it was ultimately recovered or cumulative, the harm was not irreparable and terminal sanctions were not imposed. Defendants did not contest monetary sanctions, and Rimkus was awarded reasonable costs and fees incurred as a result of the spoliation.

Turning to the earlier Louisiana state court proceeding, it was a declaratory judgment action by the defendants seeking to invalidate various provisions of their employment agreement with Rimkus, including noncompete clauses and Texas choice-of-law and forum-selection provisions. The Louisiana appellate court eventually held that all of the relevant provisions were invalid. The district court, proceeding on related claims filed by

---

57. Pension Comm. of the Univ. of Montreal Pension Plan v. Banc of Am. Sec., LLC, No. 05-9016, 2010 WL 184312 (S.D.N.Y. Jan. 15, 2010).

58. Zubulake v. UBS Warburg LLC, 220 F.R.D. 212, 220 (S.D.N.Y. 2003).

Rimkus in Texas state court and removing to federal court, gave the state court decisions preclusive effect in Louisiana but limited their geographic scope so that actions by Rimkus concerning defendants' behavior outside that state survived. However, the Louisiana state court proceeded to dismiss counterclaims by Rimkus, apparently deciding claims, including breach of confidentiality provisions, under Texas state law.

The court determined that, with respect to the motions for summary judgment on misappropriation of trade secrets and other substantive issues, all of the elements for res judicata and issue preclusion were present. In particular, although the Louisiana action was framed as a breach-of-contract claim concerning the confidentiality clause and the present action contained a tortuous misappropriation of trade secret claim, issue preclusion applied because the legal and factual questions were the same.

However, Louisiana state law, the Restatement (Second) of Judgments, and the policy underlying preclusion all allowed for an exception to be made because of the spoliation. Preclusion does not apply when material information is concealed. Such evidence is not 'newly discovered' but was affirmatively hidden or destroyed. Therefore, the court denied preclusion as to the issues to which the deleted e-mails were relevant, including the misappropriation of trade secret claims.

Under Texas state law, customer lists, pricing information, and business plans could be trade secrets. Rimkus presented evidence that all three met the criteria and the defendants failed to show that all such information was publicly available or otherwise not protected. Thus, defendants' summary judgment motion was denied.

Experts

Expert Permitted to Testify About What Constitutes a Trade Secret in the Wallboard Business

In ***U.S. Gypsum Co. v. LaFarge North America, Inc.,***[59] the Northern District of Illinois denied the parties' cross motions to exclude expert testimony regarding Gypsum's trade secret claims, finding both experts' opinions relevant and reliable.

The admissibility of expert testimony is governed by Federal Rule of Evidence 702 and the framework established by the U.S. Supreme Court in *Daubert v. Merrell Dow Pharmaceuticals, Inc.*[60] Under *Daubert*, a court must function as a "gatekeeper" in screening the admissibility of expert testimony. Rule 702 requires courts to "ensure that any and all scientific testimony . . . is not only relevant but reliable."[61] In deciding whether this standard was met, the court applied a three-element test under which: "(i) the witness must be qualified as an expert by knowledge, skill, experience, training, or education; (ii) the expert's reasoning or methodology underlying the testimony must be reliable; and (iii) the testimony must assist the trier of fact to understand the evidence or to determine a fact in issue."[62]

Applying the first element, the court found that both parties were sufficiently qualified to testify about wallboard technology and the wallboard industry, based on their extensive training and experience in the field.

---

59. 670 F. Supp. 2d 748 (N.D. Ill. 2009).
60. 509 U.S. 579 (1993).
61. Fed. R. Evid. 702.
62. *U.S. Gypsum*, 670 F. Supp. 2d at 751.

With regard to the experts' reliability, both parties argued that the opposing expert reached improper conclusions as to whether the information at issue constituted trade secrets. In rejecting the parties' arguments for exclusion, the court explained that "[w]hether something is a trade secret depends to a large extent on what knowledge is generally available in the industry and whether a new application would not be obvious to someone entering the business" and that "reliability is a function of methodology, not of outcomes."[63] The court recognized that both experts had extensive experience in the wallboard field and were aware of what information was generally available in the industry and what types of measures were taken to protect the secrecy of information not widely known. The court emphasized that even though some of the opinions offered by the experts reached conclusions as to ultimate factual issues in the case, Federal Rule of Evidence 704(a) expressly allows this sort of expert testimony. Furthermore, the court explained that the parties remained free to challenge the conclusions of one another's experts by way of cross-examination during trial.

Finally, the court concluded that the opinions of both experts would assist the trier of fact. Although U.S. Gypsum did not argue that the testimony of LaFarge North America's (LaFarge) expert would not be helpful to the fact finder, LaFarge did challenge U.S. Gypsum's expert on this ground. The court ultimately held that most of the challenged testimony would be helpful but cautioned U.S. Gypsum's expert to limit his testimony to only his own independent opinions.

---

63. *Id.* at 756.

PART VI
OTHER INTELLECTUAL PROPERTY

CHAPTER 21

OTHER INTELLECTUAL PROPERTY

Although the federal government experienced some setbacks in its attempt to regulate new methods of communication and trade, states successfully enforced their own laws dealing with unsolicited bulk mail and identity theft. Courts continued to clarify the rules for hosting content online, finding infringement by yet another peer-to-peer company, but absolving another major Web presence of liability. There were also developments related to insurance coverage of intellectual property disputes and international regulations.

Federal agencies faced limitations on their regulation of the Internet and privacy issues. In *Comcast Corp. v. FCC*, the D.C. Circuit concluded that the FCC does not have ancillary authority to regulate an ISP's network management practices because such regulations are not linked to any express authority delegated by Congress.

Similarly, the U.S. District Court for the District of Columbia held in *American Bar Association v. FTC* that the FTC violated the Administrative Procedure Act by attempting to extend the set of privacy and security regulations known as the "Red Flags Rule" to attorneys. These regulations would have required members of the legal profession to develop and implement a written identity theft prevention program.

Nevertheless, states enjoyed greater freedom to exercise control in these areas. In *Powers v. Pottery Barn*, the California Court of Appeal ruled that a California state law limiting retailers' acquisition of customers' "personal information" was not preempted by the federal CAN-SPAM Act, even if a particular retailer acquires customers' e-mail addresses. Likewise, in *Asis Internet Services v. Subscriberbase Inc.*, the CAN-SPAM Act did not preempt state law in the field of "falsity and deception." The court found that the question of whether the subject line of mass commercial e-mails is deceptive and violates state law is a question of fact for the jury, unless no reasonable trier of fact could conclude otherwise.

In a major Internet case, *Thomas Dart v. Craigslist, Inc.*, the U.S. District Court for the Northern District of Illinois concluded that Craigslist is an "interactive computer service" under the Communications Decency Act and, thus, not responsible for solicitations for prostitution posted on its Web site by users.

In contrast, content owners continued to have success. In *Arista Records LLC v. Lime Group LLC*, the U.S. District Court for the Southern District of New York entered summary judgment finding Lime Wire LLC liable for inducement of copyright infringement via its peer-to-peer file sharing software. Additionally, according to one court, even where content is originally distributed for free, its owners can recover damages for copyright infringement. In *Jacobsen v. Katzer*, the U.S. District Court for the Northern District of California held that the defendant infringed the plaintiff's copyrights in its open source code and confirmed that actual monetary damages were available for such infringement, despite the code's distribution to users at no cost.

In an insurance-related development, the Ninth Circuit in *Hyundai Motor America v. National Union Fire Insurance Co. of Pittsburgh, PA* held that patent infringement of a method patent covering an advertising method was sufficient to constitute "advertising injury" under an insurance policy, thereby subjecting the insurance company to defense obligations because the underlying action alleged "misappropriation of an advertising idea," falling within one of the policy's enumerated "advertising injury" offenses.

In *I-CONN Healthcare Solutions, LLC v. Advanced Internet Technologies, Inc.,* the North Carolina Court of Appeals affirmed the trial court's grant of summary judgment dismissing all claims by the plaintiff arising from a complete loss of its data by a server hosting service. The court excused the defendant's puffing and found no unfair or deceptive practices because the plaintiff was a sophisticated provider of Internet-based services.

Finally, in the Supplement to the United Nations Commission on International Trade Law (UNCITRAL) Legislative Guide on Secured Transactions, Working Group VI of the Commission (Security Interests) prepared a supplement to the Guide, with the intention of coordinating intellectual property law with secured transactions law.

INFORMATION TECHNOLOGY

Open Source Software

Monetary Damages for Copyright Infringement Possible for Distribution of Open Source Code at No Cost

In *Jacobsen v. Katzer,*[1] the U.S. District Court for the Northern District of California granted in part and denied in part Jacobsen's motion for summary judgment on his copyright infringement and cybersquatting claims and denied Katzer's motion for partial summary judgment on Jacobsen's claims for copyright infringement and violation of the DMCA.

Following the Federal Circuit's determination on appeal in *Jacobsen v. Katzer*[2] that open source license restrictions or "conditions" are enforceable under U.S. copyright law, the district court first confirmed that the legal standards applicable to motions for summary judgment apply to questions of copyrightability. Next, the district court explained that a compilation need only display a "minimal level" of creativity to meet the originality requirement of the copyright law.

After the district court referenced undisputed evidence in the record that Jacobsen's work had indeed met the minimum degree of creativity required for copyrightability, it denied Katzer's motion for summary judgment to dismiss Jacobsen's copyright infringement claim, finding Jacobsen's work to be original. The district court also denied Katzer's related motion for summary judgment on Jacobsen's DMCA claim, which hinged on its finding there was no underlying copyright infringement.

The district court next addressed Katzer's alternative argument that Jacobsen's copyright claim should be dismissed because Jacobsen had not suffered actual damages and was not entitled to statutory damages as a matter of law. Because Jacobsen conceded that he

1.   93 U.S.P.Q.2d (BNA) 1236 (N.D. Cal. 2009).
2.   535 F.3d 1373 (Fed. Cir. 2008).

was not entitled to and did not seek statutory damages or attorneys' fees, the district court was able to focus on the contested issue of Jacobsen's monetary damages under the Copyright Act. On this point, the district court found evidence in the record that did attribute monetary value to the source code development effort of the contributors to Jacobsen's project, holding that Jacobsen's evidence established the existence of a dispute of fact regarding the monetary value of Jacobsen's work for the purposes of his copyright claim. For these reasons, the district court denied Katzer's motion for summary judgment.

The district court also considered Jacobsen's motion for summary judgment on his claim for copyright infringement. The district court found that Jacobsen owned a valid copyright and that defendants reproduced protected elements of the copyrighted work in their own work. Therefore, the court held that Jacobsen had a claim for copyright infringement and granted Jacobsen's motion for summary judgment on the copyright cause of action as to liability.

CYBERLAW

Data Security

Dismissal of Multiple Claims Arising from Complete Loss of Data on Remote Server Upheld on Appeal

In *I-CONN Healthcare Solutions, LLC v. Advanced Internet Technologies, Inc.,*[3] the North Carolina Court of Appeals affirmed the trial court's grant summary judgment dismissing all claims by I-CONN Healthcare Solutions, LLC arising from a complete loss of its data by a server hosting service.

In March 2004, I-CONN contracted with Advance Internet Technologies, LLC (AIT) for use of a dedicated server to be housed at AIT's facility in North Carolina. According the parties' agreement, I-CONN would be able to manage the server via the Internet. The server would be used to store data, including I-CONN's Web site, and to make available Web-hosted downloadable software. I-CONN's proprietary software was used by physicians on handheld devices to access insurance companies' formularies. In September 2005, AIT informed I-CONN that the server used to store I-CONN's information had failed. In October 2005, AIT informed I-CONN that all information stored on AIT's server was irretrievably lost in a hardware crash and that the server was being returned to its third party vendor.

Contrary to AIT's explanation about the lost data, an AIT customer service employee informed I-CONN that the server at issue had been physically lost and that he had been instructed to mislead I-CONN about the hardware crash. Based on this information, I-CONN brought suit against AIT asserting claims of breach of contract, fraud, violation of the North Carolina Unfair and Deceptive Trade Practice Act, and punitive damages. AIT moved for and was granted summary judgment on each of these claims. I-CONN appealed.

The court noted that the trial court did not err in granting summary judgment on the contract claim because I-CONN did not assert how the contract provisions had been breached.

---

3.   689 S.E.2d 600 (N.C. Ct. App. 2010).

The court rejected I-CONN's attempt to raise, for the first time at the appeal, a new theory that the contract breach arose from a bailment relationship between the parties. Because this theory was not raised before the superior court, it was not proper on appeal. The court also found no err in the trial court's grant of summary judgment on the fraud and deceptive trade practices claims. As no substantive claims remained upon which to base compensatory damages, there also was no basis for punitive damages. Finding no err by the trial court, the court affirmed the trial court's grant of summary judgment on all counts.

FTC's "Red Flags Rule" Held Not to Apply to Attorneys

In *American Bar Association v. Federal Trade Commission*,[4] a federal trial court ruled that the FTC violated the Administrative Procedure Act by attempting to extend the set of privacy and security regulations known as the "Red Flags Rule" to attorneys.

In 1974, as Americans were beginning to make credit cards part of their everyday purchasing tools, Congress passed the Equal Credit Opportunity Act (ECOA).[5] ECOA prohibits discrimination against credit applicants based on their sex or marital status. By 2003, the widespread use of credit cards for purchases over the Internet and increased identity theft using credit card numbers led Congress to pass the Fair and Accurate Credit Transactions Act (FACT Act).[6] The FACT Act incorporated ECOA's definitions of "credit" and "creditor."

Under ECOA, a creditor is "any person who regularly extends, renews, or continues credit; any person who regularly arranges for the extension, renewal or continuation of credit; or any assignee of an original creditor who participates in the decision to extend, renew or continue credit."[7] ECOA defines "credit" as "the *right* granted by a creditor to a debtor to defer payment of a debt or to incur debts and defer its payment or to purchase property or services and defer payment therefor."[8]

The FACT Act also required federal agencies that regulate credit and creditors to promulgate regulations relating to privacy and security requirements that might indicate identity theft—so-called red flags. The federal agencies that regulate financial and securities firms have promulgated Red Flags Rules, which went into effect on November 1, 2008. The FTC also promulgated its version of Red Flags Rule, which was originally targeted to go into effect on November 1, 2008, but which is now scheduled to go into effect on December 31, 2010. The FTC's Red Flags Rule contains requirements that the "creditors" governed by the rules must determine whether they have "covered accounts," and if so, the "creditors" must develop and implement a written identity theft prevention program, including specific measures implemented to prevent identity theft, procedures to respond to these "red flags," and periodic review and updating of the program.

When the FTC proposed its draft Red Flags Rule in 2006 and issued the final version in 2007, the FTC did not include any statement that the regulations would apply to the legal profession. Shortly before the FTC's Red Flags Rule was scheduled to go into effect in November of 2008, the FTC delayed the effective date by six months, stating that entities were confused as to whether they were subject to the Red Flags Rule requirements.

---

4. 671 F. Supp. 2d 64 (D.D.C. 2009).
5. 15 U.S.C.A. § 1691, *et seq.* (West, Westlaw through Mar. 2, 2010).
6. Pub. L. 108-159.
7. 671 F. Supp. 2d at 67 (citing 15 U.S.C. § 1691a(e)).
8. *Id.* (citing 15 U.S.C. § 1691a(d)) (emphasis in original).

The FTC's press release listed examples of covered entities, including automobile dealers, telecommunications companies, and nonprofit companies that defer payment for goods or services, but the press release contained no mention of attorneys. The FTC again delayed the effective date for the Red Flags Rule until August 1, 2009, due to continuing confusion about its scope, but the FTC's notice at the time expressly indicated that attorneys and other professionals "who bill their clients after services are rendered" would be subject to the Red Flags Rule. The FTC again delayed the effective date from August 1, 2009, to November 1, 2009, and reiterated that the Red Flags Rule would apply to attorneys whose billing arrangements qualified them as "creditors." The ABA filed a complaint in the U.S. District Court of the District of Columbia, claiming that the FTC had exceeded its statutory authority under the FACT Act and that, as a result, the FTC's actions in extending the Red Flags Rule to attorneys violated the Administrative Procedure Act as "arbitrary, capricious, an abuse of discretion, or otherwise not in accordance with law."[9]

The district court analyzed the ABA's claims under the two-part standard in *Chevron, U.S.A., Inc. v. Natural Resources Defense Council, Inc.*[10] Under the first part of the test, the court had to determine whether Congress had delegated authority to the FTC: (1) to act in accordance with an express congressional objective; or (2) to fill in any regulatory gaps left unaddressed by Congress. The district court concluded that there was no express congressional objective to bring attorneys within the FACT Act and, therefore, cause attorneys to be subject to the Red Flags Rule. With respect to any ambiguity or regulatory gaps, the district court ruled that the "lack of clarity in the statute cannot reasonably be interpreted as either an explicit or implicit grant to the Commission to 'cure th[e] ambiguity' by regulating attorneys, given that the regulation of the legal profession has been left to the prerogative of the states."[11] With respect to the second part of the test—whether the agency's action was based on a permissible construction of the FACT Act if the law were ambiguous—the district court also ruled in the ABA's favor. The district court held that the FTC's interpretation and application of the FACT Act to attorneys was unreasonable.

The district court framed the issue with respect to the first part of the *Chevron* test as whether Congress granted the FTC the authority to regulate attorneys as "creditors" under the FACT Act. The court examined the language of the FACT Act and concluded: (1) the context of the FACT Act was inconsistent with the regulation of attorneys, but instead was intended to eliminate identity theft in the credit industry; (2) the population targeted by the FACT Act "does not correlate with the regulation of attorneys"—terms like "deposit account holders" and "consumers" were not synonymous with "client"; and (3) the FACT Act's definitions "do not apply to attorneys" because the definitions of "credit" and "creditor" "do not equate to concepts associated with the legal profession."[12] Therefore, the court concluded, "it becomes clear that the intent of Congress is unambiguous: it did not grant to the Commission the broad authority to exercise regulatory control over attorneys pursuant to the FACT Act, and accordingly the Red Flags Rule similarly cannot be properly promulgated in such a broad manner."[13] Under *Chevron*, the court found that the FTC's actions were not proper, and the analysis could have ended at this point.

---

9. *Id.* at 66 (quoting Compl. ¶¶ 61–64).
10. 467 U.S. 837 (1984).
11. 671 F. Supp. 2d at 74.
12. *Id.* at 75–76.
13. *Id.* at 82.

Nevertheless, the district court assumed "for the sake of argument" that the FACT Act was ambiguous, and proceeded to the second part of the *Chevron* test. The district court described the issue as whether the FTC's construction of the FACT Act was a permissible construction. The district court ruled that an attorney's practice of invoicing a client at the end of a month "is not delaying payment or giving a client a *right* to postpone payment."[14] In other words, the FTC's construction of the terms "credit" and "creditor" was too broad. The district court also found that the FTC's interpretation of the FACT Act "does not take into consideration how legal services must be tabulated and billed."[15] The FTC's position that attorneys created debtor-creditor relationships unless they billed clients immediately upon rendering a service and received virtually simultaneous payment was "extreme."[16] The district court found that it "clearly could not have been a result anticipated by Congress given the obvious intrusion the Commission's approach would have into the relationships between attorneys and their clients."[17] The district court also pointed to procedural issues with the FTC's interpretation, which "evolved after the period for notice and comment closed, and without any fact-finding justification for the decision."[18] Finally, the district court found that application of the Red Flags Rule to attorneys would create "another barrier for attorneys to build the level of trust necessary for clients to feel that they can openly communicate with their attorneys."[19]

In short, the district court held that the FTC's interpretation of the Red Flags Rule to include attorneys "is both plainly erroneous and inconsistent with the purpose underlying the enactment of the FACT Act."[20] Therefore, the district court ruled, the FTC's actions violated the Administrative Procedure Act.

Regulation of Internet Service Providers

FCC Does Not Have Express or Ancillary Authority to Regulate Network Management Practices of ISPs

In *Comcast Corp. v. Federal Communications Commission,*[21] the D.C. Circuit held that the Federal Communications Commission (FCC) lacked the authority necessary to regulate ISPs network management practices, including practices limiting the use of peer-to-peer, file-sharing applications.

In 2007, Comcast (the largest cable television and home Internet provider in the United States) began interfering with the ability of some of its customers to use certain file sharing software (specifically, BitTorrent) on its high speed Internet networks. After some customer complaints, a coalition of nonprofit organizations filed a complaint with the FCC challenging Comcast's practices. The coalition also petitioned for a declaratory

---

14. *Id.* at 83–84 (emphasis in original).
15. *Id.* at 84.
16. *See id.* at 85.
17. *Id.*
18. *Id.*
19. *Id.* at 87.
20. *Id.* at 88.
21. 600 F.3d 642 (D.C. Cir. 2010).

ruling that ISPs could not limit consumers' ability to access content, run applications, or use the services of their choice. Comcast contested the claim stating that its actions were necessary to manage scarce network capacity.

After a comment period, the FCC issued an order stating that it had the authority to regulate Comcast's network management practices; that Comcast's actions had "significantly impeded consumers' ability to access the content and use the applications of their choice;" that Comcast had other options available to it that would not discriminate against peer-to-peer communications; and that Comcast's actions contravened Federal policy.[22] The order further indicated that an injunction would automatically issue in the event that Comcast did not comply with the order. Comcast complied, but petitioned for review by the D.C. Circuit based on three objections: (1) the FCC failed to establish that it had jurisdiction over Comcast's network management practices; (2) the FCC's adjudicatory action was procedurally flawed because it circumvented the Administrative Procedure Act and violated the notice requirements of the Due Process Clause; and (3) the order was so poorly reasoned as to be arbitrary and capricious. The FCC's authority to regulate ISPs' network practices was the focal point of the appellate court's decision.

The court first addressed the scope of the FCC's jurisdiction and its ability to regulate common carriers, and specifically ISPs. Noting that the FCC acknowledged that it did not have express authority to manage the network practices of ISPs, the court identified the scope of the FCC's "ancillary" authority through a series of U.S. Supreme Court decisions that it recently distilled into a two-part test in *American Library Association v. FCC.*[23] The D.C. Circuit held in *American Library* that the FCC may exercise ancillary jurisdiction provided that "(1) the Commission's general jurisdictional grant under Title I [of the Communications Act] covers the regulated subject and (2) the regulations are reasonably ancillary to the Commission's effective performance of its statutorily mandated responsibilities."[24] Continuing, the court noted that "[w]hether the Commission's action satisfies *American Library*'s second requirement is the central issue of this case," but before stepping through that analysis addressed two "threshold arguments" posed by the FCC.[25]

The first threshold argument put forward by the FCC was that Comcast was estopped from challenging its jurisdiction based on the position Comcast took in *Hart v. Comcast of Alameda, Inc.*[26] Invoking the primary jurisdiction doctrine, Comcast "argu[ed] that the Commission has 'subject matter jurisdiction' over its disputed network management practices" and that, because of this, the litigation should have been stayed.[27] The *Hart* court agreed. Because Comcast prevailed in that argument, the FCC argued that Comcast should have been estopped from claiming otherwise in this matter. The *Comcast* court accepted Comcast's argument that it merely conceded in *Hart* that Internet service was a "communication by wire" but did not concede that the FCC had ancillary jurisdiction. Therefore, Comcast was not estopped from contesting the FCC's jurisdiction.

---

22. *Id.* at 645; *see also In re* Formal Complaint of Free Press & Public Knowledge Against Comcast Corp. for Secretly Degrading Peer-to-Peer Applications, 23 F.C.C.R. at 13,033–60 (2008) (hereinafter *Order*).

23. *See Comcast*, 600 F.3d at 646 (citing Am. Library Ass'n v. FCC, 406 F.3d 689, 691–92 (D.C. Cir. 2005)).

24. *Am. Library*, 406 F.3d at 691–92.

25. *Comcast*, 600 F.3d at 647.

26. No. 07-6350, 2008 WL 2610787 (N.D. Cal. June 25, 2008).

27. *Comcast*, 600 F.3d at 647.

The FCC's second threshold argument rested on the U.S. Supreme Court decision in *National Cable & Telecommunications Ass'n v. Brand X Internet Services,*[28] which agreed with the FCC's conclusion that "companies that sell broadband Internet service do not provide a 'telecommunications service[e]' as the Communications Act defines that term, and hence are exempt from mandatory common-carrier regulation under Title II."[29] The Commission argued that *Brand X* established that it "could likely 'require cable companies to allow independent ISPs access to their facilities' pursuant to its ancillary authority rather than using Title II," which in turn meant that it could assert ancillary jurisdiction over cable companies generally.[30] The court responded that the FCC has no "sweeping authority over [cable] as a whole" and "each and every assertion of jurisdiction over cable television must be independently justified as reasonably ancillary to the Commission's power over broadcasting."[31] The court continued that, although the FCC may have the authority to require service providers to unbundle the components of their services, this does not mean that the FCC may control the network management practices of these service providers.

With these two threshold questions out of the way, the court addressed the FCC's contention that the regulation of Comcast's network practices is "reasonably ancillary to the Commission's effective performance of its [statutory] responsibilities" under the Communications Act of 1934.[32] The court focused on the distinction between provisions of the Communications Act that merely set forth Congressional policy and provisions that expressly delegate authority to the FCC.

The FCC's asserted grounds for jurisdiction primarily rested on 47 U.S.C. §§ 1 and 230. Although the FCC acknowledged that these sections were statements of policy and did not delegate direct authority, it argued that sections 1 and 230 identified its "statutorily mandated responsibilities that . . . anchor the exercise of ancillary authority" over Comcast's network management practices.[33] The court disagreed, stating that "the Commission's exercise of ancillary authority [sic] derives from the 'axiomatic' principle that 'administrative agencies may [act] only pursuant to authority delegated to them by Congress.'"[34] Therefore, the court concluded that any regulatory power to regulate network management practices could not be sourced in the broad "policy" statements of the applicable statutes.

In conclusion, the court sided with Comcast, holding that regulation of network practices was not within either the expressly delegated authority of the FCC or its ancillary authority.[35]

28. 545 U.S. 967 (2005).
29. *Id.* at 973.
30. *Comcast*, 600 F.3d at 649.
31. *Id.* at 650–51.
32. *Id.*
33. *Id.* at 651.
34. *Id.* at 654.
35. *Id.*

Record Companies Prevail on Inducement of Infringement Claims against LimeWire

In *Arista Records LLC v. Lime Group LLC*,[36] the U.S. District Court for the Southern District of New York considered claims by thirteen major record companies alleging that Lime Wire LLC (LW) and several affiliated entities and individuals were liable for copyright infringement resulting from the use by third parties of LW's LimeWire peer-to-peer, file-sharing software.

The LimeWire software allows a user to scan the computers of other LimeWire users and download copies of files, including music files, which they make available through the system. The software's user interface allows a user to search for files in a variety of ways, including searching for music files by artist, album, or genre.

After addressing several evidentiary issues, the court concluded that LimeWire users were engaged in direct copyright infringement and that a very large percentage of the files currently being transmitted via LimeWire contained unauthorized copies of copyrighted music.

The court then turned to the question of whether LW was liable for inducing these acts of infringement, applying the standard set out by the U.S. Supreme Court in *Metro-Goldwyn-Mayer Studios v. Grokster*.[37] Under that standard, a plaintiff must first prove that direct infringement has occurred and then establish that the defendant: "(1) engaged in purposeful conduct that encouraged copyright infringement with (2) the intent to encourage such infringement."[38] The court found the first part of the test easily satisfied because the LimeWire software permitted users to commit a substantial amount of infringement. The court also concluded that LW intended to encourage infringement, based on a variety of factors, including: (1) defendant's knowledge of the substantial infringement that was occurring; (2) its efforts to attract infringing users, including by targeting former Napster users and purchasing Google AdWords such as "replacement napster" and "free mp3 downloads"; (3) its efforts to assist users to commit infringement, including by creating search capabilities useful for finding and copying infringing music files and providing technical assistance to users copying such files; (4) its dependence on infringement for business success in the form of advertising and other revenue sources; and (5) its failure to mitigate infringing activities, including by failing to effectively implement available filtering technologies. The court, therefore, granted summary judgment in favor of the record companies on their claims for inducement of copyright infringement.

The court also addressed, among other matters, cross-motions for summary judgment filed by both the plaintiffs and LW on the plaintiffs' contributory infringement claims and LW's motion for summary judgment on the plaintiffs' vicarious liability claims. The court declined to grant summary judgment to either party on the contributory infringement claims, concluding that there was a genuine issue of material fact as to whether the LimeWire software was capable of substantial noninfringing uses, alleged by LW to include the exchange of public domain works as well as music files released for free online distribution for promotional reasons, as well as additional uses

36. 715 F. Supp. 2d 481 (S.D.N.Y. 2010).
37. 545 U.S. 913 (2005).
38. *Arista*, 715 F. Supp. 2d at 508.

to be developed in the future. The court also denied LW's motion as to the vicarious liability claims, questioning the application of the "substantial noninfringing use" defense to vicarious liability and also finding that the existence of such substantial noninfringing uses could not be established as an undisputed fact for summary judgment purposes.

Communications Decency Act

Craigslist's "Erotic Services" Classification Is Not a Nuisance, a Violation of the CDA, or a Breach of Prostitution Laws

In *Thomas Dart v. Craigslist, Inc.*,[39] the U.S. District Court for the Northern District of Illinois granted Defendant Craigslist's motion for judgment on the pleadings, dismissing Plaintiff Dart's allegations that Craigslist's operation of a Web site that allows users to post listings for "erotic" or "adult" services violated section 230(c) of the CDA,[40] constituted a public nuisance, and violated prostitution laws.

As background, Craigslist is a popular Internet classified service provider that allows users to create and display advertisements. Although Craigslist provides a list of categories in which advertisements can be placed, users create the substantive content of their advertisements and select the category in which their advertisements will appear. The subcategory titled "erotic" (later renamed "adult") is one of most popular subcategories on Craigslist, and includes an additional "warning and disclaimer" stating that any content violating Craigslist's Terms of Use, including offers for or the solicitation of prostitution, should be flagged by users.

In March 2009, Dart, Sheriff of Cook County, Illinois, filed a complaint in federal court, alleging that Craigslist was the single largest source of prostitution, including child exploitation, in the country. Specifically, Dart claimed that the erotic-services category of the Web site operated by Craigslist for the city of Chicago, "chicago.craiglist.org," constituted a public nuisance, and that the Web site "solicits" and facilitates prostitution within the meaning of both state and federal laws. Dart alleged that Craigslist violated Illinois state law 720 ILCS 5/11-15, by arranging the meetings of people for the purposes of prostitution, and violated federal law 18 U.S.C. § 1952(a)(3), by promoting or facilitating the promotion of prostitution. In response, Craigslist argued that section 203(c)(1) of the CDA "broadly immunizes providers of interactive computer services from liability for the dissemination of third-party content."[41]

The court first addressed the CDA claims and clarified the meaning of the "good Samaritan" carveout from civil liability for providers and users of an "interactive computer service," with the parties agreeing that Craigslist provides an interactive computer service as defined by section 203(c), and that postings on Craigslist are classified and written by users. Citing primarily to the Seventh Circuit's decision in *Chicago Lawyers' Committee for Civil Rights Under the Law, Inc. v. Craigslist, Inc.*,[42] the court noted that

---

39. 665 F. Supp. 2d 961 (N.D. Ill. 2009).

40. 47 U.S.C. § 230(c).

41. 665 F. Supp. 2d at 967.

42. 519 F.3d 666 (7th Cir. 2008) (the case dealt primarily with discrimination claims under 42 U.S.C. § 3604(a), but also clarified the immunity provision of 17 U.S.C. § 230(c)).

interactive computer service providers may maintain a platform for users to provide information, but providers such as Craigslist cannot be treated as the publisher or speaker of any information provided by third parties. Following the Seventh Circuit's reasoning, the court concluded that Dart could not sue Craigslist for a third party's disclosure of its plans to engage in unlawful activity, but was free to identify and investigate the individuals responsible for these postings.[43]

Next, the court addressed Dart's allegations that Craigslist violated state and federal laws prohibiting prostitution and related offenses, and constituted a public nuisance by arranging meetings and directing people to places for the purpose of prostitution. Citing the *Chicago Lawyers'* case, the court clarified that Craigslist cannot be treated as the speaker of posted words, stating, "Craigslist does not 'provide' that information, its users do."[44] To clarify further, the court found that "[c]ourt[s] must ask whether the duty that plaintiff alleges the defendant violated derives from the defendant's status or conduct as 'publisher or speaker.' If it does, section 230(c)(1) precludes liability."[45] In this case, however, Craigslist did not induce unlawful conduct by merely providing the categories of services for its users, and the postings by users are contrary to Craigslist's Terms of Use, which repeatedly warn users not to post such content. Consequently, the court held that Craigslist is not a publisher of such information and, thus, is protected by the immunities provided under section 230(c).[46]

Electronic Mail Regulation

CAN-SPAM Act

Issue of Deceptiveness of E-mails to Be Decided by Jury; State Regulations of Falsity and Deception in E-mail Not Preempted by Federal Statute

In *Asis Internet Services v. Subscriberbase Inc.*,[47] Plaintiffs Asis Internet Services and Joel Householter, d.b.a. Foggy.Net (collectively, Plaintiffs), sued Defendant Subscriberbase for sending allegedly misleading e-mail advertisements in violation of section 17529.5 of the California Business & Profession Code. Plaintiffs alleged that, although the subject line of Subscriberbase's e-mails purported to offer the recipient "free" gifts, the e-mails and associated Web pages in fact offered gifts only to those who perform additional acts, like signing up for credit cards or submitting loan applications. Section 17529.5(a)(3), which is part of California's False Advertising Law (FAL),[48] prohibits e-mail advertisements with "subject line[s] that a person knows would be likely to mislead a recipient, acting reasonably under the circumstances, about a material fact regarding the contents or subject matter of the message."

In Subscriberbase's motion to dismiss, it argued that determining whether the subject lines in e-mails were deceptive was a question of law to be decided at the pleading stage.

---

43. 665 F. Supp. 2d at 966–67.
44. *Id.* at 967.
45. *Id.* at 968 (citing Barnes v. Yahoo!, Inc., 570 F.3d 1096, 1102 (9th Cir. 2009)).
46. *Id.* at 969.
47. No. 09-3503, 2010 WL 1267763 (N.D. Cal. Apr. 1, 2010).
48. CAL. BUS. & PROF. CODE § 17500, *et seq.*

The court disagreed and held that such questions must be left for a jury to decide unless "[n]o reasonable trier of fact could conclude otherwise."[49] Subscriberbase bore a "heavy burden" to persuade the court that no reasonable fact finder could conclude that the e-mail subject lines were likely to deceive. Because the subject lines were sufficiently ambiguous, the court concluded the issues were best left to a jury.

The court distinguished prior cases[50] where promotions indicated that recipients had won various sweepstakes, but contained adjacent language clearly stating the conditions required to actually win. Because such promotions expressly and repeatedly set forth the requisite conditions, no reasonable recipient could have been deceived into thinking he or she had won. In *Asis*, however, the subject lines in Subscriberbase's e-mails contained no such conditional language (e.g., "Review & Keep Designer Handbags worth $1500 Dollars [*sic*]—guys invited too."). Because the language was less cautious than cases with express and repeated conditions, the court was unwilling to dismiss Plaintiffs' complaint.

Finally, the court rejected Subscriberbase's argument that the CAN-SPAM Act[51] preempts Plaintiffs' arguments. CAN-SPAM was intended to create a national standard for regulating mass-commercial e-mails, and to that end it "supersedes any statute . . . except to the extent that any such statute . . . prohibits falsity or deception in any portion of a commercial electronic mail message . . . ."[52] Thus, the purpose of the preemption clause in the Federal statute is to achieve uniform regulation with respect to lawful advertisement activity while allowing states to continue regulating the field of "falsity and deception."[53] So long as Plaintiffs could establish that Subscriberbase was responsible for making knowing and material misrepresentations—as required by section 17529.5(a)(3)—their claim will sound in "falsity or deception," and would not be preempted.

California Law Not Preempted by CAN-SPAM Act

In *Powers v. Pottery Barn,*[54] the California Court of Appeal, Fourth Appellate District, held that the Song-Beverly Credit Card Act[55] is not preempted by the CAN-SPAM Act.[56]

Powers alleged that she was asked to provide an e-mail address when she visited a Pottery Barn store, selected an item to buy and used her credit card to buy it. Powers claimed that she gave the sales clerk her e-mail address and watched the clerk enter the e-mail address into the store's electronic cash register. Powers further alleged that "Pottery Barn made a practice of asking for personal identification information within the meaning of the Song-Beverly Credit Card Act and that this conduct, in addition to giving rise to a cause of action under Song-Beverly, gave rise to claims under the Unfair Competition Law (Bus. & Prof. Code, § 17200 *et seq.*) (UCL) and for invasion of privacy."[57]

---

49. Colgan v. Leatherman Tool Group, Inc., 135 Cal. App. 4th 663, 682 (2006).

50. Freeman v. Time, Inc. Magazine Co., 68 F.3d 285 (9th Cir. 1995); Haskell v. Time, Inc., 857 F. Supp. 1392 (E.D. Cal. 1994).

51. 15 U.S.C. § 7707(b)(1) (Controlling the Assault of Non-Solicited Pornography and Marketing Act).

52. *Id.*

53. *Id.*

54. 177 Cal. App. 4th 1039 (2009).

55. CAL. CIV. CODE § 1747.08.

56. 15 U.S.C. § 7701 *et seq.*

57. *Powers*, 177 Cal. App. 4th at 1041–42.

The California Song-Beverly Credit Card Act prohibits retailers that accept credit cards from requesting and recording "personal identification information" concerning the cardholder. By contrast, as noted by the *Powers* court, "CAN-SPAM imposes disclosure and 'opt-out' requirements on the senders of commercial electronic mail (e-mail) and restricts the manner in which such e-mail may be sent."[58]

The two statutes—Song-Beverly and CAN-SPAM—appear to have no relationship. CAN-SPAM preempts "any statute, regulation, or rule of a State or political subdivision of a State that expressly regulates the use of electronic mail to send commercial messages, except to the extent that any such statute, regulation, or rule prohibits falsity or deception in any portion of a commercial electronic mail message or information attached thereto."[59] But "CAN-SPAM does not pre-empt state laws that 'are not specific to electronic mail.'"[60]

The *Powers* court concluded that, "[b]ecause Song-Beverly's regulation of what may be asked of credit card customers is not a regulation of what can be sent in commercial e-mails and is not in any manner specific to e-mail, . . . Song-Beverly is not pre-empted by CAN-SPAM."[61] Even more specifically, the court concluded: "CAN-SPAM cannot be interpreted as pre-empting application of Song-Beverly to Pottery Barn's collection of e-mail from its credit card customers. Song-Beverly does not expressly regulate any Internet activity, let alone use of 'electronic mail to send commercial messages' . . . Rather, as we have discussed, Song-Beverly only governs the information businesses may collect in the course of transacting business with credit card users. Thus Song-Beverly does not fall within the scope of CAN-SPAM's express pre-emption provisions."[62] The court also rejected any implied preemption because CAN-SPAM "expressly excludes pre-emption of any state laws, such as Song-Beverly, which 'are not specific to electronic mail.'"[63]

OTHER TRANSACTIONAL MATTERS

Insurance

Patent Infringement Lawsuit Addressing Web Site Marketing Feature Triggered Insurer's Duty to Defend under Advertising Injury Coverage

In *Hyundai Motor America v. National Union Fire Insurance Co. of Pittsburgh, PA*,[64] the Ninth Circuit granted summary judgment to Hyundai, reversing the judgment of the Central District of California that National Union did not have a duty to defend Hyundai against a patent infringement claim.

---

58. *Id.* at 1041.

59. 15 U.S.C. § 7707(b)(1).

60. *Powers*, 177 Cal. App. 4th at 1041. "This chapter shall not be construed to preempt the applicability of—(A) State laws that are not specific to electronic mail, including State trespass, contract, or tort law; or (B) other State laws to the extent that those laws relate to acts of fraud or computer crime." 15 U.S.C. § 7707 (b)(2).

61. *Powers,* 177 Cal. App. 4th at 1041

62. *Id.* at 1045.

63. *Id.*

64. 600 F.3d 1092 (9th Cir. 2010).

In 2005, Hyundai was sued for infringement of two patents by Orion IP, LLC (Orion) based on allegations that Hyundai's Web site used Orion's patented methods of generating customized product proposals.

The patents at issue included Patent Number 5,615,342 ('342 patent), which concerns a method of generating customized product proposals for potential customers of an automobile dealer. The patent's abstract states that the invention is "[a]n electronic system for creating customized product proposals [that] stores a plurality of pictures and text segments to be used as building blocks in creating the proposal."[65] Because each proposal was customized for a particular customer, each proposal could have a much more persuasive effect in selling the product. Patent Number 5,367,627 ('627 patent) concerned a similar method, but was aimed at the sale of parts. The '627 patent aids parts salespersons and works much the same way as the '342 patent.

Hyundai's Web site used a build your own (BYO) vehicle feature and a parts catalogue feature. Hyundai sought a defense from its insurers, asserting that Orion's claims constituted allegations of "misappropriation of advertising ideas," which was covered under the standard "advertising injury" provisions of their policies. National Union and American Home refused to defend Hyundai.

The pertinent policy language provided:

b.   This insurance applies to: . . .
(2) "Advertising injury" caused by an offense committed in the course of advertising your goods, products or services . . .
1.   "Advertising injury" means injury arising out of one or more of the following offenses: . . .
c.   Misappropriation of advertising ideas or style of doing business . . . .[66]

After the jury in the patent infringement trial found against Hyundai and the case was subsequently settled, Hyundai brought suit against its insurers in the U.S. District Court for the Central District of California seeking a declaration that the insurers had a duty to defend.

The district court granted summary judgment to the insurers. The Ninth Circuit reversed, finding the three-element test for proof of "advertising injury" coverage to be satisfied.

First, the party claiming defense must show that it was engaged in "advertising" during the coverage period. Advertising requires widespread promotional activity to the public rather than solicitation.

The *Hyundai* court rejected the insurer's argument seeking to analogize the facts of the case to *Hameid v. National Fire Insurance of Hartford*,[67] where the court found that "advertising" should not be interpreted to include solicitation. The undefined term "advertising" was defined—purportedly in accord with the majority approach—to require "widespread distribution of promotional material to the public at large."[68] The court held

---

65. *Id.* at 1095.
66. *Id.* at 1096.
67. 71 P.3d 761, 764 (Cal. 2003).
68. *Id.* at 766.

that Hameid's agents "made telephone calls and sent mailers to [their former employer's] customers advising them of their new location and of Hameid's lower prices. These activities strongly resemble the solicitations of a competitor's customers in [one case]; the recruiting letters to a competitor's employees in [another case]; and the subcontractor's submission of bids in [a third case]—all of which were held to be 'solicitation,' not 'advertising.'"[69]

The BYO feature, according to National Union, is similar to solicitation in that it is not activated until the user inputs personal preferences, and its purpose is to create customized proposals specific to an individual user. As the *Hyundai* court observed, "In this way, each invocation of the BYO feature by a given user is somewhat similar to an individualized solicitation like the ones discussed in *Hameid*."[70]

The court found this attempt to fit the BYO feature into the framework of *Hameid* ultimately unpersuasive because in *Hameid* the court focused on the fact that the solicitations were "*limited to a discrete number of known potential customers.*"[71]

This solicitation was not widely distributed to the public at large. "Here, the BYO feature *is* widely distributed to the public at large, to millions of unknown Web-browsing potential customers, even if the precise information conveyed to each user varies with user input. All the users are still using the same BYO feature."[72]

The court then noted that the same BYO feature could have been generated in a paper-only version, featured as an insert in a general circulation newspaper, which would clearly constitute advertising, even though individual newspaper readers might each select different options and arrive at totally different final "displays."[73]

Second, the party claiming defense must show that the claims requiring defense created potential liability under a covered offense. Here the insurance agreement included "misappropriation of advertising ideas" as a covered offense. The court held that the proper test in this instance required determination of whether the patents at issue involved an invention which could be considered an advertising idea. The court distinguished prior adverse California appellate authority: *Mez Industries, Inc. v. Pacific National Insurance Co.*[74] (patents at issue "did not involve any process or invention which could reasonably be considered an 'advertising idea' or 'a style of doing business.'"), and *Homedics, Inc. v. Valley Forge Insurance Co.*[75] (actions at issue did not allege violation of a method patent involving advertising ideas or a style of doing business). Thus, the *Hyundai* court found that the suit here alleged "violation of a method patent involving advertising ideas."[76]

National Union argued that the source of the advertising idea must come from a competitor, and that Orion, as a patent holding company, was not a Hyundai competitor. The court held that there need not be a suit by a competitor because the misappropriation of advertising ideas could injure an NPE (nonpracticing entity), as the policy did not limit the identity of the claimant by its specific language. It observed, "Nor can we discern any

69. *Id.* at 769–70.
70. *Id.* at 1099.
71. *Id.*
72. *Id.* at 1099–1100.
73. *Id.* at 1100.
74. 76 Cal. App. 4th 856, 872 (1999).
75. 315 F.3d 1135, 1140–41 (9th Cir. 2003).
76. *Hyundai*, 600 F.3d at 1100.

contextual, public-policy, or logical significance to who owns the legal rights to the advertising idea in question."[77]

Third, the party claiming defense must show a causal connection between the advertising and the claimed injury. The court found persuasive the Washington Court of Appeals analysis in *Amazon.com International, Inc. v. American Dynasty Surplus Lines Insurance Co.,*[78] which observed:

> [H]ere, the alleged injury derived not merely from misappropriation of the [patented software], but from *its use as the means to market goods for sale.* In other words, the infringement occurred in the advertising itself. [The third party's] allegations therefore satisfied the causation requirement for a potential advertising injury.[79]

Accordingly, the court found "a direct causal connection between the advertisement (i.e., the use of the BYO feature on the Web site) and the advertising injury (i.e., the patent infringement). Because the use of the patented method was itself an advertisement that caused the injuries alleged in the third-party complaint, Hyundai ha[d] established the requisite causal connection."[80]

The court observed that it was "irrelevant whether Hyundai theoretically could have violated the patent in some way other than in its advertising. The proper inquiry asks, with respect to what actually occurred, whether the advertising itself caused the injury, that is, whether the advertising itself was the improper use of the patented method."[81] Having concluded that it was, the court thereby found the causal connection met.

Security Interests

Supplement to UNCITRAL Legislative Guide on Secured Transactions

In 2006, the thirty-ninth session of the United Nations Commission on International Trade Law (UNCITRAL) prepared, considered, and eventually adopted a **Legislative Guide on Secured Transactions** (the Guide). At that time, the Commission asked the Secretariat to prepare a supplement to the Guide regarding intellectual property financing. In June 2007, at its fortieth session, the Commission directed Working Group VI (Security Interests) to develop and prepare a supplement that would sufficiently coordinate intellectual property law with secured transactions law. Since that time, Working Group VI has worked with WIPO and other intellectual property organizations from both the public and private sector to develop the Supplement, and the final meeting of Working Group VI on this project is scheduled for February 2010. In the end, the Commission hopes that the final Supplement will make credit more available and at lower cost to intellectual property owners, which will thus enhance the value of intellectual property rights.

The recommendations in the Guide are not intended to be applicable insofar as the provisions are inconsistent with national law or international agreements, to which the State enacting the law is a party, relating to intellectual property. The most recent Work-

77. *Id.* at 1101.
78. 85 P.3d 974 (Wash. Ct. App. 2004).
79. *Id.* at 978.
80. *Hyundai,* 600 F.3d at 1103–04.
81. *Id.* at 1104.

ing Group VI report, issued in 2009, makes clear that issues relating to the existence, validity and content of a grantor's intellectual property rights are matters to which the Guide does not speak. In matters relating to the formation, third-party effectiveness, priority, enforcement of and law applicable to security rights in intellectual property, it may be that the intellectual property laws and the secured transaction laws provide for different rules. The Guide specifies that the guidelines contained therein only apply to intellectual property only insofar as they are not inconsistent with the intellectual property laws of the adopting State.

The Guide contains some specific provisions that clarify terminology used within the intellectual property contexts. For example, the term "acquisition security right" means a security right in a tangible asset. For purposes of the draft Supplement, the term includes a security right in intellectual property or a license of intellectual property, provided that the security right secures the obligation to pay any unpaid portion of the acquisition price of the encumbered asset or an obligation incurred or credit otherwise provided to enable the grantor to acquire the encumbered asset. In secured transactions law, the concept of a "competing claimant" is used to identify parties other than the secured creditor (created by a specific security agreement) who might claim a right in an encumbered asset or the proceeds from its sale. There is no such notion of a "competing claimant" in intellectual property law. In this realm, priority conflicts usually refer to conflicts among intellectual property transferees and licensees. The Guide does not address any of the latter type of conflicts. In regular secured transactions, the term "grantor" refers to the person creating a security right. In the Supplement, however, "grantor" can refer to an owner of the intellectual property or a licensor or licensee. Another important terminology point in the Guide and Supplement is that although the term "assignment" is used to denote not only outright assignments, but also assignments for security purposes, the term "transfer," rather than "assignment," is used in the Supplement to denote the transfer of the rights of an intellectual property owner.

Most of the work on controversial issues in the Supplement was completed at the Fall 2009 session of Working Group VI, and a final draft submission to the Commission for final approval and adoption is contemplated in 2010.

LIST OF CONTRIBUTORS AND SUMMARY TITLES

LIST OF LEGAL DEVELOPMENTS AND CONTRIBUTORS

TABLE OF AUTHORITIES

*Authorities in **bold** are the subject of volume entries.*

A

INDEX